The Wedding Book

REVISED AND UPDATED

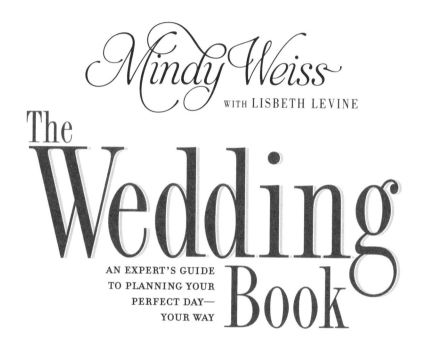

Mindy Weiss

WITH LISBETH LEVINE

The Wedding Book

AN EXPERT'S GUIDE
TO PLANNING YOUR
PERFECT DAY—
YOUR WAY

REVISED AND UPDATED

WORKMAN PUBLISHING • NEW YORK

Library of Congress Cataloging-in-Publication Data is available.

ISBN 978-0-7611-8954-1 (pb); 978-0-7611-8982-4 (HC)

Workman books are available at special discounts when purchased in bulk
for premiums and sales promotions as well as for fund-raising or educational
use. Special editions or book excerpts can also be created to specification.
For details, contact the Special Sales Director at the address below, or send
an email to specialmarkets@workman.com.

Art Direction: Janet Vicario
Design: Jodi Churchfield, Lidija Tomas, Munira Al-Khalili
Cover Design: Ariana Abud
Cover Images: comodo777/fotolia (flowers), macrovector/fotolia (lace)
Author Photo: Jay Lawrence Goldman

Thanks to B&J Fabrics/Karlé J. Meyers for the lace swatches on page 206.

WORKMAN PUBLISHING CO., INC.
225 Varick Street
New York, NY 10014-4381
workman.com

WORKMAN is a registered trademark of Workman Publishing Co., Inc.

First printing August 2016
Printed in the United States of America

10 9 8 7 6 5 4 3 2

DEDICATION

*To my man, Robert, who I knew at age twelve would be the love of my life.
Thank you for your patience.*

*To my sons, Jordan, Jesse, and Alex. I promise to be a great mother-in-law
and not to interfere in your weddings (well, unless you want me to).*

*To all the brides and grooms who have allowed me to be a part of their life
memories. I wouldn't have been able to write this book without
all that I learned from you.*

*To my granddaughter Goldie Vida. I'm already thinking about
the day you walk down the aisle! Your GG loves you.*

—M.W.

Contents

First Steps

Laying the Foundation

Making It Beautiful

The Big Event

Appendixes

Acknowledgments

Index

PREFACE TO THE SECOND EDITION

A lot can happen in eight years. That's how long it's been since the first edition of this book was published. In that time I sent two sons off to college, with the youngest preparing to fly the coop as I write. I watched my oldest son, Jordan, walk down the aisle and open a bar, bravely joining his parents in the family tradition of entrepreneurship. I became a grandmother to a darling girl named Goldie and celebrated my twenty-first anniversary with my very favorite groom. I also launched jewelry and stationery lines and helped a whole lot of couples down the aisle—too many to count!

There've been some changes in the world of weddings, too, the first and most significant being the Supreme Court decision that finally legalized same-sex marriage across all fifty states. There were more than a few happy tears in my office on that day.

I've been planning same-sex weddings for years, but of course legal recognition carries a power that a ceremony alone cannot confer. Though I use the words "bride" and "groom" and the masculine/feminine pronouns, this book applies to readers of any sexuality or gender.

Which brings me to another big change I've noticed: Where brides used to come to our meet-ings with their mothers, they're now more likely to be accompanied by the groom—who used to show up for the cake-tasting session but otherwise made himself scarce. Traditionally, wedding planning was driven by the bride and the mother of the bride. But now it's the couple who tends to handle the bulk of the planning and decision-making. Some grooms get *so* involved in wedding planning that I've nicknamed them "brooms." (Shhhh, don't tell!)

Times have changed, and that's good news. Planning a wedding as a couple is wonderful practice for budgeting, entertaining, and handling the kinds of complex social and familial dynamics you'll be facing for the rest of your lives. So again, while I generally refer to the reader of this book (and the primary architect of the wedding) as the bride, feel free to substitute pronouns as needed!

Lastly, you'll find more information in this edition about how to use tools like Pinterest, Instagram, and Etsy to help plan your wedding. I can't believe they weren't around eight years ago—how did we get along without them? I'm a full-fledged social media addict at this point, so if you're ever at a loss for visual inspiration, feel free to check out my Twitter and Instagram feeds (@mindyweiss).

INTRODUCTION

You've got a week to go until the *Big Day*. You've suddenly developed a strange rash on your shoulders, your mother-in-law is questioning your choice of main course, and a series of unexpected June rainstorms does not seem to be letting up.

First off, talk to any happily married couple about their wedding day and I can guarantee you that it's not the lukewarm entrée or the stutter during the vows they remember, but the ecstatic feeling of committing for life to the person they love, and having all their closest friends and family gathered to witness it. Things will go wrong at the last minute, but a) No one will notice, and b) Remember the old theater adage: A bad dress rehearsal means a good show.

You may be thinking that weddings are a lot more stressful these days. It's true. Wedding planning used to be simple. Typically, the mother of the bride orchestrated the wedding, and her vision, social aspirations, and budget guided the decisions. The bride was allowed some input, but mostly she went with the flow. And the groom? If all went as planned, he showed up.

Today, decisions on how to shape the wedding rest largely with the bride and groom. There are also many more choices to be made—so many that one can easily become overwhelmed. Our celebrations have gotten bigger and bigger, and ever more lavish—that's why I have the job I have, after all, and it's why so many movies and TV shows play off the notion that it's perfectly normal for a bride-to-be to go totally nuts in the process of planning her wedding.

Well, one thing you won't find in this book is any mention of those "Bridezilla" creatures everyone loves to caricature—this is not a work of science fiction! Yes, planning a wedding is a major undertaking, but so is entwining your life with someone else's. I urge you to focus on that as you go forward. It's a difficult balance to strike, I'll admit. Essentially, the challenge is to pay attention to all the details without getting mired in them.

In writing this book, I wanted to create something so complete that it would save you from having to worry about the right way to do things. (Well, there is no one right way, but there certainly are easier and better ways.) There are already tons of beautiful books on getting the look of your wedding just right. There are informative tomes on etiquette essentials. But I didn't see one book that had it all.

I've tried to encapsulate everything that I do for my brides and grooms. I take you through every aspect

1

of your wedding, from the guest list to the seating charts and the emotional highs and lows—you'll even learn how to deal with those challenging in-law situations. That's not to say that I've created a foolproof plan. There is no such thing. As I said, things will go wrong. But armed with the information you'll find here, you'll have all the tools you need to create a harmonious and meaningful wedding day—personal to you and only you—and to be able to let go and forget about all the details on the day itself. (Worried you'll forget about them before that? Use the handy stickers at the back of this book to mark pages you want to come back to.)

I'm a firm believer that prioritizing is half the battle; taken one step at a time, any task becomes manageable. But before you can prioritize, you need to identify what you're working with. What you need to do first is *identify your dream*.

Find a good time for you and your fiancé to sit in a relaxed setting and discuss your ideal wedding. Set up a time if you need to—you shouldn't be calling him while he's in line at the grocery store to say, "I've always wanted a wedding on a tugboat in Seattle. All the guests can kayak out to the ceremony. Okay with you?"

Do you see yourselves dancing under crystal chandeliers in a ballroom or barefoot in the sand? Will guests be eating off fine china or paper plates? Depending on what's important to you, the dream may involve what you'll wear, the music, or a vision of swans swimming in a nearby pond. Your goal shouldn't be to walk away with a firm place, time, and guest count, but to agree on the big picture—is it a church wedding or an outdoor ceremony overlooking the Pacific Ocean?

This conversation might reveal unknown aspects of your fiancé's personality; you're bound to be surprised by something your spouse-to-be has in mind. Different notions of taste nearly always come into play. Sometimes one member of the couple is content to leave the planning in the other's hands but feels strongly about one small element. I've seen grooms with their hearts set on pigs in a blanket, and brides otherwise lackadaisical about planning venture passionate pleas for their grandmother's lace cookie recipe.

A Note on Queen Victoria

As you read this book, you may notice a surprising number of references to Queen Victoria, the longest reigning monarch in British history. What gives? Well, on February 10th, 1840, Queen V. took weddings to a new level. First of all, she's the reason brides wear white. Before her, they would simply wear their best dresses, but a pure white dress says, "I've never been worn before and probably won't have a very long life," and the queen recognized how special that could be.

And then there was the opulence. Victoria's train was so long it took twelve train-bearers to get her down the aisle, and her wedding cake is said to have measured three yards around.

But most important, hers was the first royal wedding to take place after the advent of photography. What that meant was that brides all across England finally had something to emulate, an extravagant wedding-day dream. Beyond the lace and orange blossoms (more wedding traditions that can be traced back to her), she left an even more important legacy. The queen wasn't known for her looks, but on the day she married her Albert, she was radiant. Her appearance convinced the world that every bride could be beautiful. And that testament to the transformative power of love still holds true today.

Coming up with a shared vision may well prove to be you and your mate's first major experience in compromise, making it valuable practice for the future. If your visions differ dramatically, each of you should take a piece of paper and make a list of the three things about the wedding that are most important to you. Then compare your lists and look for common themes. If one of you wants a beach wedding and the other dreams of mountaintop vows, then at least you agree on an outdoor wedding in a natural setting. Perhaps you'll compromise by getting married in the mountains and spending your honeymoon at the beach.

Once you've sketched out your dream, write it down. Even a bare-bones description will help you communicate with parents and vendors when you're trying to shape the wedding.

But here's the rub: You don't want to get too attached to this dream, because, in my experience, 90 percent of the time it is subject to change. What happens? Your dream location may cost four times your total wedding budget. You have your heart set on a Labor Day weekend wedding but find out another wedding would preclude important family members from attending. Along the way, you might learn that September is still peak season and that your first-choice photographer was already booked for Labor Day anyway. Shift the date to early November, and guess what? Key family members can all attend, you can have your pick of photographers, and you lower your costs by 20 percent by picking a less popular month for weddings.

So don't get stuck on the original vision if it's not working. Let it go and move on. With or without lilies of the valley or the Vera Wang satin gown, your wedding will be a beautiful, extraordinarily special event. The only nonnegotiable element is your choice of spouse!

You may be wondering what exactly it is that I do. Well, first off, I don't plan weddings exclusively. I do lots of other kinds of events as well—birthdays (three a year just for my kids!), anniversary celebrations, bar and bat mitzvahs, you name it—but weddings are my favorite. They're the days with the most emotional investment behind them, which also makes them the hardest. But I love a challenge! And more important, I love feeling a deep connection between my work and other people's happiness. Can you think of a better job than making the most meaningful day of someone's life really happen?

Was I born into this business through a supernatural sense of organization and an addiction to parties? Yes and no. I got into event planning through the back door. Post college, I worked at a stationery shop. I met my best friend, Janis, there, and we both really loved the paper goods business. After a few years, we started doing custom invitations out of my house. We were getting really creative with it, and the local planners started to take notice and became clients. Back then, I thought I would never want to be a planner—they were all so grouchy and stressed! But one day, one of my good clients asked me to do his seventy-fifth birthday. I really didn't want to, but he insisted. It turned out to be a blast, and from there, I fell headfirst into party planning.

ASK MINDY

Q I wanted to elope, but my parents and friends freaked out. I'm getting so much pressure to have this big production, and it just doesn't feel right to me. Why won't people let me be? And why are weddings such a big freakin' deal?

A Every society has its own version of a traditional wedding with all the bells and whistles. And many people hold on to the idea of love and "happily ever after" as an antidote to all the hate and ugliness in the world. A wedding encapsulates those hopes.

Choose your battles. Your family just wants to see you walking down the aisle in a wedding gown. Maybe you'll only understand it when you have your own children. As a parent, one of the things you hope for is that your daughter or son marries the right person—and lets you see it happen!

You can have a beautiful event with fifty people—or less. Just give them the dress, the aisle, the traditional ceremony. That may be enough. Your mom can adorn the aisle with hundreds of roses, but you don't have to have her whole mah-jongg group there.

My mother always threw the most amazing parties, so I guess it's in my blood; my father was a lithographer, so lettering was something I grew up with, too. One of my earliest party memories is sitting at the top of the staircase with my two sisters, eavesdropping on all the laughter and conversation emanating from downstairs—I still dream about those parties.

At my own bat mitzvah, the theme was "From Lollipops to Roses," and there were lollipops and chocolate roses everywhere. My mother used *the* party planner in Los Angeles at that time, Marcia Lehr. She did the custom invites, the decorations, everything, at a time when there really wasn't a planning industry like there is now. (And now I do all my custom invitations through her daughter.)

I started working with celebrities almost by accident. Brooke Shields was my first star client, and after that things just took off. It has to do with the quality of service I offer, of course, but also with the fact that celebrities know one another and tend to hire one another's hairstylists, chefs, doctors, whatever. But although the press likes to call me the "celebrity wedding planner," and it's certainly true that I do work with a lot of A-listers, that's not what this book is about.

This book is for every bride and groom—the ones who are planning a wedding with $10,000 or ten or twenty times that, and the ones who are hiring a wedding planner and those who are not. Whether you're totally clueless about where to start or you've already mapped out your colors and tried on fifteen dresses, you'll find just what you're looking for. (Want to test your wedding IQ? Take the "What Kind of Bride Are You?" quiz that follows.)

So happy reading, happy planning, and don't forget to keep your eye on the prize—this is just the beginning of a wonderful journey. ♦

Quiz: What Kind of Bride Are You?

Before you start figuring out whether you want a church wedding or a beach wedding, lilies, peonies, or tulips, it helps to determine your overall "bridal style." As different as brides are, most tend to fall into one of four broad categories. Take this quiz and find out if you're a Dreamer, a Perfectionist, a Rookie, or a Nonconformist. Naturally, everyone exhibits some degree of overlap; even a hardcore Dreamer has a Nonconformist tendency or two. Think of each category as a different kind of shoe—each wonderful in its own way!

1. How long have you been thinking about your wedding?

A. Since I was five.

B. For two years (since I started going to so many friends' weddings).

C. For two weeks (since the day I got engaged).

D. I was never even really sure I'd have one!

2. What kind of organizational system will you use to manage the wedding?

A. Excel spreadsheets and several apps.

B. Paper files, organized by category, filled with pictures I like from magazines.

C. Honestly? Little scraps of paper floating around my purse.

D. Why would I need an organizational system? I'm planning a party, not a trip to outer space.

3. How many bridal magazines are in your home right now?

A. 0

B. 1-3

C. 4-9

D. 10 or more

4. If you had the means, would you quit your job to plan your wedding?

A. It would be lovely!

B. I've requested several weeks off and delegated my most involved projects, so it should be okay.

C. Is it really going to be all that time-consuming? I'm getting kind of nervous.

D. That's preposterous.

5. The day after you got engaged, you:

A. Went about your regular routine.

B. Hid under a blanket (it's all so overwhelming).

C. Tried on gowns.

D. Went to the health club and stocked up on celery.

6. When shopping for a wedding gown, whom do you plan to bring with you?

A. My wedding planner.

B. My mother and my best friend since childhood.

C. My husband-to-be.

D. The priest?

7. What do you think your wedding dress will look like?

A. Fitted bodice, ballgown skirt, and a train—I've been picturing it since I was twelve.

B. Something white or ivory with a poofy thing here or there?

C. No white. I want to wear a happy, celebratory color.

D. How can I possibly answer that until I've visited every bridal store within a fifty-mile radius?

8. Your ideal shower would be:

A. I'd like three: A lingerie shower, a kitchen shower, and a couples shower.

B. None—I think showers are a form of torture.

C. Does that happen before or after the wedding?

D. An afternoon get-together at a spa—there's nothing better than champagne with a mani-pedi.

9. What dishes will be on your registry?

A. I already have dishes. I don't need new ones. Do I?

B. I'm asking that people donate to charity rather than give me gifts.

C. Three sets: Formal china, everyday dishes, and patterned accent plates to vary the look.

D. The same pattern my mom registered for when she got married—I just love it.

10. Which of the following comes closest to describing your ideal wedding cake?

A. Stacked tiers—perfectly coordinated to the color scheme, of course—in different flavors so everyone goes home happy.

B. Yummy, pretty, and white. Did I mention yummy?

C. White buttercream icing, clusters of colorful flowers, and a bride-and-groom cake topper. Swoon . . .

D. An ice-cream sundae buffet! I'd rather have a sundae over cake any day.

11. What kind of shoes will you be wearing under your wedding dress?

A. White satin, of course, carefully chosen to match the exact shade of the dress.

B. Cream-colored, open-toed pumps for the ceremony and light gray skimmers for the reception.

C. Don't they just come with the dress?!

D. My favorite pair of hot-pink Converse—my wedding won't soon be forgotten.

12. Do you have an idea of who your bridesmaids will be?

A. My three best friends since high school.

B. My golden retriever.

C. I haven't decided yet, but I'll take into account length of friendship, level of enthusiasm, and general responsibility.

D. Please stop asking me questions I don't have the answers to!

Scoring

Tally up your answers to each question.

1. A-1; B-2; C-3; D-4   **7.** A-1; B-3; C-4; D-2

2. A-2; B-1; C-3; D-4   **8.** A-2; B-4; C-3; D-1

3. A-4; B-3; C-1; D-2   **9.** A-3; B-4; C-2; D-1

4. A-1; B-2; C-3; D-4   **10.** A-2; B-3; C-1; D-4

5. A-4; B-3; C-1; D-2   **11.** A-1; B-2; C-3; D-4

6. A-2; B-1; C-4; D-3   **12.** A-1; B-4; C-2; D-3

If you scored 12–20 points, you're a Dreamer.

DID YOU DRESS YOUR BARBIE DOLLS in white satin and tulle and marry off Barbie and Ken on a daily basis? Have you been planning your wedding since you were five? You're a Dreamer.

You're likely to come into one of our meetings carrying a bulging folder of pictures ripped out of bridal magazines—and there's nothing wrong with that. You're incredibly excited about the wedding planning process, and you've already done some research. Just be careful about getting too attached to any part of your vision, or you might be in for a letdown when your dreams clash with reality. It's wonderful that you're so impassioned about it all, but you're going to have to fight a tendency toward getting hung up on details. The name of the game is flexibility.

Fine-tune your ideas. Tastes evolve or change, so if you really have been clipping photos for years, you'll need to scrutinize that ten-year-old shot to see if it still speaks to you. I tell all my brides this, but Dreamers especially need to prioritize what's most

important to them. This will help them as they go along in their planning.

Don't forget about your work! I've seen many a Dreamer get so wrapped up in her wedding that she lets her job slide. Designate specific times for wedding planning and take care not to ruin your reputation with colleagues and superiors. And in that same vein, don't let the wedding planning consume you. Your happiness shouldn't depend on finding the perfect antique lace overlays—remember, above all, that you're formalizing your union with the person you love.

If you scored 21–29 points, you're a Perfectionist.

HAVE YOU ATTENDED SO MANY WEDDINGS you've become a self-proclaimed expert? Do you sample five ice-cream flavors before you order your cone? You're a Perfectionist.

You need to see a lot of choices and might find it hard to make decisions. Ideally, you should have at least six months of planning time, preferably a year. Keep notes along the way, or you're liable to forget which sauce you liked best at the first tasting.

Though there will be bumps in the road, in the end you're likely to get the wedding you really want, so try not to focus on the negative. In the initial stages, let the ideas flow freely without worrying about how they fit together. Pick out photos of what you like, not what you abhor. Then listen to the professionals you hire to execute your wedding. If you're told that peonies can't be had in September, don't waste your time second-guessing your florist. Everyone truly does have your best interests at heart. Remember that you'll have to make the inevitable compromise.

And try to have some fun. The Perfectionist's worst enemy is stress. Go on walks, drink lots of water, and don't forget to exercise. Remember, we're talking about just one day of your life.

If you scored 30–39 points, consider yourself a Rookie.

CAN YOU BARELY TELL A ROSE from a hydrangea? Are you already feeling overwhelmed by a process that's barely gotten underway? You're a Rookie.

If it seems like all of a sudden everyone around you has started speaking in tongues, don't worry: You're not alone. Not everyone is a wedding pro. That's why I wrote this book! You'll find everything in here you need in order to become educated about your choices—and, who knows, you might even have some fun along the way.

You may be tempted to lean on someone else for advice, but you'll need to overcome that instinct in order not to feel out of place on your own wedding day. You don't need to be a professional planner to pull off a lovely wedding, but, should you have the means to hire one, it might be a good idea.

I often find that the most bewildered brides are the most delightful to work with. They're open to anything, listen carefully to what I have to say, and make decisions quickly—no wallowing in the details. But the flip side of that is that you need to make sure you're not going along with something that isn't to your taste just because you don't have the confidence to have a voice in the process. Your opinion counts! Practice saying "That isn't quite what I was thinking of" in front of the mirror until you're comfortable saying it to one of your vendors.

Clip photos of things you do or don't like—even if they have nothing to do with weddings. An English garden or the sleek line of an Art Deco–inspired toaster might be the perfect way to communicate your tastes to your vendors. Think about other weddings you've attended and make a list of things you found appealing or unappealing. Visit websites of top-notch wedding planners, florists, and wedding photographers to identify styles that speak to you.

If you scored 40–48 points, you're a Nonconformist.

DOES THE NOTION OF A WHITE SATIN GOWN and a bevy of bridesmaids make your skin crawl? Do you question tradition and revel in doing things your own way? You're a Nonconformist.

You're not necessarily opposed to ritual—if a tradition has meaning for you, you'll embrace it while finding a way to add a personal twist. But if the idea of a wedding is making you nervous and you're thinking of throwing in the towel and eloping, rest assured that the proceedings can be as untraditional as you want. If you hate showers, you don't have to have one (but you might want to consider a co-ed bowling party).

In my experience, Nonconformist brides are more likely than others to have a firm grasp on their budget limitations; no going into debt on a twelve-piece band for you, and I commend you for that. Follow your instincts and funnel your funds into the aspects of the wedding that are most important to you. You might prefer to have plain wood tables rather than bad satin cloths, or you might choose a simple dress over a wedding gown.

A gentle reminder: Try not to make a statement at the expense of your guests' comfort. Some of the invitees might not be as spry as you and the groom; they may not be inclined to take three puddle jumpers and a hovercraft to reach a remote island, or may require more than the primitive bathroom facilities at your beloved summer camp.

PART I

FIRST STEPS

CHAPTER ONE

Spreading the News

FRIENDS AND FAMILY COMING TOGETHER

The first step toward matrimony is tooting your own glorious horn. You're engaged, and you probably want the whole world to know it. But before you broadcast the news across your social media feeds, think about how your parents will feel if they're not the first to hear. So call them right away (as a couple if at all possible). If you live near

them, go one better by telling them in person. Which set of parents to call first? Usually the bride's, although it's a highly personal decision.

What if he's never met your parents, or vice versa? Remember the scene in *Father of the Bride* (the Steve Martin version) where Annie announces that she met the most wonderful guy in Italy, *and* they're getting married, *and* he's on his way over to

meet them? The devastated look on Steve Martin's face says it all. Lesson: dangerous tactic. Give your parents time to acclimate themselves to the idea, then bring your fiancé to meet them.

After you've told both sets of parents, call your siblings, close relatives, and good friends. Don't let anyone who fits into these categories find out via a pic of the ring on your Instagram feed. And don't forget to call your grandparents—this is a momentous event in their lives as well.

If you already have children from a prior marriage or relationship and they're old enough to keep a secret, you may want to let them know before you tell anyone else. Or gather the three generations together and tell them at the same time. It all depends on your family's dynamics.

Snap a Pic

The question has been popped, the happy answer given, the ring placed on a jubilant hand. If you're like most couples these days, you may have followed up the tearful moment by snapping a sweetly beaming selfie.

There's something undeniably special about this snapshot, which captures the first official moments of your journey toward marriage. Many couples use this shot as the accompaniment to an informal engagement announcement via social media. One groom popped the question during an overnight stay in the desert and posted a pic of the happy campers with the caption "Check you later, bachelorhood"—a nice twist on the usual shot of the engagement ring! Other couples opt for professional engagement photos, which can run from $350 to $1,000 but are also often included as part of a photographer's wedding package. If you'd like to get a test run with a photographer to see how your personalities mesh, the engagement shot is a great way to do that. The photo can be used on social media as well as on the save-the-dates and/or invitations.

Part of the fun in getting professional photos taken lies in selecting a beautiful and meaningful location for the shoot. For some couples that could mean returning to the spot where they got engaged or had their first date. Couples who want to use the photograph on their save-the-dates or invites will sometimes arrange to have a shoot at the wedding site, in order to create a look that's unified around the location. Others simply choose beautiful outdoor spots with lots of opportunities for a variety of setups. Beaches and hilltops are perennially popular backdrops, and activities like biking or rowboat rides can make for lovely candid shots.

Choose a unified color scheme for your outfits, or have one person (usually the bride-to-be) dress in something colorful while the other wears light or muted hues. Some brides choose to use the engagement photo as a chance to do a test run on hair and makeup, but that's not necessary. No need to rack up extra expenses so early in the game.

Rather than reenacting the engagement in that classic, somewhat contrived groom–on–bended–knee shot, many photographers these days are aiming for romantic, spontaneous shots of the couple hugging, kissing, jumping for joy, or simply holding hands. There *are* grooms who hire photographers to camp out in the bushes and snap paparazzi-style pics of the engagement-in-progress, but this approach does entail some risk. What if she says no, or the photographer misses the shot or spoils the surprise? I've heard of a groom inviting friends for a pop-up celebration right after he popped the question, but turning the engagement itself into a social event is not for everyone.

To Post or Not to Post?

BEFORE YOU POST, WAIT. Again, make sure you've told your family and closest friends before you broadcast the news to the world. But consider keeping the news offline for as long as you can stand it.

You should spend the next couple of days or even weeks processing this life change and basking in the romantic moment with your husband-to-be—not fielding hundreds of Instagram comments and questions from friends. Posting the announcement too early catapults you into the public phase of your engagement right away, which is typically when things begin to get complicated. Trust me. Enjoy some private, uncomplicated moments before you launch into the planning phase of the operation.

Some couples may choose not to post the news at all, letting word flow out to their extended circles organically and waiting until the moment they are married to announce the news to the world at large.

A Formal Engagement Announcement

Not that long ago, the bride-to-be's parents sometimes sent out written engagement announcements. These days, emails and phone calls are acceptable ways of announcing one's engagement to family and friends, and posting an engagement photo to your social media feeds takes care of the rest. Formal announcements have been supplanted by save-the-date cards (see page 63), which are more useful, and/or by invitations to the engagement party (see page 17), which are usually sent via email.

If you are having a particularly long engagement and do want to send out announcements, send them only to people you plan to invite to the wedding. Announcements are usually sent by the parents of the bride, though some couples send out their own. The wording is quite simple, typically making no mention of the wedding date or location.

Making the News

SOME BRIDES SEE newspaper engagement announcements as a throwback. (Engagement announcements run well in advance of the wedding, while wedding announcements run shortly afterward.) But an announcement in the newspaper can be a wonderful keepsake, and sometimes parents or grandparents are attached to the notion. If so, I vote for making them happy on this one. Save your battles for something bigger! If it's not a priority for you, send a photo of the two of you to the set of parents who want it published, and let them handle the rest.

You can place an announcement in your hometown paper, even if you moved away years ago. You can also submit the announcement to a paper serving your current address. Check the paper's individual guidelines, usually available on its website, to find out what information is required. The article might include information about what you and your fiancé do and your parents' occupations, along with a photograph. No need for studio head shots or anything fancy here; announcement photos, both for engagements and weddings, can be as casual as you like. Just make sure your heads are lined up on the same plane.

Some newspapers print announcements for free as part of their community or social news; others treat them as advertising and charge a fee; and some offer a combination of both. If the newspaper treats announcements as news, they have no obligation to run your announcement, and in some national publications the selection process can be quite competitive.

Ideally, an engagement announcement would run three to eight months before the wedding. If you're planning a very small wedding, you may want to skip the announcement, since it might increase the number of people dropping hints that they want to be invited.

Publications tend to differ on their stance toward the timing of wedding announcements. Some will run them only the day after the wedding, while others will run them months after the fact.

A Complex Response

Most of us expect our happy news to be met with shrieks of excitement. But congratulations are rarely the last word—and not always even the starting point. Your parents might immediately assail you with questions: when, where, how many, and "the big one"—how much is this thing going to cost? They might seize on differences—religious, cultural, or geographical—between you and your fiancé and ask how they'll be resolved.

Steel yourself (after all, this is only the beginning). Just because people demand immediate answers doesn't mean you have to provide them. Do you answer every email as soon as it comes in? For your sake, I hope not. Until the two of you have hatched a firm plan, don't attempt to answer questions from inquiring relatives—you could find yourself in a serious quarrel over

What Happened to the *Friend* in *Girlfriend*?

Most of your friends will undoubtedly scream, squeal, jump up and down, or otherwise let you know how happy they are for you when you break the news, but don't be shocked if some people, particularly girlfriends, sound less than thrilled.

What's going on? Perhaps a little envy—maybe your grumpy friend has been waiting for a ring from a noncommittal boyfriend since your first date with Mr. Wonderful. Even if she's already married, maybe she envies your blissful state. Or perhaps she's already jealous of all the attention you'll be getting in the coming months.

Try to cut the naysayers and the sulkers a little slack, and then tune them out. Yes, you're disappointed in their reaction, but don't dwell on it and let it escalate to anger—you'll only be hurting yourself. Unless people are bringing you paperwork documenting criminal charges against your beloved, remember that this is your bubble and you shouldn't grant anyone the power to burst it. Give your less-than-elated friends a few weeks to get used to the idea. Then go out for drinks or dinner and assure close pals that while your relationship with them might change, you're still friends . . . good friends. Most of them will come around eventually. And if you were thinking of asking them to stand up for you? Wait. Indeed, wait on choosing all of your attendants, for reasons I'll go into in chapter 4, "Building Your Team."

---

something you don't really care about or unintentionally backed into a corner. Before the two of you have agreed on some basics, tell everybody the same thing: We're just enjoying this time and we will start planning later.

Your Worst Nightmare

IF YOU ANTICIPATE a negative reaction from your parents, make sure that your future spouse is out of earshot when you tell them about your engagement. There's no reason why your fiancé should be subjected to their response.

But what if they scream "What are you thinking?!" or "Are you out of your mind?" or some more colorful variation on the theme? Just make it clear that your plans to marry are nonnegotiable. Tell them how important it is to you to share this wonderful experience with them. Keep your tone respectful—they are your parents, after all, even when they're not behaving like adults. And if they carry on in front of your fiancé, take them aside and let them know they're embarrassing you.

If the screamers are your future in-laws, try not to take it personally. Though this will be very difficult, realize that their negativity could have nothing to do with you—it might stem from separation anxiety or control issues. Even if they don't have the tools to control themselves, it's still in your best interest to stay calm and stop yourself from striking back.

In the long run, it is probably best not to count on the disapproving party as a source of funding. Make it clear that you love them and that they will be included in your day, but do not ask them for money, accept their money, or feel obligated to involve them in the planning in any way. It is always, *always* best to take the high road and try to preserve the relationship, no matter how angry you are, but spending someone's money on something they don't believe in sets you up for all kinds of awkwardness and heartbreak.

Let's hope, however, that the reaction is happy. In any case, be prepared for a profound response. Even if you've been dating for years and see the engagement as a predictable next step, this is still life-changing news from your parents' point of view. It means that you're officially creating a family of your own, and that's a very big deal.

If It's Not Your First Trip Down the Aisle . . .

IF THE MARRIAGE isn't your first, how do you tell an ex-spouse about your new engagement? Well, it depends on your relationship and on whether you have children together. If you have children, I suggest you don't let them break the news first: Your ex will naturally have questions and concerns about the family shift that's about to occur, so you should set up a time to talk about any changes in living arrangements. If alimony will be affected, you may bring this up in person or through a lawyer. By the same token, take pains to be totally up-front with your children; you don't want them to resort to pumping your ex to find out how their life is going to change.

If you don't have children together but have a cordial relationship with your ex, by all means call to share the news within the first few weeks. These days, it's not all that uncommon for exes to be invited to the wedding, especially if there are children involved.

ASK MINDY

Q My parents are going through a painful divorce as I plan my wedding—and it seems to be bringing out the worst in them. I feel like they're not even happy for me, and I'm constantly jumping through hoops, trying to smooth over conflict. Why can't they act like grown-ups? This is supposed to be about me!

A I've seen this happen, and often. But believe me, they're just angry that their marriage didn't work—they don't mean the things they're saying. Your wedding has given them an opportunity to face each other again—to get mad again—and unfortunately the emotions are directed toward you. This tension especially comes up around issues of money. I've heard fathers say, "I gave your mother enough money," and mothers say, "He's using his money to buy your loyalty."

If you keep focusing on the fact that you're going to make it down the aisle with the man of your dreams, your clarity will jar them into behaving better. One way or another, they will realize their error by the end. But if you want to deal with it earlier in the planning process, have a private meeting with each of them. I'm a big advocate of not bottling anything up, and letting people know how you feel. But don't threaten—that's a plan that's bound to backfire.

The Merging of the Clans

I f you haven't met your future in-laws by the time you get engaged, you need to set up a meeting ASAP. Both sets of parents should also connect to congratulate each other, first by phone and then, if at all possible, face-to-face.

Historically, the bride left home to join the groom's family, so tradition holds that the groom's parents call the bride's, essentially to say they are thrilled to be welcoming their daughter into the family—though it doesn't really matter who initiates the connection as long as the call is placed. It should preferably be done within a day or two of the engagement; otherwise it gets awkward, and one side might think that the other isn't happy about the news. If either set of parents is divorced, calls should be made to all parents.

Not every parent is schooled in the social graces, and some parents may just forget these sorts of niceties in their excitement; so when you share the news of your engagement, plant the idea of calling your future in-laws with your mom and dad. If you hear nothing more, follow up and remind your parents to call.

If all of the parents live nearby, the next step would be for them to get together with the couple for a celebratory dinner. Parents can also get together on their own, without the couple. It's really up to each family.

The first gathering can take place at either of the couple's homes, at a parent's home, or at a neutral site, like a restaurant. If you have any reason to think that your spouse-to-be or his parents will be uncomfortable in the suggested setting (for example, if your parents have invited everyone to join them at "the club" and your intended comes from a blue-collar background), shift things to a more neutral location where everyone will be on equal footing.

In my experience, about 50 percent of the time, the parents have already met, but even so, the fact that you're now engaged calls for an official get-together. Ideally, this is simply a time for parents to get to know one another and celebrate the occasion. Some parents will want to roll up their sleeves and tackle the details; if so, the subject of money will come up, I promise you, along with the inevitable question: Who will be paying for all of this? Unless you have experience in wedding or event planning, you probably have no idea of the actual costs involved, so it's best to stay away from numbers until you have some real ones in hand. (The *average* cost of a wedding in the United States has skyrocketed since the 1980s, nearing $30,000.) So I advise you to read through chapter 2, "Creating the Budget," before this meeting occurs.

Headed for Harmony

GUESS WHAT: Everyone experiences some degree of culture shock upon getting married. It happens when you visit your fiancé's family home, when your families meet for the first, second, or third time (and beyond), and when you begin to blend customs and traditions into the new family you're about to start.

Though the potential for misunderstandings and conflict is definitely higher if you're marrying someone of a different religion, race, social background, or even region of the country, no one is immune to culture clashes. Because what is a family if not a little country of its own, complete with customs, rituals, and taboos?

Here are a few tips for *every* first meeting, no matter how different or similar the families seem:

> Remember that your families are going to have to work together on the wedding—and have at least some kind of relationship after you're married, especially if you're planning on having children. So it's in everyone's best interest to invest time and energy in sending the relationship down the right path from the very start.

- If you and your fiancé live together and have the space to entertain comfortably, host the first meeting. If you're serving food, consider offering something that's representative of each side of the family. If you can't host, have the first meeting on neutral territory, such as a restaurant, and pick up the tab to save your parents the awkwardness of fighting over the bill. Choose a place you know and like that's comfortable, unpretentious, reasonably priced, and quiet enough for conversation.

- If both parties are traveling into town for the meeting, don't feel that everyone needs to spend the entire weekend together. One or two group events would be fine. Each of you should spend the rest of the time hanging out with your individual family. It's amazing how far a little one-on-one attention goes at a time when parents are bound to be feeling sadness and loss about you growing up and "moving on."

- Keep conversation to neutral topics. If there's something that you know shouldn't be discussed, warn each party separately beforehand. Prepare a few funny, endearing stories to tell if there's a lull—it's always good to remind everyone why the people at the table are special.

- Arm your families with some positive, interesting information about the people they'll be meeting. The further apart your families are culturally, the more education each side will need, and you two are the teachers. But you debrief your family; he debriefs his. (This is also a good rule to remember going forward, in cases of conflict. "Blood talks to blood" is the way some therapists put it.)

- Write a gracious note afterward to both sets of parents, thanking them for coming and mentioning how much fun you had— and how much fun the other parents told you they had. (Even if they didn't!)

In short, summon all the rules of social savvy that you'd employ while hosting a dinner party for people who don't know one another well, blend them with what you know about your families, and trust your gut on how to proceed. And whatever you do, do it with panache. Be enthusiastic, and take the lead. You're the reason for these families coming together, and it's up to you to set the tone for a harmonious wedding and a successful, loving future. Do it with confidence.

ASK MINDY

Q I am a wreck just thinking about my parents meeting my fiancé's. Mine drink half a glass of wine at Thanksgiving, but his pull out the cocktail shaker as soon as the sun goes down. They're all really nice people, and I think they would discover they had a lot in common if they could get to know one another, but I can already see that judgmental look in my mother's eyes that means she's made up her mind—and she's not going to budge.

A Go in with your fiancé as a tough, together team: No matter what happens with the families, you guys are getting married. That's the attitude you want to have. Your fiancé can ask his parents to be on their best behavior, but this isn't really something you can control—if this is the man you want to spend the rest of your life with, your parents are going to have to meet his. They are adults, they'll deal with it. And you may be surprised. Go in telling yourself: They don't have to like each other, but wouldn't it be great if they did? In any case, there's nothing you can do but hope for the best.

The Engagement Party

The first public celebration of your new status is the engagement party. There's no obligation to have one, but it can be a lovely way for family and friends on both sides to start getting to know one another. Although engagement parties date back centuries, there's little formal protocol governing them, which means you have plenty of latitude. Cocktails and hors d'oeuvres at a parent's home, dinner in a restaurant, a Sunday brunch, or an outdoor barbecue would all fit the bill.

Traditionally, the parents of the bride gave the engagement party, inviting guests to cocktails at their home without noting the occasion. The cornerstone of the event would be the moment when the bride's father stood up to announce the happy news and propose a toast to the couple. And while this is still an important gesture, it's often not the surprise that it once was.

These days it's not always practical to have the bride's parents throw the party, especially if the couple doesn't live near them. Other likely hosts are the groom's parents or any close family member on either side. More and more often, a close friend offers to host the event. In theory, you shouldn't host your own unless you're going to make it the occasion for a surprise announcement. (But it really needs to be a true surprise—not an open secret—and the first time that anyone is hearing your news, with the possible exception of your parents.)

In keeping with such notions of secrecy, traditional etiquette prescribes that guests be invited to an event "in honor of" the couple, not an "engagement party." But I almost always use *engagement party* or *engagement dinner* on the invitations sent out by the couples I work with. I think people appreciate knowing exactly what type of event they're being asked to attend.

There are no hard-and-fast rules about when to hold the party, but it usually takes place at least two months after the engagement and no later than six months before the wedding—after that, it's simply too close to all of the showers and the wedding itself, and guests may feel like they're being "hit up" for too many gifts. A lot depends, of course,

17

Visit a Flower Shop

If you get engaged a year or more before the wedding, pay a visit to a local flower shop during the month you plan to be married and familiarize yourself with the flowers that are in season. If you're a flower lover, the buckets of peonies, hydrangeas, or parrot tulips might even inspire a theme or color palette. But remember that you're dealing with Mother Nature here, and she offers no contracts and no guarantees. Depending on weather conditions, the precise dates when a particular blossom will be in season can shift from year to year. For an extensive list of flowers by season, see page 297.

on the length of the engagement. If the engagement is six months or less, there usually isn't time for a party.

Speaking of gifts, there is no formal tradition governing engagement gifts, other than between the couple (remember the ring?). Although some people—particularly close family members, close friends, and long-standing friends of your parents'—may bring or send gifts, you should not expect them and they shouldn't be opened at the party. Obviously, since you're not supposed to expect gifts at the party, you don't need to register before the event. From a practical standpoint, you don't want to register in a rush or before you've had time to decide on what you like. (Many brides just can't be stopped, though, and that's fine, too.)

Can you have more than one engagement party? Absolutely, but not in the same city. If the couple lives in Los Angeles and the bride's parents live nearby, but the groom's parents live in Minneapolis, it would be perfectly fine (but not necessary) for the bride's parents to host an engagement party in Los Angeles and for the groom's parents to introduce the couple to their family and friends at a party in Minneapolis. And if finances and schedules allow it, it's wonderful if both sets of parents can attend both parties.

The guest list should be limited to people who will be invited to the wedding, though of course there can be exceptions to the rule. If you're unsure about the size of the wedding, play it safe and invite only family members and your closest friends, or hold off on the party until you have a clearer idea of how many people you'll be inviting to the wedding.

At one time, it was traditional to have a receiving line on the way in, but this seems dated to me. It's unnecessarily formal and tends to create a logjam at the door, which gets the party off to an uncomfortable start.

And that's exactly what you don't want. The goal of your engagement party is to get the two sides mixing and mingling. The better people get to know one another, the easier all of your other pre-wedding events—and the

ASK MINDY

Q For financial reasons, my fiancé and I are having a very small wedding—but between the two of us, we know a lot of people. We were thinking of having a casual engagement party for all of the people we can't afford to invite. Is that bad form?

A In theory, anyone invited to the engagement party should be included in the wedding. These days people are much more understanding. But rather than invite them to an engagement party, have a great, inclusive get-together after the wedding.

Fun, descriptive name tags are one way to break the ice at an engagement party.

wedding itself—will be. Consider making name tags that specify the wearer's relationship to the couple, like "Bill's uncle" or "Jennifer's college roommate." Even if you're having passed hors d'oeuvres, make sure there's at least one food station where people can congregate. It could be as simple as crudités and dip or a cheese tray, or something a little more elaborate like a Mediterranean station with raw vegetables and pita with a yogurt dip, hummus, tabouleh, and baba ghanoush. A station for making ice-cream sundaes is a great gathering place. A wine-tasting bar—either manned by someone knowledgeable about the subject or labeled with detailed descriptions of each wine—works wonders as a conversation starter.

Activities are another way to bring people together. If you're having a backyard barbecue, set up croquet and volleyball. Consider drawing up a quiz or a crossword puzzle about the bride and groom, and have prizes for the highest scores on each side. The engagement party is also a great place to incorporate any ethnic or family traditions, whether that means Greek baklava for dessert or an ultracompetitive game of charades.

If you want something more low-key, you could also opt for a small dinner at a restaurant. Forget the activities, but go around the table and have all the guests introduce themselves, or say a little something about each person yourselves. It's a nice way to break the ice and create a sense of ceremony.

The Toast

AFTER MOST OF the guests have arrived at the engagement party, or about an hour into the event, it's time for the father of the bride to make his toast. If he isn't available, another significant family member can do the honors. Other likely candidates are the mother of the bride, either parent of the groom's, a grandparent, or a close friend. Either wine or champagne can be poured for the toast.

You may not be used to being toasted, so bone up on the etiquette involved. When the person giving the toast asks everyone to raise their glasses, don't raise yours. You're also not supposed to drink to yourself after the toast, but today, many couples clink their glasses and take a sip. No one would look at them askance.

After the toast, the bride and groom should briefly address the gathering to thank the person who gave the toast, the host of the party, and the friends and family members who came out to celebrate their happy event. If either or both sets of parents haven't already been introduced to everyone, it's time to make the introductions. You can talk a little bit about how excited you are to be getting married, but save the "I knew you were the one for me" speech for the rehearsal dinner or wedding. All these people will presumably be attending your other wedding celebrations, so don't use up all your good material this early in the game!

After the Party

SEND A HEARTFELT note and a gift to the host the day after the party. If a parent hosted the party, you don't need to send a gift (parents always get the short end of this stick). Flowers make a wonderful gesture, especially if the host is difficult to buy for. Candles, chocolates, beautiful soaps, a picture frame, or a special bottle of wine or champagne also make fine gifts. A couple of my favorites are personalized stationery for the host or a monogrammed throw blanket. You can also bring the gift with you to the party, but you should still send a note afterward.

And all those gifts you weren't supposed to get? Each requires a thank-you note. They should be sent out as soon as possible, preferably within two weeks. Think of it as a good warm-up for all the thank-you notes to come. (One of the first things you should buy early on in your engagement are notes with both your first names on them, so you can use them before and after the wedding.) Either the bride or groom can write the notes—I strongly encourage equal opportunity note writing! (See chapter 20, "The Invitations," for more information on types of stationery, fonts, and designs, and chapter 15, "Saying Thank You," for more about my philosophy of writing thank-you notes, along with sample notes.)

ASK MINDY

Q One of my best friends didn't show up at my engagement party. She lives in a town about two hours from me. My feelings are really hurt, especially since I was going to ask her to be a bridesmaid. I feel like she's not excited about my wedding. Am I overreacting?

A Yes, you are. Maybe she had a financial issue or a previous obligation. Or, indeed, she might be feeling a little envy, which she's going to need some time to deal with. But if you were going to ask her to be a bridesmaid, and you changed your mind for this little thing, she must not have been that special a friend.

Give her a second chance and the opportunity to come to some other event. You'll find that all your bridesmaids may not be able to attend all your events; that doesn't mean they don't care or aren't excited.

As you've probably guessed, I am an advocate of the dying art of the handwritten thank-you note. But don't get me wrong: If for some reason (it better be a good one!) you can't make time for that, it's better to call or email than to do nothing at all.

Engagement: What's It For, Anyway?

The contemporary year-plus engagement is just that: contemporary. Yes, various faiths and cultures have betrothal periods and accompanying traditions that have evolved over time, all designed for more or less the same purpose—making sure that the two of you really want to seal the deal, and that your families and friends are on board—but the secular, across-all-faiths "engagement" most of us practice today bears a distinctly North American stamp. And we've definitely given the engagement period the same treatment we've given weddings (and all other rites of passage in our culture), making it ever bigger, more action packed, more commercialized, and longer. At no point in history have couples waited so long between "Yes!" and "I do."

Conventional wisdom might suggest that we wait so long these days because it takes that long to plan a wedding of the size and complexity to which we've become accustomed. (Or to accumulate the funds to pay for a wedding of the size and complexity to which we've become accustomed!) Or because there are now so many steps in the process, so many milestones and parties that dot the path to the altar.

Or maybe we stretch things out because there aren't as many reasons for speed. Women make their own money and aren't being handed off from parent to husband, and these days the shift between dating and being married is (or appears to be) less intense. A couple may already be living together and chances are good they're already sleeping together. What's the rush?

A Transitional Time

NO MATTER HOW long or short your engagement, or your reasons for making it so, using this period solely for shopping and sipping champagne is a missed opportunity—for you, for your spouse-to-be, and for your families. When else in life do you have a nice chunk of time to get used to something before it becomes your reality? If you're having an engagement of any length, try to prevent the planning and partying from eating up all of it. Savor your in-between status and explore the far corners of your mind, and your husband-to-be's. Kick those tires: Think carefully about everything from the communication patterns you want to implement in your marriage (it's easier to form good habits than to break bad ones), to how the two of you will handle in-laws, to where you're going to live and how you're going to work your finances.

Focus on yourself, too. Think about the enormous transition you're going through and acknowledge all the feelings—elation, love, and security, yes, but also perhaps fear, anxiety, and sadness at having to kiss your single life good-bye. Then find healthy ways to process them.

Talk to friends, married and single, about what lies ahead and what went before. Take extra-good care of your single friends, who may be feeling bereft about "losing" you. Reach out to them, make plans, and don't let your wedding dominate the conversation.

Above all, if you find yourself feeling sad, angry, or upset during your engagement, or fighting more with your fiancé, don't fret. It's completely normal to have doubts, fears, anxieties, and an increased level of conflict, even though these are not things we like to talk about in public. If you don't have any doubts, fears, anxieties, or fights, you're probably not being honest with yourself.

Ceaseless fighting, unshakable feelings of remorse or doom, infidelity, or abuse are different matters—see page 159 if you're experiencing any of those, as you might need to give your plans some serious thought. But if it's more like the occasional panic attack about the groom—or if you're beginning to suspect that your battles over his tuxedo might be about something other than haberdashery—you're in good company.

Rest assured: For every kind of upset you experience during your engagement, there are many other brides (and grooms) who have faced the same issues. They've also had trouble sleeping and blue (or black!) moods. They've also become obsessed over a particular wedding detail, or been unable to relax, or felt utterly exhausted. Still, try to be as self-aware as possible. Take good care of yourself, and if the stress reaches new heights, try to track down the cause and address it. Keeping a journal is a great help in monitoring yourself and blowing off steam in a way that's completely private and won't come back to haunt you. (Though do be careful not to leave it lying around if you share a home with your husband-to-be!)

And now that you've dealt with how *you* feel, it's time to consider the effect your wedding is having on other people. Getting engaged and then planning a wedding puts stress on *all* your relationships—including, and

ASK MINDY

Q I can count on one hand the number of times we've had sex since I proposed to my girlfriend exactly two months ago. I feel like she's been taken over by some wedding demon who feeds off guest counts and discussions (endless discussions) about table settings and linens! Where did the woman I fell in love with go? And am I just getting a taste of married life?!

A Being preoccupied with all the exciting plans is a normal part of being engaged, and yes, that can sometimes zap sexual energy. But this should be a temporary problem—and a good excuse for learning more about each other. Sit down and talk to your fiancée about what's going on, and then plan to have a date night once a week when you put a moratorium on wedding talk. Take heart: That wonderful woman you remember will definitely be there on the honeymoon.

perhaps especially, your relationship with your fiancé. Most couples report feeling less close, fighting more often, and having less sex than they did when they were just dating. It may sound depressing and unromantic, but it's true.

Think about it: Before the proposal, all you had to worry about was enjoying each other, or maybe about *getting* to the proposal, if the timing was a source of debate. After you agree to marry each other, however, all kinds of guests show up at your previously cozy party: your family, his family, the future, and all the challenges it will bring. Throw in planning the wedding, which is a significant and time-consuming project, and you've got a lot of things just waiting to intrude on domestic bliss.

Premarital Education

THE ENGAGEMENT PERIOD can be full of stress, but luckily, there are plenty of places to go for support. If you're getting married within a faith, you might be required to attend a premarital program of some kind. Though these classes have an element of religious doctrine in them, more and more of them are also adopting curricula that emphasize what's known as "premarital education." Exercises will help you learn communication and listening skills, build empathy so you can see the other person's point of view, and compile inventories that will help you see how well your and your fiancé's values—about everything from money to family to sex to what constitutes infidelity—line up.

If your church or temple requires such courses, don't turn up your nose, or be cynical. Be grateful. Learning how to openly and clearly ask for what you need; listening to and truly understanding what the other person is saying; fighting fair; making up after arguments; reaching compromises; and compensating for inevitable differences (what two people in the world agree on everything?) increase your odds of marital success over the long haul. These skills are acquired, not innate. Taking a class with a group of other couples can also help you see the challenges in your relationship in a larger context. You're less likely to feel alone and despondent when trouble arises.

If you're not getting married within a faith, these courses are still available to you—and may even get you a discount on your marriage license! (It depends on the state.) PAIRS (Practical Application of Relationship Skills) and PREP (The Prevention and Relationship Enhancement Program) are two great programs with national scope.

If you believe that an ounce of prevention is worth a pound of cure, you can also pursue some form of premarital counseling—even if you aren't grappling with serious issues. That may entail speaking with your pastor, priest, or rabbi, working as a couple with a therapist who one of you is already seeing individually, or finding a couples' therapist in your area.

Congratulations! You are now officially engaged, with all the bells and whistles. The first step toward the wedding of your dreams? A solid budget. Read on to find out how to assess and manage your funds. ♦

CHAPTER TWO

Creating the Budget

A REALISTIC FRAMEWORK

Take a deep breath: Before you can start choosing colors and wrapping yourself in acres of silk, you're going to have to face some spreadsheets. But don't worry about the math—all you need to do is plug in some numbers. This chapter is short, and there's a reason for that. Managing a wedding requires neither a graphing calculator nor a hundred-page tome.

Budgeting is first and foremost a matter of organization, and all you really need is a good tracking system. Set things up correctly from the get-go and you'll save yourself some serious headaches.

In this chapter, you'll find traditional and modern approaches to sharing expenses and learn how to set up a wedding budget and keep track of expenses. I'll also cover the perils of going into debt to finance a wed-

ding and tell you why it's so important to stick to your budget—though I will allow you to go 10 percent over, because everyone is entitled to a few splurges.

No matter who's footing the bill, a wedding is very much a family affair, so it's best to make everyone feel a part of things—though the dynamic will be quite different if you are the ones shelling out the cash. But if you do expect parents to foot part or all of the bill—or if they've already volunteered to do so—it's time to have a conversation about what they wish to contribute.

The bride and groom often choose to call or visit their own parents individually to discuss money matters; for a larger wedding, I think it's a good idea to meet as a group after that as well.

Sometimes parents announce that they can contribute a fixed amount; sometimes they detail what they'll pay for. Many parents ask to see some estimates before they agree to anything or even decide how much they can put toward the event. Some may not be able to help out at all. And some will want to know what the other side is contributing before they commit to anything.

Be prepared for a possible reality check. Your dream wedding may cost $200,000, and you may come to find out that you can't spend a penny over $50,000. Parents may be willing to pay more money for a hometown wedding—a tried-and-true bribery tactic!—or may want to pay for the country club but skimp on the food, while you'd settle for a less tony location with better catering.

If you find yourself stalled over specific items in the budget, keep in mind that it's likely you're arguing about priorities rather than money. And the best way to prevent such arguments, and help them pass more quickly when they do arise, is to get absolute clarity about those priorities. What are the two or three things that are most important to you? (And no, you can't make everything "high priority"— you must rank some things over others.)

You should ask anyone who's funding part of the celebration to complete the same exercise. If you find yourself in a disagreement over a money issue, look back at your priority lists to see if the thing you're fighting about is really worth going to the mat for. Is it in your top three? Your mom's top three? Might it be okay to let her have her way on this one, or do you really need to stand firm?

> If budgeting disagreements arise, identify your top two or three priorities. Stick to your guns about them and make concessions elsewhere.

Who's Paying?

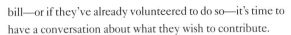

For many families, a relatively simple and fair way to split expenses is by using what I call the FLOP. The groom's family pays for flowers, liquor, orchestra, and photography (not including videography). In addition, they also typically cover the cost of the rehearsal dinner. (While the groom's family used to pay for the honeymoon, about half of the couples I work with pay for it themselves, often using some of their wedding gift money.) The bride's family pays for the rest.

That said, any division that works for the couple and the families is a good one. At one of my weddings, the couple and each set of parents covered the costs for "their" guests, a strategy that worked miracles in terms of keeping down the guest list. Parents may also wish to divide the expenses based on their interests or connections. If the groom's mother has a longstanding friendship with the best caterer in town, covering the food would be a natural fit for her. Some parents like to know the traditional breakdown as they decide on their contributions, so I've included it as a point of reference (see box, opposite page). But more and more often, I see my brides and grooms covering the cost of the wedding themselves, or accepting a fixed amount from parents who give the couple free rein to allocate funds as needed. And for same-sex couples, the old-school breakdown won't come into play, though again, it may be helpful as a reference for how to split the bills between families.

A Plea for Restraint

DESPITE TENDENCIES to the contrary, a wedding shouldn't send you or your parents (who are probably nearing retirement age) into years of debt. If you absolutely must borrow, don't take on more debt than you can pay off in a year. You don't need to put additional strain on your new marriage, especially if you're paying off student loans or buying a new home.

And don't fool yourself: Charging things that you can't afford on your credit cards is just foolish. Credit card interest is about the highest you can find, so if you need to borrow, find less expensive financing, such as a home equity loan.

One last thing: Open a separate bank account for wedding expenditures. It will help you keep track of how much you're spending and know if you're over budget.

Setting a Budget

And now for the meat-and-potatoes part of this whole experience: You'll need to keep track of every expense related to the wedding, from vendor deposits to facials and manicures—but it's not as hard as it sounds. You can copy the worksheet I've sup-

plied on page 440 in the appendix, create your own chart in Excel, or use one of the many wedding software programs or apps on the market. *Note: These and other similar charts contain a wide range of possible wedding expenses—no one wedding would have all of them.*

If you're creating your own chart, make sure you have a column for estimated cost, another for actual cost, and a third for deposit amount. Leave yourself room for notes regarding deposit due-dates or the cost of upgrades or extras. If you need to trim the budget, you can delete items easily. Once you've settled on an organizational tool, you're going to have to work it into your routine. For some brides, that means saving up receipts and recording purchases once a week, maybe over coffee on Saturday mornings. For others, a more immediate system may work better.

THE TRADITIONAL BUDGET BREAKDOWN

You and your families will need to work out a system that works for you—but if you're curious as to the most traditional way to divvy up the tab, here it is.

GROOM'S SIDE
- Accommodations for the groom's attendants (optional)
- Bride's engagement and wedding rings
- Bride's bouquet, corsages for mothers and other honored family members, and boutonnieres for fathers and men (other than the groom) in the wedding party
- Gift to the bride (optional)
- Gifts to the groom's attendants
- Honeymoon, including transportation to the airport
- Liquor
- Marriage license
- Officiant's fee or gratuity
- Rehearsal dinner (all costs)
- Transportation for the groom and best man to the ceremony
- Transportation or lodging expenses for the officiant if invited by the groom's family
- Transportation and lodging for the groom's parents

BRIDE'S SIDE
- Accommodations for the bride's attendants (optional)
- Gifts to the bride's attendants
- Gift to the groom (optional)
- Bride's gown and accessories
- Bridesmaids' luncheon (two or three days before wedding)
- Church costs, such as the sexton's fee
- Flowers for the ceremony and reception, plus bridesmaids' bouquets and groom's boutonniere
- Groom's ring
- Invitations and other paper goods
- Music at the ceremony and reception
- Photography
- Reception expenses
- Rentals for the ceremony or reception
- Transportation for the bridal party to ceremony and reception
- Transportation or lodging expenses for the officiant if invited by the bride's family
- Videography
- Wedding consultant

It's All Relative . . .

WHATEVER ACCOUNTING METHOD you choose, your budgeting is going to require forethought. If you're working with $30,000, it would be extremely foolhardy to plunk down $20,000 on a venue and $5,000 on a dress you fell in love with on the spur of the moment. That's a drastic example, but you see my point: you can't cover food, music, transportation, and so on with the remaining one-sixth of your budget. Though I do encourage you to allocate funds according to your priorities (within reason, and taking into account your guests' comfort), you also need to think about the big picture. As a very rough guideline, I've included a chart below representing the *average* wedding's budget allotments. Go ahead and sticker this page. You'll want to refer to it as you move ahead with your plans to see how your choices fall in line.

The Splurge Cushion

INEVITABLY, THINGS WILL COST more than you think. Inevitably, you will face temptation, whether it be monogrammed cookies (so sweet!) or the champagne with the finer bubbles. And, yes, inevitably, you will succumb to some of those urges. That's why you should build a 10 percent cushion into your budget—it will also help cover any expenses you overlooked or couldn't have foreseen.

Making Choices

No matter how big or small their budget, every couple has to make decisions about their priorities. Great music might be one couple's top priority; in order to afford the band they want, they'd be happy serving Kentucky Fried Chicken. On the other hand, two foodies who want to serve a five-course meal might be willing to forgo a DJ and use a playlist. But always keep in mind the comfort of your guests. Don't skimp on areas that will leave them hungry, tired, cold, or waiting in a long line for the bathroom.

Here's one good way to gauge how essential something is: Ask yourself, "Will anyone notice if we *don't* have it?" No one is going to grumble, "I can't believe there's no caviar" or "Why aren't the tablecloths silk?"

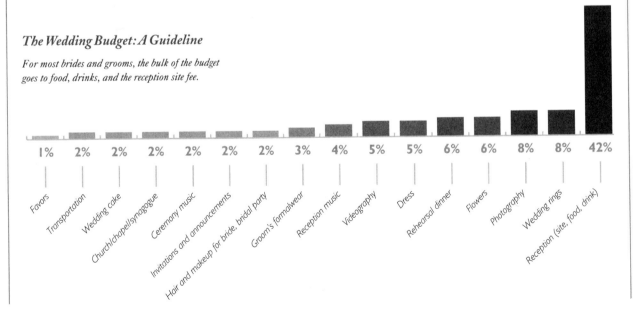

The Wedding Budget: A Guideline

For most brides and grooms, the bulk of the budget goes to food, drinks, and the reception site fee.

Favors	Transportation	Wedding cake	Church/chapel/synagogue	Ceremony music	Invitations and announcements	Hair and makeup for bride, bridal party	Groom's formalwear	Reception music	Videography	Dress	Rehearsal dinner	Flowers	Photography	Wedding rings	Reception (site, food, drink)
1%	2%	2%	2%	2%	2%	2%	3%	4%	5%	5%	6%	6%	8%	8%	42%

The little niceties—monogrammed cocktail napkins, favors—should be the first things to go, because nobody but you will ever know they were in the picture. If you need to cut out the welcome bags, write a welcome note. Just always think: Guests first. If you make this your mantra, people will rave about your wedding for years.

The Ten Best Ways to Cut Costs

OBVIOUSLY, THERE ARE as many ways to scrimp as there are to break the bank. But the key to a great wedding is knowing where to spend and where to save. Here are the ten best ways to keep the bills down without compromising the integrity of the event:

1. Trim the guest list. Your cost per head is your biggest expense.

2. Choose a gorgeous setting, whether it's a conservatory or a Tudor ballroom. You'll save a bundle on decorations.

3. Skip the off-site location and go with a reception site (a hotel, club, or restaurant) that comes with tables, chairs, flatware, and staff. Tents and other rentals add up to a substantial expense.

4. Start the wedding earlier in the day. Breakfast, lunch, afternoon tea, or heavy hors d'oeuvres cost less than dinner, and earlier in the day, people drink less, lowering your liquor costs.

5. Limit the alcoholic offerings to wine, beer, and a signature cocktail. Also consider sangria or punch as a festive but cost-effective alternative to mixed drinks.

6. Move the wedding from Saturday to Sunday; if you need to bring down the price even more, move it to a weekday. Vendors lower their fees for days that are less in demand.

7. Eliminate the champagne toast. Most of the bubbly will be thrown out anyway. Have guests toast with whatever they're drinking at the time.

8. Instead of a band, hire a DJ or have a friend create a playlist.

9. Opt for an inexpensive printing method on your invita-

TIPPER'S TABLE

Some vendors include gratuities in their bills, so read contracts and bills carefully, and keep in mind that these guidelines aren't set in stone. You might choose to add or subtract based on the quality of service, the size and location of your wedding, and the role played by particular vendors. Though in many cases tipping is optional, it is the norm to tip coat check attendants, bartenders, waiters, valet parkers, and drivers. A tip isn't always appropriate for professionals who own their own businesses, but a personal note and a gift—even something as simple as homemade cookies—are always much appreciated.

- *Bartenders:* 10 percent of the total liquor bill (to be split among them)
- *Bathroom attendants:* $1 to $2 per guest
- *Catering manager:* $200+ or a personal gift
- *Chef:* $100+
- *Coat check attendants:* $1 to $2 per guest
- *Hairstylist:* 15 to 20 percent
- *Hotel chambermaids:* $2 to $5 per room; $10 to $15 if you used a suite as your dressing room
- *Limo or bus drivers:* 15 percent
- *Maître d'hôtel or headwaiter:* 1 to 3 percent of food and beverage fee
- *Makeup artist:* 15 to 20 percent
- *Musicians:* 15 percent of fee for ceremony musicians; $25 to $50 per musician for reception
- *Photographer/videographer:* If you're paying a flat fee with no overtime, $100
- *Valet or parking attendants:* $1 to $2 per car; 15 percent for valet parking
- *Waiters:* $20 and up each (distributed by the catering manager or maître d')
- *Wedding planner:* 15 percent of fee or a personal gift

tions. You can get a great effect from offset printing, for a fraction of the price of letterpress or engraving.

10. Skip favors. Write a personal note instead.

The Five Best Splurges

BY THE TIME you invite your parents' friends and hire a band and pay the florist for twenty centerpieces, there's rarely any money left for extras. But should you have the funds, these are the splurges that deliver a lot of bang for your buck:

1. Extra waitstaff at the meal. A hotel or caterer will typically provide 1.5 waiters for every three tables. When staffing is light, one side of the room might be finished eating while some tables are still waiting for their main course. Make it two waiters for every three tables and you'll get much faster service.

2. Professional lighting. Lighting can make a setting come alive by highlighting the standout features in a room and adding dimension. It also casts a flattering glow that makes everyone look great in photos. See chapter 21, "Creating the Look," for more information.

3. Continuous music or an after-hours DJ. Most bands will take three to four breaks throughout the evening, during which they'll typically plug in a playlist. If you can afford the extra fee, they'll add extra musicians and play seamlessly. Or for those younger guests who want to burn up the dance floor late into the night, hire a DJ.

4. Guest menus. A printed menu really ups the ante and makes a wonderful keepsake for your guests.

5. Extra prints. Have your photographer make extra prints you can send out to select guests with your thank-you notes.

Now, was that so hard? I didn't think so. Your budget is not only a way to keep your spending in check, but it's also a handy organizational tool that can help remind you of what's left to be done. But you won't be able to get a sense of how things stack up until you've solidified the two most important elements of your wedding: the date and location. ◆

ASK MINDY

Q I live in an expensive city, and my fiancé and I are trying to save for a down payment on an apartment. Our goal is to have a wedding and a celebration for $5,000, but we've been told that's basically impossible. Help!

A Having a wedding in a church or other place of worship is not that expensive. But once you start adding in food, costs spiral: The more your guests eat, the more they drink. And it's hard to invite them to sit down at a table with no flowers. Well, you see where it goes from there.

So here goes: The only way you can have a wedding with some degree of formality in a major urban center for $5,000 is to invite guests for wine and dessert, no table seating. But that's okay. It will still be your wedding—unique to you—and you can buy your apartment when it's over. You may be able to pull off something more elaborate in a small-town setting and/or with a very small guest list (thirty people or less), so if that's an option, it's something to consider. For the latter, seek out inspiration on sites like intimateweddings.com.

Wedding Seminars

If you can find a wedding planning seminar or bridal fair in your area during the early stages of your engagement, go . . . and take your mother with you. It's a good bonding experience and will help bring your mother up-to-date on wedding trends and styles.

CHAPTER THREE

SETTING THE SCENE FOR YOUR MEMORIES

Your wedding date will be with you for the rest of your life, a sentimental reminder of your union. But it's also a critical decision. The date is the linchpin for so many key steps—you can't firm up commitments for a location, officiant, or other vendors until you have a date—and it also affects your budget. Though in some cultures,

an astrologer, numerologist, priest, or monk chooses a favorable wedding date, for our purposes I'll assume the choice is in your hands (you can always call in an astrologer to serve as a tiebreaker).

Remember that vision you and your fiancé outlined? Now is the perfect time to revisit your dream. Ask yourself what you consider the most important thing about your wedding day. There's no right answer.

For many couples, it's the location, but it could also be an officiant who has known you since childhood, a particularly gifted photographer, or something as personal as carrying lilies of the valley down the aisle. Whatever you come up with should be your first consideration—will the family friend you want to officiate be spending the month of July in the Adirondacks? Will lilies of the valley be unavailable in late August? If your dream is a weekend wedding in Northern California wine country with 100 to 150 guests and an outdoor ceremony, then you'll need to choose a time frame based on the weather (not too cold, not rainy season), then zero in on locations that can handle 150 guests.

Remember that "location" can refer to the location of the ceremony, the reception, or both. Churches book up early, so if you're only going to be happy at one church, that should be your first call. If you know that the only place on earth where you could possibly hold your reception is on the lawn of that charmingly weathered inn on Nantucket where you spent a romantic weekend, you need to find out the dates it's available before doing anything else. And if your friend, the best caterer in town, has offered to cut you a break on her services, you better check on her schedule right away!

Some lucky couples wind up with a choice of dates in their time frame. If that's the case, investigate the second priority on your list (perhaps a photographer whose style you love) or run both dates by your closest friends and family members before making a final decision.

PICKING A DATE

A General Time Frame

How many June weddings have *you* attended? Sometimes it seems as though the whole world has decided to marry in a single month! Why? Well, it actually goes back to ancient Roman tradition. The goddess Juno, after whom the month of June was named, was said to protect those married during her watch.

And June has hung on as the most popular wedding month for over a thousand years, no doubt helped by its warm weather and the plethora of flowers—particularly roses—blooming then. It also follows May, a month traditionally thought to be unlucky for weddings—perhaps because it was the month for planting and sowing the fields, and not one with much time for courtship and celebration. July, August, and September follow close behind,

and October is growing ever more popular. The slowest month is January, with February, March, November, and December tied for second slowest.

Why am I throwing these rankings at you? So you can take into account the relative popularity of the month when deciding on a date. If you're going for a Saturday wedding during one of the top months, know that you'll have to compete to get the location and vendors you want, and you'll need to plan as far in advance as possible. Some couples intentionally opt for one of the slower months, knowing that it will be easier to get their pick of photographers or reception venues. Choosing a slower month can also be a money saver.

> If you're considering a destination wedding in another country (that includes most Caribbean islands), be extra vigilant in researching your date—you don't want your Riviera wedding to fall on France's Labor Day.

Weather accounts for much of the popularity of any given month, but other factors come into play as well. No one factor need absolutely rule out a wedding; I'm simply cautioning you so you don't inadvertently alienate family and friends or select a date when hotel rooms are impossible to come by in your town.

Is it a holiday? Consult a standard calendar first for major holidays. You should do additional research on religious holidays, taking into consideration your faith and the religions of the majority of your guests, or at least your closest friends and family members.

Also consider significant holidays surrounding your date. Holy Week (Palm Sunday through Easter) and any weekend during Passover are not good choices. For Jewish couples, any weekend that overlaps Rosh Hashanah or Yom Kippur is out of the question, but even weddings too close to the High Holidays can pose travel problems for family members. It's also worth a call to your clergy before you make a final decision. Some churches won't hold weddings in late December or during Lent;

Think Twice

Beyond major religious holidays, also consider the ramifications of the following dates. Keep in mind that some holidays are more regional in nature—Columbus and Presidents Day are much more likely to be days off on the East Coast than in the Midwest, and Patriot's Day is a big deal in Boston. Do an online check for any huge local events or conventions on your proposed date—hotel rooms are scarce (and pricey) during the weekend of the New York City Marathon, and it's close to impossible to find a hotel room in Chicago during the National Restaurant Show. If scheduling a wedding during a daylight savings time weekend, be prepared to send out lots of reminders about the time change.

April 1, April Fool's Day

Christmas and the surrounding days

December 7, Pearl Harbor Remembrance Day

Father's Day

Final Four/March Madness

Fourth of July weekend

Friday the 13th

Halloween

Lunar New Year

March 15, the Ides of March

March 17, St. Patrick's Day

Martin Luther King Jr. Day (or weekend before)

Mother's Day

New Year's Day

New Year's Eve

Oscar night

September 11

Super Bowl Sunday

Thanksgiving weekend

Valentine's Day

Weekend before April 15, tax day

you may consider yourself well versed in Jewish traditions but still be surprised to learn that you might not be able to get married on Sukkoth or between Passover and Shabuoth, a seven-week public mourning period in the spring. Muslims usually avoid weddings during the sacred months of Muharram and Ramadan.

Is the date notable for any other reason, good or bad? All dates are connected to something, but it's a good idea to review what happened on that date in history—recent or distant—before deciding.

The Holiday Wedding

I'VE PLANNED Fourth of July weddings, New Year's Eve weddings, St. Patrick's Day weddings, even Purim weddings. Why get married on a holiday? For many couples, it's a convenient way to save guests and family from having to take days off from work.

Week of May 21, 2018

M	T	W	T	F	S	S
30	31	1	2	3	4	5
6	7	8	9	10	11	12
13	14	15	16	17	18	19
20	21	22	23	24	25	26
27	28	29	30	31	1	2

21 Monday
Get Aunt Millie from the airport

22 Tuesday
Call the florist about the delivery

23 Wednesday
Call the airline, confirm the flight

24 Thursday
Dinner at Mom's

25 Friday
Rehearsal dinner, leave at 6 pm

26 Saturday
The Big Day!

27 Sunday

A date makes it all seem much more real.

Valentine's Day Weddings

It's no surprise that February 14 is an enormously popular date for weddings—in Texas, it's typically the number one wedding date of the year. While it does make for a great anniversary date, Valentine's Day presents several major drawbacks as a wedding day.

For one thing, even if you sign a contract many months in advance, flower bills soar into the stratosphere. (It isn't unheard of for prices to triple.) Some florists won't book Valentine's Day weddings at all or will book only on a limited basis, as they expect to be frantically busy with individual orders. Restaurants—typically packed with diners on Valentine's Day—may be reluctant to host a reception or may charge a premium. Because it's such a popular time to get married (even the weekend closest to Valentine's Day is a crowded market), there's heated competition for reception spaces, officiants, bands, photographers, and limousines.

Though the rest of February is one of the slowest times of the year for weddings—and a month when prices may be negotiable—forget getting any kind of break around Valentine's Day. Know, too, that some guests may not take kindly to having their own romantic plans take a backseat to yours. If your wedding is very small or doesn't require much in the way of flowers, the obstacles might be surmountable. Otherwise, think hard before choosing such a competitive, expensive date.

Though a holiday wedding can be festive and handy (he'll never forget your anniversary!), I think it's possible to muddle your wedding date with multiple associations. Your anniversary should be about the day you officially began your lives together as husband and wife, and that's what you should be celebrating in the years to come. A holiday wedding could also get a mixed reception from guests, who may prefer to celebrate the holiday in their own way.

Before making a final decision about any holiday weekend, run it by close family members and friends, especially ones you hope to have in your bridal party.

Because these weekends are so popular for various events and vacations, they're best suited to weddings planned at least a year in advance. If you ultimately decide on a holiday weekend, send save-the-date cards or otherwise get the word out as early as possible.

What's in a Day?

If you've identified a possible time bracket, check out some day-of-the-week strategies.

Saturday is the most popular day of the week for weddings, usually being the most convenient for guests. But because Saturdays are so popular, it's difficult to strike any deals. Churches, reception sites, and vendors book up early on, so it can be quite competitive to get the vendors you really want.

Sunday weddings typically cost less, and there's less heated competition for vendors. Of course, be mindful that your out-of-town guests may have to give up a day of work; avoid the imposition by holding the wedding in the late morning, followed by a luncheon reception.

Don't rule out other days of the week, which can be terrific cost-savers. What better way to kick off a summer weekend than a Friday afternoon wedding? Many weddings begin with a rehearsal dinner on the first evening, are followed by get-togethers and outings the next day, and conclude with an evening ceremony; but go ahead and mix it up. You could hold a Friday wedding and still have everyone gather on Saturday for golf, volleyball, or a clambake.

There's a growing number of Thursday evening weddings in cities like New York, where Thursday is widely considered the "new Friday." Some couples have personal reasons for choosing a certain day of the week. Broadway actors or symphony musicians might choose a Monday night, when the theater or the symphony hall is dark, so that their fellow actors and musicians can attend. Granted, this will be less convenient for your accountant uncle, but when you've got such a wonderfully personal starting point for a wedding, you're already on your way to setting the stage for a warm and special gathering.

Of course, the day of the week may be determined by your religion. Jewish law doesn't allow weddings on the Sabbath, which begins at sundown on Friday and ends at sundown on Saturday. Churches differ in their policies regarding Sunday weddings; some embrace them and others believe they interfere with the day of rest.

PICKING A LOCATION

Find a Place You Love

Once you've got your date, your wedding will seem much more real to you. You're not just getting married anymore, you're getting married on September 21. (How different does *that* sound?) It's time to start the process of narrowing in on venues and signing contracts.

Think about other weddings you've attended and how much the setting influenced the feel. A wedding at an art gallery has a completely different ambience than a beach wedding. Many spaces can, of course, be transformed: A formal ballroom can be turned into a lounge, a 1940s supper club, or a formal indoor garden—but it is always more economical to work *with* the location rather than against it.

And there's so much more to the decision than the ambience. You'll need to evaluate the number of people the site can hold and the total cost of having your event there, taking into account not just the rental fee, but all the auxiliary costs as well. You should also consider your guests' travel expenses and investigate weather and overall convenience.

A House of Worship

If you are considering a ceremony in a house of worship —whether it's a church, synagogue, or mosque—you will most likely need a separate location for your reception. Another thing to know is that churches book up

early (more so than synagogues) and times are often non-negotiable, so you may wind up with a wedding at 3 p.m. If you're planning a reception for 6 p.m., you've got yourself an awkward gap.

The upside of such a break is that it gives the photographer plenty of post-ceremony time with the bridal party, and guests have a chance to change clothes if the two events have different dress codes.

ASK MINDY

Q Within two months of my engagement, my little sister dropped a bomb on us—she's engaged, too, and to make matters worse, she scheduled her wedding a month before mine. I'm so angry I could kill her, and I've even thought of canceling my wedding altogether. Part of me thinks we should just bite the bullet and do a double wedding. It seems ridiculous to invite the same group of guests to two ceremonies such a short time apart. What's entailed in a double wedding? Do you think that's a bad idea?

A Yes, it's definitely a bad idea. You need to have your own memories. There are very few days in your life when you are the star, and this is one that belongs to you and your fiancé. And you just can't have pictures of two brides together! (When we do weddings at hotels I always have a lookout person whose job it is to make sure that my bride doesn't see any other bride that day.)

If your sister isn't willing to change her date, either go ahead with your plan or postpone your wedding for six months, so at least it's a different season, with different flowers, in a different environment.

I don't really get why sisters do this, but it does happen. Underlying jealousy, I guess. Get pregnant first and beat her at her own game!

If there isn't time or a need for the guests to go back to their rooms, the most gracious solution is to fill the gap with some sort of hospitality or entertainment—a tea party at the reception site, for instance. (For one church wedding with a hotel reception, I even set up a casino in one of the ballrooms, complete with faux gaming chips and real prizes for the winners—the guests had a great time and got to go home with their wallets intact!)

The One-Stop Wedding

An integrated ceremony and reception space will make your wedding easier to plan, give you better control over timing and flow, and make things more convenient for your guests. Hotels, private clubs, banquet halls, estates, museums, and wineries are common dual-use venues, and some churches and synagogues also offer reception space.

A single location can also be kinder to your budget. You have only one location rental fee, you don't have to worry about transportation between sites or filling downtime, and it's easier to reuse flowers and other decorative elements from the ceremony at the reception.

A common downside: If such a site hosts multiple parties at once, it can feel a bit like a wedding factory. Make sure to find out whether other weddings are taking place at the same time as yours and factor that into your choice.

If you'll be using the same room for the ceremony and the reception, you'll need to factor in the changeover—the time it takes to transform the room. During this time, you'll generally have cocktails in another area; if, for religious or personal reasons, you're having a dry wedding, you're still likely to need this changeover time, but you can serve an appealing variety of nonalcoholic offerings (see page 135 for details). Places that handle changeovers regularly have it down to a science, but you'll need to make sure they're planning on enough staff to remake the room within an hour. When cocktail hour turns into ninety minutes, guests get antsy and your bar and appetizer bills escalate.

A lovely and budget-friendly gesture is to offer guests refreshments when they leave the church. Think fresh lemonade and juice spritzers, cupcakes with pastel frosting, or cookies decorated to look like wedding cakes.

Entertaining guests for the entire gap may be beyond your budget. If the reception is at a hotel where many guests are staying, a hospitality room where they can gather during the downtime doesn't have to cost much, especially if you're allowed to stock it from outside sources like a warehouse club. You can account for some of the time gap by stretching cocktail hour at your reception site to an hour and a half, but the extra drinks and appetizers you'll be serving during that time will add to your costs.

Speaking of timing: Many churches are very strict about starting on time. If you're someone who is perpetually late, you'd be better off with a ceremony site where the start time is a little more relaxed. I've done Catholic weddings where a late bride meant that the couple didn't get their full mass! These are the types of situations you want to avoid whenever possible, so know yourself and your limitations.

A Hotel

The hotel wedding is a perennial favorite, and with good reason. It's the easiest type of event to arrange, and it wins my nomination for "Most Likely to Run Smoothly." Although there is no such thing as a glitch-free, hitch-free event, hotels present the fewest risks, since their staff are pros at handling weddings.

One of the biggest advantages of a hotel is that nearly everything you need is already there, from the tables to the dance floor to the employees who will staff the wedding. If you run short on plates at the buffet, there are undoubtedly more to be had. There are likely to be multiple spaces you can adapt to your needs for the ceremony, the reception, and cocktail hour. If a fuse blows, there's an engineer on staff to fix it.

All of this comes at a price, which is built into the cost of food and beverages—many hotels have a minimum food and beverage charge. Aside from the catering and bar, you can usually bring in your own vendors, but make sure to ask, as some hotels require you to use their florist or lighting staff. When comparing the cost of a hotel wedding to that of an off-site wedding, compare the total price tag attached to the event, not simply the cost per meal. A catered meal should cost substantially less than a hotel's, but the caterer's price doesn't include the cost of china, flatware, tables, linens, glassware, or labor, all of which (and more) are included in the hotel fee.

If there's a negative about hotel weddings, it's that they can feel impersonal, particularly if the ballrooms are nondescript and the property puts a heavy emphasis on meetings and conventions. The good news is that any room can be totally transformed. The walls and ceiling can be draped in fabric to create a tentlike feel, unattractive chairs can be hidden under chair covers, and you can add texture to a square room with trees or an undulating wall of flowers. But there is an absolute correlation between the drama of the transformation and the size of the budget required to pull it off.

There *are* ways to personalize the occasion without upping your costs. A hotel chef is usually willing to make a family recipe, whether it's your grandmother's Italian wedding soup or your Filipino uncle's pancit. And do some research: If the hotel you're considering has multiple ballrooms, look at how they're positioned and find out the numbers of other weddings taking place there on the same day as yours. You don't want your guests to have to pass three other receptions on their way to the bathroom.

Another plus: A good hotel catering manager can make your life easier. Catering managers are familiar with many of the local vendors for flowers, linen rentals, and cakes. Some hotels and resorts retain their own wedding coordinators: If they're top-notch, they can fill the role of a wedding planner. Find out who your contact person will be and how involved she will be on the day of the wedding. How long does he plan to stay at the event to ensure that everything is running smoothly? Most stay until the entrée is served, at which point the captain takes over. Some very upscale hotels actually require couples to hire

Booking Space for the Rehearsal

While you're booking your ceremony location, try to book time for the rehearsal as well. In theory, it should take place one or two nights before the wedding, but many venues have set times when they permit rehearsals. (Don't hold it too early or people are likely to forget what they're supposed to do.) If you can't get access to the space until the day of the wedding, hold the rehearsal in the morning.

Aim to hold the rehearsal at the ceremony site so that participants can see the length of the aisle, where they'll wait before they go down the aisle, and where they'll stand during the ceremony. At off-site and outdoor weddings, the space may not be ready the day before—use an extra room or outdoor area at the rehearsal dinner site, or hold the rehearsal in a park or someone's backyard.

independent wedding planners. (Since a high-end wedding requires a ton of personal attention, these hotels are wisely ensuring that they're not overstretching their staff while giving their clients the best possible experience.)

A Restaurant

Best suited to weddings of 125 or fewer guests, restaurants are often chosen for superb food, a distinctive setting, or a special ambience—all of which can make for a chic and intimate wedding. Some restaurants may have a patio, courtyard, or other space that lends itself to a ceremony, but most commonly, the ceremony is held elsewhere and the reception follows at the restaurant.

The downsides: Your guests might be spread over multiple rooms, and space limitations often preclude a large dance floor.

On the plus side, a restaurant can deliver great food, usually less expensively than a hotel (the restauranteur will have you choose from a couple of preset meals). Whether it's a Tuscan villa, a southern mansion, or a Victorian conservatory, the look will be particularly distinctive. With features like French doors, dark wood floors, or sculptural chandeliers already in place, you'll be buying into a concept you adore, which is always a money saver, rather than trying to create one from scratch.

If you're taking over the entire restaurant, the owner will typically expect you to match the revenues he would bring in on a regular business day. And don't be surprised if you still need some rentals. A restaurant doesn't usually deliver a hundred servings of soup at a time, so you may have to rent some bowls.

An "Off-Site" Wedding

First, a bit of wedding lingo: Whether it's indoors or out, an event is considered "off-site" if the place doesn't have a commercial kitchen or stock items like tables, linens, china, and flatware. The setting could be anything from an estate, a beach, or a park to an urban loft or cultural center. Open fields are common wedding spaces in rural areas where ballrooms or large indoor spaces are nonexistent. A home wedding is almost always considered off-site, unless it is such a small event that you don't need to bring in rentals.

Off-site weddings can be gorgeous, but (counterintuitively) can come at a high price. An off-site location means bringing in everything you'll need, from ice cubes to chandeliers—not to mention tables, chairs, china, linens, and lighting. Often you'll need to construct one or more tents, which entails floors, portable toilets, and generators. You may need to rent the site for additional days to cover the setup time (particularly if you're building subfloors for the tent). Depending on the location, you may need to obtain a municipal permit or monitor some very un-bridelike concerns: tide times, lawn watering, and the ins-and-outs of bug control.

Find out from the site whether you must use a particular vendor or work from an approved list of vendors. Inquire about any restrictions; art museums often limit the areas that can be used and the beginning and ending times for the event. Find out how long you get the space for and what the additional fees are if you need more time for setup and knockdown. You'll also need to look into whether the rental fee covers insurance or whether you will need to purchase extra. (For more information about insurance, see chapter 12, "Making It Legal.")

The Great Outdoors

An outdoor wedding can be absolutely magical. It won't look like any other wedding, and for many, there's no space more sacred than nature. Another bonus: No photographer's trick can match the glow of a sunset against the smiling faces of your family and closest friends.

If you're planning a year or more out, try to visit the site during the same month and at the same time of day that you're envisioning your wedding. This will give you a taste of the weather, the light, the foliage, the flowers, and the insect situation. (You may discover that your dream site in New Hampshire is under siege by blackflies in June.) Do an Internet search for the average temperature and rainfall for that time of year, and check out what allergens are typically in the air.

The cardinal rule for outdoor weddings is to have a backup strategy. Rain, high winds, extreme heat or cold, and bug infestations are just a few of the tricks nature can dish out to foil your plans.

You might be thinking a back-to-nature wedding will simplify your planning and lower your costs, but costs can actually add up quickly. On the other hand, outdoor weddings tend to have a playful, magical quality you just can't re-create indoors. An improvisational approach can work wonders—that willow tree off to the side can make an excellent canopy for your guest-book table, and a neighboring hedge might make a wall for your outdoor "room."

Before you commit to an outdoor wedding, consider your personality. Make sure you can handle the uncertainty that comes with an unpredictable location. If you must have every detail under your control, if you can't laugh off frizzy hair or mud stains, if you have difficulty making last-minute changes, you'd probably be happier with a more controlled environment. (For more information on the rentals often involved in outdoor weddings, see chapter 11, "The Nitty-Gritty.")

Home, Sweet Home

A SENTIMENTAL FAVORITE, the home wedding is personal and intimate. You won't see any other brides in the halls. You can choose any day and time you like. If privacy is a concern, it's a top choice (when major celebrities want to pull off secret weddings, they often go the at-home route).

If you're taken with the idea of a home wedding but there isn't a suitable property in your family, you might consider renting a home. If you're lucky, a close friend or relative with a spacious home might offer to host.

Like outdoor weddings, home weddings tend to have hidden costs. Sure, there's no rental fee, but you're going to need the same equipment you would for an off-site reception—tables, chairs, china, glassware, and, depending on the size of your wedding, portable bathrooms and generators. You might wind up constructing a tent in the backyard or installing landscape lighting, taking out extra insurance on your home, or hiring valet parkers. Expect some fix-up costs like cleaning bills for the carpets

What does your version of paradise look like?

and upholstery, paint touch-ups, and minor repairs after the wedding. If it's within your means to hire a one-time consultant, have a professional caterer evaluate the home to make sure it will work for your wedding size and advise on the kitchen setup. Even professional-style home kitchens often can't accommodate all the people it takes to cook, plate, and serve your food, which is why caterers sometimes create a kitchen in the garage.

Now that I've disabused you of the notion that at-home weddings are practically free, let me tell you about their biggest budget bonus: You can buy the alcohol yourself through a liquor store, cutting the bar bill in half (sometimes even more) and actually upgrading the quality of the product. To increase your savings, shop around for a store that lets you return unopened bottles.

The Destination Wedding

Since destination weddings involve some amount of travel, they also tend to last longer than the average wedding: Festivities might go on for two to three days. Because of the degree of planning involved in a destination wedding, I've devoted a special appendix to the topic (see page 417), but here are some preliminary considerations to help you assess whether such a wedding is a good match for you.

Typically, you're essentially taking care of guests from the moment they arrive until they depart. You might be coordinating everything from airport transportation to a welcome party, activities during the day, the wedding itself, and the reception, plus a day-after brunch—and possibly more. You may find yourself negotiating airline and hotel rates, assembling welcome gift baskets, matching up foursomes for golf, booking spa appointments, and printing detailed, individualized itineraries for guests.

Assuming you're inviting people outside of your immediate family, a destination wedding requires a lot of lead time, so it's not a good choice if you're working with a short engagement (though if the wedding is limited to a few close family members, you have a lot more latitude). Full information packets should go out six to eight months before the wedding. If a prime holiday weekend is involved, you should get save-the-date cards out even earlier.

LOCATION 411

Whenever you visit a potential site, take notes and photos to help jog your memory. Places will blur together rapidly, especially with everything you've got on your mind! At each location, whether it's for the ceremony, the reception, or both, you should ask the following questions.

☐ How many people can the space hold? Be clear about whether that number represents standing or seated guests.

☐ Are there any restrictions on event times, what I can and can't serve (some locations may not permit alcohol), or who can officiate? Are there any other restrictions that haven't been mentioned?

☐ Can I use any vendors I want, or must I work from an approved list or with in-house service providers?

☐ If there's a rental fee, what does it cover and for what time period? What does the rental fee exclude?

☐ When do I get access to my site for the setup? If you're planning to install extensive decorations, you may need access the day before.

☐ What type of deposit is required, when is the balance due, and what is the cancellation policy? Always read the contract before committing to a location!

☐ If you're planning an event with an outdoor element (even a cocktail hour on a hotel terrace), what is the location's backup plan in case of bad weather?

☐ Is my date available? Are there any other weddings that day?

☐ Is there a place at the site for the bridal party to get dressed? Are there separate rooms for the bride and groom and their attendants? Are they included in the fee? Look at the rooms to make sure they meet your needs. If there isn't a room, you'll have to make arrangements to get dressed elsewhere.

☐ Are there restrictions on photography or videography? Applies mostly to houses of worship, but a museum may also have areas where flash photography is not allowed.

☐ Can I see the plate, glassware, and linen selection? Renting your own will significantly alter your budget projections.

☐ If the ceremony and reception are to be held in the same space, how long does the location need for the changeover (the time it takes to convert the space)?

☐ Is there sufficient parking for my guests? Will I need to arrange for valet parking, or off-site parking and a shuttle?

☐ Are any permits required? Who obtains them?

☐ Are there any noise restrictions? Are there residences close by that might be disturbed by a live band or DJ at night?

☐ Is any specific type of insurance required?

☐ Are there sufficient bathrooms, or will I need to bring porta-potties in?

☐ Is there enough power at the site, or will I have to supply a generator?

☐ Are there any other rules that haven't been covered? It's hard to conjure up every possibility, so ask this question in an open-ended way. I know of hotels that require you to work with a wedding planner, venues that specify you use their in-house florist, estates where you must arrange for valet parking, beaches and parks with detailed rules about garbage removal, and properties that require you to hire security. Many places have specific rules about where and how candles can be used.

☐ What form of payment does the location accept?

While a destination wedding tends to be pricey for guests, it isn't necessarily ultraexpensive for the hosts. Nothing affects costs more than head count, and destination weddings are traditionally small affairs. An entire weekend in a beautiful setting lets you play a theme to the hilt, so if you're detail oriented and like to include lots of personalized touches, nothing will let you do it better than a destination wedding.

One of the most frequent questions I get about this type of wedding is who pays for the bridal party and the guests to attend. As with any other wedding, guests and bridal party members attend at their own expense, though you may want to help out the bridal party by covering some or all of their airfare, hotel room, and wedding attire. Some people with the means to do so fly in all of their guests and pay for their hotel rooms, but this is, understandably, not something most of us can afford.

If you're not in that fortunate minority, consider which people you most want at your wedding and whether they're likely to be able to afford to attend. Also consider mobility issues among older relatives and whether your choice of location might prevent them from being at your wedding. If your dream location is going to keep some of your most cherished guests away, maybe you're better off with a less exotic wedding closer to home—it could still be a weekend-long event, and you can save the dream location for your honeymoon.

For planning purposes, count on making at least one trip to the destination prior to the wedding, though some couples go two or three times. In any case, you'll need someone who can act as a liaison with the local vendors. Your hotel may be able to help out; if not, you'll probably need a wedding coordinator.

Another thing to take into account are local customs and the availability of goods and resources. If you're planning a wedding on a tropical island or in Mexico, you'll have to accept that everyone works on "island time," which can be frustrating, even infuriating, for a type A urbanite. Your choices in flowers, cakes, and music might be limited, so you have to be flexible. Oh, and one more thing: If you don't like to travel, *please* save yourself the headache and plan a wedding closer to home.

CEREMONY SITE

The following location questions apply exclusively to the ceremony site.

- What are the restrictions on flowers and other decorations?

- Is an aisle runner provided? Is an aisle runner permitted? (Some churches don't allow them.)

- Are there fees for the organist, soloist, choir, or musicians? Is there a customary fee or donation for the minister, priest, or rabbi, and how is that handled? Is there a fee for the sexton (the church groundskeeper)?

- Can the flowers customarily used in the church be removed?

- Will a traffic officer outside the church be necessary or required?

- Who is the contact for the florist, photographer, and other vendors?

Guest Accommodations

As you're going through the process of choosing a venue, you should also be keeping an eye out for places where your out-of-town guests can stay.

If you're having a destination wedding at a resort, the whole crowd should stay at the same place or they won't feel like part of the festivities. Otherwise, whenever possible, you want to offer guests choices in a few different price ranges. Also make sure to offer lodgings that appeal to your parents' friends as well as your own. While your friends might love a place that celebrates retro motel chic and has a lively bar by the pool, your aunts and uncles might be much happier at a more predictable, full-service hotel where they can be sure to get a good night's sleep.

Soon after you choose the location, you'll want to reserve blocks of rooms. If part of your wedding is taking place at a hotel, a staff catering manager or wedding coordinator can assist you. Otherwise, call the sales department to negotiate a group rate. Typically, you have to book at least ten rooms to get a discounted rate. If you're holding your reception, rehearsal dinner, or other wedding-related events at the hotel—especially if these represent significant expenditures—you'll have better leverage for negotiating a deeper discount. (This is not the moment to get shy—no one is going to offer you a special rate if you don't ask. At the same time, you're going to be working with these people for months, so you don't want to get an early reputation for being difficult.) The rooms will be held at that rate until a set date, at which point any that aren't booked will be released.

Let guests know about the rooms you've booked on your website and your save-the-date cards (see page 63).

Now that you've got the parameters in place, it's time to start filling in the gaps. To do that, you've got to assemble the team of knowledgeable experts who'll be filling your wedding day with flowers, food, music, and more. It's time to start meeting vendors. ♦

CHAPTER FOUR

Building Your Team

THE PEOPLE WHO WILL MAKE IT HAPPEN

Whether you've got the means to assemble an army of helpers or are working on a do-it-yourself budget, you're going to need help pulling off a full-scale wedding. But how do you gather your team? Brides often feel as if they're flying blind. How do you find a high-quality florist when you've never done more than grab a bunch of daisies

at your local deli? Well, your catering manager might be able to help you find a great one—so it's important to get your hiring priorities straight. Your first consideration should be whether you want a wedding planner, since she will guide you through the process of selecting your vendors. Even if you do know you will be working with a planner, you should still read this section to be sure

you're asking the right questions and covering all your bases in your vendor contracts.

Too often I see couples throw a wrench in things by taking a high-handed attitude or working with their vendors in a disorganized way. Follow my advice on working with vendors and, chances are, they'll bend over backward to deliver the wedding of your dreams.

The first rule for choosing vendors is to avoid those who suggest that your budget isn't sufficient. The planning process should be about taking your ideas and making them work. Another thing to be wary of is vendors with such a strong outlook that they're really not interested in your opinion. If you admire the person's vision, then it's usually fine; but if you find yourself feeling intimidated, that's not the relationship you want.

A WEDDING PLANNER

What Is a Wedding Planner, Anyway?

Part gal pal, part mother, part shopping buddy, a wedding planner should be a gifted organizer, diplomat, time-management guru, psychologist, and style consultant. Some planners have specialties, like floral design. I'm full service—I really care about creating a complete experience—and I think for most people that's the most useful kind of planner.

As recently as twenty years ago, a wedding consultant was viewed as an indulgence reserved for the rich. But as weddings have become more involved, more costly, and filled with more choices, the need for someone to manage it all has increased. Contributing to the need for help are couples with demanding jobs, brides who don't live in the same town as their mothers, and the increase in destination weddings.

Although a planner represents a significant cost, she can frequently find you better deals than you could get on your own and can come up with creative ways to allow you to achieve your dream wedding within your budget. You will get better service. As a wedding client, you are a one-shot deal, but a wedding planner is a repeat customer, so vendors have an incentive to do a better job for her. They often throw in some nice extras and work harder for you.

A planner should also be able to save you from costly mistakes and cut down on overtime charges. You see a

photographer's contract that allows for eight hours of shooting time on the wedding day, and you probably think that's plenty for a six-hour event—I know better. Most weddings require more time, and a planner will negotiate for it up front so you won't be left with a tough choice about overtime on your wedding day. Conversely, your father might be twitching for a twelve-piece band, but I can look at the size of your space and guest list and tell you that that much sound is going to blow out the room.

Best of all, a planner makes everything happen on your wedding day. With her running the show and serving as the point person for all of the vendors, you get to enjoy your day to its fullest.

Planners, Designers, Coordinators—Oh My!

As you've probably noticed, there is a fair amount of flexibility within the wedding world as to who does what—sometimes a florist or a catering manager can play quite a strong organizational role. Still, there are distinct categories, even within the world of wedding planners.

An *event designer* might play the role of a planner but probably has more experience transforming a space into an Arabian Nights fantasy than creating time lines and schedules. If you're looking to an event designer for full-service planning, ask specific questions about his experiences, the services he offers, and who will handle what.

Many full-service wedding planners also offer truncated versions of their services. A *partial-event planner* gives advice and vendor recommendations on an hourly basis. Similarly, a *day-of coordinator* will give you a specific number of hours for a set fee and, despite her job title, will typically see you for two meetings prior to the wedding; she should be in attendance at the rehearsal and the wedding itself.

For the DIY set, there are *wedding libraries*, upscale, by-appointment-only boutiques where couples can review portfolios from photographers, florists, invitation designers, and cake makers. There is no charge, but the library most likely will receive fees for referrals or for representing the vendors.

A Planner's Services

The services offered by planners cover a huge range. Some planners (including me) will do the big-picture design stuff and the teensy-weensy details, like bringing an extra pair of shoes to the wedding in case someone forgets theirs or a strap breaks. All planners will help you time the flow of the wedding and make sure the elements come together, and that nothing important has been overlooked. Here are some of the concrete things a planner might offer her clients.

- Recommending, hiring, dealing with, and confirming vendors
- Setting up a budget
- Keeping track of deposit due dates and nudging you when it's time to pay up
- Helping you get your legal documents in order
- Assisting the rehearsal dinner hosts with planning and execution
- Coming with you to shop for a gown, bridesmaids' dresses, and groomsmen's attire

- Selecting or designing invitations (some planners will address and send them out for you, some won't)
- Putting together the look of the wedding, from flowers to tabletops
- Making musical recommendations and helping with menus
- Booking hotel rooms
- Working through the processional and recessional
- Creating welcome bags and favors

- Arranging transportation
- Creating a wedding day schedule

. . . and so much more. A full-service planner might even help you through difficult family situations; she'll certainly be there on your wedding day with all those little things you might have forgotten to bring—a pen, an emergency kit, and years of experience.

Finding a Wedding Planner

A TOP-NOTCH HOTEL is one of the best sources for great planners. Even if you're not considering using the hotel as a venue, call the catering manager, who witnesses dozens of weddings a year. Tell him that you're a big admirer of the hotel; that you've just gotten engaged; and that you're wondering if he could recommend some local planners. He should be useful to you even if you have no idea whether you want a wedding in Nebraska, in Hawaii, or at the inn down the street—many planners, especially those at the higher end, handle both local and destination weddings.

Other vendors may also have an inside track on good planners. Don't hesitate to seek recommendations from any vendor you know (that includes your friend who works part-time for a caterer) or whose work you've admired at other events.

You can also get referrals to planners from the Association of Bridal Consultants and the Association for Wedding Professionals International. (A caveat: Many of the top-tier planners do not belong to associations like these, so double-check your findings against another source.) A simple web search for "wedding planner" and the name of your location will also turn up results; check out the planners' websites to get an idea of their work.

How Much Will It Cost Me?

FEES MAY BE structured in several ways. Some planners charge a flat fee based on your plans. A standard fee is often based on eighty hours of service and will go up as much as 15 percent for an off-site wedding. The same goes for a destination wedding, and you'll need to pay expenses for the planner's scouting trips and wedding travel.

Though a significant number of planners base their fees on a percentage of the entire cost of your wedding (typically 15 percent to 20 percent), I think it's best to find a planner who bases her charges on the job, rather than the budget—that way you won't run into planners whose incentive is to sell up at every turn.

Fees span an enormous range, and as with any other service, you get what you pay for. A planner charging $2,000 to handle your entire wedding will help hook you up with vendors but isn't likely to go to every meeting, every tasting, and every fitting. She's also likely to stick with a tried-and-true formula instead of venturing out

The best days to reach a planner are Tuesdays, Wednesdays, and Thursdays. Fridays are hectic preparing for rehearsal dinners and weekend weddings, and many planners use Mondays to regroup after working for most of the weekend. (I make it a point to return all calls on Mondays, but every planner works differently.) Don't even think of trying to reach a planner on weekends. If she can take your call then, she's not busy enough!

of the box. At the high end, planners are under pressure to justify the fee by making the wedding dazzling and original. They offer many more levels of customization—they'll design invitations instead of picking them out of a book, or they'll find a special box to mail them in and track down postage stamps that fit the theme.

The Planner's Contract

FIRST THINGS FIRST: Read the contract. If there's anything you don't understand, call for clarification. Take a look at my standard contract (opposite page) to familiarize yourself with the terrain.

The contract should specify how many hours of work are included in the fee and how overtime is

Is a Wedding Planner Right for Me?

Though most every bride can benefit from the help of a planner, these situations call for one more than others.

- **Destination weddings.** It's no coincidence that 25 percent of those embarking on destination weddings hire a planner.

- **Weddings at an off-site location**—meaning any location where you're dealing with tents and all manner of rentals. This includes a home wedding, since you'll have to adapt the home and grounds to accommodate a crowd.

- **Large weddings** (more than two hundred guests). More people equal more work.

- **Difficult family dynamics.** The planner can serve as a neutral point person, negotiator, and mediator.

- **Inflexible work schedule.** If you can't devote ten hours a week to wedding planning for the first two months, five hours a week for the next few months, and ten to twenty hours a week for the last ten weeks before the wedding, a planner could be a lifesaver.

- **Organizational phobia.** If organization isn't your strong suit, a planner can be a godsend.

handled. (See clause 2, opposite.) It should include the number of staffers the planner will provide at the wedding. If you're expecting the name planner (as opposed to an associate) to attend the wedding, get that spelled out in the contract.

The deposit amount and due date should also be specified, as should the due date for the balance.

Though a planner will help you find and hire vendors, note that it's the couple, not the planner, who signs the contracts with the vendors. The planner assumes no liability if a vendor doesn't deliver. (See clause 5, opposite.)

Sample Contract

This is a general contract I use for simple parties. If your planner's contract is already leaving you confused or if you are working with someone informally and want to draft an agreement, this should be a helpful point of reference.

This Special Event Consultant Agreement ("Agreement") is entered into by and between ("Client") and Mindy Weiss Party Consultants ("MWPC")

1. SERVICES. Client desires to hold a special event and MWPC agrees to provide professional event planning consulting services for this event.

2. TERMS. MWPC agrees to provide Client with eighty (80) hours of consulting services for a base price of _____ dollars ($____). Services provided by representatives of MWPC in excess of the base number of eighty (80) hours will be paid by Client, in addition to the base fee, at the rate of _____ dollars ($____) per hour. The above base fee includes three experienced and qualified representatives from MWPC at the event from commencement to completion of the event. The representative will be Mindy Weiss and/or a representative unless otherwise agreed to with Client. MWPC will provide design concepts for the event and develop and implement a schedule for the event. All costs and expenses incurred by MWPC for planning events outside the Los Angeles limits as defined by MWPC, including but not limited to, long distance telephone bills, travel, daily per diem, and lodging, will be paid for by Client. Lodging for MWPC staff shall not exceed a daily rate of _____ dollars ($____) per night unless agreed upon with Client.

3. FEES AND DEPOSIT. A non-refundable deposit equal to fifty percent (50%) of the base consulting fee is to be paid upon execution of this Agreement. The full balance of the unpaid base consulting shall be received by MWPC no later than ten (10) days prior to the date of the event. If the event is held outside the Los Angeles limits, the full balance shall be received by MWPC within ten (10) days prior to the event or prior to MWPC's departure for the event, whichever is sooner. At the time the balance is paid in full to MWPC, Client shall also pay for the estimated costs of travel and lodging, if the same are required by MWPC. The actual costs and expenses incurred for events held outside the Los Angeles limits will be determined upon completion of the event. For all weddings, fees exclude consulting services for bridal showers and engagement parties unless specifically included in base fee by MWPC and Client. Rehearsal dinners and brunches are included in the coordination fee.

4. INDEMNITY. Client agrees to indemnify, defend and hold harmless MWPC and Mindy Weiss including their officers, directors, employees, agents and heirs and assigns, from any and all liability, costs, damages and attorneys' fees resulting from or relating to any claims in any way connected with this event, except to the extent of any negligence or misconduct by MWPC, its employees or agent. This indemnity, defense and hold harmless provision extends to any damages caused by the Client or the Client's guests or attendees in connection with the event.

5. VENDORS. MWPC agrees to recommend vendors for such needs as rentals, catering, floral design, photography and entertainment; assist in vendor selection; assist in negotiations with vendors if desired by Client; and supervise vendor performance at events. However, the final selection in hiring any vendor is at the sole discretion and responsibility of the Client. MWPC assumes no responsibility in any way for any negligence, non-performance or other misconduct by hired vendors. Each vendor contract with Client will be subject to review and approval by Client.

6. LOSS BY GUESTS. MWPC assumes no responsibility for damages or losses incurred by the Client or Client's guests or attendees at the event. MWPC also assumes no responsibility for any food, beverages, floral arrangements, décor or items, either personal or professional, or any other items whatsoever brought by anyone to the event prior to, during, or after the event. Client agrees to be solely responsible for all guests and attendees at the event and the acts of the guests and attendees. Client agrees to pay for any and all damages arising out of the event, except to the extent of any negligence or misconduct by MWPC, its employees or agents.

7. INTERVENTION OR TERMINATION OF EVENT. If MWPC is unable to provide services under this Agreement for reasons outside of its control; including but not limited to termination of the event by the Client, for any reason including bad weather conditions; acts of God; or government intervention, Client will not be entitled to any refund of the consulting fees due under this Agreement.

8. LIMITATIONS ON DAMAGES. In any action or legal proceeding of any kind brought by Client against MWPC for any alleged negligence or any other form of misconduct on the part of MWPC, its employees, or agents in connection with a claim for any failure to provide consulting services or for providing consulting services in a matter unsatisfactory to Client under this Agreement, in no case shall MWPC's liability exceed the amount paid by Client under this Agreement.

WITH THE SIGNATURES OF THE PARTIES HERETO, THIS DOCUMENT BECOMES A BINDING LEGAL INSTRUMENT

Client _____ Date _____

Mindy Weiss Party Consultants _____

THE WEDDING PLANNER

Choosing a wedding planner has a lot to do with compatibility. You're entrusting a lot to this person, so go with your gut—you should like her! And you should like her style, too, so make sure you can see yourself, or some version approaching it, in her promotional materials and samples. At your first meeting, make sure you cover all your bases. Here's a list of helpful questions.

- *When did you start doing weddings? How many did you plan last year?*

- *How many weddings do you book in a day? In a weekend? If you book more than one per day, will you be at my wedding? Ideally, you want a planner who books one wedding per day, but that's not always an option. And you want the person you've been working with to be the reassuring face you see at your wedding. If she won't be at your wedding, find out who will be.*

- *Will you be at the rehearsal?*

- *How many staffers will you have at the wedding? The answer will depend on the size of your guest list, but what you're trying to determine is whether she has an effective staffing strategy.*

- *For a destination wedding, ask when she'll arrive and how long she'll stay. Some planners leave once the final brunch is set up—there's nothing wrong with that, but it shouldn't come as a surprise to you.*

- *What is your fee and how much is required as a deposit? When is the remainder due?*

- *Precisely what services are included in the fee? What isn't included? You may find out that showers and bachelorette parties are not included in the fee.*

- *If it's an hourly fee, how often am I billed?*

- *Beyond the planner's fee, are there expenses for which I will be billed?*

- *Can you provide three references? Ideally you want to talk with other brides she has worked with, not clients from corporate events or birthday parties.*

THE VENDORS

In Search of the Best

I t's likely you'll have few contacts as you embark on the search for vendors. Not to worry. There are multiple ways to make inroads into the wedding network, and once you're in, you'll find it easier to connect with other talents.

Start by gathering recommendations from your wedding planner (if you're using one), your point person at your reception location (usually a catering manager), and from friends and family members who recently got married. The more you like someone's taste, the more these recommendations are worth. If you have any friends or contacts in any related businesses who interact with vendors, tap them for recommendations—a friend who works in the restaurant or catering business could be a great resource for florists, cake makers, bands, and DJs.

Look up the websites of any prominent local vendors. If you find one that makes you take notice, check to see if the site offers links to other vendors. They're likely to share a similar aesthetic and to offer a similar level of quality.

Do you have a florist who comes up with amazing arrangements every time you call? Then feel free to abandon my prioritized vendor contact list (see opposite page) and talk to him first. If the florist's style exemplifies what you're looking for, chances are he'll be part of a network of like-minded vendors.

Whether your wedding is local or far-flung, don't forget to check in with the hotel concierge, even if you've already spoken with the catering department. Sometimes the concierge has additional resources; if you're booking a block of rooms at the hotel, he should be happy to help.

Be creative in how you think about sources for referrals. Weddings aren't the only events that rely on florists, bands, and linen-rental companies. So if your fiancé's aunt is on countless committees for charitable fund-raisers, you can be sure she'll know that Amoré Flowers won't touch a centerpiece for less than $200.

Order, Order!

THERE'S AN ART to the order of booking your vendors, some of which is based on the importance of the service to the wedding (that's why the officiant is way up there), some on how many weddings the vendor can handle in a day, and some on old-fashioned supply and demand. Photographers come way before florists simply because a single photographer can commit to only one wedding on a given day (although a large photography studio may have a stable of photographers), but a major florist can book several events for the same day.

First Priority

Planner. If you've decided to hire a planner, she'll recommend vendors directly.

Officiant. If there's a special officiant you want for your wedding, this becomes your first call.

Photographer. Many of the top photographers, particularly the independent photojournalist types, book only one wedding a day—or one wedding a weekend, for a destination wedding. With so few slots available, the good photographers book up very early, sometimes more than a year in advance.

Caterer. They can only handle a limited number of events in a given weekend. The more you care about the food, the higher your caterer moves up your list.

Reception band or DJ. Because they are so important to creating the mood of the event, they get snapped up early. The competition for bands comes not only from other weddings but also from fund-raisers and corporate parties.

Second Priority

Videographer. Some planners give the videographer higher priority, but I find there are enough good ones around that it doesn't hurt to wait a bit. Many of the video companies have a number of cameramen on call, so they can book several events in the same weekend.

Florist. A large florist can handle several events in a weekend. If you're booking eight or nine months in advance, you should be able to get your choice of florists.

Cake maker. Should you want to hire a specialty cake designer, get on his schedule. The top ones limit the number of cakes they make in a week, and they won't bake ahead and freeze cakes. Commercial bakers do bake ahead, allowing them to turn out more cakes in a weekend; you can book them later in the process.

Hairstylist. The most talented stylists book up early, and those who come to you can generally handle only one wedding a day.

Transportation. The availability of limos, shuttles, and other vehicles depends on the locale and the season. If it's spring (prom season), book your limo earlier.

Third Priority

Invitation designer. If you're having invitations custom designed, you want to start the process about four months before the wedding.

Ceremony musicians. There's no shortage of talented classical musicians, so you can usually wait until a few months before the wedding to put down your deposit.

Lighting company. They set up ahead of time and can handle multiple events in a day.

Makeup artist. Most brides want a classic look for their wedding—which the average makeup artist can handle. There are many deft makeup artists, so unless you're attached to a particular person, you should be able to find one a few months before your wedding.

A Picture Speaks a Thousand Words

No matter what type of bride you are, one piece of advice remains constant: Find and save photos you love from across the web, the world of bridal, craft, and design magazines, and beyond. Seek out and collect pieces of visual information that convey something about how you want your wedding to look and feel. That could mean the whimsical ombré wedding cake or elegant crossback dress that catches your eye, or a flower, color, landscape, or room that reflects a particular mood. The social media feeds of wedding planners and vendors are obvious places to visit, but a site or magazine dedicated to a hobby or personal interest of the bride or groom (think travel, horses, gardening, collecting) can become another source of inspiration.

Over the past few years, Pinterest has emerged as a particularly useful tool for wedding planning. Bursting with ideas and easy to use, the site is both a virtual scrapbook and a place for discovery. I tell the brides I work with to start pinning everything they love in the early stages of the process—but often they've already been doing just that. Where brides and grooms used to bring me magazine clippings, now they show me their Pinterest boards, which I find incredibly helpful. Sharing your boards or physical clippings with wedding planners, florists, cake makers and caterers can provide valuable guidance about your personal aesthetic. A single picture of a chair cover might be the clue that tells a vendor or planner what direction your wedding should take—ethereal and romantic,

modern and tailored, or homey and rustic. Very often I'm able to pick out a color story from a bride's Pinterest boards, and I've found ideas and inspiration there myself (like the apples carved with the words "I love you" that we used for my best friend's daughter's wedding shower!).

Brides will often juggle several wedding-related Pinterest boards for dresses, décor, locations, and more. Once we get further along into planning, I like us to sit down together and create a single, pared-down board that then acts as our visual master plan. Whether you're working alone or with a planner, you can do the same. (Since you don't want to spoil the *ooh* and *aaah* factor when guests walk into the venue on the big day, make this one a "secret" board.)

Rentals such as tents, chairs, china. Barring a huge convention in the area, you shouldn't have a problem reserving rentals.

Internet Wisdom

OF COURSE, the Internet is a wonderful resource for finding vendors, but a listing on a site should not necessarily pass for a recommendation. On some sites, people pay to be listed; on others, resources are culled on the basis of merit. Clear enough, you think? Well, no. Wonderful vendors may choose to advertise on a site because it brings them business, and merit-based lists may be limited by the taste and research abilities of the person who compiled them. But if you find a particular florist listed on a multitude of paid sites and can't find one positive editorial mention, you can probably skip an interview with him.

You should also do a web search that includes both the type of vendor you're looking for and the location, for example, "wedding cakes" and "Houston." Try adding "best" to the search and see what comes up.

Once you have a list of resources to investigate, take a look at their websites and social media feeds. Many vendors post photos of recent events on their websites and Instagram feeds, and you should be able to determine from the photos and the overall style of the site whether you want to set up an interview. Most vendors do not put any pricing information on their sites, and many won't discuss pricing over the phone, so you'll need to talk face-to-face to determine if they're within your budget.

Should you judge a company by its website? Yes and no. If everything about the site (from the typeface to the photos) strikes you as cheesy, cross the place off your list. But if the site's only crime is simplicity, that could merely

||||||||||| **MEETING AND GREETING** |||||||||||

The Vendors

As a rule of thumb, you should interview no more than three vendors per category. In some categories like lighting, you probably won't have that many choices. Fine. But if you have dozens of options (like florists), interviewing too many vendors will just confuse you and waste everyone's time.

Ask yourself whether the styles you see in a vendor's photos and samples resonate with you; whether he is asking you relevant, knowledgeable questions and making on-target suggestions; and whether the vendor acts pleasant and professional.

Make sure to ask the following questions during your meetings, but also trust your gut as to whether the vendor seems knowledgeable and inspires confidence. These apply to nearly every vendor.

- *How long have you been in business and how many weddings do you do per year?*
- *Are you available for my wedding date? Even if they or their assistant told you they were available over the phone, double-check during your meeting. If the answer is no, there's no point in continuing the conversation.*
- *How much is the deposit? When is it due? When is the balance due?*
- *Will you be on-site at my wedding?*
- *How is the pricing established and what is it based on?*
- *Can you provide three references, preferably recently married couples?*
- *How do you get most of your business? The best vendors get most of their business via referrals.*
- *What is your cancellation policy?*

indicate a vendor who is busy doing what he does best and who hasn't found time to devote to his site. If a site is astonishingly beautiful and elegant, though, that's a promising sign that the business pays attention to detail. Fly-by-night companies don't expend a lot of effort on developing a website that wows you.

ASK MINDY

Q A friend of mine runs a catering company, and she's offered to cater my wedding at a reduced charge. The problem is, she's very busy and hasn't made time to sit down with me and talk about the menu. The months keep ticking by, and I'm starting to wonder whether it's safe to depend on her. I feel weird asking her this, but I wonder if maybe we should draw up some kind of informal contract.

A The contract may be insulting to her. Instead, voice your concern, and tell her you appreciate her offer but you are an excited bride, and the more you can get checked off your list the better—so can we please schedule an appointment? If at that point you don't see any forward motion, you might want to consider going with another option and inviting her as a guest.

Business 101

APPLY THESE BASICS of business to your dealings with each vendor:

- Get a written estimate.

- Sign a contract. If a vendor doesn't have one, write a letter stating all the terms. Both of you should sign and date it. (See the contract points outlined in the individual vendor chapters to find out what you need to include.)

- Read the entire contract before signing, paying special attention to deposit and cancellation terms. Make sure the contract names the person who will be at your event. You don't want to be surprised by someone you've never met on your wedding day.

- Double-check the wedding date, time, location, price, attire of the vendor's staff, and overtime fees stated in the contract.

Make sure the contract specifies exactly what the vendor will provide. It should describe any product with potential variations, such as a cake, a bouquet, or an invitation.

Check references. Ideally you should talk to couples who have hired the vendor within the last eighteen months. The vendor should be willing to give you three references. If she isn't, walk away. It's also worth a call to the Better Business Bureau to find out if any complaints have been registered against the company.

Without a Deposit, You've Got Nothing

If there's one mistake that couples make over and over, it's in thinking that they've somehow reserved a vendor's services before they've put down a deposit. No matter how deep your personal connection during the interview, no matter that you were told the date is clear, *you are not even penciled in* on a vendor's calendar until you've put down a deposit. And nothing is officially reserved until you've both signed the contract. Do not assume that the vendor will contact you before accepting another event for the same date. On the contrary, if they haven't heard from you, vendors assume that you're not interested in booking them. When you wait to send in the deposit, you risk losing some of your top choices.

Firing a Vendor

If one of the members of your team isn't working out (maybe he's so far behind schedule that he's missing opportunities, or he's not in step with your vision), it could become necessary to break off the relationship. The first step is to speak calmly with the vendor to discuss your concerns and dissatisfactions. If you have enough time, try to give the vendor one month to address your planning concerns. If not, explain why you don't think the relationship is working and terminate it. Do it in a businesslike manner—no hissy fits allowed. Many of these vendors belong to the same professional circle and may be friends with one another, so you don't want to go ballistic and gain a reputation for being difficult. For these same reasons, you also don't want to bad-mouth the vendor.

Your contract should specify the financial ramifications of firing a vendor. In some cases, you will lose your deposit, but it may be the best solution to keep your wedding on track.

Don't Forget Your Manners!

TEAM SPIRIT is the key to a great relationship with your planner, florist, photographer, DJ, and other vendors. Treat them as professionals, not as members of your personal entourage. Good vendors put their heart and soul into their work. I've seen photographers stay for an extra hour at no extra charge for a couple they like, and I've seen florists throw in something that the bride had to cut when she was over budget. When the band is happy to be part of your day, you feel the extra energy in the room.

The flip side is that florists, caterers, and cake makers are human, so it's inevitable that at times they will make mistakes. But if you don't like the first sample you see, there's no faster way to torpedo the relationship than to say: "This is the ugliest thing I've seen in my life!" If you want great relationships with vendors, remember these rules:

Say "please" and "thank you." This will go far.

If you don't care for a sample your florist or caterer puts together and there's still time for changes, convey your feelings without insulting them. And if there isn't, repeat the following to yourself: "Nobody will notice but me. Nobody will notice but me."

Try to find something positive to say ("the color is fabulous") before discussing what you want to change.

Pay vendors promptly.

On your wedding day, go up to the band (and any other vendors working to make your day special) and thank them for being part of your day. Show them a little appreciation and they'll work their tails off to do a good job for you.

LGBT-Friendly Vendors

For same-sex couples interviewing potential vendors, it's important to ensure that they—and their employees—are LGBT-friendly. I've personally never had an issue with this in all my years of planning, but I live in a major urban center and work with a trusted network of vendors whom I often bring along to destination weddings.

Sadly, in some places, discrimination can still be an issue. That's obviously never okay, but particularly not on this most special of days. It's one of the most important celebrations in your life, and you want to be certain that nothing is going to spoil the vibe. So do your research before interviewing a vendor. Gay-wedding resource sites allow you to search for vendors in your area online, and referrals from within your community of friends and colleagues are another great way to go.

If you're interviewing someone who didn't come through vetted channels, dispel any chance of miscommunication by asking her directly whether she's done same-sex weddings before. It's also a good idea to make sure the vendor is confident that all the people she'll be hiring to staff your wedding are LGBT-friendly as well.

■ If someone does a great job for you, write a thank-you note. You'll be glad you did.

You're relying on these vendors to make your memories. Behave badly, and you jeopardize the goodwill. Why would you risk that on such an important day? The wedding business is a very personal one, so connecting with your vendors is key—the better you get to know one another, the better your chances of ending up with a wedding that feels true to who you are.

THE WEDDING PARTY

Choosing Your Wedding Party

Bridesmaids and groomsmen serve as helpers, witnesses, and confidants. They symbolically ease the way down the aisle for you, representing by their presence a belief in your union shared by your peers, your community, and your family. And, last but not least, they tend to know how to get the party started.

How to choose your wedding party? First off, don't do so before your venue plans are finalized. Even if you're sure you couldn't possibly get married without all of your college roommates standing up for you, you really can't make good decisions about the wedding party until you have booked your location. Remember, you can always add to your wedding party, but it's horribly awkward—and possibly permanently damaging to a friendship—to have to rescind an invitation once it's been issued.

As you're considering which friends and relatives to include, imagine looking around as your ceremony begins. Will you feel supported by them and grateful to have them in your life? Those are the people you really want in the wedding party. Another question to ask yourself: Will your parents know who all of these people are? Naturally, there are exceptions to this rule, but the friends who know your parents are generally the ones who have stood the test of time.

Some people are only happy when they're surrounded by a large number of friends, while others are more comfortable with an intimate group. (I consider six or more attendants on each side a large wedding party.) Be aware that the larger the wedding party, the higher the cost. A large party can make it harder to reach a consensus on anything, from the bridesmaids' dresses to the style of shoes. There will be more chaos getting dressed, it may be harder to arrange transportation—in short, you're worrying about the welfare of that many more people.

TRADITION PRIMER

Bridenapping, Evil Spirits, and Other Dangers

While groomsmen and bridesmaids serve largely ceremonial roles today, it wasn't always so.

During the Middle Ages, when robbers were common and a young woman needed an entourage to protect her virtue, the groomsmen, known as "bride's knights," were charged with safely escorting the bride from her home to the wedding.

Similarly, the tradition of having a best man goes all the way back to the days of marriage by capture among Anglo-Saxon tribesmen. It was too dangerous for a man seeking a mate to attempt the heist solo, so he brought along a comrade (usually a brother who was a skilled swordsman) to help fight off angry relatives or to create a diversion while he grabbed the maiden and rode off on horseback. The best man also helped protect the couple from being found by the bride's family before they consummated the marriage; today, this custom translates into last-minute help in getting the couple off on their honeymoon.

As for bridesmaids, their origin stems from a perception of spiritual danger: In early European society, it was believed that evil spirits would try to ruin the happiness of the bride and groom. To fool the demons, the bride and her bridesmaids dressed alike, making it harder to identify the bride (the same went for the groom's side). This ruse also proved useful for fooling ex-suitors or a groom attempting to spirit away the bride without making it legal. By the end of the Middle Ages, the bride's attire stood out from the bridesmaids' dresses, but the custom of having the attendants dress alike remains. To this day, however, the groomsmen dress nearly identically to the groom—but that's probably the result of a lack of fashion options for men.

Some couples choose not to have attendants at all. I know of one unconventional couple who had so many close and cherished friends that they didn't want to have to rank them. During their Jewish ceremony, it was just the two of them under the chuppah with the rabbi and the cantor. At one point, the rabbi had them turn around and look at their guests for a moment, a beautiful way of making everyone feel part of the ceremony. Many couples choose to have their close friends walk down the aisle and light candles. In any event, if you don't want any attendants or only want honor attendants (maid of honor and best man), those are both valid choices.

Don't be afraid to think outside the box when it comes to creating a wedding party. If a groom is close to his father, he may opt to make *him* the best man. A grandmother or godmother can make a wonderful matron of honor. If you have a close male friend, you could ask him to be a "bridesman."

In addition to the nature of your relationship to any potential bridesmaids and groomsmen, you should also stop to consider whether they have the stuff to be a supporting member of the wedding party. Are they going to be responsible enough to be there when you need them, show up on time for the wedding, and remember to deliver the in-room gift baskets? Or will you end up having to babysit them through the planning process and track them down the morning of the wedding while they're off nursing a hangover? You could always consider giving that type of person a less critical role—that drama queen friend can probably deliver a terrific reading, and if she flakes out, hardly anyone will know.

What to do when you're not able or willing to invite every member of a group of girlfriends to be a part of the wedding party? This is always a stressful issue for brides, but it need not be. One possibility is to find other ways to include friends in the ceremony (see page 56). But if not including someone is going to become a sore spot or a political land mine, I suggest erring on the side of inclusion (unless space or money are an issue or having the person there is truly going to cause you distress). You don't want to create a whole brouhaha early on if it can be avoided.

Maid of Honor or Matron of Honor

SHARING WITH THE BEST MAN the distinction of being an honor attendant in a traditional wedding party, the maid or matron of honor is responsible for organizing a shower and bachelorette party for the bride; witnessing the marriage license; holding the bride's bouquet and the groom's wedding band during the ceremony; arranging the bride's train and veil; and making a toast at the reception. She helps the bride get dressed and assists her if she changes clothing before the reception or the send-off. She also helps with other wedding-related tasks. A few centuries ago, this meant stitching the bride's trousseau together; today it might mean going dress shopping with the bride, writing the seating cards, or delivering in-room gifts, though her list of tasks has tended to shrink as brides and grooms have gotten more and more involved in all aspects of the planning process. She's in charge of the bridesmaids, making sure they arrive on time for the ceremony and photos, are properly dressed, and fulfill any tasks assigned to them. A matron of honor is married, while a maid of honor is single. It's more common to have one or the other, but you can have both.

Bridesmaids

THESE ATTENDANTS HELP the bride with pre-wedding tasks and organize a shower and bachelorette party. They can be married or unmarried, despite the *maid* in the name. They may also be assigned small tasks at the reception. Their main purpose in modern weddings is to offer the bride any support she needs, whether it's listening to tales of florists who just don't get it or matching the loops to the right button when bustling the train. And they should absolutely, positively signal the bride if she has lipstick on her teeth.

How many bridesmaids is too many? And how to choose without hurting feelings?

This is such a difficult issue for so many people. I always say to my brides who haven't picked the wedding

Will You Be My Bridesmaid?

There isn't any particular ceremony attached to asking your friends to stand up for you, but some couples come up with sweet and unexpectedly clever ways to pose the question. One bride made miniature cakes for each of her bridesmaids, and iced them with the quip "Being my bridesmaid? Piece of cake!" A groom named Jonathan presented his groomsmen with bottles of Johnny Walker Scotch and a card that read, "Will you be Johnny's walker?" Yet another bride stickered her message on boxes of homemade popcorn: "He popped the question. Will you be my bridesmaid?"

It's an Instagram-worthy moment, to be sure, but before posting, check your instincts. Might the pics make other friends feel left out? If so, it's best to keep the special moment private.

party yet, "Can you picture these girls in twenty years looking at your wedding pictures? They'll all be there, still your friends? Friends not of the moment, but for a lifetime?"

The most I have done is fifteen, and that was hard. Not only does it add more issues, it's like a sorority—it's hard to find fifteen girls who all like the same dress.

Some people will feel closer to you than you do to them, but there are other ways to include them. Put them on the guest book, make a job for them, make them part of the experience. If they get angry and start up with you, know that they won't be at that little party in twenty years.

My philosophy is always to face it head on; don't avoid talking about things. If you get to that eighth person and you don't want to go there, sit down with her and say, "I love you, and I hope you understand. I can't have such a big wedding party; I'll include you in all my wedding stuff."

And remember, just because your fiancé has eight groomsmen, you don't have to have eight women standing up for you. It doesn't have to be even. Go with who feels right. If it's all too overwhelming and you really are concerned, just have your siblings. Or if all else fails and you can't handle disappointing anybody, go with just a maid or matron of honor and best man. If you're getting married for a second time or much later than the majority of your peers, your girlfriends might actually thank you for sparing them the time and expense. (Not that *I* could ever imagine being sick of weddings, but I have *heard* that at a certain point, some people do just max out!)

Treat Them Right

Have you ever noticed how you sometimes reserve your worst behavior for your closest friends? Now, I hate to call on that awful, overused word that starts with *bride* and rhymes with *gorilla*, but I have tended to see that type of behavior come out toward bridesmaids. Lest your comfort level lead to lapses in judgment, try to remember that each of your bridesmaids is giving up a significant chunk of free time and money to go dress shopping with you, get her dress fitted, throw you a shower, and so on. These are the wrong people on whom to take out your stress.

Caring for Your Bridesmaids

While the time leading up to your wedding can be stressful and emotionally taxing, don't go hormonal on a bridesmaid who hasn't bought her shoes yet if what's really upsetting you is the fact that you're $5,000 over on your flower budget. Treat her like the precious friend she is. To help you get off on the right foot with your bridesmaids, take to heart my list of dos and don'ts.

Don't put too much pressure or too many expectations on your bridesmaids. You've asked them to be in your wedding because they are special to you. Don't make it another job for them.

Do start things off right with a great dinner or get-together.

Don't expect your bridesmaids to bring a gift to every wedding-related event. In fact, you shouldn't necessarily expect them to attend every wedding-related event. Remember, being a bridesmaid involves an enormous outlay of funds.

Do budget enough for gifts that show you appreciate all they've done for you.

Don't behave badly. You can ruin lifelong relationships.

Do provide sufficient information regarding what type of jewelry, hairstyle, and nail color you'd like to see on the wedding day. If you take everyone out for manicures and hire a hairstylist for the wedding, you can tiptoe around some of the more delicate areas. Gifting your attendants with jewelry, a handbag, or a wrap is not only generous but also a great way to exercise some control over style.

Don't email your graphic artist bridesmaid the day before she leaves for your wedding, asking her to design your programs in the next twelve hours.

Do give your bridesmaids plenty of notice regarding dates and deadlines. If you want them to attend a fitting with you, help you assemble gift bags for out-of-towners, or have their shoes dyed a particular shade of apricot, give them a proper heads-up.

Don't choose bridesmaids' dresses that only a runway model could wear.

Do consider the various dress sizes, body types, and skin tones of your bridesmaids when choosing a style and color for their dresses. While finding an outfit that's universally flattering is virtually impossible, there are some choices that are kinder than others. And unless you're paying for the dress, consider their budget limitations. If you can find a comparable style in a less expensive fabric, go for it.

Remember that your bridesmaids have busy lives of their own and can't make their world revolve around your wedding. Be as organized as you can so that you're giving them enough time to take care of wedding-related tasks. Whether you're asking them to help you glue bows onto votive candles or listen to your woes about the caterer, treat them with courtesy and respect. If a bridesmaid has less-than-perfect highlights or a penchant for overdoing the self-tanner, keep your thoughts to yourself—it's more important to maintain the friendship than it is to emerge with a wedding party that perfectly conforms to your ideal. Take time to listen to your bridesmaids when they're expressing opinions, especially where it concerns their attire. And after they've gotten through the ceremony, don't overburden them with so many jobs that they feel like they're working the wedding. Give them plenty of time to enjoy the festivities; you want them to have wonderful memories of this day, too.

The Best Man

As THE GROOM'S right-hand man, the best man will be asked to take on a number of major responsibilities. He's there for both moral and practical support, helping to keep the groom relaxed, making sure he gets to the ceremony on time, and safekeeping essentials from the ring to the marriage certificate. Like the maid of honor, the best man signs the marriage certificate.

At modern weddings, the best man is in charge of the ring. Even if there's a ring bearer, the best man usually holds the *real* ring. He also makes sure the other groomsmen and the ushers get everywhere they need to be on time and in the proper attire; assists the groom in getting dressed by tying his tie or helping with the cuff links; coordinates with the rental shop and picks up the tuxedos for the groomsmen; holds on to checks given to the couple at the wedding and keeps them safe or deposits them while they're on their honeymoon; and passes out payments and gratuities to clergy and vendors at the reception.

The best man gets the most notoriety for organizing the bachelor party and cohosting it with the groomsmen, but he's most visible to guests for offering the first toast

at the reception. He's also charged with assisting with the getaway—which typically means rounding up the groomsmen to decorate the vehicle with empty cans, balloons, shaving cream, and whatever else it takes to make it say JUST MARRIED.

Groomsmen and Ushers

GROOMSMEN OFTEN SERVE as ushers, escorting guests to their seats. But in some parts of the country, it's customary to have dedicated ushers. Though traditionally ushers are men, it's now become common for women to act as ushers, too. If you're trying to include a large number of friends in your bridal party, you may want to make the ushers a separate entity. If you're having a large wedding and want ushers, make sure you have enough so that guests won't have to stand in a long line. A good rule of thumb is one usher for every twenty-five guests.

Ushers get to the ceremony early, escort guests to their seats and, just before the ceremony begins, unroll the aisle runner. Ushers can hand out the programs, or you can assign a sole person to the job. They sit with the other guests during the ceremony.

If the groomsmen are ushering, then they fulfill all of those duties. Otherwise, their main role is to throw the groom a bachelor party, help keep the groom calm

ASK MINDY

Q Does the number of attendants for the bride and groom have to match?

A Absolutely not. And you shouldn't invite someone you don't really want in the wedding party just to even out the numbers. For aesthetic purposes, it's better if the count on each side is close, but there are creative ways to structure the procession if the numbers are lopsided. Two bridesmaids can walk down the aisle together, or, if the aisle is wide enough, a groomsman could walk two bridesmaids down the aisle.

throughout the proceedings (and the days leading up to them), and assist in whatever way they can on the day of the wedding. That may include rounding up relatives for photos, directing guests to the various places they need to go, and taking gifts from the reception to a parent's or attendant's car. Famously, groomsmen also help decorate the getaway vehicle.

Groomsmen will often need to rent matching formal attire, while ushers don't necessarily wear specific attire other than a boutonniere and a tie in an assigned color.

Other Special Roles

THERE ARE SO many ways to include a special person in your wedding day that there's no reason to feel badly about not asking someone to be a bridesmaid or groomsman. Believe me, many people are relieved not to be asked to make that kind of time and financial commitment. Some people might be too shy to feel comfortable in such a visible role but would be pleased to man the guest book. Here's a look at other roles you can invite people to fulfill (but feel free to invent your own tradition if there are special people you want to include).

- Welcoming guests to the ceremony.

- Handing out programs.

- Doing a reading or performing a piece of music.

- Lighting a candle. You can have honored guests hold candles during the ceremony or light candles on stands along the aisle right before the ceremony begins.

- Holding the chuppah at a Jewish wedding.

- Serving as witnesses to the ketubah signing at a Jewish wedding: Two or more people stand by you while you sign the wedding contract, or ketubah, before the public

ceremony, and add their names to the document. Ask your rabbi about requirements for the witnesses—in some branches of Judaism, they can be Jewish men or women, but some will only recognize men.

- Manning the guest book.

- Delivering a toast at the reception or rehearsal dinner.

- Saying grace or offering the Jewish prayer for the wine or the bread before the meal.

Children in the Wedding Party

CHILDREN CAN BE an absolutely charming addition to a wedding party. You can never predict what they'll say or do, and they often turn into the talk of the wedding. Whether you view these possibilities as pros or cons says a lot about whether you should have kids in your wedding party. In many European countries, it's customary for the wedding party to be comprised exclusively of children, which creates a beautiful image—the bride and groom surrounded by an array of girls in starched dresses and boys in little suits, brimming with innocence and hope.

If you have children of your own, younger siblings, half-siblings, nieces, nephews, or godchildren, you may want to incorporate them into the ceremony. Don't worry about creating a balance between boys and girls. You can have a ring bearer but no flower girl, or four flower girls and no ring bearer.

A ring bearer is typically between the ages of three and seven, and it's his job to bring the ring (or a facsimile if you don't want to entrust your platinum band to a preschooler) down the aisle. Sometimes couples have younger ring bearers, but unless the boy is a child of the bride or groom and so integral to the wedding that you want him to have a featured role, I don't recommend it.

A flower girl brings a touch of innocence and playfulness to the proceedings.

Pets in the Wedding Party

Many couples can't imagine getting married without their pet being present. (About a third of the weddings I do involve dogs.) Dogs often play the same role as ring bearer, walking down the aisle with the ring tied to their collars. To be on the safe side, use a faux ring and put the real thing in the groom's pocket. A flower dog goes down the aisle in a collar or leash made out of flowers, which your florist can make for you. Frequently, the bride or groom wants their pooch in a special outfit for the occasion, from a tux to a tulle veil—that's a matter of personal taste.

You'll have to assign one of your maids or groomsmen the task of ferrying the pet down the aisle; they should also be in charge of pet sitting during the ceremony as need be.

Flower girls are anywhere from three to seven years old, and they walk down the aisle just before the bride, wearing a wreath of flowers in their hair and scattering petals from a basket. There can be more than one flower girl—in which case they dress alike—but you really only need one ring bearer. However, if there are two boys you're trying to include, you can have them share the duty by both walking down the aisle, each holding pillows. You can tie rings to each pillow, or have one ring bearer escort the ring and the other carry a garland.

Girls and boys between eight and fourteen are given the role of junior bridesmaids and ushers. The girls wear modified versions of the bridesmaid dresses more suitable to their age and walk down the aisle after the bridesmaids

> Don't forget to include your grandparents in the ceremony. They'll be so touched to be asked to do a short reading or man the guest book for a while.

but before the flower girl. The boys wear tuxedos or suits, in keeping with what the groomsmen are wearing, and walk down the aisle with the groomsmen.

Pages are not very common. They're borrowed from a royal tradition of having two young boys corral the bride's ultralong train—which would look out of place at most modern weddings. But if you're having a grand, formal wedding, and you're searching for a way to include two boys in the wedding party, you might consider making them pages.

There are other roles that you can create for children. A child can be designated as the bell ringer. Just before the bride walks out, the child stands at the top of the aisle and rings the bell—a great role for a child who is too bashful or young to walk down the aisle—or the child

ASK MINDY

Q I have a very demanding job but can't afford to hire a wedding planner. I really can't take time off in addition to the time I'll need for the wedding and honeymoon, and I'm having trouble getting everything done.

A Be careful whom you choose as your maid of honor. You can really use her to help you do some of your busywork. And thank God for the Internet; there's so much you can do online. You can buy bridesmaids' gifts, order samples of flowers, choose music for your band. But it's really important to meet face-to-face with the photographer, because if he turns out to have an abrasive personality, you're going to look uncomfortable, and that's going to show up in the pictures.

Also, choose people who can see you after hours. A lot of times in the wedding world people can't see you Saturdays, but maybe they can make some time for you on Sunday. Look for people who can work around your schedule.

can walk down the aisle, ringing the bell and announcing, "The bride is coming!"

You can also incorporate the special talents of a child you're close to. Some have had a younger sister play the piano or sing a song that's special to the family. Keep in mind that the purpose of such little performances is more sentimental than theatrical; a cracking voice or slipped line only adds that extra bit of charm.

Who Pays for What?

Bridesmaids and groomsmen (and any other members of the wedding party) customarily pay for their own outfits or rentals, along with their airfare and hotel expenses. But the cost to be a member of a wedding party seems to rise each year. It's not unusual for a pair of bridesmaids' shoes to cost $100; fifteen years ago, $35 shoes from Dyeables would have done the trick. There are also the travel costs to consider, and bridesmaids usually help pay for the bridal shower and bachelorette party, while groomsmen pick up the tab for the bachelor party. Today, that bachelor or bachelorette bash may not be an evening of entertainment, but an entire weekend in Las Vegas. Before you know it, the cost of being in someone's wedding has escalated to several thousand dollars.

Many couples realize the burden exceeds what the wallets of their attendants can bear and try to find ways to defray the costs. They might pick up the room tab or the airfare for a destination wedding. Brides who can afford the expense may pay for the dresses. Look for creative ways to help with costs—maybe it's asking if some attendants would like to share rooms or finding a friend who can put them up. I see a lot of brides giving their bridesmaids the shoes as part of their gift, especially if they want them to wear a pricey style. Making a gift of a wrap, jewelry, or a special handbag to go with the bridesmaid dress is very much the norm, so much so that a whole business has sprung up of designers offering jewelry and handbag-making fêtes for bridal parties.

Whatever you choose to do, it's important to be up front about the expenses so that no arguments arise later. If attendants will be paying their own way, you need to tell them so directly and give them an estimate of what everything will cost. Have this discussion when you ask them to be part of the bridal party and before they decide whether to accept. Their financial position may be such that they can't afford to be in the wedding party, no matter how close you are. Remember, these are your closest friends and family. If they tell you that being part of your party is beyond their means, thank them for their honesty—and then try to find another role for them in your wedding. Above all, be gracious.

It takes a village to make a wedding happen, even for the most frugal couples. If you feel overwhelmed by all the scuttling about that you're bound to be doing, think of it as a learning experience: You're not just preparing the party of your dreams, you're also building up valuable "project management" experience (to use a bit of business lingo), along with a trove of high-quality contacts.

Now on to more familiar territory: your nearest and dearest, the cherished guests you'll be inviting. ◆

CHAPTER FIVE

The Guest List

THE WITNESSES TO YOUR UNION

A wedding is anything but a solitary affair. But why all the guests, really? Though a fantastic party is a wonderful draw, it's not what weddings are fundamentally about. Your guests are there to witness your union, giving it their seal of approval through their attendance, and to savor this wonderful, momentous event with you—and I believe that

sharing in the happiness of others puts us in touch with something essentially human.

To me, there's also something especially poignant about weddings in these disconnected days. With family and friends increasingly spread out to the far reaches of the globe, a wedding is one of the few occasions when it's possible to get everyone (or almost everyone) you love in the same place at the same time.

Don't let anyone fool you, however: Preparing the guest list is nowhere near as simple as pulling out a legal pad and writing down the names of every relative, work friend, and college pal you'd like to invite. It's often one of the most harrowing steps of the wedding process, sometimes turning into a territorial battle or a heart-wrenching exercise in emotional prioritizing. But before you get undone about it, let's look at the facts. The precise size of the guest list will be highly dependent on your budget and the size of your ceremony and reception venues. It may also reflect your religious, ethnic, or cultural background; you may be expected to invite the entire community, congregation, or half the town to your wedding. But let us not forget this: The number of guests you include affects your costs more than any other element of the wedding. So you can trim away all you like by cutting out an hors d'oeuvre at cocktail hour, forgoing premium liquor for the house brand, or skipping the overlays on the tablecloths, but a wedding boils down to a cost-per-head affair, and eliminating some of those heads is the single most effective way to bring a wedding in on budget.

Whom to Invite?

B egin by jotting down a list of all the people you would love to have at your wedding; you and the groom can do this together or on your own. As you move ahead, start to draw lines between which groups you're inviting and which you're not. You may decide to invite first cousins but not second cousins, or that you'll give up your book group if he lets go of his Saturday afternoon hockey league. Then, have every party involved—you, the groom, and both sets of parents—submit a list of the people they want to invite; if someone has a sense that their list is a touch ambitious, they should star the high-priority people. If any of the parents are divorced, each party submits their own list.

When you merge the lists (and I recommend you do this electronically rather than by hand), remove the duplicate names and then add up the remaining names. You will come up with a number that will invariably exceed your budget. This is true across the board, whether your wedding is budgeted at $5,000 or $500,000.

Now it's time to cut. If you're on the fence about someone and can't decide whether or not to invite them,

> Be prepared for some possible prickliness between you and your fiancé over the guest list. But even if you've hated his friend Rick since day one or find his college buddies insufferable, my advice is to keep the peace.

here's what you do: Imagine that after the wedding, you bump into them on the street. Think about how you'd feel if you hadn't invited them. Absolutely horrible or just a tiny pang of guilt? Let your reaction guide your decision. You may need to have a discussion about people you don't want at the wedding—estranged family members or friends, an ex-girlfriend or ex-boyfriend, a relative famous for behaving badly at parties. If a particular person's presence is truly going to ruin the day for you, then calmly state why you don't want him or her at the wedding and be prepared to hold your ground. But if it's a matter of a cousin you don't much care for, let family harmony prevail. Perceived wedding invitation injustices seem to have no statute of limitations, so remember that these decisions can cause lasting repercussions.

In the end, listen to your heart. If it comes down to a choice between a relative you've never met and a good friend, I say go with the friend, though of course it depends on you and your particular family. Part of what makes a wedding so special is the sensation of being surrounded by people you care about. Don't fill the room with virtual strangers out of a feeling of obligation.

Two people you won't want to forget on the list: you and the groom. You are, after all, part of the head count. It's also a common courtesy to invite the officiant along with a spouse or partner.

The Magic Number

IF YOU'VE FOLLOWED my plan, you've already booked your location. To come up with a more accurate idea of the number of people you can afford to host, you need to figure out your fixed costs—the costs that don't change with the number of guests. Those include location rental fees, music, photography, video, officiant fees, and the like. Then you'll need estimates for the costs that will fluctuate: these include food, alcohol, flowers, invitations, and the cake. So, as you can see, as you get further along in the process, your initial ideas about the size of your guest

The "B-List"

You may have heard talk among other brides of their B-list, the second round of potential invitees they don't have the room or budget to accommodate but would love to have at the wedding. Couples usually put friends and coworkers on their B-lists, thinking that they'll be more amenable than older guests to receiving last-minute invites once the no's from the primary guest list start trickling in.

But in my opinion, it's tricky territory. No one wants to be relegated to the B-list, no matter how distant a relative or how tenuous a friend. The smoothest approach is to only send save-the-date cards to your "must-invite" list. Though save-the-dates don't call for a response, you will get advance notice from some of the people who can't make it; should you start hearing regrets in a few weeks, you can send out save-the-date cards to B-listers, but if it's later, just wait and send them an actual invitation.

list may change. Many couples group their guest lists into three categories—the "absolutely essentials," the "almost absolutely essentials," and the "it would be nice's" or "do we have to's." That way they can make changes as they go along without reinventing the wheel.

If yours is a hotel wedding, the catering manager will be able to estimate the price per head or give you the average cost per person early on. For an off-site wedding, a caterer should be able to give you a per-head estimate that includes food, beverages, and rentals. Subtract your fixed costs from your total budget, see what's left (hopefully, it's a positive number), and divide that figure by the cost per head to figure out how many guests you can invite. You may realize you need to reevaluate the budget, come up with some additional funds, or trim the list.

How Many Regrets Can I Count On?

Not everyone is going to be able to attend your wedding, which brings me to one of the most common questions of engaged couples everywhere: If you have room for 200 guests, how many people can you actually invite? The

answer is 10 percent over your capacity, or 220 people in this scenario. If it's a destination wedding, or if more than half of your invitees live far enough away to need to book a flight to attend, you can go 20 percent over.

You can always keep a wish list or B-list of people to invite should you have more people decline than expected, but proceed with care (see the box at left).

Dates and Children

YOU'RE UNDER NO OBLIGATION to invite single guests with a date, unless the single person is in a serious relationship. However, in some communities, single people are routinely invited with dates. Take into account how many single people are being invited—if they are few and far between, you'll probably want to extend "plus one" invitations so you don't end up with any wallflowers.

Children are another issue you'll want to tackle. If either you or the groom already has children, obviously you'll make them a part of the wedding and perhaps extend invitations to other families as well, so that you build a child-friendly event; the same goes for young step-siblings or half-siblings, nieces and nephews, or a slew of godchildren. It's perfectly fine to invite only the children of very close family and friends and not invite others. If you have the means, you may want to have special children's goody bags or a separate children's room with babysitters and activities.

Some couples don't want to risk a toddler screaming through the ceremony or servers having to circumnavigate games of tag during the reception. If you don't want children at the wedding and one or more parents is pressuring you to include them, you'll have to weigh your desires against keeping the family peace. You can also try to hammer out a compromise by having children at the ceremony and cocktail hour but not at the reception.

No matter what your decision, some guests will disagree with you; smooth the way by letting people know early on that you've made an overall decision and are not just singling them out. That will also give them time to adjust to the idea and make the necessary arrangements for child care.

His Side and Her Side

IN THE PAST, the bride's side and the groom's side got an equal number of invitations. Nowadays, it's common for the invitations to be divided in thirds, with a third going to the bride's parents, a third to the groom's parents, and a third to the couple. If either set of parents is divorced, they split their share. This isn't a hard-and-fast rule, but it seems simple and fair to me. Footing the bill doesn't entitle a party to invite more people, though the person writing the checks doesn't always share that sentiment. You also have to account for logical exceptions. One side may have a huge family, and the other side a small one. As with all aspects of your wedding planning, flexibility and a spirit of compromise are key.

In order to prevent disagreements over the guest list from morphing into awkward, family-to-family disputes—usually carried out by (guess who?) the bride and groom—the best approach is to ask both families for their guest lists very early in the process.

ASK MINDY

Q My fiancée is inviting not one but three ex-boyfriends to the wedding. I think it's not only awkward, but disrespectful to me. She says she values her past relationships and that I have nothing to feel threatened about. What gives?

A It could be that she's looking for closure by inviting her exes and having them witness her union to another man. It could be that she thinks of them as friends and wants to share the experience with them. No matter: If it bothers you, then it should be brought up and discussed. You don't want the day after your wedding to be tainted with resentment over whether she took a spin with one of them on the dance floor. It shouldn't be so hard for her to disinvite them—such a decision would be easy enough for anyone to understand.

Say your future in-laws have legions of friends and relatives whom they insist on inviting—more than your own parents, in fact, and it's putting you way over your number—yet they're not offering any financial contributions to the wedding. If you have room for additional guests, have the groom approach his parents and ask them if they want to cover the costs of some or all of the guests that are putting you over budget. If that isn't an option or you don't feel comfortable with that scenario, the groom will simply have to explain that for budget reasons, they are going to need to trim their list. (Try to do this before *your* parents even get a look at his parents' list.)

If an increased financial contribution is not forthcoming, and they are still refusing to bend, you are in an uncommon and uncomfortable situation. If you have to tell them that their list must be cut drastically, try suggesting that you work with them to plan some kind of event, no matter how modest, in their hometown for their friends. In many cases, people just need to feel like they've included others in the festivities in some way, and a compromise like that can fit the bill.

Too Many Guests!

LET'S FACE IT: Most couples go over budget on their weddings, to varying extents, as they get caught up in the excitement of all of the choices available to them; they may love the hue of a particular hybrid rose, or they may decide that the tables look infinitely better with overlays on them. But if you're already over budget based simply on a rough estimate of costs from your guest list—before you've been faced with all of the temptations waiting for you down the line—you're headed for the kind of serious debt it takes years to pay back. Winnow down that guest list or change the reception concept to bring it in line with your budget. No matter how many people do it, I don't believe in hosting a wedding that is beyond your means.

How to get the count down? First off, get rid of extraneous "plus ones"; let the singles mingle! If that doesn't do it, it may be tempting to shave the lion's share from your parents' lists, but that's sure to set you up for some conflict. Likewise, the groom may not be too thrilled if your list is longer than his. Be prepared for some discussion, and try to keep your emotions out of it—if you can bring your closest friends and family together, you're already pretty lucky.

Staying Organized

Once you've got the list, type the names into a spreadsheet. Creating a master list in Excel or a similar program will help you manage the list and keep track of everyone's status. Set up columns noting that you've sent the save-the-date cards and the invitation, that you've received the RSVP, and for the number of guests in each party. It's also a good idea to set up columns to record gifts and thank-you notes. You can also set up columns for other events such as showers or the rehearsal dinner and indicate which ones each guest is invited to.

Remember to back up your files frequently as more RSVPs come in. Share the list with your fiancé and your wedding planner, if you have one, but beware of giving too many people access—that's a recipe for accidental hijinks. If you make changes after you've already given vendors or your planner the count, be sure to communicate with them. Do *not* assume they will simply notice that the document has been updated.

Should you not be inclined to create your own spreadsheet, several apps and websites offer complimentary guest-list managers.

Send a final copy of the entire guest list to both sets of parents and ask them to proofread their guests' names; it will help them feel included in the invitation process, prevent them from wondering who got invited and who didn't, and lower your chance of error.

If you plan to hire a calligrapher to address your invitations or write out seating cards, keep a list of names in a simple text program like Word; most calligraphers do not like to work off spreadsheets.

Plan Ahead

As you're compiling the list, make sure you're getting the full name of each guest, with its correct spelling; any professional, military, or political titles; and a mailing address, email address, and phone number. Even if you're sticking to paper invites for all of your events, email addresses will prove handy if you need to contact guests to find out where they're staying, and it's great to have the phone numbers in case guests don't RSVP.

If you are inviting a guest with a boyfriend or girlfriend whose name you don't know, get the date's full name; if you're inviting a single guest with a date of his or her choice, no need to inquire about whom they're bringing. Make sure to get the names of any children you're inviting as well.

Save-the-Date Cards

Once you've put together the guest list, it's time to give people a heads-up about your wedding date and location.

In the days of simple hometown weddings, invitations were mailed six weeks before the event. The save-the-date card, giving guests ample opportunity to request time off from work and make travel arrangements, emerged with destination weddings. As everyone has gotten busier, with schedules ever more packed, the save-the-date has become standard for all kinds of weddings, and I think it's a nice courtesy to give guests as much time as possible to plan. (The only reason *not* to send one is for a very short engagement, with the wedding less than two months away.)

More and more often, people are choosing to save money and time by sending out virtual save-the-dates using services like Paperless Post or Minted. I'm doing very few printed cards these days, but in the interest of upholding tradition (and because I love all things stationery), I'm including information on old-school cards.

Save-the-date cards do not need to echo the style of the invitation. Some people prefer a cohesive style statement that continues through to the favors and thank-you notes; others see the save-the-date card as an opportunity to get creative or go casual; and still others opt for simplicity in the interest of saving time and money. You may choose to design your own cards on a computer and print them on a laser printer. If you're not creatively inclined, there are some wonderfully stylish lines of imprintable stationery out there

Beyond virtual or printed cards, the save-the-date notification can be as informal as an email or a telephone call, though telephone calls are more time-consuming and email, like virtual invites, might not be the best option for some of your elderly invitees.

A Question of Timing

THE IDEAL TIME to send out save-the-date notifications is six or seven months before the wedding. (For a destination wedding, they can go out as early as nine months prior.) Any earlier feels premature, and you risk giving people too much information too soon. If you're

> If you order save-the-date cards through a stationery store or invitation designer, whether in person or online, go ahead and order your thank-you notes. You'll need them sooner than you think for engagement and shower gifts.

behind in your planning, you can send them out as late as four months before the wedding. You don't want the invitation to follow on the heels of the save-the-date, so if it gets any later, simply send your invitations out on the early side, about two months before the wedding.

The earlier the save-the-date notification goes out, the less information you need to include. Generally, you include the name of the couple, the date of the wedding, and the general location—it's more fun to leave the precise location a surprise so guests will learn something new when they receive the invitation. So the save-the-date might say

Though save-the-dates are informational, they can also be a place for the bride and groom to express their personalities.

We hope to see you in June!

June 16, 2018
Madison, Wisconsin

Please save the date
Invitation to follow

Save the Date

CARRIE and PETE
are finally
tying the knot!!
#carrieandpete

Some of My Favorite Save-the-Dates . . .

- Use photo booth shots of the two of you holding signs with the message "Save the date," and mount them on the front of a fold-over note.

- For a beach wedding, take a photo of your names and the date in the sand with a heart traced around them. Have the photo printed on cards.

- Buy up postcards from your location (vintage ones are particularly great) and turn them into save-the-date cards. Flea markets are a great source.

- If you're not using a lot of text, have the information printed on magnets. Whimsical artwork or a photo can turn the magnet into a keeper.

- Choose a graphic element that will be used on all of your wedding stationery and incorporate it on the save-the-date card. You could use a monogram, a palm tree, a flower, or an image that's particular to you as a couple.

"Santa Barbara, California," whereas the invitation would say "Bacara Resort, Santa Barbara, California." Let people know if it's a morning, afternoon, or evening celebration so they can plan accordingly. If you're planning to do a wedding website or already have one, include the URL on the save-the-date; see page 289. If it's not ready yet, reserve the domain and alert guests to "watch for mindyandrobertwed.com." And if you plan to give guests a sneak peek of your wedding prep, include your wedding hashtag (e.g., #mindyplusrobert) so that guests can start following—and eventually posting their own pics of the festivities. (See page 104 for more on social media.)

For a destination wedding or a weekend-long event, include the dates and enough lodging and transportation information so that guests can begin to make their plans. Typically, lodging information would include the hotel names, phone numbers, rates, and the name on the block of rooms; for transportation, include the names of the airlines that serve the destination.

No reply cards are used with save-the-dates, and guests aren't expected to respond, though some will let you know if they definitely can't make it. Before ordering or printing save-the-date cards, figure out how many you'll need by calculating the number of households on the guest list. Don't make the mistake of thinking that the number of guests is equal to the number of invitations, which is a common—and costly—blunder.

Now reach around and give yourself a pat on the back: You've made the biggest decisions, and you've spread the word. From here on out, the work is in the details. ◆

ASK MINDY

Q I'm having trouble whittling down my guest list. Whom should I cut first? Am I obligated to invite certain relatives, even though I don't know them?

A I always say there are two things that I find most difficult: the guest list and the seating chart. Family is such a touchy issue. Your parents will bring up some cousin and say, "You haven't met her, but you'll love her!" This is a moment where you really have to sit down and talk about priorities. On your wedding day, you should be surrounded by people you pretty much know. A good goal is to make it so that you've met everyone there at least once, so you're familiar with them and can introduce them to your fiancé.

PART II

Laying the
Foundation

CHAPTER SIX

Planning the Ceremony

TRADITIONS NEW AND OLD

The ceremony is the cornerstone of the wedding, the reason you've all gathered together. Sadly, I've seen brides get so wrapped up in their party planning that they give the ceremony short shrift. The vows and readings demand as much attention as—actually, much more attention than—the choice between salmon and sea bass. There are so many ways to make the ceremony about the two of you, your families, your cultural heritage, and your traditions, from vows and readings to discreet, personal gestures meant for you and your immediate family. Truth be told, some religious ceremonies don't allow much wiggle room. Even in those cases, you can add another layer of meaning, whether it's carrying your grandmother's Bible down the aisle or adding a family ring ceremony to include children from a previous marriage.

The planning starts with decisions about the type of ceremony (religious or civil) and type of officiant, both *very big* questions where most families are concerned. And if it's religious, will it adhere to a particular faith, combine elements of two faiths, or be spiritual but nondenominational?

Whatever road you choose, plan your ceremony with heart. Whether the traditions you incorporate are ancient or newly minted doesn't matter—what's important is that they symbolize love, union, and the coming together of families.

Religious Ceremonies

Some religions give you opportunities to personalize the vows, readings, or music but limit your choices to sacred material. Others, such as Unitarian Universalism, let you devise the ceremony—a nice option for couples struggling to find a religious service that meets interfaith needs. But if you really want to control the entire ceremony, you may want to opt for something secular (see page 74).

It's also important to know that in some religions, including Buddhism, Islam, Hinduism, and Sikhism, the ceremonial power vested in the official may fall short of being legal; if it does, you'll need to make a civil ceremony part of your plans. If you're getting married outside of the United States, see chapter 12, "Making It Legal," for more information on making sure your union is legally recognized.

Keep in mind that most religions vary from sect to sect, or sometimes from one minister to the next, so it's impossible to generalize all of the customs and rituals. The ceremonies also differ depending on where you are—a Buddhist ceremony in Japan is likely to be quite different from one in the United States. Many religions have Westernized their ceremonies to a great extent and been influenced by other cultures as they've worked their way around the world.

What follows is an overview of what you might expect at each type of religious ceremony in the United States. But be sure to check with your officiant to get all of the requirements of marriage for your religion.

> If you have a say in the length of your ceremony, keep timing in mind when writing vows, choosing readings, or adding songs. Anything over thirty minutes starts to feel long to your guests.

Buddhism

IN BUDDHISM, marriage is a secular arrangement, so there is no prescribed ceremony or liturgy. This has made Buddhist weddings increasingly popular, as it leaves a lot of leeway for the couple to make the ceremony personal to them, as long as it doesn't contradict the spirit of the dharma or the teachings of the Buddha. Traditions vary from one sect to the next, and each strain of Buddhism has been influenced by the geographic path it has taken as it traveled through Asia or India. The Japanese ritual of *san-san-kudo*, the sharing of sake, for instance, is now part of many Buddhist ceremonies, whether or not the couple is of Japanese descent.

A priest or Buddhist preceptor usually conducts the ceremony, though in some cultures, the union may be blessed by a monk. (For the wedding to be legal in the United States, make sure that the officiant is ordained.) You'll find that most Buddhist officiants—priests and monks—are flexible as to where the ceremony takes place. But wherever the marriage occurs, incense is typically offered to the Buddha at the beginning of the ceremony, which may be announced by the sounding of a gong. Usually a shrine holds flowers, a candle, incense, an image of the Buddha, and possibly a bowl of fruit. In most ceremonies, you'd hear at least one sutra chant—a means of expressing gratitude to the Buddha.

Some priests emphasize the six virtues, or paramitas, as a way of cultivating and maintaining a relationship. Each virtue has a symbol, which may be incorporated into the ceremony: flowers for exertion, incense for patience, a candle for meditation, perfumed water for discipline, food for generosity, and music for knowledge.

Although Buddhist priests are open to many traditions, some do object to the use of a unity candle (see page 84) because Buddhists value and respect individual differences in marriage and don't subscribe to the notion that two people should become one.

Eastern Orthodoxy

EASTERN ORTHODOX CEREMONIES overflow with rituals—many of which are performed in threes to represent the Holy Trinity. Marriage is a sacrament, so weddings take place in a church and last about an hour. The bride and groom generally do not recite any vows.

The ceremony begins with the exchange of rings, which go back and forth between the couple three times and are actually placed on the ring finger of the *right* hand. After the priest's initial blessing, the couple's hands remain joined for the rest of the ceremony.

The highlight of the ceremony is the crowning, wherein the male sponsor, known as the *koumbaros*, swaps the crowns (yes, three times) between the bride and groom. As soon as the priest removes the crowns, the couple is married. The bride and groom take sips of wine from a shared cup as a reminder that they will henceforth share everything, and the priest leads them in walking three times around the altar for their first steps together as a married couple.

Episcopalianism

THE FAMILIAR OPENING, "Dearly beloved, we are gathered here today in the presence of God . . . " is a mainstay of many Protestant weddings, but it originated in the Episcopalian Book of Common Prayer. Episcopalians consider marriage a sacrament, so the marriage ceremony must take place in a church, unless you're able to get an exemption from the local bishop, and the music must be religious in nature.

Though Episcopalian weddings are similar to other Protestant weddings in many respects, they tend to hew closer to what you would expect from a Sunday service. Rings are blessed before being handed to the couple, and the celebrant leads the congregation in blessings like "The peace of the Lord be always with you," to which the congregation responds, "And also with you." If the couple wishes, the ceremony may include the celebration of the Holy Eucharist, and all baptized Christians may receive communion.

Judaism

TWO IMPORTANT CUSTOMS take place before a traditional Jewish ceremony. First, the couple, rabbi, parents, and designated witnesses gather in a chamber to sign the ketubah, the Jewish marriage contract—a wonderfully intimate, sacred pause before the larger ceremony gets under way. Then comes the *bedeken*, in which the groom veils the bride in order to symbolically ensure her identity; the roots of the ritual come from the biblical story of Jacob, who was tricked by a heavy veil into marrying the wrong woman.

The bride and groom are each escorted down the aisle by both of their parents. At the front of the aisle stands the chuppah, a canopy attached to four poles under which the bride and groom are married. The chuppah has a dual purpose, representing both the presence of God and the couple's first home. (For more information on the chuppah, see pages 87 and 305.)

Toward the end of the ceremony, the bride may circle the groom seven times; this tradition, which once symbolized the centrality of the groom in the family, fell out of favor for a while. Popular once again, it now signals completion and carves out a magical circle around the couple. And at the very end comes the famed moment when the groom (or the couple) stomps on a glass and all the guests shout "Mazel tov!" This riotous gesture heralds the end of the serious stuff and the start of the festivities.

In conservative or orthodox Judaism, the couple goes into seclusion, or *yichud*, for about fifteen minutes immediately following the ceremony. If they've fasted prior to the wedding, this is when they break their fast.

Hinduism

THOUGH A TRADITIONAL Hindu wedding encompasses more than a dozen rituals and can last for several days, it can be condensed—a North American ceremony typically lasts about an hour and a half. My description here focuses on some of the highlights of the actual wedding day, but customs vary widely among ethnic groups, families, regions, and castes.

No matter what type of ceremony you're having—religious or civil—read over the service and the vows well ahead of time to make sure you're comfortable with the language, especially any references to God and the responsibilities of the man and the woman in the marriage.

Weddings are conducted by a Hindu priest, or pandit, who chants Sanskrit mantras from the Vedas, the books of holy scripture. The groom wears white, while the bride wears a red and gold sari.

Under the *mandap*, a flower-bedecked canopy, the bride and groom exchange floral garlands to wear for the duration of the ceremony. After the father of the bride gives his daughter away, the priest ties the couple's right hands together. The heart of the ceremony, the *mangalfera*, also involves a binding ritual, wherein the groom's scarf is tied to the bride's sari and the couple circles a sacred fire seven times. With each round, they pray for a blessing—from food and prosperity to strong and virtuous children.

Once the steps are completed, the marriage is sealed. The groom puts a red powder called *sindhoor* on the part in the bride's hair to show that she is a married woman.

Mormonism

THERE ARE TWO KINDS of ceremonies for members of the Church of Jesus Christ of Latter-day Saints. A temple ceremony or sealing ordinance takes place within a Mormon temple and may only be attended by Mormons in good standing; they need a temple "recommend" to attend, just as the couple must meet a series of requirements to get their "recommend" for a temple wedding. The ceremony seals the couple together "for time and all eternity," meaning for this life and the afterlife. Details of the ceremony are sacred and not shared with non-Mormons.

In a civil ceremony, still religious, the couple is married by the local bishop, usually in a church or a home.

The marriage is intended to last until death but does not extend to the afterlife; non-Mormons may attend. Many couples marry in a civil ceremony and have a temple wedding later.

Islam

THOUGH MUSLIM CEREMONIES are short and simple, nuptial celebrations may last for a week. Customs vary greatly according to region; Muslim weddings in India, for example, share many traditions with Hindu weddings. Generally, the offer of marriage is extended by a male representative of the bride, called a wali, to the groom. If accepted, a *mahr* is negotiated between the two sides; it's a specific sum of money or other valuable gift (such as property) that the groom gives the bride to guarantee her security and independence within the marriage. The first part of the mahr, "the prompt," is paid at the wedding—today, it usually takes the form of a wedding ring. The deferred part of the mahr is paid during the marriage.

The only aspect of a wedding specifically prescribed by Muslim tradition is the *nikah*. During this ceremony, the bride and groom are separately asked if they agree to the marriage and to the mahr. After they agree, the marriage contract is signed by the two sides; two to three Muslim witnesses must be in attendance. The imam oversees the signing of the contract and also reads from the Qur'an. The couple may or may not exchange vows, which aren't required in the Muslim faith.

Following the nikah (but not necessarily on the same day), the marriage is made public by a celebration with a large feast called a *walima*; at some Muslim weddings, men and women celebrate in different rooms.

An additional civil ceremony is usually required for legal recognition.

Protestantism

LOVE, HONOR, CHERISH. In sickness and in health. These are phrases from the vows of a Protestant wedding, familiar to most Americans due to its frequent depiction in movies and television. Whether the service

Mixed-Faith Ceremonies

As couples who come from different religions and backgrounds join their lives together and attempt to honor traditions from both camps, mixed-faith ceremonies have become common.

There are several ways to handle a mixed-faith ceremony. You can have coofficiants, assuming both religions permit the practice (not always the case), a nonreligious officiant like a judge, or an officiant deemed "neutral" by the couple—an ordained friend, a Unitarian minister, or a flexible clergy member.

You can also hold two separate ceremonies, one following the other. The ceremonies might take place on separate days, if need be.

Before jumping into the logistics, the bride and groom should talk about what's important to them about their respective religions—maybe it's some of the traditions rather than the religious elements. Then they should have a meeting with their families to find out what's important to *them* and make everyone feel included. You may not be willing or able to accommodate every wish, but if it's a simple matter of carrying rosary beads to make your grandmother happy, I say go ahead and keep the family peace.

When bringing together families and guests from very different backgrounds, make an extra effort to explain the traditions in your program. It will make people feel more comfortable, and

everyone loves learning the origin of wedding traditions. One side may have grown up watching couples jump the broom or get lassoed together, but for many in the crowd, it will be a first.

If you're planning to have two religious officiants, you're obviously going to have to find ones who are willing to marry interfaith couples and cooofficiate. Independent rather than affiliated officiants are more likely to fit the bill, though it depends on the religion, the sect within that religion, and the specific congregation.

A mixed-faith ceremony is likely to be unique and memorable, but what's most important is that you design a ceremony that honors both families and makes both sides feel embraced.

is Presbyterian, Methodist, Baptist, or Lutheran, the processional, the welcome from the minister ("we are gathered here today . . ."), the vows, the exchange of rings, and the final "you may now kiss the bride" don't vary much. Leeway in vows, musical choices, and readings depends upon the religion and the minister, but most allow some flexibility. The service can be as short as fifteen minutes, and can include Holy Communion. Unity candles are a popular tradition but not mandatory. Because marriage is considered holy but not a sacrament, you can usually hold the ceremony outside of a church, and many ministers will co-officiate. (Also see the entries for Episcopalian and Unitarian weddings.)

Religious Society of Friends

TO GET MARRIED among the Quakers, you must write a letter of intent to the clerk of the meetinghouse. If the

marriage, actually referred to as a meeting, is approved by the "clearness committee," the Friends appoint an oversight committee to help with arrangements; it plays much the same role as a wedding party, or even a wedding planner. Both "unprogrammed" and "programmed" weddings exist among Quakers according to the branch, though the former is the better-known style.

At an unprogrammed wedding, there is no officiant, music, or service. The couple and the oversight committee sit on benches facing one another before the guests. All worship silently until the bride and groom stand, hold hands, and exchange their vows. They can write their own vows, but many like the directness and simplicity of the traditional Quaker vows: "In the presence of God and these our friends I take thee [name of intended spouse], to be my husband/wife, promising with Divine assistance to be unto thee a loving and faithful husband/wife so long as we both shall live."

The couple sits down and signs the Quaker marriage certificate, which is then read aloud, after which guests may stand up individually and say a few words to express support for the union. At the end of the meeting, guests turn to one another and shake hands. Everyone in attendance signs the Quaker marriage certificate, making it a most meaningful keepsake for the couple.

Military Weddings

The protocol governing military weddings varies according to the branch of service, so members of the military should always check with their base chaplains or consult their service manual.

Commissioned officers—whether they're men or women—may wear full dress uniform, which is extremely formal. They may also wear the somewhat less formal dinner or mess dress, which corresponds to a tuxedo. There's a no-flower rule on uniforms, so men should not attach a boutonniere to their uniform, though female officers may carry a bouquet. Both can wear civilian dress if they prefer. An American flag and the unit's standard should be displayed.

The ceremony itself doesn't vary from a regular civil or religious service and often takes place at a base chapel. The highlight of a military wedding is the arch of swords or sabers during the recessional—swords for a navy wedding and sabers for an army wedding. The attendants form two rows and make an arch out of their swords or sabers for the bride and groom to pass through. Only members of the military, in uniform, can draw swords; civilian members of the bridal party should stand at attention in the lineup. The arch can occur on the aisle, or on the steps outside the chapel. (Cake cutting can also take on a military edge if the couple choose to cut the cake with the sword or saber.)

Military titles for the bride or groom on active duty are used on the wedding invitation; for guidance on matters of wording, see page 280.

Roman Catholicism

AS ONE OF THE SEVEN sacraments of the Catholic Church, the marriage ceremony follows a strict set of rules, but the structure doesn't differ significantly from a Protestant ceremony. The main difference is that a traditional ceremony includes a nuptial mass after the exchange of rings, which means the ceremony lasts about an hour. (You *can* opt for a shorter ceremony that does not include a mass.)

After the marriage rite, the priest has everyone make a "sign of peace" by shaking hands with their neighbors. Holy Communion follows, but only for the Roman Catholics among your guests.

Ceremonies must take place in a church or chapel unless permission is received from the vicar-general's office, and music and readings must typically be religious. Before the wedding, you must announce your intention to wed by publishing banns (wedding announcements) in the church bulletin for three consecutive Sundays.

Nondenominational Ceremonies

Some couples believe in a higher power but don't feel comfortable with all the rites of a particular religion. Some come from different religious backgrounds or cultures or are prevented from marrying within a faith by sexual preference or prior divorce. Or perhaps their beliefs don't conform to those of a single religion.

For these couples, what may feel right is a very personal, spiritual wedding ceremony that isn't linked to a single religion. They often write their own vows, and some of them write their entire ceremony and include their own spiritual beliefs.

If that's the case for you, a New Age minister or an ordained friend can work well as an officiant, but there are also some religious organizations you can turn to. Again, check your state laws to find out whether a particular ceremony is legally binding; you may need to supplement the service with a civil ceremony.

Unitarian Universalism

A PLURALISTIC RELIGION with Judeo-Christian roots, Unitarian Universalism doesn't have prescribed rituals and rules, which allows couples to work with a minister to design a ceremony that fits their beliefs and personalities. The ceremony can be in a church or secular space, the service can be short or long, the couple can be of the same faith or hold different beliefs.

You can take inspiration from whatever source you like, divine or otherwise, and you don't need to belong to a Unitarian church to be married by a Unitarian Minister.

Humanism and Ethical Culture

THE AMERICAN HUMANIST ASSOCIATION, more akin to a philosophy than a religion, has celebrants who are authorized to perform weddings. Among other things, humanists believe in equality, and the vows reflect that. Related to humanism, the Ethical Culture movement is recognized as a religion in the United States, and its leaders are legally authorized to perform weddings. Both of these inclusive philosophies value the worth of every individual, which makes them an option worth investigating for those who don't find religious doctrines a good fit.

Civil Ceremonies

A CIVIL CEREMONY is presided over by a legal official rather than a religious official. People often choose civil ceremonies when they're getting married on short notice; if they come from different faiths and want a neutral ceremony; for encore weddings; or for destination weddings.

A civil ceremony isn't necessarily an impersonal choice. If you have a judge in your family or circle of friends, she may be quite capable of bringing warmth and depth to the ceremony. She might also be amenable to working with you to personalize the ceremony.

The classic civil wedding takes place at city hall, but it can take place just about anywhere, as long as you find an official who is willing to travel; some are more willing to leave the office than others.

Civil ceremonies in the United States are usually based on the Episcopalian Book of Common Prayer. The officiant would not necessarily include religious prayers or blessings, but some may allow the couple to make them part of the ceremony.

Couples who choose a civil ceremony due to time constraints or who head to a wedding chapel on an impulse trip to Las Vegas can often get their marriage blessed at their church at a later date.

Same-Sex Ceremonies

Now that same-sex marriage is legal across the United States, these weddings don't entail quite the same thicket of complications they did in the past, such as unions that were recognized in one state but not another, or frequent and confusing changes to the laws.

Supreme Court Ruling for Same Sex Marriage

"No union is more profound than marriage, for it embodies the highest ideals of love, fidelity, devotion, sacrifice and family. In forming a marital union, two people become something greater than once they were. As some of the petitioners in these cases demonstrate, marriage embodies a love that may endure even past death.

"It would misunderstand these men and women to say they disrespect the idea of marriage. Their plea is that they do respect it, respect it so deeply that they seek to find its fulfillment for themselves. Their hope is not to be condemned to live in loneliness, excluded from one of civilization's oldest institutions. They ask for equal dignity in the eyes of the law. The Constitution grants them that right."

Still, some challenges are unique to an LGBT wedding. While gay weddings are legally recognized in the United States, the views of various religions on same-sex weddings are still in flux. As of this writing, clergy from more than a dozen religions are permitted to organize some sort of wedding, commitment ceremony, holy union, or blessing—but not every clergy member will necessarily comply. So along with the task of finding LGBT-friendly vendors (see page 51), one of your first priorities will be finding the right space and officiant for the ceremony.

Some gay couples choose to sidestep the issue by having a friend or family member get ordained online through organizations like the Universal Life Church Monastery or the American Marriage Ministries; such an ordination may not hold water in your particular state, however, and some states require the applicant to become both an ordained minister *and* a "temporary officiant." It's worth poking around among your circle of friends and acquaintances, as you may find someone within six degrees of separation who fits the bill.

Another option is a ceremony at city hall, which can have special significance as a political statement, highlighting the legal recognition accorded to the couple by federal and municipal entities. Often followed by a full-fledged reception or an after-party at a separate site, a city hall wedding can either supplement or take the place of a nonbinding ceremony. Attended by only the couple, a witness, and perhaps a handful of family members and friends, it may be held a few days or even weeks before the reception in order to simplify things.

Wherever they are married, many gay couples choose to write their own vows, inventing their own rituals rather than cleaving to traditions that might not feel inclusive enough. Some choose to read bits of poetry or literature without any particular political overtones (see page 84), while others opt for choices that overtly celebrate their legal right to marry. Lines from the powerful closing statement of Justice Anthony Kennedy's supreme court ruling (see box at left) make a poignant choice for many couples.

To answer the question that's surely at the top of your list—yes, the creative spirit that surrounds same-sex ceremonies *does* extend all the way from the procession to the dress code. If both brides want to wear white lace, let them wear white lace! There are no fixed rules as to who should wear what in a same-sex wedding, though ideally the degree of formality should be matched.

Who wears the engagement ring? The person who proposes is usually the one who purchases the ring—often to be surprised by a reciprocal gesture a few weeks later. Instead of exchanging rings, one male couple decided to exchange engraved watches prior to their Massachusetts wedding. Another couple, two brides-to-be, found a single ring they loved in Mexico City and had a jeweler split the band into two. The custom of gay couples wearing wedding bands on their right ring fingers has fallen away with the legalization of same-sex marriage, but some couples still prefer the less heteronormative option. The real question is: Who asks?

A note on destination weddings outside the United States: Sadly, homosexuality is still considered a crime in many places in the world, so be sure to do your research when selecting a location.

Finding an Officiant

You may already have a strong feeling about who you want as your officiant. And if you're getting married in your hometown church, your officiant will be part of the package.

But those getting married in a place where they don't have ties to a church, synagogue, or local judge must find an officiant. Explore the rules governing who can marry you and what constitutes a legal marriage in the state or country where the wedding will take place (for more information on local marriage laws, see chapter 12, "Making It Legal"). In most states, ordained members of the clergy and civil servants such as judges and justices of the peace can officiate; in some municipalities, mayors and court clerks can, too. In Florida, Maine, and South Carolina, a notary public can legally wed people. In Colorado and Kansas, a couple can even get special permission to officiate their own union!

A ceremony will feel so much warmer if you have a strong connection with the person leading it. For that reason, many couples opt to have a friend or family member get ordained online (it's free) by the Universal Life Church. Again, check local laws: The state of New York, for example, doesn't recognize the Universal Life Church.

If you're active in a church or temple but your minister or rabbi isn't able to travel to your wedding, ask if he or she can recommend someone. The catering manager or other contact at your reception site should be able to provide local recommendations; at a destination wedding, the hotel staff can often arrange for the officiant.

Encore Weddings

Second marriages (and beyond) used to have their own set of rules that essentially revolved around toning down the celebration and banishing any references to virginity. But encore nuptials now make up more than a quarter of all weddings, and brides and grooms are fully entitled to have whatever kind of celebration best suits them. For some, that may be a low-key affair with the bride in a simple sheath, a small destination wedding, say; for others, it may be a pull-out-all-the-stops formal dinner and reception for two hundred.

Encore weddings often involve children, so making them feel part of the union might be what distinguishes the ceremony. You can make them part of the bridal party—for roles children can play see page 56. If children are old enough, they can even walk their mother or father down the aisle. After the exchange of rings, it can be especially poignant to add a jewelry ceremony involving them; they might receive a special necklace or ring that in some way represents the creation of a new family. Or they can take part in a unity candle ceremony or similar ritual; see page 84.

Family vows are particularly moving, especially when the officiant can incorporate a family prayer mentioning each child by name into the ceremony. Ask him for ideas—one that I have seen and love is to have the officiant ask, "Who will support this new family?" to which the children reply, "We do." A wedding doesn't get more beautiful than that.

Who Sits Where?

How many times have you attended a wedding and been asked if you were on the bride's side or the groom's side? And been tongue-tied for an answer because you were friends with both of them? Reserved seating for close family members aside, the tradition of seating guests on the bride's side to the left of the aisle at a Christian wedding and to the right at a Jewish wedding deserves to be retired. (The sides, by the way, correspond to the position of the bride during the ceremony.) Many couples have already done away with the practice, so it may not have even occurred to you. In my opinion, a wedding is about bringing two people and two families together, so it should likewise bring guests together. Making a distinction as to which side invited them serves no purpose.

THE OFFICIANT

If you're shopping for an officiant, you may need to interview several. You can get some idea of their views through their websites, which are increasingly common with unaffiliated officiants. Call to determine if your date is available, then set up a meeting or a phone interview if you're long-distance. You'll want to talk at length about their approach to the ceremony, how much latitude you have to personalize the proceedings, and what kind of language they use about God—if you don't believe in a savior, you don't want one invoked during your service; if you're extremely religious, you want to make sure your officiant honors the same beliefs you do.

Instinctively you'll know if you feel comfortable with the officiant and if you have a good rapport. You'll also learn a lot by the way he answers your questions and by how much time he is willing to give to the discussions. Ask yourself if this is the person you want delivering a sermon about the two of you. If he's cracking bad jokes during your conversation, he's likely to be equally off-putting at the ceremony. If he's always cutting you off or saying "Don't worry about that," you have reason to worry. You want an officiant who takes a thoughtful

approach to the wedding, not someone who shows up at the last minute and phones in a performance (or worse, doesn't show up at all!).

These are topics and questions that you'll want to bring up with potential officiants. Some of them apply to all officiants, while others are specific to officiants-for-hire, and still others pertain to clergymen affiliated with a house of worship.

QUESTIONS REGARDING THE CEREMONY SITE

☐ *Are there restrictions on the choice of music? Do I need to work with the church's organ player or choir, or can I bring in outside musicians?*

☐ *Are there any rules about amplification of sound?*

☐ *Are photography and videography permitted? Are there any restrictions on lights or where they can be set up?*

☐ *Are there any restrictions regarding clothing? Some houses of worship may require arms and shoulders to be covered. What about head coverings?*

☐ For a Jewish wedding, ask who will provide the chuppah. *Are there any restrictions on how it is decorated? Who will provide the ketubah (Jewish marriage contract)?*

☐ If you're having an off-site wedding, *what will you need to provide for the ceremony? An altar, chuppah, table, altar cloth, kneeling cushion, candles?*

QUESTIONS REGARDING THE CEREMONY

☐ *How many readings are customary? Are there any restrictions on the choice of readings?*

☐ *Is premarital counseling required?*

☐ *Do you have a contract? (This may be needed if you're working with a paid officiant outside of a house of worship.)*

☐ *How long is the ceremony?*

☐ *How much flexibility is there in the ceremony script? Can I write my own vows? Add a blessing or a unity ceremony?*

Having guests sit wherever they like also keeps you from ending up with one side of the church three-quarters full and the other side three-quarters empty, an imbalance that can prove awkward and cause people to draw inaccurate conclusions.

Older guests will often tell the ushers which side of the family they're on and ask on which side they should sit. The ushers should simply tell them that it's open seating and they should sit wherever they like.

Reserved Seating

THE FIRST FEW ROWS of seats should be reserved for close family members. This is one of those small details that's really important—you want those closest to you to feel like they have an honored place and a good view.

Some churches mark off the first few rows of pews with ribbons; guests to be seated in those rows receive a separate "within the ribbon" card or a pew card in their

What is the fee, honorarium, or requested donation? Is a deposit required? With an unaffiliated officiant, it's usually a fee. For others, it's usually a donation or honorarium. If you pay a deposit, make sure you get a receipt.

What does the fee include?

Are there additional charges for travel time, the rehearsal, or saying a blessing at the reception meal?

If the officiant is traveling for your wedding, discuss how to handle travel expenses, for which the couple pays. Also ask what he needs to do to legally officiate at your wedding location; he may have to register there or get a license.

If you've never met the officiant and he's not a civil servant, ask him to provide a couple of references from couples he has married. You don't want to be scammed by someone who has set up a minister-for-hire website.

Will you conduct the ceremony outside of a house of worship? If so, does that change any of the restrictions?

If I want to include a pet, is that acceptable?

If you have children, ask about ways he might make them feel part of the ceremony.

If you're pregnant and working with a religious officiant, make sure he is willing to marry you.

Interfaith couples should ask about any limitations regarding interfaith marriages. If you want to use cofficiants, find out if he'll perform alongside another clergy person. In Roman Catholic weddings, the priest has to be the one performing the marriage if it takes place in a church; outside of a church, he may agree to cofficiate. If you're still seeking a second officiant of a different faith, ask if he's worked with anyone he'd recommend. It really adds to the ceremony when the cofficiants feel comfortable with each other.

How many other weddings are you doing that day? What happens if an earlier wedding runs late?

If the ceremony is Christian, will it include Communion? If it's Catholic, will it include a nuptial mass?

Will you lead a rehearsal? When does it typically take place? How long does it last?

How many meetings will we have about the ceremony?

If one of you is divorced, tell the officiant and ask if that poses any problems or if you'll be required to produce special documentation or get a dispensation.

If you're contacting an independent officiant, ask what authority he has to perform legal ceremonies. For your own peace of mind, find out what church ordained him. Also check his references through the church offices.

Are there any rules regarding the religion of the attendants?

When do you sign the marriage license? At the ceremony or beforehand? (It's easier to get it out of the way before the ceremony.)

invitation, or after they RSVP, to hand to the ushers. In most churches, the wedding director automatically reserves the first few rows by putting RESERVED signs on those rows and roping them off with ribbon. If you are detail oriented, you may choose to take it a step further and have a calligrapher write each guest's name on a card to be placed directly on the seat. Or you can print the cards from home. (If you put cards on seats, you don't need ribbons marking off the reserved area.)

Ask all of the parents for a list of people they'd like to seat, so you won't leave out anyone important. If you have a flower girl, ring bearer, or other children in the wedding party, remember to reserve them and their caregiver a seat.

If you're not sending out pew cards, tell these guests in advance that you've reserved a seat for them. And don't forget to give the ushers a list of those with reserved seats.

Cell Phones at the Ceremony

Ringing cell phones are one of those modern concerns that must be addressed. Hence, the recent addition of the cell phone announcement to the pantheon of wedding etiquette. (It's also the perfect time to announce any rules about photos and flash photography.)

For the guests, post a sign or have the wedding planner or a family member or friend make an announcement before the officiant enters; I prefer posting a sign, which I find more subtle. Have it penned in calligraphy, with a pretty border, or at least take care in choosing a nice font, and put it where guests will see it as they enter; some churches will already have signs in place. Don't forget to remind the wedding party beforehand as well.

I like to inject a little humor in the wording so it doesn't sound heavy-handed. (See samples.) An image of a cell phone with a diagonal line running across it also helps get the message across.

If you choose to make an announcement, appoint someone to welcome everyone to the wedding and ask that they turn off their cell phones. If you have a wedding planner, she typically makes the announcement; otherwise, a family member or friend who is comfortable in front of large groups (like your cousin the actor) can fill the bill. This should happen right before the ceremony begins, before the officiant enters. The announcer can also remind guests about any restrictions on photography. Again, a little levity can help. I usually have someone say: "The only bells that the bride and groom want to hear are wedding bells. Please take a moment to turn off your cell phones."

Joining the ringtone issue is the current phenomenon of guests waving their camera phones around at the ceremony. If you'd like to keep your ceremony private, you'll be joining a growing contingent of brides and grooms who've opted to do just that. The ceremony is an incredibly special and meaningful moment, and you've invited guests not as amateur videographers but as witnesses to that moment. Asking them to honor the spirit of the occasion is completely appropriate, and wording such as "We gratefully request that no pictures be taken and nothing be posted to social media during the ceremony—and please remember to silence your phones!" should cover your bases. Post the message on signage outside the ceremony site, and print it in your programs for good measure. Though there's no way to fully police your request, in my experience guests are happy to comply. For more on social media and privacy concerns, see page 104.

> IN HONOR OF THIS
> ONCE-IN-A-LIFETIME MOMENT,
> PLEASE TURN OFF ALL
> CELL PHONES.

> The only "ring" we want to hear about is ours.
>
> Please turn off your cell phone.
>
> Love,
> the Grooms

Where Parents Sit

At Christian weddings, the bride's mother is the last person to be seated. She sits in the first seat in the front row, on the left side of the aisle. The seat beside her is left open for the bride's father to occupy once he has walked his daughter down the aisle. In Jewish weddings, both sets of parents traditionally stand under the chuppah with the couple; but if parents are seated, they would sit in the front row, across the aisle from each other. If your parents are divorced, seating depends on their relationship. If they get along, you can seat them next to each other. However, if one or both of them is remarried, they should be seated next to their spouses.

If the relationship is not cordial, seat them at opposite ends of the front row. Or the father can be seated one or two rows behind the mother.

Note: In a Jewish wedding, only parents are allowed to stand under the chuppah; any spouses or dates would sit in one of the first few rows.

The Aisle Runner

The aisle runner is meant to be kept pristine for the bridal party. Traditionally, that means it's not unfurled until the moment before the processional. (In a Christian wedding, the runner is placed after the bride's mother is seated.)

Two ushers unroll the runner and, if necessary, tape it in place. (Your florist can provide the right kind of tape.) When possible, they should practice laying it down at the rehearsal—it's harder than it sounds.

I should say that I find this tradition fraught with problems. Aisle runners can be quite unwieldy, and the groomsmen don't always get out those treacherous lumps and bumps. I nearly always have the aisle runner rolled out and tacked in place ahead of time. To keep it absolutely spotless for the wedding party, guests are directed to walk down the side aisles to their seats, or the center aisle is ribboned off.

Ceremony Components

When planning your ceremony, think about all of the standard components of a wedding:

Prelude music

Honored guests are seated

Processional music

Processional

Officiant's opening remarks

Vows

Exchange of rings

Other unity customs

Pronouncement

The kiss

Recessional music

Recessional

The Processional

At a mainstream Protestant wedding, the music begins, and the officiant enters from the side. The groom and best man follow and stand to the right side of the altar. The groomsmen then walk down the aisle in pairs, escorting bridesmaids, or solo. In some cases, they enter from the side and take their places at the altar.

While it used to be customary for bridesmaids and groomsmen to walk down the aisle in pairs, now more couples are choosing to have the groomsmen go down the aisle one by one, followed by the bridesmaids—a terrific approach if the numbers of attendants don't match up. If you have a very large wedding party (six or more attendants on each side), it's better to have them walk in multiples, or the processional will drag on too long.

The maid of honor is the last of the bridesmaids. The ring bearer is next, followed by the flower girl. Finally, the bride and her father appear, with the bride standing to the left of her father. In most congregations, everyone rises when the bride appears.

At a Jewish wedding, there are no set rules, but the processional usually involves the wedding party walking down the aisle. It's led by the rabbi (and the cantor, if one is present). The grandparents follow and take their seats in the front row. The placement of the groomsmen and brides-maids can vary, but at my weddings, the best man follows the grandparents, then the groom is escorted down the aisle by both parents. The groomsmen and bridesmaids come next, then the maid of honor, ring bearer, and flower girl. The bride, like the groom, is escorted by both parents, with her father on her left and her mother on her right. All four parents stand under the chuppah during the ceremony.

While in traditional weddings the groom walks first and the bride's trip down the aisle is the big moment, in same-sex weddings there's no clear answer to the question of who goes first. Some couples circumvent the question by happily marching down the aisle arm in arm; others widen the aisle so they can fit as a foursome, with a parent on either side. One set of brides wove their way around the outside of the aisles and met in the middle, beneath the chuppah.

Procession Order for Catholic and Protestant Weddings

There's no reason you couldn't modify the traditional processional order to suit your needs, but here it is for reference:

- Officiant enters.
- Groom's grandparents are seated.
- Bride's grandparents are seated.
- Groom's parents are seated.
- Bride's mother is seated.
- Best man usually enters from the side.
- Groom usually enters from the side.
- Groomsmen and bridesmaids come down the aisle.
- Maid of honor comes down the aisle.
- Ring bearer comes down the aisle, then takes a seat.
- Flower girl comes down the aisle, then takes a seat.
- Bride and her father come down the aisle.
- For the recessional, the order is reversed. It's led by the bride and groom, followed by the flower girl and ring bearer (though if they took seats during the ceremony and miss their place in line, it's not a big deal); the maid of honor and best man; then the other attendants—they usually pair up to make the recessional more time efficient.
- Guests file out, starting with the front row.

At the Altar: A Christian Wedding

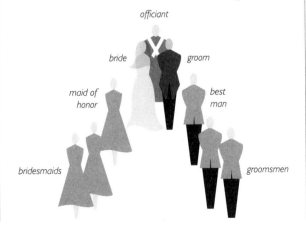

Procession Order for Jewish Weddings

There are no hard-and-fast rules, but this is the order I think works best:

- Rabbi (and cantor, if you have one) enters.
- Groom's grandparents are seated.
- Bride's grandparents are seated.
- Best man comes down the aisle.
- Groom is walked down the aisle by both parents.
- Groomsmen and bridesmaids come down the aisle.
- Maid of honor comes down the aisle.
- Ring bearer comes down the aisle, then takes a seat.
- Flower girl comes down the aisle, then takes a seat.
- Bride is walked down the aisle by both parents.
- The recessional is led by the bride and groom, who are followed by the bride's parents, the groom's parents, the attendants, and the rabbi and cantor.

Under the Chuppah: A Jewish Wedding

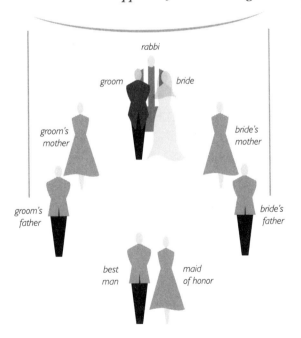

Walking the Bride Down the Aisle

IT'S TRADITIONALLY the role of the father of the bride to walk his daughter down the aisle, but it's not a one-size-fits-all world. Sometimes the father is deceased, doesn't have a role in his daughter's life, or is unavailable for the job. In that case, the bride can ask her mother or a male family member like an uncle, grandfather, godfather, or brother to walk her down the aisle. Some brides have asked close male friends to do the honors. If a stepfather has a strong presence in a bride's life, he often walks with her.

In a Jewish ceremony, both parents traditionally walk their child down the aisle. If only one parent is still living or available, that parent can do the honors alone or ask a relative to join in on this momentous walk.

If your parents are divorced and not on good terms, it may be difficult to envision them taking on a joint role. But even in extreme cases where parents aren't on speaking terms, it's sometimes possible for them to pull out good behavior you didn't know they were capable of—just for you. But I've also seen brides choose to walk unescorted, meeting the groom on their own terms. This is a tradition, not a rule, so do whatever feels right to you.

Making It Yours

The main areas where you have leeway to alter the ceremony are the music, the vows, and the readings, but simply spending the time to get to know your officiant can make his service that much more heartfelt. Don't be afraid to embrace traditions from other cultures or religions that speak to you, as long as they have the blessing of your officiant. (One Christian couple incorporated a chuppah into their outdoor ceremony at a golf club in Wisconsin. The bride's parents built and decorated the chuppah themselves, and both sets of parents joined the couple under the canopy during the ceremony.)

Make a Wish

Brides and grooms are finding increasingly inventive ways to involve the guests in creating a warm cocoon of good wishes for their marriage. At one of my weddings, each guest received a flower upon arrival and was asked to make a wish on it and tuck it into arches lining the aisle. Other couples have handed out river rocks or wishing stones and had guests make a wish and place them into a special vessel during the ceremony; later, the stones can be incorporated into the couple's garden or given a special place in their home. At a beach wedding, you might ask every guest to collect a shell. It's a great way to incorporate any object that's meaningful or spiritual to you.

Write Your Vows

DOES WRITING YOUR OWN vows make them more personal? It does for some people, while others wouldn't even consider a marriage official without traditional vows. If you're not particularly religious, read over the vows your officiant normally uses. Do they make you well up with emotion or leave you flat? That will tell you how to proceed.

Many modern couples modify the vows just a bit in order to get rid of sexist language, starting with having the officiant declare them "husband and wife" instead of "man and wife." Or the bride may object to being "given away" and ask the officiant to omit these words. Some couples also find that modifying the language to give it a more contemporary feel makes the vows that much more real to them.

Should you decide to write your own vows, don't fly blind—head to a bookstore or library. There are several books full of detailed guidelines and inspiring samples. If you're getting married by a member of the clergy, remember that he may need to approve your vows in advance.

Have a Reading

A READING IS A WONDERFUL WAY to share something that's sacred or meaningful to you with your guests. It can also give a special role to a person you're close with. Don't overdo it, though; including more than two

---

Some of My Favorite Readings

If you're looking for inspiration, you can't go wrong by starting with these traditional wedding favorites.

Apache wedding prayer—known by this title, but it's not an authentic Apache poem—author unknown
   ("Now you will feel no rain . . .")

"Sonnet 43," by Elizabeth Barrett Browning
   ("How do I love thee?")

The Bible, Book of Ruth 1:16
   ("Whither thou goest . . .")

"The Passionate Shepherd to His Love," by Christopher Marlowe *("Come live with me . . .")*

Eskimo love song, author unknown
   ("You are my husband/wife . . .")

The Bible, First Corinthians 13:4–8
   ("Love is patient, love is kind . . .")

The Prophet, by Khalil Gibran
   ("Love one another . . .")

Letters to a Young Poet, by Rainer Maria Rilke (various)

The Bible, The Song of Songs (Song of Solomon) 2:8–10
   ("Listen! My lover!")

"Sonnet 116," by William Shakespeare
   ("Let me not to the marriage of true minds . . .")

"Give All to Love," by Ralph Waldo Emerson
   ("Give all to love; Obey thy heart . . .")

"Sonnet 17," by Pablo Neruda
   ("I do not love you as if you were salt-rose . . .")

---

readings will make the ceremony drag. If you're getting married in a house of worship, you may be limited in your choices, so ask the officiant before you do anything.

You can either choose a passage yourself or allow your reader the choice; in the latter case, make sure to give some guidance.

Beyond the Bible, there are endless rich sources for readings—poems, passages in a favorite book, song lyrics, or famous love letters. Couples have used everything from treasured children's books like *The Velveteen Rabbit* to Anne Morrow Lindbergh's *Gift from the Sea*. There are wonderful words to be found in Eskimo love songs, Shaker hymns, Buddhist marriage homilies, Native American wedding poems, and Chinese proverbs. And would it really be an Irish wedding without an Irish blessing? Make sure to identify any readings in your ceremony program (see pages 287 and 439).

Special Songs

THE OTHER MAJOR WAY to personalize the ceremony is through the songs you include. You've got the processional and recessional music to play with, and you can also include a meaningful song at another point in the ceremony. It can be instrumental or vocal, performed by the church organist or by your favorite niece. (Note that a house of worship is likely to put constraints on the music selections.) For more detailed information, see page 122.

Light a Candle

SYMBOLIC UNITY CEREMONIES, representing two people and families becoming one, are among the most moving rituals I've seen. The most common version is the lighting of a unity candle. Although the ritual is particularly popular at Protestant weddings, its origin is secular; lighting a unity candle is appropriate at any type of wedding. (Just make sure your house of worship allows the candles, as some do not.)

Though this modern ritual is ever evolving, in the most traditional approach the mothers of the bride and groom each light a taper candle at the beginning of the ceremony and place the lit candles on either side of the central pillar candle. After the "I dos" and ring exchange, the bride and groom each take one of the taper candles and use them to light the large pillar candle, extinguishing the taper candles to symbolize that the single, united flame is now more important than the individuals. Some couples, however, prefer to keep their tapers lit to symbolize the fact that their individuality burns strong alongside their union.

If the marriage will also serve to blend families, the children can participate by getting their own tapers. And the ritual can easily be broadened to represent family and friends coming together. At a small wedding, a couple may ask every guest to walk down the aisle with a candle and place it in a candelabra. I've also seen couples choose to forgo attendants, instead inviting family members and friends to participate in some form of candle lighting.

Incorporate an Heirloom

KEEPING A REMINDER of a relative close to you underscores the sentiment that a wedding is about you and your families. If the item belonged to a deceased relative who was particularly dear to you, it can help you feel as if that person is present and taking part in your wedding.

Unattended Children

If children in the wedding party also have a parent in the wedding party, you'll need to make sure that an adult they know can not only look out for them after they walk down the aisle but also do the all-important, preceremony bathroom reminder and be prepared to take the child out of the ceremony area if he becomes too loud. I recommend having treats on hand for bribing! (For more on keeping children occupied during the ceremony, see page 333.)

After children walk down the aisle, they shouldn't be expected to stand, so make sure you've reserved a seat for them and their "keeper" somewhere in the front.

More than likely, it will fulfill your "something old" at the same time.

Many brides choose to make a family Bible part of their ceremony. Rosary beads can serve the same purpose. Men can incorporate a family watch, cuff links, or a wedding band, and either the bride or groom can find a use for a handkerchief from a beloved relative.

Wearing family jewelry is another time-honored tradition. For a bride to walk down the aisle in the same pearls her mother or grandmother wore on her wedding day truly makes her feel like she's following in the footsteps of the women in her family.

If there's a meaningful piece of jewelry in the family that doesn't quite work for you, find another way to make it part of the day. Some brides have a family ring sewn into the hem of their gown. You can put a baroque brooch on display by pinning it to the fabric cuff on your bouquet (discuss ideas with your florist ahead of time) or by attaching it to a fabric handbag. If all else fails, you can always tuck a special memento into your handbag.

Your mother's gown may not work as your dress, but could part of it be turned into a ring bearer's pillow or an inset on your train? Many brides cherish the chance to wear a veil from their family, but it can also be used as part of a chuppah or turned into a shrug or handbag. On the guy's side, tallith (Jewish prayer shawls) from a grandfather or other relative make a wonderful covering for the chuppah.

Don't be limited by convention. The mother of one bride surprised her daughter the night before the wedding by presenting her with a teddy bear made from her late grandmother's fur stole. The stole's monogrammed satin lining became the bear's paw pads, and he occupied a front-row seat at the ceremony.

Be a Lucky Bride

Every bride wants to attract good fortune and ward off "evil spirits" on her wedding day. Here are some traditions from around the world for bringing luck—one of them might have your name on it.

Honoring the Deceased

Many couples want to honor deceased relatives by symbolically representing their presence at the wedding. Traditionally, one might leave an empty chair with the person's name on it, but I think it preferable to find a way to honor the family member in a more private manner; after all, this is a celebration, and you don't want to sadden everyone. This could mean wearing something that belonged to the person, visiting the cemetery before the wedding, playing his favorite song, carrying her favorite flower, or wearing a charm or locket with a photo of the deceased.

If the death was very recent, it might be appropriate to add a note or dedication to the program, such as: "Even on this day of joy, we want to remember those who are no longer with us," then giving the person's name and relationship to the bride or groom. If the officiant knew the family member, he might be able to weave him into his speech.

Put a sixpence in your shoe. A tradition with English brides, who tuck a sixpence into their left slipper. In fact, the entire "something old" saying goes like this: "Something old, something new, something borrowed, something blue, *and* a silver sixpence in her shoe." Several Internet retailers actually specialize in silver sixpence just for this purpose, but many people substitute a U.S. dime, even though they're no longer made of silver. Swedish brides slip a silver coin from their father into their left shoe, and a gold coin from their mother into their right; the coins ensure that the bride will always have money.

Carry a horseshoe. Irish brides believe carrying a horseshoe will bring luck to the marriage. Some wear a horseshoe charm, but you could also attach a horseshoe pin to the cuff of the bouquet. A horseshoe should always be positioned so that it's open on the top—that's how it holds the luck it catches.

Wear an eye charm. At Greek weddings, the bride, her attendants, or guests often wear a *mati*, a blue glass bead shaped like an eyeball, to ward off evil spirits. It's usually a charm or pin; some brides slip it inside their dress.

Carry a lump of sugar. Greek brides slip a sugar cube into their glove, believing it will bring them a sweet life.

Get henna tattoos. *Mehndi* is the Hindu word for the intricate henna designs painted on a bride's hands and feet. Henna has been heralded for its magical properties since ancient times and is believed to ward off evil spirits. It's customary for Indian, Pakistani, Persian, North African, and other Muslim brides to have a mehndi party a day or two before the wedding. (For more about mehndi designs and parties, see page 89).

Kiss a chimney sweep. Easier said than done today, but in Great Britain, it's considered lucky for the bride to kiss a chimney sweep on her wedding day. He has special powers, and when he makes the chimney safe, he also sweeps away evil spirits.

Have 1,001 cranes. Cranes, a symbol for peace, happiness, and longevity, are thought to live for 1,000 years; at Japanese weddings, the presence of 1,001 white paper origami cranes is said to make a wish come true or to wish the couple good luck more than 1,000 times over. The cranes can be placed at the ceremony or reception.

Get sprinkled with sugar. At Iranian wedding ceremonies, happily married women hold a cloth over the bride and groom, then scrape elaborate sugar cones over them, letting sugar rain down on the cloth for good luck.

Tradition, Your Way

Every culture and religion has its own wonderful twist on wedding traditions, and increasingly, couples are reaching into their own histories or the customs of other cultures for meaningful rituals to incorporate into their weddings. In our hyperglobal, fusion-loving world, it's become as natural as hopping on a plane.

Jewish Traditions

Breaking the Glass

The ancient custom of stomping on a glass at the end of the ceremony is laden with symbolism. There is no single, agreed-upon meaning to the act—some say it's a reminder that destruction and loss should be remembered even at a joyous moment, others that it specifically represents the destruction of the Temple in Jerusalem, and still others that it's a foreshadowing of the impending loss of the bride's virginity. One thing is certain: It signals the end of the solemnity and the beginning of the celebration. The glass is traditionally stomped on by the groom, but modern couples may choose to break it together. Be sure to wrap it in a cloth (use a napkin or a specially designed pouch) to prevent foot injuries, and don't use very cheap glass; it's too hard to break. A thin crystal glass will shatter with much less effort.

The Chuppah

The chuppah is a canopy attached to four poles, under which the bride and groom are married. It's open on all four sides, as a reference to Abraham's tent and hospitality, representing God's presence at the wedding and the couple's first home. If the couple has a custom-made cover for the chuppah, they might choose to display it at home after the wedding. For more direction on constructing and decorating a chuppah, see page 305.

Down the Aisle

In Judaism, both parents escort the bride and groom to the chuppah, symbolizing the union of the families. It's a way of acknowledging that both parents have played an important role in their son's or daughter's life, making it a more egalitarian option than having the father alone walk the bride down the aisle.

Yichud

In ancient times, the purpose of this fifteen-minute period of seclusion, immediately following the ceremony, was to consummate the marriage. Today, it's when the bride and groom share their first meal as husband and wife or enjoy a few private moments together to consider the ceremony. Providing the couple with both emotional and physical sustenance, *yichud* is a tradition that can benefit a couple of any faith.

ASK MINDY

Q I come from a nonpracticing Episcopalian family, and my fiancé is Jewish. Not a problem— or so I thought—since religion has never come up as a serious topic. I happily agreed to a reform Jewish wedding, but it seems like a much bigger deal. The wedding is becoming more religious by the minute, to the point where I'm worried the service may exclude my side of the family. What can I do to even the score gracefully? (His family is paying.)

A Speak up: Remind your fiancé that you agreed to a reform wedding. Point out anything that's making you uncomfortable, and ask for his help in making a change. You may also want to ask the rabbi if he or she can incorporate something from your culture to balance things out. Use the program to explain the Jewish traditions to guests who might not be familiar with them. That should go a long way toward making your side of the family feel more comfortable. Try to incorporate your family's traditions or heritage in the reception, too. Strive for balance. If you're doing the hora, follow it up with a traditional dance from your culture. Even though his family is paying, it should be about what the two of you want.

African Traditions

Jumping the Broom

This ritual has been reclaimed from its sinister roots in slavery, when African Americans were denied the right to legally marry and performed such symbolic acts to solemnify their unions on their own. To signify their leap into a new life together, the couple jumps over a broom (often decorated with some combination of ribbons, flowers, and cowrie shells) at the end of the ceremony.

Crossing Sticks

The bride and groom each hold a branch of a tree and cross them while saying a prayer. The trees symbolize strength, a rooted family, and the desire for a grounded marriage. To give them personal meaning, the branches can come from the respective homes of the bride and groom, or from another place that is special to the couple. If they met in college, for example, the branches could come from their campus.

Tasting the Four Elements

In a tradition of the Yoruba people in Africa, the bride and groom taste sour (lemon), bitter (vinegar), hot (cayenne), and sweet (honey), to represent the different stages and facets of a relationship. The tasting symbolizes the couple's willingness to journey through both good and hard times together.

Sharing a Kola Nut

A symbol of healing (due to its medicinal qualities) and fertility, the kola nut has long been linked to weddings in African societies. At Nigerian weddings, the couple and their parents share a kola nut to conclude the ceremony. Some couples choose to create a kola nut communion, having everyone partake of the kola nut at the ceremony. After the wedding, the nut can be kept in the couple's home to remind them to heal their rifts.

Celtic Traditions

Tartan Sharing

Strongly associated with culture and kinship, tartan plaid has an important place in Scottish wedding rites. At the end of a Scottish ceremony, the groom takes off the tartan sash bearing the family pattern and places it over the bride so it runs diagonally from shoulder to hip. It's a lovely way of demonstrating that she is now part of the family.

Handfasting

This pagan Celtic tradition once constituted a legal wedding ceremony. The couple's hands are crossed to create an infinity symbol and tied together with a cord to represent union. The cord is tied into a knot—one possible origin of the phrase "tying the knot." Handfasting is often used at pagan and Wiccan ceremonies and is popu-

What to Toss

The tradition of throwing rice at the bride and groom as they exit the church actually stems from an ancient fertility rite. (Today, it's more common to do it at the end of the reception, but with more couples skipping the grand exit, it might make sense to shift it back to the end of the ceremony.)

Uncooked rice can be harmful to birds, so have guests throw rose petals instead—they'll make for a gorgeous photo, and they're relatively easy to clean up. Any florist should be able to supply them. If real petals prove impractical, you can buy fabric petals from a florist supply house, chain craft store, or party supply company. You can even order freeze-dried petals in a choice of colors from some specialty stores. Other tossing alternatives include birdseed and confetti; guests can even blow bubbles at the bride and groom.

Check with your site about restrictions. Some places have rules against tossing anything, some may charge an additional cleanup fee, and some may require you to arrange for the cleanup yourself.

lar at less traditional unions, especially those not legally recognized. However, it's also used at Christian and non-denominational ceremonies.

Spanish and Mexican Traditions

Wrapping the Couple

This intimate, quietly celebratory Spanish tradition shifts some of the ceremony's focus to the families, giving them an active role in the proceedings. Both sets of parents come up to the altar to wrap the couple in a mantilla (a long rectangular veil) for several seconds as a symbol of the unification of the families. Afterward, the mothers fold up the mantilla together.

The Lasso

After the bride and groom have said their vows, a "lasso" of rosary beads, orange blossoms, or white ribbon is draped in a figure eight around their shoulders. The loop is a symbol of love and unity. At the end of the ceremony, it's presented to the bride as a keepsake.

Thirteen Gold Coins

Though this tradition originated in Spain, it migrated to the New World. A godparent holds a dish containing thirteen gold coins. (The number thirteen is a representation of Christ and his twelve apostles.) The groom takes the coins and pours them into the bride's cupped hands—entrusting her with all of his worldly possessions and showing that he's committed to providing for her. The priest blesses the coins, which later become a keepsake in the couple's home.

Asian and Indian Traditions

Tea Ceremonies

Many Asian couples hold tea ceremonies on their wedding day to honor their families. The bride and groom kneel in front of older relatives and family friends and offer them a cup of tea as a sign of respect. Honorees typically respond by giving the couple an envelope containing money or gold jewelry.

Sharing Sake

Shinto, Buddhist, and Christian Japanese weddings tend to have one thing in common: a sake-sharing ceremony called *san-san-kudo*. To formalize the union of their families, the bride and groom, followed by their parents, take three sips from each of three sake cups.

Henna

Adorning the bride with henna, or mehndi, is common practice in India and in the Middle East among Muslims, Hindus, and Sikhs. The bride's hands and feet are painted with intricate designs a few days before the wedding, sometimes at a mehndi party with her female friends and family members. The deep red natural dye stains the skin and lasts two to four weeks. Legend holds that the darker the stain, the deeper the love of the mother-in-law for the bride.

You've paved the way for an unforgettable ceremony; to make sure it lives on beyond *your* treasured memories, read on. Photography, and sometimes videography, are the indispensable tools that will enable you to pass on those memories to future generations—not to mention the pleasure you'll get out of thumbing through the photographs and reliving it all yourself. ♦

CHAPTER SEVEN

Making Memories

PHOTOGRAPHY AND VIDEOGRAPHY

Who doesn't remember being totally transfixed by her parents' wedding album as a child? Even the biggest cameraphobe has to admit: A wedding isn't an event to entrust to memory. It's just one day, that's true, but it's a day that changes the course of your life. That's where photos and video come in. And that's why you want to hire

a professional. You want images that don't simply record the events, but evoke the emotions of the day. A good photographer can even capture details that might escape you and your guests—the way the bride's father looked into her eyes one last time before handing her over to her groom, the bashful excitement of the five-year-old flower girl.

Video adds another dimension, bringing the wedding to life over and over again—the slip of the tongue during the vows, the toast that had everyone in the room chortling, the bride's shrieks as her chair was lifted up for the hora.

Photography and videography have been transformed in recent years by a new degree of professionalism and a wave of technological advances. The advances have led to more choices—and to couples spending more money on their photography and videography. These days, you can commission artists to create a narrative of your day worthy of a gallery wall or an art house cinema. That's why it's so important to learn how to evaluate a photographer's book, what to look for in a video, how to choose between black and white or color, film or digital. You'll find suggested shot lists and tips for developing a strong rapport with the photographer and videographer. Once you're done, you'll be ready for your close-up.

PHOTOGRAPHY

Choices, Choices

Before you start interviewing photographers, you should think about what kind of photography you want: portraiture or action shots, film or digital, color or black and white. Some photographers offer a combination.

Because one size doesn't fit all—especially when family opinions get factored into the equation—some couples hire a photographer proficient in several styles. If you hire only one type of photographer to cover more than one base, make sure that he's willing to shoot in the other style and that you review the quality of his work in both areas.

Photojournalists or *documentary photographers* strive to document the day as it unfolds, to tell a story. Their unscripted photos have a more modern look than traditional wedding photography. A photojournalist who shoots on the fly may not be skilled at lighting portraits; some documentary photographers won't set up portraits at all, while others are more flexible. Find out, and also ask if they'll work with a shot list, as some may not.

Traditional or *classic photographers* tend toward posed photos that need to be set up, with time spent on portraits and wedding-day milestones (first dance, cake cutting, and the like). The photographer will bring lighting and possibly a backdrop for photos. He'll shoot a lot of frames to get the perfect picture and interact fairly heavily with

guests. When evaluating the book of a traditional wedding photographer, see if you like the composition of the photos, the backdrops, and the poses. If the poses make you groan or you find the setups trite, it's not the right match.

Fine art photographers take an artistic approach, producing dramatic photos with a particular point of view or style. They often shoot on film, which can create stunning results but offers less flexibility for low-light settings and takes longer to process. They typically shoot what they find compelling, so find out if they're willing to work with a shot list. Photos are printed on archival photo paper, and the photographer often brings specialized equipment and a broader array of lenses. While the results can be gorgeous, you may need to supplement their work with that of a traditional wedding photographer if you want to keep the family happy. (See opposite page for more on the choice between digital and film.)

Color vs. Black and White

BLACK-AND-WHITE photography is perennially popular in the bridal world, and justifiably so. The format makes for dramatic, artful, evocative pictures with a timeless look. Black-and-white film is particularly wonderful at capturing a mood and letting shadow and light create the drama. And among other upsides, it can help prevent Aunt Trudy's bright-pink gown from sticking out like a sore thumb in perpetuity! But the main reason people love the medium so much is plain and simple: Everyone looks better in black and white.

Still, most photographers will offer you a mix of black and white and color, and with good reason. You've spent time creating a harmonious color scheme—don't you want to be able to see it once the wedding day is over? Color will capture the dusky red of the roses, the blue of the ocean, the pale-green sash on the flower girl's gown.

Photographers who work digitally shoot everything in color and then process images to achieve the desired effect (black and white, sepia, "bleached") after the fact. With film, you and the photographer should discuss your preferences in advance, as making black-and-white prints from color film will compromise the quality.

The Rise of the Photo Booth

Photo booths, one of the most fun recent wedding trends, can bring a whimsical and interactive touch to a reception. Though totally optional, they're almost universally beloved. Frequently stocked with lighthearted props, they tap into guests' desire to vamp it up in their party clothes while striking seriously silly poses with friends. They give guests a physical memento to take home, one that's way more special and concrete than that six-hundredth selfie. And, when combined with a guestbook, they leave the bride and groom with a wonderful keepsake filled with candid pics and heartfelt messages.

Photo booths aren't something your wedding photographer will offer, so if you're interested, you'll need to go through a photo booth company or consider the DIY route.

You can opt for an old-school booth with a curtain and a small seat, but these days, couples tend to go the open-booth route, with guests posing in front of a backdrop. You can crowd more people into an open-booth setup, and there's more room for action shots, too! Many of today's photo booths also offer guests the option of instantly sharing their pics on social media, so they're getting the best of all possible worlds. The machines will usually come staffed by an attendant and may include a variety of props—think fake mustaches, boas, funny glasses, and oversized picture frames.

A four-hour-long photo booth rental will run anywhere from $650 to $1,200, but a DIY version can be made for much less. Photo booths are a great choice for DIY, given that they don't require duplicating your efforts across fifty dining tables or two hundred chair backs—but you may want to deputize a tech-savvy friend to help with setup and to check on the operation every once in a while.

You'll need some kind of a backdrop, a tripod or easel, and either an iPad or smartphone outfitted with a photo booth app (for shareable digital photos) or a Polaroid camera with a timer (for hard copies). But of course the real pleasure in creating a DIY photo booth comes in creating the backdrop and stocking the prop table.

Pinterest is a great source for inspiration, but common props include big block letters guests can use to spell out messages, paper parasols, and the aforementioned mustaches and picture frames. My personal preference is to keep things simple by focusing on a beautiful backdrop—a gorgeous length of patterned wallpaper, a wall of colorful streamers, or rows of gold fringe that catch the light. Oversized chalkboards or signage featuring the couple's names, the wedding date, the wedding hashtag (see page 104), or some combination thereof are other popular choices. If you're going to go that route, I think it's worth hiring a professional chalk artist or calligrapher to make those pieces—you'll be seeing a lot of them! Lastly, a photo booth is also a great place to play to any themes, visual or otherwise, that are present throughout your wedding day.

Going Old-School

LIKE THE VINYL RECORD, the roll of film is here to stay—both in the realm of high art and in the wedding world. Though most wedding photographers shoot in digital, some favor film photography for its ability to render contrast, texture, and light. Individual photographers tend to make the artistic choice to shoot with either film or digital and then stick to their guns, so the choice of photographer and format will go hand in hand. There are upsides to both schools of thought (and hugely talented artists in both camps), so before you commit to a photographer it's worth considering the pros and cons.

The biggest advantage to going digital, of course, is that the photographer can peek at the screen to see if he got the shot, a great feature when you're talking about a once-in-a-lifetime event. It shortens the time needed for group portraits, since he doesn't have to overshoot to make sure he was a decent shot of all twenty-one people. And yet it means that he *can* snap a hundred frames of the group shot if that's what it takes, since digital photographers aren't limited to a certain number of shots by the

Booking a Pro

In some cities, wedding "libraries" will let you come in and browse through the books of recommended photographers. Magazines and blogs featuring local weddings are another great place to scout for photographers. (Check the photo credits.) But many of the photographers will be in Los Angeles and New York, with fees commensurate to their names. Most wedding photographers routinely travel, though, so if you're willing to pay travel expenses, you don't need to limit yourself by location.

Your other vendors, especially the florist and the contact at your venue, are likely to know the good local photographers. Also ask at the bridal salon, since there's a close link between fashion and photography.

Act Fast

Many top photographers book a year out, so nail one down as early as possible. You'll need to have settled on your wedding date and the general location, but you don't need to have the venue booked or know the size of the guest list. Photography is so important to some people that I've actually seen couples change their wedding date to get the photographer they wanted!

Understandably, not everyone can book so far ahead, but your choices will start rapidly diminishing once you're within six months of the date.

cost or available quantity of film. Digital photographers also devote a significant amount of time to editing: cropping, retouching, or adding special effects. This means the blemish that appeared on your chin the morning of the wedding won't be making the history books. And unlike film photographers, who are hampered by processing time, digital photographers are able to send you a handful of preview pics in the days right after the wedding. Brides who want to update their social media feeds and change their relationship status directly after the wedding often find that last point to be a deciding factor.

But generally, the differences between the two mediums have diminished as equipment and technology have improved over time. Professionals use digital cameras of a much higher grade than what you might use at home, resulting in digital prints that are comparable in quality to film; they may also use effects designed to replicate the look of film, giving you the best of both worlds. One area in which film photography may not be able to compete with digital, however, is in the latter's ability to produce crisp, clean images in low light. For purists, though, the particularly rich texture of film can never be matched.

You may find that the photographer you like best shoots with film, and the choice will have been made for you. Though prints from film tend to be more expensive, the additional time digital photographers spend on effects and retouching may make up the difference.

Do You Need an Entourage?

THE NEED FOR multiple photographers depends on the size of your wedding and what kind of album you want. Any wedding with more than two hundred guests will benefit from multiple photographers. If you want pictures of yourself getting ready at home *and* of the groom and his attendants getting ready in their hotel suite, you're going to need more than one. For photos of the ceremony, having a photographer up front and another in back allows you to get pictures from more than one angle. If you're hiring photographers through the same studio, there's an additional charge for a second shooter, but it's less costly than hiring two unrelated photographers.

Quite a few husband-and-wife teams are well known in the field, and what could be better on your wedding day? You've got a guy to go to the groom's dressing room, and a woman to shoot the girls getting ready, and you have the positive karma of a married couple working together.

A photographer may also bring an assistant who shoots for part of the time, which is less expensive than hiring two full-fledged photographers.

Sticker Shock

DUE TO THE TIME and skill involved in shooting a wedding, photography will rank as one of your major expenses. Though together with videography (if it's involved), it often amounts to at least 10 percent of the overall budget, some couples allot 30 percent.

When you're trying to find funds for everything you want at a wedding, it's tempting to go with the immediate gratification of a dessert table rather than investing in something that doesn't contribute to the enjoyment of the day. But you want to cherish your photos, so this is not the place to cut corners—eliminate the chocolate-covered cherries to cover the photographer's assistant.

Fees vary widely across the country, but expect to pay anywhere from $2,500 to $5,000 for a basic package, and from $5,000 to $10,000 for a top photographer. Most require a deposit to hold the date (anywhere from $500 to half of the entire fee) and full payment two to three weeks before the event.

When comparing prices from photographers, look closely at charges for proofs, prints, and albums. Some photographers charge an artificially low fee to shoot the wedding but heavily mark up the price of prints, so you're paying more at the back end.

All the Precious Moments . . .

DO YOU WANT a photographer there for the rehearsal? The rehearsal dinner? Is the photographer visiting the bride's dressing room? Are you going to a separate site to shoot portraits? Will the photographer leave after the cake cutting or not until the last guest leaves? What about photos at the brunch the next day? If you're having a destination wedding, is it important to you to have a photographer there for the whole weekend, or just for the wedding itself? Your answers to these questions will affect your costs.

> If you can, book the photographer for the rehearsal or rehearsal dinner. You'll give him a chance to learn who's who before the big day.

Photography fees are based on the number of hours worked, so you may have to compromise and scale back on your dream coverage in order to be able to afford the photographer you love. You can always supplement the professional photos by having a talented relative take photos at pre- or post-wedding events.

Keep in mind, too, that photography is intense, physically grueling work, especially when you factor in the weight of the equipment—a high-end photographer might carry no less than *five* cameras around her neck. So you don't want to wear her out by expecting her to work twelve hours straight.

You don't need a photographer there the minute you start putting on makeup. Have her show up when you're putting on your dress and getting your face and hair touched up.

One last thing: Many couples choose to have the photographer leave soon after the cake cutting. Not everyone can afford to have the photographer stay till the end, but if you can manage it, that's often when you get the best pictures: the barefoot bride's arms wrapped around the groom's neck as they sway to a slow song, or a group of friends sitting on the floor with crystal flutes and a bottle of champagne.

Checking Out a Portfolio

After you've gathered recommendations, start checking out photographers' websites. If a photographer you like is booked, ask if there is someone else he would recommend, since the approach and quality are likely to be in the same vein.

Meet the photographer in person before making a decision. Personality is critical—you're going to be spending the entire day with him (whereas you may not even see your florist on your wedding day). If you're booking a photographer at your destination and it's not possible to meet in person, have a lengthy phone conversation.

A PHOTOGRAPHER

Though a photographer may provide most of this information without being asked, the following are all important points to cover with him during your interview.

- *What style of photography do you prefer?* Some photographers pride themselves on their photojournalistic style and are loath to do posed portraits.

- *Do you prefer to shoot film or digital?*

- *Do you prefer to shoot/process in black and white or color?* If he does a mix, what's the typical breakdown? Do couples have a choice in this percentage?

- *Do you bring an assistant?* The definition varies from one photographer to the next. Some photographers call a second shooter an assistant. Others have the assistant carry lights around.

- *What will the assistant do?* If the assistant will be taking photos, ask to see samples of his work.

- *Where will you and/or your assistant stand during the ceremony?* If you don't want them in the aisle where they may obstruct guests' views, make that clear.

- *How many hours are included in the package?*

- *What's the rate for extra hours?*

- *Is film included in the price, and is it limited to a certain number of rolls?*

- *Is film processing included in the price?*

- *How soon after the wedding will I get proofs* (small prints of selected photos)?

- *Will you post or send a teaser image or two for social media sharing in the days following the wedding?*

- *Are proofs part of the package or do they cost extra?* (They can run an extra $400 to $500.)

- *Will the proofs be posted online, delivered to me, or require a visit to your studio?*

- *Is an album included? If so, how many photos are included as part of the package?*

- *How much do additional prints cost?*

- *Are you willing to follow a shot list?*

- *Are the prints on archival quality paper?* Archival fiber paper lasts much longer than resin-coated paper.

- *Will there be a way to share photos online?* Some photographers post on photo-sharing sites or have their own password-protected sites.

- *Will guests be able to order prints directly?* This is a wonderful time-saver and convenience for the bride and groom.

- *Will you stand by the quoted fees, even if you raise your rates before my wedding?* If you're booking a photographer a year out, this is a particularly pertinent point.

- *Do you bring lighting?* Ask about the photographer's approach to lighting. Some use available light, others use "slave setups," positioning multiple lights in a corner of the room—but these can be obtrusive. Lighting is an important skill and deeply affects how you look in pictures, so you want to assess the photographer's knowledge. Indoor portraits nearly always require some extra lighting. Be skeptical of a photographer who tells you that he can shoot strictly with available light. Expect a very different approach to lighting between classic wedding photographers and photojournalists.

- *What type of clothing will you and your assistant wear? What kind of footwear?* If you have preferences, make them known. You want the photographer to be comfortable because he'll do better work, but you don't want a khaki photo vest in the midst of your black-tie reception. If he's going to wear sneakers, specify that they be black so they'll blend in.

How many photographers do you think I need for my wedding? See what the photographer says. If you have more than two hundred guests and want extensive coverage of your reception, you usually need two photographers. Some people want two at their ceremony to capture more than one angle.

What are my choices in albums? Are the photos mounted with photo corners? Slipped behind plastic? Printed directly onto the pages of a bound book to look like a coffee-table book? How much are extra albums? Is there a smaller album available? (These are sometimes appreciated by grandparents, close family members, and the maid of honor and best man.) Do you like the way the album is put together and the sensibility, or are there too many cheesy special effects for your taste?

Who owns the copyright to the photos? Typically, the photographer retains copyright and grants you certain usage rights. That means you'll have to go through the photographer for additional prints, which is more expensive than getting them printed on your own. Find out how long the photographer keeps the negatives—you may be able to buy them after a certain period.

How many weddings do you book per day? At the high end, photographers usually limit themselves to one per day, but some may try to squeeze in two a day. If yours is not the only wedding of the day, find out where he will be coming from and what happens if the other wedding runs late.

How long will you need for formal portraits of the couple and of family and friends? Make sure you adjust your wedding day schedule accordingly.

If you get sick and can't be at the wedding, what's the backup plan?

How many pictures can I expect to see? There is no magic answer; the purpose of the question is to establish clear expectations so that no one is disappointed. A photographer should have no problem telling you how many frames he averages, based on the length of the event. He might shoot 1,200 photos at a six-hour wedding, for example. More isn't necessarily better, but if you're the type of person who wants a lot of choices, don't go with a minimalist, "one perfect shot" photographer.

Will you visit the ceremony and reception sites before the wedding day? If he hasn't worked there before and he's in the area, it's a plus if he's willing to do a site visit.

Who gets the photography guidelines from the church or synagogue? It's often the couple, but make sure you're both clear on this. Some places don't allow a photographer at the altar, some don't allow flash, and some may not allow photos during the ceremony at all.

Ask for a couple of references. They should be clients who got married within the last year. Wedding photography is a very particular skill, so other types of clients aren't as relevant. If it's a studio or a company with multiple photographers, make sure the references worked with the same photographer. Ask former clients how the photographer acted at the wedding. *Did he draw a lot of attention to himself or stay in the background? Did he crack jokes in poor taste with the relatives? How long did he take to set up portraits? Did he capture the moments or try to put them on hold while he got his shot?*

Is there a minimum order for prints?

Photographers will sometimes offer discounts for putting down a higher deposit, for ordering prints early, or for weekday weddings. Ask if you're eligible for any price breaks.

How much of a deposit is required to hold the date?

When is the balance due?

What is the cancellation policy?

Will images from my wedding be posted to your professional website or social media feeds? If privacy is a concern, make sure you discuss how and where you photographs can be used.

Some of My Favorite Shots

Some of those less-expected shots can be the most memorable, setting a contemplative or whimsical tone to round out your book.

- Still life of the bride's shoes. There's something so pure and hopeful about those shoes before they get danced in and dirtied—it's all about new beginnings.

- The wedding gown on its hanger. A peaceful, beautiful shot.

- The rings. This detail shot is always touching, and if you're crafty, it makes for a lovely graphic on thank-you notes.

- The church or temple door. If there's a wreath on the door, all the better. This pre-festivities shot makes a great opener for your book.

- End-of-reception shots. The bridesmaids have kicked off their shoes, some of your friends are sitting on the floor, and only the most dedicated partygoers remain. . . .

When you make the appointment, tell him you want to see a set of proofs from a single wedding (not the greatest hits from many weddings). Just about anyone can get a great shot or two, but you want to see whether there's consistency all the way through. The advance notice gives him time to pull together the proofs in case he doesn't have them ready to show. He will show you a book of wedding photos or possibly a PowerPoint presentation. Evaluating the book is perhaps the most important part of the process.

If you're dealing with a photo studio, ask to look at the work of the photographer who would shoot your wedding, rather than a mix from the various photographers in the studio's stable. If they're not prepared to show you the individual photographer's work, move on.

When evaluating the book, look at the percentage of color to black and white and portraits to candids. Are both portraits and candids well done, or does the photographer have a clear strength? Is the composition pleasing? How do the subjects look?

If you like a photographer but haven't yet made the decision to hire him, book him to take an engagement portrait (see page 12). It gives you a chance to see his working style. And there are so many uses for a great engagement photo, from social media to save-the-dates or programs.

Working with a Photographer

Once you've hired a photographer you feel good about, it's likely you won't be in contact for a while. One to two months before the wedding, have a meeting, in person or by phone, to get reacquainted. Go over all of the points you agreed upon many months before, including the format, style, whether there's an assistant, the hours, and the location.

When creating your wedding day schedule, allow a meal break for the photographer. It's exhausting to be on your feet and lugging around equipment for hours on end, so make sure to give the photographer a chance to refuel. At a sit-down meal, have the photographer eat while the guests are eating, since you don't want shots of your nearest and dearest with their mouths full. There's usually a separate room for the vendors to eat in, but if you've gotten close with any of the vendors, asking them to join guests at tables can be a nice gesture.

Consult him on when he thinks you'd have the best light for photos, and build his recommendations into your schedule. Whenever possible, you want to use available light, not flash, which isn't as flattering or realistic.

Review dress with the photographer, and if your event is casual, by all means, let the photographer know. The photographer wants to blend in, which he won't do if he's in a dark suit when the guests are in jeans—or vice versa.

Once you've finalized the schedule, send a copy to the photographer and go over it together. Also give the photographer a shot list (see box, facing page) and a seat-

THE SHOT LIST

The shot list includes all the combinations of people you want the photographer to capture at the wedding. I've laid out the traditional shot list as a guide, but don't forget groups of family or friends who are rarely in the same place at once—college friends, high school friends, and cousins. Send the list to the photographer a few days before the wedding, and bring an extra copy with you on the wedding day.

A note: Step-parents should be included in the photos, with the frequency and combinations dependent on family dynamics. Ditto for step-siblings and half-siblings. If the bride or groom has children, they should be incorporated in as many shots as they can stand.

BEFORE THE BRIDE AND GROOM SEE EACH OTHER

- Bride
- Bride and father
- Bride and mother
- Bride and sister(s)
- Bride and brother(s)
- Bride, mother, sister(s)
- Bride, mother, sister(s), grandmother
- Bride and grandmother
- Bride, mother, mother-in-law
- Bride and mother-in-law
- Bride, mother-in-law, groom's sister(s), groom's grandmother
- Bride, groom's sister(s)
- Bride, bridesmaids
- Bride, flower girl

- Groom
- Groom, mother, and father
- Groom and father
- Groom and mother
- Groom, siblings, mother, father
- Groom and sister(s)
- Groom and brother(s)
- Groom, mother, siblings
- Groom, mother, siblings, grandmother
- Groom and grandmother
- Groom, grandmother, and grandfather
- Groom and grandfather
- Groom, mother, mother-in-law
- Groom, mother-in-law
- Groom, sister-in-law
- Groom, groomsmen

AFTER THE BRIDE AND GROOM SEE EACH OTHER

- Bride and groom
- Bride, groom, bride's mother and father
- Bride, groom, groom's mother and father
- Bride, groom, both sets of parents
- Bride, groom, wedding party
- Bride, groom, grandparents
- Bride, groom, each set of grandparents
- Bride, groom, siblings
- Bride, groom, maid of honor, and best man
- Bride, groom, flower girl, ring bearer

UNMISSABLE MOMENTS

- Room shots at ceremony
- Ketubah signing (Jewish)
- Signing of marriage certificate
- The bride walking down the aisle
- The groom's face as he waits/sees her
- Flower girl walking down the aisle
- Ring bearer walking down the aisle
- The vows
- The first kiss as husband and wife
- The recessional
- The first dance
- Father/daughter dance
- Mother/son dance
- The toasts
- The cake cutting
- Bouquet and garter toss
- Couple being showered with petals
- Couple's departure
- Room shots at reception
- Bride and bridesmaids getting ready
- Groom and groomsmen getting ready
- The "reveal"—when the couple sees each other for the first time before the wedding
- Close-up of seating-card display
- Parents of bride dancing
- Parents of groom dancing

seating chart so he can locate his targets—better yet, put table numbers next to the names on the shot list. Go over any special things you're doing at the wedding that you want documented—a special dance, a surprise that one of you has planned for the other, or the anniversary cake you're sending out to your aunt and uncle. If there are any unusual family dynamics, give him advance notice. Tell him whether you have children, and if there will be exes there or divorced parents.

VIDEOGRAPHY

A Plug for Wedding Videos

Wedding videos have come a long way. There were a lot of valid reasons they got a bad rap in the first place: in-your-face videographers putting guests on the spot to say something about the couple, the camera's bright light, poor sound quality, uneven lighting, and unsophisticated editing techniques in the finished product.

Today, digital technology and editing software have made it possible to get a video that elegantly captures your wedding, turning your story into a narrative that can make you laugh and cry at all the *right* places. The field is now staffed by creative and talented cinematographers, filmmakers who take an artistic approach to your wedding and will spare no effort in creating the effects they're looking for. They may use black and white for drama, intersperse it with color, and digitally alter sequences to give them the look of old home movies. And they may employ drones, steady-cam rigs, and sliders to capture crowd and overhead shots while giving their productions a richly cinematic feel.

For many couples video still plays second banana to photography, but it's worthwhile in its own right. You may not think it's a big deal now, but in ten years, you'll treasure the chance to see Grandma Rose smiling and chatting on your wedding day. You'll be able to replay your video on your anniversary and hear yourselves saying your vows all over again. If you have children in a few years, they will get a big kick out of seeing Mom and Dad tying the knot. And you'll be so busy on your wedding day that you won't even realize all of the things you miss—the wedding video will show those moments, from the guests greeting one another on their way into the ceremony to the shenanigans you missed while your back was turned for the bouquet toss.

That said, if your budget is tight, videography is probably something you can do without—or delegate to a friend.

Choices, Choices

Think about whether you prefer color, black and white, or a mix. Would you like to see an opening montage of shots (possibly including old photos) followed by the day's story? Would you rather have a series of vignettes or just watch the day unfurl? Would you like the video to have the choppy look of an old home movie or do you prefer smooth camera work? Do you want a video that's set to music?

How many cameras? Having two adds dimension to your video by giving you different angles, which is particularly effective for filming during the ceremony. (Find out the video rules at your ceremony site—some churches don't permit a video camera at the altar.) If the bride and groom are getting ready in different locations, two cameras will get you footage of both. You can negotiate to have two cameras for the preparations and the ceremony, then one camera for the rest.

Do you want interviews? "Interviews" are the man-on-the-street comments from your guests about you as a couple. They may be your favorite part of a video or they may make you painfully uncomfortable. If you decide you want them, tell the videographer if you want him to approach people randomly or whether you're going to

Dollars and Sense

As noted in the photography section, photography and videography account for 10 percent of the typical wedding budget.

For video, fees vary widely, depending on the area of the country, the skill level of the videographer, and the quality of his equipment and editing programs. At the low end, four hours of shooting will start around $850, but adding a second cameraman increases the expense. The more highly skilled the videographer and the more rigorous the editing, the pricier he's likely to be. (Editing is a time-intensive process.)

Film is much more expensive, because film itself is pricey. A forty-five-minute film shot in Super 8 (based on a full day of coverage) starts around $12,500 but could easily run much higher.

Most videographers require a deposit to hold the date; a typical videographer might ask for a third of the fee up front, and the balance a week or so before the event.

give him a list of people (with table numbers) to interview. You can take a different approach by announcing that the videographer will shoot interviews at a designated spot; anyone who wants to be on camera can approach him on their own. Don't pull people out of the reception room to do interviews, as it takes them away from the wedding.

How many videos? Do you want a short version (twenty to thirty minutes) and a long version (an hour or more)? Do you want a ten-minute video of your love story to show at the rehearsal dinner? In these "he said, she said" videos, the videographer weaves together childhood photos with current video, interviewing both members of the couple separately. The process gets you better acquainted with the videographer before the wedding, which should give you a stronger rapport on the wedding day.

How much video coverage? Do you want the videographer at the rehearsal dinner? In the bride and groom's dressing rooms? The time spent shooting correlates to the fee, so use it wisely. Couples trying to contain costs keep the videographer until a half hour after the cake cutting. But if budget is not a problem, have the videographer stay until the very end, when you'll get wonderful footage of the party winding down as everyone wishes the bride and groom well.

Do you want drones? When drones were first introduced, they were big and loud and expensive. Now they're small and affordable, and more and more filmmakers are using them to incorporate cinematic overhead shots of outdoor locations into their work. Drone shots may be priced as add-ons or by the hour; some videographers don't charge extra for the service, but may require additional staff.

Be sure the person you're hiring has had sufficient experience using drones, as an amateurish operator could mean having your ceremony music overwhelmed by the sound of a swarm of honeybees—or even worse, risking the possibility that your event is interrupted by a very unromantic crash.

Used tastefully, they shouldn't attract unwarranted attention. But for some couples, an unmanned aerial device is most definitely an unwanted wedding guest.

Photographers and videographers are both competing for the same moments, so tensions can arise if the videographer steps into the photographer's shot. Set up a conference call to go over the wedding day schedule with both of them. If they can discuss in advance who is setting up where, things should go more smoothly on the wedding day.

A VIDEOGRAPHER

Videographers' websites will give you a good idea of their style, so winnow down your list of names by visiting the sites. Once you've identified three with potential, call to check their availability. Ask to see a full-length video of one wedding, not just highlights from multiple weddings. You want to see the quality of the production all the way through—a two-hanky departure sequence is great, but if you can't hear the vows, that's a problem.

THE DEMO

Lost as to what to look for in a demo? Here are some key points:

- Are the images sharp? Are the colors crisp and clear?

- How is the sound quality? Can you hear the vows and the toasts? Or does the videographer try to cover up the lack of adequate sound by setting these parts to music?

- Study the lighting. Is it clear what's going on at all times? Can you see faces, or are they dark shadows against a bright background? Are the people bright but the background a sea of darkness? You don't have to be a lighting expert to know whether the lighting is pleasing to the eye or of poor quality.

- Are the effects tacky or the edits ungraceful?

THE MEETING

- *What kind of equipment do you use?* Don't worry if the answer means little to you—odds are he'll tell you all about it. Quality videographers travel with both prime and zoom lenses and bring back up equipment. Also ask why he likes this particular equipment; you'll get a sense of whether he sounds knowledgeable about the latest developments.

- *How do you handle lighting?* Lighting should be contained in the camera and shouldn't require an outlet, a sign of outdated equipment. Also, on-camera lighting *will* be necessary in low-light situations.

- *How do you handle sound?* Good sound during the ceremony is critical so you can hear the vows—most videographers put a microphone on the groom, but some work in creative ways like hiding a microphone in the altar flowers. If there's no microphone within three feet of you, you're not going to hear the vows.

- *Have you used drones before?* If you're interested in having a videographer shoot overhead shots of your wedding, make sure he has experience.

- *Will you be doing a practice run at the rehearsal, or require early access to the site?* Ask about any additional setup time that drones might entail.

- *Are you familiar with drone regulations at my wedding location?* Both you and the cinematographer should check with the location to find out whether they have rules in place about drone use on the property. In this case, it's worth having two parties confirm the answer. Most churches and many hotels prohibit drones, but sometimes the site itself will be unclear on its own regulations—and one thing you don't want is a team of law enforcement officials storming your ceremony.

Getting Great Video

A videographer is one vendor who won't be standing on the sidelines. Since he'll be interacting with you and the guests, personality is important, so it's best to get a direct referral from friends or your other vendors.

Photographers can be an excellent resource, given that they often have to coordinate with videographers at weddings, though you should know that many photographers aren't terribly fond of videographers—so don't expect a wealth of names. Videographers and photographers are not typically employed by the same studios, though a few of the larger studios offer both services.

What form of editing do you use? In-camera editing is usually the province of amateurs—it's essentially the footage as it was shot and involves little postproduction work. It's the least expensive option, and it will give you a rudimentary video. Professionals use editing software such as Avid, Premiere, or Final Cut Pro.

In what format will my final video be? Will there be a way to share videos online?

Do you provide an early, rough version of the video? Some videographers are able to have a rough video uploaded to your iPod in time for the day-after brunch.

Who is responsible for getting the videography guidelines from the church or synagogue?

How long have you been doing weddings, and how many have you done? You want somebody with wedding experience.

Have you worked in my ceremony and reception locations before? If so, do you have suggestions for how to get the best results? If he hasn't, will he visit the site in advance? He should know ahead of time where he is going to set up for the ceremony and how he is going to mike it.

If he shoots film, ask what type of film and why he likes that format. Super 8 is the norm, but some filmmakers work in 16 mm as well.

Is an assistant necessary? What does the assistant do? If the assistant is shooting part of the wedding, ask to see samples of his footage.

Can I be involved in the editing process? Do I get to choose the background music used in the video?

Ask him what special effects he uses and who chooses them. This is a good time to talk about what you specifically liked and disliked in the demos you viewed.

If it's a package, go over exactly what you get for the fee. How many hours of filming, if there will be an assistant, in what format you'll receive the video, and the video's finished length. While many package deals net you a five-minute highlight reel, a twelve-to-fifteen minute edit will have a much better chance of capturing the spirit of the day.

How long does it take for you to edit and finish the video?

Go over his attire. If he's going to wear sneakers, request that he wear black, which will blend in better with the look of the guests.

How much of a deposit is required to hold the date? When is the balance due? What is the cancellation policy?

Are references available? Get a few names of recently married couples. Ask them whether he was obtrusive at the wedding, how he interacted with guests, how long they had to wait for the video, and whether they were happy with the final product. Were there any technical problems or misunderstandings?

Who owns the copyright to the video? It's typically the videographer, so if that's the case, ask what kind of usage rights you have.

Discuss the general structure of the video. Will it open with a montage of photos, will it be broken into chapters, will it be chronological or will it jump around?

The wedding libraries that were mentioned in the photography section of this chapter are equally excellent for videography referrals.

You can also try associations such as the Professional Videographers Association or the Wedding and Event Videographers Association International. In addition, wedding sites list local videographers, usually those who have paid for the privilege.

You can wait a bit longer to hire a videographer than a photographer; try to book one three to six months before the wedding. If video is an extremely high priority for you, or if you must have a certain videographer to make your day complete, then move it up on your priority list.

Working with a Videographer

I f you booked your videographer more than six months in advance, have a meeting to get reacquainted one to two months before the wedding. Go over all of the points you agreed upon, and ask if he's added any new equipment or editing software that might improve the video.

Send the videographer a detailed schedule of events ahead of time, and discuss any highlights, special family traditions, or anything else he might not know is important to you. On the schedule, build in a meal break for him so that he won't be eating dinner just as you're cutting the cake.

Give him a list of the people you want in the video, along with a seating chart or their table numbers. Fill him in on any uncomfortable or unusual family situations. If you have children, let him know so he can get good footage of them.

Although you'll have an ending time in the contract, ask him not to leave without checking in with you. Sometimes weddings get off schedule, and you might want to go into overtime.

Your Wedding Hashtag

C apturing those quiet moments of intimacy or that epic dance floor scene, candids have become the darlings of professional wedding photographers—as well as a favorite pastime for your nearest and dearest. With nearly every guest toting a camera phone around in their pocket, your wedding day is likely to be documented in an exponential number of these fleeting shots. And since the advent of Instagram and the rise of the wedding hashtag, there's been a whole lot of sharing going on, something most of my couples love.

For those who are comfortable having pictures of their wedding shared publicly, there's nothing like waking up the day after the wedding and getting to relive the night as the photos roll in. For others, a social media trail is an unwelcome nuptial by-product, which is why some couples ask their guests to refrain from posting (or even taking) photos altogether. As you decide how you'd like to handle the issue, it's worth considering the reasoning.

Celebrities aren't the only ones with privacy concerns—many people simply aren't comfortable having their likenesses out in the world at all. Some brides and grooms specifically don't want prospective clients or employers (or exes, for that matter) having access to their intimate, unguarded photos. Others may be comfortable sharing photos to their own social media feeds, where the privacy settings are under their control, but are wary of letting friends with feeds set to "public" share wedding photos far and wide; once a photo has been posted publicly, it's very hard to take it back, particularly if like-minded brides start reposting. Then there's the issue of privacy within your own circles. Couples having a small wedding may wish to avoid offending the friends and relatives they weren't able to invite—could your work buddies or the members of your book club be hurt when they see pics of the big day? Couples hoping to create an authentic, memorable event may simply want their friends and families to be as present as possible, instead of scrolling through their feeds or watching the proceedings through a screen; for some, it's enough to ask that guests refrain from posting during the ceremony only (see page 80).

If you choose to go the lo-fi route, simple signage outside the ceremony and reception spaces, along with a note in your printed programs, should get the message across; wording needn't be more involved than something like, "We gratefully request that over the next six hours, no pictures be taken or posted to social media." Similar language can be posted on your website and sent out in an informational email a few days before the wedding.

If you're a sharer, welcome to the club! Selecting and broadcasting a wedding hashtag is a great way to ensure that you and your guests will be able to see and enjoy

THE PHOTOGRAPHY AND VIDEOGRAPHY CONTRACTS

Make sure these points are addressed in your contracts with photographers and videographers.

- The date of the wedding, the arrival time, and the full address of the location.

- The number of hours of photography or videography included in the fee.

- The deposit amount and the date the balance is due; the cancellation policy; the rate for overtime.

- The assistant(s), if there is one, and the hours he will work.

- The fee, and a detailed list of everything it includes. There should also be a price list for extra prints, albums, and the like.

- For photography, the format or formats to be used. It should also include the percentage of black and white versus color.

- What the photographer or videographer will bring or provide.

- For videography, the number of hours of raw footage he'll shoot and the length of the edited video.

- What the photographer or videographer will wear to the wedding.

- The backup plan in case the named photographer or videographer falls ill and can't make the wedding.

the weekend's photos as they're posted to Instagram. To choose a hashtag, type some options into the app to see whether they've already been taken; if obvious choices like #EmilyRobertWedding or #TheAndersons are gone, try a cute amalgam of your names like #Robily. To establish a wedding hashtag early in order to share sneak peeks of wedding décor or pre-wedding festivities with your guests, include it in your invitations or save-the-dates or post it to your wedding website. (Just be mindful of whether you might be inadvertently hurting feelings by sharing photos of showers or bachelorette parties.) To share your hashtag with guests on the day of the wedding, print it on framed signs placed on the bar, in the bathrooms, and/or on the guestbook. If you're going the photo booth route (see page 93), make sure the hashtag is displayed on the prop table.

A final piece of advice from an Instagram addict who's had her share of bloopers: Please *don't* let anyone share a photo of the bride getting ready before she has walked down the aisle. Remember how the dress is supposed to be a surprise? Unfortunately, I speak from experience. (And even more unfortunately, the culprit was me!) *Do* feel free to share this advice with your wedding party or anyone snapping pictures while you're getting ready.

A Balancing Act

f photography and videography are stretching you beyond your budgetary means, take the amount allotted, put it into one of the categories, and get the best you can afford. It's better to do one thing well. You might be the lucky one who gets a film school student to do your wedding on the cheap and come out with a brilliant video, but more likely, the student's inexperience will show.

Photography is timeless, and that's where I'd put my money, but these days some couples will feel a greater affinity for video. You *can* print stills from high-end video, though they won't be of the same quality as photographs. Whatever your medium, try these tricks to trim your costs:

- Have the photographer arrive when the bride is putting on her dress, not the moment she arrives for hair and makeup.

- Don't travel to different locations for portraits; it adds a lot of time.

- As a last resort, cut the assistant.

■ Send the photographer/videographer home thirty minutes after the cake is cut.

■ Limit the videographer's time at the wedding to the ceremony and essential parts of the reception.

■ If you can't afford a videographer, have your photos turned into a slideshow set to music.

Now that we've tackled the subject of preserving the wedding, let's turn to the pursuit of a more fleeting pleasure: food. Whether you already have some idea of what you would like to serve or are starting with a blank slate, the next chapter will guide you through the process of working with a caterer and choosing a menu. (A bonus: Tastings are involved.) ◆

CHAPTER EIGHT

Planning the Menu

CHOOSING THE RIGHT MENU FOR YOU

The wedding feast goes back as far as weddings themselves. In the Middle Ages, the entire community was invited to a couple's feast, which often lasted for several days. Food still remains central to a wedding celebration, and with good reason. Breaking bread has always been synonymous with conviviality—and good times. For most couples,

food is the number one expenditure. One of the worries people have about wedding food is that it's going to cost a lot and end up tasting . . . well, not so good. But if you approach it thoughtfully, the menu at the cocktail hour and the reception can be just as much about you as the dress. Even if you're on a challenging budget, you don't need to settle for a generic rubber-chicken meal.

Know, too, that the influence of the caterer goes beyond the food—in the past, the term *caterer* was used interchangeably with *wedding planner*, illustrating the broad role that the caterer plays in the wedding; many caterers and hotel catering managers still assume that role if no separate wedding planner is involved. They oversee not only the menu but also the staff and the setup of the room. If there's no wedding planner, the caterer runs the cocktail hour and reception, directing the timing of everything from the first dance to the cutting of the cake. All the more reason why you want to make sure you choose your caterer wisely.

A Season for Menus

Your time line for menu planning depends on whether you're working with an in-house or independent caterer. If the food is being handled by the hotel, club, banquet hall, or restaurant where you're holding the reception, you'll start getting into menu specifics about three months before the wedding. On the other hand, if you're having a wedding at home, at a museum, or at any off-site location where you bring in your own caterer, you'll want to begin the interviewing process as soon as you've lined up a location, an officiant, and a photographer. (If food is far more important to you than photography, by all means, choose the caterer first.) This could happen as soon as eight months before the wedding.

Although many caterers can handle multiple events in a weekend and might not necessarily book up that far in advance, you want to get one on board early because caterers often have an insider's knowledge of your reception site and can offer invaluable advice on room setup and logistics. The caterer may be the one to let you know that you're going to need outdoor lighting, extra portable toilets, a backup generator, or air-conditioning for the tent. If you have a short engagement or another reason why you can't book a caterer sooner, not to worry: Three months before the date is plenty of time to plan the menu and schedule a tasting.

It's ideal to plan the menu and conduct the tasting when the foods you'll be serving are in season, so you don't want to tackle the menu too far ahead of time. This timing also allows the caterer to give you more accurate pricing—food is a commodity, and the prices of ingredients fluctuate considerably, depending on the season and market conditions. You can certainly request sample menus earlier and start jotting down ideas for what you

like. You'll want to make some of the major decisions about the style of food service early on, because those will affect the room setup, flowers, and decor.

Food Service

The first step is to determine what meal you're serving. You'll need to think about the time of the reception and your budget, taking into account any cultural expectations. In some regions and cultures, punch and cake in the church basement will suffice, but in others, it would be an affront to offer anything less than an abundant buffet.

While dinner is probably the most common meal, it's also the priciest. Shifting the meal to lunch can help you save significantly on both food and alcohol. You should also consider brunch, cocktails and hors d'oeuvres, afternoon tea, or a dessert reception. All of these variations on a traditional reception should be noted on the invitation—"please join us for cocktails and hors d'oeuvres following the ceremony"—so that guests can plan accordingly.

Once you've figured out whether you're holding a lunch, dinner, or dessert reception, you'll need to focus on the type of service; it affects your budget and also strongly influences the formality, the atmosphere, and the pacing of your reception.

Think about ways to combine different styles of service throughout the event to mix things up. Too much of the same gets dull, even when the service is impeccable. If you're having a sit-down meal, consider having a buffet at cocktail hour, serving the first course family style, or setting up a few dessert stations. Even within a sit-down meal, you can offer a plated appetizer and "Russian service" (see page 110) for the main course.

Each style of service has its own set of considerations, so read on for what to know about each before making a decision. Always ask the caterer or catering manager about the space needed for each before signing a contract—you don't want to commit to a sit-down meal and later find out that you only have room for a standing reception.

Budget Cutters

IF YOU KNOW your food budget is tight, consider these pared-down—but still elegant—options.

Cocktail reception. Heavy hors d'oeuvres and cocktails can go a long way. Try for a mix of tray-passed hors d'oeuvres and stations (anything from an antipasto display to sushi), which add excitement to the food component, especially if a chef in a white toque is making the preparation a performance. It's a money saver because you're not serving a full meal and the reception won't last as long—two and a half to three hours is ideal. Dancing isn't usually a big part of this type of reception. It's a good fit for those who have a large guest list and can't afford to serve everyone a full meal, for those who have chosen a space that won't seat everyone comfortably, and for couples who have eloped or had a small destination wedding and then invited everyone to celebrate at a later date. Some older couples—whether it's a first marriage or an encore marriage—also feel more comfortable with this format.

Breakfast/brunch. While it's officially a meal, the food is significantly less expensive than dinner, and people drink less, which keeps the bar bill down. Morning ceremonies followed by a wedding breakfast are a long-standing tradition in England, though a rather elaborate lunch is typically served. It may be hard to entice people to dance early in the day, but if you bring in a great jazz band and have a receptive crowd, people will get up on their feet. You can serve a sit-down meal, but I prefer the variety and abundance of stations and a buffet for a brunch. Try an omelet station, a waffle station, a buffet with sausages and fresh fruit, and a build-your-own-bagel display. For beverages, champagne and juice cocktails such as mimosas or Bellinis are a natural, as is a Bloody Mary bar.

Afternoon tea. Hold an early afternoon wedding followed by tea in a ballroom or lounge. Seat everyone at tables and offer a tea menu with individual pots of tea, giving guests a choice of loose-leaf black teas, green teas, white teas, and herbal teas. (You should also offer coffee to those who want it.) Champagne or another sparkling wine makes a lovely tea accompaniment. Put out tiered platters of finger sandwiches, biscuits with ham, scones, and petits fours. And, of course, you should make the wedding cake part of the tea service. You don't need a full bar with an afternoon tea—if you're serving alcohol at all, wine and champagne should be sufficient. A jazz or classical quartet, pianist, or harpist would provide the right musical note.

Dessert reception. Start your wedding at 7 p.m. or later, and follow it with a dessert reception. Set up a buffet or stations with crepes, an ice-cream sundae bar, and deep-fried beignets. Or offer ice cream pounded on a slab with the guest's choice of candy, cookie crumbs, or other mixings. Serve miniature tortes, pies, cookies, cupcakes, and crème brûlée, so everyone can sample a variety. In addition to regular bar service, offer a coffee bar and, if your budget allows, after-dinner liqueurs. Music should get guests up and dancing.

Sit-Down Service

A FORMAL RECEPTION almost always involves a sit-down meal, although you can certainly offer it at less formal events as well. What doesn't work so well is to have men in tuxedos and women in evening gowns trying to negotiate plates and sauces at a buffet. A sit-down meal features assigned seating, with guests picking up their table numbers during cocktail hour. At the tables, you can either specify where everyone sits by putting place cards at each seat or let guests work it out for themselves. It's a matter of personal preference, though control-happy hosts tend to opt for place cards. (You should know, however, that some guests aren't above rearranging them.)

Within the realm of sit-down meals, there are several different options for service. Always ask your catering contact to spell out the definition of each type of service, as some venues use the term "French service" to describe "Russian service," and "table side" can also have several meanings.

Plated Service

The course is plated in the kitchen, and plates are often covered by domes to keep food warm on its way to the table. Sometimes referred to as American service, it's efficient and leaves little to chance. Standard staffing at higher-end weddings is three waiters for every six tables; if it's any lower than that, try to allocate the funds to increase the number of waiters. Otherwise, you risk one section of the room finishing the main course while another section is still waiting to eat. To truly pamper guests, hire extra staff to bring the ratio to one waiter per table.

Russian Service
(*Service à la Russe*)

Waiters bring the course to the table on platters and serve each guest individually. One waiter may bring the entrée (or choice of entrées), and another the vegetables. It's often incorrectly referred to as French service. Russian service costs more than plated service because it requires more staffing. It has an elegant, Old World feeling.

French or Table Side Service

True French service involves waiters or chefs with portable butane stoves on trolleys who set up table side cooking stations. You can employ table side prep for anything from tossing and serving a Caesar salad to flaming steak Diane in brandy. Guests are then served individually. (French service can be combined with Russian service by putting the just-prepared food onto platters, then having a waiter serve guests.) Table side service brings elegance and dramatic flair to the meal, but it requires a lot of staff, and highly trained staff at that, so it's pricey and not all that common.

Family Style
(*Table d'Hôte*)

Food is brought out on large platters, and guests help themselves. It works particularly well at long tables and creates a warm, convivial atmosphere. Family-style service is a wonderful icebreaker for the first course, as it compels guests to interact with one another. It's also

There's no real butler involved in the service term "English butler," which simply describes tray-passed hors d'oeuvres. If the waiters wear white gloves, it's referred to as "white-glove butler service."

become an increasingly popular option for health-conscious couples, allowing them to offer their guests the freedom to customize their meal to fit their particular dietary constraints. Though it seems like it would require fewer waiters, so many platters have to be brought out simultaneously that you need the same number of waiters as if you were serving a plated meal.

Table Side Selection

Table side selection is not exactly a type of service but an elegant alternative to having guests check the chicken or beef box on their response cards. When guests sit down, the waiter takes their order for the main course, typically from two or three choices. The entrées aren't prepared until the orders are taken, so it's closer to restaurant-quality food than to banquet-style meals. It's more expensive than preselected entrées because more food has to be purchased to allow for choices.

Buffet Service

THERE'S A PERCEPTION that buffets are less expensive than plated meals, but that's not necessarily the case. True, you save on staff, but you have to order more food because you can't predict how much guests will eat, and you have to have enough food to create an appealing presentation. Guests don't want to be scraping the bottom of the chafing dish for their chicken Parmesan.

Although it's more expensive, you should have a server at each chafing dish for three reasons: to exert a measure of portion control, to move the line along more quickly, and to make it easier for guests to negotiate the buffet—it's a tricky business balancing a plate and trying to serve yourself pasta with one hand. To avoid long lines, have the maître d' call a few tables up at a time, and try to have at least two identical buffet lines.

Stations

Stations are a great way to bring a room to life. You can set them up for cocktail hour, a cocktail reception, or a full meal. They can be used imaginatively to showcase your favorite foods or offer a culinary tour of the city or of the places the two of you have lived. And the showmanship of the chefs manning the stations turns them into conversation starters.

The cost is about the same as for a buffet. They take up space, so make sure your room is big enough to accommodate your vision. If you're having an off-site reception and renting plates, keep in mind that stations will require more plates than a seated meal.

The Menu

First things first: Feeding a crowd isn't the same as planning a dinner party. You're serving people who typically represent three or four generations and a wide range of tastes. And, you're serving more of them, which shapes food preparation choices.

The secret to a successful meal is creating a menu that plays to your crowd. You might think a raw-food tasting menu is the latest and greatest, but how is that going to go down with your meat-and-potatoes grandma and grandpa? This is not to say that your menu has to be totally bland and middle of the road, but you should try to find ways to inject personality into the meal that aren't too challenging for the majority of your guests.

If it's a full meal, you're generally serving three courses—an appetizer, entrée, and dessert, unless you add in extras. Your aim is to choose foods that work together but don't weigh guests down. If they eat too much, it's hard to get them out of their chairs for dancing!

There used to be a strong correlation between the formality of the wedding and the food, but no longer. You can have a black-tie wedding and serve soul food or red-sauce Italian favorites. As a courtesy to guests, I wouldn't offer messy food such as a whole lobster or crab (items generally served with a plastic bib) if they've been asked to dress in their best clothing.

Start by looking at the sample menus offered by the venue or the caterer. In most areas of wedding planning,

No matter what type of service you decide on, give guests a place to congregate besides the bar and the dance floor. Consider a cappuccino and coffee bar, an ice-cream sundae bar, or a cookie station with milk shooters.

you begin with your dream vision, but when it comes to food, I find that it turns into a more successful partnership if you study the chef's strengths and then personalize the menu from there. Get a sense at the outset of how much leeway there is for creativity—some kitchens welcome the chance to experiment and break out of their mold, while others discourage too much variation from their menus.

A few guidelines to keep in mind:

- Unless you know everyone loves spicy food, avoid highly spiced dishes. And unless there's an Indian contingent at the wedding, avoid serving East Indian food if other options are available.

- A lot of people have an aversion to fish, so don't make it the main course unless there is a choice of entrées.

- Choose the menu for the main meal first, then figure out hors d'oeuvres for cocktail hour. Avoid repeating central ingredients—if you're serving beef for the main course, don't carve mini roast beef sandwiches at cocktail hour.

- Ethnic food can add character to a menu, but offer some simpler preparations for the unadventurous. You and your friends may live on sushi and Thai food, but those may be considered "out there" by certain family members. Ask yourself if your grandmother will go for it. What about your thirteen-year-old cousin? Not every guest has to like every dish, but they shouldn't leave your reception hungry, either.

- Realize that the size of your guest list is going to affect the menu. Some dishes can dazzle a dozen guests but don't work when there are 250 to feed—a soufflé, for instance, wouldn't be a good idea. Listen to the caterer or catering manager when he tells you what will and won't work.

- Expectations about how much food will be served can vary widely in different parts of the country and in other parts of the world, so make sure to discuss portion sizes and quantities with your caterer.

- If you're having an off-site reception, accept that there will be limitations on the menu. The caterers are often working out of makeshift kitchens and usually have to partially cook items in advance and finish them at the site. They also may not have room to assemble three hundred small plates, especially if they all need to be finished at the site. Again, listen when the caterer tells you what will and won't work.

- An outdoor reception will have some food limitations, especially in warm weather, when food spoils quickly.

Making It Yours

MANY COUPLES DON'T REALIZE how many ways there are to put their stamp on their meal. Look to these suggestions for inspiration. It will make planning your meal more fun, and your guests will delight in savoring food that reflects your tastes, your history, and your background.

Before you do anything, though, stop to make a list of foods that you are passionate about. Even if you think you could never in a million years serve it at a wedding, write it down. Show the list to your caterer or catering manager. You'd be surprised at the ideas your favorites could spark in a creative food professional. If you love waffles, perhaps he'll suggest adding a Belgian waffle station to dessert. If you adore cherries, you can serve a chicken or pork dish for the main course with a cherry sauce. Other places to look for inspiration:

- Is there a favorite family recipe? Ask if the chef is willing to make Grandma Helen's carrot soufflé or Aunt Shula's Persian rice.

- Explore your cultural history to find out if there's a food traditionally served at weddings to bring good fortune to the marriage—Iranians serve sweet jeweled rice (*shirin polo*); Italians serve twists of fried dough sprinkled with sugar; and Indian weddings make recurring use of eggs to symbolize fertility.

- Ask the chef to re-create a dish that's part of your love story. Maybe it's an appetizer you ate on your first date, or a side dish from the night you got engaged. Does the groom always order the same dish at your favorite restaurant? The chef may be willing to share the recipe for the occasion.

- Find a way to showcase your favorite foods. From a ravioli station to a meat-carving table, the options are endless.

- Bring out your regional background via the food. For a New York groom, that could mean mini pastrami sandwiches at cocktail hour and black-and-white cookies on the dessert buffet. For a Texas bride, you could carve barbecued brisket onto small rolls at cocktail hour.

- Showcase the location by selecting a menu that highlights seasonal, local produce. Some venues are known for favoring this approach, but often a creative hotel chef will be willing to bring some farm-to-table touches to the venue's standard menu.

- Whenever you incorporate a personal element in your food, a note on the menu, the table, or the buffet explaining the significance of the dish is a lovely touch. If you're serving an ethnic food that will be unfamiliar to some guests, write up a description of the food and the tradition behind it.

Menu Manners

I often see family disagreements related to generational issues surrounding the menu and timing of an event. The bride and groom might want an eclectic menu that speaks to their own tastes; or in the interest of keeping things going late into the night, they want to stall on serving dinner. Parents often want a more traditional menu that's not going to offend anyone's palate, and they're thinking less about the dance floor and more about how your great-aunt is going to make it to the cake slicing if the salad course isn't served until nine-thirty.

I have to side with the parents on these matters. It's important to be courteous to all your guests—even the ones whose presence might not be as thrilling to you as that of your college buddies. The best approach here is compromise.

In general, consider the comfort and needs of your older guests above that of your peers. Eating earlier won't upset the young folks, but eating later could put a major damper on the enjoyment of some older guests. If you want to keep the party going late, serve a fun dessert course near the end of the evening, or a midnight snack.

First Course

THE FIRST COURSE is often preset at a large wedding—when guests walk into the room, the salad is waiting at each place setting. This saves on time, but it tends to look like a charity event, not a wedding, so it's not my favorite way to do things. Many venues will try to steer you to a preset first course. One way around it is to begin the reception with the first dance. Once the first dance is over, other guests can get up on the dance floor. While people are dancing, waiters can bring out the first course. Most likely, people will have just eaten during cocktail hour, so there's no need to feed them the moment they walk into the reception.

The Main Course

SHOULD YOU OFFER guests a choice of main course options? It adds some cost to the menu, but it makes the meal more enjoyable for them. If I can swing it from a budget standpoint, I love to offer guests a choice—not that anyone will grumble if you don't. (Even if you're technically serving a single option, make sure to have a vegetarian selection as a backup.)

There are several ways to offer a choice of entrées. Most venues have you list the options on your RSVP cards so the guests make their choice in advance; if your numbers change, you can usually change the order up until the time you have to give your final guest count, three or four days before the wedding. (Guests will forget what they ordered or change their minds, of course, but at least your caterer will have a sense of whether yours is a chicken or fish crowd.) Some venues have guests mark their entrée choice on their seating card.

The most elegant option, but also the priciest, is table side service. It's often found at five-star hotels and isn't always available at other venues. Guests receive menus describing three entrée choices, and waiters come around and take their orders. Table side service requires more time because the waiters need to get the orders into the kitchen and the kitchen needs time to prepare the meals, so plan on having lots of dancing before the main course. You might need to serve both a soup and a salad or add an intermezzo to fill in the time.

One final option: You can place two entrées on the plate ("a duet"), pairing, for example, a small steak with salmon.

Dietary Accommodations

Besides having a vegetarian alternative, you should be prepared for guests with food allergies and special dietary requests. Some guests will tell you on their response cards or call to let you know that they have a nut or gluten allergy. You can't accommodate every diet plan, but if you've got guests who need a gluten-free, dairy-free, nut-free, or a kosher meal, talk to your catering contact about options. Be sure to give the maître d' a list of special meals with table numbers for these guests before the reception so the service can remain as seamless as possible. If you know your crowd is full of people on unusual food regimens, consider having a buffet or stations instead of a plated meal.

Dealing with dietary accommodations is no longer the struggle it once was. Most venues offer options for everyone these days, and more often than not I find myself arguing with brides for the *inclusion* of gluten. I've done fully vegetarian and vegan weddings and tricked wedding guests with a gluten-free cake (no one was the wiser), but I say, let the people have their starch!

Children's Meals

MOST CHILDREN aren't going to be wowed by shrimp risotto or pistachio-crusted halibut with a side of broccoli rabe, so arrange kids' meals with the catering staff for anyone under the age of twelve. The venue or caterer will usually discount these; often, they won't charge for children under five, though you'll still have to rent place settings for them at an off-site location.

If you're expecting enough children to create a separate kids' table, plan a special menu for them. Even better, set up a separate buffet for them with kid favorites such as chicken nuggets, macaroni and cheese, pasta, mini hamburgers, and french fries. Make the buffet a child-friendly height and decorate it to appeal to younger sensibili-

> A buffet allows the kids to eat sooner than the adults—if you're having separate activities for them (see page 333 for ideas), they can eat and head for the playroom while the adults enjoy the reception, then come back for dessert. If you have a significant number of children at the reception, have sugar cookies shaped like brides or wedding bells ready for them to decorate after they eat, and serve them with ice cream.

ties—with teddy bears dressed as brides and grooms, for instance. The buffet should be staffed, both to avoid accidents and to make it easier for the little ones.

Dessert

THERE'S NO QUESTION that the wedding cake should be the star dessert. (See chapter 23, "The Sweet Finale," for all you need to know). But couples often want more. Some couples love sweets so much that the dessert spread outshines the meal!

If you are going to have a dessert table, make sure to balance rich, elaborate confections with simpler, homier favorites. Chocolate chip cookies, lemon bars, and ice-cream sandwiches are likely to be snapped up while the petits fours and fancy tortes linger, and there's nothing cuter than an updated version of a junk-food classic like Twinkies or HoHos. If there are favorite family recipes for a blueberry crumble or Key lime pie, see if the chef will make them or allow you to bring in a few made by a family member. Ditto for desserts that represent the family's heritage, whether it's rugelach or baklava. Miniature-size goodies let guests sample several options and are easier to serve. It's always a good idea to have fruit on a dessert buffet—it offers guests who don't indulge in pastries an alternative and adds a healthful, colorful touch.

Dessert lends itself to stations, set up in different parts of the room. They're a wonderful way to get guests circulating after dinner, so think about your favorite desserts or any local specialties that could be turned into stations. Attune your choices to the setting and the weather—if it's hot, a snow cone or gelato cart will be enthusiastically received. A coffee and cappuccino bar is practically a must, and a cookie shop complete with to-go bags is irresistible.

If you don't want to spring for a buffet but wish to serve something in addition to cake, put out plates of chocolate truffles or cookies on each table.

Although dessert tables are popular, they're an extra expense. If you need to trim your budget, stick with wedding cake. No one is going to say, "I can't believe she didn't have individual soufflés." Your caterer can help you come up with ways to make the cake extra special on the plate, from painting your initials in raspberry coulis to rounding out each plate with a tuile (a thin, crisp cookie) and a small scoop of ice cream.

A Taste-Off

Definitely one of the highlights of the wedding planning process, the tasting gives you an opportunity to preview the food you plan to serve at the wedding. Even if the groom has shown little interest in other aspects of wedding planning, he is usually just as eager to sample the meal as the bride. A tasting is essentially the same whether you're working with an in-house or outside caterer; the only difference is that a hotel will also show you the full table setup.

A tasting is normally included as part of the catering fee. If you're working with a wedding planner, you should invite her to the tasting; if you're working with an in-house caterer, make sure the catering manager is with you for the tasting. Both can offer valuable suggestions on the flavors, presentation, and combinations based on their experience. Remember, they know which dishes are perennial crowd-pleasers and which ones get left uneaten; they know what the kitchen is capable of turning out; and they've seen a dozen different ways to present the haricots verts.

The caterer or catering director will tell you whether you can bring guests to the tasting and how many. If you *can* have a few guests, it's a nice gesture to invite parents to the tasting (particularly if they're footing the catering bill), but it's by no means necessary.

The tasting should take place close enough to the wedding so that the ingredients are in season, typically six to eight weeks before the event. Don't wait until the

With some venues, a cake will be part of the caterer's package.

Tweaking the Menu

A chef can't transform beef stew into filet mignon, but there are plenty of things that can be changed. Sometimes things won't be to your liking or you'll want to taste a different sauce, salad, or side dish. In that case, you can usually set up a second tasting just for those elements. Some examples of reasonable tweaks to suggest:

- The way the food is seasoned.

- The way it's presented. Maybe you'd like a platter of shoestring fries for the table rather than having them directly on the plate, where they get soggy from the beef juices.

- Changing the side dishes. Once you taste the chicken, you may decide that it's crying out for a side of sautéed tomatoes and artichokes.

last minute, because you want to allow time for a second tasting if a dish or sauce needs to be tweaked. Typically, you'll get to try two selections from each course. Then you'll make your final decisions. If you're having a buffet or stations, the caterer will prepare a variety of dishes for you to try. They won't necessarily reflect the final presentation, but they should taste like what you'll get at the reception.

The purpose of a tasting isn't to feed you, though you should certainly walk away full! Be sure to pay attention to the following:

- How the dish is presented on the plate. Take a digital photo or a Polaroid of each course. It will let the catering manager know that you are expecting what you're seeing at the tasting.

- The portion size. Is what you see representative of the portion that will be served to guests?

- How it tastes. Is the seasoning to your liking? Could it do with less salt? Would a few sprigs of rosemary make the roasted fingerling potatoes more interesting?

A Comfort Food Menu

These no-fuss, familiar foods are great for a casual wedding and if you have a lot of kids in attendance. These are the kinds of dishes that will surprise and delight.

Two Worthwhile Splurges

Should your budget have some leeway, consider these two ways to make your meal memorable.

Have a cheese plate brought out after the main course and before dessert. A typical assortment might include a soft cheese like Brie, a hard cheese like cheddar or Emmental, and a flavorful blue cheese like Gorgonzola. Serve with thin slices of French bread and fruit. The cheese course can be plated in the kitchen, or, for a more elegant option, a waiter can roll a trolley around to each table and cut individual wedges for guests. Cheese is such a personal taste, so I like the latter method because it allows guests to choose what appeals to them.

Serve a midnight snack, one of my favorite ways to keep the party going late. Obviously, that won't be an option in venues where the kitchen shuts down early or in rural areas where outside food sources aren't available. But if bringing out late-night munchies is feasible and you expect the party to be going strong at 1 a.m., it's always a crowd-pleaser. The food refuels guests for more dancing and steers guests who've been overfrequenting the bar in another direction. Popular choices are burgers and fries (I've brought them in from McDonald's and had waiters pass them on silver platters), breakfast burritos, or cookies with milk shooters. The snack should be something that people can eat with their hands; the revelers don't necessarily want to sit down, and tables have probably been cleared at this point. There's a lot of room for playing here, particularly since not everyone will still be around and not everyone will partake—if you're known for chowing down on chicken biscuits or hitting a diner for grilled cheese at 2 a.m., that's what you should serve.

I don't care whether you're wearing a three-piece suit or shorts and flip-flops—everybody loves pigs in a blanket.

This retro salad has made such a comeback. You can also do it with Thousand Island dressing— my absolute favorite!

Serve these in plastic baskets set directly on the table.

Throw in whatever other toppings you like on a sundae.

· PASSED APPETIZERS ·
Miniature Hamburgers with
Caramelized Onions

Pigs in a Blanket
Spicy Mustard

Individual Crudités in a Shot Glass
Green Goddess Dip

Crab Cakes

Grilled Cheese Sandwiches

· SALAD COURSE ·
Iceberg Lettuce Wedge Salad
Crumbled Blue Cheese, Bacon
Red and Yellow Cherry Tomatoes
Creamy Blue Cheese Dressing

· ENTRÉE ·
Boneless Short Ribs
Red Wine Sauce

Crispy Fried Chicken
Peach Chutney

Salmon with Leeks
White Wine Reduction

French Fries and Onion Rings
Ketchup, Mustard, and Ranch Dip

Grilled Vegetables
Herb Marinade

· DESSERT ·
Hot Fudge Sundae
Vanilla Ice Cream
Hot Fudge, Crushed Almonds,
Whipped Cream
Bing Cherry Topping

A Formal Menu

Formal doesn't have to mean boring. This is a creative take on a traditional, four-course menu. You can do away with either the first course or the salad course if you wish, although sometimes a four-course menu is part of a package deal.

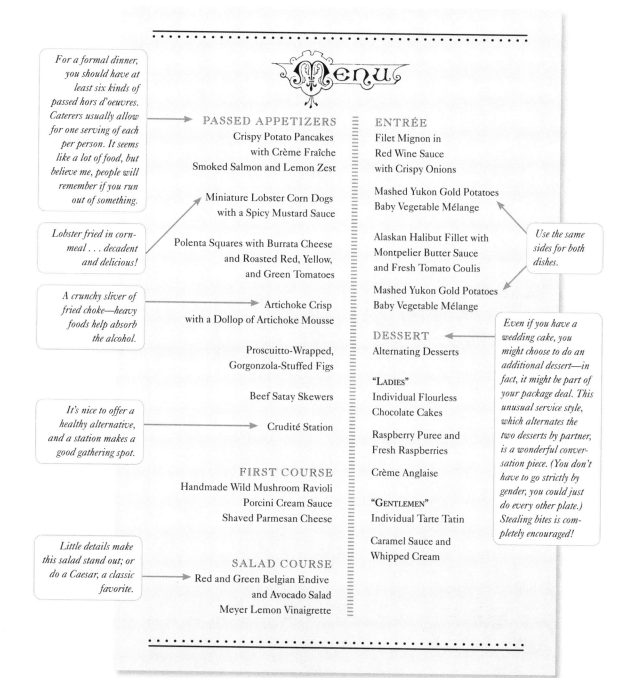

Menu

For a formal dinner, you should have at least six kinds of passed hors d'oeuvres. Caterers usually allow for one serving of each per person. It seems like a lot of food, but believe me, people will remember if you run out of something.

PASSED APPETIZERS
Crispy Potato Pancakes
with Crème Fraîche
Smoked Salmon and Lemon Zest

Miniature Lobster Corn Dogs
with a Spicy Mustard Sauce

Lobster fried in corn-meal . . . decadent and delicious!

Polenta Squares with Burrata Cheese
and Roasted Red, Yellow,
and Green Tomatoes

Artichoke Crisp
with a Dollop of Artichoke Mousse

A crunchy sliver of fried choke—heavy foods help absorb the alcohol.

Proscuitto-Wrapped,
Gorgonzola-Stuffed Figs

Beef Satay Skewers

Crudité Station

It's nice to offer a healthy alternative, and a station makes a good gathering spot.

FIRST COURSE
Handmade Wild Mushroom Ravioli
Porcini Cream Sauce
Shaved Parmesan Cheese

SALAD COURSE
Red and Green Belgian Endive
and Avocado Salad
Meyer Lemon Vinaigrette

Little details make this salad stand out; or do a Caesar, a classic favorite.

ENTRÉE
Filet Mignon in
Red Wine Sauce
with Crispy Onions

Mashed Yukon Gold Potatoes
Baby Vegetable Mélange

Alaskan Halibut Fillet with
Montpelier Butter Sauce
and Fresh Tomato Coulis

Mashed Yukon Gold Potatoes
Baby Vegetable Mélange

Use the same sides for both dishes.

DESSERT
Alternating Desserts

"LADIES"
Individual Flourless
Chocolate Cakes

Raspberry Puree and
Fresh Raspberries

Crème Anglaise

"GENTLEMEN"
Individual Tarte Tatin

Caramel Sauce and
Whipped Cream

Even if you have a wedding cake, you might choose to do an additional dessert—in fact, it might be part of your package deal. This unusual service style, which alternates the two desserts by partner, is a wonderful conversation piece. (You don't have to go strictly by gender, you could just do every other plate.) Stealing bites is completely encouraged!

THE CATERER

If you're interviewing an in-house catering manager at the venue you've already chosen, you're likely to have less leeway, so not all of these questions will apply. If you or the groom has any food allergies or particular aversions, make sure to mention those up front; while you won't be able to please everyone, you might as well please yourselves!

- Ask about their philosophy or approach to food preparation. Does it align with your vision? Most caterers are jacks-of-all-trades, but some might espouse a strong commitment to using organic, locally raised foods whenever possible or have a strong affinity for cross-cultural influences in sauces, herbs, and spices. Can they accommodate special dietary restrictions?

- Look at the photos in their portfolio and/or check out their social media feed. Are you impressed with the style of presentation and the setup? Look at the vessels on a buffet and the way food is arranged. If you're seeing disposable aluminum tins, that's what you'll see at your wedding.

- *How large is your staff? Do you know all of the waiters who will be working at my wedding?*

- *How many weddings have you done? If you're having a wedding for 250, you don't want to risk using a caterer who primarily does in-home dinner parties for 30. It's not necessary for them to have wedding experience, but definitely ask how many events the same size as yours they've handled.*

- *Have you done events at my reception space? It's not a requirement, but it's helpful. If they have, what suggestions would they make based on their experience?*

- *On what date is the final guest count due?*

- *Can I provide my own alcohol? Is there a setup fee for the bar?*

- *Can guests have a table side choice of entrées? How many choices can be offered?*

- *How much do staff meals for the vendors cost?*

- *What's the charge for children's meals?*

- *If it's an off-site wedding, does the site impose any limitations on the menu? Where will they set up the kitchen?*

- *When will the tasting be held?*

- *If there's a buffet or stations, do you decorate them? (If the caterer doesn't, you'll need to talk to your florist.) Will the buffet stations be staffed?*

- How long it takes to serve each course. This will give you an idea of how to plan the schedule for your reception.

If you're not sure about a flavor or whether the beef should be that chewy, speak up. Ask questions! This is your opportunity to make comments and get input from the kitchen staff. Be sure to remain courteous—sometimes couples go in with the attitude that the caterer is trying to shortchange them in some way, and this can damage the working relationship.

Take notes during the tasting. If you and the catering manager agree on changes—whether it's something as simple as adding a lemon wedge to the plate, substi-

tuting grape tomatoes for tomato wedges in the salad, or deciding to serve the sauce for the lamb on the side—follow up with an email outlining the changes to make sure they're not forgotten.

Finding a Caterer

f you're in the market for a caterer—meaning that your location doesn't require you to use an in-house company or work from an approved list—you'll probably have an easier time gathering recommendations

How much time do you need for the setup and breakdown?

What's the ratio of waiters and bartenders to guests? How much would it cost to hire additional waiters or bartenders?

During cocktail hour, how many waiters will be passing hors d'oeuvres? There should be at least four waiters for every hundred guests.

What do you provide in terms of china, flatware, glassware, and linens? If the caterer offers them, ask to see a setup. What colors of linens are available?

Do you bring chairs and tables? What styles do you offer?

What types of props and unusual serving pieces do you have?

How many events do you typically book in a day? What's the maximum number you'll take on?

How will the waitstaff be attired?

How are leftovers handled?

Is insurance for china and glassware breakage included?

Do you have a pastry chef who makes wedding cakes? If I bring in an outside cake, is there a charge to serve it?

Get an estimate of the number of rentals needed for place settings (especially if you're doing a buffet or stations) so you can factor it into your budget.

How much of a deposit is required to hold the date? When is the balance due?

Are you licensed by the state? Do you have a health certificate?

How much liability insurance do you carry, and does it include liquor liability insurance?

How much is the additional charge for service, gratuities, and taxes? Depending on where your reception is, this can add 25 percent to your food costs. If you hear the term "plus-plus," as in "the meal will cost $50 a head plus-plus" that's $50 before taxes and service.

When do overtime charges apply? What are overtime rates?

What's the cancellation policy?

Are setup and cleanup fees included in the estimate?

Are there delivery charges?

than you did with your other vendors; unlike a florist or cake maker, a caterer's work doesn't need to be specific to weddings.

To find caterers, look to:

- Friends who have gotten married.

- Friends or relatives who enjoyed the food at a special event or fund-raiser.

- The manager at the reception site, who is in a position to see the work of multiple caterers.

- Other vendors who interact with caterers—if you already have a photographer, cake maker, florist, or linen-rental source, ask them who does the best work.

- Your favorite restaurant. Ask if the chef caters outside of the restaurant; if not, ask if there's a caterer he admires.

A Proposal and a Contract

AFTER YOUR FIRST MEETING with a caterer or catering manager, you should receive an initial proposal—you'll get the final proposal after the tasting. You want to receive the proposal early in the process so that you can budget appropriately. It should include:

- The cost per person for the food, with detailed descriptions of what's included in each course.

- Estimated alcohol charges (if caterer is providing alcohol).

- Estimated charges for staffing (from a caterer or from a hotel if you're hiring extra staff).

- Power charges (from a caterer for an off-site reception).

- Any additional charges for an engineer (at a hotel or other on-site location) to fix anything that's gone wrong, from a blown fuse to a broken ice machine.

- Bathroom staffing and charges for bathroom attendants.

- Charges for coat check attendants.

If you agree to the proposal, you'll be asked to put down an initial deposit. Make sure to find out whether the price you're quoted includes tax and service charges, which can add thousands of dollars to the bill and will throw off your budget if you haven't accounted for them. Your contract, which comes a bit later in the process,

Find out what happens to leftovers; with a caterer, they're usually yours to keep. Make arrangements to have them picked up by a soup kitchen or local organization that can use them to feed the less fortunate.

Dollars and Sense

Over budget on your food? Here are some ways to cut your costs.

- Serve fewer courses.

- Stay away from meat entrées, which are usually more expensive. No one is going to complain if you serve chicken instead.

- If you love a particular ingredient but it's pricey, ask the chef or caterer about a less expensive way to bring it to the table. Instead of rack of lamb, you could serve lamb stew or shepherd's pie.

- Skip the dessert buffet and stick to wedding cake.

should include the refined information from the initial proposal—an in-depth description of each course and any tableware items the caterer will provide—along with the following: the wedding date; time of the event; time the caterer will arrive; the number of guests; the deadline for guaranteeing the guest count, after which you'll be responsible for paying for that number; and cancellation and refund policies. If the caterer is decorating the buffets, that should be stated as well.

There is one essential accompaniment to all that yummy food that doesn't come from the caterer: the music. The following chapter takes you through the musical options for your whole wedding (not just the reception), from the moment your guests arrive to their departure. ◆

CHAPTER NINE

Music & Dancing

SCORING THE MOMENTS, FROM FIRST TO LAST

Think of music as the conductor who sets the pace of your wedding—scoring each sequence, adding another layer of meaning to your ceremony, setting an upbeat, convivial mood at cocktail hour, and getting everyone into the groove at the reception. At some junctures, music will fade into the background, but you still want it to be part of the

environment. (I once made the mistake of doing a wedding with no music during cocktails, and, trust me, you absolutely notice when it's not there.)

And, let us not forget, music provides the impetus for dancing, which has been at the heart of wedding celebrations for centuries. In fact, the quality of a wedding is often measured by the amount of dancing —when the guests dance till 2:30 a.m., the affair is universally considered to have been a great success.

My philosophy? Yes, it's about the choices you make, from the prelude to the last dance, but it's equally important to calibrate the music to the rhythm of the event—and to make your selections with an eye to getting every generation up on the dance floor. (As with all aspects of your wedding, it's essential that you communicate your tastes to the people you work with—hence the infamous Do-Not-Play list.) It's always possible to give a portable digital device a budget-friendly role in the festivities. And a couple with four left feet between them should *not* be afraid of a few dance lessons. (Come on, it might even be fun!)

First Steps

Some couples are so eager to book the band that they jump the gun. Don't start listening to demos until you've done some homework, or you could learn too late you've booked musicians who aren't right for your location. They may, in fact, not even be *allowed* at your location.

Find out whether your ceremony site has any restrictions on music. Many churches and synagogues have rules about whether music is allowed, whether you can bring in outside musicians or must use the ones at the church, and what type of music is permitted. Catholic churches usually allow only religious music; many reform temples permit secular music but may ask you not to use particular songs. The church organist might be part of the package, in which case you don't need to shop around for ceremony musicians; your song choices may be limited by the organist's repertoire, though some are willing to tackle new pieces. If you're having a religious wedding outside of a house of worship, ask the officiant if he has any restrictions.

For an outdoor ceremony or reception, find out from the site whether there are any noise regulations. At a public park or in the backyard of a private home, music may not be allowed past a certain hour and amplifiers may not be permitted at all. Also ask your site contact about electrical outlets, the size of the stage, and how many musicians are usually needed to fill the space with sound.

Once you've identified any limitations, start thinking about the types of music you

want for the ceremony, the cocktail hour, and the reception. Do you want a classical quartet as you walk down the aisle? At the reception, would you prefer a little of everything or a single genre such as R&B, klezmer music, or salsa?

Next, consider the size of the location and the number of guests. In general, a large wedding demands a larger band—a quartet will be drowned out by the din of three hundred guests; a small space can't handle a large band, for both space and volume reasons. Outdoor weddings of any substantial size require a good sound system, and instruments will need some protection from the sun. Also find out what type of acoustics you have at each location where you'll have music. Good acoustics might mean you'll need fewer musicians to fill the space with rich sound.

Scoring the Ceremony

There's a lot to be said for adhering to tradition in ceremony music. Walking down the aisle to "Trumpet Voluntary" or "Jesu, Joy of Man's Desiring" connects you to the millions of brides before you who have walked this same path and can make this rite of passage feel even more sacred. But some brides and grooms aren't moved by tradition and need to choose music that they connect with in a more personal way. My son Jordan and his bride, Tali, had a twelve-piece orchestra playing classical renditions of '90s hip-hop songs as they walked down the aisle. I'd been apprehensive, but even I had to admit that it worked!

On the classical front, Wagner's "Bridal Chorus" from *Lohengrin* (most people know it as "Here Comes the Bride") remains the most divisive of processionals. Some brides have dreamed of using it since they were girls, and some think it represents everything trite and outmoded about weddings. Though not everyone knows about its origins, it's frowned on by some because its composer was a known anti-Semite.

> Popular bands and big-name DJs get snapped up early, so you should be aiming to book a band at least six months before the wedding. If you don't have that much time, you will certainly be able to find a talented band through an agency, but you may not get your first choice.

Sound Check

You want to make sure that guests can hear not only the music but also the ceremony itself, so ask questions about the sound system at the ceremony site—only small weddings can get away with not using amplification. If the sound system isn't adequate, find out what you're permitted to have in the space; you may need to rent speakers, an audio board, a microphone, or lavaliers (wireless clip-on microphones). If your budget allows and you're having a large wedding, it's a good idea to put speakers at both the front and back of the ceremony space.

If you have choices open to you, first decide on the style of music you want for the ceremony—classical, Latin, Caribbean steel drums—then start looking at song selections. A string quartet (two violins, viola, and cello), a duet of Latin guitars, a string trio (two violins and a cello), a flute trio (flute, violin, and cello), and voodoo lounge (four-piece ensemble that plays traditional music rock 'n' roll style) are popular choices. Caribbean steel drums sound wonderful at a beach wedding. At the very high end, a ten-piece orchestra of winds and strings provides a full, rich sound. Gospel choirs, which can often be hired through your church or through a college or high school, lend a beautiful note. And of course there's nothing wrong with using recorded music at the ceremony. If you're hiring a DJ for the reception music, find out if he's willing to handle the ceremony as well. (Big-name DJs won't do this, so you'll need to find a stand-in.) Just make sure he's using the right versions of the songs you've selected.

The Prelude

THE PRELUDE is the ambient music played as guests arrive and are seated. When booking musicians, plan on thirty to forty-five minutes of prelude music, even if you think you only need twenty: This buys you time in case the wedding starts late. Since this is the first music guests will hear, it sets the tone for the ceremony. You might not have anything in mind, but your musicians will usually have excellent suggestions for suitable pieces.

The Processional

THE SWITCH to processional music signals the beginning of the ceremony. It's grander, designed to get guests' attention. You'll choose as many as four songs for the processional, with different tunes to use while the grandparents and parents are being seated, when the wedding party goes down the aisle, and finally for the bride. Some weddings feature as many as six songs, but that seems excessive to me. You can use fewer than four tunes, but switch the music to announce the bride's entrance. This is, after all, the moment your guests are waiting for.

The Interlude

SOME CEREMONIES feature a song during the lighting of the unity candle or at another point in the ceremony. The song can be instrumental or vocal; if there aren't rules restricting it to religious music, it could be a love song special to the couple. A talented friend or family member could sing or play an instrument. Consider giving a child or teen a special role by having them play something simple but meaningful.

The Recessional

ONCE THE GROOM KISSES the bride and they turn to walk back up the aisle, the recessional music comes on to herald the triumphant, joyous moment. Although there are several classical choices that do the job, nothing better expresses the spirit of the moment than a gospel rendition of "Oh, Happy Day"; or a Motown song like "Signed, Sealed, Delivered." This is another ideal place to personalize the ceremony by choosing a song that says something about the couple—one bride had "Take Me Out to the Ball Game" played as a surprise for her baseball-obsessed groom. Scottish couples may want to honor tradition by having a bagpiper escort them out of the church.

The Postlude

KEEP THE MUSIC PLAYING until every last guest has exited the ceremony area. Music should revert to the background, but it should be a little more exuberant than the preceremony selections. Plan on fifteen minutes' worth of music.

Music for the Reception

Assuming that you're planning a reception with dancing, you should aim for music with broad appeal. Naturally, you want a band or DJ whom you're truly excited to hire, but keep in mind that you'll have three, four, or even five generations represented at your wedding. And you want them all out on the dance floor. If you hire a Clash cover band, your punk rocker friends will be over the moon, but older family members and friends of your parents will be left out in the cold. A DJ who specializes in electronic music or hip-hop might be a better choice for the after-party than for the reception.

The term "wedding band" doesn't always have a positive connotation, but what a wedding band does extremely well is play to an all-ages crowd. Think about the kind of mix that's going to appeal to your guests—perhaps some jazz standards along with rock 'n' roll, Motown, and disco. When choosing songs from the playlist, one way to go is to think about hitting each decade from the 1930s on.

When guests enter the reception, music should already be playing. Nothing kills a party mood like watching the

Tried-and-True Ceremony Tunes

Many brides want something classical for the ceremony but are at a loss in the world of classical music. If that's the case for you, use the following lists as a starting point. (You'll also find a couple of contemporary surprises.) Many of these pieces are readily available online for a quick listen.

THE PRELUDE

"Jesu, Joy of Man's Desiring" (Bach)

"Air on a G String" (Bach)

Trumpet Concerto, 2nd Movement (Torelli)

"Vocalise" (Rachmaninoff)

"On Wings of Song" (Mendelssohn)

THE PROCESSIONAL

"Bridal Chorus" from *Lohengrin,* known as "Here Comes the Bride" (Wagner)

"Trumpet Tune" (Purcell)

"Trumpet Voluntary," also called "The Prince of Denmark's March" (Clarke/Purcell)

"Canon in D" (Pachelbel)

"Here Comes the Sun" (The Beatles)

THE INTERLUDE

"Hymne a l'Amour" (Josh Groban)

"Wedding Song (There Is Love)" (Peter, Paul and Mary)

"The Prayer" (Andrea Bocelli and Celine Dion)

"Ave Maria" (Schubert)

"Clair de Lune" (Debussy)

THE RECESSIONAL

"Wedding March" from *A Midsummer Night's Dream* (Mendelssohn)

"Ode to Joy" (Beethoven)

"Hallelujah Chorus" from *Messiah* (Handel)

"The Arrival of the Queen of Sheba" (Handel)

THE POSTLUDE

"Water Music: Air" (Handel)

"Exsultate Jubilate: Alleluia" (Mozart)

"Waltz in A Flat" (Brahms)

"Wedding Day at Troldhaugen," Op. 65, No. 6 (Grieg)

"All You Need Is Love" (The Beatles)

band set up. I like to start off with mellower music to ease the transition. Think Frank Sinatra and Harry Connick Jr.

Stick with low-key music until after the first dance. If you're having dancing between courses, you can throw in some Motown and disco to lure people to the dance floor, but save the really high-energy dance tunes for the time between dinner and dessert, with a small break for cutting the cake. While people are eating, the music should be a backdrop; you may want most of the band to take their break then, leaving a pianist to play during dinner.

For the overall flow of things, I like to have dancing between courses. It gives everyone, especially the older set who may leave on the early side, a lot of opportunities to dance. It also makes it easier to integrate traditional dances like the tarantella into the flow of the reception. The other way to structure a sit-down reception is to serve the full meal, then begin the dancing. Some people feel that this is a more elegant option, but in my experience, the guests are so stuffed by the end of the meal that it's hard to get them to dance. It also makes for a late evening, and the older guests and children may not last until the father-daughter dance.

Since many couples choose to play standards at their weddings, I'm including some classic favorites for specific moments in the reception to inspire and guide you, but I encourage you to follow your heart on this one. If the two of you go swing dancing on weekends, hire a swing band. If you share a love of The Beatles, why not plan an all-Beatles event? One couple I know has a serious thing for movies, so they used music from their favorite sound tracks. Calypso, reggae, zydeco, country-and-western, bagpipers, or klezmer music can all make your celebration stand out.

The First Dance

MY FAVORITE WAY to start a reception is to have the newlyweds introduced and have them head straight to the dance floor, while the evening is still young and guests will give you their full attention. Follow the first dance with the father-daughter and mother-son dances, then invite the rest of the guests onto the dance floor, and you'll get your party off to a great start.

Or take a page from some of ties who've kicked off their recepti mobs featuring the entire bridal pa a different song to announce eacl party and had them come out dancing.

If you're going the more traditional route, pick a first-dance song that couldn't belong to anyone else. Yours should be a song you love, one that has special meaning for *you*. Some of the most popular first dances, like "At Last" and "It Had to Be You," are gorgeous in their own right, but people have heard them at so many weddings that they cease to feel special.

Many couples immediately know what their first dance is going to be, the same way the bride recognizes the gown she's meant to wear. But if you don't, not to worry. Your bandleader or DJ will have great ideas.

You should also consider what type of music lends itself to your dancing abilities—one couple had just mastered the waltz together, so they asked their bandleader which waltzes his jazz ensemble knew. He immediately

Music and Cocktails

A transitional period between the ceremony and reception, the cocktail hour shouldn't claim a lot of your music budget. You want to go for something a little livelier than the ceremony sound, but it should still remain in the background, as you don't want the musicians to drown out conversation. A string quartet, jazz trio or pianist, Spanish guitar players, a calypso group, or a Latin quartet all make great choices.

What usually works best is to have the ceremony musicians keep playing for cocktails—since you probably have to book them for a minimum of two to three hours, it's a good way to get your money's worth. You can also work out a deal with your reception band for a few members to arrive early and play for cocktails. If you're on a tight budget, program your own cocktail hour music and hook up your MP3 player to a sound system.

Music to Dance To

Including dances in your reception schedule is not just a sweet nod to tradition; it's also a way to inspire wallflowers to get onto the floor, as well as a nice pacing mechanism. I really think you should choose music that's close to your heart, but if you're drawing a blank, take a listen to some of these.

FIRST DANCE

"At Last" (Etta James)

"Here and Now" (Luther Vandross)

"Can't Help Falling in Love" (Elvis Presley)

"Have I Told You Lately" (Van Morrison)

"It Had to Be You" (Frank Sinatra)

FATHER TO DAUGHTER

"Can You Feel the Love Tonight" (Elton John)

"Daughters" (John Mayer)

"Father's Eyes" (Amy Grant)

"Hero" (Mariah Carey)

"My Girl" (The Temptations)

MOTHER TO SON

"Beautiful Boy" (John Lennon)

"In My Life" (The Beatles)

"Through the Years" (Kenny Rogers)

"You Raise Me Up" (Josh Groban)

"What a Wonderful World" (Louis Armstrong)

LAST DANCE

"Let's Stay Together" (Al Green)

"Save the Last Dance for Me" (Michael Bublé)

"The Best Is Yet to Come" (Nancy Wilson)

"Fly Me to the Moon" (Frank Sinatra)

"Save the Best for Last" (Vanessa Williams)

suggested "Some Day My Prince Will Come," which had long been a sentimental favorite of the bride's. It was the perfect choice.

Father and Daughter, Mother and Son

AFTER THE FIRST DANCE, it's time for the touching rituals of the father-daughter and mother-son dances. The bride takes to the dance floor with her father either following the first dance or just after the entrée has been eaten. Then the groom and his mother dance. In these song choices, sentimentality is fully embraced—just go there.

The Last Dance

YOU WANT TO GO OUT on the right note, so handpick the last dance. Nothing beats "Last Dance" by Donna Summer, but there are endless options. "At Last" makes a wonderful way to end the evening, and while it's overplayed as a first dance, it's a less expected choice for the last dance.

Traditional Dances

IN MANY CULTURES, celebratory group dances are traditionally performed at weddings, and they're often remembered as the high point of the reception. Many are danced in a ring, to symbolize eternity—just like the wedding band.

If either of you has a link to a culture with a special dance, do make it part of your celebration. When everyone joins together in a dance, you truly feel like two families are being united. And if one side of the family has never attempted the Italian tarantella or the Greek handkerchief dance, you're probably in for some good laughs.

There's no protocol governing when you start a group dance. Some couples like to do it right after the first dance and the parent-child dances. It brings everyone together early in the reception and gets the energy up in the room. I always think it's best to do the hora on a light stomach, so I advise couples to do it before the meal! You can also do these dances later in the evening, after guests have had a few glasses of wine and loosened up a bit.

Some of these dances have become popular far outside of their native cultures, so if there's one that appeals to you, feel free to make it part of your celebration.

If you're planning on any ethnic dances, make sure the band knows the music or is willing to learn it.

Hora. This joyous Jewish circle dance has the bride and groom lifted in chairs, each holding ends of the same handkerchief to stay joined together. If it resembles other Eastern European dances, it's because it's derived from a Romanian folk dance.

Mezinka. A Jewish circle dance that celebrates parents who have married off their last child. The lucky set of parents is seated in the middle of the dance floor, with family and wedding party members forming a circle around them. The band starts off playing the mezinka melody very slowly as people circle and congratulate the parents. The tempo gradually quickens until it segues into a festive hora romp.

Hasapiko and Kalamatiano. Both are popular Greek circle dances in which guests lock arms to form a circle, then wind their way around the room. There's a specific foot pattern to these dances, so if they're not known to members of your community, you could have your wedding party sign up for a lesson—it's simple enough.

Tarantella. Legend has it that this Italian circle dance was named for a spider whose bite could only be cured by a round of frenetic dancing. Guests intermittently take turns dancing in the center of the circle. The circle itself moves in a clockwise motion until the music speeds up; with every change in tempo, the circle switches direction.

Mexican snake dance (*La Vibora*). The couple stands on chairs facing each other and turns the groom's jacket into a bridge. The single women in attendance form a conga line that passes under the jacket. When the music stops, the couple drops the jacket. The woman on whom it falls receives the bride's bouquet. The dance is repeated with the single men; the winner gets the bride's garter.

Music for Other Types of Receptions

NOT EVERY RECEPTION consists of a cocktail hour followed by a meal and dancing. If you're having a cocktail party, an afternoon tea, or a late-night dessert buffet, you need to think about your music differently. Much will depend on whether you're planning to have dancing.

The music should fit the mood of the party. The earlier in the day your reception, the smaller the band should be, and the more low-key the music. A ten-piece band with horns is too much at a brunch or an afternoon tea, but a jazz quintet, a harpist, or a pianist would be perfect.

For cocktail parties, choose a lively band if you're planning to have dancing. But if the focus is on food, drink, and conversation, a smaller ensemble can provide ambient music. Late-night parties usually place a heavy emphasis on dancing, so if you're inviting everyone at 8 p.m. for drinks and dessert, you're free to go all out in your music choices.

Bands, Orchestras, and DJs

A band brings the excitement of a live performance to your wedding. I love the elegance of the big band sound, with the musicians all wearing white dinner jackets and a trumpet player doing solos. But your tastes might run to rock 'n' roll, bossa nova, salsa, zydeco, reggae, or country-and-western bands. A "wedding band" typically plays a little of everything, from 1930s big band and 1940s boogie-woogie to disco and current hits.

The main advantages of hiring a live band are the rich sound and the spontaneity. The bandleader should be able to adjust the tempo, extend the set, or switch from jazz standards to Motown to keep the crowd dancing. The downside is the expense; a live band costs considerably more than most DJs and requires more breaks. Many bands have wide-ranging playlists, but don't expect a swing band to be able to toss in a set of downbeat lounge music. The size of the band should correlate to the size of your guest list. Too large a band will overwhelm guests; too small a band won't make an impact. But the more musicians you hire, the steeper the fee.

Once considered a low-rent alternative to a band, DJs have emerged as a desirable alternative. The main draw: You can book a DJ for one-third to one-half the price of a band, though celebrity DJs charge more. Beyond price, there are several advantages. A DJ has thousands of songs at his fingertips and should be able to get his hands on any songs you request ahead of time. So if you want to alternate between West Coast swing and alt-rock, he can do it. With a DJ, you're getting the original big-name artist singing your favorites instead of a cover band. Club-style DJs add their own style to the music, blending, scratching, and remixing songs to create an entirely new sound.

Pay attention to your DJ's onstage persona. DJs range from cool club kids who don't say much of anything to in-your-face "hosts" in sequined tuxedos, so find out what kind of role they usually play at weddings and check their references to make sure you know what you're getting.

The Best of Both Worlds

WHEN IT COMES TO BANDS and DJs, it doesn't have to be an either/or situation. If your budget allows, book both and get the best of both options. Alternate the band and the DJ, having the DJ play while the band takes its breaks, and get the benefit of distinct styles of music. Or start off the reception with a band and change to a DJ when you want to shift the party into gear. Having a DJ on hand will also prevent you from going into costly overtime with the band; in some cases, the entire cost of a DJ can work out to less than band overtime pay.

Finding the Talent

THE REFERRAL ROUTE for musicians differs, depending on what type of talent you're seeking. Friends, family members, and the catering manager at the best hotel in the area are good sources. Wedding websites, wedding libraries, and vendors can also provide names.

Many bands are booked through entertainment or music agents, which you can find in the Yellow Pages. You may be able to get a lower price by negotiating directly with a band, but an agency has the ability to find a substitute should there be any sort of last-minute emergency with the band you booked.

For recommendations about specific categories of musicians, look to where they ply their trade. For ceremony musicians, ask your contact at the church or synagogue for a recommendation. If you want classical musicians, call your local orchestra or chamber music society. For a break on price, contact the nearest music conservatory, where you can often hire students for a fraction of the cost. For a jazz quartet, ask the booker at a local jazz club. Likewise, for the coolest DJs, get recommendations at clubs.

Any concert venue is a viable resource for finding musicians. If you've heard a singer, Spanish guitarists,

ASK MINDY

Q *Between the two of us, my fiancée and I have four left feet. To put it mildly, we're not looking forward to the idea of doing a first dance. Will people miss it if we don't? And is there some other way to get the party started?*

A People probably won't miss it; I think it's optional. Personalizing your wedding also means not having to do something that you don't want to do! Get the party going by having the bandleader start off with high-energy music and invite everyone up to the dance floor.

or a steel drum band you love at a local coffeehouse or bar, get their contact info from the manager. If these groups aren't accustomed to playing weddings, they may be better suited to cocktail hour or a special set at the reception—they may not have the experience to direct the tempo of your entire reception.

Another thing to know: Wedding bands tend to play at corporate functions, black-tie fund-raisers, and other social events. If you know someone on the social circuit or who sits on committees for fund-raisers, she'll be able to reel off a list of the bands that get people on the dance floor.

For a reception band or a DJ, you want someone with wedding experience, but that's not critical for ceremony and cocktail hour musicians.

Vetting the Talent

THE BAND OR DJ is going to play an integral, visible role at your wedding, so you want to meet them in person if at all possible. If that can't be arranged, set up a telephone interview and make sure you see a video of a performance. If booking long-distance, make sure that you've at least seen a photo of the band so you have some idea of their appearance.

If you can possibly hear the band perform, that's the best way to judge whether you like their music, their style, and their stage presence. Some bands play at local clubs, so it's just a matter of getting their schedule and catching a performance. But if they're strictly a wedding band, it's more difficult to see them live.

A video can give you an idea of how they look and sound when performing, and a playlist is also helpful. Many bands now feature music and video clips on their websites. With both, however, find out whether the number of musicians is the same as what you're booking. That twelve-piece band you listened to online isn't going to sound the same as the five-piece band you're hiring. Also ask whether all of the players will be the same. Many bands pick up musicians for bookings as they need them—this isn't necessarily a bad thing, especially with a jazz band that's used to improvising, but do ask if they've played with all of their pickup musicians before. You

Dollars and Sense

The amount spent on ceremony and reception music at a $26,000 wedding should be about $1,800, which works out to 7 percent of the budget. But it's not unusual for couples to put music at the top of their list and allot a much higher percentage of their budget to getting a band that rocks.

Prices vary dramatically according to the location and reputation of the band. If you're going to hire a famous band or singer, you're going to pay dearly for their presence. Fees for bands and DJs are generally based on four hours of work and are predicated on the number of musicians; they vary widely, depending on geography.

Expect to put down a deposit of 50 percent and to pay the balance two weeks prior to the event.

should always know who you're booking—if an entertainment broker won't provide a photo of the band and there's no way to listen to them, keep looking.

Don't forget to ask for and check references. Ask if the band showed up on time, whether there were any substitutions in the lineup, if they brought everything they promised. Did they agree to learn any new music for the couple? If so, how well did they perform it? How well did they play to the crowd? If the bandleader or DJ served as the emcee, what kind of personality did he project? Did they adhere to the Do-Not-Play list (see page 132)? Did they take requests?

After you book a band, you'll typically have one more meeting four to six weeks before the wedding to discuss the schedule and playlist in more detail.

The Playlist Wedding

OVER THE PAST DECADE, digital music devices have emerged as the DIY music alternative for couples on a budget. While they're not ideal as the main source of reception music—you need someone to man the device and it's hard to sync them with the flow of the party—

THE BAND OR DJ

Don't let yourself get intimidated by that cool musician vibe—you're still going to need to ask some questions.

- *What's your overall approach to playing weddings? How do you pace the event?*
- *How many hours of playing time are included in the contract?*
- *What are the options for the size of the band and the number of vocalists?*
- *What do you typically wear to play a wedding?* Some bands bill for tuxedo rentals if they need to wear black-tie, while others own tuxes, so find out if there's a charge.
- *Will you learn a song I request if you don't know it? How much advance notice do you need? Is there a fee for arranging the music?*
- *Do you require any equipment or instrument rentals, such as a piano? Is there anything else I will need to provide for you, such as a table for equipment or a speaker?*
- *Do you bring your own sound system?*
- *Do you need extra electrical power for your equipment?*

- *Do you need a certain style of stage? What size stage do you require?*
- *Do you want the bandleader to be the emcee of the reception or to stay in the background?* If he's going to play the emcee, ask him how he views that role and make sure you're both on the same page.
- *Discuss their typical playlist and identify your favorite songs.* It's a good way to get a feel for each other's tastes.
- *Discuss whether they take requests and how you want to handle it.* You may not want guests taking the music into their own hands.
- *Ask how long they've been performing at weddings. How many have you done in the last year?* Ask for references from a couple of weddings they've done.
- *How many breaks will you take? How long is each break?* Many bands need a fifteen- to twenty-minute break each hour.

- *How is music handled during breaks? Is continuous music an option?* Some bands can leave one or two musicians onstage to play during breaks. *If not, do you bring recorded music to play? Does a DJ bring a set of recorded music?*
- *What kind of backup plan do you have if one or more band members falls ill or has an emergency on the day of the wedding?*
- *Do you have liability insurance?*
- *Find out how long they need to set up.* Emphasize that you want them set up and playing before the first guests walk in. Some bands like to arrive at the last minute, and they're still setting up as guests arrive.
- *Would you like a meal?* It's customary to provide one but worth checking, in case they prefer to bring their own food.
- *If you have a special theme, ask if they have song suggestions.*

they're a fine way to provide music at the rehearsal dinner, after-parties, and even during cocktail hour. At a destination wedding, using a digital device can eliminate the stress of booking a band you've never heard and can offer vastly greater variety than a local band.

If you decide to go this route for the reception, appoint a friend to play DJ. You'll want separate playlists for the ceremony, cocktail hour, and the reception.

You'll need to hook the digital music player up to a sound system. Most hotels can supply speakers, or you can rent a sound system from a party supply company, an audio rental company, and even through some DJs. A few DJ agencies and audio rental companies also rent digital music devices programmed with wedding music.

Find out in advance what equipment you'll need to provide. Plan on bringing a mini-stereo-to-RCA cable to hook up the device to the speakers. It's also a good idea to bring a "male to female" RCA extension cable.

Music Lists and Schedules

For everything to go smoothly at the reception, get the band or DJ a detailed schedule of events four to six weeks before the wedding (see page 348 for details). If you don't have a wedding planner, the bandleader can often help you create the schedule. It should include the songs you've selected for the first dance and the father-daughter and mother-son dances; it should also make clear whether you're having music between courses or everyone is dining and then dancing. If the band hasn't played in the space before, the schedule should allow time for a sound check, but remember, you'll have to pay for that time.

Don't forget to include breaks for the band or DJ, and indicate which one is the meal break. Also include the name and cell phone number of the person they should check in with when they arrive.

If the bandleader or DJ will be serving as the emcee, write down phonetic pronunciations of the names of anyone you want introduced, including the bride, groom, parents, best man, and maid of honor. Also note how you want to be introduced—as Mr. and Mrs. Thomas? As Jennifer and Mark?

ASK MINDY

Q How do you feel about hiring entertainers at a wedding? My fiancée is planning a really elaborate affair, and I thought it might be nice to surprise her by booking a magician for the children and possibly some professional dancers to get things going on the dance floor. Is that tacky, though?

A I've done both. It's a wonderful idea to do something for the kids, if you can afford it. It keeps them busy, the dancing adds fun for everyone, and it's great to let part of your personality come through like that. But it all has to be kept in the spirit of the wedding. Break dancers probably wouldn't be the best choice for a reception in a formal garden.

I would advise against the surprise element, though. It's great to want to chip in, but talk to your fiancée beforehand to make sure you're on the same page. After all that careful planning, she might not appreciate being thrown for a loop.

THE MUSIC CONTRACT

No matter what type of band or DJ you choose, the following points should be addressed in the music contracts.

- Date of event, address of location, arrival time, starting and ending time, number of hours the band will perform. (If they're available to stay longer if needed, write it into the contract.)
- Deposit amount and date the balance is due.
- Frequency and length of breaks, and anything they'll provide during the breaks, such as recorded music.

- Fee, detailing what it includes and what equipment they're supplying. Also list any equipment they've agreed to supply, such as chairs and amplifiers.
- Overtime rate.
- Cancellation policy.
- Attire of musicians or DJ.
- Names of the performers.

- For a band, the number of musicians and number of vocalists. Note the instruments they'll be playing.
- If the Do-Not-Play list is of utmost importance to you, make it part of the contract.
- Statement that they have valid liability insurance.

Go through their playlist and mark the songs you like. Send them a Do-Not-Play list of songs you positively don't want to hear. If the bandleader has agreed to learn a few songs for you, send him the choices at least three months before the wedding so they have time to find the music and rehearse it.

Not everyone chooses specific songs for all of these reception moments, but you'll want to note your selection for at least some of the following:

- Introduction of the bride and groom
- Introduction of the wedding party
- First dance
- Father-daughter dance
- Mother-son dance
- Cake cutting
- Bouquet toss
- Garter toss
- Last dance

> If you're having an after-party or lounge, keep it basic with a DJ or a digital device. (Couples with sky's-the-limit budgets have been known to bring in big-name entertainers for a late-night set.) The crowd will have thinned out, so the music can be geared strictly to the couple and their contemporaries: It's all about dance music.

Dance Lessons

You're likely to feel self-conscious out there during the first dance, so why not boost your confidence with some expert instruction? Taking dance lessons can also offer a welcome respite from the stresses of wedding planning, giving the two of you time to connect. Even if one of you has to be talked into lessons, you'll both end up having a blast.

You can sign up for a group class at a dance studio or take private lessons. If you just want to learn a few basics, a couple of lessons should cover it. Start them about two months before the wedding—if you take them too early,

The Do-Not-Play List

When you hire a band or DJ, you don't dictate every song they play. You'll have conversations about your tastes to steer them in the right direction (and I hope you're hiring a band or DJ whose tastes jibe with yours to begin with), but you need to make sure they don't accidentally play a song you happen to be allergic to. Even if you think of yourself as someone who's not that picky about music, I'm pretty sure you can come up with at least five songs that make you cringe.

That's where the Do-Not-Play list comes in. If your band or DJ has a playlist, ask to see it; take a look and simply cross out the songs you don't want played. (And don't worry about seeming controlling; the Do-Not-Play list is standard in the world of weddings.) If your band or DJ is working without a playlist, you'll have to come up with some of those wince-worthy tunes on your own. Write them down. Then think about it for a few days, and you'll doubtless come up with a few more. Give the list to your DJ or bandleader and breathe easier knowing the Hokey Pokey won't be making an appearance on your wedding day.

you run the risk of forgetting what you've learned.

You can also go a step further by learning a choreographed routine. Contact a dance instructor to get an estimate of how many lessons you'll need; a dozen is fairly typical for untrained dancers. You don't need to have already chosen your first dance—the instructor can help you identify the style of dancing you like and can make song suggestions.

To find dance lessons in your area, try the National Dance Council of America or check out available options on sites like Yelp. Your bandleader may also be able to point you to a gifted instructor.

With all the dancing and carousing going on, your guests are bound to work up a thirst. In the following chapter, you'll learn about all your cocktail options, from a full bar with signature cocktails to wine and beer. ◆

CHAPTER TEN

Spirits, Wine & Bubbly

PERSONALIZING THE COCKTAIL HOUR

Weddings were so closely intertwined with spirits in England in the Middle Ages that wedding feasts were called bride-ales, which gave rise to the word *bridal*. At bride-ales, the drinking of ale or beer could go on for days. Today's toasting seems sedate by those standards. Still, a wedding tends to be thought of as an occasion

for lifting a glass or two (or even three).

I'm not advocating overindulgence, but unless your friends and family are unusually abstemious, you've got to plan on alcohol constituting the single largest expense after food.

Liquor helps to grease the wheels of social interaction, to be sure—all your careful work on those seating charts will come to naught if your friends Patty and

Bill can't get beyond the "where are you froms" and "what do you dos." Alcohol can also help turn a dinner party into a dance party. I guess it's a little sad that most of us need to have our inhibitions loosened a little before we find the courage to break into a Greek circle dance, but it's true.

Last but not least, your guests are going to need something to toast you with. *Salud!*

Cocktail Hour

The cocktail hour is certainly a time for guests to get a glass of wine or a mixed drink, but it also serves as a buffer between the ceremony and the reception. It creates a window for the bridal party to get their photos taken—if they haven't done so before the ceremony—or, possibly, to greet guests in a receiving line. For guests, it's a time to contemplate the ceremony, find their seating cards for dinner, and pick up a few nibbles to keep their hunger at bay. Cocktail hour may be the best chance they have to mingle. If the ceremony and reception will take place in the same room, cocktail hour is an absolute necessity, allowing time for the room to be transformed (the "turnover" or "changeover"). Since it's a stepping-stone between the ceremony and the reception, the music, food, and drinks should ideally introduce the mood your guests will see next.

Despite the name, cocktail hour doesn't have to involve alcoholic beverages. Some couples choose to have a soft bar for personal, cultural, or budgetary reasons. You should know, however, that many guests do like to have a celebratory drink or two at weddings, and some will be disappointed to find they can't get a glass of wine.

Changing Times

In the past, people didn't expect to see much of the bride and groom during cocktail hour. Tradition and superstition dictated that they not see each other before the ceremony, so the cocktail hour was their chance to pose for pictures. But more couples are choosing to do their photos before the ceremony so they don't miss out on the chance to mix and mingle with their guests. The upshot: The bride and groom feel more a part of their own wedding, gain more time with their guests, and may even get a sip of their own signature cocktail.

How Long Is Cocktail Hour?

THIS IS NOT a trick question. Although cocktail hour most commonly lasts sixty minutes, it doesn't have to. A shorter cocktail "hour" of forty-five minutes works better at a daytime wedding, when people don't tend to drink as much and the reception doesn't last as long. Trimming fifteen minutes from the cocktail hour will also lower your expenses, as guests typically consume one less drink in that time.

If the room where you had the ceremony is being completely transformed for the reception, the staff may need as long as an hour and twenty minutes for the changeover. This is a long time for guests to stand around, so bring in extra seating and consider creating a lounge area. Also try to have an activity to keep people engaged—set up a photo booth by the guest book so friends and family can ham it up for the camera and paste their photos in the book with a clever caption; or hand out a quiz about the bride and groom, with a prize going to the winner.

Timing the Interval

THOUGH MOST PEOPLE sandwich cocktail hour between the ceremony and the reception, some couples serve cocktails before the wedding ceremony. Preceremony cocktails are particularly common at Saturday evening Jewish weddings; in a traditional ceremony, the marriage cannot take place until sundown, which can be as late as 8:30 p.m. in summer, so preceremony cocktails keep the event from running very late. The practice is also common in cultures where invitation times are viewed in a more fluid manner—latecomers have a better chance of getting there in time for the ceremony.

Forget preceremony cocktails at a church wedding or at any house of worship, as they're not allowed. And take a minute to think about the nature of the families: Serving alcohol too early in the event is not a good idea if the guest list includes a heavy contingent of people who regard drinking as a competitive sport.

Making It Work

INCORPORATE THESE INGREDIENTS into your cocktail hour. Stir gently. Serve immediately.

Make sure you have music. It instantly lifts the mood and sets the tone for the party, and you'll always notice if it's *not* there. Cocktail hour music is more low-key than the reception music—it's about creating a mood, not getting people on the dance floor. Turn to chapter 9, "Music & Dancing," for more specific suggestions on types of music that lend themselves to cocktail hour. If there's no budget for musicians, talk to the catering director about hooking up a portable music device.

Greet guests with drinks. You don't want your guests' first impression to be a twenty-minute wait at the bar. Have waiters welcome guests with trays of sparkling water and wine or champagne. Or fill the trays with a signature cocktail in a striking color to create a vibrant style statement. Always offer a nonalcoholic option to incoming guests. Getting a first drink into everyone's hand should prevent an initial rush at the bar and keep everyone in a good mood.

Offer some seating. It's very important to have at least a few tables and chairs for older guests; an hour is a long time for them to stand. At a minimum, set up two tables with four chairs at each. Also plan on having one high-top cocktail table for every twenty guests. You don't necessarily need chairs for these tall tables; they're mostly there to give people a place to rest their drinks and plates, but they definitely make guests feel more comfortable. For those who have the budget, adding a grouping of upholstered furniture creates a modern living-room vignette that instantly makes people feel as if they've come to a great party.

Set up at least one food station in addition to serving passed hors d'oeuvres. Stations let you create a visually arresting presentation and give people a place to congregate, which is key to the flow of a party.

Have one bar staffed by two bartenders for every one hundred guests or more, if you have the means—it will keep the line down. Study the floor plan to decide on the best placement. You want to put at least one of the bars

---

Sipping Pretty

I
n addition to sparkling water, offer alluring nonalcoholic drinks other than the usual juices. You might serve blackberry-sage iced tea garnished with a skewer of blackberries, or a sparkling mango-lime cooler. Put out different flavored waters (each a different hue) in carafes and let guests conduct their own tastings. This will make nondrinkers and underage guests feel as if they're getting a special treat and will encourage everyone to drink more nonalcoholic beverages, so they're less likely to overindulge.

far away from the entrance so that guests will fill out the room. Position the bars away from any areas that provide passage to guests or the waitstaff. You don't want the line for the bar to block the path of waiters carrying trays of glasses to the kitchen.

Attune the cocktails and food choices to the season. Mojitos in the summer and warm cider in the fall feel more festive than a standard selection of bar drinks. Likewise with tray-passed shot glasses of gazpacho in July and teacups of roasted butternut squash soup in October.

Design the cocktail hour as an extension of the ceremony, so it creates a transition to the reception. If the wedding color is pink, the ceremony could be done in traditional shades of white and ivory with the bridesmaids carrying pink bouquets. At cocktail hour, you retain the pink-and-white color scheme but introduce more pink, using pink cloths on the bar and cocktail tables and serving a rosy-hued signature cocktail. The reception shifts even more toward pink.

Add an unexpected twist. Instead of simply having wine poured, set up a wine-tasting bar with five or six varietals and notes about each. Find unusual ways to present the food and drinks. Rent special glasses for drinks or garnish them with striking flowers, fruit skewers, or half a dozen pomegranate seeds. Lay out tray-passed appetizers on stalks of bamboo, banana leaves, a bed of (uncooked) white beans, or a mound of flower petals. Outstanding presentations make a big impression—gussy up french fries by serving them in paper cones printed with a mock-up of a newspaper page about your wedding.

Don't skimp on the mixers. It's better to spend more on quality mixers (including liqueurs) and less on liquor. Good mixers can boost so-so alcohol, but a bad mixer will bring down good alcohol.

Speed up bar lines by having pitchers of premixed drinks like a white sangria or a rum punch behind the bar. Also set up a table with glass decanters of nonalcoholic beverages such as lemonade and hibiscus iced tea. Put out tented cards identifying the drinks and let guests help themselves.

Hors d'Oeuvres

You want to offer enough variety in hors d'oeuvres to keep guests from getting bored and just enough quantity to take the edge off their hunger. Ideally, you would serve six to eight different hors d'oeuvres and count on guests eating one of each during cocktail hour. For sushi, calculate three pieces per person.

When choosing appetizers, avoid repeating ingredients that will be featured prominently in the meal. If you're serving steak as the main course, don't serve sliders at cocktail hour.

Cocktail hour food can be edgier and more experimental than the main meal, so it's a wonderful opportunity to showcase foods that reflect the ethnic background or culture of one side of the family or that reflect the character of your wedding location. For example, you could set up a taste of Seattle with a raw bar (a bar of raw *and* cooked shellfish) and dim sum. Because it's not the main meal, you don't have to worry as much about pleasing a crowd.

Appetizers are an often-overlooked opportunity to show another side of yourselves. Besides sharing family traditions, think about your own favorites. Don't worry about whether they're elegant enough for a wedding. Tell your caterer about the foods that make you happy, and you might be surprised at how the mundane can be transformed into something special. For a midwestern groom who wanted hot dogs, a hotel chef created pigs in a blanket with a special herbed pastry served with six different types of mustard in dipping bowls. These are the touches that add personality to a wedding and make it memorable.

Bar Basics

Your choice of location will factor into your bar and alcohol options. If your reception is at a hotel, catering facility, private club, or restaurant, your venue will most likely be your supplier. Alcoholic beverages are a high markup item, and the bar tab for cocktail hour and the reception amounts to one of your more significant reception expenses.

You'll have a choice of a bar package or a consumption bar, where you'll get a by-the-drink tab. Packages provide an open bar for a set number of hours and are available at several levels: A "soft" bar includes beer and wine only; a "house" bar or "standard" bar would include house brands or lower-priced name brands; next up is a "premium" bar, which features higher-end brands; at the top levels are "deluxe" and "super-deluxe" bars, which would be stocked with the priciest liquors. At a house bar, the vodka might be Smirnoff; at a premium bar, Absolut; at a deluxe bar, Ketel One; and at a super-deluxe bar, Grey Goose.

With a consumption bar, you're charged by either the drink or the bottle. (Wine and champagne are always by the bottle.) You can mix and match the plans, opting for a bar package for cocktail hour, and per-consumption pricing for the rest of the reception. With a consumption plan, many venues charge you for a bartender but waive the fee once the bar bill hits a specified amount.

Packages are not inexpensive but can be a good choice if your guest list is filled with hearty drinkers. Consider how many underage guests you have on the list and how many known teetotalers. You can negotiate

How Much Will They Drink?

At a typical wedding, figure that each guest—minus children, of course—will consume two cocktails and two and a half glasses of wine. Another approach is to allow one drink per guest per hour.

For a cocktail and hors d'oeuvres reception, which typically lasts two and a half to three hours, estimate four drinks per person—five if your crowd runs to heavier drinkers. Although there is more focus on drinking, it's counteracted by the fact that the reception doesn't last as long as a full dinner.

In terms of yield, you'll get five glasses of wine from a 750-ml bottle, five and a half to eight glasses of champagne from a standard bottle, and eighteen to twenty cocktails from a one-liter bottle of liquor.

a reduced rate for those guests. Also take into account the time and day of the week, knowing that people drink more on evenings and on weekends.

If your reception will be held at an off-site location where you can bring in your own caterer, depending on the rules of the venue you may have the advantage of being able to purchase your own alcohol; the retail price of a bottle of wine is often one-third to one-fourth of the price charged by a hotel or club—plus you'll get a further discount for buying by the case.

The caterer should be able to provide bartenders and the bar setup, the definition of which varies from one caterer to the next. Some caterers include only ice, bar equipment, and bar fruit (lemons, limes, olives, cherries) in the setup, while others include mixers and bar fruits but charge separately for ice. They'll typically charge a setup fee, anywhere from $100 to $350.

You'll have the freedom to structure the bar any way you like, offering three types of tequila and five brands of single malt Scotch if that's what makes your crowd happy. Buy from a store that allows you to return unopened bot-

tles. But be aware that stores will not accept returns on unopened wine that's been chilled on ice, because the labels suffer in the process. Bring some local flavor to the bar by including beer and wine from regional microbreweries and wineries or freshly squeezed juice from a regional fruit.

The Signature Cocktail

A COUTURE COCKTAIL has become a staple of many a modern wedding. Although their novelty has worn off, they deserve to remain a fixture on the bridal bar scene. They make a statement about your style, become part of the wedding ambience, and give you an opportunity to share something about yourself or your love story with your guests. Best of all, signature cocktails can curb your bar bill when combined with a soft bar.

Contact your catering director or bartender to brainstorm ideas for a special drink. You might adapt your favorite cocktail, bring the location or the color scheme into the concoction, or choose a variation of a drink with a meaningful name (a Manhattan for a New York City groom, a Sazerac for a New Orleans bride). Make sure you sample the concoction before the wedding to make sure the combination works.

You can further personalize the drink by rimming the glass with colored sugar or salt, adding a striking flower or fruit garnish, or using candy sticks or lollipops as stirrers. I love clear cocktails (try vodka mixed with white cranberry juice and triple sec) garnished with a white flower—they look gorgeous and modern. And if they spill, they won't create an immediate stain on a wedding gown. The stain is likely to oxidize and appear later if it's not properly cleaned, but at least you won't have a red splotch on your gown at the wedding.

Don't forget to give that signature cocktail a name and feature it on a tented card at the bar.

Specialty Bars

WANT TO GO ONE STEP further than a specialty cocktail? A specialty bar can be a wonderful touch. One

Stocking the Bar

When setting up a bar, you need to think not only about your friends, who may be happy with martinis and beer, but also about the guests who might want a Scotch on the rocks. The following quantities apply to a four-hour reception of a hundred people. (If you know you have a crowd of heavy drinkers, increase the liquor quantities by 25 percent.) You'll need a full selection at each bar, so add accordingly.

Vodka: 6 liters

Gin: 1 liter

Scotch: 1 750-ml bottle

Bourbon: 1 liter

Tequila: 1 750-ml bottle

Light rum: 1 liter

White wine: 12 bottles

Red wine: 12 bottles

Champagne (optional): 12 750-ml bottles

Beer: 1 case (24 bottles)

Light beer: 1 case (24 bottles)

Sparkling water: 15 25-oz bottles

Bottled water: 15 1.5-liter bottles

Tonic water: 6 liters

Club soda: 6 liters

Ginger ale: 6 liters

Cola: 8 liters

Diet cola: 8 liters

Lemon-lime soda: 8 liters

Cranberry juice: 8 quarts

Orange juice: 4 quarts

Grapefruit juice: 2 quarts

Margarita mix: 2 liters

Margarita salt: 1 container

Dry vermouth: 1 375-ml bottle

Triple sec: 1 liter

Blue Curaçao: 1 750-ml bottle

Lime juice: 1 25-oz bottle

Grenadine: 1 25-oz bottle

Bitters: 1 jar

Olives: 1 jar

Maraschino cherries (optional): 1 jar

Lemons: 4

Limes: 8

Ice cubes: 250 lbs

SUPPLIES

Corkscrews and bottle openers

Garnish bowls

Ice buckets

Ice tongs

Ice tubs

Knife and cutting board

Citrus squeezers

Lemon zester

Long-handled spoons for mixing

Shot glasses (for measuring)

Measuring cups

Cocktail shakers

Strainers

Cocktail napkins

Sponges

Garbage can

Extra trash bags

GLASSWARE

All-purpose wineglasses

8-oz highball glasses

Champagne flutes

Martini glasses

note of caution: Think long and hard before setting up a shot bar or any bar where people are downing a high-proof alcohol at a rapid rate. You don't want guests sloshed before they get to the reception.

A martini bar is one elegant option; wrangle in guests who aren't seasoned martini drinkers by featuring an array of flavors, from apple to chocolate. For a tropical flavor, try a margarita or daiquiri bar. Or set up a wine bar with six different varietals and tasting notes by the bottles.

For nonalcoholic options, try a hot chocolate or coffee bar. Include Kahlúa, Irish whiskey, sambuca, and amaretto for those looking for a little extra kick.

What About a Cash Bar?

ASKING GUESTS TO PAY FOR their libations is less than gracious. You invited people to experience something special in your life, and what they're going to remember is that they had to pay for a drink—not how beautiful your vows were, the work you put in, the flowers, or the music.

To me, it's simple: When you're doing the inviting, guests shouldn't ever have to pull out their wallets. If an open bar is out of your budget, limit the offerings to wine or a signature cocktail or serve a tantalizing array of nonalcoholic drinks. Neither should guests be expected to tip bartenders. Be clear with the catering manager or bartenders that you'll take care of gratuities and that you don't want to see tip jars on the bar.

This is not to say that you'll never see a cash bar, but I think it's the wrong way to handle what's essentially a budget issue. You'll find great ideas for trimming the bar bill on page 142.

Champagne and Other Sparklers

T o some, love and bubbly are like a horse and carriage. Champagne has long been considered one of life's luxuries, and its tiny, elegant bubbles have been associated with celebrations since champagne was invented in the seventeenth century.

Genuine Champagnes like Taittinger and Veuve Clicquot come from the Champagne region of France, and you pay a premium for that distinction. Technically, anything else cannot be called Champagne, even if it's made by the *méthode champenoise* or *méthode traditionnelle*—a second fermentation inside the bottle that gives Champagne its fizz. You can, however, find delicious alternatives to Champagne that are kinder to the budget and may actually be more appropriate to the setting. Sparkling white wines, especially dry varieties such as brut, *blanc de blancs*, or *blanc de noirs* (categories that also apply to Champagne), can be lovely if chosen carefully.

But don't think it's a *must* to serve Champagne or sparkling wine at your wedding. Although it's a lovely tradition, the Champagne toast is the first thing I cut from a

Q How much alcohol will people drink? I'm not a drinker myself, and I'm considering having a dry wedding. Will people resent me?

A I've done one dry wedding, and it was my hardest. The bride and groom were both recovering alcoholics and I understood why they wanted to do it that way. But it turns out that it really affected the energy of the wedding. People didn't dance. It's unfortunate that we have to depend on alcohol to let loose, but we do. It took so much time to get people out and dancing, so much energy to get everyone laughing. People are inhibited; they don't want to be first in the buffet line or on the dance floor.

I would consider just serving wine. Or you could always try a morning wedding and a brunch, when people won't expect a band and dancing. (Serve great coffee.) If you do an evening wedding, the expectation is that alcohol will be served.

budget. Why? Because it can cost $2,500 to pour everyone a glass of Champagne at a large wedding, and many guests will hardly take more than a sip. (At a wedding for two hundred people, you'll need twenty-four bottles, or two cases, if you pour them a half glass each for the toast.) Furthermore, good Champagne is expensive, and mediocre sparkling wine can be vile; everyone will be better served if you pour a fresh round of whatever wine you're serving before the toasts begin.

Think Pink

ALTHOUGH IT WAS on the outs for years, pink Champagne makes a wonderful choice for weddings. The color lends itself to the occasion, and the fact that you don't see it as often makes it feel special. In recent years, I've seen many more offerings in rosé Champagnes and sparkling wines, along with great improvements in the quality. In addition to Champagne, you can find rosé sparkling wines from California, along with Spanish cava and Italian Prosecco.

A Champagne Glossary

YOU DON'T HAVE TO BE a sommelier to understand the basics of bubbly. Read on for a crash course.

NV. Stands for nonvintage and accounts for at least 75 percent of Champagne production. NV is blended from several vineyards and harvests. (For a Champagne to qualify as a vintage, at least 80 percent of the grapes in the blend must have been harvested in the same season at a single vineyard, and the rest from reserves from prior seasons.)

Rosé. Two methods are used to make rosé. More commonly, a small amount of red wine is added to the blend, but macerated red grape skins can also be used.

Blanc de blancs. Champagne made solely from chardonnay grapes, giving it a lighter, more delicate taste than traditional Champagnes, which are made from a blend of white and black grapes.

Blanc de noirs. Champagne made only from black grapes, pinot noir and pinot meunier, with a more robust taste.

Here's how Champagnes rank from driest to sweetest. You'll hear a lot of talk about dry, but most Americans actually prefer something a bit sweeter, even if they won't admit it. Warning: The terms can be utterly confusing, since *sec* means "dry" in French but "sweet" in the Champagne lexicon.

Extra-Brut. Very dry. In my opinion, too dry to be popular with a crowd.

Brut. Dry, not sweet. This is by far the most popular style of Champagne. Contains less than 1.5 percent sugar.

Extra dry or extra sec. Sweeter, sometimes fruitier, than brut. Moët & Chandon White Star is a popular extra-dry Champagne. Contains 1.2 to 2 percent sugar.

|||||||||| MEETING AND GREETING ||||||||||

THE BAR MANAGER

Ask the following questions of whomever is handling your liquor and bar, whether it's a caterer, an independent supplier, or an in-house contact

- *If the ceremony and reception are in the same room, how long does the staff need to "turn over" or "change over" the room?* This will affect the length of your cocktail hour.

- *How many bars and how many bartenders will be in place?*

- Discuss bar setup. Ask to see samples of the glassware. If ice will be stored in view, find out how it will be housed. (You don't want gray plastic garbage cans at your bar.)

- *How will I be charged for sodas, juices, and bottled water?* Some places charge per consumption, others don't charge at all.

- *How will I be charged for opened bottles of liquor?* Some venues charge by the bottle, and some charge by the tenth of a bottle.

- *How will bartenders deal with guests who have had too much to drink?*

- Find out the best way to handle gratuities for the bartenders; be clear that you don't want to see tip jars.

- Ask how much the venue or caterer carries in host liquor liability insurance. Find out if the reception site requires the host to take out an additional policy. (For more info on liability insurance, see chapter 12, "Making It Legal.")

Dry or sec. 1.7 to 3.5 percent sugar.

Demi-sec. 3.3 to 5 percent sugar. Considered a dessert wine.

Sweet or doux. An extremely sweet dessert wine that contains more than 5 percent sugar. (It would be highly unusual to serve it at a wedding.)

Sommelier for a Day

Most couples offer guests a choice of a red or white wine for the meal, though if you're serious about wine, you may want to pour a different offering with each course. The more wines you serve, the higher your costs—you'll have to open enough bottles to pour everyone a fresh glass. If you're on an extremely tight budget and it's a warm-weather wedding, you can sometimes get away with serving only white, though you can't do the reverse—too many people have aversions to red. For a summer wedding, consider serving a red, a white, and a rosé.

Once you've settled on your menu, you should discuss wine possibilities with the catering manager or sommelier. You're looking to complement the flavor, weight (light or heavy), texture, and acidity of the food. In general, lighter fare goes well with white wine and heavier food with red (white with chicken or fish and red with red meat). Some people consider those rules to be outdated, and in any case there are many exceptions, so get some recommendations and try them at

THE COCKTAIL HOUR CONTRACT

The following points should be addressed in the bar contract.

- Type of bar plan.
- Number of hours the bar will be open, and the time the bar will close.
- Number of bars and bartenders.
- Number of waiters.
- Number of and descriptions of hors d'oeuvres.
- Date, time, and place of the reception.
- Description of specialty cocktail, if applicable.

ASK MINDY

Q I saw in a magazine that these days some brides are finagling free stuff from companies (liquor, favors, etc.) by displaying their logo somewhere in their wedding. Is this kosher, or does it look tacky? I know celebrities do it, so why can't I?!

A You just can't. It's tacky, unless a magazine is sponsoring the proceedings and guests already know they're going to be in the public eye. You don't want your wedding to be a sponsored charity event. And believe me, your guests will notice it.

your menu tasting. Most venues will have you taste two whites and two reds.

If you're having an off-site wedding and buying your own wine, get recommendations from a trusted wine store after you've chosen your menu. Also ask the caterer if he has any specific recommendations on wine pairings. Buy several different reds and whites and try them at your food tasting.

It always adds a wonderful touch if you can personalize your wines, and there are more and more ways to accomplish that. You can order wine with custom labels printed with your names and wedding date. You can also choose wine with a meaningful name—maybe there's a vineyard that shares the groom's last name—or origin. It could be a wine from a place where the two of you vacationed together or from a country that relates to your family's heritage. When there is a personal reference, don't keep it a secret: Put tented cards or menus on the tables explaining the meaning.

Before you start sipping those cocktails, flip the page for tips on keeping those bar bills under control. Next up: some essential elements that may not involve as much fun, but can truly make or break a wedding. ♦

Dollars and Sense

Not only is alcohol a hefty expense, it can also be a tough one to predict. Use these strategies to keep the bar bill in line without sacrificing graciousness.

- Forgo a full bar. Instead, offer a soft bar with wine, beer, and soft drinks, which can cut your bill by 50 percent. If you have the budget, you can add either champagne or a signature cocktail to the menu. This is an option that's become more and more common in the wedding world.

- Look for French sparkling wines from outside the Champagne region. The closer you can get to the Champagne region (Burgundy being one of the close regions—look for Crémant de Bourgogne) the more likely they are to share a similar style.

- Serve sparkling wines from other countries. Prosecco and sparkling Moscato from Italy and cava from Spain are favorites for bargain-priced bubbly. Cava usually costs less than $10 a bottle at wine stores (Freixenet being the most common but far from the only option), while there are lovely Proseccos for $10 to $15.

- Instruct waiters to refill wineglasses upon request instead of automatically topping off glasses.

- Ask bartenders and the catering staff to open bottles only as needed. Some bartenders open every type of liquor bottle on the bar, meaning you're committed to a bottle of tequila even if no one orders a single margarita. Some also preopen wine before the reception to speed up the service, but if they overestimate, you're paying for unpoured wine.

- Ask waiters to clear drinks only if they're "complete," meaning the glass has been drained or is clearly abandoned. When waiters whisk away glasses the minute a guest puts one down, it increases your bar consumption.

- Schedule your wedding during the day. The earlier the wedding, the less alcohol people consume. Or schedule it on a weekday, when guests drink less than on weekends.

- Mix sparkling wine into a champagne cocktail. A sugar cube, bitters, and lemon peel can turn a mediocre sparkling wine into an elegant sip, or try other classics like kir royale (champagne with crème de cassis), Bellini (champagne and white peach puree), or mimosa (champagne with orange juice). You can, and should, buy a less expensive sparkling wine if you're using it as a mixer. Stick with a brut, which is dry, when you're going to add sweet ingredients.

- Consider having an off-site wedding where the caterer allows you to buy your own alcohol. (Many caterers will.) You bypass the markup, paying only a setup fee and the hourly fees for bartenders; buy by the case to nab discounts of 10 percent to 15 percent, and shop around for a store that will allow you to return unopened bottles. Don't forget that warehouse clubs often offer excellent prices on wine, champagne, and liquor.

CHAPTER ELEVEN

The Nitty-Gritty

DEALING WITH THE DETAILS

Behind every gorgeous, breathtaking wedding you see in a glossy magazine layout lies a lot of basic, down-and-dirty planning. It may not be so much fun thinking about portable toilets and car rentals, but if you don't, your wedding will suffer the consequences. Remember, your motto should always be "guests first." In keeping with that, I recommend

that you visualize your event from start to finish—*from a guest's point of view*. That's why I put so much emphasis on the "site inspection"—the physical walk-through of your ceremony and reception sites. It's the only way you can map out the flow of your event, from guest parking to the location of the dance floor, from vows to good-byes. Will guests have a place to hang their coats when they walk into the ceremony and

reception sites? Will they have to wait in long lines to use yucky outdoor toilets? Do the shuttle bus drivers know the route that avoids rush-hour traffic?

This is one area of planning a wedding in which just about everyone can count on the occasional surprise—who knew you needed to rent a separate tent for the caterers? Or that a tent will probably need a floor? Keep your eyes open and stay flexible.

The Site Inspection

As soon as you've confirmed your location for the ceremony and reception, preferably six months prior to the wedding, make a site inspection the first order of the day. For an elaborate off-site wedding involving tents, do your site inspection as far in advance as possible. If the ceremony and reception are in two separate locations, you'll need a site inspection for each.

At a venue that frequently hosts weddings, the inspection might be quite informal. The catering manager points out the room where you'll have the ceremony, the patio for the cocktail hour, the ballroom for the reception, the placement for the bars and the buffet. If you're happy with what she's proposing, you're as good as done.

At an off-site wedding, however, you're designing the event from scratch, so you'll need to map out all the stages. Is that massive oak tree going to be the focal point for your ceremony, or would you rather erect a flower arch in an open field? You already know that guests will move into a tent for dinner, but where are they going to have cocktails?

If you're working with a wedding planner, she'll likely bring in a representative from a party rental company. At fragile or persnickety locations, like museums or historic estates, you'll want a site representative on hand to advise on their rules and to share examples of what's been done before. It's in your best interest to find out early on in the game if nothing can be attached to the walls or if food can't

> Given the number of vendors involved, a tent wedding requires someone on site to supervise, sometimes for several days. Unless the bride, groom, or someone in the family has the time and organizational skills necessary to coordinate the operation, I'm of the opinion that a tent wedding calls for a wedding planner. One exception: a site with a semipermanent tent in place and access to on-site facilities.

be set up in any of the galleries. If you're already working with an event designer or florist, they could be present to brainstorm ideas, but if you don't yet have them lined up at this point, they might opt to do a separate visit later.

Do a walk-through of every moment of the event, from the guests' arrival to departure. Considerations will vary according to the location—if there's a parking lot for three hundred cars in front, that's crossed off the list—but see the list of walk-through questions opposite to make sure you cover your bases.

Once you've completed the walk-through, a rental company consultant or hotel catering manager will devise a floor plan; this might also fall under the purview of a wedding planner. (See page 146.)

All About Tents

Nearly any venue or combination of venues classified as off-site (see page 36) will involve a tent. At-home weddings almost always necessitate tents. Sites such as estates and wineries often do too, and depending on their size, country clubs, hotels, and resorts might as well.

An important thing to know: A venture into tent territory may involve more than one tent. Depending on the proximity of large-scale cooking facilities, your caterer is likely to need a separate tent for cooking. If the ceremony and the reception are any distance apart, the walkways between them might need covering—if you need to build walkways from scratch, turn to the section on subfloors, page 146—and the tent itself will require lighting.

Tent construction often requires a permit from the city or town, especially for a large tent, which in rare cases might even manifest the need for a crane—and with it, crane access to the property.

Once you have a firm location, date, and a general idea of guest count in hand, preferably at least six months before the wedding, you can contact a rental company to figure out what style and size of tents you'll need. Rental companies are usually listed under Party Supplies, Party Rentals, or

THE WALK-THROUGH

If you're using a wedding planner, she should most definitely accompany you on your walk-through. Make sure to bring a pen and notepad with you so you can jot down any salient details. As you perform your site inspection, keep an eye to the following questions.

- By what means will guests arrive? If they're driving, where will they park? Will you need a valet service? Will you need to run shuttles from a remote parking lot?

- For an evening wedding, will you need to light the way to the ceremony, the path to the cocktail hour, the route to the portable toilets?

- Where will you hold the ceremony? How will you set up the altar area? How many aisles will you have? Will guests be seated in traditional rows of chairs or in the round, with patio furniture providing some of the seating? Where will the musicians be seated? Will you be able to run power to mike the officiant during the vows?

- Where will guests go after the ceremony? If it's directly to the cocktail hour, do you need to build a walkway?

- How will the cocktail hour be set up? Think about where to place the musicians, the bars, the buffet, the guest book, the gift table, and the seating-card table.

- Will you need to provide a coat check?

- Will you have a receiving line? Where will it take place?

- Where will the reception be held? Is it a seated meal with dancing? A buffet? Cocktails and several food stations? Think about where to place the band or DJ, the dance floor, the bars, any buffets or food stations, the cake, and the guest tables. If you've booked your band, ask in advance what kind of space they need.

- Where will the caterers set up their kitchen? What do you need to provide for them in terms of power, water, and equipment?

- Will you need tents?

- Do you want a postparty? Will it take place at the same site or elsewhere? Do you need to rent a separate tent?

- When do you get access to the site? How does that correspond to the setup time required? Can you get more setup time by paying an additional fee?

- What's the deadline to have everything cleared out?

- Will you need portable restrooms?

- If it's outdoors, are there insect issues? Will you need to spray pesticides the day before? Set up citronella torches?

- Does the landscaping need any cosmetic improvements before the event?

- Does any of the space have problems that need to be fixed or disguised (ugly columns or stained wallpaper)?

- Does any part of the room need special attention? Perhaps the room is too large and you need to make space "disappear" by bringing in trees, playing with the lighting to darken the perimeter, or fabricking the room.

- How much power will you need for the caterers, the band, lighting, and heat or air-conditioning in the tent? Will you need to rent a generator?

- For every part of the proceedings slated to take place outdoors, what is your Plan B?

- Will guests need a shuttle to get back to their cars?

Tents in the phone book or on the Internet. You're bound to encounter some costs you couldn't have imagined, so it's best to get these expenses factored into your budget as soon as possible. (See page 148 for more about rental companies.)

When determining the size of the tent, figure on fifteen to twenty square feet per guest. For two hundred people you'd need at least a forty-by-hundred-foot tent (factoring in space for the band, the dance floor, the cake table, bar, any special stations, and perhaps a lounge area).

Tent Terminology

Frame tent. Supported by a frame (think of an umbrella minus the handle), its center is free of poles for an unobstructed view. Significantly more expensive than most push-pole tents, frame tents can fit into tighter spaces.

Pole tent. Center poles support the tent and quarter poles hold up its sides; its stakes require a fair amount of space. Consider talking to your florist or event designer about disguising the metal poles—there are plenty of clever ways to play with them. Note: A "century tent" is a high-end pole tent characterized by dramatic peaks and valleys.

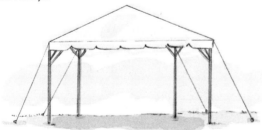

Canopy. A canopy is a simple canvas top supported by four poles. A canopy is typically used to protect guests and food in mild weather—you might erect one over the ceremony seating or the buffet at an outdoor wedding. Several can be put together to create a larger space.

Subfloors

A PLYWOOD OR VINYL FLOOR constructed underneath the tent, a subfloor levels off sloped ground, creates smooth, firm footing for guests, and offers protection from soggy terrain. (Any rain within a few days of the wedding can create problems when water seeps into the ground, even if the tent is already up.) I generally cover mine with carpeting and add a dance floor on top.

Subfloors add substantially to the cost, primarily as a result of the labor involved and installation time, and I know that some brides love the simple allure of plopping the reception tables directly on the grass—but I almost always recommend them. One common exception: A tent installed over a tennis court doesn't need a subfloor—though you'll want carpeting or artificial turf—unless it's in a low-lying area where water pools. If the land is very flat, you can sometimes get away with not installing a subfloor, but it will be awkward for women in heels. (Be sure to let them know about the terrain in advance so they can choose appropriate footwear.)

Subfloors can also be used to create architectural detail. I've placed uncovered subfloors outside of the main tent to serve as deck lounges. They can even be raised to multiple levels to set off sunken dance floors or lounge areas.

A Floor Plan

Though it's a very simple document, a floor plan is also very necessary. This computer-generated sketch of the reception area layout lets the various vendors know where to set up; you'll attach it to the wedding-day schedule you'll eventually create for your vendors and anyone else involved with the wedding.

You may notice a resemblance between the floor plan and the seating chart (more on that later), but their purposes are unique. The seating chart indicates who sits at what table, while the floor plan determines the overall layout of the room. If there's a choice in the matter, where

RENTING A TENT

When you speak to or meet with the rental representative, ask to see photos of the styles of tents the company offers. (For more general questions to ask party rental companies, see page 148.) Make sure your discussion covers the following points.

☐ How much setup and breakdown time the company will need. Know your site's specifications and any restrictions before this meeting so you can accurately assess your options. If you want subfloors (see opposite page) and the company needs to start building the tent on Wednesday, that's going to be a problem if your venue doesn't grant access until Friday. (Some sites will grant earlier access for an extra fee.)

☐ *Does this rental company design and install lighting?* If so, what are their lighting recommendations?

☐ *Will I need heating or air-conditioning?* Space heaters aren't terribly expensive, but air-conditioning gets costly. However, this is one of those areas where you shouldn't shortchange your guests' comfort.

☐ How much power you'll need, and whether a generator is required. Also discuss the cost of a backup generator, which sounds like an extravagance but provides insurance in case the first generator breaks down or gets overloaded.

☐ *Do you also rent portable restrooms?* You might be able to rent them from the same company. (See page 148 for more information.)

☐ *Will I need a permit for the tent?* Determine how much it costs and who obtains it. Typically, a full-service rental company will handle permits, but don't assume anything.

☐ If you're considering a tent as a Plan B in case of rain, by what day do you need to confirm or release the tent? What's the deadline for the company to begin installation?

☐ Subfloors: Does the tent rental representative recommend them for your site? *How much will it add to the cost and to the installation time?* If you're putting in subfloors, you'll still need to account for the price of renting a dance floor. (See below for more information.)

☐ *What products or services does the rental company offer besides the tent?* Some companies offer full-service party rentals, and many can act as your subcontractor to arrange lighting, portable toilets, generators, and possibly even tables, chairs, linens, dishes, and lounge furniture.

will the bars be stationed? Where can the sushi chef set up so that he doesn't interrupt the flow of traffic from the kitchen? The floor plan may also show the placement of any key decorative elements.

Who makes the floor plan? It depends on the situation. It might be the catering manager, the tent rental person, or your wedding planner—whoever has the most knowledge of the site and rises to the occasion!

Last but not least, make sure that someone takes measurements of the space so the floor plan is accurate. You need to make sure that the banquet tables *can* actually fit along the east wall.

The Dance Floor

For many couples, the dance floor is a preexisting element of the venue: it's right there in the room in all of its parquet glory. But at a tent wedding, or in any space where you determine the size and placement of the dance floor, you'll need a little know-how.

Position the floor in front of the band or DJ. To give as many tables as possible a good view, arrange them around the other three sides of the floor, with the bride and groom's directly across from the band.

THE RENTAL COMPANY CONTRACT

Party rental companies vary greatly in their scope—some rent everything from tablecloths to tents, while others focus solely on the infrastructure elements.

As with any vendor, check for references before signing a contract. Make sure you get a contact and a cell phone number in case there's an issue at delivery time with items that are missing, damaged, or incorrect. Make sure your contract with the rental company covers the following points.

- Deposit due date, amount, and balance due date. A 50 percent deposit is typical.

- Delivery date. Make sure this corresponds with the site's restrictions on access. Build in some leeway in case the delivery runs late.

- Disassembly and pickup date. Again, make sure it agrees with your contract at the site.

- Delivery and pickup fee, if applicable.

- Insurance policy. Is supplemental insurance required? It could be a good idea if your rentals are pricey—for more information on insurance, see chapter 12, "Making It Legal."

- Charge for lost or damaged items.

- Detailed description of goods, including quantity.

- Setup policy. Can the company provide someone to stay on site throughout the setup and the event in case a gust of wind knocks over a canopy or something else goes wrong? How much extra will that cost?

- Overtime policies and fees. Some of these extra charges are negotiable, especially if you're placing a large order.

Lately, dance floors have been turning into showpieces. They can be raised or lowered to allow guests a good view; place plants or candelabra on each of the corners so guests won't forget about the height differ-ence. You can also rent illuminated floors. (The most stunning—and the most expensive—dance floor I've ever done actually revolved!)

Like tents, dance floors come through party rental companies. Typically, you'll have a choice of parquet wood or a laminate. Though not widely available, clear acrylic floors are another great option; they look especially amazing when laid over a swimming pool and lit from below.

The size of your dance floor should be proportionate to the number of guests. The rental company can do the math, but if you want to be vigilant, here's how I do it: Figure on 2.25 to 2.75 square feet of dance floor per guest—for 250 people, I typically use a 24-foot-by-24-foot dance floor. (I prefer a crowded floor—it entices people to dance.) If you know you've got a dancing crowd, tell your rental consultant so you can plan for a larger-than-standard dance floor. If the band or DJ will be sharing the dance floor (rather than having their own stage), find out how much space they'll need and factor that in.

Portable Restrooms

Not as much fun as choosing your flowers, true, but being sure you have sufficient bathrooms at your site is essential. Portable toilets are available through many party rental companies; in the best of all worlds, you'll be able to rent your tent, dance floor, and toilets from the same company, but that may not be possible in remote areas.

Most off-site locations, even residences, require portable restrooms—that handful of toilets in a home can't handle a crowd; if you are using residential restrooms, though, make sure you have the septic tank emptied and the pipes cleared before the wedding to preempt any problems.

Figure on at least one toilet for every fifty guests. For an event longer than four or five hours, you'll need additional restrooms. Rent the plushest ones your budget will allow. "Executive trailer" toilets are the most luxurious. They come with piped-in music and stalls. The sinks are within the trailer, so women have a private place to freshen up. Individual bathrooms are unisex, of course, but if you choose to designate men's and women's, allocate more for women. If you have guests with special needs, make sure that one of your bathrooms is handicapped accessible or "ADA compliant."

Consider placement when doing your site inspection. You want them close enough for convenience and far enough away for discretion. Light the path to the toilets, and post signs as needed.

Before you make any decisions, find out if your site has any restrictions about the type of toilets allowed.

Transportation

ow for rentals of an entirely different order: transport for the bride and groom, the bridal party, and the guests, if necessary.

Providing transportation for the wedding party, even for a local wedding, shows that you're taking care—and it's in your best interest, since you want to make sure everyone gets there on time. At a minimum, you should also arrange transportation for both sets of parents to the ceremony site, and it's very thoughtful to give grandparents the special treatment. As for the bride, if she is already dressed, she usually arrives at the ceremony site with her father; if she's getting ready on site, she arrives earlier, perhaps with her bridesmaids. When coming up with your vehicle-occupancy counts, you may

> If guests are driving to the wedding, have a plan in place should some overindulge. Call a taxi company or ridesharing service and make arrangements in advance (see page 152).

want to leave room for a photographer in the vehicle carrying the bride, since those photos often become keepers.

The groom and the groomsmen drive to the ceremony together. Any other members of the wedding party, including junior bridesmaids and ushers, ride along. If you have young children in the wedding, they're probably going to be more comfortable with their parents; you can certainly provide transportation for the family if you're so inclined.

Although you don't want to order too many cars only to have one sit idle, you also don't want to cut corners. I had one bride decide to save money by having a single limo pick up the wedding party in shifts to get to the ceremony. The driver got stuck in traffic on one of the trips, and the ceremony couldn't start on time because we were waiting for half of the wedding party to arrive. Timing is too important to take this kind of risk.

Vehicle Occupancy

ake a look at the following occupancy guidelines to figure out which type of vehicle best suits your needs.

Bus. Seats 45 to 60 (a school bus will seat more).

Double-decker bus. Seats 65.

Limo bus, limo coach, or party bus. Seats 18 to 28.

Golf cart. Seats 2 to 6.

Limousine. Seats 6.

Lincoln Town Car, luxury sedan. Seats 2 to 4.

Minivan. Seats 7.

Passenger shuttle. Seats 15 to 33.

Stretch Hummer/Lincoln Navigator/ Cadillac Escalade. Seats 12 to 22.

Stretch limousine. Seats 12 to 14.

SUV. Seats 5 to 7.

Trolley. Seats 22 to 30.

Van. Seats 12 to 15.

If the ceremony and reception sites are separated by more than a very short walking distance, you'll also need to get all of the people you transported to the wedding over to the reception. And, last but not least, you'll want a special vehicle for you and your groom to depart in. (See "The Getaway Car," this page.)

Ferrying the Guests

DO YOU NEED transportation for your guests? Think of their comfort, both physical and mental. Guests should feel taken care of, and providing a shuttle in an unknown city or arranging for everyone to get back to the hotel together can make all the difference—they don't have to worry about directions, where to park, whether they'll be on time, or how many glasses of champagne they can safely imbibe at the reception.

Give serious consideration to providing transportation to guests if:

- Yours is a destination wedding. They're already going to great expense to attend your wedding, so don't give them the added burden of paying for a twenty-dollar cab ride to the wedding site.

- You have a high percentage of out-of-towners.

- The wedding is taking place in a city where parking is difficult to find or expensive, especially if the ceremony and reception are in two different locations. Guests shouldn't have to worry about parking or hailing a cab twice.

Although it may seem like an unnecessary extra expense, guest transportation can make such a difference in everyone's mood that I recommend providing it when possible, even if it means cutting out favors or trimming another item on your budget.

The advent of ride-sharing services such as Uber and Lyft, available in more and more cities and countries, has made wedding transportation an infinitely cheaper and simpler proposition. Among their many great qualities? The flexibility they allow you and your guests. Contact the ride-sharing company of your choice, and you can arrange for a group discount at no cost to you. You offer guests the discount code, they plug the code into the app on their devices, and everybody gets a cheaper ride. Often guests who've never used the service before will be eligible for a ride that is completely free—the best price of all!

The next level up is to defray a portion or the entirety of your guests' ride in combination with that group discount. You get to offer your guests a break, while customizing your contribution to your budget. Your guests have the flexibility of coming and going as they please, along with the option to ditch the car they drove if they've had one too many drinks. And once you've done the initial setup, you don't have to coordinate a thing.

Guests are usually on their own for getting to and from the airport, but for a destination wedding in a remote spot, you may want to coordinate van service.

Whatever you do, make sure to communicate clearly with guests about transportation. Let them know well in advance whether you're providing transportation, and if not, give them names, phone numbers, and websites of car rental agencies, airport shuttle services, and taxi companies. Include details and discount codes in your information packet, on your wedding website, or in any newsletters you send.

The Getaway Car

THE MOMENT when the happy couple departs in a special car, a JUST MARRIED sign attached to the back, ranks as one of my favorites. This is a tradition worth preserving.

Tunes for the Ride

An easy way to make the guests' trip feel like part of your wedding? Give the driver music ahead of time—put together a compilation of your favorite songs, if you're so inclined. And don't forget to set the proper mood in your own car as well. It will help make your ride a respite from the commotion of the day.

Though there's nothing wrong with using a limo, I love to use a vintage car, like a 1950s Rolls-Royce. One of my couples even hired a 1967 red Camaro, which fit their personalities to a T. Some couples leave on a Vespa or a motorcycle (love it with a sidecar), but these options work better if you're planning to change out of your wedding dress for the departure. If your reception is by the water, you can even depart via boat.

"Just Married"

Decorating the car is a wonderful tradition, but if you have pranksters in your circle, send word to the attendants—the best man is usually in charge—that you don't want tasteless comments painted on the windows and/or a car covered in shaving cream or toilet paper.

Where does the custom of decorating the car come from? It all goes back to those evil spirits. In the nineteenth century, couples in the American South and Midwest were commonly followed home on foot by guests banging on pots and pans and making as much noise as possible, in part to disrupt intimate relations, and in part to keep the spirits away. The commotion, all part of the "shivaree," as it was known, continued once the couple was inside their home. As for the shoes, they probably date back to the Tudors, when throwing a clomper at the couple was supposed to bring good luck—if you hit either the couple or the carriage, you got an extra dose.

Booking Cars

WHEN RENTING LIMOS and other luxury transportation, you may find there's more competition than you bargained for, so it's best to reserve early. Aim for booking transportation three to four months in advance, but six to nine months ahead if your wedding falls during a time of peak demand. Prom season (April, May, and June) and summer wedding season (June through September) both find limos in short supply. Each city has its own busy period, whether it's awards season in Los Angeles or a major convention in Orlando.

If you're hyperorganized, you can book transportation as soon as you have your location nailed down. And

Dollars and Sense

Before you start negotiating with a transportation company, consider all of your needs. Will you need a car to take you to the airport the day after the wedding? Will you require transportation to and from the bachelor/bachelorette parties to prevent driving under the influence? Will you need to send a car to pick up anyone special at the airport? Are you hosting other outings over the weekend that will call for a bus or shuttle? Are you shuttling guests to the airport the day after the wedding?

Traditionally, the bride's side of the family covered the expense of getting the bride and her attendants to the wedding, and the groom's side footed the bill for getting the guys to the wedding. No matter who actually pays which bill, don't let one side of the family hire one limo service and the other side work with another. Chances are better that everything will run smoothly if all of your dealings are centralized with one company, and you want to bundle all of your transportation together for the purposes of negotiation—the more business you're discussing, the more likely you are to get a break in price.

if you're not, don't stress out: Most of the time, you can arrange rentals even a few weeks before, assuming you're flexible about the type of vehicle.

Parking

In order to determine whether or not you need to provide parking, come up with a rough estimate of how many cars you'll need to accommodate and the available number of spaces. (No need to worry about this if your wedding is taking place at a standard suburban hotel with complimentary parking—unless you choose to offer valet parking, which is appreciated by elderly guests.) Don't forget to account for vendors' vehicles.

THE VAN OR LIMO SERVICE

Always get a written contract and cost estimate from the transportation companies you're dealing with, and press for an after-hours contact name and number so you know whom to call in case no one shows up. Always, *always* get a number. Following are some other questions to check off your list.

- *Is there a minimum number of rental hours?*
- *What services does the rate include?*
- *How is the gratuity handled?* Many companies automatically build in a 15 to 20 percent tip. Some companies offer you the option of adding a tip to the bill automatically or letting you handle it yourself.
- *How much of a deposit is required?*
- *Does the company carry liability insurance that covers the passengers as well as the driver?*
- *Does the company offer any wedding packages or any discounts with multiple rentals?* But don't be seduced by the word *package*—make sure it's actually a better deal or desirable upgrade. No need to pay extra for a bottle of bad champagne.
- *If you're renting any vehicles that might bend the rules of the road, make sure they're permitted on the streets where you plan to use them. Golf carts may be permitted on a resort's grounds, for instance, but not on a public road. Also make sure any vehicle you'll be using on public streets is properly licensed.*

Guests should never have to pay to park at your wedding. Not everyone agrees with me, but I believe that if the hotel or site charges for parking, you should pick up the tab—guests are honoring you with their presence and shouldn't have to open their wallets to walk in the door.

Consider whether you need valet parking, which is commonplace in some areas of the country. Ask yourself: How far will guests have to walk from their parking spots? What's the weather typically like that time of year? If it's often ten below or scorching hot on your wedding date, hire a valet service.

If you don't need valet service but are anticipating a crowd, parking attendants can help direct guests to open spaces and keep traffic flowing. If the hotel charges for parking, they'll handle the staffing. Should you need to hire an outside service, a hotel or restaurant that offers valet parking should be able to direct you to a reputable company. Discuss the attire of the valets and attendants in advance to ensure they're dressed in a style that's compatible with your wedding.

At an off-site or home wedding, you may need to find a local parking lot to handle the cars (you can't expect to park 150 vehicles along a residential street). Sometimes a school, church, or community facility will rent out its lot. Or perhaps there's a big, grassy area for parking, but it's too far for guests to walk. You'll want attendants directing people as to where to park, and then you'll need transportation over to the reception. (You should have at least two vehicles providing continuous round-trip transportation; that way, there's one at each end most of the time.)

Should you be creating a lot of congestion at a busy intersection, you may also need to hire an off-duty police officer or security guard to direct traffic.

If you're hiring a valet company, make sure they research local parking ordinances; otherwise, call city hall to find out parking restrictions and whether you need special permits.

Now you should be starting to see your wedding unfolding in your mind's eye. Feels good, right? But without a few key pieces of paperwork, all you'll be doing is throwing a really fun party. So read on to find out how to make your wedding stick in the all-seeing eyes of the law! ♦

CHAPTER TWELVE

Making It Legal

LICENSES, PRENUPS, AND INSURANCE

nto every wedding some paperwork must fall. The legal aspects of planning a wedding are vital—though not as appealing as the tasks of choosing fonts and flowers. But you need to make sure the marriage is lawful and binding. Government agencies, fine print, lawyers, and even blood tests may be involved when it comes to obtaining a marriage license,

changing your name (if that's what you want to do), setting up wedding insurance, and tackling prenuptial agreements.

If you're thinking of having a destination wedding outside of the United States, also see page 431 in the "Destination Weddings" appendix to find out about any special steps you may need to take.

Laws vary so much—not only from state to state, but sometimes within a state

as well—that it wouldn't be possible for one book to cover all the intricate details you might encounter. What I have provided are general procedures and the tools you'll need to find out what you need to know. I've indicated which areas you can handle on your own and which ones call for an outside expert.

Armed with these tools, you should be able to slice through any red tape you encounter on your way to the altar.

LICENSE REQUIREMENTS

Since laws vary from state to state, be vigilant about gathering information when you set out to get your marriage license. Make sure not to overlook the following points.

- Do you meet the requirements? These include age of consent for the bride and groom.
- What documentation do you need to bring to the issuing office? Typically it's a birth certificate for proof of age, proof of citizenship if you were not born in the United States, and photo identification. If you've been divorced, you may need to bring a certified copy of the divorce decree. If you're widowed, you'll need to bring the death certificate. You may need to bring a witness.

- Do you need blood tests (usually to check for venereal disease), proof of vaccinations, or any other medical test? For how long are the results of the tests valid?
- What is the fee for the license? What forms of payment does the office accept? Some offices are cash-only operations. Fees typically range from $25 to $100.
- Is there a waiting period, also known as a cooling-off period, between the time you apply for the license and when the marriage can take place?

- Many states require you to wait a few days.
- How long is the license valid? In most states, it's somewhere between thirty and ninety days. You don't want to get the license too early, only to find that it's no longer valid on your wedding day.
- For religious ceremonies, ask your officiant what additional documentation you might need; for Catholic weddings, you may be asked for baptismal and confirmation certificates.

The Marriage License

There's nothing like that glorious feeling of making it official.

Start doing your homework three or four months before the wedding—you might discover that your fiancé doesn't have a certified copy of his birth certificate, which can take several weeks to obtain. Research the specific requirements of your wedding location by conducting an online search using the name of the county where your wedding will take place and "marriage license." That should lead you to the proper county clerk's office, marriage license bureau, or health department, any of which could be the office that handles marriage licenses in your given locale. Since requirements can be confusing and are sometimes subject to change, double-check by calling the proper office for clarification.

Ideally, couples should submit their application a few weeks before the wedding and have the license in hand a week or two before the big day. If you're traveling to your wedding, that may not be possible, but in some places you can submit notarized paperwork ahead of time to streamline the process once you arrive.

At your wedding, the officiant signs the license to ensure its validity; if you can, get this taken care of before the ceremony, since things get very hectic afterward. In some counties, the license must also be signed by one or two witnesses.

Your officiant will send the license to the county office for you. A few weeks later, you should receive your marriage certificate. (If you're changing your name, request three copies.)

One more thing: As of June 26, 2015, the day same-sex marriage became legal across the United States, the information in this chapter became equally applicable to all couples, regardless of their sexual orientation. Though there have been cases of civil clerks refusing to issue same-sex wedding licenses based on their religious beliefs, such an action could be punishable by jail time.

What's In a Name?

The decision to change your name is highly personal. Many women—and I was one of them—can't wait to take on a new, married name. Others view swapping their maiden name as giving up a piece of their identity. If they've established themselves at work, they might be loath to tamper with their professional standing.

One popular compromise is to retain your maiden name as a middle name or hyphenate the two names. If you both choose to take on the hyphenated name, which many couples do nowadays, your names will match your children's, cutting down on confusion. The drawback is that hyphenated names can get cumbersome; Jeffrey Hersh-David is fine, but Jeremy McSweeney-Haggerty is a mouthful.

Another compromise that some women choose is to keep their maiden name professionally but use their husband's name in social situations.

The most radical choice of all is for the couple to adopt a new name altogether. Egalitarian-minded couples going this route often combine their last names to create a new one. Some take a name that has a special meaning to them—one couple became Amato, which means "beloved" in Spanish.

While the majority of same-sex couples opt to keep their names, hyphenating or adopting new names are common practices as well.

Changing Your Name Legally

YOU CAN'T CHANGE your name until you're actually married, but the first step is to put your new name in the allotted space on your marriage license. Have your officiant sign the license after the ceremony, and ask her to request three copies. You'll need one to keep, one for Social Security, and one for the Department of Motor Vehicles. She'll send the license in for you, and you should receive the certificate a few weeks after the ceremony. If you don't get the necessary number of copies, contact the courthouse where your license was issued to request them.

TRADITION PRIMER

What Does the State Have to Do with It?

The required marriage license was established by the Marriage Act of 1753, also known as Hardwicke's Marriage Act, in England and Wales. Marriage licenses existed before 1753, but they weren't mandatory. In a move to prevent clandestine marriages and bigamy, the Marriage Act abolished common-law marriage. It mandated that banns, the wedding announcements of the time, be published, that the couple obtain a marriage license, and that the marriage take place in a church (with exceptions for Jews and Quakers). Parental consent was also required if either member of the couple was under twenty-one. Marriages from then on were officially recorded, as they eventually would be across North America, making it easier to determine if someone attempting to get married was already committed to another.

To figure out your next step, a little research can save you gobs of time and frustration. Some states require you to change your Social Security card first, while others want you to start by changing your driver's license. Look up the rules for your state on the DMV website and call the Social Security office before wasting any time waiting in line.

A marriage license, issued prior to the wedding, is legal permission for you to get married. The certified document you receive after the wedding is the marriage certificate. Keep a copy in a safe place, preferably a safe-deposit box.

Getting the Word Out

Whether one or both of you keep or change your names, you'll want to find ways to let your friends and family know how to address those holiday cards. When you enter the reception or before your first dance, have yourselves announced by the name you'll be using. Same goes for submitting a marriage announcement. Other ways to spread the word:

- Have thank-you notes printed with your married name.

- Use "at-home" cards (see page 277). If you're changing your address as well as your name, they take care of that, too. Enclose them with a wedding invitation, announcement, or thank-you note.

- Have new business cards and stationery printed.

If you are changing your name professionally, send an email to colleagues and clients. If your identity will remain obvious—say you're hyphenating your name or retaining your maiden name as a middle name—then you might not need to take this extra step.

Putting It Off

Should you be having a hard time deciding on what name you want to go by, remember that you'll always have the option of changing your name down the road. Because the marriage certificate will not have your new name on it, you'll need to petition the court for a change of name—essentially the same procedure as that described for men.

The Social Security website is a good place to start for instructions on how to request a card under your new name. You'll need a marriage certificate and your old Social Security card. It's free, so stay away from any outside companies offering to perform the service for you for a fee. Once you've received a new card, make sure that whatever name you use with the payroll department at work matches the name on file with Social Security.

To change your driver's license, find out if your local DMV takes appointments for name changes; you'll need to appear in person, and you want to avoid the lines if you can. Bring your current license, your new Social Security card or a paper stating that it's on its way (if required by your state), and your marriage certificate. Again, check your local DMV website to be sure you have the proper forms of identification—you may also need to show proof of address, such as a utility bill. If you're also changing the name and/or address on your automobile registration and title, bring the original documents with you.

Your passport is the third critical document you'll need to change. You can download a passport name change form online or pick up the form at a main-branch post office. Mail in the form with your old passport and a certified copy of the marriage certificate.

A note to honeymooners traveling internationally: Unless you're scheduling your trip for some time after the wedding, it's likely you won't be able to complete the name-change process before you go—so be sure to make your reservations under your maiden name.

Name Change Rules for Men

CALL IT REVERSE SEXISM, but it's harder for a guy to legally change his name. A woman puts her new name on the marriage certificate, begins using it, then goes through the formalities with the necessary government agencies. A guy, however, usually needs a court order to change his name, although the laws vary by state. (In New York, for instance, men can enter a new surname on the

If marriage means a new name *and* a new address, make both changes at once. And before waiting in line at any government office, find out ahead of time what you'll need to bring as proof of address. You don't want to invest all that time only to find out that you needed to bring a utility bill or canceled check.

marriage license and don't need to petition a court for the change.) It's also costlier for a man, even if he doesn't hire a lawyer. Filing and publication fees vary by state, but a legal name change can easily run a few hundred dollars. The process involves filing a "Name Change Petition" and paying a filing fee, having it published, waiting six weeks, and then appearing before a judge. Then the process begins in earnest; see page 155.

Prenuptial Agreements

True, very few people find anything romantic about a prenuptial agreement, also known as a premarital or antenuptial agreement. Just bringing up the topic can hit on so many nerves, including issues of trust, control, and sharing. But approach the conversation thoughtfully and you'll learn more about each other and gain a better idea of how your marriage will work.

What a prenup does is cover how property will be divvied up in case of divorce or if one spouse should die. It overrides state laws governing division of property, letting you craft a scenario that works for you. And should one spouse die, a prenup can protect inheritances better than a will. In the past, prenups weren't enforced regularly by courts, but now they're recognized by every state and continue to gain footing as a legally binding agreement.

Who Needs a Prenup?

CELEBRITIES AND THE SUPERWEALTHY are most closely identified with prenups, but there are several sound reasons why more ordinary couples should consider one:

- To protect assets for children from a previous marriage. Otherwise, a spouse could be awarded everything if the parent dies.

- If you have real estate, substantial investments, or a trust fund that you want to keep separate from marital property.

- If you own all or part of a family business.

Organizations You'll Need to Notify

The marriage license, the Social Security bureau, and the DMV are the most important places to change your name, but you don't want to complicate your life with the IRS, the bank, or your employer, so make sure you also change your name through the following entities and documents—though if you're feeling overwhelmed, you can actually pay a document preparation service to do much of the work for you.

Employer	Utility companies (electric, gas, water, cable)	Living will
Banks	Voters' registration office	Stock and bond certificates
Mortgage company or leasing agent	State taxing authority	Power of attorney form
Insurance companies (home, life, auto)	Department of Records or Vital Statistics (issues birth certificates)	Airline and hotel rewards programs (If you travel frequently, do this pronto.)
Credit card companies	Doctors	Magazine subscriptions
Investment companies	Automobile title	Professional associations
Post office	Will	Health club
Internal Revenue Service	Living trust	Library card
Telephone company (landline and mobile)		School and alumni associations

TRADITION PRIMER

Where Prenups Came From

Prenuptial agreements sound like a modern invention designed to protect wealthy men from gold diggers, but they actually date back centuries. They were most often associated with protecting a *woman's* property so it wouldn't automatically belong to the man. In Colonial America, such agreements were also used to protect widows who remarried. Muslims routinely draft marriage contracts before the wedding—traditionally, they cover the *mahr*, a gift of money or jewelry from the man to the woman, but they may also specify that the woman isn't obliged to cook or that she has the right to divorce if the man takes a second wife.

- To keep antiques or jewelry in the family.

- If you're responsible for the care of elderly parents or another relative.

What's in a Prenup?

A PRENUPTIAL AGREEMENT, in which both parties list all their assets and sources of income, is drawn up by an attorney specializing in family law. Essentially designed to specify what will become marital property and what will remain separate, the agreement may state whether either of you will get alimony in the event of a divorce. If the spouses are of different nationalities, a prenup can prescribe which jurisdiction will govern the divorce. (In some countries, the laws are unfavorable to women, especially if they're not citizens.)

Some couples use the prenup to lay out the ground rules of their marriage, from who will clean the cat's litter box to whether the woman will work after having children. Although there's nothing to stop you from including this type of lifestyle information, I think you should stick with financial matters. And limit the scope of the prenup to major items—don't get into who keeps the wide-screen TV. Including lifestyle choices or minutiae can adversely affect how a judge views your prenup.

Prenup Precautions

IF YOU'RE GOING the prenup route, broach the subject well before the wedding. How to bring it up? Be clear about your motivations, making sure to emphasize that it's not a sign of lack of faith on your part. A prenup is often a way to protect familial assets, so you may want to invoke the outside parties who share those assets when you broach the topic. If it's your future spouse who brings up a premarital agreement, try not to bristle.

Leave enough time for attorneys on both sides to review the agreement, and try to sign it six to eight weeks before the wedding. Prenups should *never* be a surprise. Any evidence that it was signed under duress—such as one person handing it to the other at the church and saying there won't be a wedding unless it's signed—could cause a judge to void the agreement. As a rule, it's a good idea (for both legal and emotional reasons) to sign the prenup before you send out wedding invitations.

Review the following precautions when considering a prenuptial contract:

- Each of you should have your own attorney review the contract.

- Make sure you understand all of the wording.

- The contract should be updated if you have children, if your assets change, and if you move to another state or country. If you move, make sure the agreement is legal in that state.

- If you choose a do-it-yourself version of a prenup, carefully follow local laws to be sure it's legal. Usually a prenup must be signed in the presence of a notary public.

- If it's down to the wire and you haven't signed the

prenup, consider a postnuptial agreement. It's the same thing, just signed after the wedding. In some courts, postnups are not viewed as favorably as prenups because a spouse may not have the same leverage after the marriage. That makes a prenup more desirable, but a postnup can still accomplish your goals.

Postponing or Canceling a Wedding

If you find that your negative feelings are overshadowing your positive ones, or if you're having serious doubts about the chances of your union-to-be, seek professional help immediately—certainly before you put your invitations in the mail. Very few people have the emotional wherewithal to change the plan after the invitations go out.

Any couples therapist will be glad to help engaged clients—whether that means helping to get the relationship back on track or helping you decide that you really need to call it off. And it does happen, more often than you'd think. Among my clients, I usually have at least two cancellations a year.

If you do decide to cancel, you'll have a host of practical issues to tackle along with all the emotional trauma involved. The sooner a wedding is called off, the better. But if you two are truly not meant to be, don't let anything stop you from calling it off, even if it's at the last minute.

If you decide to cancel the wedding before the invitations have gone out, let your close family and friends know by phone or email—enlist help from parents and the bridal party. There's no need to go into details. Simply say you both agreed it was for the best, and leave it at that.

If the invitations have gone out and there's time to have an announcement printed, mail one to all of your guests. It should read: "Mr. and Mrs. Thomas Scott announce that the marriage of their daughter Claire Scott to Heath Hill will not take place."

You or someone close to you should call any guests who were traveling to attend the wedding so they can cancel their plane and hotel reservations in time.

If there's not enough time to mail an announcement, round up a small committee to call guests and let them know the wedding is off. Ask for an acknowledgment from everyone (either by phone or email) that they got the message. You wouldn't want someone showing up on the wedding day at an empty church.

You will also need to notify all of your vendors as soon as possible. Each vendor contract should specify how cancellations are handled. Vendors will most likely keep the deposits, and some will expect additional payments, depending on when you cancel the wedding and the language in the contract. If you cancel the wedding the day before, your florist and caterer will have not only ordered the flowers and the food but also started preparing them, so you're likely to be responsible for the entire fee. If you cancel earlier and the vendor is able to rebook the date, you may get most or all of your money back.

When weddings are called off the day of the wedding or the day before, some families decide to make the best of it by getting together without the couple, or with just one member.

Triage

PAY CAREFUL ATTENTION to how you divide up or return the material goods in the aftermath of a cancellation. Here's what to do with:

The engagement ring. While an engagement ring is considered a gift from the groom to the bride, I like the etiquette rule that prevailed in Roman times: if the man called off the wedding, the woman kept the ring, and if she called off the wedding, she returned it. However, if it's a family ring, she should return it no matter what the circumstances. If it's a mutual decision, she should give the ring back.

Engagement, shower, and wedding gifts. All gifts should be returned with a note thanking the givers for their thoughtfulness.

Nonrefundable honeymoon reservations. Decide which one of you should use them.

The wedding dress. Your best bet is to try to sell it on eBay or through a consignment shop. Or consider donating it to a charity (see recommendations on page 220).

Postponing a Wedding

THE MOST COMMON REASONS for postponing a wedding are a death or illness in the family, or some type of natural disaster at the wedding location. The guidelines for letting guests know depend on how much time is available. If there's time to send out a printed announcement—it should arrive at least two weeks before the wedding was to have taken place—and you know the new wedding date, send a card from the hosts reading: "Mr. and Mrs. Thomas Scott announce that the marriage of their daughter Claire Scott to Heath Hill has been postponed to Saturday, the eighth of October, Two thousand and eighteen."

You don't have to give the reason for postponing the wedding on the announcement, but it's fairly common to do so, especially if it's for an illness or death in the family. (You wouldn't give a reason if, say, the groom can't quite make up his mind about whether he's ready to commit.)

Should you still have the invitations in hand, print a card with the new date to enclose with the invitations. It looks better than crossing out the date on the original invitation.

"In Case Of"

Wedding insurance, a form of "event insurance," may cover:

- Severe weather
- Lost deposits
- No-show vendors
- Lost, stolen, or damaged property
- Technical failures
- Stolen or damaged gifts
- Serious illness
- Military leave

If you need to postpone a wedding but don't have a new wedding date, formal etiquette dictates that you recall the invitation, then send out a new one. But because this gets costly for you and confusing for guests, I think it's better to call everyone to tell them that the wedding has been postponed. When you have a new date, you can either call everyone again or issue a new invitation. If calling isn't practical, use email to get the word out.

Insure It!

Wedding insurance is a fairly new development but one worth investigating. The more you're spending on your wedding, the more you stand to lose if a hurricane wipes out your wedding site, the florist goes bankrupt two weeks before the wedding, or the groom gets a sudden case of appendicitis.

Insurance fees are based on the cost of the wedding; event cancellation insurance on a $50,000 wedding runs about $400. Liability policies, which protect you from host-liquor or guest-injury liability, cost less.

Ask detailed questions about what is covered, what the upper limits are for reimbursements, what the deductibles are, and when you have to purchase the policy. For liability policies, find out what your homeowners' insurance policy covers and whether that's sufficient; some reception sites require you to carry a minimum amount of liability insurance.

Generally, you want to buy insurance when you start placing deposits, but you can usually purchase it as late as fifteen days before the wedding. Understand that insurance is sold for unforeseen problems, so once a problem has been identified (if, say, the hotel was operating under bankruptcy protection when you booked it), the policy won't cover it.

You've got all your ducks in a row, so I've got a present for you: It's time for the biggest virtual shopping spree of your entire life. That's right, it's time to organize your registry. No, you can't sign up for fifty pairs of shoes—but there are plenty of ways to gear your registry to your personal interests. ◆

CHAPTER THIRTEEN

The Gift Registry

USEFUL, BEAUTIFUL, AND JUST WHAT YOU WANT

The tradition of giving gifts to the newly married is as old as the institution of marriage itself. One of the earliest gifts was food—the newlyweds were left with a larder stocked with meat pies, cheese, spice cakes, and ale. Money or other forms of currency (livestock was once a biggie) has long played a role in helping newlyweds establish

their own households; it endures as perhaps the most appreciated gift of all (blue-chip stocks, anyone?).

Household items became popular by the Middle Ages, setting the stage for today's gifts of china, flatware, glassware, linens, and kitchen equipment. There's even historical precedent for those oh-so-modern experiential gifts—back in 1842, Henry David Thoreau planted a vegetable garden for his friends Nathaniel Hawthorne and Sophia Peabody when they married, and they got to reap the benefits at their Concord, Massachusetts, home.

Over the years, bridal registries were criticized as crass, greedy, and impersonal, even as they continued to grow in popularity among couples. But guests are now often so busy that most of them are grateful to the bride and groom for expressing their preferences. There's no absolute rule that you must register, but there's no denying that it makes the gift process convenient for everyone involved. And let's be honest: Walking through stores and creating a master wish list . . . well, there are worse ways to pass a few hours. Even if you choose to forgo gifts and want to encourage donations to charity instead, it's better to register that desire in some form than to allow guests to flounder.

In recent years, registries have proliferated at all types of stores, catalogs, and websites. Registries at home-improvement stores no longer raise an eyebrow, honeymoon registries continue to gain popularity, and certain sites let you register for anything you could wish for, from a miniature poodle to a Mini Cooper.

Through it all—and above all—you need to remain gracious about gifts. That means accepting what people have chosen to give to you with gratitude—not judging them by how much they've spent—and sending out prompt, sincere, and personal notes of thanks. Just as your choice of china pattern sends a message about your taste and style, the attitude you display regarding your gifts will telegraph the tone of your entire wedding, so make sure that you're sending a positive signal.

REGISTRY BASICS

When Can I Start?

Don't rush to register without first assessing your choices and preferences. Registering early has its benefits, but only if you're prepared. Do you want the convenience of a national retailer or the distinctive point of view of a favorite boutique? Would you rather be cooking in enameled cast-iron pots or triple-ply metal? What's most important to you: dishes, a set of outdoor furniture, or a honeymoon dive excursion?

You can register—or start a registry, adding more items later—as early as a few weeks after you become engaged, but people typically register four to six weeks before their first shower. If you're skipping showers, you

want to at least make sure that your registries are set up before you mail out wedding invitations.

How Many Registries?

WITH SO MANY CHOICES, it's tempting to start signing up at stores left and right. You could have registries at a department store, a specialty kitchen retailer, a sporting goods store, a home-improvement store . . . oh, and what about a honeymoon registry?

Registries need to be managed, so having too many can become a burden for you, especially when it comes time for returns and exchanges. To me, the ideal mix is a department store, a chain geared to your tastes and interests, and one boutique with a style that you particularly adore.

If you're using a registry aggregator site like Zola or Simple Registry, you can shop from a variety of retailers and provide one easy-to-access link for your guests, even making it possible for them to simply give you cash. Certain registry sites have a particular focus—Blueprint Registry, for example, lets you search and add gifts by room.

Where to Register

TRYING TO WINNOW DOWN your choices? Keep the following pointers in mind.

- Think about where most of your guests live. You want at least one brick-and-mortar retailer that's convenient for the majority of your guests.

- Try for a mix of physical stores and online registries. Also make sure at least one of your registries has a toll-free number for ordering. (Don't assume that everyone feels comfortable ordering online.)

- Keep in mind that you'll want to see china, glassware, flatware, and many other items in person before registering for them. Ideally, you want to put together an entire place setting in person to see if it works. So you'll want to visit a local store that carries them before committing.

- If you're registering at a high-end retailer where some guests might not feel comfortable shopping, balance it with a less lofty option. Yes, Tiffany & Co.

sells things for less than fifty dollars, but some guests will perceive that they are being asked to spend more than they can afford.

- Register at one store or site that covers a wide range of merchandise, like a department store or an aggregator site.
- Consider having one registry that offers discounted prices on china, glassware, and flatware.
- Many older relatives want to give traditional gifts for the home; if you choose an alternative registry balance it with a registry of more conventional gifts.
- When evaluating registries, look for programs with extra benefits. Some department stores offer points based on how much you register for and how much is purchased from your registry.

Setting up the Registry

Once you've decided where to register, call to find out if you need an appointment. Most stores that offer self-service scanners don't require appointments, but some stores will need to match you up with an associate.

Many couples register together. If one member of the couple is averse to shopping (forgive the stereotyping, but it's usually the guy), it works better if the other person preshops and pares down the choices to two or three china patterns. Men tend to enjoy any store with a scanner—for one, it gives them something concrete to do—and a store that carries merchandise they can see themselves using. So a bride may want to bring her man to Target and Home Depot and her mother or maid of honor to Bloomingdale's and Michael C. Fina (okay, I said I was generalizing).

When you've finished registering, request a master list from the store and the business card of your salesperson so you can follow up as needed. Take a few minutes to proofread the list—check to be sure the items, the spelling of your names, the wedding date, and the delivery address are all correct.

Alternative Registries

Looking to register outside the box? Here are some alternative registries worth considering.

Electronics stores
Furniture stores
Garden centers
General websites like Amazon.com
Home-improvement stores such as Home Depot
Honeymoon registries
Mortgage registries
Mutual funds
Sporting goods stores
Wine shops

Mismatched Tastes

IF BOTH OF YOU are actively involved in choosing items to put on the registry, you may find yourself learning new things about your spouse-to-be. Who would have thought he'd care whether the muffin tin was aluminum-coated steel or silicone? Or that she can't stand birds, ruling out the Audubon prints he wanted to put on the registry? You're in for some surprises during the registry process. It can be a great way to learn new things about each other, but it can also turn into a skirmish over preferences.

If you both have strong opinions, now is the time to start learning how to compromise. Since you'll both be living with your registry choices, you should both feel comfortable with them. You may want to divide up the categories, having the groom take the lead on electronics and small kitchen appliances, and the bride on dinnerware, flatware, and bedding (or the other way around, if that's your preference!).

A Call for Discretion

WHEN IT COMES to letting people know where you're registered, old-fashioned etiquette rules still apply. You should never enclose anything in a wedding invitation that

Nine Smart Registry Strategies

1. Register for enough stuff. Many couples do not. It's a good idea to register for two to three times as many gifts as you have guests.

2. Make sure your gifts span a variety of prices. Your registry should start at twenty-five dollars (less is fine, but don't start it higher), and you should have choices in twenty-five-dollar increments. When looking over the registry, check that you have a variety of prices not just across the board but also within each category.

3. Don't get pressured into registering for things just because they're somebody else's idea of what you need. If you don't think you'll ever use fine china, you don't have to register for it. Instead, you might want to register for two sets of everyday dishes (one patterned and one solid).

4. Even if you're combining two well-stocked households, ask yourself if you want to register for better versions of things you already own. In the registry business, this practice is called "trading up."

5. Register for more place settings than you think you need. Many store registries suggest eight, but I think you should ask for twelve.

6. You can't go wrong registering for a great set of pots and pans.

7. Register for more serving pieces than you think you need. Come Thanksgiving, no one *ever* seems to have enough.

8. Keep your registry open as long as possible. Since guests have a year to purchase a wedding gift, ask the store how long it remains active. (Also ask if it can be converted to a "special occasion" registry after a year, so you can keep filling in pieces on your anniversary and at holidays.)

9. Set up a new joint bank account at least six months before the wedding. Deposit monetary gifts in this separate account so they don't get mixed up with household funds and frittered away.

---

alludes to gifts, unless you're requesting a ban on gifts or asking for charitable donations in lieu of gifts. Even that information should be printed on a separate card, not directly on the invitation.

Guests will contact you, your parents, or a member of the wedding party to find out where you're registered. With the growing prevalence of online registries, many savvy guests don't even need to ask; they're able to find at least one of the couple's registries online by checking a few obvious sites—a department store where they live or a national chain they know the couple likes.

If you choose to build a personal wedding website, you can share all the helpful details about your wedding there, and in that context, it's permissible to post where you're registered. The difference between doing that and including it with your invitation is that people are voluntarily going to your site to get more information about your wedding; with an invitation, they're assaulted by the "gift" message right from the start.

When All You Really Want Is Money

THERE'S NO QUESTION THAT some couples desire monetary gifts most of all, whether for a down payment on a home, to defray some of the costs of the wedding, or to help ease their student debt. It's never acceptable to include any reference to money in your invitation, and traditionally, parents or members of the wedding party got the word out when they were asked about your registry. In recent years, however, wedding crowd funding sites like Honeyfund, Tender, or Hatch My House, have emerged as a perfectly acceptable means to having guests contribute funds toward big-ticket items. Link the sites to an account you've set up just for this purpose. If you don't have a site, guests will simply find out the old-fashioned way—by picking up the phone. Share the information with your mother and your bridesmaids, who'll be charged with letting people know.

Better to Give

Requesting a donation to charity is a wonderful way to do some good while letting guests give you a gift, if they so choose. You can even call your charity of choice and ask them to set up a fund in honor of your wedding.

Although you're never supposed to mention registries or gifts in an invitation, it's fine if the purpose is to alert people that you *don't* want gifts. To get the word out, have a small card printed up with the charity information and include it with your invitation.

The card should include the mailing address and website of the charity. It can read: "In lieu of gifts, a donation to [charity name here] would be greatly appreciated," or "We feel so fortunate! Please, no gifts, but if you must, a donation to [name of charity] would be appreciated."

> *Now that we've found each other, we have everything we could possibly want. No gifts, please, but if you must, a donation to [name of charity] would be appreciated.*

Displaying Gifts

Some people consider the display of wedding gifts a time-honored tradition, while others find it crass. In the Victorian era, a bride would show off her gifts by inviting friends to her mother's house for a "trousseau tea." The custom of the trousseau tea lives on in the South, but if you've never heard of such a thing, don't take it upon yourself to start up the tradition—keep your gifts to yourself!

In some cultures, money is the expected gift, and it's not uncommon for guests to simply hand over cash-filled envelopes at the wedding. Still, some guests will feel uncomfortable giving money, so you should always have at least one registry for those who want to give you a tangible keepsake.

Gift Tracking

You don't want to be thanking Aunt Bessie for the silver iced-tea spoons that came from Uncle Carl, so you'll need a system for tracking gifts. Set it up the day the first gift arrives, which is likely to be earlier than you think.

Many registries offer a gift-tracking component on their websites. Mainstream wedding websites offer complimentary guest list managers, and wedding planning software programs also cover gift tracking. If you've followed my advice in chapter 5, "The Guest List," you've converted your guest list into some form of spreadsheet that includes columns for recording gifts for each wedding-related event and marking when you sent the thank-you note. Make sure you record a detailed description of the gift and your reaction upon opening it to help you when it's time to write thank-yous.

Keeping careful track of gifts will also alert you to duplicates—which happen even with the best of registries—allowing you to get them straightened out quickly.

Maintenance

JUST LIKE YOUR HAIR and skin, your registry requires maintenance. You'll want to check on your registries once a week to make sure you still have enough items on them at a variety of prices. Some stores will call you when your registry runs low, but don't depend on them to alert you. Use your weekly checkup to delete any discontinued or out-of-stock items or anything you may have gotten from another source. (Some guests may look at your registry but choose to buy you the gift from another store.)

In the final weeks before your wedding, you should check the registry every few days to make sure that enough gifts remain at every price range.

Returning Merchandise

NO MATTER HOW carefully you attend to your registries, you will have items you want to return. To keep the process as stress free as possible, follow these steps.

- Tape receipts to merchandise as it comes in. Or create a separate folder for wedding gift receipts. An accordion file with slots for each store works well.

- When you receive a gift, check the return policy at that store. Some boutiques have thirty-day return policies, so you'll want to take care of those returns promptly.

- If you're certain you don't want to keep a gift, return it as soon as possible. Don't let the returns pile up and turn into a monstrous chore. You don't need to wait for all of the gifts to come in to decide on all of your returns.

- When returning gifts, don't feel pressured to choose another gift on the spot. Take the store credit or the refund, if it's an option. Ask whether store credits have an expiration date—believe it or not, some expire in a year. If they don't, there's no rush to spend the credit.

TO THE TABLE . . .

Dinnerware

No one says you have to register for fine china. Maybe it's not you, or maybe you've been promised your grandmother's china. If that's the case, you can register for colorful everyday dishes and a set of white porcelain dishes for entertaining. (Consider oversize ones if you serve buffet style.)

When choosing dinnerware, it's valuable to know the different types of materials. Most dinnerware is made of clay, but the type of clay and the way it's fired can make an enormous difference in the end product. Following are the main materials and the qualities that can help you decide which is right for you.

Porcelain, also known as china. Lightweight but surprisingly strong and durable, this nonporous, translucent material can be an excellent choice for everyday dishes. If you choose a design with a metallic element, know that it won't be dishwasher-safe or microwavable.

A Five-Piece Place Setting

A more formal setting includes a dinner plate, salad plate, cup, saucer, and soup bowl or bread-and-butter plate (the bowl is typically more useful).

A Four-Piece Place Setting

An everyday setting featuring a dinner plate, salad plate, cereal bowl, and mug

Bone china. A type of delicate china containing bone ash for a creamier white color. (Vegetarians beware: The "bone" in bone ash does actually come from animals.)

Earthenware. Often colorful and appealing, earthenware is what's most commonly used in everyday dishes. Though it's heavier than china, it chips easily because it's fired at a low temperature. With a five-to-eight-year life span, there's no need to aim for a timeless style.

Stoneware. More durable than earthenware because it's fired at a higher temperature, stoneware resists chipping and tends to have a rustic look. Ironstone is a type of stoneware.

Glass. Tempered glass works well for chargers and salad and dessert plates. Its versatility allows it to go from oven to microwave to dishwasher. Some makers offer gorgeous plates of recycled glass for the eco-conscious.

An Open Stock Setting

"Open stock" refers to place settings from which any item can be purchased individually. Translation: If you know you'll never use a rimmed soup bowl, you can go ahead and substitute a rimless cereal bowl. Particularly for fine china, there's often no discount for buying a standard place setting—the price is the same as buying all of the components individually. (Where you do save is when you can buy a boxed set of dishes with service for four, eight, or twelve people, but those are usually found in everyday dishes, not china.) So if you have chosen an open stock pattern, look at all the options and customize your place settings.

Glassware

You'll probably register for several types of glassware, from crystal for holiday dinners to juice glasses. Most of these tips pertain to crystal or the stemware you choose for your more formal table.

- Glass that contains 10 percent to 24 percent lead qualifies as crystal, which can be plain or cut. Cut crystal looks more traditional, while plain gives a sleeker look. If you're somewhere in between, consider a plain crystal glass with a cut pattern near the rim. Crystal is fragile, so register for extras.

- Colored crystal interferes with the color of the wine. To avoid offending oenophiles, stick with colored stems or colored water goblets.

- When it comes to wineglasses, register for at least twelve. They break easily, so you'll want backups. For champagne flutes, register for four or six if you tend to drink champagne privately, twelve if you like to serve it at parties.

- The longer the stem, the more fragile the glass. Longer stems make glasses harder to care for and

store, and, should they be dishwasher safe, less likely to fit into the top rack of a dishwasher.

- If you're wine aficionados, register for specialty wineglasses for different varietals. But if you only have the occasional glass (or are short on space), you're better served by an all-purpose wineglass

Red wine　　　*Champagne*　　　*White wine*

ASK MINDY

Q I've heard of websites that allow guests to contribute cash to your honeymoon. It seems like a great idea to me, but my mom thinks it's in bad form. What do you think?

A I like it. The honeymoon websites are very successful. If you don't need pots and pans and people want to buy you something, why not? People who aren't comfortable with that won't do it.

Do keep in mind that many honeymoon registries keep a percentage of the gift price (often 9 percent or more) for processing and handling. Whatever you're doing, you should be registered at several different places. Make sure you have some traditional options in the mix to put your mom (and her generation) at ease.

that can be used with red or white wine. Register for at least twelve. If you like to host gatherings that involve wine, put up to twenty on the registry.

- As a general rule, choose simple glassware if your dishes are heavily patterned or otherwise ornate—or vice versa. Of course, if you're a die-hard minimalist, you'll want to keep everything simple and clean.

Glassware Subtleties

A champagne flute is shaped to preserve effervescence; a white-wine glass to keep the wine cold; and a red-wine glass to allow the wine to breathe.

Flatware

With flatware, the feel is just as important as the look. Pick out flatware in person to make sure you find the size and weight pleasing to handle. There are some variations in sizes, particularly in silver; give them the touch test to find out if you really want European-size instead of the more common (and slightly smaller) place-size flatware.

Which Metal is Right for You?

Sterling silver lasts forever. It's made of 92.5 percent silver and 7.5 percent base metal to make it stronger, which is why some sterling is stamped "925." And the more you use it, the less polishing it requires. Sterling can go in

A Simple Flatware Setting

Salad fork, fork, soup spoon, teaspoon, knife

the dishwasher, provided it's not washed with stainless steel—the two create a chemical reaction that results in pits and stains. Sterling is quite expensive (easily $300

per place setting, and it can go into the thousands), and many styles are too intricate for contemporary tastes. If you have a set in the family that you might inherit later on, you don't necessarily need to register for silver.

Relatively rare, true *vermeil* is made of sterling silver plated with gold, making it even more costly than sterling flatware. Gold doesn't tarnish, so vermeil doesn't require much upkeep. It's more common to see gold plate, which is made of stainless steel electroplated with gold. Gold accents on silver serve to integrate the two metals and are an especially popular complement to gold-banded china.

Silver plate, a compromise between sterling and stainless, is created by coating a base metal with silver. Although it's much more affordable than sterling, the silver plating can wear off, especially a lesser quality brand. It's tough to discern the quality of silver plate by looking at it, though top-quality silver plate has an extra layer of silver on high-traffic spots such as the backs of spoons. The patterns typically mimic those found in sterling. Since silver plate isn't a good investment and usually doesn't have the style of stainless, it's probably your least desirable option.

A twentieth century invention, *stainless steel* is a metal alloy that resists tarnish. Quality stainless is marked 18/8 or 18/10, with the top number representing the percentage of chromium, which gives it strength, and the bottom number representing the percentage of nickel, for shine. Stainless is low maintenance, attractively priced (usually less than $75 per place setting), and often available in appealingly modern patterns.

Specialty Pieces

When you look at the full range of flatware pieces available, it's easy to get overwhelmed. Especially in sterling silver, there are some obscure pieces in the lineup that were last popular at early-twentieth-century feasts. Fruit knife? Bouillon spoon? It's safe to say that if you haven't heard of it, you probably don't need it.

Most everyone has at least occasional use for butter spreaders—either at formal dinners or for entertaining.

(They're perfect for the cream cheese at brunch or the roasted red pepper spread at a cocktail party.) The rest depends on what kind of food you serve. If you frequently cook fish, consider fish forks. Do you stir sugar into iced tea at every meal? Then you will appreciate having iced-tea spoons. Steak knives can also be extremely useful, though you'll often have to shop for those separately, as they're not always included in flatware patterns.

> **Register for extra teaspoons, which have a habit of disappearing (just like socks in the dryer). Extra salad forks come in handy if you often serve salad and dessert—that way you won't have to wash them before the end of the meal.**

Pots and Pans

In cookware, first consider which metal best suits your needs, both in terms of cooking and maintenance. Matched pieces tend to stack better, but those who really know their way around the kitchen often prefer to pick and choose pieces from different lines.

A favorite of professional chefs, *copper* is prized for cooking food more quickly than aluminum or stainless steel. It's pricey and reacts with acidic foods, so it's usually lined with tin or steel. Copper pots spot and tarnish easily and require regular polishing.

All-Clad is the standard bearer in the category of *triple-ply construction*, and many cooks swear by the brand. To make the most of the properties of each metal, its signature stainless line is made of an aluminum core sandwiched between layers of stainless steel on the base and sides, resulting in cookware that heats up quickly and evenly with a nonreactive interior.

An excellent heat conductor, *aluminum* is the most widely used metal in cookware. Avoid aluminum that's too thin, as it can heat unevenly. Pure aluminum scratches easily and reacts with food, so you want to look for either anodized aluminum or aluminum that's coated with a nonstick finish, such as Teflon. Anodized aluminum has been chemically altered to make it harder and nonreactive. It has a dark appearance, will resist sticking, and is easy to clean. (Calphalon is a well-known brand of anodized cookware.) Know that anodized and nonstick finishes can be ruined by abrasive materials and cleansers.

Nearly indestructible, lightweight, and easy to care for, *stainless steel* is a popular choice. The downside of stainless is that it isn't a good heat conductor, so an aluminum or copper base is often added to improve its performance. A nonstick surface means you can cook without oil and makes cleanup easier, but requires proper care.

Extremely heavy, *cast iron* takes time to heat up but retains heat extremely well and cooks evenly at high temperatures. In an ideal world, we'd all have a cast-iron skillet for cooking steaks and a cast-iron griddle for pancakes. Cast iron reacts with acidic foods and can absorb flavors, so it should be "seasoned" (you rub shortening into the pan, then bake it—the cookware should come with directions).

Le Creuset is perhaps the best-known brand of *enameled cast iron*, cast iron coated with nonreactive enamel. It's particularly good for stews, chili, and anything else that you braise or simmer.

There's no denying that setting up a home is one of the perks of being newly married—flip the page for the definitive list of essentials. In the same vein, the special attention a bride-to-be receives from her girlfriends and female family members is one of the special parts of being *almost* newly married. Here's to girls, parties, and only the most tasteful lingerie. ♦

REGISTRY ESSENTIALS

The following lists are intended to spark ideas and keep you from forgetting some of what I consider to be essentials. No one needs everything on the list, and some items overlap in their functions—you probably don't, for example, need both an indoor grill and a panini maker.

FORMAL TABLE SETTING

- Dinner plates
- Salad plates
- Bread plates
- Cups and saucers
- Mugs
- Chargers
- Soup bowls
- Teapot
- Coffeepot
- Sugar bowl and creamer
- Gravy boat
- Covered serving dishes
- Serving bowl
- Serving platter
- Soup tureen

CASUAL DINNERWARE

- Dinner plates
- Salad plates
- Bread plates
- Cups and saucers
- Mugs
- Pasta bowls
- Cereal bowls
- Rice bowls
- Platters
- Covered serving dishes
- Pitcher
- Buffet-size plates

FORMAL GLASSWARE

- Water goblets
- Wineglasses for white wine
- Wineglasses for red wine
- Champagne flutes
- Footed sherbet bowls or another dessert bowl

EVERYDAY GLASSWARE

- Water glasses/tumblers
- Juice glasses
- Stemless wineglasses

BARWARE

- Highball glasses
- Double old-fashioned glasses
- Martini glasses
- Margarita glasses
- Pilsner glasses
- Cordial glasses
- Brandy snifters
- Cocktail shaker
- Ice bucket and tongs
- Margarita pitcher
- Corkscrew
- Wine bucket or wine cooler
- Compact wine refrigerator

FORMAL FLATWARE

- Dinner forks
- Dinner knives
- Teaspoons
- Salad forks
- Place spoons (aka tablespoons)
- Soup spoons
- Steak knives
- Butter knives
- Cocktail forks
- Fish forks
- Fish knives
- Iced-tea spoons
- Demitasse spoons
- Serving spoons
- Pierced tablespoon(s) for serving
- Serving forks
- Salad servers
- Cake server
- Ladle
- Sugar bowl spoon
- Sugar tongs

EVERYDAY FLATWARE

- Dinner forks
- Dinner knives
- Teaspoons
- Salad forks
- Place spoons (aka tablespoons)
- Pierced tablespoon(s) for serving
- Steak knives
- Iced-tea spoons
- Salad servers
- Serving fork

Cake server

Ladle

MISCELLANEOUS ENTERTAINING ITEMS

Salt and pepper shakers

Platters

Serving bowls

Condiment dishes

Salad bowl

Bread dish

Pitcher

Electric warming tray

Butter dish

Cheese knives

TABLE LINENS

Tablecloths

Dinner napkins

Cocktail napkins

Everyday place mats

Table runner

BATH LINENS AND BATHROOM ACCESSORIES

Washcloths

Hand towels

Bath towels

Bath sheets

Bath mats

Guest towels

Shower curtain

His-and-hers robes

Bathroom scale

His-and-hers power toothbrushes

BED LINENS

Fitted sheets

Flat sheets

Pillowcases

Pillow shams

Pillows

Comforter

Duvet cover

Blankets

Bed skirt

Mattress pad

POTS AND PANS

Saucepans

Covered sauté pan

Skillets

Omelet pan

Stockpot

Roasting pan

Roasting rack

Dutch oven

Double boiler

Steamer basket

Griddle

Teakettle

Electric skillet

CUTLERY

Serrated knife

Eight-inch chef's knife

Paring knife

Carving set

Honing steel

Knife block

Electric knife

KITCHEN EQUIPMENT

Microwave oven

Toaster

Coffeemaker

Food processor

Colander

Wire whisks

Wooden spoons

Assorted spatulas

Countertop oven

Countertop convection oven

Stand mixer

Hand blender

Blender/smoothie maker

Crock-Pot

Waffle iron

Cappuccino maker

Pod coffeemaker

Juicer or juice extractor

Fondue set

Kitchen scale

Indoor grill

Panini maker

Ice cream maker

Rice cooker

Pressure cooker

Cheese grater

Mandolin

Cutting boards

Pizza stone/pizza peel

Cheese slicer

Ladle

Ice cream scoop

Garlic press

Mortar and pestle

(continued on next page)

(Registry Essentials, continued)

- Tongs
- Slotted spoons
- Cookbooks

BAKEWARE

- Half-sheet pan (aka baking sheet)
- Cookie sheet
- Measuring cups
- Measuring spoons
- Set of mixing bowls
- Cake pans
- Pie dish
- Tart pan
- Loaf pan
- Muffin tin
- Cooling rack
- Rolling pin
- Jelly roll pan

TOOLS

- Tool kit
- Phillips head screwdriver
- Flat-head screwdriver
- Needle-nose pliers
- Power screwdriver
- Drill

DECORATIVE HOUSEHOLD ITEMS

- End tables
- Bar cart
- Area rugs
- Recliners
- Candlesticks
- Cake stand
- Serving trays
- Breakfast-in-bed tray
- Vases
- Urns
- Clocks
- Lamps
- Picture frames (traditional or digital)
- Artwork
- Photo albums
- Throw pillows
- Throw for sofa
- Storage chest

ELECTRONICS AND ENTERTAINMENT

- Flat-screen television set
- Stereo
- Camera
- Speakers/docking station for digital music device
- Turntable
- Digital reading devices, tablets
- "Smart" household appliances (thermostats, video-enabled doorbells, etc.)
- Gaming system
- Board games
- Sports equipment
- Home exercise equipment
- Coffee-table books

MISCELLANEOUS

- Luggage
- Iron
- Vacuum cleaner
- Handheld vacuum cleaner
- Fireplace tools
- Air purifier

OUTDOOR ENTERTAINING

- Patio furniture
- Outdoor dishes, glasses, serving dishes
- Grill, gas or charcoal
- Decorative planters
- Stand umbrella

CHAPTER FOURTEEN

Parties, Parties, Parties

SHOWERS AND OTHER PREWEDDING FETES

The bridal shower. The bachelorette party. The rehearsal dinner. The post-wedding brunch. All sorts of peripheral celebrations surround an actual wedding. Each has its own distinct flavor, customs, and purpose. And the best part? With the possible exception of the rehearsal dinner, all involve minimal planning on your part. Why so many events dotting the way to the altar? Well, for one thing, beyond the joining of two people in matrimony, a wedding has many layers of meaning. There's the setting up of one's marital home. Even if you and your fiancé have been living together for years, you can still celebrate the cementing of your domestic life with a bridal shower.

There's the leaving behind of one's single life. For that we have the bachelor and bachelorette parties, our last big hurrahs. Obviously, that's not to say you'll never enjoy a night out on the town with your girlfriends again, but in my opinion you would be remiss not to give this important turning point its proper weight.

The rehearsal dinner and post-wedding brunch serve more pragmatic purposes. With so many guests likely to be traveling from out of town to reach your wedding, it's a courtesy to entertain them the night before and the morning after the festivities.

The Bridal Shower

The bridal shower is the party held two to three months before the wedding, during which you'll be showered with gifts to help you set up your new home. It's thrown by the people who love you—no planning on your part required. (You may be called upon to weigh in on whether you would like an all-women or coed shower—traditionally it's a girl thing.) Your main

---

TRADITION PRIMER

What's with All the Gifts?

The bridal shower dates back at least three hundred years, when a beautiful Dutch girl fell in love with a good-hearted but poor miller. Since his daughter wouldn't be properly provided for, her father refused to let them marry. Friends and neighbors wanted to see the love match succeed, so they created a procession and marched to the young woman's house, each bearing a gift to help set up her household. They showered her with enough blankets, linens, pots, and pans to rival a respectable dowry. The show of support helped convince the father to agree to the marriage.

The foundation of the shower, then, is all about gift giving. Normally, etiquette forbids us to "expect" gifts and admonishes us not to indicate in any way that a gift is expected. Not so with showers. It's fine for your hosts to include registry information in a shower invitation (*never* in a wedding invitation). Opening gifts on-site is an integral part of the party; in fact, some consider it rude if the bride doesn't open gifts at a shower.

---

role is to graciously attend the party, receive the gifts, and, of course, write thank-you notes.

Who Hosts a Bridal Shower?

THE HOSTING DUTY of a bridal shower is a hotly contested subject in the world of weddings. Traditionally, the shower was considered the maid of honor's responsibility, with the help of the rest of the bridesmaids. A friend or a friend of the parents could also host the event. It used to be considered bad form for an immediate family member to host a shower, as it could be perceived as the bride asking for gifts through her relatives.

Although some etiquette gurus will disagree, I think these days it's fine for anyone to host a shower. It's wonderful if the bridesmaids are able to do so, but it can be costly and difficult to arrange if they live far away from the bride. If a mother chooses to host a shower, it takes the financial burden off the bridesmaids.

Multiple showers are a resulting and not-so-unusual trend—but they shouldn't be overdone. A friend might throw you a couples shower, your office mates a girly tea, while your mother might organize a party for relatives and friends in her hometown. That's all right, but if two friends offer to throw showers for you with overlapping guest lists, try to persuade them to join forces.

When there are two brides-to-be, hosting a couples' shower helps ensure that neither of the brides feels left out. Most same-sex couples do choose to split up for their bachelor or bachelorette parties (see page 178), but that party has special, last-night-on-the-town connotations.

Who Gets Invited?

THE HOST WILL almost always rely on the bride to provide a guest list. Being organized about this is a courtesy. Don't even think of handing her an impossible -to-decipher list with names scrawled on the back of cocktail napkins! And accept the parameters you're given in terms of numbers. I figure that 5 percent of invited guests won't be able to attend an in-town shower, so that gives you a little wiggle room. Some planners and books will tell you to count on a higher percentage of those who won't accept, but I think it's too risky. If you're inviting people who live out of town as a courtesy, you can safely assume that most of them will not fly in for a shower. It all boils down to three golden rules:

- You should only invite people who will be invited to the wedding, unless a work colleague decides to throw a shower for office mates and it's clear to them that wedding invitations will not be showing up in the mail. If a couple holds a small destination wedding or elopes, sometimes friends who didn't attend the wedding will throw a shower for them upon their return.

- Each wedding guest should only be invited to one shower. Exceptions are mothers of the bride and groom, bridesmaids, and siblings, though they are in no way obligated to attend more than one.

- Though a shower is a treat for you, there's still a core list of people you'll need to invite as a courtesy, even if you don't expect them to attend. These are the mothers of the bride and groom, sisters of the bride and groom, grandmothers, and close aunts. If someone other than the bridesmaids is hosting the shower, the bridesmaids should be invited. Should either of you have children who are teenagers or older, they should be on the guest list. Step-parents and -siblings should be invited if the relationship allows.

With all that in mind, shower guest lists tend to be more about the bride's or couple's close friends. As with the wedding guest list, drawing mental circles around your friends and relatives will help you be consistent about who's invited and who's not. One such circle might be co-workers invited to the wedding—either you invite them all to a shower or you don't invite any of them. It's going to hurt some feelings if you pick and choose among them.

Traditionally, showers are a women-only affair; the groom makes an appearance near the end of the event, in time to watch the opening of the gifts if he's interested. In recent years, however, coed or "couples" showers have become increasingly popular.

Coed showers tend to have a different flavor. They're usually held on a weekend evening, while women-only showers typically take place in the afternoon. Cocktails might flow. (Alcohol isn't necessarily served at a girls' shower, aside from a glass of champagne or white wine, or a mimosa or two.) Coed showers frequently involve an interactive activity—popular choices include cooking classes or wine tastings. A bar shower can be great fun if you invite a mixologist (a mixed-drink specialist) to demonstrate how to make some favorite cocktails and how to set up and stock a bar.

ASK MINDY

Q I heard through the grapevine that some of my bridesmaids aren't thrilled about being asked to fly to Vegas for my bachelorette. But my maid of honor is really excited about the plans, and I don't want to meddle. What should I do?

A Weddings are expensive—and not just for you. Between outfits, travel, gifts, and the costs of attending the shower and the bachelorette party, your bridal attendants may be out thousands of dollars. That's a high price tag for friendship, so cut them a deal where you can. Be direct. Ask your maid of honor to poll the bridesmaids and find out how much they can afford to spend on the bachelorette, and then to find an event that can accommodate everyone's budget.

Shower Games

There are two kinds of people in this world, those who think shower games are fun and those who dread and abhor them. If you fall into the second category, perhaps I can entice you with a few examples—games can be a great way to bring together a group of people who might not know one another that well. And if there's no changing your mind, at least you'll have a handle on what you might expect.

Ten Favorite Shower Themes

New shower themes sprout faster than weeds after a heavy rain, but these ten are perennial winners. Play them straight, put your own twist on them, or use the list to get your own ideas flowing.

1. Alphabet Shower: Every guest is assigned a letter of the alphabet and asked to bring a gift that starts with that letter.

2. Around-the-Clock Shower: Guests are assigned a time of day and asked to bring a corresponding gift. Eight in the morning might elicit egg cups or juice glasses; 11 p.m. might mean a nightie.

3. Around-the-House Shower: Each guest is assigned a room and brings a gift for it. The living room might prompt a throw for the couch, while the bathroom might get you his-and-hers bathrobes.

4. Holiday Shower: Not a good shower for basics, but a festive option if you're having multiple showers. Everyone is given a holiday and chooses a gift in keeping with the day.

5. Kitchen Shower: Guests are asked to bring a gift to help outfit the kitchen. That could mean simple gifts like a set of dishtowels or a lemon zester, or a more elaborate pick like a mixer.

6. Lingerie Shower: Another perennial favorite, the lingerie shower is ideal as a second shower. Let the host know key sizes in case guests ask for guidance.

7. Recipe Shower: Guests are asked to bring a favorite recipe and the key kitchen tools needed to make it.

8. Stock-the-Bar Shower: A popular option at couples' showers. Guests help fully outfit a bar.

9. Home Improvement Shower: Also popular for couples' showers, this theme allows the couple to get all the screwdrivers, drills, flashlights, ladders, and other gear they'll need around the house.

10. Gadget Shower: Guests are asked to bring a gadget that changed their lives for the better.

The Toilet Paper Wedding Gown. A few designated guests serve as fit models, and it's off to the toilet paper races we go. This crafty, creative activity really brings people together, and you'd be surprised at the imaginative creations.

The Newlywed Game. This is a game for a couples party. First, choose a few couples to play alongside the bride and groom. The hosts will have prepared a set of questions for the women: What is your partner's favorite part of your body? How many other men or women would your partner say you have been with? Where were you the first time your partner said he loved you? What is your favorite color? The ladies write down their answers, keeping them facedown. The partner has to guess how his other half answered and prove how well he knows her. The couple with the most correct answers wins a prize.

Bridal Bingo. This game keeps guests entertained while the bride opens her gifts. Using bingo cards, guests fill in the blanks with gifts they predict the bride will receive. As she opens her presents, they mark off their correct guesses. The first three to call "Bingo!" win a prize.

In Her Words. Assign someone to discreetly write down what the bride says as she opens her gifts. ("How did you know I wanted that?") Once the gifts are opened, her comments are read back to her . . . as what she'll say on her wedding night. (Yup, it's dirty, and brides love it.)

Recipes for Marriage. Include a blank card in the invitation asking guests to write down their recipe for a great marriage. It can be a recipe, a joke, an anecdote, or a piece of advice. At the shower, each person reads hers aloud; a bridesmaid can later turn the cards into a keepsake album or scrapbook for the bride.

Opening the Gifts

AT OTHER PARTIES, it would be rude and self-absorbed to tie up everyone's attention while you sat there and opened twenty-five gift-wrapped boxes, oohing and aahing over each one before passing it around for everyone to inspect. Bridal showers are not like other parties. Gifts are the raison d'être of a shower, and opening them is part of the package.

As showers have grown larger, however, the gift opening has begun to take an inordinate amount of time. If you have more than thirty gifts to open—or it looks like the gift opening will exceed an hour—consider inviting each guest to open a gift.

Make sure you assign someone to sit next to you and record the gift and the name of the gift giver on a memo pad so—you guessed it—you can write thank-you notes.

Grace is of the essence during the gift-opening process. If you're opening something you registered for or a gift you like immediately, your natural reaction will probably do the gift justice. If you don't care for the gift or have no idea what it is, "Thank you, I can't wait to use it" will cover a lot of territory.

The Ribbon Bouquet

As the bride is opening her gifts, a lovely (and eco-friendly) tradition is for one of the bridesmaids to create a bouquet out of the ribbons and bows. This becomes the bouquet the bride carries at the wedding rehearsal. Superorganized hosts bring a round piece of cardboard  with holes punched in it, but one can also use the top of a box from one of the gifts. The person making the bouquet will thread the ribbons and artificial flowers or other gift decorations through the holes, tying them together on the underside of the piece of cardboard. At the end, she presents the bouquet to the bride.

What If You Don't Like the Plans?

YOU FOUND OUT that your host is placing a red rose and a spray of baby's breath at each place setting. Some brides might not care, but for you, it's totally cringe-worthy.

What do you do? You say nothing. Someone is going to a lot of trouble to throw a party in your honor. It may not be to your taste, but remember, you'll get to make your own style statement with the wedding. Think about how much effort the host is putting into the event and how much she must care about you to do all this. Think about how lucky you are to have friends or relatives who are willing to go to so much trouble and expense for you. Let them have their fun, and remember, anything they're doing for you is a gift, so you need to be showing gratitude, not attitude.

Keeping the Memories Alive

THE BRIDAL SHOWER is an event you'll want to preserve. There are plenty of wedding journals out there with sections for recording the gifts and the names of those who attended. Bring a camera with you and ask one of the bridesmaids to take photos. Make a point of getting your photo taken with the host so you can send it to her with your thank-you note. If you have a wedding website, post some photos from the shower online. A special album or scrapbook devoted to the shower makes a wonderful keepsake. Besides photos, include any special details such as personalized cocktail napkins, gift cards, and the menu. Back the photos with pieces of wrapping paper from the gifts.

A Gift for the Host

MAKE SURE YOU show your appreciation to the host of your shower by buying her a wonderful, truly personal gift. If you're stumped or don't know the host that well, consider custom stationery, a monogrammed bathrobe or guest towels, luxury soaps, or a soft throw for the sofa. In a pinch, a bouquet of flowers and a lovely note will do the trick.

Write Thank-You Notes

THE THANK-YOU NOTES don't stop with the host, obviously. Try to get to the rest of your gift givers by the end of the weekend following the shower, but if that's not possible, don't let more than three weeks pass.

If you had a couples shower, enlist the groom to do his share, particularly if you want him to write a portion of the thank-yous for wedding gifts. (Trust me, it's best to set the precedent now.)

For tips on stationery and writing thank-you notes, see chapter 20, "The Invitations," and chapter 15, "Saying Thank You."

What to Wear

YOUR ATTIRE WILL depend upon the time, place, theme, and type of crowd. But dress with care, even if it's casual. Don't arrive looking like you just jumped out of the shower (no pun intended). You want to show respect and appreciation to those who organized the party for you, and your appearance is one of the key ways to do that. Besides, you're going to be the center of attention. If you're going to be working with a hairstylist and a makeup artist on your wedding day, this is a great chance to cement your relationship with them and try out a hairstyle or new makeup. But even if that's not possible or you're not interested in making that big a deal out of it, this is a perfect occasion to treat yourself to a blowout and a mani-pedi.

Bachelor and Bachelorette Parties

sn't it nice to be able to add something fun to your to-do list, something that involves absolutely no planning on your part? I'm talking about the bachelorette party, of course. No need for blushing (or quaking in your boots)—a bachelorette party needn't involve stripping, or infidelity, or alcohol poisoning, for that matter.

It's simply a time to let go of all your worries, get together with your closest friends, and relax.

In days when wedding planning was less involved, this last hurrah was held the week of the wedding or even the night before. Your bridesmaids will be doing you a favor if they hold it closer to a month before the wedding. This not only gives the event the attention it deserves but also gives everyone more than ample recovery time. If you're going to Las Vegas or doing another sort of weekend getaway, have it four to six weeks before the wedding. (Let your maid of honor know well in advance what you would like the timing to be.)

Understandably, it's not always possible to gather college pals and long-distance friends together in advance for this party. So having it a night or two before the wed-

Bachelor(ette) Party 101

Bachelor parties are traditionally arranged by the best man, and bachelorette parties by the maid of honor. If the best man or maid of honor lives in another city, it's perfectly fine for another attendant to mastermind the festivities. Either way, the other attendants are often expected to pitch in.

The maid of honor or whoever is organizing the party should ask you for a guest list. I think smaller is better—you want it to feel intimate. But, although the guest list is pretty much up to you, keep in mind that anyone you invite should also be invited to the wedding. Depending on the type of party you're having, you can invite mothers if you're so inclined.

As for who pays, the only rule is: not the bride or groom. The attendants may all pool resources or ask each guest at the party to contribute a portion as appropriate—this might not apply if the party is being hosted in someone's home; for a spa party, however, it's perfectly reasonable for guests to pay for their own services and perhaps a portion of the bachelorette's. Any amount that guests are expected to pay should be clear on the invitation.

Setting the Tone

Your attendants are throwing this bash for you, so it's not up to you to dictate the itinerary or activities. It's a good idea, however, to have a talk with your honor attendant about tone. If you don't want strippers, say so, and you can certainly plant an idea of what you *would* like. But once you've done that and handed over a guest list, butt out.

ding might be your only option. If you do it then, opt for a tamer time with your pals (a bowling party or a spa afternoon), and take it easy on those rounds of Jell-O shots. You really, really, really don't want to be nursing the headache from hell on your wedding day.

There's no rule that bachelor and bachelorette parties need to be held on the same day, but simultaneous parties do have a few advantages: They keep each party happily entertained—no fretting about what their other half is doing—and they allow both parties to meet up toward the end of the night, if that sounds like fun.

Ten Great Parties

A BACHELOR(ETTE) PARTY can be a time to relax with your best friends or to indulge in some juvenile fun (minigolf, anyone?). In case you're asked for ideas, here are ten to inspire:

1. **Weekend in Vegas.** A visit to Sin City remains a classic for guys and girls. Gambling, clubs, great restaurants, and a spa in every major hotel make for an intoxicating combination. Atlantic City is a good alternate choice for those on the East Coast; if you can do without the gambling, Miami Beach might be your answer.

2. **Spa Day or Weekend.** There's no better way to rejuvenate yourself than through some serious pampering. Find a day spa or destination spa with group areas where everyone can hang out together in between their mani-pedis and body scrubs. Many cities now

offer mobile spas that will come to you if someone wants to host the party at her house. A variation to consider: a henna party, where artists apply henna tattoos. It's a standard girls' night out for many Indian, Pakistani, Persian, and North African brides. (Take into account that henna lasts for one to four weeks.)

3. **The Great Outdoors.** For adventurers, consider getting the group together for fishing, white-water rafting, camping, or rock climbing. Though manicured greens don't rate as wilderness, a golf outing is a classic, too.

4. **Poker tournament.** Whether or not you can get to Vegas, you can fold 'em or hold 'em in your own poker tourney. Rent professional equipment, and just add pizza and beer.

5. **Fun and Games.** All the fun of youth, along with martinis (where they're allowed). Set up an afternoon or evening of bowling or minigolf, a visit to a go-kart track, video arcade, or an amusement park, or a competitive match of paintball, WhirlyBall (like lacrosse, but in bumper cars), or laser tag.

TRADITION PRIMER

Bachelor Parties

Talk about ancient history—the bachelor party can be traced all the way back to fifth-century Sparta. The stag night involved much feasting and toasting with wine, and possibly some more explicit forms of farewells to single life. Guests even collected funds to give to the groom so that he'd be able to go out drinking with his friends once his wife held the purse strings! This custom lingers on at modern-day parties—if there's a game of poker or any activity involving a kitty, it's handed to the groom-to-be at the end of the evening.

Overindulgence isn't unheard of at bachelor and bachelorette bashes, so arrange for a limo, shuttle, trolley, or ride-sharing services to prevent anyone from drinking and driving.

6. **Sing-along.** A sushi dinner followed by a visit to a karaoke bar (one that rents out private rooms) lets everyone get silly as they sing their hearts out. Warning: A side of humiliation is practically guaranteed.

7. **Class Is in Session.** Learning something new can be a great icebreaker if your bachelorettes don't know one another that well. You can book anything from instructional makeovers with a makeup artist to a gourmet cooking lesson. Some dance studios offer pole dancing, striptease, or belly dancing classes, or you can book a mixologist to teach you how to stir up your favorite cocktails.

8. **Roadtrip.** Take to the road for a long weekend to see three ball games in three days, tour wineries, hit the beach, or visit quirky attractions.

9. **Manly Pursuits.** Something about eating red meat, smoking cigars, and sipping single malt Scotch holds timeless appeal for men. A private room in a steakhouse lets everyone indulge his inner hunter. And an old-fashioned shave lets the guys indulge in some masculine pampering.

10. **Take to the Water.** Rent a houseboat and take your crew afloat. You could even rent his-and-hers boats for simultaneous bashes.

Expectations and Limits

THE TWO OF YOU may need to have a couples talk before the bachelor and bachelorette parties (especially if that wild-and-crazy friend of yours is the organizer). This is the time to set ground rules and express any expectations. If you would be devastated to find out your partner had gotten a lap dance from a stripper, tell him that. Sending your fiancé off with a "don't do anything I wouldn't do" doesn't really set any clear boundaries.

As for your own behavior, ask yourself whether you'd mind if your spouse-to-be were doing whatever you're thinking of doing. If the answer is yes, then don't do it. And if your attendants spring a surprise on you that makes you uncomfortable, tell your maid of honor right away. Remember, you can always leave. Don't get your marriage off to a bad start in an effort not to make waves with your friends.

The Rehearsal Dinner

T he rehearsal dinner was once a formal affair hosted by the groom's parents and limited to the bridal party and the bride's parents. Nowadays, the guest list may include all of the out-of-towners, who can easily account for half of the wedding guests. That dinner for twenty at a U-shaped table is a thing of the past.

As the celebration has grown larger, it has also gotten more casual. Think of the rehearsal dinner as the kickoff to the wedding festivities, the event that gets the party started.

Despite the name, the dinner itself doesn't involve any rehearsing; but it *is* traditionally held following the wedding rehearsal (see page 359), the evening before the wedding. (For small, simple ceremonies, you may not need an actual rehearsal, but you could still have a rehearsal dinner; it's essentially a way to provide hospitality to out-of-town guests who are likely to come in the day before the wedding.)

Who Hosts?

THERE'S A LONG-STANDING TRADITION of the groom's parents' paying for and hosting the rehearsal dinner. That's still common, but as rehearsal dinners have grown larger and more expensive, other parties have come

Dollars and Sense

Looking to save some money on the rehearsal dinner? Why not limit the guest list to the wedding party and immediate family and invite everyone else to join you for a selection of desserts? For a more raucous crowd, you might even follow the intimate dinner with an open call for drinks at a local pub. If you or the host really can't afford to pick up the tab, just buy the first round; that way, you get to welcome everyone without getting stuck with a $5,000 bar tab the night before the wedding.

forward to pick up the tab or pitch in. Unlike showers and engagement parties, there is no etiquette surrounding who can and cannot host the rehearsal dinner, so the couple, the bride's parents, or another relative may take the lead.

As for who *plans* the dinner, that's another story. In the world of entertaining, that responsibility normally lies with the host. But with the rehearsal dinner, there's no clear-cut answer. As with all things, it depends on family dynamics and logistics. If, for instance, one set of parents is footing the bill but is going through an acrimonious divorce, it's far simpler all around if the planning is left in the hands of a third party; that way, all they have to agree on is how to split the bills. If there's a choice in the matter, it's easiest if whoever is planning the wedding—whether that be the couple, the bride's mother, or a wedding planner—also arranges the rehearsal dinner. It permits the planner to coordinate resources coming in from various vendors and also allows for balance in the ambience and the menu.

Even if parents are hosting, the couple may be involved in the planning to varying degrees—if the parents aren't familiar with the wedding location, they're often appreciative when the couple chooses a site for the dinner.

In some instances, parents have a very definite idea of the type of dinner they want

to host. It may be more formal or traditional than you would like, or the opposite. This is a case where it's definitely best to give over the reins. The rehearsal dinner is technically separate from the wedding, and if someone is hosting for you, you absolutely have to be gracious.

When to Send the Invites

IF TRAVEL PLANS aren't part of the equation, you can send invitations to the rehearsal dinner one month before the wedding. Otherwise, give guests at least two to three months' notice so they don't book a flight that arrives too late for the dinner. For a destination wedding, where it's likely that everyone will be invited to the rehearsal dinner, include the information on your save-the-date cards, and enclose a special card with the wedding invitation. (See chapter 20, "The Invitations," for more stationery tips.)

A Great Rehearsal Dinner

THE REHEARSAL DINNER should feel like its own distinct event—if you turn it into a mini wedding, you risk taking away from the reception you so painstakingly planned. My favorite way to distinguish the rehearsal dinner from the wedding is to make it a casual evening. The convivial atmosphere makes it easier for everyone to get to know one another, paving the way for a really fun wedding.

If you're having a sit-down dinner for your reception, think about doing stations or family-style service at the rehearsal dinner. Try not to repeat the food, the colors, the main ingredient in the specialty cocktail, the type of flowers, or the style of music.

One fail-safe way to inject the rehearsal dinner with personality is to bring the location into play. Invite guests to a clambake in New England, a fish boil in Wisconsin, a pig pickin' in North Carolina, a Tex-Mex blowout in the Southwest, or a wine and cheese tasting in Northern California. If you're set on a more

> If the rehearsal dinner is being held the night before the wedding, make sure it doesn't stretch into the wee hours. Everyone needs their beauty sleep, and you don't want your wedding party nursing hangovers on the big day.

formal dinner, choose a place with a drop-dead view that lets everyone know where they are.

If the bride's or groom's background is underrepresented at the reception, the rehearsal dinner provides an opportunity to even the score. At one of my weddings, we did the rehearsal dinner as a tea ceremony and served traditional Chinese foods in a nod to the groom's roots.

Finding a Venue

FIRST THINGS FIRST: Don't make the rehearsal dinner any more complicated than it needs to be. Restaurants, hotels, and clubs are the most popular places to hold rehearsal dinners because they're the easiest to plan. The food, the staff, the furnishings, and most of the décor are already in place, and the staff can often handle flowers for you.

Look toward your guests' convenience as well. Many will have flown in that day and might not be in the mood to navigate their way around a strange city.

There will be a lot of toasting at the event, so look for a space that can hold everyone in a single room. And since even the rehearsal dinner typically kicks off with a cocktail hour, make sure there's room enough for people to mill about, or a separate area or patio for gathering.

It's wonderfully personal if a relative wants to host the event in their home, but keep in mind that if there are more than a dozen guests, you'll have to deal with catering, rentals, staffing, and cleaning.

Warming Things Up

PROMOTE MINGLING any way you can; the more that people get to know one another, the better the wedding will be. One way to do this is to provide name tags. You can further identify people by their relation to the couple (Sadie Tomkins/Suzie's cousin), or by noting where they're from or where they went to college. If the groom loves baseball, write every guest's favorite team on the name tag. If the couple shares a literary streak, have everyone write the last good book they read below their names. Give people a conversation starter.

Where possible, set up the space so there is at least one place to gather besides the bar, whether it's a cheese tray or a photo gallery of the couple. Activities can also serve as wonderful icebreakers. A wine tasting, a round of croquet, or a quiz about the couple can all get people talking. Have a cooking school, catering facility, or hotel set up a cooking class for the group. Chopping, mixing, and tossing (with some sipping on the side) can spark a special kind of camaraderie.

Consider serving the meal family style. Making it feel like a big family dinner inspires warmth, and the passing of platters creates a genial atmosphere.

As for seating, don't leave guests to fend for themselves, even if it seems like a small enough event to do so. People will end up sitting with those they know, and you'll miss the opportunity to get the various groups together.

Toast of the Town

TOASTS ARE AN INTEGRAL PART of the rehearsal dinner—even more so, in some cases, than at the wedding reception.

Though in my experience you're more likely to be faced with an embarrassment of riches than a deathly silence, not everyone is aware of toasting etiquette or feels comfortable speaking in front of a crowd. If you've got a relatively shy family, you might speak to them ahead of time to make sure they know they're supposed to toast.

Get the toasts started during dinner. If everyone waits until the end of the meal, the evening will go on forever. Talk to likely candidates beforehand to let them know at what point in the evening you would like them to toast.

Traditionally, the groom's father leads off the toasts by welcoming the bride to the family. The father of the bride may respond in kind. Any number of toasts from bridesmaids, groomsmen, or family members can follow. Other than the parents, who may understandably want to indulge in multiple toasts, try to discourage toasts from anyone slated to make a toast at the wedding. One or both members of the couple usually closes the toasting

A Video Montage

Itching to show a video documenting your love story or piecing your childhood photographs together? Great idea. A video can also be a wonderful way to pay tribute to the marriages that made yours possible—a montage of parents' and grandparents' wedding shots symbolically summons the weight of history to bless your union.

Instead of showing the video at the wedding, roll it at the more intimate rehearsal dinner. It will have more meaning for your closest friends and family, and it won't break up the reception festivities. You can project the video on a screen near the entrance and have it rolling as guests come in; play it between dinner and dessert; or, for a low-tech approach, set it up on a TV somewhere off the beaten track—that way the guests can bump into it organically and spend some time with it if they wish.

Squeeze in the Extras

Is your wedding reception feeling a bit overcrowded with details? Streamline it by thinking about elements that you can shift from the reception to the rehearsal dinner. Serve the groom's cake there, for instance, rather than having it compete with the main cake at the reception.

by thanking the hosts, their parents, and everyone in the wedding party for attending.

Music and Favors

SINCE THE MAIN EVENT at the rehearsal dinner is generally the toasting, music plays a lesser role than at a wedding. Mostly, you want it to set the mood and stay in the background, so keep that in mind when you're programming your playlist.

If yours is the rare budget that allows for live music at the rehearsal dinner, think subtle—a pianist, jazz combo, or Latin guitars make great choices. If you can theme the music to the dinner or location by having mariachi players

at your Mexican feast or calypso music at your Caribbean destination wedding, so much the better.

Although they're not necessary or expected, rehearsal dinner favors can help build excitement for the rest of the weekend. They should be personal, fitting in with your story or location in some way. Giving away favors only at the rehearsal dinner, assuming it's smaller than the wedding reception, can also be a way to accommodate a tight budget. And you'll be giving a memento to the people who are most likely to appreciate it. For guidance on great favors, see page 328.

Post-Wedding Brunch

One final festivity for those still gathered together is the day-after brunch, a relatively recent phenomenon. There are few, if any, rules that govern this get-together. It's often fairly inexpensive, so anyone can host it—the bride's parents, the groom's parents, the bride and groom, two relatives who team up to cohost it, or a godparent.

Family members who don't often have a chance to see one another appreciate the extra time to catch up. Plus, it gives everyone a chance to indulge in some postgame analysis! (Did you *see* how young Uncle Harry's date was?! And wasn't Jane's toast hysterical?)

A Casual Get-Together

BY THE TIME the brunch rolls around, many guests will be partied-out, and some will probably be going straight to the airport, so the brunch should be an informal buffet. Make the invitation time open-ended, 9:30 a.m. to noon, for instance, so that people can come and go.

Everyone has already upheld their share of traditions by this point in the weekend, so there's no need for another toast or formalities of any kind. The brunch is simply a way to say good-bye and to feed your guests before they go on their way.

Q I don't want to treat guests who have traveled to the wedding shabbily, but the idea of yet another get-together after the wedding is too much for me. Any suggestions?

A Not all couples can socialize for days on end, and it's perfectly understandable. Instead of hosting a brunch, have boxed breakfasts delivered to the guests' hotel rooms. You can send bagels and cream cheese, croissants, Danish, or scones. Add juice and a fruit cup or yogurt. Don't forget to include a note thanking guests for coming to your wedding.

Likewise, there's no need for any special decorative treatment—everyone will have already spent enough money at this point—but you might talk to your florist ahead of time about the best way to reuse centerpieces from the reception. If you're adamant that the flowers look different, some florists, for a fee, will rearrange the flowers into new combinations.

Who's Invited?

THE BRUNCH GUEST LIST is typically the same as that for the rehearsal dinner: out-of-towners, the bridal party, parents, and close family members and friends. At a destination wedding, everyone is invited to the brunch.

What to Wear

Guests just got gussied up for your wedding less than twenty-four hours ago, so the brunch should be casual. The bride and groom should be comfortable but still pulled together, since camera shutters are bound to be clicking. Some brides aren't ready to leave behind their bridal standing just yet and choose to wear all white— something along the lines of white jeans and a T-shirt.

Going the Extra Mile

If you want to be known as the couple who thought of *everything*, send guests to the airport with a boxed lunch to take on the plane, or even a boxed snack (protein bar, trail mix, cheese crackers). Check the airlines' latest carry-on regulations before deciding what to include so guests won't have to leave their treats at security.

Guests should receive a written invitation to the brunch along with their initial save-the-date packet or wedding invitation, so they can plan for it.

It's quite a whirlwind, what with all these parties, gifts, and well-wishers. Lest the goodwill stop flowing in your direction, you'd best get going on those thank-you notes. I know, I know: The thank-you note has begun to resemble an artifact of a lost tribe—but it's an art that every bride must master. With a few pointers, you'll be well on your way. ♦

CHAPTER FIFTEEN

THE HOWS AND WHYS OF GRACIOUSNESS

The handwritten thank-you note may strike you as an antiquated tradition. But think about it this way: Thank-you notes are what you leave behind as a bride and groom—when they're received after the wedding, as most are, they're the closing impression a guest gets of your nuptials. While I understand that writing dozens (or even hundreds) of thank-you notes may not meet your definition of a good time, I can't stress how important it is.

Yes, gifts are part and parcel of getting married. But the unusual circumstance surrounding wedding gifts—namely, the fact that it's the recipient who chooses them—in no way eliminates the need for reciprocity. Each gift giver has put time, thought, and no small amount of money into your gift. (Even if it doesn't appear that way, you must use this as your working assumption.) The *least* you can do is thank this well-wisher in writing. And if the person has also invested time and money in attending your wedding, you should acknowledge that as well.

Keep in mind that thank-you notes don't apply merely to gifts. You'll also be writing notes to people who host parties for you, your attendants, and possibly your vendors.

The Burning Question: What's the Deadline?

I often hear this question phrased by couples as "How long do we have?" You'll have a much easier time of it if you adjust your attitude from the beginning. Instead of looking for ways to put off your thank-yous, put your resources into finding ways to speed up the process.

Once those wedding gifts start trickling in, build in some time several days a week to get some writing done before the trickle becomes a stream and the stream becomes a river.

For engagement gifts and shower gifts, thank-yous should go out no later than three weeks after you receive the gift. Wedding gifts can start arriving at any time after you announce your engagement, but you'll probably start to notice more activity two to three months before the wedding. While reluctant note-writers love to dredge up an old etiquette rule saying they have one year to write their thank-yous, I couldn't disagree more. Perhaps in the days when couples took off on their European tours after the wedding and didn't return home for months, a longer turnaround time was tolerated. But today, we live with texting, overnight shipping, and all other sorts of instant gratification. Your thank-yous should keep pace.

ASK MINDY

Q My fiancée and I both have extremely time-consuming jobs. I know it seems like a small thing, but handwritten thank-you notes are just an impossibility. How crude is it to send them by email? (She seems to think it's the eighth deadly sin.)

A I am a huge fan of handwritten notes. Your guests took time out of their day to get you something you wanted, and it's very important to thank them properly for it. I work full-time and have three kids and I still find time to write thank-you notes!

Three months is the absolute longest you can take to send off a note from the time you received the gift, barring extraordinary circumstances. I know you're busy, but that's not an extraordinary circumstance. Many of the people who sent you gifts and traveled eight hours to attend your wedding are crazy-busy, too.

Here's a motivator: Notes that are late need to make up for their tardiness by being longer and more eloquent. A note received two weeks after the gift was received will seem *better* to the gift giver than the exact same note received two months later. It takes a lot more literary finesse to convince recipients that their gift rocked your world if you've waited four months to tell them so.

Style and Logistics

The best time to order custom-printed thank-you notes is when you place your order for invitations—you'll often get a price break from the stationer. But if you're going to be changing your name and want the notes you send out after your wedding to reflect that, you'll need to have two batches printed up. If you're keeping your name, preprinting cards with first names only is your best bet—two different last names look awkward on a card. As for quantity, make sure to count out the number of couples or households—not individuals—so you're not overestimating your needs. Take your total and add another twenty-five percent to it to cover unexpected gifts and mistakes.

Informals and Correspondence Cards

IN STATIONERY LINGO, the standard thank-you note for weddings is called an "informal." It's folded in half at the top and measures approximately 3.5 inches by 5 inches. Generally, names or monograms are engraved or blind embossed on the front, and the inside is left blank for writing space. Historically, an informal was part of a woman's stationery wardrobe, but it's now fine for

An informal card—you may limit your note to panel A, or run over to panel B if necessary.

a couple to put both of their names on the card; however, if you're using separate cards, the groom shouldn't use a fold-over note—in men's stationery, "correspondence cards" are the standard. They're flat and heavy, with the name or monogram engraved across the top. And like informals, they are a fine choice if the bride and groom are having both their names printed on the cards.

Correspondence cards tend to have a more contemporary look than fold-over notes; they can be edged with a colored border if you're looking to inject more color. Black or gray ink on ecru paper remain the most classic choices. On a correspondence card, the writing space is limited to the front of the card. On a fold-over note, you can choose to write on two panels if you have the need. Writing on the back of a correspondence card is verboten, so if you can't squeeze it all on the front, you should throw out the card and start over.

A correspondence card

Make sure you don't order oversize notes, or you'll feel like you have to fill in the extra space. Your notes can be short and sweet, and smaller cards will help you achieve that.

What's Preprinted on the Note

THE FRONT of a custom-printed fold-over note or the top of a correspondence card is traditionally graced with a name, monogram, or initials; single initial notes are a contemporary choice, and they're often available as preprinted boxed notes. (You each get your own set.)

Boxed Versus Custom

Boxed notes cost significantly less than custom and don't require any waiting time—there's no rule that you must order personalized notes for your wedding. If you're on a tight budget, boxed cards can save you money. They're also a great stopgap if you're still waiting for personalized notes when gifts start arriving, and these days, many beautiful cards are available, often in top-quality paper. If you don't want to give up on the idea of personalized thank-you notes, buy blank notes in ecru or a color tied to your wedding and decorate them with rubber stamps, or glue a small thumbnail-size photograph to the front.

If you're going to be changing your name, thank-you notes sent out before the wedding cannot yet reflect your new, married name. So if you want to go formal and have cards that read Mrs. Brad Jones, Mr. and Mrs. Brad Jones, or Anna and Brad Jones, you'll only be able to send them out *after* the wedding. The same goes for monograms.

In general, the woman's name goes first, so the cards would read "Anna and Brad." Or you could use initials in a format like A+B or A&B. If you want something intricate, have a calligrapher or custom stationer create a design, and use it throughout your wedding.

Whether they're custom or boxed, you should have some individual notes. These are used for shower gifts to thank attendants, and for notes that are clearly from only one of you.

Some of the most personal and charming notes use images instead of initials or names. If a couple carries a motif (called a dingbat in stationery terms) like a palm tree, sand pail, pineapple, or orchid throughout their wedding, they can continue it right through their thank-you notes; your best bet for this is to use letterpress printing on cotton rag paper. You might also choose to use a photo of you and the groom—with so many quick-printing options online, it's a snap. Try black-and-white printing on paper with hand-torn edges for a vintage look.

Gift Received Cards

CARDS THAT TELL PEOPLE you've received the gift and will send a note later ("gift received cards" or "gift acknowledgment cards") may have had their place in the era of three-month honeymoons. In this day and age, they strike me as a cop-out. They don't take the place of thank-you notes and may only serve as an enabler if you're tempted to delay the task. Avoid them whenever possible.

Writing the Notes

The most important point of thank-you note etiquette is that notes must be written by hand. Email is too casual and easy to dash off, so it doesn't give your gratitude enough weight. The recipient might suspect that you were copying and pasting the note, changing a few details along the way.

Your goal is to make your notes sound warm and personal. Four or five sentences will suffice for all but your very closest friends and family members. In those sentences you want to:

- Thank the guest for the gift.

- Describe how you'll use it. If you're not sure, put your imagination to work. For a hand-painted ceramic soup tureen, you might say: "It will look terrific on our table for our first Thanksgiving dinner." Avoid vague, all-purpose phrases such as "Thanks for the great gift. It's sure to come in handy." It should be clear that you couldn't possibly be describing any gift other than theirs.

- State how lovely it was or will be to see them at the wedding. If they were unable to attend but still sent a gift, express how sorry you were that they weren't able to be there. If they did attend, add a personal observation—a compliment about how they looked, how beautifully they danced the samba, or their joke that had the whole table in stitches.

- Make a reference to a future visit or get-together, and if you can tie it back to the gift, so much the better: "We look forward to having you over for cocktails soon and putting that gorgeous martini shaker to work."

If you didn't like the gift and feel dishonest describing it in glowing detail, devote more space to how happy you were to connect at the wedding and less to the gift itself. This is the time for creative writing—but in my opinion, a little white lie never hurts.

> "Thank You" or "Thanks" should never be preprinted on a thank-you note. It's important to show that you've put some care and time into making it personal to the gift and the giver—so you should be expressing your gratitude in the actual note, not relying on a preprinted message.

Who Signs?

Old-school etiquette required that only one person, the author, sign the note. Today, couples often choose to sign both of their names to a note. It's your call; having one person sign is certainly time efficient, and it makes it easier to include personal memories that might pertain to only one of you. If you have a dual signature at the bottom, your note should be written in the first person plural, as in: "We were delighted that you were able to share our special day with us." Should you wish to make a reference to a past experience that did not include your spouse, though, this can lead to a grammatical quagmire. It's so much easier to be able to say: "It will remind me of all of those espressos we used to down at the Rathskeller while studying for finals."

Notes responding to personal gifts (such as shower gifts) should be signed by one person only.

Signing your first name is usually sufficient for a wedding gift, but if the names on the stationery (maybe you used a monogram or a symbol) don't make it absolutely clear who wrote it, then sign your last name as well.

Envelope Etiquette

Just as the thank-you notes should be handwritten, the envelopes should be addressed by hand. Although it's tempting to print off a batch of labels, the envelope is the first thing the recipient will see, and a label comes across as impersonal. You want a thank-you note, above all, to be as personal as possible. If time prohibits handwriting, at least make sure to use clear labels and print them in an interesting font and color.

The return address, however, can be preprinted on the back flap. Envelopes with preprinted addresses are a time-saver, but you must pay extra for the convenience.

A note about stamps: Thank-you notes typically require standard postage, but if yours are oversize, square, or an unusual shape, have them weighed at the post office to be certain you're affixing the correct amount. And go the extra mile by choosing a special stamp.

Getting the Job Done

Writing thank-you notes is a big job, so approach it as you would any project at work. Set aside time for it, break the task into manageable chunks, and reward yourself for milestone goals you meet along the way. And let's not forget the most effective strategy of all: delegating. In this day and age, there's no reason for the bride to carry the burden of writing the thank-you notes alone. If you are both receiving gifts, you can both write thank-yous. Divvying up the list

according to his side and her side makes the most sense. For joint friends, you can randomly split the list in half.

I know that distractions abound, so here are some strategies for even the most die-hard procrastinators:

- ▣ Choose notes you're excited about using. If there's a special pen you've been hankering for, treat yourself to it.

- ▣ Don't let yourself get behind. Keep up with the thank-you notes as gifts come in. It's easy to find the resources to write one, two, or five notes. Once you're looking at twenty-five to thirty, the project becomes a lot harder to face. It's also easier to write the notes when the gift is fresh in your mind.

- ▣ Keep scrupulous lists of who gave you what. (See page 63.) Without them, writing thank-yous can become a Byzantine process involving detective work, numerous phone calls, and pleas for discreet inquiries by parents and friends.

- ▣ Keep everything you need for thank-yous in one place so that you can start each writing session without preamble. If you have to find the list or the stamps, you may get diverted, and before you know it, you're watching a *Sex and the City* rerun (and no, the stamps aren't lurking under the television set).

- ▣ If you get behind on your notes, prioritize them. Notes to older relatives should be at the top of your list. Give high priority to people you have to face every day—colleagues, professional acquaintances, and so on. Close friends and relatives will probably be more understanding of a delay.

While I've urged you to get the thank-you notes done as quickly as possible, I draw the line at one place: the honeymoon. I've known brides who brought their thank-you notes to Hawaii with them or I wouldn't be mentioning this possibility. The two of you need your special time together—it's one of the only times in your life when you'll be this free of the constraints of the real world. If you're a type A personality with a complex about getting them done, you may work on the notes on the plane, but then put them away till you get home.

Sample Thank-You Notes

> *Though thank-you notes should be personal, they tend to conform to a certain rhythm. Take a look at the following examples for inspiration. Note: When you're using a couple's first names, the woman's name always precedes the man's. (Use first names if that's what you would use in person.)*

Dear Patricia and Bob,

I was so touched that you were able to fly in from Denver for our wedding. I so enjoyed having a chance to catch up with you, and Brad was delighted to finally meet you. The silver place setting was such a thoughtful and generous gift—we'll be appreciating it at holiday meals for many years to come. I do hope we'll be able to spend one of those holidays together soon.

It was great to see you at the wedding, and thanks again for the wonderful gift.

Love,
Anna

A General Thank-You Note

A Thank-You Note for a Monetary Gift

Dear Lara,

Thank you so much for your generous gift. Brad and I will be putting it toward a down payment on the house we hope to purchase in the next year or two. We both feel so fortunate to have a friend like you with whom we can share this amazing time in our lives. We're thrilled that you'll be coming to the wedding—it really wouldn't be the same without you. Thanks again for your thoughtfulness.

Love,
Anna

A Thank-You Note for a Charitable Donation

Dear Mr. and Mrs. Harris,

Thank you so much for your wonderful donation to the American Heart Association. This charity means a lot to us, and Brad and I try to support its research in whatever way we can.

I was so happy that you were able to share our wedding day with us. It meant a lot to us and to my parents, and it was a joy to watch the two of you take the dance floor by storm. Once again, thank you for your generosity.

Sincerely,
Anna Jones

Dear Carly and Jeremy,

We can't thank you enough for the side-by-side massages you gave us on our honeymoon. We were both so worn out after the wedding and the long trip, and the treat revived us enough to fully enjoy our honeymoon.

We were so sorry that you weren't able to share our wedding day with us in person, but we felt you there in spirit, and we feel fortunate to have friends like you. Thanks again for such a thoughtful gift, and we look forward to getting together soon and sharing wedding photos with you.

Best,
Anna and Brad

A Thank-You Note for an Experiential Gift

Other Thank-Yous

THANK-YOU NOTES aren't reserved for gifts alone. You'll want to thank your attendants for standing by you and making such a big commitment to your wedding. Thank your parents for their contributions, support, and love. Vendors also appreciate it if you write them a note after the wedding, but I know time constraints don't always allow this luxury. If any vendor went out of her way for you, do make a point of writing a note of thanks.

Signing Off

FOR CLOSE FRIENDS and family, don't hesitate to sign "Love" or "With Love." For work friends and friends of your parents, you might feel more comfortable signing off with something less personal. Choices I like include: "Sincerely," "Yours Truly," "Best," "Best Always," and "Fondly."

Thank-You Note Don'ts

What you cannot say or imply in a note:

■ That you received duplicates of the gift.

■ That you're returning or exchanging the gift, unless they already know or it's going to be glaringly obvious.

■ That the gift fell short of your expectations in any way whatsoever.

■ Any mention of money even for a monetary gift; simply allude to the generosity of the gift giver.

And now, dear reader, the moment you've been waiting for. That's right: the dress. Now that's something to be thankful for! ◆

PART III

Making It
Beautiful

CHAPTER SIXTEEN

The Dress

FINDING "THE ONE"

What bride isn't excited to step into six yards of ivory silk and see a version of herself that she has long imagined? Indeed, so much emotion is invested in choosing a wedding dress that the "right" one is often greeted with tears. The bride cries. Her mother cries. Sometimes even the sales associate and the wedding planner cry. The wedding gown

embodies all the beauty of a bride. It's love and hope and promises gathered into satin, lace, ribbons, and ruching. Ancient associations with virginity, purity, and innocence may no longer be denoted by white fabric and a veil, but they're still very much present—even if the bride in question has been living with the groom since college or is walking down the aisle with a noticeable "bump." This dress is the one that transforms a young woman into a princess for a day, a metamorphosis heightened by royal accoutrements such as a tiara and a train.

Brides are so eager to get right down to the business of finding the dress of their dreams that some don't even wait until

they're engaged to start trying them on! But with so much invested in a single dress, both emotionally and financially, the process can become fraught with doubts, tension, and pressure. For most women, this dress will cost more than any other garment they've ever purchased (on average, about $900, but many brides spend several thousand), and even the savviest shoppers will find themselves in territory completely unlike regular retail. Bridal salons turn away customers if they don't have an appointment; samples don't fit when you try them on; and the complex construction of a wedding gown brings with it terminology so obscure it can quickly confuse the nonnative speaker.

Not to worry! It will all come together by the end. If doubt creeps in at any point, remember that this is the dress in which you're going to start the next chapter of your life. And you're going to look spectacular in it.

A Game Plan

You're looking at dress after gorgeous dress. How to know which one is right for you? Start with the most basic considerations: season and location, formality, budget, and body type.

A gown that's perfect in a large church on a Saturday evening probably won't work for an afternoon harborfront wedding in Maine. For the former, you can bring on the satin ballgown, the cathedral train, the beaded bodice. The outdoor wedding in Maine calls for something simpler, like a cotton piqué A-line gown with a colored sash at the waist.

In short, the dress is a direct reflection of the formality of the wedding. And while many of the old rules are outmoded, the bride's dress still sets the standard for everyone else's attire. If she's in a short halter dress, the groom would look far better in a blazer and trousers (or even a linen shirt and tailored pants) than in a tuxedo.

If there are two brides, the only real ___le" is that their degree of formality be matched. Can there be two white, full-length, princess-style gowns at one wedding? Absolutely! If one or both of you prefers the look of tailored suiting, high-end labels like Calvin Klein, Carolina Herrera, or Jil Sander create gorgeously luxe tuxes and dress suits for women.

One of the salesperson's first questions will be about your budget, and it should be one of your first questions, too. No matter the temptation—and it will be *huge*—only try on gowns in your range, keeping in mind that alterations and the veil, shoes, and accessories will add

hundreds of dollars to the cost. So let me say it again: If your budget is $1,200, don't try on $5,000 gowns. You'll be wasting time and setting up a temptation that may be difficult to resist. One thing that helps a lot of women is preshopping. Get an idea of what's available in various price ranges by looking online and at the dresses in editorial layouts in bridal magazines. These give prices, while the ads don't.

As for body type, well . . . let's put that aside for a moment.

Now the goal is to come up with your vision of how you want to look on your wedding day. Some brides want to look like themselves, but many want to step out of their everyday personae and try on something different. Still others have no idea of how they want to look. Play around. One of my brides who did a one-eighty from her everyday look was a well-known pop singer with a punk edge. Many guests expected her to dress the part of a rocker bride, but they couldn't have been more wrong. When she sketched gowns she liked, they were all princess styles. She walked down the aisle in a fairy-tale princess ballgown from Vera Wang.

When you start dress shopping, try on lots and lots; you don't know how a dress will look until you see it on *you*. The dress you love in photos may not flatter you, and a dress that looks like nothing you'd ever wear could turn out to be dazzling. I've urged many brides to try on a dress they didn't look twice at, only for it to turn out to be "the one."

After you've done your initial assessment in the three-way mirror, pay attention to whether the dress feels good on you. No one expects a wedding dress to be as comfy as a tank top and yoga pants, but it shouldn't make you uncomfortable. Notice the weight of the gown and think about whether it's going to feel too heavy after a few hours. When you sit down, does the corset dig into your ribs? Will that strapless bodice stay put when you're kicking up steam on the dance floor? (There's only one way to know for

> If you're getting married in a house of worship, find out about any restrictions on dress before choosing a gown. Some churches and synagogues, for example, don't allow bare shoulders, and some may require the bride to wear a veil.

sure: Try out some moves in the dressing room!) Does the material feel comfortable? If it's already rubbing you the wrong way, it's going to be torture after a few hours. Likewise, you don't want to feel self-conscious. So, trust me on this one: Even if your ceremony is taking place at a beach, your dress shouldn't be too revealing or overtly sexy. You can look fantastic without peekaboo cutouts at the waist or décolletage down to you-know-where. You want your guests to be talking about you, not your booty.

Finally, when you look in the mirror, what do you see first? If it's the dress, not you, then keep shopping. You, not the dress, should be front and center on your wedding day.

The Perfect Proportion

Professional stylists can cite you chapter and verse about body types, silhouettes, necklines, and fabrics. But even the rules and guidelines that work can become overwhelming, especially to those not schooled in the laws of fashion.

Take heart: Dressing your body to perfection isn't a mystery process. It's simply a game of proportion, and a very simple one at that. You use lines and light to accentuate the things you want to play up. Don't fret about the less-than-perfect aspects of your body; if you follow my strategy, they will naturally recede. Wear a halter gown and direct everyone's eyes to your beautiful shoulders and not to your ample hips. A shorter bride can wear a dress with princess lines and vertical seaming to elongate her silhouette.

Here, in a nutshell, is all you need to know about lines. A horizontal line will make you look wider at the point where it hits. A vertical line elongates. Diagonals cut the width and move the eye to another part of the body. That's why a V-neck is so slimming. It's that simple.

Most women—and that would be 99.9999 percent of us—want to appear taller and thinner, so look for lines and proportions that get you to that goal. If your body isn't evenly proportioned—and that would describe 99.9999 percent of us—compensate! Someone with short legs can elongate her lower half by choosing an empire gown. Conversely, a woman with a short waist can balance her shape by choosing a dropped-waist gown.

If this is all new to you, educate yourself by looking at photos of wedding dresses in bridal magazines or on websites. Figure out where your eye goes first, then see how the lines of the dress direct you there. Once you've got these basics down, you can generalize the rules to find a dress that will flatter your shape.

ASK MINDY

Q My mom really, really wants to go shopping with me for my dress, but so do my sister and my college roommate. And now my fiancé's mother has started hinting that since she doesn't have any daughters of her own, it would be "so much fun" if she came along, too. Frankly, I don't trust any of them when it comes to taste, and I just can't picture the five of us traipsing around town together. What to do?

A I once heard Vera Wang say that she tells brides to come to her alone. Now that may be a little drastic, but the last thing you need while you're trying on dresses is a chorus of know-it-alls backing you into a corner. Too many opinions will just leave you confused and exhausted. But you'll undoubtedly want to share the experience with someone close to you, plus you will want a second opinion. Bring your mother and your maid of honor, if she's going to be responsible for bustling your gown. Let everyone else know that salespeople find it a nuisance when more than one or two people come along. Include your fiancé's mother for a tasting or to look at flowers. And email the rest of them links to photos of some dress options to make them feel involved.

Basic Silhouettes

No matter which way the wind of style blows, certain classic shapes remain constant in the world of wedding gowns.

1. A-line
Slim on top, fitted through the waist, and softly flaring away from the body

2. Ballerina
Traditionally thought of as a length rather than a silhouette

3. Ballgown
A boned bodice and full skirt supported by crinolines

Necklines
When choosing necklines, keep your face shape, bust size, and sense of modesty in mind.

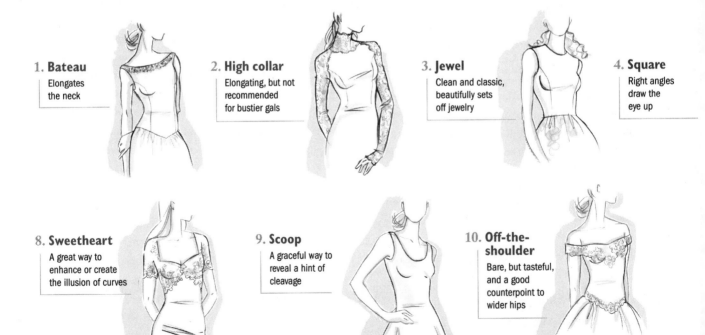

1. Bateau
Elongates the neck

2. High collar
Elongating, but not recommended for bustier gals

3. Jewel
Clean and classic, beautifully sets off jewelry

4. Square
Right angles draw the eye up

8. Sweetheart
A great way to enhance or create the illusion of curves

9. Scoop
A graceful way to reveal a hint of cleavage

10. Off-the-shoulder
Bare, but tasteful, and a good counterpoint to wider hips

4. Empire

A high waist hitting just under the bustline

5. Mermaid

Hugs the torso, then flares out from the knee or just below; great for the short-waisted

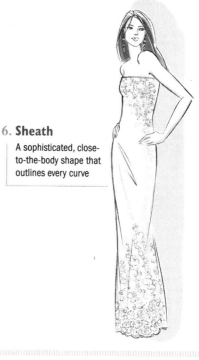

6. Sheath

A sophisticated, close-to-the-body shape that outlines every curve

5. V-neck

A streamlined, lengthening style

6. Halter

Breezy and playful—beach wedding, anyone?

7. Portrait

Somewhere between a bateau and a full off-the-shoulder line

11. Asymmetric

A sophisticated option for the small-to medium-busted

12. Strapless

Flattering to a range of body types

13. Spaghetti strap

Thin straps flatter slender frames and narrow shoulders

Waistlines

Though you'll know from experience which waistline flatters you best, some of these may be new to you.

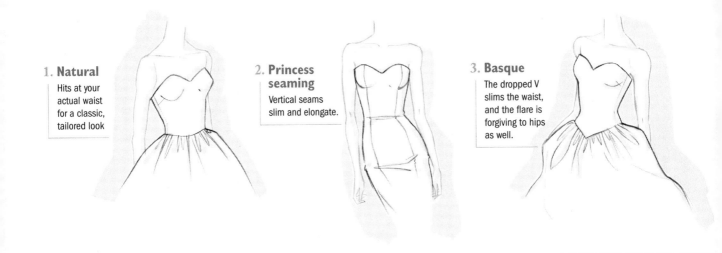

1. Natural

Hits at your actual waist for a classic, tailored look

2. Princess seaming

Vertical seams slim and elongate.

3. Basque

The dropped V slims the waist, and the flare is forgiving to hips as well.

Sleeves

Sleeve shape can dramatically alter the style of a dress, no matter the silhouette.

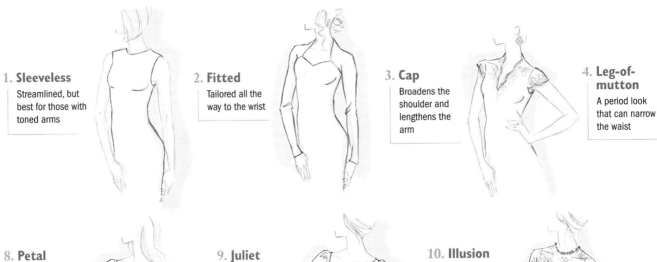

1. Sleeveless

Streamlined, but best for those with toned arms

2. Fitted

Tailored all the way to the wrist

3. Cap

Broadens the shoulder and lengthens the arm

4. Leg-of-mutton

A period look that can narrow the waist

8. Petal

A sweet detail that's lovely on a very simple dress

9. Juliet

A period look for the over-the-top romantic

10. Illusion

Sheer stretch fabric; not a great choice for heavier arms

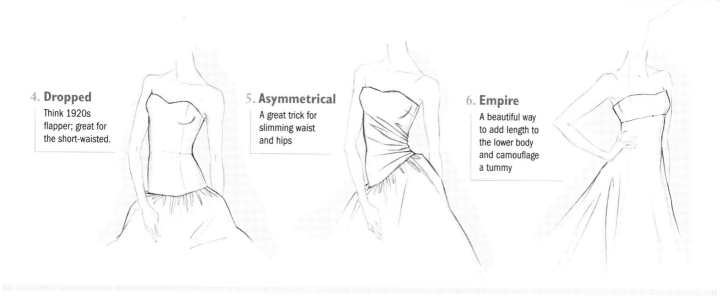

4. Dropped
Think 1920s flapper; great for the short-waisted.

5. Asymmetrical
A great trick for slimming waist and hips

6. Empire
A beautiful way to add length to the lower body and camouflage a tummy

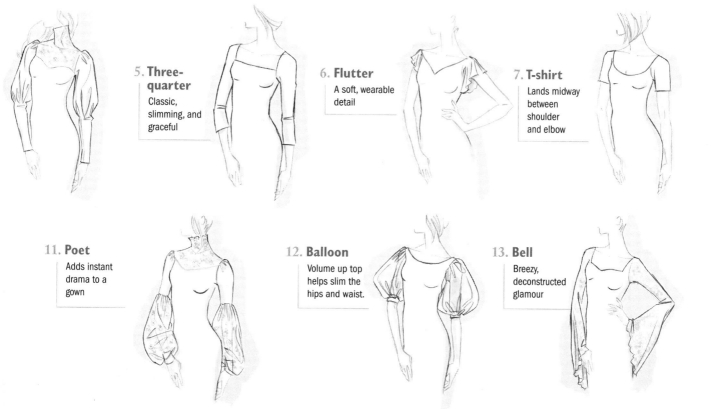

5. Three-quarter
Classic, slimming, and graceful

6. Flutter
A soft, wearable detail

7. T-shirt
Lands midway between shoulder and elbow

11. Poet
Adds instant drama to a gown

12. Balloon
Volume up top helps slim the hips and waist.

13. Bell
Breezy, deconstructed glamour

All About Figures

First off, here's what every bride-to-be should know: The most universally flattering shape is the A-line. It flares away from the hips, a typical problem area; it's kind to the tummy; and it's available in a wide array of styles.

The A-line is a particularly great choice on a pear shape, where the hips are wider than the bust. For more drama, a ballgown will have a similar effect. On the upper body, a full sleeve with a lot of volume around the upper arms (a Juliet sleeve or petal sleeve) can also help balance proportions.

If you're top-heavy and narrower on the bottom, a mermaid or sheath can show off your line to great advantage, provided the top has enough support. Ballgowns play more of a camouflage game, balancing out the top with volume at the bottom. If you feel like your chest is taking over the picture, try a dropped waist to create more space on top; that's also a good choice for the short-waisted. If you're long-waisted with short legs, you'll want to do the opposite—raise the neckline—so an Empire waist is a good choice for you. If a protruding tummy is your sore spot, try an asymmetrical cut, basque waists, curved seaming, and corset bodices. A raised waistline—that Empire waist again—can also help you skirt the issue.

Special Considerations

These days, it's not so unusual to see a bride coming down the aisle with a noticeable bump—and what of it? Times have changed. But since a pregnant body leads to its own set of aesthetic considerations, you'll find some tips for graceful dressing below. As for second-time brides, the "bump" isn't a physical one, but an emotional one. There may be a voice inside of you wondering, *What will people think?* Put those worries to rest and read on.

DRESSING FOR TWO

The Empire waist is the best friend of the pregnant bride. It's forgiving to an expanding belly and shows off a newly lush bustline. An A-line silhouette is also a good bet, though it tends to favor those in the first four to five months of pregnancy.

Stay away from extremely fitted styles, as your shape can change drastically in a few weeks. Fluid fabrics or those with some stretch to them are better bets than stiff, heavy materials. You're likely to feel warmer than usual when pregnant, so avoid long sleeves, heavy satin, and anything else that can make you too hot.

Whether or not you need a maternity gown will depend on how far along you are by the wedding date.

Several designers offer maternity sizes, and most bridesmaids' manufacturers make maternity styles. Order one in ivory and wear it as a wedding dress. Wait as long as possible to buy the dress and push alterations to the last few weeks so that it will fit on your wedding day.

STYLES FOR SECOND-TIME BRIDES

So it's not your first trip down the aisle. That used to put traditional bridal gowns off-limits, but no more. Can you wear white? Absolutely! You can even wear a veil if you choose, but skip the blusher (see page 212), which is closely associated with innocence. If veils aren't your style, find a small tiara, or put jeweled pins or fresh flowers in your

hair. A long train can seem overdone for a second marriage, and some etiquette experts maintain that any train is improper. But if your dream dress involves a train, get a train. Just limit it to a short train, like a puddle or fishtail (see page 209).

The one unbreakable rule is that you must wear something that's appropriate to your age. If you're the other side of forty, the strapless white tulle ballgown might not work on you. Still, there are many sophisticated styles you can pull off that your twenty-four-year-old counterpart cannot. (Think Jackie O. sheath or an impeccable white button-down shirt tucked into a lush ballgown skirt.)

Simple styles are a good bet if you've got an athlete's build (straight-up-and-down, with little indent at the waist); you'll probably find that you have a hard time carrying off anything too flouncy. If you want to create curves, look for styles with draping or a **V** at the waist—seaming or overskirts can do the trick. Up top, off-the-shoulder necklines can increase the differential between bodice and waist, making the waist appear smaller.

If you're a plus size, focus on your proportion and best features. Make sure that the style of the gown allows you to wear undergarments that provide support. Sheer tulle or lace overlays create movement and prevent too much attention from settling on any single body part.

No matter what your size and shape, don't forget the back of your gown. That's what all of your guests will be looking at while you're standing at the altar, and it offers just as much opportunity for drama as the front. You can even accessorize a draped or plunging back with a long necklace or a brooch pinned to the small of the back.

A Vision in "White"

There was a time when white symbolized purity and virginity (and wealth, since a white dress can be worn only a few times before it needs a cleaning). Today, third-time brides wear white, pregnant brides wear white, and brides whose children serve as attendants wear white. If white is what you want (though it's entirely appropriate to wear another color), go for it. Just know that white rarely means true white, since almost everyone looks better in ivory than in dead white. In general, beware of any shade of white that's too yellow, as it will cast your skin in a yellow glow, and few of us can risk looking sallow.

A note on lighting: The best stores take care with their lighting, knowing how important slight variations in hue can be. If that's not the case where you're shopping, bring a swatch of pure white with you. Holding it up to the dress you're trying on will give you a better idea of the actual color.

Beyond the White Dress

More and more brides consider white too predictable and choose to express themselves by wearing color down the aisle, whether it's pink, pale blue, silver, gold, or soft green. Even more opt for an ivory gown with a colored sash, embroidery, or a band of color at the bodice or hem.

But beyond that, who says you have to choose a dress? If you can't picture yourself in a long gown to save your life, there's no need to don one for your wedding. (Do yourself a favor, though, and try one on—a dream dress may be lurking in your subconscious.)

If you wear pants all the time, consider flowing pants with an off-the-shoulder top. (Take inspiration from Bianca Jagger, who wore an Yves Saint Laurent trouser suit when she married Mick Jagger.) If suits are the only thing you feel comfortable in, then find a wonderful Chanel or Armani suit for the day. There's plenty of precedent on your side: Until recent years, suits were a common choice for daytime weddings, as women were inspired by celebrities like Lauren Bacall, Marilyn Monroe, and Mia Farrow.

Though every designer names her colors differently, here are some general guidelines:

White. Stark white is a tricky shade to pull off, though it can be extremely flattering to women with cool undertones. (Not sure if that describes you? If you tend to look better in silver than gold and in colors like hot pink, blue, purple, and bluish reds, it probably does.) If you have pale skin or a yellow undertone, stay away from stark white and know that white fabric with a sheen to it looks even starker.

Ivory. A creamier shade of white, it's flattering to most women. Ivory warms up your skin and is an especially good choice for women with pale skin. There are many variations of ivory (also called eggshell); some venture into yellow territory, so try on several shades to get an idea which looks best on you.

Candlelight or champagne. Usually creamier than ivory, this color can look downright beige, depending on the designer. It's best on women with warm undertones (you look better in gold than silver, and great in coral and orangey reds), and it can look great on both pale and olive skin. Its flattering glow and sophistication also make it an excellent choice for older brides.

Pale pink or rum. Depending on the designer, this can mean white with a pink cast or a pale pink. It can be flattering on nearly everyone, though women with very olive skin tones may have a tough time finding the right balance.

Fabrics

The choice of fabric determines the shape, texture, and sheen of the dress—whether it's stiff or fluid, smooth or slubbed, lustrous or matte—and is critical to both your comfort and the price of the gown. Unless you're looking at hand-done embroidery, beading, or lace, fabric is nearly always the most costly element, so choose wisely.

All fabrics, even high-end materials like silk, vary in quality. Finer fabrics typically drape better, feel softer, and look less shiny, but you don't need to become a fabric expert to shop for a wedding dress. If you pay attention to the way a dress looks, feels, and drapes on you, it won't be long before you can spot the difference between a top-quality Italian silk and a less-expensive version from China.

You'll want to assess the wrinkle factor as well. To get an idea of how a fabric will hold up, gather a handful and squeeze it in your fist for five seconds. Release it and assess the damage. If you're a perfectionist, you won't like a fabric that looks rumpled.

One technical aspect of fabric you should know about is the difference between fibers and synthetic weaves. Silk is a natural fiber; satin, a weave, can be made of silk, polyester, or a blend. Surprisingly, you could be better off with an excellent-quality silk-and-polyester blend than with a poor-quality silk. A good synthetic blend—you'll know it's "good" by the way

One Gown or Two?

It's not uncommon for celebrities and brides with big-budget weddings to opt for two dresses, one for the ceremony and another for the reception. We can all understand the attraction—what girl wouldn't love wearing two dream dresses? But I think for most brides it's not the savviest choice. One dress is special; two dresses dilute the effect. Besides, a wedding gown is an expensive proposition; instead of fragmenting the budget, channel more money into the single dress or use it for something that will have a payoff for guests—provide transportation from the hotel to the wedding, for instance.

There's also the question of a second dress for the after-party. Brides who have planned a late-night lounge atmosphere often want a cocktail dress to change into, and that's fine, as long as it's within your budget. Choose something you love that you can wear again, but keep it in the cocktail dress price range.

To change your look without springing for two outfits, cover your shoulders with a wonderful shrug or jacket during the ceremony and ditch it for the reception, or opt for a detachable train.

it feels to the touch—can be the best choice for a destination wedding (or any wedding for which you have to pack your dress), since it will wrinkle less than an all-natural fiber. That said, since natural fibers breathe better and keep you cooler, you should stay away from synthetics if you're getting married in warm weather.

Silk has long been the preferred fabric for brides. It's luxurious and elegant, to be sure, but driving its popularity for much of its reign is the fact that it takes dyes well. Not until the last century did the wedding gown become institutionalized as a one-time-only dress; until then, it was standard for brides to turn their wedding dress into their "best dress." Wealthy newlyweds would send their wedding gowns to a dressmaker to have it restyled and dyed another color.

Among silk fabrics, none is more closely associated with brides than silk satin, a trend started by Queen Victoria at her 1840 wedding. Although high-quality satin is gorgeous and sumptuous, I find it overrated in many regards. It is a very difficult material to work with—it shows every pinhole—and can be difficult to clean. It also wrinkles. If you've ever watched a celebrity in a satin gown at a red-carpet event, you must have noticed the creases across her midsection when she stood up to accept her award. Moreover, though satin can be ravishingly beautiful at the high end, at the low end it can look really cheesy (think bad tablecloth or satin sheets). As a rule of thumb, the cheaper the satin, the shinier. So before you automatically gravitate to satin at the salon, consider some alternatives that might serve you better.

A Glossary of Fabrics

THE FOLLOWING DEFINITIONS will help you hold your own at a bridal salon and will be especially handy if you're having a gown designed from scratch.

Brocade. A heavy fabric woven to create a multitone pattern, brocade was worn by royal brides for centuries. Damask, or Jacquard, is a lightweight alternative.

Charmeuse. A lightweight satin identified with the slinky gowns of 1930s luminaries like Jean Harlow, charmeuse is the material of choice in lingerie and nightgowns. In formal gowns, it tends to be cut on the bias.

Chiffon or georgette. Sheer, lightweight, and fluid, chiffon can be a great choice for an outdoor wedding.

Crepe. Thin and lightweight, crepe is characterized by its pebbled texture. Bridal varieties are usually made of silk, but crepe can also be made of wool.

Double-faced satin. Heavyweight, with a sheen to both sides, double-faced satin is used for structured styles. It tends to be a high-end, couture fabric.

Douppioni silk. Often on the less expensive end of silk varieties, this textured silk (which sometimes naturally sports a wavy pattern) can be a good choice if you're on a budget. Since it's available in so many colors, it's a popular choice for both brides and bridesmaids.

Duchess satin. Though it can be affordable, this is the satin often favored by high-end designers. Characterized by a quiet luster, it can be made of silk, rayon, or a blend.

Faille. This finely ribbed silk or rayon blend tends to appear in couture and structured styles. Its quiet sheen also makes it a festive choice for bridesmaids' dresses.

Illusion. A sheer, mesh fabric with stretch, illusion is often used for sleeves or to fill in a bodice.

Organza. This semisheer, stiffer fabric holds a lot of shape, so it's usually used in structured styles, like full skirts or overlays.

Peau de soie. This heavyweight satin appears most commonly on shoes and handbags, but it's also used in high-end gowns.

Shantung. Like a lightweight version of douppioni with a light-catching glimmer to it, shantung has a nubby, irregular texture. It still has a fair amount of hold to it, so it tends to be used for more structured styles.

Taffeta. A crisp and lustrous fabric with a trademark rustle, taffeta is usually woven of silk or polyester. It can either be draped or structured and tends to wrinkle easily.

Tulle. A fine netting, tulle is the material that ballerinas' skirts are made of. Though the silk variety is softer than the polyester kind, it's still rough on the skin and necessitates petticoats or slips. (Beware: If tulle is in direct contact with hosiery, the hose will shred—not the tulle—in minutes.)

Velvet, burnout, panne. Though all three are forms of velvet, what's commonly called velvet is the stiffer material. Burnout is a pattern created by burning out the pile with chemicals, so you get a brocaded effect and a thinner, more drapeable material. Panne is a supple, glossy version in which the pile is flattened in one direction.

The Romance of Lace

Good lace is the product of true craftsmanship, and its styles are heavily influenced by region.

1. Alençon

A delicate needlepoint lace featuring solid motifs on sheer netting

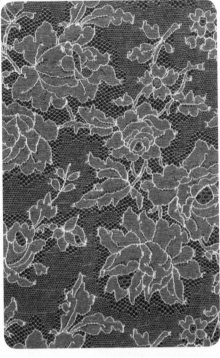

2. Chantilly

A fine mesh with delicate botanical motifs, it was reputed to be Marie Antoinette's favorite. Its edges are often scalloped.

3. Duchesse

A very fine bobbin lace with heavy, raised floral motifs

4. Honiton

This English lace's floral and leaf pieces are bound together by small braids.

5. Guipure

A heavier, sculptural lace that features large patterns in needlepoint or bobbin

6. Venise

Heavy raised floral, foliage, or geometric designs give this lace its trademark chunkiness. The designs are joined by connecting threads called "brides."

7. Schiffli

This machine-made lace has delicate floral embroidery. Designs can vary greatly.

SIGNS OF QUALITY

Before making a decision based purely on the look of a gown, you should also evaluate its quality. Use the following checklist to determine if a particular dress is well made.

- Seams are neat and even and lie flat.

- Embellishments are sewn on, not glued. Beads, sequins, and pearls are sewn on individually, not in strands.

- Crystals are clear all the way through. (Rhinestones have a dark backing and can appear black in photos.)

- The dress is properly lined, so that a scratchy crinoline isn't touching bare skin.

- Zippers are hidden and glide smoothly.

- The inside of the dress looks completely finished, with no raw seams.

- Fabric is matte or lustrous, but not shiny.

- With a structured gown, the corset should be built in and boned; if it's strapless, the boning should run the length of the bodice.

- A ballgown hem should be lined with horsehair so it appears to be rolled under instead of stitched—this gives body and structure to the skirt.

- Buttons are operable, not just sewn on top of a zipper. Buttonholes are cleanly finished; at the high end, they're hand-bound to create a frame around the opening.

- The dress feels great when you put it on.

Lace

TREASURED BY BRIDES for its delicacy and beauty, lace has long been associated with weddings. Because all lace was handmade until the nineteenth century, it was costly, and the amount of lace worn by a bride symbolized her wealth and social standing—so much so that more than a hundred lace makers reportedly worked for six months to produce the lace on Queen Victoria's dress and veil.

There are so many styles of lace, from fragile Chantilly to crunchy guipure, and each has its own look. The one characteristic all lace shares is that it's romantic. Though some brides write it off as old-fashioned, it certainly doesn't have to be. Sure, a bride in long lace sleeves and a high collar looks more Victorian than Queen Victoria herself, but a lace plunge halter gown is another story altogether.

Good lace is still expensive. (The best comes from Europe.) Since it's made on narrow looms, price per yard isn't necessarily a good indicator of cost. If you can't afford beautiful lace, I urge you to stay away from it altogether. There's nothing good about bad lace—in fact, it can cheapen your whole outfit. Many people will notice shiny, tacky lace, but not one person will say: "I can't believe she's not wearing any lace."

Embellishments

Some brides adamantly want their gowns stark and simple, and others go for all the trimmings. Beading and embroidery *can* add richness and glamour, but they can also detract from a dress when done poorly. If you don't have the budget for quality embellishments, skip them in favor of a gorgeous fabric or add embellishment via the veil.

If you're looking for a dress with beading, make sure the beads are sewn on individually. If they're just strung together and tacked on, it's a disaster waiting to happen.

(Don't know what I'm talking about? Close your eyes. Picture your wedding day. Hear the processional start. Then imagine snagging that string of beads just as you begin to walk down the aisle. Need I say more?) To add interest without the glimmer, embroidery or appliqués can be beautiful alternatives.

Dressmaker touches like pleating, lacing, and ruffles can also add texture and detail. Trapunto stitching, done on the underside of the fabric, creates a raised but seamless design. Ruching, a technique that produces gathers, can be used to highlight décolletage or to add texture. Pickups gather the material in bunches to create a bustle-like effect that brings in a lot of movement.

Employ embellishments strategically to direct the eye where you want it to go. If you have beautiful shoulders, beading along the upper edge of the bodice or straps will help draw attention to them. Embroidery on the bodice lures eyes up, away from the hips and thighs.

Trains

For royalty, trains have been de rigueur since the Middle Ages. Outside of childhood dress-up, the walk down the aisle might be the only chance the rest of us get to don this regal accoutrement. If, that is, you choose to wear a train at all.

You may think that the time of day and the formality of the wedding will determine the length of your train. You're right to the extent that there are "rules" regulating what is "done," but I certainly don't think you need to follow them to the letter. What's important is that you choose a train that suits you and your location.

Dragging on the ground as they do, trains are not terribly compatible with outdoor weddings—from both a practical and aesthetic standpoint—though a short train is fine, as long as you're using an aisle runner. Another consideration is the length of the aisle. Let me tell you—if the aisle is short, your train may be at the back of the church while you're at the altar. Not good! There's a reason it's called a cathedral train. A long train also means

that you'll need attendants (either bridesmaids or pages) to help manage it, so if you've chosen not to have attendants, don't go ordering a twelve-foot train.

Finally, think about the train in proportion to your body. If you're petite, you could be swallowed up by a long satin train. Opt instead for one that's shorter and made of a lighter fabric such as organza, lace, netting, or silk charmeuse.

Bustling a Gown

If your train isn't detachable, the alterations staff will design a bustle for you at one of your fittings. There are many creative variations on bustling, but the dominant styles are a standard bustle and a French bustle. A standard bustle is hooked, looped, or buttoned to rest on top of the skirt. A French bustle is looped under the skirt, creating a cleaner look; it's more intricate, and you'll need a patient bridesmaid to help you with it, but it's more flattering and holds up better than a basic hook. With a standard bustle, have the hooks reinforced to hold better. I've often seen them tear when someone steps on the bride's skirt as they're coming up to congratulate her.

A standard bustle

A French bustle

Trains

What kind of train do you see yourself in? (And will it suit your location?)

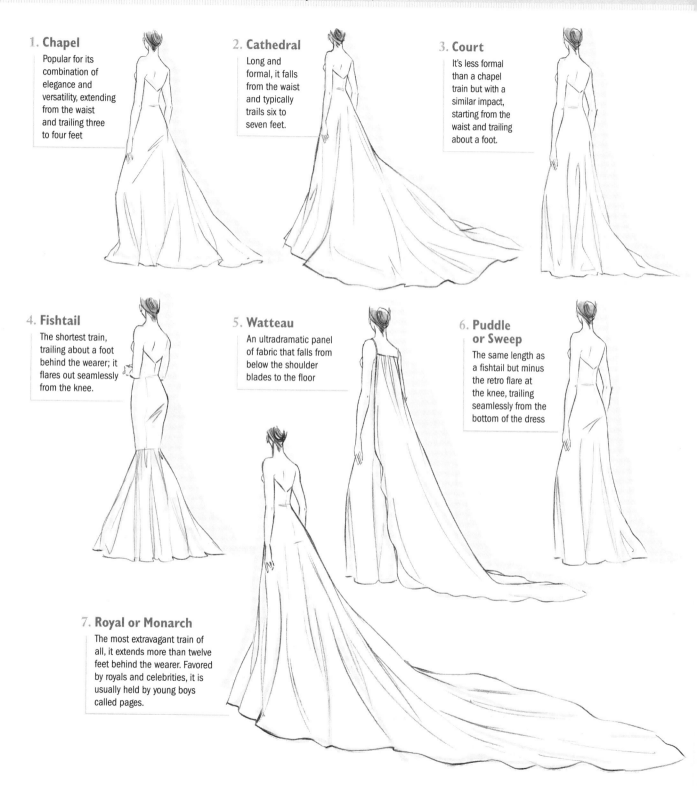

1. Chapel

Popular for its combination of elegance and versatility, extending from the waist and trailing three to four feet

2. Cathedral

Long and formal, it falls from the waist and typically trails six to seven feet.

3. Court

It's less formal than a chapel train but with a similar impact, starting from the waist and trailing about a foot.

4. Fishtail

The shortest train, trailing about a foot behind the wearer; it flares out seamlessly from the knee.

5. Watteau

An ultradramatic panel of fabric that falls from below the shoulder blades to the floor

6. Puddle or Sweep

The same length as a fishtail but minus the retro flare at the knee, trailing seamlessly from the bottom of the dress

7. Royal or Monarch

The most extravagant train of all, it extends more than twelve feet behind the wearer. Favored by royals and celebrities, it is usually held by young boys called pages.

After the ceremony, the train is bustled or detached so it won't get in the way at the reception. Some trains can also be looped over your finger (but this isn't the most convenient option), attached at the waist via buttons or hooks, or designed as separate overskirts that you remove for the reception.

If you love the look of a train but find it too cumbersome, you can create the same effect with a long veil that trails behind you as you walk down the aisle. After the ceremony, you simply remove the veil—no bustling involved.

Dollars and Sense

If the gowns you love are all beyond your budget, you may simply be trying on styles that are expensive to produce. Focus on less costly styles to bring down the price.

■ Ballgowns require more fabric than slender silhouettes, so they cost more. If you're on a budget, look for a narrower silhouette.

■ Trains mean additional fabric, which means additional cost. If the train is scalloped, embroidered, or beaded, that adds even more to the price tag. Bypass a train to bring down the price. (You can always wear a long veil.)

■ A heavily constructed gown (the kind that stands up by itself) costs more to make than a gown without built-in boning, corsets, and multiple layers of lining and fabric.

■ Any type of handwork, from beading to pickups, adds to the price. Look for dresses without embellishment.

■ Lace is expensive and ups the price of a dress. Stick to lace trim or skip the lace altogether.

■ Try on separates to get a better fit without so many costly alterations.

Veils

The father of the bride raises the blusher of his daughter's veil and kisses her "good-bye." The bride and groom look into each other's eyes, as if for the first time. This is the stuff that romance is made of. So, do yourself a favor: Even if you think a veil isn't for you—and they aren't for everyone—try one on, just to make sure. A veil connects a bride to the tradition of marriage. It enhances her beauty, bringing a soft-focus halo of light to her face. And, not to be underestimated, it makes a bride feel, well, *bridal*.

The custom dates back to Greek and Roman times, when veils were thought to protect the bride from evil forces. Then, in Europe, when so many marriages were arranged, they were used to prevent a groom from changing his mind when he saw his bride for the first time—the bride's veil wasn't lifted until the marriage was finalized. In America, the tradition took off when one of George Washington's nephews walked by a window and was enchanted by the vision of a lovely young woman behind a lace curtain. The woman was Nellie Custis, and she donned a lace veil at their wedding to honor the moment their romance began. The Jewish custom of wearing a veil is documented in Genesis, when Rebekah first sees Isaac and covers herself with a veil out of modesty. A veil also leads to perhaps the most famous Biblical wedding mix-up, when Jacob is tricked into marrying Leah instead of Rachel because he can't see under her veil. To this day, in a traditional Jewish ceremony the groom visits the bride before the ceremony to lower the veil over her face (in a ceremony called the *bedeken*), to ensure that he is marrying his intended.

The Right Veil

CHOOSE A VEIL TO complement your gown and face shape and to create a smashing silhouette. Look at the volume, length, and structure of the veil over your dress to determine if you're elongating your body or cutting it off at an awkward point. The bottom edge of a veil is a horizontal line, so you don't want it to end at your widest body part, as it will only emphasize it. (Edging a veil with ribbon further emphasizes this horizontal line.)

The fabrics in the dress and the veil should be compatible. In general, a more structured dress needs a stiffer veil, while a fluid gown looks better with a softer veil with more of a drape. On the other hand, sometimes the contrast is what makes the look. A spare white silk gown paired with a hand-embroidered veil can be a knockout; a voluminous veil can dazzle over a slender column.

Tulle, the fabric most commonly associated with veils, creates a structured, full silhouette; it can be made of silk or nylon, silk being more expensive but also softer and finer. If you want a soft, fluid veil, consider lace or chiffon. Organza veils are somewhere in between: They have structure and body but aren't as stiff as tulle.

Also try to use the veil to balance your face shape. A fuller veil will flatter a narrow face, while an angular face will be softened by a fluid veil. If you have a short forehead, choose a veil and headpiece that add height at the crown. But if you're sensitive about being taller than the groom, go with a flat veil or one that attaches at the back of your head.

How to balance the train and veil? If your gown has a long train, you should either go with a short veil that doesn't touch the floor or a veil that trails several inches beyond the train. You don't want them reaching the same point on the floor, or you'll wind up with a lot of material without definition.

A delicate tiara

Borrowing a veil can save you hundreds of dollars and give you your "something borrowed" at the same time. A recently wed friend or relative is usually the best source. Make sure the veil owner is in a good marriage: Superstition has it that her happiness will rub off on whoever wears her veil.

Headpieces

MOST VEILS NEED to be attached to a headpiece, which can be as simple as a comb or as elaborate as a tiara. (Mantillas are the exception, as they're pinned on.) The veil can be sewn to the headpiece, but if you want to remove it, have it attached via Velcro or loops and hooks. If you're skipping the veil entirely, you can still wear some of this hair jewelry on its own.

Since a comb can be positioned at the top or back of the head, it's the most versatile option, and often the least expensive as well.

Tiaras sit across the top of the head, princess style. They're often used as a showcase for crystals or diamonds but also exist in unadorned versions. The look is similar to that of a crown, though a crown circles all the way around the head, while tiaras go only halfway; a half-crown sits like a tiara but has more height.

For a look that's both regal and ethereal, try a wreath. Usually made of natural materials like flowers or greenery, it wraps around the head like a crown. You can have your florist make a wreath to match your bouquet.

Another option is a headband, covered in fabric similar to that of your dress or embellished with beading, flowers, or jewels. (A backband or backpiece is a straight barrette that fastens onto the back of your head.)

Headpieces have gotten more streamlined over the years, but if you're going for a vintage look or just something different, try a Juliet cap, which fits tightly to the head. Another option, if you're wearing your hair in a bun, is a snood or bun wrap; it fits over the bun, and the veil attaches beneath it.

Now Take That Thing Off!

ALTHOUGH MANY BRIDES can't bear to take off their veils for the reception, I think it's far more elegant to remove it. I promise you, everyone will know you're the bride, veil or no veil.

Veils

A veil may seem like a simple proposition, but there are many styles to choose from. Which one is right for you?

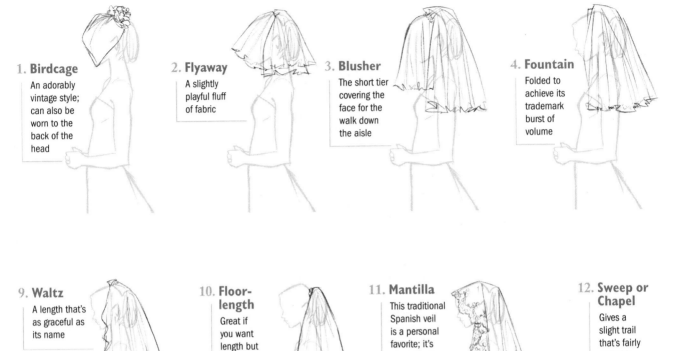

1. Birdcage
An adorably vintage style; can also be worn to the back of the head

2. Flyaway
A slightly playful fluff of fabric

3. Blusher
The short tier covering the face for the walk down the aisle

4. Fountain
Folded to achieve its trademark burst of volume

9. Waltz
A length that's as graceful as its name

10. Floor-length
Great if you want length but fear getting tangled up

11. Mantilla
This traditional Spanish veil is a personal favorite; it's pinned to the crown of the head.

12. Sweep or Chapel
Gives a slight trail that's fairly walkable

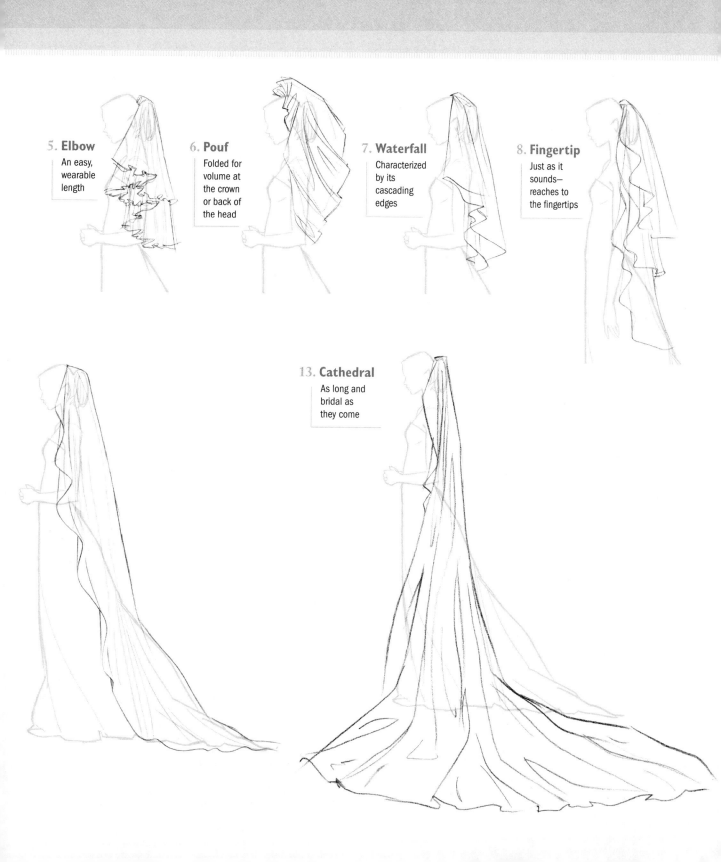

5. Elbow

An easy, wearable length

6. Pouf

Folded for volume at the crown or back of the head

7. Waterfall

Characterized by its cascading edges

8. Fingertip

Just as it sounds— reaches to the fingertips

13. Cathedral

As long and bridal as they come

Make sure your veil is readily detachable from any headpiece you want to wear at the reception. If you're determined to keep your veil on, opt for a breakaway, which allows you to remove the long part and leave a short veil in back. You can bustle a long veil for the reception, but they don't always hold. One compromise is to leave the veil on for the first dance, then take it off.

A Unique Shopping Experience

Shopping for a wedding gown is unlike any other clothing shopping you'll ever do. Most bridal salons don't stock gowns in a variety of sizes—the inventory would be far too expensive—so they keep samples in only one or two sizes. Brides try a dress on, commit to it without ever seeing how it will fit, have their measurements taken, and wait for the designer to cut the gown to order.

Another oddity is that the size of the dress will bear little relation to your regular size. For one thing, bridal gowns run one or two sizes smaller than other clothing. For another, the salon will order the size based on your largest measurement, because it's much easier to take in a dress than to let one out. Once you order, the gown typically takes four to six months to arrive at the salon, though a gown with heavy hand-beading done overseas could take up to ten months. Salons try to schedule it so the gown arrives eight weeks before the wedding, allowing time for multiple fittings.

Bridal shops aren't generally set up for browsing. (A traditional salon will not let you in without an appointment, even if the store is empty.) They cultivate a rarefied atmosphere—chandeliers and Vivaldi on the sound system are more conducive to selling $2,500 ball-gowns than fluorescent lights and Aerosmith—and book appointments so that a sales associate can focus on one bride at a time.

You should ideally start shopping for your gown eight to eleven months before the wedding, but if possible it's best to wait until you have decided on a date and location—these factors will affect your decision.

Shopping Around

YOU MAY HAVE FANTASIZED about walking into one particular bridal salon since you were sixteen years old. Good for you. But if you're like the rest of us and you don't have any stores in mind, start asking friends who recently got married about their experiences with particular stores. Do try to visit three stores. That should be enough to expose you to a range of different designers and to varied opinions from different salespeople. It's not unusual for a bride to fall head over heels in love with the

SHOPPING 101

- Bring pictures of dresses you like. Bring pictures of dresses you don't like. If you like the neckline of one gown and the draped back on another, point out exactly what you do and don't like to the sales associate.

- Wear underwear you won't be embarrassed to be seen in! Trying on wedding dresses is not a solo operation, so this isn't the day to wear a peekaboo thong.

- If you're shopping a sample sale or the Filene's Basement bridal gown sale, wear a body stocking, unitard, or swimsuit under your clothing so you can change in the aisles if necessary.

- Bring a camera. Not every salon will allow you to take photos, but if possible, get a photo of yourself in the dress you're buying, not only for showing your mother (if she's not with you) but also for your florist, cake maker, and other vendors trying to assess the style of your wedding. Remember, the dress sets the tone for the wedding. A photo will also help you when shopping for accessories, though a fabric swatch is important, too.

first dress she tries on, but most people will feel better if they've shopped around a bit before making such a major commitment.

Shoppers have different personalities, and you should take yours into account when deciding where to shop. If you love pawing through racks of clothes in search of a bargain, you'll be in your element at a sample sale or at the Filene's Basement bridal gown sale. But if you abhor that kind of hunt and really value service above all else, then such bargain stores will probably prove a huge waste of time for you.

When making appointments, don't be shy about asking the price range of gowns carried in the store. You want to make sure you're shopping at places that fit your budget. If your budget is really tight, ingenuity can fill in the gap. Try consignment stores, Craigslist, eBay, bridesmaid dresses, or the after-five section in a department store.

Bridal Salons

Offering the highest level of service, bridal salons require a hefty deposit, often 50 percent, when you place your order. On-site alterations and an extensive array of accessories, from tiaras to shoes, are some of the perks you might find. You'll almost always need to make an appointment, and you'll be slotted in for forty-five minutes to an hour. At a high-end salon, a consultant should be assigned exclusively to you. (Bring magazine clippings with you to give her a general sense of your taste.) You'll have to use a certain amount of imagination, since you'll be looking at yourself in sample gowns that don't fit.

Department Stores

For brides outside of urban areas, a department store may offer a better chance of landing a contemporary gown than the mom-and-pop bridal store in town. Department stores are similar to bridal salons in that they often require appointments and 50 percent deposits. Many also offer on-site fittings and alterations.

A Snapshot of Kleinfeld's

Famous as the setting of the show *Say Yes to the Dress* and arguably the single most recognizable bridal salon in the United States, New York City's Kleinfeld's is a bridal salon with 35,000 square feet entirely devoted to bridal gowns, shoes, and accessories. They have a thousand samples, twenty-eight dressing rooms, and seventeen fitting rooms for alterations. A custom-made overhead Railex system that is one city block long stores gowns on order until the bride arrives for fittings, and mirrors and lighting are specially designed to give an accurate view of the dress and its hue. All alterations are done on-site, and specialists will even realign beading after major alterations or add beading to a gown or veil.

Along with the personal attention, a selection of accessories will also come with the territory. Another bonus: If your bridal party is small enough to allow you to shop for bridesmaids dresses off the rack (see page 226), you can make it a one-stop shop.

Single Designer Salons

A designer can either make a gown to order from his collection or create a custom-made dress for you. A custom gown from a big-name designer is very costly, but you might be able to find local designers whose gowns don't cost any more than the ones in a bridal salon. The designer will make sketches for you based on photos you've shown him during your conversations. He'll cut a shape out of muslin and fit it to you before making the actual gown. The fee should include at least three fittings, and you should walk out with a one-of-a-kind gown that fits you flawlessly. The drawback? You won't really get a feel for how the dress will look on you until it's practically finished. And since the process can take several months, it's not a good choice for a bride in a hurry.

> Bridal salons are extremely busy on weekends, especially in the peak shopping months of January through April. If you can shop on a weekday, you'll get an appointment sooner and get more attention.

Vintage Boutiques

Does the thought that other brides might be wearing the same style dress as yours make you cringe? Vintage boutiques, some of which specialize in bridal attire, can be a wonderful way to find one-of-a-kind gowns for a bargain. Sizes have changed a lot through the ages, so you won't be able to judge a dress by its number. (And take care to find a very good tailor, as vintage fabrics are delicate and some vintage cuts don't lend themselves to easy alteration.) Avoid *really* old dresses—the fabric on anything made before the 1920s is too likely to rip.

Consignment Shops

Upscale bridal consignment shops are a growing trend; some are as plush as bridal salons and even feature on-site alterations. They offer brides on a budget a chance at designer labels, with prices 30 to 70 percent below the original retail. Inspect gowns carefully for stains, rips, or cigarette burns before buying. Styles are usually a few seasons old, so your best bet is a fairly classic style that doesn't scream last year. (On the other hand, if you're buying a new designer gown, consider recouping some of your investment by selling it through a consignment shop after the wedding.)

Mass-Market Chains

Bridal chains carry most of their dresses on-site, so you can usually try one on in your size and take it home as soon as the alterations are done. Chains carry more budget-friendly options; appointments are encouraged but not usually required, and sales associates typically

> If you're on a tight budget, check out the bridesmaids' dresses at department stores and bridal salons. Many can be ordered in white. The styles tend to be simpler and less embellished, but that suits plenty of brides perfectly.

help a few brides at once. Alterations may or may not be done on-site and may be limited to basics, such as hems and side seams. They're a great option if you're looking for a dress in a hurry or if you want a fairly simple dress.

Discount Stores

Discount stores primarily carry samples from previous seasons, often selling well-known designer labels at significant markdowns. On-site alterations are a rarity. Dresses may be soiled (though surface dirt at the hem will usually come out in a cleaning). Inspect them carefully, because once you pay for one, it's yours. You won't be able to order alternate sizes—many of the dresses will be samples.

You've got to be a fairly self-sufficient shopper if you're going to go this route, as the degree of personal attention varies greatly. But if you're a savvy shopper, you may walk out with a great bargain.

Sample Sales

If you have your heart set on a particular designer, the sample sale can actually be worth the cost of travel to another city, since gowns from a previous season could be at least 50 percent off. Though some sales are heated free-for-alls, in other cases you might be making an individual appointment with the designer. Most sample sales are held in New York City, once or twice a year; visit the designer's website for sample sale info.

Inspect the dress carefully for damage and for dirt. If it's been worn in a runway show, it will be a little bit dirty but can often be successfully cleaned. You'll have to look elsewhere for alterations and accessories, and all sales are final. Dresses will mostly be in sample sizes.

For shopping mavens, some of the large wedding dress retailers (like Kleinfelds) hold annual warehouse sales. Samples, overstock, and unsold dresses from bridal boutiques are priced at $249 and $499. Labels range from so-so to top of the line. You'll need to be prepared to arrive early and to change in the aisles, but if you excel at competitive shopping—it is not for the faint of heart— you might walk out with a fabulous bargain.

Shopping Online

The web allows you to shop at any hour, but obviously you won't be able to try on the gown until you own it. You can buy online from retail stores like J.Crew and BHLDN (Anthropologie's bridal site), which give you the ability to return and don't involve a deposit; or from individual designers like Joanna August, whose terms and timeline mirror those of traditional bridal salons. Craigslist, eBay, and message boards on sites like theknot.com are good sources for once-worn dresses at a great price. But do some research to make sure you're getting a good deal; it's not uncommon to see sellers asking full retail for a used dress or lying about the original cost. Do an online search for "once-worn bridal gown" to find leads. Make sure you get detailed photos and measurements before buying. And pay with a credit card or via PayPal to have some protection in case the seller doesn't deliver.

Rentals

Not thrilled about the notion of plunking down a significant sum for an item of clothing you'll never wear again? Many brides feel the same, which is why the wedding dress rental business has blossomed in the digital age.

Renting from sites like Get the Gown and Borrowing Magnolia may mean you can afford that haute couture designer you wouldn't have been able to look at otherwise. Rent the Runway features a bridal section that caters to brides looking for simpler, more modern styles at bargain-basement prices, which can make it a great option for rehearsal dinner attire. Several of the sites will send you a backup size for free and/or let you order several dresses at once so you can see which one you like best. As a bonus, renting saves you on the other end as well—cleaning and/or storing a dress (see page 389) are expensive propositions. With a rental, you just pack the dress up in the shipping materials it came with and head off on your honeymoon.

Another option is to buy a "nearly new" dress. The site Nearly Newlywed makes it very easy to purchase their never-worn designer samples and once-worn gowns, and then to relist your purchase for sale once you're ready to pass it along to the next bride.

GET IT IN WRITING

When ordering a dress from a bridal salon, ask for a fabric swatch (it will help you match shoes and accessories) and get the following points in writing.

- [ ] Description of the gown ordered, including the name of the designer and the style number, fabric, size, and color. Any changes that you've requested from the designer should be noted as well.

- [ ] Delivery date.

- [ ] What happens if there's a problem? If the dress doesn't arrive in time, your agreement should state that the salon will refund your deposit.

- [ ] Number of fittings.

- [ ] Estimated alterations fee, deposit amount, amount due, due date for remainder of balance.

- [ ] Cancellation and refund policy.

Not the thrift-shop type? Consider the fact that wedding dresses are a unique breed among used items, as they've generally only been worn a handful of times. The new rental sites pride themselves on featuring immaculate clothing and include guarantes limiting the total number of times a dress can be worn before it is retired.

Scouring the Attic

Wedding gowns were once carefully stored away in hopes that yet-to-be-born daughters would wear them one day. But both body types and dress styles change dramatically from one generation to the next, so it's not all that common to see a bride wearing her mother's gown anymore.

It's a loving sentiment, though, and can be an especially meaningful tribute if the bride's parents have had a long and happy marriage. If your mother's dress isn't quite to your liking, you can take it to a skilled seamstress who may be able to alter the style of the neckline, sleeves, and back, or change the width of the skirt. Those skilled in working with vintage gowns are sometimes able to match lace and other fabrics in the dress to replace stained areas or add more fabric as needed.

Know that though dresses can be taken in, it's almost impossible to let out a dress significantly. Also check for stains, discoloration, fabric deterioration, rips, and any other wear and tear. If either the size or the condition of the dress makes it unwearable as is, think about creative ways to incorporate part of the dress. A good seamstress can remove the lace or some of the fabric and use it to create flutter sleeves for your dress or a jacket for the ceremony. If there are appliqués or beading on the dress, you may be able to salvage them and add them to your bodice. Lace can also be worked into an inset in your train, turned into a veil, or wrapped around your bouquet. If nothing else works, cut out a swatch of fabric and sew it inside your hem or to your petticoats as your "something old." You could also use a length of the fabric as a wedding canopy or, in a Jewish ceremony, for your chuppah.

Don't have the dress cleaned until you get an expert evaluation—cleaning can cause a vintage gown to fall apart and can even bring out stains that weren't visible before. Check with the best vintage clothing store in your area for referrals.

Fittings and Alterations

'll let you in on a secret of Hollywood style: When a celebrity walks down the red carpet looking oh-so-fantastic, she owes as much to a skillful tailor as she does to the designer who created the gown. Alterations are *that* important to how a dress looks on you. You can be wearing duchess satin that costs a hundred dollars a yard, but if it bags where it should sculpt, you might as well be wearing a Hefty sack. Likewise, a great fit can elevate an inexpensive dress into something that feels and moves as if it were much pricier.

FITTINGS 101

☐ Bring all undergarments that you'll be wearing under the dress—bra, body shaper, crinoline, petticoat, hosiery; for the best fit, you need to be wearing the exact undergarments you'll be wearing on your wedding day. That means you'll need to buy the items you need before the first fitting. For more on undergarments, see page 221.

☐ Bring the shoes you'll be wearing to ensure you'll get the correct hem length.

☐ Bring a second pair of eyes. Your mother, a bridesmaid, or your wedding planner are all good candidates.

☐ You can get light-headed from standing still for so long, so stash a bottle of water or Gatorade and a high-protein snack in your bag. Just take care not to let the food get anywhere near the gown.

☐ Bring a camera so someone can take photos of you at your fitting. It's a wonderful experience to document and to share with the groom later.

☐ Skip the foundation and lipstick. You don't want makeup to rub off on your gown. If you're coming from work, the salon can usually provide a mesh makeup protector hood that prevents makeup from coming off on the dress.

☐ Have the front of the dress hemmed an inch shorter than the back to help prevent you from catching the toe of your shoe in the hem and tripping.

This is one area where you don't want to scrimp. Unless Aunt Sally works in the back room at Reem Acra, don't take her up on her offer to alter your gown. And whatever you do, don't head to the corner dry cleaner where you take your pants for hemming. Find someone who specializes in wedding gowns. You might spend as much as $150 to $500 on alterations alone, so it is crucial that you budget them in when choosing your gown. (If you're buying at a bridal salon, alterations should be included in the estimate you're given.)

Choosing the Right Tailor

IF POSSIBLE, have the dress altered where you bought it. It will not be the least expensive option, but it assures you a certain level of quality while giving you some protection in the event that a problem emerges in the alterations. Once you take the gown outside the salon, the store is not going to assume responsibility for anything that goes wrong. The best salons have a staff working on the gowns within the building. Some charge a flat fee for alterations, while others price them à la carte.

If you find the dress in a city other than where you live, making two or three extra visits for your fittings may not be practical. In that case, check the designer's website to find out where he sells in your area, and call that salon to see if they'll alter the dress.

You can also go with an independent alterations specialist. To find an experienced one, ask at your city's best fabric store—they'll often keep a list of local tailors. If there's a local wedding gown designer, ask if he does alterations on other designers' gowns—some do and are very skilled at it.

The Fittings

UNLESS THEY'RE CUSTOM-MADE, bridal gowns are cut to standard measurements, so they typically need significant alterations. How significant? Well, let's just say that since the size of the gown you'll get will be based on your largest measurements, you may be shocked at the first fitting to find there's a gap the size of the Columbia River Gorge between your bodice and your chest. Alterations can—and will—make a world of difference.

Most brides need two to four fittings. At high-end salons and with custom-made gowns, three or four is standard; at chain retailers, two is standard, with the second fitting really just an excuse to try on the dress and make sure it fits. Start your fittings in plenty of time; you want to have your dress ready three weeks before you need it.

During your fittings, make sure to move around in your dress and point out anything that doesn't feel right. Put your arms above your head, as if you're dancing, and

check to see what happens with the bodice, particularly if it's strapless. If you're uncomfortable with anything, this is your chance to speak up.

With a full-length gown, pay close attention to the length. Many brides have their dress hemmed to brush the floor, but they fail to realize how many people are likely to step on their gown. Have a full skirt hemmed to land about an inch off the floor. A narrower skirt looks better when it's hemmed shorter, just covering the ankles.

ASK MINDY

Q My fittings are dragging on for longer than I thought they would, and I'm starting to get worried. Is there a chance that my dress won't show up on time? Is there a chance it won't show up at all?

A It's an incredibly slim chance, but you do want to protect yourself in case it happens. What I would suggest is that if your dressmaker seems to be getting off schedule, you take action by buying an off-the-rack inexpensive safety dress somewhere. When your beautiful gown comes in (it will, I promise, I'm just making sure you cover your bases!), you can simply send the safety dress back for a refund.

Shoes

When it comes to choosing wedding shoes, it's not just about looks. Think about what kind of surfaces you're going to be walking on—no one ought to be wearing stiletto heels on grass, for instance. Then consider your fiancé's height—you may not be comfortable towering over the groom, but if he's super tall, you may want to give yourself a

SHOES 101

- Consider buying two pairs of shoes, one with a lower heel, so you can do a changeover when it's time to hit the dance floor—even an inexpensive pair of satin slippers or jeweled flip-flops could do the trick. You absolutely want to avoid killer foot pain.

- If you're on a tight budget, no one is going to notice if you bypass the Christian Louboutins under your long gown and wear basic satin sling-backs, which you can buy for about fifty dollars.

- If your feet are prone to swelling, buy your shoes a half size larger than usual, and bring along pads, just in case.

- If the shoes have a smooth sole, scuff it up for traction: Take a pocketknife and make a series of shallow crisscross cuts on the soles.

- Put in extra pads wherever they'll help. In sandals, place them under the ball of the foot. In pumps, you may also need pads under or behind the heel.

- Walk around in your shoes at home for two to three weeks before the wedding to break them in. If you're taking dance lessons, wear your shoes so you'll be comfortable in them on the dance floor.

- Look for a style you can wear again, especially if you're spending a lot. If you're going with ivory satin shoes, you can dye them black after the wedding.

- If you're not a habitual heel-wearer, you might be better off opting for platforms.

lift. Next, think comfort. No matter how gorgeous the shoes, do not buy them if they're painful. You're going to be standing and dancing for at least five hours—maybe eight—and you don't want footwear that's going to turn into a torture device. To best assess comfort, shop late in the day when your feet are larger.

Now it's time to think about style. My secret? Look for shoes that help create one lean, uninterrupted line from head to toe. Beware of any shoes with horizontal lines that stop the eye, or of anything pancake flat. Only those blessed with runway-ready physiques can pull off a ballet flat with a long gown; the rest of us need a heel to boost the derriere and create a longer line.

With the exception of metallics, formal shoes are generally made of fabric, rather than leather. Because it dyes easily, satin is the most common

Don't wear them fresh out of the box— break them in at home before the big day.

material for wedding shoes, but you'll find a range from silks to linens or synthetics in a variety of finishes.

As for budget, take into consideration how visible your shoes will be under the dress you've chosen. The more visible the shoe, the more you can rationalize a splurge.

Timing It

SHOP FOR YOUR SHOES soon after you've chosen your gown, as you'll need them by the time you go in for your first fitting. You might have the good luck of finding the shoes of your dreams in the same store where you purchase your gown, but if you want to get the lay of the land before making a choice, you'll find options anywhere from department stores to bridal salons to special wedding accessory boutiques.

In terms of timing, know that many stores, particularly bridal salons, only stock samples and will have to order the shoes in your size. Many stores

> If your gown has lace at the hem or is made of a gossamer fabric, beware of shoes adorned with jewels and rhinestones. They may look dazzling, but there's a chance the stones will snag on the inside of the gown and tear it.

also don't allow returns on bridal shoes, so ask about the return policy before buying.

If you're getting them dyed to match your dress, allow two weeks for the process. It can be quite tricky to get the right shade of ivory, so leave extra time in case you have to send them back to be redone.

Shopping Online for Shoes

YOU MIGHT BE ABLE to find your dream shoes online. There are many great websites offering a wide selection of styles, prices, and sizes. Internet retailers often have less restrictive return policies than brick-and-mortar shoe stores, and some even offer free return shipping.

Assuming there's a friendly return policy, order every pair you think might work—in more than one size if necessary. Don't hesitate to contact the customer service department to get guidance on sizing. (Some brides have been known to trace their feet onto paper and email them over to customer service!) When you receive the shoes, make sure to try them on with your gown before making a decision, even if it means paying an extra visit to the bridal salon.

Undergarments

The right foundation garments can spell the difference between flabby and flawless. Like alterations, these are the unsung (and unseen) heroes of red-carpet dressing, so you should buy the best you can.

A wedding gown may require undergarments you've never worn before, much less even heard of, like all-in-ones, slimmers, and cinchers. Once you've selected your dress, get advice on the best undergarments from the salesperson. Consult with your alterations person to determine whether a bra or any other necessary foundations can be sewn into the gown—if that's possible, do it. The last thing you want to be doing on your wedding day is tugging at straps and adjusting your bodice to hide the wayward edge of a bustier.

With a ballgown, most everything you need for support should be built into the bodice of the dress. But if you choose a slimmer, slinkier dress, then you need to make sure you have all of your bases covered. No matter what your body type, you need to create a smooth layer for the dress to glide over, otherwise it will stick where it shouldn't, and it won't hang right. If the fabric is slinky or very lightweight, look for seamless undergarments, especially the newer laser-cut panties and bras. Depending on the style of the dress, you may need an allover smoother like a strapless minidress or a seamless bustier or body shaper. Make sure a shaper doesn't create a visible line at the waist; if it does, you need a seamless all-in-one.

Although lacy undergarments seem like a natural for a bride, they tend to show through, so stay away from them. Go even smoother by choosing boy-shorts or boy-cut thongs instead of bikinis.

While you're shopping for undergarments to wear with your wedding gown, be sure to think about any specific undergarments you might need for your rehearsal dinner outfit and any other wedding weekend outfits. And while you're there, pick up something special for the honeymoon!

> For "something blue" that's an alternative to a garter, wear pale blue panties. (A pale blue flower in your hair is a lovely way to go, too.)

The Myth of the Pearl

Iridescent white, with a warm glow from within, a strand of pearls at the neck can be a simple and lovely finishing touch. There's a long tradition of fathers giving pearls to their daughters as wedding gifts—so long, in fact, that it's recorded in an ancient sacred Hindu text, the Rig Veda. According to the legend, the god Krishna dove to the bottom of the sea, unearthed the very first pearl, and triumphantly offered it to his daughter on her wedding day.

Though many cultures associate pearls with innocence and purity, there is an entire web of superstition that surrounds them. The ancient Greeks called pearls the "wedding gem" and believed they would prevent newlywed brides from crying—but some brides wouldn't be caught dead in pearls as they're also thought to *cause* tears and bring a marriage bad luck. Nobody's really sure where that belief comes from, but it has stuck around. To further muddle the topic, legend also goes that it's *good* luck for a bride to shed tears on her wedding day; that way she gets it all out at the altar!

Superstitions aside, many a bride opts for the classic look and elegant shimmer of a pearl necklace or a pair of pearl earrings. And how could she go wrong with a gem once thought so precious it could only be legally worn by a member of the English royal family?

Hosiery

HOSIERY GENERALLY MAKES SHOES more comfortable and puts legs in their best light, but if you're wearing a sandal or an open-toed shoe, skip it. Ditto if you're wearing mules—backless shoes and hose were never meant to be worn together.

With a wedding ensemble, you want hose to be simple. There's no need for extra adornment. Look for a pair that blends seamlessly with your outfit, a sheer nude or a sheer with a hint of pink or ivory. Sheen can look lovely, but know that it adds weight to your legs.

Give your hosiery a trial run with the dress. If there is any tulle or netting next to your legs, it will shred your hosiery in minutes. If that's the case, get an extra slip or petticoat to protect the hose and your legs from the scratchy material.

If you choose traditional pantyhose, make sure the waistband doesn't create a visible line. Also check to see that no seams down the center of the panty are showing through. Thigh-highs and hose worn with garters can be a very sexy look, as long as they don't show through the dress or through a slit in the skirt.

And buy yourself peace of mind by buying an extra pair or two of hosiery to take with you on your wedding day in case of a run or snag.

Accessories

Between the wedding gown, the veil, and the bouquet, there's a lot going on. Throw in a necklace, earrings, and a shrug, and it just may be too much. My advice? Make sure that any accessories you *do* choose to wear on your wedding day are simple and discreet. They should enhance you, rather than steal the attention.

If you have a hankering for extravagant accessories like fine jewelry and fur wraps or shrugs, look into renting. Some bridal salons and bridal accessory boutiques rent white furs, and some high-end jewelers will rent diamonds, sapphires, and other gems for the occasion.

Jewelry

JEWELRY IS CLEARLY INTEGRAL to the wedding day (remember the ring?), but this is not a day to overdo the bling. All eyes should be on you, not on your jewelry. A full suite might be too much, especially when combined with a wedding ring and a tiara or other hair jewelry.

Heirloom Jewelry

Y ou may have planned to wear a piece of family jewelry only to realize that it just doesn't work. Your late grandmother's diamond necklace might be gorgeous, but if it's the wrong length and size for your dress, you'll have to think of another way to wear it. Perhaps you can have it turned into a brooch that you can pin on your bodice or at your hip; maybe you can ask your hairstylist to work it into your updo (think Audrey Hepburn in *Breakfast at Tiffany's*). If the style of the jewelry clashes with your dress, consider pinning it to your bouquet (the stems would be wrapped in fabric that holds the pin) or attaching it to your handbag—I've even seen brides have a family member's wedding band sewn into their gowns. If you're wearing valuable jewelry at your wedding, assign a reliable member of the wedding party to keep track of it while you're getting ready.

As with anything else you wear on your wedding day, use jewelry to move the eye where you want it to go and to balance the overall picture. Prominent earrings help draw attention to your face; a long necklace elongates your upper body; a bracelet helps anchor bare arms.

On your fingers, wear only your wedding and engagement rings. You don't want other rings to dim their luster. Leave your watch at home, as even a proper evening watch won't look right with a wedding gown. (Anyhow, once you've gotten to the ceremony on time, you shouldn't be concerned with the hour on your wedding day.)

Factor in any sparkle you plan to add to your hair, as well as the amount of embellishment on your dress. If it's heavily beaded and embroidered, you want your jewelry to be simple. And if there's any jewelry accenting the top of the dress, such as sparkling brooches anchoring your straps, or embroidery on the bodice, don't let a necklace compete. Wear earrings instead. They'll bring all eyes up to your face, where they belong.

Handbags

NOT A NECESSITY, but a nicety, a bag or clutch comes in handy for keeping a lipstick, handkerchief, and breath mints—but realize that a bag will probably spend most of the reception sitting on your table. Ask your maid of honor to hold it for you when necessary.

Like shoes, handbags for formal occasions are generally made of fabric, not leather. A bridal bag should be petite and discreet so it doesn't draw attention away from your gown.

As a rule of thumb, if your dress is a clean, tailored style, it will look best with a structured handbag. A soft, flowing gown will look better with a drawstring pouch or a bag with curves to it. Ballgowns work with just about any delicate handbag, from a jeweled minaudière to a fabric pouch on a chain strap. If your dress is vintage or draws its inspiration from a particular era, you can't go wrong by choosing a bag from the same period.

Most bridal bags are white satin, but you can also inject a touch of silver or of color—this is another great opportunity for your "something blue."

An unstructured fabric bag is typically the least expensive option. You can often find bargain bags in satin at nonbridal stores, sometimes even at discount stores. As long as you stick to a simple style, no one will know the difference. If the timing works, shop for a dressy bag around New Year's, when stores are well stocked with bags at all price levels. Want to gussy it up? Add a rhinestone pin or clip.

Wraps, Shrugs, and Boleros

IF YOU'RE WEARING a strapless or bare-shouldered dress, you might want a cover-up for the ceremony (if it's in a house of worship) or the reception (if it goes into the evening and may get chilly). For the ceremony, you want a shrug or bolero that stays in place, not a shawl that you have to constantly adjust. For warm-weather weddings, look at cover-ups in organza, silk, lace, or lightweight cashmere. For a cold-weather wedding, you can go with satin, velvet, cashmere, or white fur. Designers are con-

The Rehearsal Dinner

Did you think I'd forgotten about a dress for the rehearsal dinner? Though for guests, rehearsal dinner clothing is much more casual than attire for the main event, I've yet to meet a bride who *didn't* want to make a mini-grand entrance on the night before her wedding. (Note that while your degree of formality needn't match your guests', you do want to make sure that your groom follows your lead.)

Many brides choose to wear white the entire weekend, from the rehearsal dinner through the morning-after brunch. No better way to make sure that you're the center of attention. But what you don't want to do is steal your own wedding-night thunder. If you're wearing a dress, particularly a white one, stay away from shapes or embellishments that look too bridal. Or opt for a pantsuit or jumpsuit, a gutsy and stylish move that looks really modern and clean. One of my brides recently took things up a notch by wearing a scarlet-red jumpsuit, complete with towering heels, to her rehearsal dinner. There's no question that all eyes were on her!

Depending on where you're shopping for a gown, you may find a rehearsal dinner dress in the same shop. If not, head straight to your favorite retailer or check out one of the bridesmaid-dress designers you'll be reading about in the following chapter.

stantly coming out with innovative styles that address the need to cover shoulders in a house of worship.

Gloves

TREAD CAREFULLY WHEN it comes to gloves, but if you're so inclined and gloves work with your dress, go for it—though I'm of the opinion that they tend to clash with today's styles. Choose a length that complements the style of the gown and the setting. With a sleeveless gown, over-the-elbow gloves are elegant, but wrist-length gloves create an awkward line; save them for a three-quarter sleeve. Then rehearse how you're going to handle the ring part of the ceremony. The ring should always be placed directly onto the finger, not over a glove. You can either remove the glove when it's time for the ring or purchase gloves that let you fold back the ring finger.

Use Your Dress to Do Good

Get more mileage out of your gown by buying from a store or sales event where the proceeds benefit charity. Or donate your gown to a special organization after the wedding.

Brides Across America accepts mail-in donations of gently worn bridal gowns and passes them along to military brides in need. Donations of gowns and accessories can be written off as a tax deduction. Adorned in Grace, a Portland, Oregon, bridal store, sells used wedding dresses and donates the proceeds to supporting victims of sexual trafficking. The Bridal Garden in New York City sells designer samples and leftover inventory from bridal shops at a major discount (by appointment only), and the proceeds benefit Sheltering Arms Children and Family Services. You can also donate your gown to a local thrift shop that benefits a hospital or church that's meaningful to you.

If you feel like gown shopping has taken you back in time, what with the layers upon layers of fabric, the tight corsets, and the endless fittings, you're not alone; it's the closest most brides will come to Old World couture.

Bridesmaids' dresses, on the other hand, are more reminiscent of the kinds of frocks you might wear for a fun night out. Though the shopping process is still likely to involve sample sizes and alterations, the styles should be much more familiar to you.♦

CHAPTER SEVENTEEN

Dressing the Women

BRIDESMAIDS, FLOWER GIRLS, AND MOMS

There's no doubt about it: Bridesmaids' dresses have gotten a bad rap over the years. And with good reason. There have been weddings where each bridesmaid was dressed in a different hue to create a rainbow, where sleeves were poufed and waists were dropped, and where giant bows were placed on hips, sleeves, and, most famously, on derrieres.

Wearing "a bow on your butt" became a euphemism for a bad bridesmaid's dress.

But times have changed. Serving as a bridesmaid is an honor, and the styles in stores have grown to reflect that. Talented designers have brought a fresh focus to bridesmaids' dresses, resulting in offerings that are simpler, cleaner, and more attractive.

Still, there are challenges to outfitting a posse of BFFs and relatives. Unifying the group without getting that costume vibe; finding a way to integrate the bridesmaids into the overall look of the wedding; addressing differences in body type and skin tone; and coordinating fittings and alterations. It's likely that the mothers of the bride and groom will need help finding their special something to wear as well.

In the past, bridesmaids were dressed identically. But it's far more modern (and

The Wearability Factor

I've met enough bridesmaids to know one question that is likely to be weighing heavily on their minds: *Will I be able to wear it again?* Especially these days, with designer bridesmaids' dresses all the rage, your friends might have to spend a fairly large sum of money on what's likely to be a one-time-only garment.

No matter how modern the style, a bridesmaids' dress that can be repurposed is indeed a rare thing. But if you're dedicated to the cause, consider the following options: Dress the bridal party in black; select a color range and let the bridesmaids wear mismatched dresses of their own choosing for an effect that is modern and fresh; or go with off-the-rack separates. If you want more uniformity, select a color from a designer like Joanna August, who features a stunning variety of graceful fits in a lovely and modern palette.

flattering) to strive for a unified, rather than a uniform, look. Letting bridesmaids mix it up a little makes for a prettier, happier bridal party. And at the end of the day, a happy bridesmaid makes for a less stressful wedding.

When and Where to Shop

The wedding gown sets the tone for the attire of the bridal party, so try to choose your gown before you start focusing on your bridesmaids'. Bridal salons encourage you to order bridesmaids' dresses four to six months before the wedding, allowing two to four months for the gowns to arrive and another month for alterations. If you're buying them off the rack in a department store or boutique, purchasing the dresses three months before the wedding gives everyone plenty of time to get alterations done and find accessories.

There's a direct correlation between the number of attendants in a bridal party and the length of the shopping and alterations process, so if you have eight bridesmaids, allow as much time as you can.

Options abound in terms of where to shop, but the more bridesmaids you have, the more sense it makes to take the conventional route of ordering through a bridal salon or bridesmaids' dress boutique. Finding off-the-rack dresses in a regular retail store can be fuss free with two girls, but if you're trying to fit and flatter eight bridesmaids, it may be more than you bargained for.

Bridal salons stock samples of bridesmaids' dresses in a range of styles and prices, with an emphasis on traditional looks. They require appointments and typically order the dresses in one batch so they'll be cut from the same dye lot of fabric. They generally require a deposit of 50 percent, and take eight to sixteen weeks to deliver an order. For those in a hurry, some salons carry a limited number of styles in stock so they're available on short notice. Salons also offer the benefit of on-site alterations. Just like bridal gowns, bridesmaids' dresses are nonreturnable, whether you've made alterations or not.

Chains like David's Bridal offer a wide array of budget-friendly and high-end styles. Most are stocked rather than made to order, so it's a great option for those without much time; some even do on-site alterations. Chains are also convenient for geographically dispersed bridal parties, as the bridesmaids can visit the store closest to them to pick up their dresses.

A few boutiques specializing in bridesmaids' attire, Joanna August and Bella Bridesmaids among them, have emerged in major cities, and the trend continues to grow. Some of these stores feature online ordering, while others do not. They cater to fashion-conscious bridal parties who don't mind spending more to get up-to-date styles and quality fabrics. The colors, silhouettes, and details of dresses in these boutiques and brands are more in touch with runway trends, so bridesmaids are more likely to be able to wear them again.

A long skirt and camisole

A floaty, graceful alternative to a dress, this cami-skirt-shawl combo is a guaranteed hit with bridesmaids and a great choice for outdoor weddings.

A cap-sleeved wrap dress

The cap sleeves offer coverage and balance out broader hips, while the wrap's diagonal lines nip in the waist. A pretty, totally wearable look that doesn't bare a lot of skin.

A strapless A-line dress

There's no cut more universal than the A-line, and for length, at or just below the knee gets my vote. A contrasting sash gives an added bit of interest and flatters the waist.

Some popular retailers like Anthropologies' BHLDN and J.Crew also carry bridesmaids' dresses. Often these offerings are sold only online, which is actually an advantage, as you can order a lot of styles, get them within a week, and return what you don't like. It's also easy for all the bridesmaids to view the possibilities. Styles are appealingly clean and simple. You'll be on your own, however, for alterations. The same goes for designers like Nicole Miller and ABS, who offer lots of bridesmaid-friendly choices in their regular collections.

If you're going the department store route, don't restrict your browsing to just the bridal department. Sometimes the formal or evening wear department can yield just the dress you're looking for. If you're having a less formal wedding, cruise other departments, too. You might find the perfect beaded camisole or A-line georgette sundress. Department stores are often able to order the sizes you need from other stores, and they have more liberal return policies than independent boutiques. You'll probably need to go elsewhere for alterations, though some stores offer them on-site. Look for deals during sales, particularly after New Year's Eve and prom season.

Finding a Bargain

You never know when you might strike gold. One savvy bargain hunter I know happened to be out shopping in New York City the day after she got engaged—New Year's Eve. She walked into H&M and spotted full-length chocolate satin dresses marked down to $25.

We've all been to weddings where the $250 bridesmaids' dresses are hideous, and she was determined not to do that to her friends. She and a shorter friend tried on the bargain gowns, and they both looked great in them, so she bought eight for her six bridesmaids, thinking she might need a different size or could use the extra material for purses (total cost: $200). She even bought one in a size sixteen for the fabric, which turned out to be a godsend: By the time her wedding date rolled around, one of her sisters was seven and a half months pregnant, and they were able to alter the dress to fit.

Moral of the story? Stay on your toes, and don't be afraid to act on an impulse. You could end up with the deal of a lifetime.

If you love the style of a particular store, whether it's a fancy boutique or a big chain, check it out when shopping for bridesmaids' attire. By shopping sales, you can sometimes nab a bargain at a nonbridal store.

If you're going custom, allow five to seven months for the process, timing it so that the dresses are scheduled to be ready four weeks before the wedding.

Whose Choice Is It, Anyway?

t's a fact of life: At least one of your bridesmaids will not be in love with her dress. That said, your goal is to make everyone as happy as possible with the choice. To that end, bridesmaids—or one representative bridesmaid—should have a say in the dresses.

Typically, a bride and her maid of honor shop together. More bridesmaids can come if it's practical, but too many opinions make it that much harder to reach a decision. If your bridesmaids represent a range of body types, make sure that someone other than the five-foot-nine swimsuit model tries the dresses on.

The most diplomatic way to handle the process is for you and one attendant to narrow down the choices, then get input from the entire bridal party on your top three picks, either in person or via email. Some brides who aren't attached to a uniform look are comfortable giving their bridesmaids the essential criteria—color range and perhaps length—and sending them shopping; see box on page 230 for more details.

Assuming the bridesmaids are paying for their own dresses, price can often be a sensitive issue. Give them an idea of the cost ahead of time, then strive to stay in that range. The average bridesmaid dress costs over $150, and that's before you factor in alterations, shoes, and undergarments. If you choose a top-tier price range—$350 and up—I suggest you subsidize the cost as a courtesy to your friends.

Does the Maid of Honor Dress Differently?

THE MAID OR MATRON OF HONOR is often distinguished by wearing a slightly different style or color, but with so many wedding parties mixing up their looks, this distinction becomes trickier to accomplish. If you want to vary the color, it looks pretty and still unified if she wears a different tone in the same color family. If the bridesmaids are in forest green, she can wear olive. Many times it works well if the maid of honor's outfit sports a different color sash or type of trim. If making her stand out via her attire isn't practical, you can always opt to have her carry a different bouquet.

Not Your Mother's Separates

BRIDESMAIDS' LINES TEND TO offer a fair number of separates, and with good reason—they are far more likely to fit and flatter than dresses. They give you varied options for bodices and skirts, a great route if you have

---

Virtual Shopping

Your bridesmaids are busy people. But don't worry if you can't get them all together; take advantage of technology to make long-distance shopping a group experience.

Some ways to share the shopping process:

■ Use sites like Pinterest to aggregate and share styles that catch your eye.

■ Scan photos from magazines or take photos while shopping and email them to your bridesmaids.

■ Set up a conference call with your bridesmaids and cruise online photos together, weighing in with thoughts and opinions.

bridesmaids with a wide range of figure types. One could choose spaghetti straps to show off beautiful shoulders, and a bridesmaid who hates her upper arms could opt for three-quarter sleeves. You can even vary the lengths of the skirts if you wish. You'll end up with figure-flattering options and a modern looking bridal party.

Separates may also cost less to alter, since you can order different sizes for the top and bottom. And they double your chances of getting something that can be worn again. Even if the skirt screams "bridesmaid," perhaps the beaded camisole top can be paired later with jeans.

Alterations

Since bridesmaids' dresses are so often purchased as samples, alterations are almost always necessary. (As with bridal gowns, samples are ordered according to the bridesmaids' largest measurements, so they'll probably need to be taken in.)

Each bridesmaid is responsible for getting her dress altered, though she may need some reminding (which is a good job for the maid of honor to take on). Ideally, alterations should be done where the dresses were purchased, so you have more recourse in the unhappy case of a mistake. If that's not a possibility, see page 219 for tips on finding a good tailor you can trust.

The price of alterations depends on the style of the dresses and the fabric and work involved, but expect to spend anywhere from $30 to $150. Remember to factor the alterations fee into the budget when you are choosing dresses. Urge your bridesmaids to try on their dresses when they pick them up to make sure they fit. You wouldn't believe how many times a dress doesn't fit on the wedding day because bridesmaids neglect to take the simple precaution of trying on a dress after it's altered. The bride or maid of honor should make sure the bridesmaids are leaving enough time for alterations (and re-alterations, if necessary); ideally, the bridesmaids should have the finished dresses in hand a week or two before they need to leave for the wedding.

Figure and Tone

No single color or style is universally flattering, but some choices are kinder than others. Black, chocolate brown, and navy can be worn by the vast majority of women. Yellow—and anything with a strong yellow undertone, like certain shades of green—isn't so versatile.

As for shape, high-waisted A-line dresses get my vote for the closest thing to a universal fit. For tips on how to flatter particular body types, see page 202.

Dressing Pregnant Bridesmaids

A bridesmaid who becomes pregnant is one of those not-so-uncommon wedding wild cards. Before you start worrying about her dress bursting at the seams, remember to congratulate her on the happy news—this is definitely one of those cases in which it is *not* all about you.

Then you'll need to do some strategizing. If you've already ordered the dress, call the store to assess options, which will vary depending on the store, manufacturer, and timing. You might be able to change to a larger size or switch to a maternity dress or an empire-waisted style in the same fabric.

If none of those options is available, some manufacturers will sell you fabric to match the other dresses; you can then hire a local seamstress to create a flattering style that reflects the other bridesmaids' dresses.

It's possible that you may have to order a second dress and still pay for the first one. If you haven't ordered a dress yet, look for bridesmaid dress designers such as Thread and Watters & Watters, which offer maternity styles. Or designate a color and have your bridesmaid pick out an off-the-rack maternity dress.

Unlike other bridesmaids, she should wait as long as possible to have alterations done.

Accessories

Accessories are key to unifying the look of a bridal party, but it doesn't take many to do the job. Bridesmaids' outfits already have a lot going on—often the dresses are embellished, ruffled, or sashed with a contrasting color, and the girls are holding bouquets. Additional accessories beyond shoes and jewelry add cost and shopping time, and they can have the unfortunate effect of turning a perfectly lovely bridesmaid into a child playing dress-up—so skip the lavender stretch satin gloves or fishnet stockings.

Shoes

ALLOW BRIDESMAIDS TO CHOOSE their own shoes, since they'll be wearing them for hours on end; some women can wear three-inch mules as if they're house slippers, and others can't walk in an inch-and-a-half heel to save their lives. Matching color and material is more important than enforcing a uniform style. But even here, a perfect match isn't essential. Though dye-able shoes are part of the bridesmaid tradition, they seem like a waste of time and money to me—after all, nobody is going to be staring at your bridesmaids' shoes while you're up at the altar exchanging vows.

Send your bridesmaids guidelines specifying color and material (satin, faille, silver leather), and let them know what kinds of surfaces they'll be walking on so they don't show up for a lawn ceremony in four-inch stilettos.

Do them a favor and consider whether black or metallic shoes could work. Your maids might already own a pair, and even if they end up having to buy black silk evening shoes, they'll find other occasions to wear them.

Jewelry

BRIDES OFTEN GIVE their attendants a piece of jewelry to wear at the wedding—it's both a diplomatic way to sidestep questions of taste and a token of thanks. Whether you're going the gift route or letting them

BRIDESMAIDS' DRESSES 101

Follow these suggestions for a smoother, crisis-free shopping and alterations process.

☐ Have everyone get measured (height, bust, waist, and hip), and know that bridesmaids' dresses run one to two sizes smaller than ready-to-wear. If in doubt, order larger—it's easier to take in a garment than to let one out.

☐ Order all dresses at the same time and through the same store.

☐ Check in with the store occasionally to find out the status of your order.

☐ Tell bridesmaids early on that there will be an extra expense for alterations, so they can budget for them.

☐ When you place the order, get the style number, manufacturer, fabric, color, sizes, delivery date, deposit, and balance due in writing. Also get the cancellation and refund policy in writing.

accessorize on their own, provide guidelines ahead of time—you might write them a friendly email telling them what they need to know about their dresses, accessories, and alterations. One item of jewelry is often enough, and you don't want bridesmaids showing up in chandelier earrings and wristfuls of bangle bracelets.

Wraps and Handbags

WHEN A WRAP or cover-up is needed for the ceremony, the bride typically gives it to her bridesmaids as a gift. If it's the reception that's outdoors, no need to go all out unless you want to. Since they won't be wearing wraps down the aisle, matching isn't necessary and they can wear their own.

Handbags that complement the outfit are another popular gift; they're not going to be carried down the aisle, so they're not a necessity. If you don't plan on giving handbags, don't impose a host of restrictions; your bridesmaids shouldn't have to buy new bags just for the wedding.

Flower Girls

The bride typically chooses the flower girl's dress, but it's also fine to send the flower girl's mother shopping with a list of criteria. If you're a stickler for detail, you might want to make sure she's willing to send you photos of the dress before making a nonrefundable move. You might specify the color, length, or the type of fabric, or simply tell her the colors being worn by the bridal party and leave it to her discretion. Send her a photo of the bridesmaids' dresses so she can see the style; the formality of the flower girl's dress should be in keeping with the wedding.

If you're not paying for the dress, be sensitive to price issues, as it will probably only be worn once before the flower girl outgrows it. Many brides pick up the tab, but that's optional.

Junior Bridesmaids

The color of the junior bridesmaids' dresses should echo or match that of the bridesmaids', though the style can stand on its own. First and foremost, keep the ages of the junior bridesmaids in mind when choosing dresses. They shouldn't bare too much skin. As a courtesy, show the mother of the junior bridesmaid the dress style and accessories before finalizing them. Your idea of what's appropriate on an eleven-year-old may be at odds with her mom's.

You may be able to fit your junior bridesmaid into a small adult size; if not, many bridesmaid's dress manufacturers offer dresses especially for juniors.

Once the province of specialty children's designers, flower girls' dresses are increasingly included among the offerings from top bridal designers. Accordingly, some bridal salons carry flower girls' dresses, but you can also shop at department stores and children's clothing stores; if you're shopping for only one or two flower girls, it may be more convenient to simply buy something off the rack. If you are able to shop near Easter or the holidays, you'll find a wide selection of dresses at discounters like Target—I've seen adorable holiday dresses at Costco for less than $25. Or look into renting formal dresses online.

A note on accessories: While it's easy to get caught up in all those darling trimmings, remember that kids fidget and take things off and lose them, so keep the number of tchotchkes low. Flower girls do traditionally wear flower wreaths in their hair; your florist can make the wreaths for you, or you might opt for a bow or headband instead.

A purse can make a sweet gift, and if it's the right shape and size, it can substitute as a basket to hold the flower petals on the walk down the aisle.

For more on the flower girl's accoutrements and her role in the ceremony, see chapter 4, "Building Your Team."

Dressing the Mothers

Dressing the mothers of the bride and groom can be tricky territory. They shouldn't fade into the background in a beige suit, nor should they look like they're trying to steal the spotlight. Plus, in my experience, shopping can be a fraught experience for fifty-plus women, who have a hard time finding things that aren't either too young or too dowdy.

In my opinion (though you may hear otherwise in some quarters), the mothers shouldn't match their colors to those of the bridesmaids, and they shouldn't match each other. White will look competitive, and black might be taken as a subliminal message about the union. Any other color is fair game.

If the mothers wish to coordinate their outfits, etiquette holds that the mother of the bride choose hers first, then communicate what she's wearing to the mother of the groom; then the mother of the groom can pick something of similar formality in a color that doesn't clash. It makes sense to give the mother of the bride the home-court advantage at a traditional wedding, where the bride's parents are paying and hosting. But these days, everyone may just choose to go out on her own—it all depends on the dynamic. The most important thing is for the mothers to feel comfortable and attractive in what they've chosen; to some extent, they'll be in the limelight on your wedding day.

As for exactly what to wear, many mothers lean toward structured suits in dressy fabrics rather than dresses, though a dress with a matching, tailored jacket is also a nice option.

If you have time, helping your mother shop for her outfit can be a fun outing and a great bonding experience. Many bridal salons carry styles for the mother of the bride, so if your mother is with you while you're shopping for your wedding gown, have her try on some dresses, even if she isn't ready to get serious about shopping. It's a convenient way to open a dialogue about what you both like and think will work well.

Now that we've got all the girls taken care of, it's time to turn our attention to the other party who'll be gracing the altar in his finest: the groom! True, he may not have been dreaming of his wedding tux since early childhood, but he'll want to look his best on this important day, too. ♦

CHAPTER EIGHTEEN

Dressing the Men

THE FINE ART OF FORMAL SUITING

Though the groom's clothing isn't freighted with the same mythology as the bride's, for centuries it was just as spectacular as hers. In ancient Greece, the bride and groom both donned white togas; later on, throughout Europe, men's finery involved velvets, brocades, and satins. There also used to be a whole host of strict etiquette rules tying

the formality of the attire to the time of day, but those have largely fallen by the wayside.

The options in menswear now hinge on two things: the bride's gown and the setting. The bride and groom should look as if they belong together. If she's in an understated slip dress, he shouldn't be in a gold brocade jacket and vest, and if she's wearing a satin ballgown, he can't get away with a linen shirt and shorts. The same principle

works for the setting—a grand ballroom dictates a formal suit.

The groom's attire also correlates to any dress code specified on the wedding invitation—he should be at least as formal as the specified dress, though he has the prerogative to dress a degree more formally than the guests. Translation: If the invitation calls for cocktail attire, he could wear a suit or ramp it up a notch and don a tuxedo.

The groom's comfort and personal style are also factors, of course. The outfit should allow some measure of self-expression, even something as subtle as the choice of studs and cuff links—though by no means is a wedding the time to go ballistic. Robert Downey Jr. can get away with a lavender shirt, tie, polka-dotted scarf, and sneakers, but the investment banker who lives in Brooks Brothers should probably stick to classics.

For two grooms, the only "rule" is that the degree of formality is matched.

The Mighty Tuxedo

Most men opt for tuxedos on their wedding day, and with good reason. I have yet to meet a guy who doesn't look dashing in one.

The tuxedo jacket is actually a relative latecomer to formal attire. A cross between a tailcoat and a velvet smoking jacket, it was originally known as a dinner jacket and was worn only in someone's home or in a private club. (Anyplace more public demanded white tie.) When Griswold Lorillard wore the style to the autumn ball in Tuxedo Park, New York, in 1886, it was considered downright scandalous—until the Duke of Windsor adopted it.

Though the jacket is what it first became known for, a tuxedo has many elements. The key to proper tuxedo dressing is that the pants' waistband should never be visible; that's where a cummerbund or vest comes into play, though a double-breasted tuxedo jacket, worn closed, negates the need.

To find a tuxedo that best suits his body type and style, the groom will need to familiarize himself with the various jacket, shirt, vest, trouser, and accessory options. This may sound more complicated than it is; the illustrations on pages 236–238 will make it easier to understand.

Tuxedo Jackets

THE MOST POPULAR and versatile style, single-breasted jackets look great on everyone. Slimming and elongating, they're especially great for shorter grooms. Double-breasted jackets are a stylish, somewhat more dashing choice, and they're worn without a vest or cummerbund.

With either of these jackets comes a choice of lapels. The peaked lapel is the most classic and versatile of all. It's flattering on most everyone, but the sharp lines make it an excellent choice for men whose middles or faces are somewhat round; it looks best paired with an equally angular wing collar. A notch lapel doesn't have quite the same drama, but it's another highly wearable option; it looks the most like the lapels you might see on an everyday suit. Evocative of the lapel on a smoking jacket, a shawl lapel creates a softer, rounded look.

Tuxedo Shirts

TUXEDO SHIRTS are usually white. Hollywood types like to shun tradition by donning black on black, but they're missing out on the wonderful contrast of a white shirt against a black tux, which looks sharp and also photographs well.

Detailed front panels, either in the form of vertical pleats or a stiffer bib of cotton piqué, are another traditional touch. A plainer front is a better choice for a waistcoat pairing, however, as the combination of pleats and vest tends to look a little busy; some shirts come with covered plackets for a more streamlined look. One feature that's unique to many formal shirts is a tab with a buttonhole that attaches to a special button inside the trouser waistband to prevent the bib from billowing out.

The shirt collar should complement the cut of the suit jacket, so the two should be tried on together. Though collar cuts will vary by designer, there are three

Men who are getting married in a hot climate or tend to perspire heavily should bring a second dress shirt for the reception— it can be a lifesaver.

Q *If the wedding is at 11 a.m., is it appropriate for the groom to wear a tuxedo?*

A Strictly speaking, morning coats or strollers (see pages 236–237) are worn till early afternoon and tuxedos aren't worn till 6 p.m., but only a very few grooms heed these old-school rules these days.

basic styles. A winged collar is high and pointed, standing away from the neck and framing the jaw. It's an elegant showcase for a bow tie but not a great choice for a T-shirt addict, as it's fairly stiff. The softer turndown collar would be a better choice. (The style was actually popularized by the Duke of Windsor as part of his mission to make clothing more comfortable.) A banded collar has no collar points at all and is held closed with a stud; it must be worn without a tie, so it's a bold, minimalistic choice.

And one more thing that might be unfamiliar to many grooms: cuff links. A formal shirt practically cries out for them. When assessing fit, keep in mind that cuffs should extend about a half-inch over the wrist.

Tuxedo Pants

TRADITIONAL TUXEDO PANTS sport a satin stripe down the outside trouser leg and should never be cuffed—you want to avoid breaking the line of the stripe. Some updated tuxedo pants may not have a band, but they should still hang straight, without a cuff. The pants should skim the top of the shoe.

The Cummerbund

IN THE DAYS WHEN formal attire was de rigueur, cummerbund folds were a handy place to store theater or opera tickets. Today, the pleats still face up to honor their original function.

Though black silk is the traditional fabric for a cummerbund—which should match the bow tie—some grooms

White Tie Confidential

A notch above black-tie in formality, white-tie, or full dress, is typically seen at consular balls and very formal evening weddings—but with the right attitude, a groom can certainly pull off this vintage look in more relaxed surroundings. The centerpiece is a black wool tailcoat with a split tail that hits the middle of the knee. It's paired with black side-striped trousers, a formal white shirt with a winged collar, a white piqué bow tie, and a white piqué vest.

Pinning on the Boutonniere

A boutonniere should be worn only on a jacket with a special boutonniere buttonhole on the lapel—pin a boutonniere directly onto a satin lapel and you'll leave lasting holes in the fabric. (A handkerchief should be worn instead.) Pin the flower to the left lapel, on the side with the breast pocket.

take the opportunity to make a statement. A wedding isn't the time for a novelty pattern like the Texas state flag, but a tartan print or kente cloth can be a wonderful way to honor a heritage, and a subtle seasonal nod like green velvet for a holiday wedding can look rich and elegant.

The Vest

A FORMAL VEST, also called a waistcoat, can be either single- or double-breasted. Though it often matches the dinner jacket, it's another good place to add interest via color, fabric, or texture. While the traditional vest has a deep **V** front designed to show off the shirt, some contemporary vests button high, showing only a small triangle of shirt; these work better with a long necktie.

The backless vest was invented for hot weather by the Duke of Windsor (he truly was on a mission) with the intent to keep the wearer cooler; but in that era, a gentleman never would have dreamed of taking off his jacket for dancing.

ormal Menswear

Contrary to the saying, it's the cut and the suit that make the man. . . .

1. Black tie
The standard bearer of wedding attire

2. Classic suit
An exquisite suit can carry the day.

3. White tie
A tailcoat worn with a white vest and bow tie

The Jacket *The jacket styling is where much of the suit's personality comes through.*

1. Single-breasted tuxedo
The classic—a slimming, elongating style

2. Double-breasted tuxedo
Always worn closed, without a vest or cummerbund

3. Stroller
Similar to a tuxedo jacket, without the satin accents

The Icing

With formal suiting, it's all in the details.

1. Waistcoat
If your vest is backless, keep your jacket on.

2. Suspenders
A belt should never be worn with a tuxedo.

3. Scarf
A dashing cold-weather complement to a tuxedo

4. Tie
A simpler approach to neckwear

5. Bow tie
The absolute classic in formal neckwear

6. Ascot
A plush, Old World touch

7. Cummerbund
Finishes the line of the suit by disguising the pants' waistband

4. Morning coat/ Cutaway
The most formal option for a daytime wedding

5. Full-dress tails
Usually worn only at the most formal evening events

Button Stance

A fairly technical term from the world of men's tailoring, the "button stance" refers to the placement of the first button in relation to the top of the jacket. A button stance can be "high" or "low," a factor that greatly affects the look of a suit. A jacket with a high button stance tends to look better on men with a slim to average build; closed, it negates the need for a cummerbund. A low button stance is more traditional. It's worn with a bow tie and exposes more shirt or waistcoat; paradoxically, the wider **V** makes it more flattering to heavyset men.

The Lapel

Pay close attention to how the lapel, shirt collar, and neckwear work together.

1. Notch lapels
Closest to the lapel that you would see on an everyday suit

2. Peaked lapels
Dramatic peaks can give a round face more definition.

3. Shawl lapels
A softer, rounded line with vintage appeal

The Collar
An element so close to the face should be chosen with care.

1. Banded collar
This bold choice cannot be worn with any neckwear.

2. Winged collar
Elegant and structured, it pairs well with a bow tie.

3. Turndown collar
A more contemporary look, it lends itself to a simple necktie.

The Shoes
Pull it all together, from head to toe.

1. Oxford
In black patent or very shiny leather, the natural choice with a tuxedo

2. Opera pump
A now unusual choice that harkens back to the origins of formalwear

3. Buck
Paired with a light suit, a more casual choice for a summer wedding

4. Velvet evening slipper
What used to be paired with a tux—a very dashing choice

Signs of a Good Fit

When assessing the fit of a suit or tuxedo, whether purchased or rented, look for:

- On a suit, trouser hems that break over a third of the length of the shoe and brush the top of the heel in back. With a tuxedo, the pants should hang straight and just brush the top of the shoe. (The side stripe looks terrible when rumpled.)

- A jacket collar that lies evenly at the back and sides of the neck.

- A shirt collar with space for one finger between the collar and skin of the neck.

- Jacket shoulders that don't extend too far beyond the natural shoulder line (if they do, the jacket is too big), and that fit smoothly over the shoulder blades in back.

- Jacket sleeves that hit the wrist bone. Shirt cuffs that extend a half-inch beyond the jacket sleeves.

- A back vent (if there is one) that doesn't pull open, a sign that the jacket is too tight.

Rental tuxedos often come with backless vests, but the fact is, a backless vest is not attractive without a jacket. For grooms who imagine taking off their jackets on the dance floor, a full vest is preferable.

Suspenders

A **BELT IS NEVER** worn with a tuxedo. Suspenders, also known as braces, allow pants to hang evenly without breaking the line at the waist. (They are especially important in getting pleated pants to hang correctly.) Though they don't have to be standard-issue black, it's the most elegant option with a tuxedo. With white-tie attire, white suspenders are the classic choice.

Neckties and Bow Ti

A "FOUR-IN-HAND" TIE (the te lar old necktie) is worn with a notch lape cummerbund. Peak lapels and shawl collars, on the o hand, are designed to be worn with bow ties. Recently, many style-conscious grooms have been eschewing the traditional bow tie for a full-length tie. It makes sense, as a four-in-hand necktie is naturally elongating and easier to deal with. But the bow tie will always have its place.

How to Tie a Bow Tie

1. Start with left side extending 1½ inches below right.

2. Cross longer end over shorter end.

3. Pass longer end up underneath shorter end.

4. Form loop by doubling hanging end horizontally. Hold loop with left hand. Drop long end down over front.

5. Fold long end under itself and bring folded edge up through gap in horizontal loop.

6. Gently grasp both folded edges and pull until knot is tight and edges are even.

Ideally, the fabric of the bow tie should echo the facing on the jacket's lapel. That can mean either a fabric match (satin on satin) or a play on texture (a silk twill or otherwise textured tie with a grosgrain lapel). For four-in-hand ties, solid satin looks wonderful in neutrals like ivory, white, silver, or black, but a narrow stripe can also look quite dashing.

Morning Coats and Strollers

Though evening and day wear used to be two separate categories, they've melded together over time. Still, some grooms wish to honor tradition by donning the proper suit at the proper time.

A morning coat, or cutaway, is a black, charcoal, or dove-gray tailed coat that sweeps into a long, wide "tail" in back. Worn for only the most formal of daytime weddings, it should be paired with a wing-collared shirt, gray vest, a four-in-hand tie, and gray striped pants. Though it's a natural look for Princes William and Harry, it can be a challenge for the less blue-blooded groom to pull off. Still, some men love the old-fashioned elegance.

A more wearable, but still dignified, daytime option is a stroller, a hip-length jacket in black or gray that's cut like a tuxedo jacket, minus the satin accents. It's paired with striped pants and a shirt with a turndown collar. At the neck, an ascot or a wide, formal tie is folded over and fastened with a stickpin or tie tack.

Beyond the Tuxedo

Weddings aren't always highly formal affairs, and if the bride has decided to forgo the wedding dress, there's no reason the groom shouldn't have a choice in attire as well.

The White Dinner Jacket

Often overlooked as an alternative to a black tuxedo, the white dinner jacket is a wonderful classic. Think Humphrey Bogart in *Casablanca* or James Bond holding a martini. The summer version of a tuxedo, it's more suited to country clubs and outdoor weddings than to church affairs. It comes in both single- and double-breasted versions, always with a shawl lapel. Worn with a bow tie and cummerbund rather than a vest, it's generally paired with a black or midnight blue trouser.

Sleek, dark suits continue to gain popularity among fashionable grooms, especially for destination weddings or anywhere a tuxedo would look too stuffy. A single-breasted suit worn with a solid necktie, a white dress shirt, and French cuffs and cuff links is a perfectly acceptable alternative to a tux. (The shirt fabric should be a smooth broadcloth, not an oxford, which is too casual.) It's also a great investment, since a wonderfully tailored suit will never go out of style.

Light-colored suits in sand or off-white can be wonderful choices for outdoor weddings; they tend to look more natural with open-collar cotton or linen shirts than dress shirts and ties.

Shoes and Other Accessories

The shoes traditionally paired with a tuxedo are patent or very smooth calfskin leather; wing tips or styles with perforations are considered too casual. (Old-school formality used to call for velvet evening slippers, but that's a little too Hugh Hefner for most grooms.) With white pants or a seersucker suit, white bucks are a natural.

The groom should specify what type of shoe the groomsmen wear; formal-wear stores typically offer four or more styles. If at all possible, though, the groom should wear his own shoes or buy shoes to wear with his outfit. Rental shoes in general may not be comfortable, and the patent versions available at rental stores aren't usually made of real leather, so they're not very breathable.

Shoes can also be a way to make the groom and groomsmen stand out. I've seen wedding parties in black Converse high-tops, and in Texas, many a groom walks down the aisle in cowboy boots. If the shoe fits, it can be a great signature style element. (But if it doesn't, it *will* look kooky.)

> If the groom is buying new shoes for the wedding, he should wear them to any dance lessons he takes with the bride. It's the perfect way to break them in. To make sure the shoes are kept in pristine condition, they shouldn't be worn outside the dance studio.

Socks

THERE'S A GOOD REASON hotel gift shops sell men's dress socks. If there's one thing guys forget to bring along on a trip, it's the socks. With that in mind, the groom should bring several pairs of socks on the day of the wedding, just in case any of the groomsmen forget. A playful option is to give all of the groomsmen socks in the same pattern—for a golf-loving groom, that might mean black-and-blue argyle socks.

In theory, though, dress socks should match the color of the pant—not the shoe—in order to create an unbroken line. They should be made of finely woven, semisheer silk, cotton, or wool and should reach over the calf. Don't try to get away with shorter socks that stop at the bottom of the calf—you might think they cover everything, but they don't. When you sit down, especially if you cross your legs, there will be a flash of bare calf, which is exactly what you don't want to happen. It's one of the cardinal sins of menswear.

<hr/>

Major Menswear Don'ts

In menswear, less is more, so it can all be boiled down to three simple rules:

Don't wear socks that are too short. They should come up over the calves so that no skin is exposed when you sit down and cross your legs.

Don't wear a belt with formal clothing. Use suspenders to hold up trousers.

Don't overaccessorize. You don't want to look foppish or overly flashy.

Jewelry

MEN SHOULD LIMIT JEWELRY to their wedding band and a watch. Certain men can pull off a stud earring. Anything else is too much. A pocket watch, as opposed to a wristwatch, is traditionally paired with white-tie attire but should only be worn by a groom who's comfortable carrying one.

Cuff Links

I ADORE A GOOD CUFF LINK; it pulls a suit together and provides a great way for a man to express his personality. I always urge my grooms to buy quality stud sets—which include cuff links—rather than wear the ones that come with the rental shirt.

Cuff links also make a wonderful gift for the groomsmen, or a gift from the bride to the groom.

Onyx, gold, and silver links and studs are classics. With white-tie or a white dinner jacket, mother-of-pearl is traditional. For a subtle, personal touch, there are cuff links with initials, Superman logos, golf motifs, race cars, motorcycles, martinis—pretty much every sport, hobby, or icon you can imagine.

If the groom is giving cuff links as a gift to the groomsmen, they don't have to match—it makes the gift

Multipointed fold

 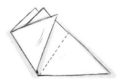 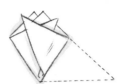 

1. Fold kerchief into an uneven triangle.

2. Bring triangle's lower left corner up to meet triangle's top, slightly overlapping the edges.

3. Repeat with right corner.

4. Fold point of kerchief into the center.

5. Insert into breast pocket and adjust as needed.

Triangle fold

1. Fold right corner slightly past middle of kerchief.

2. Repeat with left corner.

3. Holding shape in place, bring bottom half of kerchief under to meet top.

4. Insert into breast pocket and adjust as needed.

Puffed fold

1. Pinch kerchief at center of square.

2. Gather end of kerchief.

3. Bring pinched and gathered ends together.

4. Insert into breast pocket and adjust as needed.

more personal if each groomsman's cuff links are specific to his interests. Cuff links can also be monogrammed; just be sure to allow a month for engraving.

The Kerchief

EVEN IF YOUR usual style tends to be very casual, you might want to think about a handkerchief or pocket square for your wedding day as a finishing touch. With a tuxedo, you should stick to a starched white linen or cotton handkerchief folded into the pocket. With a suit, you could also consider a silk pocket square, which has a softer look than linen, in a color or a pattern. Stiff handkerchiefs in linen or cotton look best folded into a style featuring triangles or points, while silk handkerchiefs look more natural as a soft puff. Keep in mind that the handkerchief will be close to the boutonniere, so you should make sure they don't clash. Believe me, you don't want a spray of stephanotis and lavender next to a profusion of purple and green paisley.

AT THE RENTAL SHOP

No one should ever, ever pick up a tuxedo at a rental shop without trying on every last piece of it. (That goes for the groomsmen as well as the groom.) Problems are extremely common when men send in their measurements on their own. Who knows if they've measured right? If you find out in advance that the pants are too short or the zipper is stuck, you've avoided the crisis.

Before leaving the rental shop, the groom or groomsmen should try everything on and check for the following.

- Is everything in the correct style and color?

- Are the jacket sleeves the right length?

- When the jacket is buttoned, are all of the buttons in place? If it's a double-breasted suit it should include an inside button. *When the inside button is closed, does the jacket hang correctly? (If the inside button is loose or sewn into the wrong spot, it will throw off the fit of the jacket.)*

- Is the suit too big or too small?

- Are the buttons in place for attaching suspenders?

- On the shirt, is the sleeve length correct? Is the neck comfortable, neither too loose nor too tight? Are the buttons all there? If there are buttonholes for studs, are all of the studs in hand and do they fit into the buttonholes? Examine the cuffs: Are the buttons in place or do cuff links fit into the buttonholes?

- Are the tie and cummerbund or vest provided?

- Do the shoes fit? Do they match? (This is a good time to make sure the groom and all the groomsmen have the right socks for the suit!)

- Does the zipper on the pants work properly? Does the waistband fit and does it fasten correctly?

- Are there any stains, holes, cigarette burns, or frayed edges?

To Rent or to Buy?

I f the groom has cause to wear a tuxedo at least once a year, it probably makes more sense for him to buy than to rent. He won't have to rent each time another one of your friends gets hitched, and he'll be ready for an impromptu formal event (how about a romantic dinner for two?).

While alterations on rentals must, by definition, be minimal, a purchased tuxedo will be tailored to fit perfectly, and the higher quality fabric will drape better from the get-go. Though prices can start as low as $200, a good quality tuxedo is in the $500 to $600 range, and a top-of-the-line designer suit costs $1,000 and up. To find out how many wearings it will take to pay for itself, add the cost of the tux, shirt, and accessories and divide that by the rental fee.

Where to shop? Designer outlet stores like Polo Ralph Lauren, Hugo Boss, Ermenegildo Zegna, Brooks Brothers, and Burberry can be a great source for discounted tuxedos, as can off-price stores like Filene's Basement.

Rentals are the perfect solution for many grooms, a lot of whom respond very warmly to the price, which can vary from $50 to $125. That's just for the suit; the accessories are extra, and though they're available at rental stores, I urge grooms to seriously consider buying their own shirts, cummerbunds, bow ties, studs, and shoes. They'll upgrade a look for a relatively small investment, and these accessories can be used again and again.

But the fact that you're renting doesn't mean you don't have to plan ahead. Formal-wear shops may have to order in a quantity or particular style, so it's best to give them three months' notice. (Suits can be found on much shorter notice, but reserving in advance guarantees more choices in styles.) There are also rental websites, but the groom and

Measurements

If any of the groomsmen are coming from out of town, they'll need to communicate their measurements to the best man.

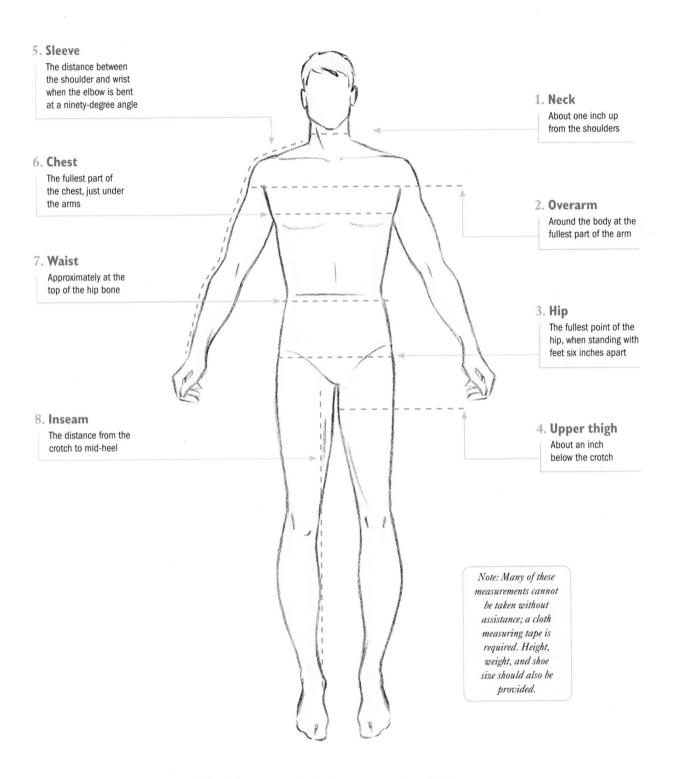

5. Sleeve

The distance between the shoulder and wrist when the elbow is bent at a ninety-degree angle

6. Chest

The fullest part of the chest, just under the arms

7. Waist

Approximately at the top of the hip bone

8. Inseam

The distance from the crotch to mid-heel

1. Neck

About one inch up from the shoulders

2. Overarm

Around the body at the fullest part of the arm

3. Hip

The fullest point of the hip, when standing with feet six inches apart

4. Upper thigh

About an inch below the crotch

Note: Many of these measurements cannot be taken without assistance; a cloth measuring tape is required. Height, weight, and shoe size should also be provided.

Honoring Your Roots

One great way for a groom to honor his heritage or tap into the vibe of the place where he's getting married is to skip the tux and wear a traditional wedding costume. Another great option is to have a jacket made out of a fabric that reflects the groom's heritage, such as kente cloth, *bògòlanfini* (mud cloth), or colorful cloth from Guatemala or Peru. You can go with western-inspired styling or come up with a hybrid. The ethnic wedding-outfit market is booming, and you can buy both garments and fabric directly from their country of origin over the Internet. Just remember to allow for plenty of shipping time! And remember to make sure that whatever you choose matches the setting and feel of your wedding. Traditional clothing has evolved because it makes sense in its home climate—you wouldn't wear a guayabera to a ski-season wedding on a mountaintop. Here are a few ideas.

- **Kilts** and all the other accoutrements of full Highland dress are extremely popular for people of Scottish or Irish descent, though wearing a kilt is a bold move. It's worn with a tuxedo shirt and special versions of a jacket and waistcoat called "Prince Charlies."

- People of Mexican descent or who are marrying in Mexico may want to opt for a **guayabera**, a traditional lightweight Mexican dress shirt that often features beautiful, detailed embroidery. It is also a great option for any casual wedding in a beach or tropical setting.

- At an Indian wedding, the groom's attire depends on which region he hails from. For a modified Indian look, opt for a suit with a **Nehru jacket** or other ethnic styling.

- At traditional Japanese weddings, both bride and groom wear a **kimono**, the male version of which is called a **haori-hakama**.

- In the Philippines, a **barong tagalog** is the formal wear of choice for men. It is a very lightweight and often transparent embroidered shirt that is worn untucked, over an undershirt.

groomsmen will need to provide their own measurements, which can be trickier than it might seem. (See the previous page for a list of common measurements.) If the fit isn't right, sites like The Black Tux will offer you a small credit for alterations at a local tailor of your choice, or they'll ship you a replacement suit in a different size, free of charge.

Formal wear usually needs to be returned the first business day after the wedding; if the groom will be away on his honeymoon, this is usually a responsibility that the best man takes on.

Dressing the Groomsmen

Though the groomsmen essentially dress like the groom, one element of their outfits should differ in order to make him stand out. The groom can wear a vest or tie that contrasts with the groomsmen's cummerbunds or bow ties. The groom's boutonniere is also typically different from the groomsmen's.

A note of warning, though: If there's one thing I've noticed from all my years of wedding planning, it's that brides tend to like to match things. In dressing the groomsmen, beware the high-school prom syndrome—turquoise bow ties and vests to match the sashes on the bridesmaids' dresses (which match the tablecloths at the reception). Some color is fine, but it shouldn't overpower the bride or the flowers. The same goes for patterns, which tend to jump out in photos. So when in doubt, stick with basic black and white. (All of this applies to anyone else who needs a tux—the dads, the ring bearer, and any man at the wedding with an honorary role.)

Fathers of the Bride and Groom

TYPICALLY, FATHERS MATCH the groomsmen in attire. But they always have the option of wearing a tuxedo, even if the groomsmen are wearing something different. In an ideal world, the fathers' tuxes would match the groom's, but by that stage in life many men own their own tuxedos and are reluctant to rent one or to change their ways. If they're easily persuaded to go with the flow, then have them match, but if they're dead set on wearing their own duds, don't stress out about the differences in style. Do check on the dads' accessories to make sure they're somewhat up to date. (Some fathers are all too happy to seize the opportunity to wear their own tuxedo shirts, purchased in 1981 and complete with pink ruffles.)

Ushers and Ring Bearers

USHERS—assuming they're distinct from the groomsmen in your wedding party—should dress similarly to the groomsmen and should match one another. If they're renting tuxedos, they should rent the same style; but if they're wearing their own suits, at the very least tell them what color of suit, shirt, and tie you would like them to wear. (This is a good opportunity to make a gift of ties.) Set ushers apart from groomsmen in photos by giving them different boutonnieres.

The ring bearer's outfit traditionally relates to what the groomsmen are wearing, but there's a lot of leeway—especially if he's very young. There's room for play here. At a seaside wedding, with the groomsmen in navy blazers and white pants, the ring bearer could conceivably wear a middy-collar sailor suit. But beware of the Little Lord Fauntleroy look (black velvet tunic with knee pants, sash, and lace-trimmed shirt), knickers, and anything with an Eton collar. I find that kind of thing just a wee bit too precious.

A cotton or linen suit with either trousers or knee-length shorts, on the other hand, is quite darling; with shorts, the ring bearer wears kneesocks and dress shoes. Tuxes (which even come in infant sizes) are a fine option, too.

Do consider the child's comfort when choosing the outfit. A comfortable ring bearer is more likely to be a cooperative, non-tantrum-throwing ring bearer. And on the day of the wedding, don't get him dressed too soon—the longer he has the outfit on, the more likely it is to come into harm's way.

All right, enough about him—now back to you! In fact, this next chapter is all about you: Taking care of yourself (inside *and* out) in advance of the wedding, and showing yourself off to your best advantage on the big day. ◆

CHAPTER NINETEEN

Just Gorgeous

GETTING BEAUTIFUL—INSIDE AND OUT

n your mind's eye, you've seen yourself walk down that aisle at least a hundred times since you were a little girl. And, of course, you've never looked more beautiful. Your skin is radiant and you're glowing with happiness. Your eyes sparkle. Your hair is soft and shiny, and your arms look great in that strapless gown. Best of all, you're so blissfully

happy, you can't stop smiling—and by the way, your teeth look great! But now that it's really happening, you're terrified. The truth is, most brides aren't nearly as nervous about getting married as they are about looking fabulous for the wedding.

Whether you are a seasoned beauty diva or an ingenue, you may need some help navigating through the pleasures—and potential pitfalls—of creating an absolutely beautiful

look for your wedding day. It's not so easy whipping your skin and body into shape, zeroing in on the prettiest hair and makeup looks for your big day, and finding the best team to make it happen, especially if you are far from home. Most important, you'll want to discover healthy ways to approach beauty from the inside out: how to relax and manage stress, eat well and boost your energy, and make sure you feel as beautiful as you look.

Skin Care

Good habits yield great results, but don't wait until the last minute—start now. When you begin to shop for bridesmaids' dresses and think about your floral arrangements—around six months ahead of your wedding—start to focus in on your skin-care regimen, too.

No matter what your skin type, the secret to healthy, great-looking skin consists of four steps: cleanse, exfoliate, moisturize, protect your skin from sunlight.

Look for products that are geared toward your skin type—oily, dry, normal/combination, sensitive—and fit comfortably within your budget. Clear skin starts with good nutrition, so you may want to look at cleaning up your diet to ensure a clearer complexion in the months before your wedding.

If your skin tends to break out, is sensitive or allergic, or if you have other common conditions like eczema or rosacea, you might want to consult a dermatologist and/or a facialist and map out a master plan leading up to the wedding. A skin-care professional can recommend treatments and a product regimen specifically geared toward great results for the big day.

If your skin is already in good shape, and you've been following a regimen, now is not the time to change it. As the saying goes, if it ain't broke, don't fix it. But if it is, facials are a great way to get your glow going. Plan a year ahead, and book a facial every two months, adding an extra appointment two weeks to a month before the wedding. (Don't have a facial less than a week before the wedding, just in case your skin has a reaction. Even if you've been fine all along, your hormones may act up.)

There are all types of facials, and the trick is to find the one that's best for you. If you are prone to blackheads, look for a facialist who will do extractions. A microdermabrasion treatment or a glycolic peel will also help unclog blemished skin and improve your skin's texture, but it may leave your skin slightly irritated for up to twenty-four hours. If your skin is dry, a moisturizing facial will keep it looking plump and juicy.

If a professional facial is beyond your budget, give yourself an at-home mini facial. Wash with your cleanser, exfoliate, and apply a mask for ten minutes while you relax around the house or in the tub. Rinse with warm, not hot, water and moisturize.

Oily Skin

IF YOUR SKIN IS OILY, wash twice a day with an oil-free or gel cleanser. If you suffer from breakouts, use a beta-hydroxy cleanser, which will add a little extra firepower to the process. Exfoliate four or five nights a week with a beta-hydroxy lotion or a gentle scrub. (If you use a scrub, do not rub it into your face—gently press it into your skin.) Apply a clay (aka "kaolin") mask once a week to help remove dead skin cells and absorb excess oil.

Dry or Normal Skin

WASH ONCE A DAY, using a creamy cleanser and warm water (hot water dries the skin). Exfoliate gently once a week to control flakiness, and apply a rich moisturizer at least once a day, more often if needed. Apply a moisturizing mask once a week.

> Here's a great dry-skin tip I picked up from makeup artists: Give your skin a spritz with a "hydrosol," a floral water often used in spa treatments. It will help your moisturizer penetrate the skin, and its botanical scent will perk up your spirits.

Sensitive Skin

WASH WITH A GENTLE, nonfoaming cleanser, and avoid products with a heavy fragrance or that contain essential oils, as these can irritate sensitive skin. Moisturize with a light lotion formulated for sensitive skin. If you have rosacea, avoid spicy foods, alcohol, caffeine, and sun exposure.

Blotchiness and Rashes

THE DAYS AND WEEKS leading up to the big day can be stressful, and stress *will* show up on your face—especially if you have sensitive skin.

Whatever you do, do not change your skin care routine in the days and weeks leading up to your wedding. It's much too risky—your skin could be sensitive to an ingredient in a new product and you could develop a rash, or even hives. To soothe a rash, apply a thin layer of over-the-counter hydrocortisone cream. If you have hives or swelling, check with your doctor first, but an over-the-counter antihistamine should make them disappear in a couple of hours.

If your face is blotchy, apply an anti-inflammatory lotion on affected areas.

Bridal Breakouts and Blemish Treatments

A BIG GUST OF WIND may not knock down the tents at *your* backyard wedding (true story), but chances are pretty good that either the bride or the groom will wake up the day before the wedding with a pimple. Even if you've had regular facials and have been scrupulous about your skin care, the stress can make breakouts seem almost inevitable—especially if your skin is oily to begin with.

When you're stressed-out, the oil glands work in overdrive, clogging pores and causing breakouts. Hormones are another trigger, which is why birth control pills are a factor to weigh. The pill can either clear up or cause breakouts, and it can take several weeks to find out how starting or stopping it will affect *you*, so keep your doctor in the loop about your wedding plans.

Finally, switching to a new brand of makeup—if your skin is sensitive, or if the makeup is oily—can cause "cosmetic acne," which is why it's always important to try out your makeup at least a month or two before your wedding.

If you're prone to blemishes, you might want to schedule a backup appointment with your dermatologist a day or two before the wedding, just in case. As a last resort, he can inject the blemish with cortisone, which will make it disappear in a couple of hours. If you have

Bridal Beauty: The Rules

1. Keep it simple. As makeup artist Bobbi Brown once said: "Most brides want to look pretty, but all brides end up looking beautiful." You will too, and it doesn't have to be complicated.

2. Your wedding is not the time to reinvent yourself. Your hair and makeup should enhance your natural beauty—not transform you into someone else.

3. Relax! You are the superstar. This is your day to look and feel beautiful—so prepare to enjoy it.

a red spot the night before, apply an antibiotic ointment or a spot acne patch to reduce redness and swelling overnight.

Or try this makeup artists' trick for the day-of: Use a Q-tip to dab a bit of Visine on the blemish for one or two minutes to bring down the redness and swelling. Then take a small brush and dab a thick cream concealer on top of the pimple, working toward the center. Use the brush to blend around the edges. Apply another layer, then add a light dusting of loose translucent powder (pressed powder is too cakey) to set the concealer.

If you've got a few pimples in the weeks leading up to the wedding, try any one of these tried-and-true remedies: salicylic acid cleansers and over-the-counter spot treatments to unclog pores; tea tree oil to kill bacteria and dry up pimples; beta-hydroxy acid lotions, which exfoliate the top layer of pore-clogging dead skin cells; or moisturizers with retinol, an over-the-counter vitamin A derivative that smooths and exfoliates the skin.

If you have blemishes that you've lived with—minor acne, sun-damage, surface pitting or scars—now may be the moment you decide not to tolerate them any longer. With a deadline in sight (you need to start six months ahead of time), you can virtually obliterate them with lasers, retinol creams, skin lighteners, glycolic or fruit acid peels, or microdermabrasion, which may be best for sensitive skin.

That Time of the Month

Worried your period will unexpectedly arrive on your wedding day? Join the club—it's an almost universal concern among brides. If you want to take preventive measures, consult your gynecologist. She should be able to tweak an existing birth control prescription or set you up on a new schedule to make sure your period bypasses your wedding date by a week or two; there are also prescriptions that suppress your period so that it comes only several times a year.

You should know, though, that even brides who take precautions are sometimes taken by surprise; a case of nerves and overwrought hormones can actually bring on early menstruation. (That's why, no matter where you are in your cycle, you must pack those tampons in your emergency kit.)

Some women suffer from extremely severe cramps, nausea, or even migraines during or just before their periods. If that's the case for you, see your gynecologist or doctor far enough ahead of your wedding date that you can experiment with the proper medications and find something that helps you feel more comfortable.

Consult a dermatologist to figure out the best treatment protocol for your skin. Your doctor may decide to prescribe a retinoid cream to keep your pores unclogged and dry up blemishes; these can also cause redness, flakiness, and seriously dry skin, so it's very important to give your skin time to adjust.

Extreme Beauty

THIS IS YOUR BIG DAY, and, of course, you want to look your absolute best. The fact is, most brides do, without going to any great lengths to get there. It's the oldest cliché in the book, but when you're feeling this happy—bolstered by the love of friends and family—the glow you feel on the inside will inevitably radiate outward.

Nonetheless, some brides feel the pressure to look "perfect" and are willing to go to great lengths, from cosmetic dermatology to surgery, to reach their goal. I would strongly urge against taking any drastic steps—implants, Botox, liposuction, gastric bypass, face-lifts, etc.—in the months leading up to your wedding. But if you do, make sure to plan ahead. Surgical procedures, obviously, require downtime for recovery, and you need to talk to your doctor to build enough time—generally, at least six to eight months—into your schedule. (And if you are going to do anything to alter the shape of your body, do it before you order your dress.)

Even minor facial treatments can result in inflammation for up to a couple of days. I'll never forget the bride who walked through the door to discover that her friends and family had thrown her a surprise bridal shower. Her surprise was only too obvious, because she'd just had Restylane injections, and her lips were bumpy and swollen. (If she'd known, of course, she would have timed it better.) As a result, her memories of that happy event—not to mention her photos—are forever tinged with embarrassment and discomfort.

Certain skin conditions can be treated with lasers in the dermatologist's office, with minimal downtime and discomfort. If you have forehead wrinkles, adult acne, scars, chronic puffiness under the eyes, spider veins, or reddish stretch marks, you may want to discuss laser treatments with your dermatologist. Laser treatments involve application of a topical anesthesia or gel. There's a feeling of warmth or slight burning during the procedure, with aftereffects similar to sunburn: a few days of redness,

In the weeks leading up to the wedding, drink six to eight glasses of water each day. It may help clear up blemishes and will definitely give your skin a more luminous quality. While you're drinking more water, cut back on caffeine. It will calm you down, and it's good for your skin.

Pearly-White Teeth

To get your teeth really sparkling, have them cleaned one to two weeks before the wedding. And look into the following options for extra oomph.

DO-IT-YOURSELF

■ Drugstore Strips. Peroxide-coated whitening strips and gels are applied directly to teeth for 30 to 50 minutes (read the instructions) twice a day and take approximately three weeks to work. Be attentive! They can move around in your mouth, which may result in uneven bleaching ($30 to $40).

■ Whitening Toothpastes. These can subtly lighten teeth over time—it takes at least two months, once or twice a day ($15 to $20).

PROFESSIONAL WHITENING

■ Laser Bleaching. A one-hour in-office treatment that combines light with hydrogen peroxide bleaching solution ($500 to $2,000). Results are immediate and can last up to five years.

■ Power Bleaching. Two in-office bleaching treatments supported by a week or more of at-home bleaching with custom trays. Results take at least a week and last up to two years ($500 to $1,500).

■ Custom Trays. Your dentist makes special trays filled with bleaching solution for you to wear at home. Results take a few weeks (up to $500).

■ Porcelain veneers. These are not, technically, whitening treatments but will cover any cracks or discolored teeth ($1,500 to $3,000 per tooth).

swelling, or flaking. Look for a board-certified dermatologist (check the American Academy of Dermatology website) with expertise in lasers. Treatments can run from $750 to $1,500, but many conditions require several sessions. All that said, I'll reiterate my earlier point: I've never seen a bride who *didn't* look beautiful on her wedding day. What's more, your fiancé is pledging to love and honor *you*, not a woman out of the pages of a magazine. So, please, take it easy on the drastic alterations!

ASK MINDY

Q My fiancé and I had a passionate night, and I woke up with a bad case of beard burn. It won't go away! What can I do?

A Next time, make him shave first! Seriously, though, beard burn is the cumulative result of tiny abrasions in the skin. The best thing to do is rinse your face with cool water, gently pat it dry, and apply an over-the-counter hydrocortisone cream.

Makeup

Though you may never be nominated for an Academy Award, your wedding day is your walk down the red carpet. And at that moment, all eyes *will* be focused on you, so you'll want to choose your makeup with care.

That said, there's no need to go overboard. Approach your wedding makeup the way you would think of makeup for a date. You don't want to load it on—but you don't want to go bare-faced, either. (Remember, the photos!) Be realistic, and be yourself. If your style is fresh, healthy, and low-key, don't suddenly transform yourself into a stylized Parisian coquette. I've seen grooms do a double-take (and not in a good way) when the woman walking down the aisle—the bride!—is someone they hardly recognize. It's not a great idea to go for anything too trendy, either. Take the long view. How dated will that lime green shimmer shadow look in your photo album ten years down the road?

Skin Dos and Don'ts

Although skin condition is largely genetic, there *are* simple things you can do (and some no-nos to avoid) to stack the odds in your favor:

Do drink lots of water—six to eight glasses per day.

Don't sleep with your makeup on; it can make your skin break out.

Do keep hands away from your face—dirt and oil cause blemishes.

Don't squeeze a blackhead or a pimple.

Do build in enough time—at least a week—to give your skin a rest after a facial or waxing.

Don't booze it up or eat salty foods the night before the wedding—you'll look puffy.

Do try on your makeup a month in advance to make sure your skin doesn't have a negative reaction.

Don't try a new skin-care product within a month before the wedding—you may have an allergic reaction.

Do use sun protection, every day, even when the sun doesn't shine. And if you go to the beach, be extra diligent.

Don't get a spray-on tan or apply self-tanner the day before. You can develop streaks or orange palms.

Your makeup needs to mesh not only with your personal style but also with the rest of the wedding. Smoky eyes, for example, might look overdone at a beach or garden ceremony, while sheer, neutral shades might be too low-key for a formal evening affair.

Style aside, there are also practical concerns. Your makeup will need to last for many hours. You'll want it to work both live and on camera. And as the star of the show, you won't have much time to nip away for touch-ups, which means you'll want hair and makeup to last.

Some brides choose to apply their own makeup, but most play it safe by working with a professional makeup artist. Unless you are highly skilled, I would strongly advise that you at least consult with a pro, and, if you can afford it, hire a makeup artist for the big day. Believe me, it's worth it.

When you go for a trial run with your makeup artist, wear a white T-shirt to ensure that the makeup colors will flatter you in your wedding gown. (Obviously, if your gown is fuchsia, wear a pink T-shirt.) And take advantage of your camera-ready face— a really good time to do a trial run is right before your bridal shower.

Finding a Makeup Artist

WELL-KNOWN MAKEUP ARTISTS in cities like New York, Los Angeles, Dallas, or Atlanta book up fast. Start shopping around at least five or six months in advance if you want to have the pick of the litter; you'll also have time for a "trial run" to experiment with different looks and new products.

Start by asking friends, friends of friends, other brides, and the stylist at your local salon for recommendations. Many salons employ makeup artists who are also trained in brow shaping. Call your local cosmetology school, where instructors may be available for private bookings; you can also hire a student at a lesser rate. Ask the staff at your bridal shop, your wedding planner, your photographer, your local day spa, or the salespeople at the makeup counter in your favorite department store—many do makeup on the side, or can refer people who do. Search online for local agencies that book freelance makeup artists for weddings.

Doing It Yourself

UNLESS YOU'RE REALLY A PRO, you'll want to shop around for some guidance. Even if you choose not to book a makeup artist for your wedding day, it's a good idea to hire one in advance to create a look, make a diagram of it for you, and teach you how to do it yourself.

Or you can take the bargain route. Go to the makeup counter at your local department store and find a salesperson whose makeup you think looks good. (If you like the way she's applied her own makeup, you'll probably like what she'll do for you.) Tell her what type of look you're after, or, better still, bring tear sheets from magazines to show her. Have her do your makeup. If you like it, buy the products and ask her to map out what she did.

Foundation

IF YOU'VE BEEN FOLLOWING a healthy skin-care regimen, your skin should be in pretty good shape. Your foundation can take you the rest of the way to flawless. A good foundation covers up imperfections, smooths out your skin tone, and imparts a healthy glow to your skin without feeling heavy or artificial. But you'll have to experiment to find the right type. No one should hide behind a heavy mask of makeup, especially not a beautiful bride on her wedding day. The most important factors when it comes to foundation are comfort, that it feels (and looks) natural, and that it lasts.

If your skin is normal/dry and clear, try a tinted moisturizer for the lightest lasting coverage. If it's oily, you'll want an oil-free liquid foundation or oil-free "gel" foundation—look for a "semi-matte finish," which will give the skin a luminous, velvety look (see page 255 for shine-proofing). Airbrushed makeup, which you spray onto a sponge then dab onto your face, offers light, even

> If you choose to do your own makeup— especially if you're looking for a natural, healthy look—check out some of the "bridal" palettes or kits designed by makeup artists for the occasion. Most makeup artists recommend soft, neutral shades, and that's what you'll find in these kits.

|||||||| **MEETING AND GREETING** ||||||||

A MAKEUP ARTIST

Once you have a list of makeup artists, you'll want to start scheduling consultations. (Some makeup artists offer these for free, others charge. It's important to ask.) Before your meeting, look through magazines and tear out shots of makeup looks you like. Having a picture always helps—your "neutral" may be another person's "moss green." Ask her to bring her portfolio, if she has one, so that you can see what her style looks like.

But loving her work is not enough. Assess whether you feel comfortable talking to her, and expressing your ideas. No one wants to be bullied or intimidated on her wedding day! Determine whether she's dependable. Does she return phone calls promptly? You don't want to have to worry that she may not show up. During your meeting you should cover the following questions:

- *Do you have experience working with brides?*

- Ask about her philosophy—what does she think a bride should look like on her wedding day?

- *What do you think would be best for me?* She may be completely in sync with you, or she may come up with something totally different—and you may love it!

- *What if something happens and you can't make it at the last minute? Do you have a backup person to send?*

- Find out if she'll bring her own supplies (brushes, tweezers, etc.), or if she expects you to take care of it. (Most bring their own—one less thing for you to worry about.)

- *Will I need to purchase and bring my own makeup?*

- *How do you charge—by the hour? By the job?*

- *How many events do you do in a day?* (Will she be rushing off to someone else?)

- *Will you come to me?*

- *Will you stick around for touch-ups? If not, can you teach me how to do my own?*

- *Finally, do you have references I can call?*

coverage for the long haul. Mineral makeup—a natural option made from powdered minerals—is great for all skin types, but doesn't last as long as liquid foundation.

Some makeup artists recommend applying a foundation primer underneath foundation to help your makeup last longer. It's certainly not necessary, but it does help to fade-proof your face and create a smooth base for foundation. But if you're not really comfortable wearing makeup, skip this extra step and look for a water-based foundation, which won't separate like an oil-based product, or for makeup with silicone (its ingredients will end in –one), which feels silky and lasts forever.

How to apply? Unless your skin is oily, use a tiny bit of moisturizer to plump up lines and smooth over any dry patches. Use a small brush—or fingers, so your body heat can help "melt" the product into the skin—to dab concealer over blemishes or broken capillaries. Apply foundation with a clean sponge, brush, or very clean fingers. Dip a big, pouffy brush in loose, translucent powder, shake off the excess, and lightly stroke around the face, pressing lightly into oily areas, like the T zone.

A light dusting of powder helps "set" the foundation so that it lasts longer (especially if you have oily skin), but if powder makes your skin look dry, spritz your face with mineral water after you apply it or skip this step entirely.

Bronzers, Highlighters, and Illuminators

IF YOUR SKIN looks dull or pale and you need to warm it up a bit, these products make it easy. A *bronzer* is a great alternative to self-tanning, which can be a risky business unless you really know what you're doing (see page 269). Apply bronzer (cream, powder, or gel) sparingly to cheekbones, the top of your forehead, and your jawline—wherever the sun would naturally hit. If using powder bronzer, apply with a big, fluffy brush, shaking off the excess first. Apply cream or gel with a sponge or fingers, and blend really well.

Also blend your bronzer into your neck and décolletage so that you lose the lines of demarcation. But be careful not to get too close—you don't want to stain your gown.

Highlighters and *illuminators* contain bits of light-reflecting minerals, which really can create a trick of light and shadow to give you that "lit from within" look, a faux glow that almost glistens. Be very judicious when applying such products. Dab a bit on your cheekbones and the bridge of your nose. If your gown is low cut, apply a bit along the collarbone, into the cleavage, and over the tops of your shoulders.

To build a subtle glow slowly, try a *glow lotion*, a moisturizer infused with a tiny touch of self-tanner, to enable you to apply a bit each day and control your glow.

The Blushing Bride

THE MOST IMPORTANT THING to remember with blush is that a little goes a long way. The second is to blend really well, and third, to choose the right color, and keep it soft.

If you're using powder blush, throw away the brush that comes in the compact immediately—it's too stiff and won't blend well. Use a fluffy, natural-bristle blush brush or a Japanese-style fan brush instead.

To avoid streakiness or stripes, smile and apply blush to the apple of the cheek in short, vertical strokes, outward and upward toward the ears.

Contract Points

Once you've found your makeup artist, negotiate a rate and get it in writing—even if you're working with someone who doesn't usually draw up a contract. The contract should cover the date, arrival time, number of hours, price, location, and any extra expenses (for example, parking, products, etc.). On average, makeup artists (and hairstylists) usually take about forty-five minutes to work their magic, which doesn't include time to travel and set up their tools.

Shine and Dark Circles

Excess facial shine and under-eye circles are *not* a bride's best friends. Not to worry, there are simple ways to address both of these common issues.

SHINE-PROOFING

To make sure that your skin is shine free, forget about moisturizing on the morning of your big day—unless you have truly dry skin—and reach for a mattifying lotion. Apply only on areas where you're oily, like the T zone. Look for oil-free foundation or a water-based gel formulation and make sure to dust with loose translucent powder—use a big, poufy brush—to set. For touch-ups, pack blotting papers (choose a brand without powder to avoid buildup when you blot) and extra mattifying lotion in your makeup bag.

DARK CIRCLES

Some women have a natural tendency toward that dark, smudgy look under the eyes. If that's you, start at least a month in advance with one of these two remedies: Twice a day, apply a vitamin K eye cream, recommended by many cosmetic surgeons to help control bruising after surgery. Or try a product called Hylexin. It's pricey—about $90 for a tiny tube—but, applied sparingly twice a day, it really works. To camouflage dark circles after a night of partying, of course, you'll want to reach for a concealer. The trick to avoiding white circles under your eyes is to choose a product that's one to two shades lighter than your foundation, and use just a bit. If your skin is dark, look for a yellow-based concealer, which won't turn ashy. For a more perfect match, look for a split-pan concealer, so that you can blend the colors together. Use a tiny brush or your fourth finger (the least pressure) to apply, patting from the tear duct in an outward direction.

For cream, gel, or cheek stain, use your fingers or a makeup sponge. Dab a tiny bit on the apples of your cheeks, and massage in round, gentle, circular movements. Blend very well. (Stains look really sweet and natural, but they dry quickly, which means you need to blend fast—it may take some practice—in order to avoid splotching. Wash your hands to avoid staining your fingertips.)

To choose cheek color that complements your skin tone, look for light pinks if you're pale, brown-pink or peach if you're medium, or golden brown, burgundy, or deeper peach if you have a darker complexion. Red shades that look too dark in the palette or tube may look really soft and subtle on your cheek—these can flatter all skin tones, but the only way to know if they work for you is to try them.

Eye Openers: Three Great Looks

EVEN THE SUBTLEST eye shadow should, if applied correctly, make your eyes look bigger, brighter, and more beautiful. Here are three looks, all simple, that signal totally different moods while managing to complement any eye color. A note: Lighter color eye shadows make eyes pop, while darker shades add depth. If your lids are translucent or veiny, you should apply an eye base—which is really just a concealer for the eyelids—before applying shadow.

The Natural

A soft, natural look is perfect for an outdoor or daytime wedding and looks beautiful with either strong or subtle lip color.

1. Brush a light or neutral shade—vanilla, suede, pale lilac, buttercream—on your upper lids and into the crease with a medium, natural-bristle eye-shadow brush.

2. Stroke on black or brown mascara.

The Shimmer

A subtle shimmer shadow is perfect for evening and adds a gleam and sparkle to the eyes. It works especially well with a matte or sheer lip color.

1. Choose a light shimmer shade with a hint of copper, bronze, gold, champagne, pink, or silver and brush onto the upper lids and into the crease with a medium, natural-bristle brush. (Don't overdo it.)

2. Use a brown or charcoal gel eyeliner (these have staying power) and a small brush to press a line close to your lash line.

3. Stroke on black or brown mascara.

The Gamine

This graphic, sophisticated French style manages to be bold but not over the top. It looks beautiful with a simple matte-red lipstick.

1. Brush a light, pale shadow on the upper lids and into the crease.

2. Use a black or charcoal gel eyeliner and a small brush to press a line close to the lash line.

3. Stroke on black mascara.

Lush Lash

MOST BRIDES who want a fabulous fringe reach for a magical mascara wand—waterproof, of course! But before you do so, try an eyelash curler, which is easy to use and really opens up your eyes. (Always curl lashes *before* applying mascara; if you decide not to wear mascara, simply curling your lashes will make them look thicker.) Apply two coats to the top lashes (let them dry for a minute in between) and one coat to the lower (to minimize smudging). Go

Eyeliner Elegance

Liquid liners can look too harsh, and pencil liners tend to smudge. Try a long-lasting gel liner instead. Black may look too severe against a white gown, so try dark brown or charcoal for a softer look.

To use, dip a small, flat brush into the pot, wipe against the sides to remove excess, hold the outer corner of the eye with one hand, and apply—in small, close-together, dotlike motions, working outward—as close to the lash line as possible.

Don't start at the inner corner of the eyelid, or you'll actually make your eyes look smaller. Instead, start the line near the beginning of your iris.

through your lashes with a lash brush/comb immediately after application, as waterproof formulas can be clumpy.

If you're worried about raccoon eyes and your budget allows, you may want to consider professionally applied eyelash extensions. Unlike false eyelashes, they look subtle and natural (diamond-studded mink lashes aside, of course). False eyelashes also run the risk of ending up on your cheeks if you cry and the binding glue dissolves.

Eyelash extensions take two to three hours to apply, last for up to two months, and cost anywhere from $150 to $500. They're labor intensive: Unlike false lashes, which come in a strip, each lash is applied individually with a tweezer and surgical glue. Though the results are beautiful, sitting through the procedure requires patience. Afterward, you can't shower for a day and must initially be careful about not getting too much water around the lashes when you wash your face. Of course, you can't—and won't need to—wear mascara.

Brows

A BEAUTIFUL ARCH not only frames the eyes, but also creates a polished, well-groomed finish to the face. Even if you usually do your own brows, it's a good idea to consult a professional before the wedding. If you

The Lighting

Apply your makeup in natural light, preferably near a window. Artificial light will encourage you to overapply, and you may wind up looking overdone, especially in the bright light of a daytime wedding. If you're getting married outdoors, go with creamy makeup, which looks fresher in natural light than powder formulations. Natural light can also make shimmery products look overly frosty, so go easy on the shiny stuff.

don't already have a brow routine, start five months in advance of the big day, in case your brows need time to be reshaped. In most large cities you can find "eyebrow experts" or "brow salons" where talented brow shapers have carved out their niche; makeup artists are also trained to shape brows. Brows can be tweezed, waxed, or threaded (a Middle Eastern technique where thread is wrapped around each individual hair and pulled). I recommend tweezing. It's the gentlest, least irritating method and offers the greatest control.

Your last shaping should be a week before the wedding. If you choose to wax, you don't want any residual redness. If you wax your brows and they do get red, apply lavender oil directly to the area or take an antihistamine to reduce redness. If your brows need extra definition, lightly go over them with a brow pencil or a bit of shadow one to two shades lighter than your brows, and blend with your fingers or a Q-tip.

Lips

LAYER ON THAT LIP BALM in the week before your wedding to avoid waking up with chapped lips on the big day. If you do experience chapping, apply Vaseline or lip balm and gently massage your lips with a soft toothbrush to loosen dry skin.

As for lipstick, makeup artists have lots of clever tricks to keep it where it belongs (a major concern with so much hugging, kissing, eating, and drinking going on throughout

the day!). Color in your lips with a nude lip pencil before applying lipstick. The color will adhere to the pencil and last longer. Applying your lipstick with a lip brush will also help it last, and the brush offers more precision.

Lip stains are another great option but can stain fingers, so use a lip brush. Long-lasting lipsticks will keep you covered throughout the day, but can be drying. Layer a bit of clear or tinted gloss on top to help keep lips looking moist and add a lovely bit of shine.

ASK MINDY

Q If I wake up on the day of the wedding and my eyes are red, what should I do?

A If your lids are red, apply a yellow-based concealer—yellow neutralizes red. But if your eyes are irritated, apply redness relief drops, preferably a brand that you've used before. Or try blue eyedrops, which are popular with brides, as they not only soothe the eyes, but are also tinted to make whites look whiter, especially in photos.

Picture Perfect

To master your makeup so that it looks fresh and pretty in person *and* in photos, you'll need to keep a few things in mind. Follow this tip sheet, relax, and smile!

1. To diffuse harsh light in photos, look for light-reflecting foundation, or one that contains ingredients that end with *–one* (for example, silicone)—these last a long time, and give your skin a soft, dewy quality without the shine. Or, mix your normal foundation with highlighter before you apply it. If your skin is oily, obviously, look for oil-free foundation.

2. Use cream blush, rather than powder or gel, to add warmth to your skin tone. It lasts longer.

3. For shine-free photos, don't forget your powder. Dust lightly on your T zone.

4. If you use powder, continue it down onto your neck and chest to prevent the lines of demarcation that can appear so vivid in photos.

5. Make sure your mascara is waterproof—for obvious reasons!

6. Avoid lipstick shades with brown undertones, which can look really flat in photos. Steer clear of really dark lip shades, which will dominate the photos, or very pale shades, which will wash out.

7. Lip gloss is fine, but not super shiny—it will reflect too much in the photos.

8. Blend your makeup really well, especially your blush, concealer, and eye shadow. The camera can exaggerate visible makeup lines.

9. Keep your chin up—it's the most flattering angle.

10. Stand up straight—your mother was right.

11. If you're wearing a sleeveless gown and you're concerned about the way your arms look, take a tip from the stars: Angle your body slightly away from the camera and place the hand closest to the photographer low on your hip.

12. To make your hips look narrower, angle your lower body at a slight diagonal and swivel your head and torso around to face the camera.

Hair

Most brides want their hair to look soft, healthy, beautiful—but not too trendy. And most stylists agree. Beyond that, there are several other things to consider: your personality, the location, your headpiece, and your dress. If you're getting married on the beach, a loose, natural style may feel more appropri-ate than a chignon. But it's hard to predict what your hair will do when you wear it loose—especially in the great outdoors. If you're the type of bride who needs to have everything under control, you may be more comfort-able with the structure of an updo. And remember your dress: If you're wearing a full-skirted Cinderella gown, for example, a style that's tight to the head may not create the most flattering proportion.

Finding a Hairstylist

LIKE MAKEUP ARTISTS, good hairstylists can get booked up months in advance. If possible, start checking out your options six months ahead of time to give your-self enough time for a "style trial" where you'll consult with the stylist, discuss ideas for your hair, and actually have her style you. Most hairstylists charge separately for a consultation and trial run, and depending on where you live and the stylist's level of expertise, their fees usually start at $150 and go up as high as $1,000. Junior stylists are always more affordable, and many are extremely talented.

If you don't have a hairstylist you would like to work with on your wedding day, ask your wedding planner or caterer for suggestions. (Even if you're not using a wed-ding planner, call the best one in your area and ask for a recommendation.) Or ask friends and makeup artists at your favorite cosmetics counter. Once you have your list of names, speak with the hairstylists by phone to help narrow down your options. Make sure you're comfortable with the stylist's manner before you book an appoint-ment for a trial run.

The Logistics

IT'S ALWAYS LESS EXPENSIVE to go to the salon than to have a stylist come to you, though having your stylist "on location" can be a worthwhile splurge. If you aren't going to the salon, find out whether the stylist will bring tools and products or if you need to supply your own. Some stylists also do makeup, which is not only conve-nient but can cut back on the cost.

A Hairstylist

Before you meet with the hairstylist, look through magazines for inspiration—don't limit yourself to bridal books. Rip out pages from women's magazines and hairstyling magazines, and bring these tear sheets along. Of course, your hair may not turn out just like the photo in the end, since everyone's hair texture is different, but at least you'll start with a level playing field.

Also ask your stylist if she has a bridal portfolio and take a look. Make sure you address the following points:

- *Do you know how to work with veils, headpieces, and hair jewelry?*

- *Do you work with a team, or with assistants?*

- If you want her associates to style anyone else in your bridal party—mother, sister, attendants, etc.—find out what she would charge.

- *If I want you to do my hair for the rehearsal dinner—or other related events—what would the price be?*

- *Do you have backup, in case you get sick?*

- Do you want her to stay to help you transition from the ceremony to the reception?

- *What style will work best for my hair type—thick, thin, curly, etc.?*

- If you love to dance, what styles will stay put while you're showing off those cha-cha moves you learned in your ballroom dancing class?

- *Will this style look good from a 360-degree angle, not just from the front?* Take the neckline and silhouette of the dress into consideration.

- If you have already selected a headpiece, bring it to the trial. If not, discuss your ideas with the stylist, and then set up another appointment when the headpiece comes in.

- *Do you have references I can call?*

Once you've found your stylist and negotiated the rates, you'll need to get a contract and put down a deposit. The contract should cover the date, arrival time, number of hours, price, location, and any additional expenses (parking, products, touch-ups for pictures, veil removal, etc.).

To find a stylist for an out-of-town wedding, ask your home stylist for recommendations. (If cost is not an issue, some brides choose to fly their stylists out to their weddings.) Check with day spas, wedding planners, and bridal shops near your wedding venue. And when you are scouting locations, take advantage of your proximity and go for trial runs with hairstylists in the area.

Six Great Wedding Hairstyles

THE FOLLOWING HAIRSTYLES aren't just great looks; some are also "convertible," giving you the option of changing your style between the ceremony and the reception. It's always quicker and easier to put your hair

up in a loose ponytail or twist than to take out all those pins and let it down. Everyone's hair texture is different, so give your style a test run before you decide. An updo is easy, elegant, cool, and comfortable—especially if you plan on working up a sweat on the dance floor or your wedding is taking place in a hot, humid location; on the other hand, for some brides, nothing says romance like flowing locks.

For a destination wedding, consider doing as one client of mine did: Have your local stylist do your hair, photograph it (close up and from every direction), and bring it to a good salon near your venue to replicate. Even if the local stylist tends toward a dated look, given some guidelines she should be able to replicate a style that's more to your liking.

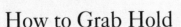

How to Grab Hold

Hairspray is essential if you want your style to last for hours and hours. Even if you never use it again in your entire life, you've got to have it on your wedding day. That said, you get to choose what type of spray will suit you best. Nonalcohol, nonaerosol hairspray is the least drying and sets to a softer finish than traditional sprays. Plus, it's much more eco-friendly. The downside, of course, is that it won't hold your style as well as a little spritz of the old-fashioned beauty parlor stuff. Another thing to keep in mind: Updos hold better when your hair isn't squeaky clean, so don't wash your hair the day of the wedding unless you have a fairly oily scalp.

The Chignon

A chignon is an easy, elegant style for a more traditional bride who wants to look impeccably groomed. It's also perfect if you're a worrier—it's a long-lasting style with great hold.

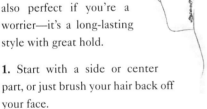

1. Start with a side or center part, or just brush your hair back off your face.

2. Gather the hair in a ponytail with an elastic at the base of the neck.

3. Loosely twist hair, and wrap around the elastic. (For a fresher, less formal style, let the ends stick out a bit.)

4. Use wide hairpins to hold hair in place.

5. Spray hair or slick on a dab of gel for extra hold.

Note: A chignon that sits low on the nape of the neck is easy to wear with a tiara. You can also accessorize a chignon with a bun wrap, or use combs—embellished with jewels or tiny pearls—to hold shorter pieces of hair back off the face.

A French Twist

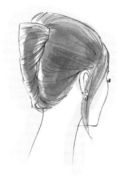

A French twist is a structured, sophisticated style that keeps your hair off your face and works beautifully with a veil or tiara.

1. Brush your hair back with a tiny bit of pomade (aka hair wax) or gel. (Or part it on the side.)

2. Gather your hair at the nape and gently twist, pulling it upward and securing with wide hairpins as you go. If your hair is supersilky, you may want to wrap your twist around a "hair rat," a soft, mesh bun that's available at drugstores. Hair rats come in all shapes and sizes: A larger rat will create more depth and make your hair look fuller. Hold the rat where you want to place the twist, roll your hair around it, and pin it in place with wide hairpins.

3. Tuck the ends in, or if you want a younger, looser look, let them hang loose.

4. Spray for extra hold.

Note: A brooch at the top is a beautiful way to glam up a simple French twist.

A French Braid

It may sound retro, but for a wedding, a French braid is a simple, romantic style that works well with straight or wavy hair (so long as your hair is not too thin).

1. Take a section of hair at your crown and divide it into three equal pieces.

2. Start to braid and add in more hair to each of the three sections as you go. You can make the braid as loose or tight as you like.

3. When you reach the bottom, all of your hair should be woven in.

4. Fasten with an elastic, and top with a ribbon. Or if you like, separate a section of hair from the bottom, wrap it around the elastic, and tuck in the end. Tuck in any strays with bobby pins.

Note: Wrapping a silky ribbon around the elastic a few times then tying it in a flat bow adds a touch of color.

Half Up/Half Down

This is a romantic, almost universally flattering style. It's less controlled than an updo, but still keeps your hair off your face.

1. Pull a section of hair back from each side of your head, and fasten it in back with a pretty clip, barrette, or brooch—but don't let your hair accessory interfere with your veil.

2. Gently pull your hair through the barrette from the bottom. Brush the ends.

Extensions

It used to be that women would start to grow their hair out for their wedding as soon as they got engaged. I still see many brides doing the same—seems like there's just something about a short, choppy do that doesn't look right with a full-length ballgown. If you're very patient or are planning on a really long engagement, growing your hair out may work. But now there's a much easier way: extensions.

Extensions are synthetic or real hair that's braided, sewn, woven, bonded (glued), or clipped into your hair to make it look longer and thicker. There are extensions available for all hair types, from silky, straight Caucasian strands to curly African-American hair. Aside from clip-ons, popular for brides because they're so easy to remove, extensions can be left in until they fall or are cut out.

Braided extensions have a shelf life of about three to four weeks, after which they need to be redone because they pull on the hair.

If you're considering extensions, you'll need to have an initial consultation with a hairstylist so that she can order them to match your hair. Extensions can take anywhere from one to six hours to put in, so you will need to book the hairstylist a few weeks in advance, and the cost ranges from about $75 to $1,200. (Clip-on extensions, of course, take much less time and are less expensive.)

Loose Hair

Most stylists agree that loose, flowing hair is an extremely pretty, romantic look for a wedding. But it can be hard to control, especially if the weather is hot or humid, or if your wedding is at the beach. (Though nothing makes hair look thicker and sexier than sea air and salt water. If you're going for a wildcat look—and you don't put any styling products in your hair—that's exactly what you'll get!)

If you're planning to wear your hair loose, consult with a stylist who will advise you on how to control your locks and create the best style for your hair texture. In general, heat-styling—blowing your hair out and making sure it's not the slightest bit damp—will help control the texture and prevent frizz before you set it, curl it, or straighten it with a flatiron.

> **If your hairstylist is not going to stick around until after the ceremony and you want to take off your veil, make sure you have someone around who knows how to do it without messing up your hair. If you can keep your stylist—or an assistant—around until then, it's a good idea.**

Hair Dos and Don'ts

Because healthy, shiny hair never goes out of style, get yours in mint condition for the big day:

Do give your hair a deep conditioning treatment in the months leading up to your wedding.

Don't wash your hair the day of the wedding if you're going for an updo—unless you have fairly oily hair; it won't hold the style as well. Shampoo and lightly condition the night before.

Do go for your final haircut one to three weeks before the ceremony, so that it looks natural and not too-new.

Don't dig the comb (for the veil or headpiece) in too deep—you'll get a headache.

Do use a heat-protection spray when you style your hair to reduce dryness and damage.

Don't get your hair permed less than a month before the wedding. A bit of time will soften the style.

Do bring a picture of your dress to the consultation with your stylist.

Don't do anything drastic—for example, Japanese straightening, perming, chunking, relaxing—in the weeks before the wedding.

Hair Accessories

HAIR JEWELRY can add an elegant, unique touch to your style, but it's important to make sure that whatever accessory you choose doesn't compete with your veil or your headpiece. Remember Bridal Beauty Rule No. 1, Keep it simple? Many brides go over the top with clashing hair accessories, jewelry, veil, etc. Make sure to bring your hair jewelry choices—brooches, hairpins, combs, barrettes, ribbons—to your consultation and the style trial with your hairstylist. If you haven't selected any yet, be ready to discuss your ideas and, of course, ask your stylist for hers.

Coloring Your Hair

HAIR COLOR can be heavenly, but your wedding is not the best time to experiment—especially not with a do-it-yourself product from a box.

If you decide to color your hair, go to a professional colorist. Start slowly and give yourself a six-month trial period: See how you like it and correct things if necessary.

Highlights around the face catch the light and give your skin a glow. (If you're a dark brunette, talk to a colorist about lowlights—a few light pieces that break up dark brown hair.) If you plan to wear your hair up, give your colorist a heads-up so she can add a few highlights in the bottom layers, too. To add extra shine to your hair, consider asking your colorist to put a glaze or a gloss in your hair along with the color. These clear treatments coat the hair cuticle and add amazing shine to colored hair. Visit her again two weeks before the wedding to freshen up your color.

Dull Hair and the Frizzies

ONE THING you *don't* want is to wake up on the morning of your wedding to find that you've stumbled into a—gasp!—Bad Hair Day. I've got you covered.

Frizz-Proofing. If you are planning a summer or outdoor wedding and your hair poufs up when you sweat, you'll need to plan for frizz control. Starting a month before the wedding, use a deep conditioner once a week, but have the last treatment a week before the wedding, or your hair will be too soft to style. On the day of the wedding, pat a bit of styling cream on damp hair if your hair is curly. If straight, mix a dab of gel in your palm with pomade and pat through. Spray towel-dried hair with hairspray, which acts as a barrier to humidity.

Dull Hair. Give your hair extra shine with a shine-enhancing spray. Look for ingredients (at the top of the ingredient list) that end in *–one*, which contain silicone. Unless your hair is greasy, you can also pat a shine serum or botanical hair oil lightly through your hair.

Q Which fresh flowers will hold up best in my hair?

A Certain blooms tend to hold up better than others. Avoid overly delicate flowers like hydrangeas and lilies of the valley. Tulips and calla lilies are too big and tend to look clumsy and awkward. The best choices are baby roses, dendrobium and cymbidium orchids, stephanotis, freesia, Million Star baby's breath, and gardenias; East Indian brides traditionally work jasmine into their hair.

Once the flowers are in, don't touch them too much, as they might turn brown. Apply hairspray *before* you put the flowers in, so the spray won't wilt them. And if they have a strong scent, remember that it will increase as it picks up heat from your body.

Taking Care of You

Most brides agree: Planning a wedding is more stressful than they ever could have imagined. In addition to generalized prenuptial jitters, there's the juggling of hundreds of tiny little details, negotiating family politics, and dealing with the changing nature of your relationship. That said, there are many easy and effective ways to manage stress. The key is to build a regular stress-management regimen into your routine before you crash and burn. Devote one or two nights per week to a relaxing, stress-relieving activity like the ones below.

Get a massage. If it works into your budget, treat yourself to a weekly massage, which helps the muscles relax and slows the sympathetic nervous system. If you can't afford a professional massage, ask your fiancé to help you out (you can return the favor). Last resort: Place a rolling pin on the floor, lie on your back on top of it, and do it yourself—it really helps!

Yoga, yoga, yoga. There's no better stress reliever than yoga, and it will tone you up, too. Make a commitment and sign up for a series. If you're a newbie, start with a beginner class. Try a yoga DVD if you prefer to practice at home.

Try acupressure. A traditional treatment in Chinese medicine, acupressure is based on the belief that the body has energy pathways, or meridians; when the energy is blocked, you feel stressed and out of whack. An acupressurist applies pressure to points throughout the body to release the flow of energy and restore balance. A session will leave you alert and energized.

Drink some tea. If you have only a minute, make yourself a cup of herbal tea. Chamomile is calming, and peppermint is rejuvenating. Sit down and sip it. Stare out the window. Feel the warmth through the cup. Breathe in the aroma. Relax!

Take a bath. Wash your cares down the drain with a relaxing aromatherapy soak. Keep the water warm, not hot—too drying—and sprinkle in some fragrant botanical bath salts (lavender, sandalwood, jasmine) to lift your spirits, and a few drops of bath oil to soften your skin. Light a candle and settle in.

Head for the spa. The spa is the mother ship for those of us who need to beat back stress. Try a body wrap, a hydrotherapy treatment, or a facial. If you really want to get away from it all, consider "floating," or spending time in an isolation tank—a small tank filled with body-temperature water infused with Epsom salts. You float, and light and sound are minimized. Devotees swear by it for deep, lasting relaxation.

Sing it, sister. Singing at the top of your lungs is transporting; backing tracks takes it to a whole new level. You'll feel so much better after belting out something soulful, either at your favorite local karaoke emporium, or at home, if your cable provider offers Karaoke on Demand. Mic sold separately . . . but the clicker makes a fine substitute.

Pop in a Movie

Whether you watch with the husband-to-be or indulge solo, a movie with an element of romance—be it gooey, racy, or refined—makes a perfect break in the planning process. Here's a mix of guilty pleasures, classic four-hankie specials, and truly good films that fit the bill.

- *Breakfast at Tiffany's:* Audrey, Tiffany's . . . What more could you ask for?

- *Moonstruck:* Cher and Nick Cage and Brooklyn—oh my!

- *Four Weddings and a Funeral:* Hilarious weddings galore and Hugh Grant at his most charming.

- *Monsoon Wedding:* The most sumptuous on-screen wedding of all time.

- *When Harry Met Sally:* For your Billy Crystal-and-Meg Ryan fix, with lovely New York as backdrop.

- *You've Got Mail:* Another New York Meg Ryan movie—it's totally irresistible.

- *The Sound of Music:* A romance on a grand scale, there's really no limit to how many times you can watch this one.

- *Mystic Pizza:* Sisters with gorgeous hair, a young Julia Roberts, pizza, and love, sweet love.

- *An Affair to Remember:* The movie on which *Sleepless in Seattle* is based—the ultimate tearjerker.

- *My Fair Lady:* Audrey again, in what's actually quite an unusual tale of hate, love, hate, and love again.

Make something. Reach for easy, satisfying creative outlets. Bake cookies or muffins. Make a collage. This probably isn't the best time to pick up a complicated new hobby, but perhaps you can go back to something that gave you pleasure when you were younger—knitting, crocheting, photography, origami. This kind of fun is especially good therapy for times when it feels like nothing is getting done: Completing even one task start to finish gives you a great sense of accomplishment and makes the larger projects feel more manageable.

Ladies' night. There's nothing better than hanging out with your girlfriends when stress is threatening to send you over the edge. And while bars and restaurants are fun, you can't really kick off your shoes and relax the way you can when you're in someone's home. So why not open yours to the gals in your life? Invite everyone over for something simple like takeout or pot-luck with board games. (P.S. Steer the conversation away from weddings!)

Pump up the jam. Any activity that involves music, sweat, and boogying is a surefire way to leave the world of weddings far behind and bathe your brain in endorphins. Go dancing at a club, find a place to roller-skate or ice-skate, or take an aerobics class. Or just put on the stereo in your living room and dance up a storm. Partner optional!

Take a walk. Know the expression "There's nothing a cold beer and a hot shower can't cure"? Same goes for walking—and you'll spare yourself the beer belly. So put this book down immediately and go outside. Take a hike, power walk, or just stroll aimlessly.

Go back in time. Go ahead—regress a little. All this looking forward can really freak a person out. So rewind. Blow bubbles. Bounce on a trampoline. Play with paper dolls. Go outside and get muddy. What's that? Forgot how to play? Find some little kids and take their lead.

You and Your Food

Though it may be tempting to cut back on meals to stay slim or lose weight for the wedding, it's more important than ever at this time to eat a healthy diet, keep your energy up, and build strength to fight stress. Some brides-to-be find they're too nervous to eat. But there's nothing worse for a case of the nerves than an unhealthy diet—and too much caffeine. If you want to eat less, look for foods with a high water content—vegetables, fruits, water-based soups and stews, and cooked whole grains—which are low in calories but highly satisfying. Start your meals with soup or a salad, and stay away from foods with a lot of refined sugar.

Keep your eye on high-energy foods—protein bars (minimum five grams of protein), honey-sweetened yogurt, antioxidant fruits and vegetables, protein drinks, low-sugar smoothies, and healthy fats. Fruit will also boost your energy. And, of course, make sure to keep yourself hydrated by drinking six to eight glasses of water each day. Try an electrolyte-filled coconut water, avoid soda, and limit coffee and caffeinated tea to two cups or less per day—they will not only make you jittery, but they are also diuretics, which means they pull moisture out of the body.

Beat the Bloat

SALTY FOODS make your body retain water, so cut back on salt, processed food, soy sauce, and junk food at least a week before the wedding. If you're sensitive to wheat or dairy, hold off on bagels, breads, and ice cream, too. Also avoid gassy foods like beans and broccoli, and don't skip meals—when there's less food in your system, more air gets trapped there, which creates gas.

Whatever you do, this is not the time to be tempted by diuretics. They deplete your body's potassium supply, which can lead to fatigue. To keep your energy up and stimulate your digestive system, work out at least thirty minutes every day. Make sure you consume fruits, vegetables, lean proteins, and green tea to flush out excess water.

Hangover Helpers

OKAY, SO YOU PARTIED too much the night before your meeting with your officiant, and you need to pull yourself together fast! Mix a packet of Emergen-C, an energizing vitamin blend available at drugstores, into a glass of water and drink it down to replenish what your body has lost. (If you don't have Emergen-C, take a multiple vitamin.) Splash a few handfuls of cold water

on your face. If your lids are bloodshot, apply a cool compress dipped in raspberry tea or green tea. If you're puffy—alcohol dehydrates the skin and can make it look swollen—lie down for ten minutes with a bag

ASK MINDY

Q I'm wildly in love with my fiancé and there's no question in my mind that I'm marrying the right person. But what I'm marrying into—that's another question. Since we've started planning this thing, I receive multiple calls a day from his mother giving me unsolicited advice on everything from the menu to the punctuation on our invitations. Worse, his sisters have drawn me into their sibling feuds over the bridesmaids' dresses, the bachelorette party venue, and my choice not to change my name. I'm trying to keep my cool, but I'm beginning to hate his family. Please tell me they'll start to behave better after this thing is over. And should I confront them or just suck it up? I don't want to establish weak boundaries with people I'm going to have to deal with for the rest of my life.

A Be polite, but don't suck it up. You'll be dealing with holidays, babies, and more for the rest of your married life. And you're right: It's easiest to set boundaries at the beginning of a relationship. I suggest you confront the situation with your future in-laws directly: "I so appreciate all your advice and opinions, but Joe and I have a very specific vision for this wedding." Start with the positive—thanking her for taking an interest—and if the calls don't cease, try diverting her by assigning her a specific task or area of the wedding. You'll keep her busy, and she'll get to feel that she has some control over the proceedings.

of frozen blueberries, peas, or corn on your face. For nausea, drink a cup of chamomile or peppermint tea, with a slice of dry toast. Avoid acidic juices, fatty foods, caffeine, and, most important, stay away from the hair of the dog! Next time you're out on the town, alternate every drink with a glass of water, it will keep you hydrated and slow you down.

The Wedding Workout

It may take some effort, but you're going to look toned in your gown, even if you've got to sweat a little to make it happen. Whether your goal is to shed a few pounds or spot-tone specific areas like your arms or torso, if you set realistic goals, it's certainly doable. It will take discipline and determination, but there's no need to panic. Like any good reporter knows, having a deadline will help you organize a game plan and map out your goals week to week—the best way to achieve results. The added benefit of exercise, of course, is that it's a terrific stress reliever. So let's get moving!

The Buff Bride

A cottage industry in "bridal boot camps" has recently sprung up, and many brides are taking advantage of gyms, personal trainers, and spas that offer "wedding workout" programs promising to maximize results in a specific time frame (usually twelve weeks). If you can afford it, sign up for these personalized workouts to target whatever body parts you want to whip into shape. If a full program is beyond your budget, register for a few sessions and ask the trainer to create a program that you can do on your own.

If you need a little extra motivation, sign up with a friend, or a group of friends. Turn your workout sessions into a girls' night out. Or, if you prefer to work out in private, shop around for a "wedding workout" DVD.

A Call to Arms (and Back and Shoulders and Torso)

MAYBE YOU'RE DREAMING about a strapless sheath, or a sleeveless gown with a fitted bodice. Beautiful strapless, sleeveless, and corset styles have upped the ante in arm- and torso-toning wedding workouts these days.

If you are going to showcase your arms, plan to devote fifteen minutes a day to a targeted workout, and start three to six months before your wedding. Even if you only have four to six weeks, you can still achieve great results.

Beautiful Bodice

Here are three exercises that will tighten up your torso. Start with two sets of each, and when you're comfortable, increase to three sets.

Sit-ups. Lie down on the floor or on a mat, with knees bent. Tuck your feet under the side of a couch to anchor them. Link your fingers behind your head, and, taking deep breaths, do twenty-five sit-ups.

Torso twists. Stand with your feet hip-width apart. Bend your knees slightly, making sure that you have a little bounce in your legs. Pretend you're holding a ball

Torso twists lengthen the abdominals while strengthening the obliques.

Ab crunches target the lower belly without straining the lower back.

Those Last Ten Pounds

Looking to shed those few extra pounds before the wedding? Join the club. Almost everyone wants to lose weight in the months and weeks before their big day. (Bridal salons are used to making gown alterations for this reason.) Whether you sign on for a weight-loss program or do it yourself, there are certain unshakable rules: exercise, avoid processed foods, don't skip meals, control your portions (use your palm as a guide to a serving of protein), and include protein with every meal and with every carb—for example, half an English muffin with a spoonful of peanut butter—to fill you up faster and slow the digestive process so that you feel full longer. If you're prone to overeating at meals, drink two glasses of water or a cup of broth before you eat. It's good for you, and it fills you up.

Let's face it, the earlier you start, the more you can lose. But as a general rule, any healthy weight-loss program will recommend that you lose not more than two pounds a week. If you have less to lose, it may come off more slowly, and it might be more realistic to count on a pound per week. Though you may be tempted to sign on for a drastic diet or extreme exercise, don't. The resulting fatigue, energy loss, and stress to your system is the last thing you need; you want to feel vibrant and full of energy for the big day. Plus, losing weight too quickly can leave you looking haggard.

---

between your thighs. Tighten your thigh muscles, pull your belly in, and tuck your pelvis. (You'll be in somewhat of a sitting position.) Link your fingers behind your head and slowly twist from side to side, turning your upper body from left to right. Keep your shoulders back, and don't rush—slow and steady! Do forty twists.

Ab crunches. Set yourself up in the same position as you did for the torso twists, without the imaginary ball. Lift your left knee toward your right arm, with your elbow coming down to meet your knee. Hold for a few seconds, then return to your starting position. Repeat on the right side, with a total of twenty reps on each side.

Sensational Shoulders

Here are three exercises that will sculpt your shoulders and upper arms. If you're a beginner, use two- to three-pound hand weights. If you're further along, use five- to eight-pound weights. Whatever you do, don't strain yourself. The last thing you want is to pull a muscle before the wedding.

Bicep curls. Hold a weight in each hand. Keep your arms at your sides with your fists facing forward. Tuck your elbows in to your waist. Slowly bend your elbows and raise your fists to your shoulders, and then back down. Don't rush, and repeat fifteen times.

Arm raises. Stand with your legs shoulder-width apart, holding a weight in each hand, with your palms facing inward. Without bending at the elbows, raise both arms until they're parallel to the floor. Lower. Repeat fifteen times.

Push-ups. If you can do the traditional-style push-ups (on your hands and toes), go ahead. Otherwise, get down on your hands and knees, and push up from there. Repeat fifteen times.

Arm raises are not to be skipped—so basic, but so important.

Allover Beauty

Now that you've put all that effort into sculpting and toning, you'll want your arms and shoulders to look—and feel—as smooth and silky as they do in your mind's eye when you see yourself floating down the aisle!

Whether you start a month or a week before the wedding, use a moisturizing body wash in the shower. Soap—even the most moisturizing triple-fatted vegetable soaps—can be drying. After your shower, apply body oil or a rich body cream, while skin is still damp, for the most intensive hydration. If your skin is oily and tends to break out, apply an alpha hydroxy lotion, to help exfoliate the skin. To soften rough and flaky elbows and knees, apply moisturizer. Massage it in with an old, soft toothbrush.

> On your wedding day, make sure to eat a healthy breakfast. I've seen brides faint from hunger! And pack a light snack—crackers, cheese, almonds, dried cranberries, celery sticks with peanut butter—to munch on while you're in hair and makeup.

Bacne

IF YOU ARE PRONE to bacne (breakouts on the back and shoulders), start focusing on that area at least two to three months before your wedding, depending on the severity of the breakouts. To control excess oil, apply a salicylic-acid- or benzoyl-peroxide-based body wash with a synthetic body scrubber. Follow with a topical acne lotion. Twice a week, apply a clay (kaolin) mask to the area.

Red Bumps

SOME WOMEN are prone to breaking out in a swath of hard little red bumps (known as keratosis pilaris, or KP) on the back or on the backs of the upper arms. The best way to treat KP is to keep the area really clean and exfoliate regularly with a body scrub or a synthetic body scrubber or sponge—but be gentle. After your shower, apply an alpha- or beta-hydroxy gel or lotion. You may want to try an at-home chemical peel twice a week. If the bumps don't go away within a month, see a dermatologist for treatment.

Arm Hair

TO ELIMINATE dark hair on your arms, you have several choices. You can bleach it with an at-home bleaching kit. It's relatively easy and effective, but you'll still have hair on your arms. Do a patch test first, at least a month before your wedding: Apply a tiny bit of bleach on a small patch of skin, and give it a day to make sure you don't react. Another option is to wax. Most day spas offer professional arm wax treatments that range from $35 to $75 and take about half an hour, lasting up to four weeks.

Or you may want to try laser hair removal. It's expensive, but it can be permanent. You'll need several sessions, four to six weeks apart, at approximately $500 per visit. Start treatment six months to a year ahead of time.

No Sweat

IF YOU SWEAT a lot, experiment ahead of time with antiperspirants—not deodorant—to see which works best for you. Dress shields are an option if you're wearing a dress with sleeves. If perspiration is a serious problem for you, consult a dermatologist about Botox injections, which were approved by the FDA for that purpose a few years ago.

Tattoo Coverage

IF YOU'VE DECIDED not to flaunt that skull and crossbones tattoo on your left shoulder in your Great Aunt Mattie's face, a little makeup artistry is all it takes to cover that thing up.

You'll need two shades of cream foundation or concealer: one that's a shade lighter than your body skin—to

GROOMING THE GROOM

Every guy wants to look his best for the big day—he just may not know where to begin. If your man is a little clueless when it comes to the grooming department, you might want to give him a little nudge. Consider the following:

- *Is his skin in good shape?* Make him an appointment for a facial a couple of weeks before the big day.

- *Is he using the right products for his skin type?* Men's skin is thicker and oilier than women's, so look for special men's skin-care products like cleanser, exfoliant, and moisturizer.

- *Does he occasionally get dandruff?* If so, he should start using a dandruff shampoo at least four weeks in advance of the wedding.

- For blackheads, he should use pore strips a day or two before the wedding.

- If he is prone to razor burn, make sure his blades are clean and sharp. He should shave in the direction the hair grows, not against it. To beat the burn on the morning of the big day, he can soften his stubble prior to shaving by applying warm towels to his face—it feels great.

- If he generally sports a five o'clock shadow, he should pack an electric razor and shave between the ceremony and the reception.

- *Do his ear or nose hairs need trimming?* If his brows are crazy wild, he should use a comb to tame them.

And yes, a wedding *is* an occasion for a good haircut. He should get one about a week before the big day so it has time to settle in.

neutralize the ink—and one that matches your skin tone. Apply the lighter shade directly to the tattoo with a brush. Cover it with the darker shade and blend well. Top with a layer of powder.

Scars and Bruises

TO COVER A BRUISE or scar, use a stick concealer a shade lighter than your skin. Apply a dab to your palm. Your body heat will warm it and enable it to blend nicely into the skin. Then take a small, flat brush, dip it into your palm, and apply the concealer to the area. Pat it down gently with your fingers. Apply another layer, pat it down, and dust lightly with loose, translucent powder. To fade scars and bruises, apply a vitamin K cream twice daily for two months.

The Faux Glow

SELF-TANNING or spray-on tanning treatments at the spa are wildly popular, but I've seen enough orange brides walking down the aisle to know that it isn't always a great idea. A tan can make you look slimmer and healthier—especially against the contrast of a white wedding dress—but proceed with caution.

A tan should be a subtle glow. Exfoliate first for a smoother, more even color. To build a tan slowly, use a glow lotion instead of a self-tanner, or mix a dab of self-tanner with moisturizer in your palm before you apply it—the moisturizer will also smooth out dry patches so your tanner won't streak. Wash your hands immediately afterward, or you'll "tan" your palms. Whether you are "tanning" yourself or having a spray tan applied, have it done four to five days before the wedding to give it time to tone down.

If an old-fashioned suntan has left you with some unsightly tan lines, try this trick: Dip a barely damp makeup sponge in liquid bronzer, and dab over tan lines. Blend very well with the sponge, and top with a light dusting of bronzing powder.

Hands (and Feet)

NOW THAT YOU'VE GOT that rock on your finger, your hands will be attracting more attention than ever. If you're wearing strappy sandals, ditto for your feet.

Keep a tube of hand cream in your drawer at work, in your purse, and at your bedside, and massage into your hands, around your cuticles, and into your feet several times each day. Wash your hands with warm water—not hot, which can be drying—and apply sunscreen to the backs of your hands to protect them from developing spots and dryness. For especially dry hands, treat yourself to a paraffin treatment at a day spa or nail salon; your hands will be exfoliated, dipped in warm wax, and placed in heated mitts. It feels amazing and leaves skin incredibly soft. (The same treatment is available for feet.)

To get your nails in great shape for the wedding, plan ahead. Dry cuticles and chipped nails don't heal themselves overnight. Start going for regular, weekly manicures three months before the wedding—or give yourself a deluxe treatment every week—and book a mani-pedi for the day before (not the day of) the wedding. It will be one less thing to do, and you won't end up with smudges. (The longer you let your nails dry, the fewer smudges you'll have.)

Starting six months in advance, strengthen your nails with protein-packed specialty products, and make sure to eat a diet rich in protein (chicken and fish) and biotin (carrots and eggs). To protect your hands in the days and weeks leading up to the big day, wear gloves when you're washing dishes, cleaning the house, or gardening. If your nails are prone to tearing, it means they are dehydrated. Make sure to drink your full dose of water each day and invest in a good cuticle oil. If you're a nail biter, reach for the hand cream every time you feel the urge.

As for style, long nails can snag the lace on your wedding dress or veil. It's best—and more universally

ASK MINDY

Q Is there anything I can do to avoid stubble on my underarms? I'm wearing a strapless gown.

A If you use shaving cream and a high-quality razor, you should be fine. But if you want to be really smooth, try waxing. Experiment a few months ahead of time to make sure your skin doesn't have a reaction. If you're good to go, make an appointment at a local day spa two days before the wedding. Your hair won't grow back for a couple of weeks, which means you'll still be smooth for your honeymoon.

flattering—to keep your nails short, with tips one quarter the length of the nail bed. And unless your usual palette is rich and deep, avoid the latest trendy purple nail polish and stick with neutral shades—pale pink, beige, coral, lilac, or French manicures—which always look great.

That takes care of one very special package (you, of course). Now for the invitations and other paper goods—a means of conveying vital information, but also a delightfully tactile pocket of surprises. For your guests, the stationery is the first entrée to your wedding day. ◆

CHAPTER TWENTY

THE TIMELESS BEAUTY OF STATIONERY

nvitations embody a central premise of the wedding itself: the public recognition of a private commitment. But for many brides-to-be, marriage marks a first introduction to the world of stationery. Maybe you're a pro at writing thank-you notes for birthday presents and particularly fabulous dinner parties—I hope so—but the truth is that few of us

take the time to write letters. And most of our stationery, if we have any, is bought boxed. But trust me, once you've experienced a few close encounters with cotton rag, deckle edges, and letterpress printing, you may find yourself falling hard. Fine stationery is simply so *beautiful*.

Until recently, the rules of the wedding stationery—what type to use, how to engrave it, when to send it, how to sign it—

were set strictly by etiquette, not by style. These days, invitations and other wedding stationery are fully initiated members of the wedding party, giving guests a preview of what's to come and helping to bind the look of the event together.

There's another important consideration that goes beyond aesthetics: Invitations give you an early opportunity to help your guests feel taken care of.

Invitations and Timing

Plan to mail invitations about eight weeks before the wedding. You'll usually receive them within three to six weeks of ordering them—up to eight weeks for engraved invitations—so start the process four to six months before the wedding.

Leave time to review a proof of the invitation—it slows down the process, but it's absolutely critical. Can you imagine your invitations going out with the wrong date or the groom's last name misspelled? Also build in time for assembly, especially if you're planning an elaborate presentation. You'll need to allow at least a week for addressing invitations (if you're working with a calligrapher, find out her turnaround time), proofreading addresses, and stuffing envelopes, particularly if you have a lot of inserts.

If you have a shorter time line, there are plenty of options. Try a local designer, and go with flat printing rather than engraving or letterpress—it's a faster process. Some websites for invitations guarantee quick turnarounds, even on engraving and letterpress, so that's another avenue worth pursuing.

Shopping for Paper

Invitations are typically priced by the set—the invitation, the reply card, and envelopes for each. Additional enclosure cards will cost extra. Prices vary greatly, from $2 per set at the low end to more than $70.

Traditional stationers tend to stock books of invitations, with an emphasis on conventional styles. Some department stores and wedding planners also carry books from standard-bearers like Crane & Co. and William Arthur. At the high end, jewelers like Tiffany & Co. and Cartier are renowned for their classic engraved invitations and high level of customer service.

Custom designers have become very popular of late. Working by appointment, they listen to your ideas, show you samples, and either design invitations for you or modify an existing design. Many are experts at wording and can suggest creative solutions to any dilemma. Though the word "custom" might lead you to believe otherwise, prices actually vary widely.

Specialty stationery stores are great places to get inspired, especially if you're not sure what you like. They carry invitation and stationery books and offer custom design services. They often feature good selections of modern designs, and their staff members are generally knowledgeable.

You can also order invitations online, either from traditional stationery companies such as Crane & Co. or from online boutiques. Be sure to get a sample of the paper to feel the texture and weight for yourself. (Any good company should be willing to send you a sample;

TRADITION PRIMER

From Monks to Typefaces

Although written invitations are perhaps the most tradition-bound element of a wedding today, they rank as relative newcomers to the universe of wedding customs. Until the Middle Ages, weddings in the English countryside were announced by a crier.

When weddings evolved from community events into by-invitation-only affairs, noblemen and wealthy people turned to monks, who were already keeping records of royal marriages, to create handwritten invitations. Their elegant calligraphy was a given; if the bride's family had the means, they commissioned illuminated drawings as well, making the invitation a true work of art.

After the invention of the printing press, copper plates were etched with typefaces designed to mimic the monks' calligraphy styles, and the engraved invitation was born. In fact, some of the fonts that remain popular today, including Antique Roman, Shaded Roman, and Fancy Gothic, closely followed the monks' calligraphy.

some will charge a fee.) Though shopping online is convenient, its disadvantage is the lack of personal assistance; and if you make a mistake and something is printed wrong, it's unlikely that you'll be able to return or redo anything.

Choices, Choices

The key components of invitation styles are the format, type of paper, paper color, printing method, font, and ink color. Don't focus on the extras—things like borders, dingbats, beveled edges, and ribbons—until you've made the big decisions. A deckle edge wouldn't apply to a card, for instance, and a beveled edge wouldn't apply to a fold-over, so your decision-making process will be all over the map if you don't do first things first.

The Format

A STANDARD CARD, either square or rectangular, makes for a classic statement. It's rather stark, so treat-

ment is important—engraving or letterhead looks best. (For a more formal feel, print your announcement vertically; text printed across the length of the card tends to look more modern.) A *script card*

A standard card

is shaped like a long, narrow rectangle and fits into a standard no. 10 envelope. This minimalistic style doesn't mesh with lots of enclosures or embellishments, but looks wonderful with colored paper, colored ink, and letterpress printing.

One of the most popular styles, a *fold-over*, *folder*, or *bifold* is folded vertically to open like a book. A fold-over invitation was once considered the most formal of choices, but today such distinctions don't really hold water—it's the overall style of the invitation, rather than the format, that indicates the tone. The traditional treatment is to engrave the information on the front and

A fold-over card

leave the inside blank, but you can also print a monogram on the outside and the invitation on the inside, allowing for a response-card pocket on the inner left panel (see page 284 for more detail).

A *gatefold*, also known as a barn door invitation, has two panels that open from the middle. The doors are held closed with a ribbon, band, or tie. Inside the "doors," you can attach pockets for enclosure cards, making the gatefold a great choice for destination weddings and/or weddings with multiple stages.

A gatefold card

An invitation that folds into three panels is called a *trifold* or *three-paneled folder*. One panel contains the invitation wording and the others may contain reception details, directions, or a map. Some use a perforated third panel as the reply card. If you want to print your invitation in two languages, this is the perfect format.

A trifold card

Boxed invitations are elaborate confections usually put together by custom designers. They make a lavish first impression but are generally quite expensive, and you've also got to factor in the extra postage. The invitation itself is printed on a series of cards, often accompanied by a decorative element—a starfish for a beach wedding, for example. Box materials can range from paperboard to silk, velvet, and even suede.

A boxed invitation

The Paper

PAPER IS a very personal choice. Even at the highest end of the stationery spectrum, there's no consensus on whether the ideal paper for letter writing is hefty or onion thin, so don't let anyone steer you to a certain type of paper out of snobbery if you don't find it pleasing to the eye and the touch. A note on stock: Paper ranges from three to nine ply, with nine ply being so heavy that it hardly bends at all.

As for color, your choices are no longer limited to white or ecru—in fact, choosing a colored paper is a great way to make an impact without adding cost.

The Printing Method

A CRITICAL ELEMENT of the invitations, the printing method profoundly affects their look, turnaround time, and price. Paper aficionados will actually tell you that printing quality is everything, but the focus has moved from type to overall effect as tastes have become more adventurous. Don't get me wrong: A traditional ecru three-ply card calls for quality in printing and paper. But if you've got lavender paper matted onto chocolate card stock and wrapped in iridescent organza, offset printing will probably do the job. What's most important to you? If switching from letterpress to offset is going to allow you to back your invitations with that dreamy imported paper from Thailand and add silk threads with hand-tied crystals, it could well be a worthwhile trade-off.

There are also practical considerations. Some printing methods aren't compatible with certain papers or fonts, or require a longer turnaround time. Read on to learn more about the primary printing methods.

Engraving

This elegant Old World technique never goes out of style; in fact, more and more of my clients are asking for engraving, which immediately telegraphs a certain cachet. An intricate, costly process, it can take up to eight weeks. Text is engraved onto a copper plate or "die" that's dipped in ink, and paper is forced into the plate, creating a raised design that beautifully transmits detail. It requires substantial paper stock, so it's not a good choice if your tastes run to the diaphanous. Added bonus: You can keep the plates as souvenirs.

Letterpress

Letterpress is the opposite of engraving: A cast-iron plate with raised lettering is dipped in ink (think of a stamp) and pressed onto the paper, creating an impression. Though it can work on a range of papers, letterpress

The Most Delicate Enclosure

What's with the slip of tissue paper found in wedding invitations? It originated at a time when ink was oil based and took much longer to dry than it does today—the paper protected the type from smearing. People either mistakenly kept the tissue paper intact or liked the look of it, and a tradition was born. Today we use water-based ink, which dries much faster, and even engraved invitations don't necessitate a protective slip of paper.

If you're attached to the notion of tissue paper, it's all right to keep it with a traditional invitation, though it is pretty wasteful. But don't go there if you're sending a contemporary invitation, where tissue paper would look like an anachronism.

Always feel paper before committing to it. Is it cottony, flimsy, crisp, substantial? Some people prefer a definite texture to their paper, others want it smooth.

Beyond issues of taste, you'll need to hone in on paper that works with your choice of printing method. Cotton makes for creamy, soft stock that's naturally acid free and doesn't yellow with age; heavy cotton lends itself perfectly to letterpress printing but won't make it through a laser printer. Wood fiber, which can achieve similar effects, used to be reserved for lower quality papers but has been improved to the point where it's now used by some of the high-end companies. For a textured, luxurious finish, linen is a wonderful and underused option; it can range from durable to extremely delicate.

You'll probably also run into the term *vellum*: It's a thin, translucent parchment that's often attached to card stock for a layered effect. Flat printing is the way to go, as vellum and other ultrathin papers can't stand up to engraving or letterpress.

stands out better against smoother varieties. A high-end printing process, it can take three weeks to a month. It lends itself well to graphics and is used by many custom designers. There's been a renaissance of this vintage technique among small printers.

Thermography

This modern process was designed to mimic the look of engraving at a more affordable price. The design is flat printed (see next entry) and dusted with resin powder while wet; it's then heated up, causing the letters to rise. Though paper snobs will miss engraving's telltale indentations and might detect a telltale sheen left behind by the resin, the average guest won't know the difference. Turnaround is two weeks to a month.

Offset or flat printing

Offset printing provides the same effect you would get from a personal printer, but it's done at a commercial printing house with higher quality and quicker machines. As I mentioned, it's becoming more popular as invitations stray from tradition, but it wouldn't be a good choice for a very simple design on high-quality paper. Turnaround time is significantly lower for this least expensive of methods. One caveat: The heaviest paper won't fit through a printer.

The Font

UNLESS YOU'RE USING unusual paper, the font affects the look of the invitation more than anything else. The typeface conveys a mood, an era, even the formality of the event. If you're doing an Art Deco wedding, head straight for Parisian or Kingsbury. If you're having a casual beach wedding, think about a sans serif style such as Engravers Gothic rather than a traditional font like Edwardian Script. Make readability a priority—flourishes lose their effect when guests have to struggle to read the print.

Ink Color

THOUGH STATIONERS' RULE BOOKS long maintained that black or dark gray were the only acceptable

Some of My Favorite Fonts

FOR ENGRAVING, THERMOGRAPHY, AND OFFSET PRINTING

Script:

Helinda Rook Font
This is the font I've chosen.

Snell Roundhand Font
This is the font I've chosen for my wedding.

Fine Hand Font
This is the font I've chosen for my wedding.

Print:

Engravers Roman Font
THIS IS THE FONT I'VE CHOSEN.

ITC Eras Font
This is the font I've chosen for my wedding.

Florens Font
This is the font I've chosen for my wedding.

FOR LETTERPRESS

Script:

Stuyvesant Font
This is the font I've chosen for my wedding.

Shelley Script Font
This is the font I've chosen.

Print:

Mrs Eaves Font
This is the font I've chosen.

Cloister Font
This is the font I've chosen.

ink colors for an invitation, times have changed. Colors like chocolate or champagne are simple ways to stylize; soft greens are lovely for spring and summer weddings; and deep cranberry sets a rich, festive tone for fall and holiday weddings.

As with font choices, when it comes to color, readability needs to be a high priority. Light-colored inks, especially in letterpress, can be difficult to read. Do try to save a few surprises for the wedding. You might use one of your main wedding colors in the ink, but don't give away your entire color scheme. Also, be careful not to overdo it. If you opt for purple ink on ivory paper, you can pick it up with a purple envelope liner, but don't add a purple wrapper or matte the paper on purple card stock.

> When assessing fonts, look for one that's versatile enough to use on your seating cards, table numbers, and other paper goods. Keeping your font consistent will help tie all of your wedding elements together.

Dingbats, Monograms, and Other Decorative Touches

A GRAPHIC FLOURISH that relieves the eye from an overabundance of text and adds an immediately recognizable flavor to your stationery, a *dingbat* is a typographical term for a motif or symbol. Choose one that's related to your wedding or personalities; many stationery books offer an array at no extra charge, or you can even have one custom designed. Often centered at the tops of invitations, they can also be placed on the lower right-hand corner of thank-you notes or incorporated throughout the wedding—where there's a budget, they can reappear on napkins, coasters, and more.

Timeless, elegant, and personal, monograms can be a lovely way to illustrate the joining together of two lives. For not a whole lot of money, a calligrapher can design a custom monogram for you, which you can continue to use

post-wedding on personal stationery (or pillowcases and bathrobes, for that matter). One complication: If you are changing your name, the monograms can't incorporate the first letter of your new last name until after the wedding—in that case, have a monogram made using only your first initials.

Photographs and drawings can also be used to great effect on certain types of stationery. I would urge you to steer clear of photos of you and your groom—it gives off a bit of a self-centered vibe; an image of the wedding venue, however, can be lovely. Stick to black-and-white photos or screen the image in a single color. You can also hire an artist to create a line drawing or watercolor of the site.

If you're springing for a boxed invitation, you may want to include a physical decorative element that's somehow tied to your wedding. A gatefold or an invitation with several components—vellum layered over card stock, for instance—may require a method of closure. Organza or satin bows are lovely choices, but unusual touches like grommets, suede cord, or even paper clips in stylized shapes are fun and festive ways to pull things together.

Enclosures

IN ADDITION TO the invitation, reply card, and reply card envelope, you may need to include one or more enclosures to convey additional information to your guests. Many of these enclosures can be merged into single cards as space allows—directions and hotel information often are, for instance—but a formal stationery treatment should never look crowded. Of course, many couples opt to keep the paper invitations simple and send out emails with all the details closer to the date. There's nothing wrong with that (though you'll need to make sure older guests get the message by following up with calls), but I've included the traditional breakdown for reference.

Maps and directions. For the ceremony, the reception, or anything else that requires directions. If you can afford to, order the map and the invitations from the same company; or look for compatible paper you can use for offset

Calligraphy

The artisan craft of penmanship, calligraphy is thought of as an Old World technique, but many calligraphers work in a wide range of styles. Consider harmony. Though you may be seduced by a precious Renaissance script with oodles of flourishes, it will look out of place if you're using a stark sans serif font on your invites and doing an all-white loft wedding; a calligrapher may be able to duplicate the über-modern font you used on your invitation.

Calligraphy is generally used to address the invitation's outer and inner envelopes; it's worth looking into if you earned poor handwriting marks in grade school or if you just want to make a great first impression. Prices vary from three to ten dollars per invitation, so for a wedding with 150 guests, you'll be adding hundreds of dollars to your budget. You'll also need to allow for more time in your schedule while the calligrapher is working.

The best way to find a calligrapher in your town is through word of mouth. People tend not to have much use for calligraphy outside of weddings, so ask other married couples you know for a recommendation; the stationery shop where you purchased your invites should also be able to provide a reference.

Find out in what form the calligrapher wants you to submit names and addresses; some prefer Word documents to Excel charts. While you're at it, look into the cost of having her do table card numbers, seating cards, place cards, and any other paper goods; it will certainly help give your wedding a cohesive look.

Though a calligrapher's sweeping brushstrokes have a texture and spontaneity that's difficult to duplicate digitally, computer calligraphy has gotten fairly advanced. Cheaper and faster than hand calligraphy, it offers a choice of many different styles. The downside: You won't be able to make last-minute changes or additions. Look online to find reputable digital calligraphy websites.

---

printing. Try to avoid sticking a piece of copier paper inside your gorgeous invitation!

Accommodation cards. Listing names of and information about the hotels where you've blocked off rooms.

Transportation cards. If you're providing transportation to or from any of the venues, a transportation card lets guests know you're taking care of them. The cards generally read: "Transportation will be provided from the ceremony to the reception." If you're using a ride-sharing service, be sure to include the discount code (see page 150).

Rain cards. Giving an alternate location or plan in case of rain.

Pew cards. Letting relatives and close friends know they have a reserved seat in the pews; they should hand the card to an usher upon arrival. (Also known as "within-the-ribbon" cards, which indicate that certain guests should sit in a reserved area marked off by ribbons.)

Website address. If you've created a wedding website, put the address on a small enclosure card so guests can keep it handy. It shouldn't be on the invite proper, though it can appear on the save-the-date card.

Ceremony cards. If you're opting for a very intimate ceremony, followed by a larger reception, a separate ceremony card lets your special guests know they're invited.

At-home cards. Originally a way to inform friends and family of the couple's new address, they've been resuscitated with the newfound purpose of letting everyone know whether the bride is keeping, hyphenating, or changing her name.

Rehearsal dinner. If the groom's family is hosting the rehearsal dinner, the traditional school of etiquette holds that they send out a separate invitation. However, if all the guests are being invited to the rehearsal dinner (see page 180 to find out more), it's less expensive and more

How Many Invitations?

Unless every guest is single, two hundred guests does not equal two hundred invitations. One caveat: Children eighteen or older should receive their own, whether they live with their parents or on their own. Younger children (if invited) are simply included on the envelope of their parents' invitation.

Calculate the number of households, then order fifteen extra invitations, in case you've forgotten anyone, and twenty-five extra envelopes, to allow for mistakes in addressing. (Add or subtract a handful, depending on the size of your wedding.) If you're doing a "B-list," make that twenty-five extra invitations and thirty-five envelopes (see page 61).

If you're not sure of the precise number of invitations to order, make your best guess and place the order. When the proofs come in, you can change the number before they go to the printer.

Proofs

Always request proofs at the time you place your stationery order. Once the various components have been printed, you own any errors, along with the paper they're printed on.

Some custom designers automatically send proofs to you, but you'll have to request them from larger companies, and pay extra to see them. Ask your sales contact when to expect proofs and how long you have to read them. Make sure you return them quickly, or you'll delay your invitations.

Have a bridesmaid or your mother help read the proofs. And make sure to double- and triple-check the time, year, date, and venue addresses.

efficient to include a small card in the invitation packet. (If only select guests are invited, it's too easy to make mistakes when stuffing the invitations and to invite your friend Dan when you meant to invite Uncle Dave, so I do recommend mailing a separate invitation.)

Peripheral events. Prepare cards for any peripheral wedding events. For a casual morning-after brunch that doesn't require an exact head count, you can skip a separate invitation and let everyone know about it by word of mouth or on your website. If you do need a precise head count, include a card and some way to RSVP in the invitation. For multiple events like golf outings or tours, create a single card that allows room to RSVP to each.

When the invitations arrive, count every card, enclosure, and envelope to make sure they're all there. Otherwise, you might not discover that you're missing five rehearsal dinner invitations and ten response cards until you're stuffing the envelopes.

A Stationery Glossary

THE LANGUAGE of stationery isn't complex, but it does feature some terms with which you may not be familiar.

Beveled edge. A slanted edge, usually used on heavy card stock or inside embossed panels.

Borders. A band of color that frames your invitation or other stationery. It's most often used on cards but can also work on fold-overs. A border design can be carried through all of your printed items, helping to create a signature look.

Bruise. A by-product of engraving, the bruise is the ultrasmooth area around the lettering on the front of an invitation. It's created by the pressure of the die.

Cotton rag. Rich, creamy paper made from cotton fiber. (Everyday paper is made from wood pulp.) It's used in many top-quality invitations and is naturally acid free, which means it won't discolor over time. The softness of the paper lends itself to letterpress printing.

Debossed. Like embossing, except that the image is depressed instead of raised.

Deckle edge. Rough, uneven edges on paper that give it an Old World look. They were a natural by-product of papermaking in the days when paper was handcrafted on frames, but the deckle edges you see today are more often torn or die cut to make them look unfinished.

Die cut. A precision cut mainly used in folder cards to create a "window" for text or images behind the first card. Lasers have made die cuts easier to execute.

Dingbat. A typographical term for a decorative motif used on stationery. A palm tree, pinecone, or eternity symbol can convey something about your theme, location, or personality.

Embossing. A raised image created when the paper is squeezed between a die and a counter-die. If there's no ink involved, it's known as blind embossing, and the effect is subtle. Embossing is typically used for monograms and return addresses on envelopes; a panel can be embossed on a card, creating a frame around the edge.

Foil stamping. Metallic foil that is heat stamped onto paper. It's typically used for borders and dingbats, often in conjunction with embossing.

Font. The style of typeface used on the invitation. The font can speak volumes about the style of your wedding.

Inclusions. Embedded flower petals, leaves, or seeds that impart color and texture to handmade paper.

Panels. A frame that's blind embossed on either card stock or fold-over notes, with the lettering inside the frame. *Panel* also refers to the number of printable surfaces on the invitation—a trifold invitation has three panels.

Invitation Etiquette

You'll hear a lot of dos and don'ts when it comes to stationery. There are endless rules about how to address people, what you can and can't say—and exactly how, down to the period, you should

---

TRADITION PRIMER

The Inner Envelope

Have you ever wondered why you sometimes open an envelope holding a wedding invitation only to encounter another envelope? Rewind to the Victorian era, when streets were muddy and outer envelopes were often sullied in transit. After a servant received the mail, he would remove the invitation from its outer envelope and place the pristine inner envelope on a silver tray for the mistress of the household. (Which also explains why the inner invitation omits the address and has no glue on its flap—it doesn't need sealing.)

Silver trays notwithstanding, inner envelopes can still be useful for inviting family members, as putting the names of parents and their four children on an outer envelope can present space challenges. If you're sending traditional invitations, go with whichever style you prefer. A modern invitation, however, demands a single envelope.

---

say it. Why can't you just write what you want and be done with it? Well, first off, using colloquial language on a gorgeous card you've gone to the trouble of engraving would be like showing up at the opera in overalls. Moreover, a wedding is a public event, which means that you need to be respectful of etiquette—in essence, the specially designed code that smooths social interaction. All that wording has been honed over the years to ensure that not one word in your invitation could offend any one of your guests! (And if you think I'm exaggerating, take my word for it—I couldn't even begin to count the squabbles I've seen over invitation wording. . . .) That said, along with the standard wording options, there are plenty of ways to make the invites more personal or casual while still maintaining the requisite form.

The Dos . . .

■ Do use the third person for formal invitations: "Mr. and Mrs. Robert Craig Smith / request the pleasure . . ." ("Mr. and Mrs." being the parents of the bride.) For less formal invitations—and this is still considered radical by etiquette gurus—you can use the first person plural, which seems more natural if the couple is hosting the wedding: "We invite you to celebrate our wedding," etc., with your names on the last line.

■ Do use the phrase "request the honor of your presence" for a ceremony in a house of worship; for a ceremony in a secular venue, use the phrase "request the pleasure of your company."

■ Do be consistent in your spellings. If you opt for the British *honour*, put the *u* in *favour*. There's no reason to go British: If you're going for a contemporary style, *honor* and *favor* have a cleaner look.

■ Do spell out numbers in the date and year ("the twenty-fifth of September, two thousand and ten"), but not in addresses.

■ Do spell out numerals in times. For weddings on the half hour, write "half after five o'clock," not "half past five" or "five thirty in the afternoon." Rather than "a.m." or "p.m.," a formal invitation should read "in the morning."

■ Titles for medical doctors (but not PhDs) are generally included, both for parents and for the couple. On a formal invitation, "Doctor" should be spelled out, though for fit purposes the abbreviated form is fine. If one parent is a doctor, list that parent first; if both are, use "The Doctors Smith."

■ For Jewish weddings, invite guests to the marriage of the bride "and" groom, not of the bride "to" the groom.

■ Capitalize the first word of the invitation and all proper nouns. Capitalize any line that stands alone if it *would* be the first line of a new sentence—"Black-tie" and "Please respond," but not the "and" you might use between clauses.

The Don'ts . . .

■ The line breaks in the main body of the invitation act as punctuation, so don't use commas or periods at the end of a line. The only punctuation typically used is a period after a social title (Mr., Mrs.) and any commas used to separate phrases in the middle of a line.

■ Never include any reference to gifts or the registry. If you would prefer that guests make a donation to charity, you may include that information on a separate enclosure card. For suggested wording, see page 165.

■ If you've chosen not to include children, you may not mention that on the invite—it could strike some as rude. Convey who's invited on the inner envelope. If you have reason to suspect they won't pay attention, call them to say how sorry you are that you couldn't invite Ben and Emily, but that the place isn't set up for children.

■ Never include information about post-wedding events on the invitation itself. Day-after brunches and afterparties belong on a separate insert or on wedding websites; rehearsal dinner information should either be relegated to an insert in the invites or communicated by phone or email.

Military Titles

If either the bride or groom is on active duty in the military, include their military title and service designation. If they are senior officers—captain or above in the army, air force, or marines, and commander or above in the navy—their title goes before their name; junior officers should have their name on one line and their title and branch of service on a separate line; noncommissioned officers do not use their rank, only their branch of service. For parents, use titles whether they're on active duty or retired.

The Wording

Invitation language should always be graceful and clear.

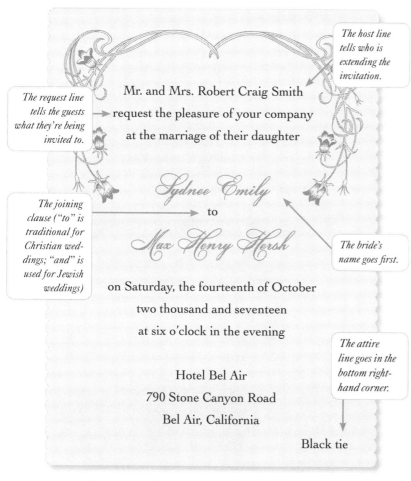

The host line tells who is extending the invitation.

The request line tells the guests what they're being invited to.

The joining clause ("to" is traditional for Christian weddings; "and" is used for Jewish weddings)

The bride's name goes first.

The attire line goes in the bottom right-hand corner.

Mr. and Mrs. Robert Craig Smith

request the pleasure of your company

at the marriage of their daughter

Sydnee Emily

to

Max Henry Hersh

on Saturday, the fourteenth of October

two thousand and seventeen

at six o'clock in the evening

Hotel Bel Air

790 Stone Canyon Road

Bel Air, California

Black tie

A standard invitation in which the parents of the bride invite guests to the wedding. Since their last name appears at the top, hers is omitted.

If the bride's parents are hosting but you want to recognize the groom's parents, too

Mr. and Mrs. Robert Craig Smith
request the pleasure of your company
at the marriage of their daughter
Sydnee Emily
to
Max Henry Hersh
son of Mr. and Mrs. Spencer Ross Hersh (etc.)

If you prefer to skip social titles

Mindy and Robert Smith
request the pleasure of your company (etc.)

If the groom's parents are hosting the wedding

Mr. and Mrs. Spencer Ross Hersh
request the honour of your presence
at the marriage of their son
Max Henry
to
Sydnee Emily Smith
daughter of Mr. and Mrs. Robert Craig Smith (etc.)

If the couple is hosting the wedding

Sydnee Emily Smith and Max Henry Hersh
request the pleasure of your company
at their marriage
on Saturday, the sixteenth of October
two thousand and seventeen (etc.)

If the couple is hosting but wants to include their parents

Together with their families
Sydnee Emily Smith and Max Henry Hersh
request the pleasure of your company
at their marriage (etc.)

If parents are divorced and not remarried or are hosting without their spouses

Mrs. Mindy Smith / Mr. Robert Smith
request the pleasure of your company
at the marriage of their daughter (etc.)

If parents are divorced and remarried

Mrs. Mindy Harris and Mr. John Harris
Mr. Robert Smith
request the pleasure of your company
at the marriage of their daughter (etc.)

Alternative Wording

As with every other aspect of your wedding, the invitation is a chance to express yourself while still keeping an eye to the solemnity of the event. I love invitations that are warm, friendly, or romantic. I don't love invitations that resort to second-grade humor or that sound too casual about a lifetime commitment. And unless you're a recognized poet or lyricist, you should not attempt rhyming verse!

Don't forget that wording on even the most mundane aspects of the invitation can be personalized or tweaked. Instead of "reception to follow," you can write "dinner and dancing till dawn to follow." You can also apply this idea to your response cards.

If a couple wants alternative, modern wording, the possibilities are boundless, but the two templates below are warm and moving in their simplicity.

In celebration and ceremony
please join us at our marriage

Saturday, the fourteenth of October
two thousand and seventeen
at six o'clock in the evening

Hotel Bel Air
790 Stone Canyon Road
Bel Air, California

Sydnee Smith
and
Max Hersh

For a reception only, such as one held after a small destination wedding or an elopement

Just Married!
Please celebrate our marriage
Cocktails, Dinner, and Dancing
Saturday, the fourteenth of October
at six o'clock in the evening
Hotel Bel Air
790 Stone Canyon Road
Bel Air, California
Sydnee Smith and Max Hersh

ASK MINDY

Q My parents and my fiancé's parents are contributing equal amounts of money. Do I need to reflect that in the invitation? How?

A It's optional, but it's a lovely thing to do, and I would recommend it. The bride's parents' names go first. You can say: "Mr. & Mrs. Joe Smith and Mr. & Mrs. John Doe request the pleasure," or you can just say "Together with their families, etc."

We would love you to share
this special day with us
as we join hands in marriage

Saturday, the fourteenth of October
Two thousand and seventeen
at six o'clock in the evening

Hotel Bel Air
790 Stone Canyon Road
Bel Air, California

Sydnee Smith
and
Max Hersh

Two simple, modern invitations

Rehearsal Dinner and Day-after Brunch

If the guest lists for the rehearsal dinner and the brunch are the same, I like to combine the invitations to keep things simpler—even if the events are being hosted by different people.

LET THE CELEBRATIONS BEGIN!

The Night Before...	*The Morning After...*
Please join us and share in our excitement at a Rehearsal Dinner in honor of	It's not over till you have Brunch! Come Celebrate with the Newlyweds
Sarah and James	Sunday for Brunch
Friday, September twenty-second seven o'clock in the evening	Ten-thirty in the morning at our home 1219 Elm Street Pasadena
Lawry's 1234 La Cienega Boulevard Los Angeles	Lovingly given by Jill and David Ascroft
Given with love by Mildred and Jake O'Neill	Kindly respond to both celebrations at 310-555-1234

In the itinerary, remind guests about the brunch, and include directions and a map if necessary.

Dress Codes

IN MORE FORMAL DAYS, you didn't need to specify a dress code: A wedding after 6 p.m. WAS ALWAYS black-tie, and a morning wedding called for—what else—a morning coat. These days, few people are even aware of the old rules; if you want a casual evening clambake where your guests wear white linen, that's your choice. Likewise, no one would bat an eye at an 11 a.m. black-tie wedding. But

DRESS CODE 101

Though dress codes have become more and more elastic with time, it's still helpful to bone up on the proper wording.

- **White-tie.** Tails for the men and full-length gowns for the women; it's rare to see this most formal of dress codes at a wedding these days.

- **Black-tie.** Men wear tuxedos and women wear formal gowns of any length.

- **Black-tie optional; Black-tie invited; Formal attire.** A very common middle ground, this indicates that the bridal party will be in formal dress, and it's optional for the rest of the guests. For men, dark suits or tuxedos are appropriate; women wear dresses or formal evening pants in colors of their choice.

- **Cocktail attire.** Men wear suits or sports jackets and pants. Women wear dresses or dressy pants.

with all these options comes a certain degree of uncertainty, and that's where the dress code comes in.

Strive to make your dress code helpful and clear. One of my pet peeves is the cryptic dress code: resort formal, country club casual, beachside chic, retro Hawaiian dress, postmodern picnic attire. All designations like these do is leave guests scratching their heads and calling other guests or the hosts for clarification. If you're going to use a nontraditional guideline, make sure it's clear, like "casual picnic attire." And a line that guests *will* thank you for is this: "The service will be held on grass. Please wear appropriate shoes."

If your ceremony and reception are in the same location, the dress code goes at the bottom right or center of the invitation. If the reception venue is separate, attire is specified on the reception card; it's not considered proper to tell people what to wear to the ceremony, which is a legal or religious proceeding as opposed to a social occasion.

RSVP

YOU REALLY NEED TO KNOW how many people plan to attend your event, so make it as easy as possible for them to respond. That means enclosing a response card and a pre-addressed, stamped envelope.

The RSVP request—which stands for "*répondez s'il vous plaît*," the French phrase for "please respond"—appears at the bottom left corner of the invitation; unless you're sending out a separate reception card, in which case that's where the request goes. Indicate that you want a reply with the text: "The favo(u)r of a reply is requested before the seventeenth of June," "RSVP before the seventeenth of June," or "Kindly reply by the seventeenth of June."

If someone other than the host is collecting replies, their name should be included as well: *RSVP / Mr. and Mrs. Robert David / c/o Mindy Weiss Party Consultants.* (Reply card envelopes should be addressed to the person keeping track of responses and managing the guest list, be it the bride and groom, a parent, or the wedding planner—the address need not match the return address on the invitation.)

Choose a reply date that leaves you enough time to call any stragglers and adjust arrangements to your guest count. If you're mailing out invitations eight weeks before the wedding, the reply would be due four weeks before. If you mail them out six weeks before the wedding, ask for replies by the three-week mark.

> To figure out the mystery identities of guests who reply but neglect to sign their names, assign each response card a number. Write the number on the back of the card, in pencil, and on your response-tracking sheet. When you get the inevitable reply without a name, you'll be able to match up the numbers.

The reply card itself should follow the same style as the invitation in terms of spelling and grammar. Though the stationery should echo the shape of the invitation, it's generally a much smaller size; you save on postage, and guests don't feel as if they need to write a novel in response to your invite.

As for the content on the reply card, you have two options. You can choose a minimalistic format that simply states the reply date at the top of the card and leaves blank space, an approach I love because it encourages creative or heartfelt replies that make wonderful keepsakes. Or you can make things extra easy for your guests by including a line for their name above a line of text reading "will ____ attend."

Return Address

THE RETURN ADDRESS should be blind embossed or printed on the back flap of the outer and response card envelopes. Blind embossing (raised letters with no ink) saves the beauty of the engraving for the moment guests open the invitation.

Traditionally the return address belonged to the hosts (the bride's parents). Before registries were so common, you could also use the address to indicate where you wanted gifts to be sent. Today it often makes the most sense to use the couple's address.

Addressing the Envelope

The envelope makes the very first impression, so choose a good quality paper with some heft to it. The next most important thing? It should be hand addressed, whether by a calligrapher or by the couple—I'm adamantly opposed to the printed-labels shortcut. (For information on calligraphy, see page 277.) A wedding invitation should arrive looking personal,

RSVP
The favour of your reply
is requested by the
fifteenth of September

_____
will ____ attend

A traditional response card does almost all of the work for the guest.

and a printed label somehow seems tossed off to me, as if it came from some computer-generated spreadsheet. You want your guests to feel that your heart is in this thing, and that all of the pieces add up to a carefully considered choice (that of your soul mate, of course).

Addressing Invitations

IN LIEU OF THE real thing, computer calligraphy is a suitable form of trickery (see page 277). You *can* also laser print the envelopes (harder than it might sound), but again, please stay away from printed labels.

Follow these guidelines in addressing your envelopes to make sure you give guests a great first impression.

■ Spell out *street, avenue, apartment*, etc. Spell out state names, unless the state name won't fit on one line. *Mr.* and *Mrs.* are abbreviated, but spell out *Doctor.* Use numerals in addresses.

■ The names of married couples belong on the same line, unless there's a fit issue. The names of an unmarried couple go on two separate lines, with the name of the person you know first; if you know both, put the woman's name first. For gay couples, if you know both of them well, rely on alphabetical order.

■ The treatment of family invites depends on whether you're using an inner envelope. If you are, you can simply write the couple's names on the outer envelope, then go into further detail on the inner envelope, either by stating the children's names—from oldest to youngest—or by writing "and family."

■ If you're inviting someone with a guest, find out the guest's name and write it on the envelope. (Mail it to the person you know.) The words "and guest" come across as impersonal, unless you come from a community or culture where enormous weddings of four hundred or more are the norm. Some of the older etiquette books maintain that a "plus one" should get his own invitation if he doesn't live with the primary invitee, but it's much less confusing and wasteful to send a single invitation to the guest you know.

■ Write the return address on the back flap of the envelope (if you didn't have it printed or blind embossed), even if the post office asks you to put it on the front. Put apartment numbers on a separate line *above* the street address (*Apartment 3C / 750 Park Avenue*).

■ Use titles and full names for formal invitations. The most formal invitations use middle names, never initials.

■ Medical doctors should get *Doctor* before their name. Also use titles with judges, government officials, clergy members, and military officers. If one member of a couple has a title and the other doesn't, the one with the title goes first.

The Inner Envelope

ASIDE FROM SERVING as a vehicle for further detail than you might be able to fit on an outer envelope, the inner envelope is mostly decorative. (It bears repeating that I think it looks out of place in a modern invite.) Unless you're inviting children, it simply repeats the guests' names, without the address, of course. In theory, where the outer envelope would read, "Mr. and Mrs. Robert Craig Smith," the inner envelope would simply read, "Mr. and Mrs. Smith"; but I find that too formal. The inner envelope is more intimate, so I think that if you want to be more casual there, you should be. Go ahead and write "Mindy and Robert" or even "Aunt Mindy and Uncle Robert." It's a sweet touch.

The inner envelope is also useful if you're inviting

Envelope liners can make a big impression and convey a certain level of quality. They might pick up the ink color or border of the invitation or even carry a pattern. It's a worthwhile decorative splurge, but only if there's room in your budget—no one will notice if you skip it.

someone who will be bringing a date. If you made the effort to find out the date's name and weren't successful, the outer envelope would be addressed to the person you know, and the inner envelope would be addressed: "Ms. Bernstein and Guest."

Putting It All Together

The goal in assembling invitations is to put your best face forward. Invitations should be placed in envelopes so that the front faces the back flap. If there's a fold in the invitation, it should be at the bottom of the envelope. When in doubt, remember that a right-handed recipient should be able to slide the invitation out of the envelope and read it. If you're using tissues, they're placed on top of the lettering on the invitation.

Enclosure cards are stacked on top of the invitation. Place the largest one next to the invitation and proceed in order of size, with the smallest card on top. (Typically, the reception card is the largest, followed by the reply envelope, then the reply card.) The reply card is tucked under the flap of the reply envelope, with the lettering facing out.

If using double envelopes, the inner envelope will have the guest's name written on it. Insert the invitation and enclosures in the inner envelope and place it inside the outer envelope with the name of the guest facing out. Do not seal the inner envelope—it should remain open, with the back flap facing the front of the envelope. In cases where a wrap or band encircles the invitation, place the enclosures on top of the invitation, inside the band.

The Humble Postage Stamp

DON'T FORGET the postage! Obviously you're going to need to put stamps on all these envelopes, so why not use something that adds, rather than detracts, from the look of the invitation? It's a little detail that not every guest will notice, but a stamp that's just so provides a terrific finishing touch.

Vintage commemoratives can add a lot of personality. You might find old "Love" stamps, stamps that celebrate the state where you're getting married, or a beautiful floral design. You'll probably need multiple stamps, as these commemoratives will have been issued in lower denominations. Go ahead and combine different vintage stamps as long as they look harmonious. You can find vintage stamps at stamp shops or online.

The post office also sells special wedding stamps in coordinating designs to cover the postage for a typical invitation with enclosures and a reply-card envelope. Order them online if you're having trouble finding them or getting the quantity you need at your post office. Also take a look at the other offerings for the year: If you like the Valentine's Day stamps, buy them in early February, even if your wedding isn't until June.

Custom photo stamps, available online, are another popular option. They can be ordered in any denomination, so if you need seventy-four cents in postage, you can get that in a single stamp.

When you're ready to put everything in the mail, pay the extra charge to have the post office hand-cancel your postage so that black ink won't be smeared across the envelopes. To be extra safe, mail an invitation to yourself. It will assure you that invites are getting through the post office unscathed and give you an idea of how long it takes them to get to the recipients.

> Don't use guesswork in choosing your postage amounts: Take a sample invitation to the post office to have it weighed.

Your Stationery Wardrobe

Beyond the invitation, there's a whole slew of other paper goods with which you'll need to acquaint yourself. What follows are descriptions of some of the most common varieties.

Thank-You Notes

THANK-YOU NOTES are such a key part of the wedding experience that I've devoted an entire chapter to the subject. See chapter 15, "Saying Thank You," for guidelines on card styles, how many notes to order, and effective strategies for sounding as grateful as you are for the lovely gifts.

Programs

WHILE NOT REQUIRED, programs serve several useful functions. They're a great way to let guests know who's who in the ceremony and give them something to read while waiting for the ceremony to begin. If you're having a church wedding, a program also lets guests know which readings are included. For the couple and immediate family, it makes a treasured keepsake.

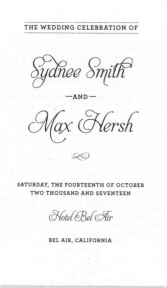

THE WEDDING CELEBRATION OF

Sydnee Smith

—AND—

Max Hersh

SATURDAY, THE FOURTEENTH OF OCTOBER
TWO THOUSAND AND SEVENTEEN

Hotel Bel Air

BEL AIR, CALIFORNIA

Though this wedding program cover is highly designed, it's perfectly fine to use offset printing.

The program also offers the couple a place to express their appreciation of their families, of the guests who attended their ceremony, or of the fates that brought them together in the first place. It's yet another opportunity to share a piece of themselves with those attending their union. (See page 439 for samples of program interiors.)

(See page 439 for samples of program interiors.)

ASK MINDY

Q What's the difference between cold feet and a case of nerves? I can't sleep, I can't eat, and I find myself crying uncontrollably. Is this normal? How do you know when to pull out? And will I ever live it down if I do?

A Brides with serious second thoughts often think they've gone too far to cancel, especially once the invitations have been mailed. But concerns about public opinion are not a reason to get married. And about twice a year, I get people who do reconsider and call it off—it *can* be done.

I strongly urge you to get a third-party opinion. Talk to someone about this, and soon. You may wind up concluding that what you're really concerned about is spending the rest of your life with one person, or about having sex with only one person— or you may decide to get out. If you go to a therapist, go alone, not with your fiancé. (At that point, he may be unaware of how you feel, and if it's just a case of cold feet there's no sense in riling him up.)

In the event that you do decide to cancel, you have my deepest sympathies. It's not an easy choice, but it is a brave one—marriage *is* supposed to be forever, even if a lot of people seem to have forgotten that these days. For information on how to cancel a wedding, see page 159.

For information on how to cancel a wedding, see page 159.

Programs can be designed and printed inexpensively, either on a home laser printer or at a printing shop. At a minimum, the program should list the order of events, the names of people with roles in the ceremony (from the officiant and attendants to anyone doing a reading), and the music that will be played. If you're incorporating any religious, ethnic, or even self-invented rituals, devote a few lines to the meaning behind them. For cross-cultural weddings, a play-by-play guide helps everyone feel included.

For a Roman Catholic nuptial Mass, the program typically outlines the liturgy and lists the readings, prayers, and responsorial psalms.

Personalize the program as much as possible by including a note of thanks and sharing a favorite quote or blessing. This is also the place to remember a deceased relative or friend.

Guest Books

THE STANDARD GUEST BOOK nets you a list of names and addresses of those who attended—not terribly useful or sentimental in the long term. Perhaps in the age when people in the community simply showed up for a wedding, this was a helpful record, but nowadays, we've got our spreadsheets. Still, the guest book is a tradition worth keeping, especially if you turn it into something that you'll treasure. A few of my favorite twists on the tradition:

- Use a leather or cloth scrapbook with blank pages and set up a table with Polaroid cameras, colored markers, glue sticks, and stickers. Put up a sign encouraging guests to snap a self-portrait, glue in their photo, and write and decorate a message to the couple.

- Place note cards and pens on the guest-book table and ask guests to write a special wish or share their advice for a happy marriage. Set up a bowl or box for the completed cards. After the wedding, you can glue them into a scrapbook or have them bound into a book.

- Have something special for everyone to sign. You can order a pewter or silver platter or picture frame (you may need more than one, depending on the size of your wedding) and an engraving pen that allows guests to inscribe their names. You can also find ceramic platters that guests can sign with special ink.

Menus

MENUS ARE OPTIONAL, but the more gourmet the meal, the more likely you are to see them. They look most elegant when printed on heavy card stock in a style that's in keeping with your other stationery. Place three on each table (passing them around forces guests to interact). Or try one of my favorite twofers, the menu and seating card in one—have a calligrapher pen each guest's name at the top of the menu, and leave one at each place setting.

Seating or Table Cards

SEATING CARDS let guests know where they're seated and are generally picked up before the reception. These small cards can be handwritten, scripted by a calligrapher, or printed.

In my opinion, the best all-around version is a flat card inserted in an envelope. The guest or couple's name is written on the front of the envelope, and the table number appears on the inside card. This format allows you to make last-minute switches without anyone knowing, because the calligraphy on the outer envelope isn't affected. The other popular style is a tented card, with the guest's name written on the front, and the table number inside. Note: Though you may hear the term "escort card" used interchangeably with seating cards, escort cards were originally designed to tell a gentleman which lady he would carry on his arm into dinner.

Place Cards

THESE SMALL CARDS, often tented, indicate each person's seat at a table. (This means your guests would first receive a *seating* card designating their table and then find a place card at their designated seat at the table.) Place cards are entirely optional, as many people prefer to let guests choose their own seats at their given tables.

Table Numbers

THIS IS HOW YOU IDENTIFY the table, by name or number. Use square cards on heavy stock and incorporate them into the tabletop décor so that they're a design element, not an eyesore. (To that end, avoid using the plastic table numbers that come with most function spaces.) But make sure they're actually visible, or your reception will start off with a roomful of confused, wandering guests.

Maps and Directions

PROVIDING MAPS and directions is a helpful and sometimes absolutely essential gesture if guests are responsible for transporting themselves to the ceremony or reception. If you're mailing them with the invitation, try to print them on the same or similar paper and in a similar color and font.

A Wedding Website

The wedding website has become as much of a mainstay as the save-the-date announcement—they're both helpful tools for any wedding, but none more so than a destination wedding. (In fact, a wedding website domain name has become a popular engagement gift.)

In purely practical terms, clicking on AudreyandOliver.com allows guests to:

- Find out how to get from the airport to the hotel.

- Get directions from the ceremony to the reception site.

- Obtain names and phone numbers for airlines that fly to the destination, along with group discount codes.

- Get hotel rates and contact info.

- See the complete weekend itinerary so they can figure out when to arrive and leave.

- Learn about area attractions.

- Find out details like suggested dress for peripheral events.

But a site also serves a more personal purpose. It gives you a forum to let everyone know how you met and share the story of the proposal, making guests who have never met your intended feel close to both of you. You can post photos of you and the groom and update the site with engagement party or shower pictures as the months pass. (Be sure not to put up any pictures that could make some guests feel left out.) The site builds a community among your guests, which will help everyone make connections sooner.

Keep the look as clean and uncluttered as possible. Fonts should be easy to read; avoid reverse type (white against a black background), which is notoriously hard to decipher. And keep the text short and sweet. There's no need to introduce every person in your sixteen-member wedding party.

You'll want your site up and running as early as possible, at least six months before the wedding. Reserve a domain name (more on that below) even earlier so you can include it on the save-the-date card. When gathering addresses for your guest list, get email addresses as well, so you can send an email blast when your site goes live.

> Have your journalist or English major friend proofread the text before you go live. Spelling errors and typos make you look careless, and you want everyone thinking that you've taken care of every detail.

Types of Sites

WEBSITES CAN BE FREE, paid, or do-it-yourself, and all can serve you well. Read on to find out which best suits your needs.

Free sites. The downsides are that you may get an awkward domain name or a site that looks overly "wedding-ish." One of the main advantages—besides the price!—is that they're easy to use, even for the technologically challenged.

Paid sites. Several companies offer paid sites that are a notch above the free sites in terms of design. You also get more space for photos and personalized features.

You often have the option of purchasing a more concise, personal domain name—no awkward hyphens for you.

Website designers. If you've got the money to spend, you can hire a designer to create a site for your wedding that fully expresses your style. Carry through the color, style, or motif from your invitations so that you're presenting a consistent style statement. Wedding planners usually know of an independent designer (some even offer the service themselves), or you can search online to find one. Remember to check references and to ask if there are additional charges for updating the site.

DIY. If you've got the skills, you can buy a domain name and create your own site. Or if you're lucky, a friend will offer to design your site as a wedding gift. You can make it look any way you like and you'll have far more storage space. But keep in mind that designing a site and keeping it updated can eat up a lot of time.

The Content

CONFUSED ABOUT THE PURPOSE of a wedding website? These are some of the elements you should consider including on yours:

- Detailed attire guidelines for each event. You cannot be too specific—women want to know that the temperature drops thirty degrees at night, so they should bring a wrap, and that the rehearsal dinner will take place on the beach (sand affects shoe choices). If the golf course, tennis courts, or any of the hotel restaurants have a dress code, note that as well.

- Weather guidelines.

- Links to your registries.

- Registration for an email informing them when the site is updated.

- Your love story, your proposal story, or the story of how you met. Knowing more about your history will get guests more excited about your wedding. (Some people feel that sharing these stories is in poor taste; it's a personal choice.)

- A detailed itinerary.

- At least one photo of the happy couple. The photo will be the first thing people see when they visit the site, and it leaves a big impression.

- Travel information, including flight and hotel details. Include the hotel's website address so guests can learn more about the property. Also include a link to a good travel website that covers the destination for those who like to do their own advance research. Put in a list of local activities, attractions, and restaurant recommendations for those planning a longer visit.

- Local transportation details, such as directions from the airport to the hotel, contact info for car rental agencies, etc. If you'll have shuttles all weekend to transport guests, let them know.

- An RSVP list, giving guests the option to RSVP to the wedding or to specific activities. If you're offering a choice of entrées, some sites are set up to let guests enter their choice.

- Directions to the wedding, reception, and any other events, along with maps.

- A guest book. Visitors sign it and leave you messages, allowing you to see if people are checking the site; if they're not, you may need to send a newsletter via snail mail.

- Your wedding hashtag.

You've set the scene with the first design element of your wedding. Now on to the wider world of design choices, from flowers and tabletops to ice sculptures and chandeliers (also known as: The Juicy Stuff). ♦

CHAPTER TWENTY-ONE

Creating the Look

THE FLOWERS! THE TABLES! THE LIGHTS!

When you picture your wedding, what do you see? A canopy of flowers and ferns over the ceremony area? A bridal bouquet of mini calla lilies? Guests lounging on sofas near the bar? Hundreds of candles setting a room aglow? Colorful Japanese lanterns hanging from a tent? Décor is what brings your wedding to life,

encompassing all the visual elements that pertain to the event—down to the plates your guests will eat from. From flowers to candles, tableware, and some unexpected props, your choices should add up to a cohesive picture. It may seem like you're dealing with many disparate details, but your goal should be to bring it all together to create a unique experience.

There's no limit to what you can do. I've set up living rooms on the beach, enchanted gardens in a ballroom, and funky discos in a tent. You can rent just about anything today, from iconic modern furniture to antique cake stands. Ice artists can carve an entire bar out of ice, and floral designers can make sculptures worthy of a float in the Tournament of Roses Parade.

What ultimately ends up taming the fantasy factor is budget. Transformations are dazzling, but they come at a price. Rather than being able to create something from the ground up, most couples have to work with what they have.

But even if your budget allows only for centerpieces, personal flowers, and a few small touches to personalize your setting, you can learn how to create focal points, unify a space, and maximize your resources. A few creative touches can work wonders, and you'll be surprised to discover how many of them don't come with big price tags.

Who Does What?

The roles of the people helping you with the look of your wedding can get murky. There are no hard-and-fast rules—some florists are also event designers; some wedding planners conceptualize the vision while others leave that to vendors; and some florists or linen rental services provide props.

Here are descriptions of how various vendors may be able to help you. You probably won't have all of them involved in your wedding, and some of them may play a lesser or greater role than described below.

Full-service florist. There are different types of florists, and a "full-service florist" is typically a retail shop that can provide centerpieces, altar arrangements, bouquets, and boutonnieres.

Floral designer. Offers a wider range of flower design services than a full-service florist and may or may not have a retail shop. A floral designer should have a large studio space for constructing chuppahs and large quantities of centerpieces. They typically have a variety of props available, including vases, baskets, urns, candelabra, candles, trellises, and arbors.

Event designer. Conceptualizes and executes the overall visual design of a wedding, including flowers, props, fabric, and lighting. Event designers are primarily needed at high-end, off-site weddings, especially those that involve tents. They're also brought in if you're totally transforming a space. Some florists and wedding planners do the work of event designers, while others work in conjunction with them; it's a fluid term.

Wedding planner. Wedding planners differ in how much they design and how much they simply coordinate. Some point you to the vendors you need and then oversee them, while others will work closely with you to design the flowers and décor, then locate the vendors who can bring the vision to life; see page 42 for more information.

Rental company. The scope of rental companies varies widely. Most areas have at least one rental company that delivers a broad range of basics (chairs, tables, chafing dishes, coatracks), but rental companies in major metropolitan areas also handle tents, subflooring, carpets, dance floors, and basic lighting. Some companies specialize in linens or china, furniture, and props (these may be called prop houses). If you're doing an off-site wedding or any wedding involving a tent, a representative from the rental company can often help determine the layout of the event and devise the floor plans. The company will also make suggestions and tell you what's required in terms of rentals, which make up a very significant part of the budget at an off-site wedding.

Where to Begin?

Before you can even think about how to decorate your wedding spaces, you need to think back to the layout and flow of your event. (See page 146 for a refresher on floor plans.)

During your site inspection, you should have asked about any restrictions governing décor. Some venues won't let you attach anything to walls, many churches have strict rules about what you can and cannot do, and some places may not allow candles. Know the limitations before you start thinking about the wide world of options. Also find out what comes with the site: What sizes of tables are available, what do the chairs look like, what are the choices (if any) in linens, china, glassware, silverware? Does the venue have any containers to offer for flower arrangements? This will help you figure out what you do and don't need to rent. You may not have planned on renting chairs, but if you learn that the hotel's only chairs are upholstered in a mauve-and-lavender patterned fabric and have brass legs, you may decide that you'll be renting chairs or full-length chair covers. You may also discover that the hotel staff is willing to move upholstered furniture from another area into your late-night lounge, saving you from renting sofas and upholstered chairs.

Don't forget the in-between spaces: the walkway from the ceremony to cocktails, the hallway to the restrooms, the area guests see when they step off the hotel elevator to get to your ballroom. You may want decoration there, or maybe just a pretty sign pointing the way to your reception.

Assess each area of your venue. You're looking at what it needs, and then thinking about what kind of effect you want to create. In each space, you'll see features you want to play up, and others you want to hide. If you notice ugly supports in the middle of your loft space, you can think about ways to disguise them.

You'll need to form a vision of what you want to create. This can be a daunting prospect, especially for those who don't have a lot of background in decorating or fashion. The best way to start is by returning to those photos you've been pinning all along.

If you want to go the extra mile, break down your boards (or physical clippings) by category:

Color. Show your vendors both the colors you love and the ones you detest.

Flowers. Types of flowers and styles of arrangements.

Ceremony elements. Items such as a gazebo, flower arch, chuppah, or aisle treatment.

Props. Vases, linens, china, chair covers, furniture, statues, and chandeliers. Put any photos that don't fit into other categories into this folder.

Share these photos with vendors when you meet with them, discussing what you like and don't like. Don't worry that it will lead to a carbon copy of what's in the photo—you can say "I love the color in these flowers, but

The Color Palette

Usually, I recommend working with two main colors, sometimes bringing in a third as an accent. Those who dream of a romantic, very bridal-looking wedding tend to prefer white and cream plus a soft accent such as pink, peach, or celadon. But there's no need to stick to neutrals anymore. A room decorated in orange and a deep red makes everyone feel like they've walked into a fantastic party. Even if you want to go with white, consider using a strong color like lime green or chocolate brown for the accent; you'll immediately create a very modern look. If one or both of your cultures has a "lucky" color, work it in.

hate the texture," or "I like the idea of weaving ribbons into table runners, but I can't stand shine."

All of this will help your vendors craft a vision for your wedding. They can start attaching price tags to the vision, which will give you an idea of what's possible and not possible on your budget. This is often one of the more painful reality checks in the wedding planning process, because brides may have no idea that creating a replica of the Trevi Fountain out of flowers will cost thousands of dollars or that using ice sculptures at your tent wedding means you have to bring in costly air-conditioning.

Create a thematic framework—whether seasonal, color based, or regional. Once you have a big picture in place, most of your decisions will flow naturally.

FLOWER POWER

The World of Flowers

Flowers have been linked with romance and fertility since time immemorial. They lend grace and natural elegance to any setting, but they're especially central to weddings, accounting for anywhere from 6 to 15 percent of the total budget.

Often, brides-to-be don't realize how expensive a really lush floral treatment can be—on a $28,000 wedding, 15 percent comes to $4,200. So when you're working with a tight budget, it's important to keep your eyes open about the costs. Still, within any budget there are many ways to create beautiful centerpieces and effects.

The first step is to figure out your floral style, or give your florist enough clues to allow her to figure it out. Often, the first question she'll pose is whether you have a particular color in mind. Then she'll try to establish whether you like arrangements that are tight, or loose (for more of an unkempt garden look). I find that whether a bride considers herself to be a "flower person" or not, she probably has a pretty defined idea of what she likes and doesn't like.

Floral Styles

Most FLOWER ARRANGEMENTS fall into one of the following categories; if you recognize which one appeals to you the most, you'll have a head start in planning.

Architectural. A clean, contemporary look that makes use of sculptural flowers like tulips, calla lilies, and orchids. Flowers are typically white or green, and the style can also be achieved with foliage, snake-grass, or bear grass. Clear glass vessels naturally complement the style, but you can also cover boxes with snake-grass or leaves if you want a warmer look. A single type of flower is typically used in each vessel. This minimalist look can be budget friendly because you can get away with using just a few stems in each vessel without looking chintzy, and arranging a few sprays of orchids in a glass container doesn't incur heavy labor charges.

English garden. Fluffy and full, but with more color than romantic arrangements, English garden styles burst with a prolific variety of flowers such as roses, hyacinths, muscari, and Iceland poppies. They usually contain a trailing element, like jasmine. Colors tend to be some combination of pink, white, lavender, periwinkle, and green. It's a traditional look that is less formal than romantic and can look lush in silver containers or charming in a basket.

Romantic. Fluffy arrangements in white, blush, cream, with perhaps a touch of pink. Roses, peonies, and hydrangeas lend themselves to this style. Most often used in traditional, somewhat formal arrangements in silver containers and accented by lots of candles (think tall urns, low bowls, mint julep cups, and candelabra).

Tuscan. Warmer and earthy, Tuscan arrangements rely on sunny shades of yellow and orange as well as some deeper reds; they often incorporate fruit, such as grapes or kumquats. Flowers could include sunflowers, ranunculus, dahlias, oncidium orchids, poppies, and hypericum berries. Terra-cotta containers are a natural, and the arrangements mix well with natural wood tables, rust-colored or verdigris candelabra, and fat cylinder candles.

Color Choices

FLORISTS ALSO HAVE a way of talking about color that you may not be familiar with; read on for a list of commonly used terms.

Cool. Deep colors from the cool end of the spectrum, mainly blue, green, and purple.

Graduated. A light-to-dark spectrum of a single hue. It could start out as a wash of blush pink and graduate to fuchsia or red.

Hot. Intense colors on the warm end of the color wheel, such as orange, red, and coral.

Monochromatic. One color is used throughout. The effect is tailored and orderly, but it can still add a pop of high-contrast color if you're using hot pink flowers against white linens.

Tone-on-tone. Similar hues worked together, such as light pink and medium pink, or white and cream. Adds sophisticated depth to arrangements.

Variegated. Spotty patches of different colors, usually used in relation to the patterns found on leaves.

A Design Philosophy

How do you tie all the pieces together to create a cohesive and pleasing whole? That's often where I come in, translating clients' personalities into details that will make their weddings memorable. I ask them about their likes and dislikes, favorite foods, hobbies, and places to go. I'm going to show you how to do it on your own; to begin, you can't go wrong by probing the following aspects of your wedding for ideas.

The *location* of your wedding can serve to inspire everything from the colors and food to the flowers and table settings. If you're getting married by the water, you might build your look around shades of blue and choose nautical motifs like fish, seashells, or mermaids; you would serve some seafood, of course. If there's a unique preexisting feature like a gazebo on the grounds, it can be incorporated into the invitation and paper goods.

Likewise, *season* is in and of itself a ready-made theme. A fall wedding can incorporate oranges and yellows and sheaves of wheat, and feature squash soup or other harvest foods that reflect the bounty of the season. Hollowed-out white pumpkins could be the vessels for your centerpieces. One advantage of this approach? Seasonal flowers and foods are less expensive and fresher than out-of-season products.

Without descending into total sappiness, there are also many ways to incorporate your *love story*. Have you traveled together extensively? Name tables after the places you went. Did the proposal take place over a memorable meal? If so, ask the chef to re-create the appetizer and include a brief explanation on printed menus.

If you take pride in your *culture*, work it in. Even if you consider yourself familiar with your roots, spend some time researching wedding and hospitality customs to learn about ways to enhance the day. Maybe you'll find out about a special dance or lucky food. If the two of you come from different backgrounds, look for ways to incorporate traditions from both cultures.

Finally, if there's something that everyone associates with one or both of you, work it in. Your collection of rubber ducks or snow globes or your love of all things Art Deco could bring just the right touch. Weddings can be constructed around a favorite flower, a personal collection, an animal, a hobby, or any other passion.

The bottom line? If you have fun with the visual elements of your wedding, you'll end up with a picture that is entirely your own—and that's the best look of all.

My Favorite Flowers

Flowers are delicate, living creatures that need to be chosen to suit the season and the setting. Some can't withstand heat or direct sun. Some are available only two months out of the year. Some will prove too costly to ship to your wedding in Mexico. If flowers are going to be without water for many hours (those used in hair, bouquets, and boutonnieres), you need to stick with less thirsty varieties. Generally, for reception flowers, you want to stay away from anything with too strong a scent; it could interfere with the flavor of your food and become cloying over time in a crowded room.

Specific conditions aside, I've developed some all-around favorites over the years.

Roses. The best all-around wedding flower, roses are showy, romantic, hardy, and come in so many colors that they can be worked into any color scheme. An ancient symbol of love and passion, roses are available year-round. They're easy to ship, which makes them a smart choice when you're planning a wedding in a place with limited flower choices. They'll last outdoors in the heat, and they're well priced for such a high-impact bloom. I love a full-blown garden rose, which lets you get by with fewer flowers. Yves Piaget, Dolce Vita, and French Anna roses are some of my favorites. For a vintage, tea-dyed look, try Sahara and Message roses.

Peonies. Feathery and lush, peonies are among the most romantic of flowers. Because they're so full, you don't need a lot of them. Peonies have a limited season from May to June and a flip season from October to December, when they're imported from New Zealand. They're available in white, pale pink, magenta, and red, so they can be a neutral or part of a bold color statement. Although they're scented, they're so beloved that it's rare for anyone to object to them in centerpieces.

Tulips. Clean, simple, and fresh, tulips can look innocent or impossibly chic. French tulips have long stems and are the most elegant, but they droop quickly and need to be wired. Tulips need a lot of water, so bouquets should be made at the last minute. Tulips also grow after they're cut, so centerpieces that look perfect the night before the wedding may have to be readjusted on the wedding day. They come in a staggering array of colors, and some are available most of the year, but the best colors start appearing in mid-January and last through May.

Orchids. Bold and beautiful, orchids can look sleek or exotic. They can stand on their own or add texture to an arrangement. Hardy and available year-round, they hold up well outdoors and can live without water for long periods, making them a good choice for bouquets, boutonnieres, and, of course, the classic corsage. There are dozens of varieties, but cymbidium, dendrobium, and phalaenopsis are my favorites for weddings. Try suspending individual orchids upside down from the ceiling to utterly change the landscape of a room. Orchids can be pricey, but if you're paying by the stem and you have twelve to fifteen blooms per stem, you're getting a lot for your money.

Carnations. Ignore the stereotype of carnations as filler flowers. They're wonderful, hardy, budget-friendly blooms that can captivate when used in a creative way. Arrange them in a pavé style (massed together as closely as possible) for centerpieces and other decorative elements and you've got major flower power.

Hydrangeas. Big, round, snowball-like flowers, hydrangeas come in stunning colors like blue, burgundy, light pink, green, and variegated antique shades. Their size, impact, and romantic look make them a perfect match for the ceremony, and they're hardy enough to withstand an outdoor summer wedding. Because of their English country garden look, hydrangeas work better at a semiformal wedding than at a black-tie event. You can get them from spring until fall, and now they're commonly imported from New Zealand in winter and early spring.

Lilies of the valley. A wedding favorite for its bell-shaped flowers and beguiling scent, the lily of the valley has a very limited early spring season (April and May); even then, it can be hard to obtain. For this scarcity, you pay a price. To get the most out of its blooms, use them in the most visible places of all, such as the bride's bouquet, or sparingly in mint julep cups surrounding a big centerpiece.

Calla lilies. Sleek and stylized, long-stemmed white calla lilies are a classic bridal bloom dating back to the 1920s. These days, mini calla lilies are also available in colors like mango, blackened red, and purple. They're hardy and versatile, making them a great choice for modern-looking bouquets, centerpieces, and napkin treatments. Their distinctive shape creates a lot of impact.

Dahlias. Midsummer to early fall flowers, dahlias aren't usually the first option a bride thinks of, but they're both sturdy and graceful, with a touch of the exotic. Their sculptural petals add a lot of texture to arrangements, and they are available in a range of sizes and colors and realistically priced. They also hold up well in the heat.

Great Accents

THE FOLLOWING BLOOMS work best in a supporting role. Chosen wisely, they can create special effects or help tame a runaway budget.

Amaranthus. When you need a flower that drips from high urns, baskets, or arbors, amaranthus fits the bill. It's most often used at the ceremony and in tall centerpieces.

A Season for Flowers

Ordering flowers in season will keep your costs down and give your wedding a lovely, natural feel.

SPRING	SUMMER	FALL	WINTER	YEAR-ROUND
Cosmos	Anemone	Aster	Amaryllis	Anemone
Flowering branches such as apple, cherry, dogwood, forsythia	Aster	Calla lily	Camellia	Asiatic lilies
	Calla lily	Chocolate cosmos	Flowering branches like cherry and quince (late winter)	Baby's breath
Hyacinth	Casablanca lily	Chrysanthemum		Bachelor's button
Hydrangea	Cornflower	Dahlia	Freesia	Bells of Ireland
Jasmine	Dahlia	Fuchsia	Heather	Calla lily
Lilac	Daisy	Hydrangea	Holly	Carnation
Lily of the valley	Delphinium	Lavender	Ivy	Gardenia
Mimosa (acacia)	Garden rose	Marigold	Lisianthus	Hypericum berry
Muscari (grape hyacinth)	Gerbera daisy	Parrot tulip	Mimosa (acacia)	Iris
Peony	Hydrangea	Snowberry	Narcissus	Orchid
Poppy	Larkspur	Statice	Ornamental berries	Rose
Sweet pea	Lavender	Sunflower	Paperwhite	Stephanotis
Tulip	Marigold	Sweet William	Poinsettia	Sweet pea
Viburnum	Sunflower	Winterberry	Ranunculus	
Violet		Zinnia	Snowberry (early winter)	
			Tulip	
			Viburnum	
			Violets, winterberry	

hyacinth   *violet*   *daisy*   *marigold*   *aster*   *tiger lily*   *ivy*   *ranunculus*   *gardenia*

It's a very distinctive-looking flower, so people tend to either love it or hate it.

Chocolate cosmos. A brownish red hue makes it a hit with brides using chocolate in their color scheme, and its cocoa scent never fails to delight. The flower makes a cool counterpoint to pale green or pink blooms and a sophisticated mix with red. Delicate and expensive, it has to be used judiciously.

Lisianthus. A sweet-looking flower that can resemble a rose or a poppy, lisianthus comes in white, pink, and purple. Considered a filler flower, as it's not assertive enough to stand on its own, it beautifully rounds out a romantic or garden-style arrangement. It looks delicate but is actually long-lasting.

Ranunculus. A surreal shape and amazing color range—white, yellow-gold, bronze, orange, scarlet, and vivid green, among others—make ranunculus a standout accent in arrangements. It looks a bit like an exploded rose, and it's kind of a shape shifter: It can go from formal to supernatural and earthy, depending on the treatment. It's lush, lovely, and incredibly sturdy.

Stephanotis. Small star-shaped white flowers with a slightly waxy look and a light fragrance, stephanotis are closely linked with brides. They have no stems, so florists insert a wire and tape them to other blossoms in order to make them functional; the labor involved makes them a pricey flower. They last well without water, so they're ideal as accents in hair and in bouquets, boutonnieres, and corsages. They mix well with roses in romantic arrangements, as their star shape breaks up the unmitigated roundness, and they can also work with orchids for a tropical or architectural look.

Viburnum. A sometimes overlooked accent flower, viburnum can fill space in an arrangement or create a fluffy backdrop for roses, peonies, or lilies. Pale green viburnum can look ultramodern when mixed with burgundy or hot pink blooms, but can look equally at home in a country garden arrangement. It's most commonly available from February into June.

Bouquets and Other Personal Flowers

A long with the dress and the veil, the bouquet is one of the most symbolic and treasured elements of the wedding day, and it's one that many women fantasize about from the time they're young girls.

Roses are a mainstay of bouquets for their strong association with love and romance, but so is myrtle (also known as periwinkle), which Queen Victoria incorporated in her bouquet; to this day, members of the British royal family honor that tradition by carrying myrtle cut from the royal gardens in their bouquets. In the American wedding tradition, the bridal bouquet used to be a vision in white, but color is often used these days. If you love coral and green, there's no reason you shouldn't carry a bouquet of coral roses and green viburnum at your black-tie wedding.

While your bouquet will be gorgeous and layered with meaning, it also has to meet practical criteria. Personal taste is one consideration, but for optimum effect you should also factor in the formality of your wedding, your wedding colors, any colors in the wedding gown and the bridesmaids' dresses, the style of the wedding dress, and your height and weight.

The flowers themselves need to be available—many brides come in asking for lily of the valley, but this April and May bloom is prohibitively expensive the rest of the year, if you can even find it. Any flowers should also be hardy enough to withstand time without water. Scent is something to think about as well—a whiff of fresh flowers can be wonderful, but too strong a scent can be cloying.

First and foremost, the bouquet takes its style cues from the bride's dress. As a rule of thumb, simple, spare gowns look more natural with a simple bouquet (perhaps a nosegay of one or two types of flowers tied with a ribbon), and more elaborate gowns serve as a perfect backdrop for elaborate bouquets with lots of texture. This isn't a hard-and-fast rule, however. A ballgown can work with a simple nosegay of lily of the valley, for example, but it

The Language of Flowers

The romantic Victorians assigned meanings to particular flowers and established an actual language of flowers; the giving of flowers thus became a highly developed way for lovers to communicate their feelings to each other. If you're looking for inspiration, draw on these definitions to assemble your very own love poem.

anemone	anticipation		**lily, yellow**	walking on air
apple blossom	hope		**mimosa (acacia)**	friendship
aster	elegance		**myrtle**	love and remembrance
baby's breath	pure-heartedness		**orange blossom**	purity
calla lily	beauty		**orchid**	rare beauty
camellia	perfect loveliness		**peony**	bashfulness
carnation	devotion or pure and deep love		**Queen Anne's lace**	trust
daisy	gentleness		**rose, coral**	desire
forget-me-not	remembrance		**rose, red**	love, passion
freesia	innocence		**rose, white**	innocence
gardenia	purity		**rose, yellow**	friendship
heather	future fortune		**rosemary**	remembrance
heliotrope	devotion, faithfulness		**stephanotis**	marital happiness
hibiscus	true beauty		**thyme**	courage
ivy	eternal fidelity		**tulip**	passion
larkspur	laughter, openheartedness		**violet**	modesty or faithfulness
lavender	luck		**zinnia**	affection
lily of the valley	happiness			

should be an unembellished fabric—heavy beading and embroidery at the torso will swallow up the simple flowers instead of showcasing them.

The silhouette of the gown should work with the shape of the bouquet. A cascade looks better with a train and long veil than it does with an ankle-length sheath. Long-stemmed calla lilies go with a long and lean silhouette. (Don't overthink it, though—if you choose a dress you love and gravitate toward a bouquet you love, chances are they'll work together.)

Proportion is also something to consider. A posy of pansies is going to be lost on a five-foot-ten bride, and a bountiful cascade that trails to the calves will overwhelm a five-foot-two bride in a size two gown. Think about

where you'll be holding the bouquet, and make strategic choices to best complement your figure. A teardrop shape can elongate the hip area instead of widening it, which is a flattering sleight of hand for a pear-shaped figure; if you have robust hips, don't accentuate them with an enormous pavé of red roses.

There are dozens of ways to make a bouquet about you. You could incorporate a flower that your husband-to-be sent you after your first date; choose flowers that correspond to your initials (foxglove for Fiona and astilbe for Anthony) or that match your sentiments (see "The Language of Flowers," above); add wired seashells to the arrangement for a beach wedding; tie meaningful charms or family jewelry onto ribbons trailing from the

Q How can I save money on flowers? I can't believe how expensive they are.

A I get this question all the time. A good way to save money is to make sure you're picking flowers in season. Out-of-season or short-lived varieties are more expensive. If you have the time, buy them directly from a flower market and hire someone to make them up for you. And use a small number of flowers with beautiful greens for filler. Everything looks better when it's fuller.

Remember that candles are inexpensive. You need clusters of them to get any real effect, and they usually cost about a dollar per votive. Another tip: Don't bother sprinkling rose petals! They're not cheap, and they don't look that good.

The bottom line, of course, is that the less decoration your space needs, the less you'll spend. If you really want to save money on flowers, get married in a garden!

---

bouquet; or wrap the stems in special ribbons or fabric. If you're all about sparkle, you could add crystals to the center of some flowers. If you're unconventional, feathers or compact fruit might add just the right touch. Herbs add scent and, often, a special meaning—rosemary has been used in bouquets for centuries because it signifies remembrance.

One note of caution: Bouquets might not be the best DIY project. There's a lot more to the construction of even a simple bouquet than meets the eye. Flowers are often individually wired and may need to be treated beforehand to last through the ceremony and reception. There are other areas where you may be able to do some of the flower arranging yourself, but I think you're best off leaving the bouquets to a professional florist.

If you want to hold on to this memory by preserving your bouquet, turn to page 390 to see the options.

A Bouquet Glossary

FLORAL ARRANGEMENT is a technical skill—and the plethora of bouquet styles reflects that.

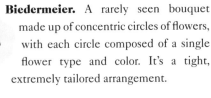

Biedermeier. A rarely seen bouquet made up of concentric circles of flowers, with each circle composed of a single flower type and color. It's a tight, extremely tailored arrangement.

Breakaway. A tricky bouquet to construct, the breakaway comes apart to form several individual bouquets. In an earlier era, the bride's going-away corsage formed the center of the bouquet, but today, the technique is more likely employed for the bride to give part of her bouquet to an honored relative or to break into individual bouquets for tossing.

Cascade. A longer, looser bouquet that trails. The flowers are wired into place to create the shape, and the stems are wired and wrapped in ribbon to form a handle. The style cycles in and out of fashion but was very popular in the 1980s, thanks to Princess Diana's copious cascade. A shorter, more tamed cascade is often referred to as a teardrop bouquet, which is what style icon Jacqueline Bouvier carried when she married John F. Kennedy.

Collar. The outermost ring around the bouquet. It can be made of a particular flower, leaves, feathers, or fabric.

Composite. Individual petals are glued or wired to create the look of one giant bloom, such as a rose. It's a labor-intensive bouquet that doesn't really work with the natural beauty of the flower, making it pricey, even if inexpensive petals are used.

Cuff. The ribbon, fabric, or leaves that circle the stems of a bouquet. The cuff can be personalized with jewelry, charms, or embroidery.

Dome or Nosegay. This is the first image most people hold of a bridal bouquet: round, dome shaped, possibly trailing ribbons. "Nosegay" technically denotes a smaller bouquet, but the term is often used by florists to describe the bridal bouquet. The bouquet can be tightly packed or loose, and stems are typically hand-tied. It can be composed of one type of flower or several, but rarely more than three types. A very small nosegay is called a posy and may be carried by bridesmaids, flower girls, or mothers.

Hand-tied. Most bouquets today are hand-tied, meaning that the stems are arranged in the palm of the florist's hand and tied together with ribbon, fabric, a handkerchief, or leaves for a serendipitous, natural look. The more stem left exposed, the more casual the bouquet.

Pavé. French for "paved," these are flowers arranged to create a flat, even surface. It's a controlled, tailored look. Inexpensive flowers such as carnations can often be massed into a pavé arrangement to stunning effect.

Presentation. Long-stemmed flowers carried in the crook of the arm, Miss America style. For brides, the bouquet is usually made of calla lilies.

Sheath. A handful of the same type of flowers tied together with a ribbon, leaving much of the stem exposed. It's usually done with clean flowers like tulips or miniature calla lilies. An unprepossessing, natural look, its linear shape goes well with a simple dress. Although the term is not widely used (you may need to describe it to the florist if you get a blank stare), the style is very popular.

Toss. A smaller, simpler version of the bride's bouquet made expressly for the bouquet toss. Bedecking it with streaming ribbons makes for pretty photos when the bouquet is captured in midair.

Tussie-mussie. A tiny nosegay of flowers arranged to fit into a conical silver holder on a chain. It dates back to the Victorian era. It's too small for brides but can be charming when carried by bridesmaids or the bride's mother.

Love Knots

Streaming ribbons from a bouquet is a centuries-old tradition to bring good luck. The ribbons, called "love knots," are tied to represent the lives that are about to be intertwined. Three knots (many brides use more) symbolize the bride, the groom, and their future offspring.

Wired. Wires are inserted into stems or taped to flowers in order to create a particular silhouette or make the flower work in an arrangement. Each flower is wired by hand, so it makes a bouquet more costly.

Bridesmaids' Bouquets

THE BRIDESMAIDS' BOUQUETS should be smaller than the bride's but should echo a feature of hers, whether in shape, color, or type of flower. They should also complement the color of the bridesmaids' dresses, so bring your florist a fabric swatch for reference. If you're

Bouquet Alternatives

There's no law that requires you to carry a dome of flowers on your walk down the aisle. For out-of-the-box brides, here are some alternatives to a typical floral arrangement:

- Ditch the flowers and carry only greenery for a fresh, contemporary look. For an uplifting fragrance, add herbs to the arrangement.

- For a vintage, high-fashion look, carry a pomander, a ball of flowers suspended on a ribbon. It also makes a wonderful alternative for bridesmaids or flower girls.

- Adorn yourself in a flower muff or stole: Your flowers become a living accessory that covers your hands or circles your shoulders.

- Wear a floral garland for an ethereal, timeless look.

- Carry a Bible with a single flower attached.

- Incorporate fibers and feathers into your arrangement. Faux flowers may sound unappealing, but some designers can craft couture concoctions of silk or dried flowers paired with feathers, crystals, and natural flora like dried pods and berries. Best perk: The arrangement becomes a keepsake that looks beautiful on display in your home.

- Carry a strand of rosary beads. They have religious significance for the Catholic bride, and they won't hide the front of your gown.

planning to have the bridesmaids place their bouquets on the cake table during the reception, keep the cake and linen colors in mind as well.

Although you want everyone in the wedding party to look like they belong together, the bridesmaids don't have to carry identical bouquets. With a small bridal party of up to three bridesmaids, it looks better if the bouquets are alike. With a larger bridal party, you can explore some variation.

The color of their bouquets might match, but each could be composed of a different flower—tulips for one, roses for another, dahlias for a third. Or the colors could graduate, starting with palest pink and deepening to magenta. If the bridesmaids' dresses vary in style, keep the bouquets more uniform so that the effect doesn't get out of hand.

The maid of honor's bouquet can be slightly different so that she stands out from the other bridesmaids. You might use the same flowers but have different color ribbons trailing from her bouquet or wrapping the stems.

Boutonnieres

THIS CLASSIC ACCOUTREMENT for men has tended to cycle in and out of popularity, but there are ways to successfully pair a modern suit with a flower. Smaller, sleeker boutonnieres with fewer elements look more

Five Great Blooms for Boutonnieres

1. Stephanotis

2. Orchid (dendrobium or cymbidium)

3. Rose

4. Mini calla lily

5. Lavender

THE FLORIST

Luckily, it's relatively inexpensive to sample the work of florists. You may already have a family or neighborhood florist you know you want to work with. If not, and you find yourself intrigued by a flower shop you pass on the way to work, order an arrangement to see how you like it. Paying for a few arrangements is the simplest way to get a feel for the style of several florists without committing a lot of time (theirs and yours) to interviews. Once you find an arrangement you like, make sure the florist is available on your wedding date, then go in for an interview.

You'll find that the business of flowers is fairly personal, so it's important that you have a good feeling about your florist. You should feel comfortable enough to say "This isn't what I was thinking" if you don't like a test centerpiece.

At the first meeting, you won't decide on every last inch of your floral design; you'll get to know each other and talk about matters of style, taste, and scope. (Some couples only need bouquets and centerpieces, while others want arbors, aisle treatments, and a thicket of trees.) Before the meeting, find out if the florist has been to your wedding site. If not, bring photographs to show her. During this meeting, you should:

- Confirm that the date and time are available.

- Discuss the size and floral needs of your wedding party.

- Discuss the location of the wedding and reception. If possible, you may want to have the meeting at the site. Some florists will want to do a walk-through before creating a proposal; it may require a separate meeting.

- Go through your flower and related décor needs for the ceremony, cocktail hour, and reception. Include any pre- and post-events where you'll want flowers, from the rehearsal dinner and hospitality suite to the late-night lounge. If you know that you're having buffets or stations, let her know.

- Look at the florist's portfolio or "book" to see examples of other weddings. Do you love what you see? To get an idea of what you can get for your money, ask what particular centerpieces, bouquets, and altar arrangements in the photos would cost. If you like particular flowers in an arrangement, find out what time of year the wedding took place—if it was a spring wedding, and yours is in September, you're less likely to have access to the same flowers.

- Discuss budget. Not every couple knows their flower budget at this juncture, but florists find it very helpful when crafting a proposal to have a ballpark idea.

- Ascertain that the florist has done other weddings and events of a similar size.

- Convey a sense of your style. Don't worry about whether you know the names or types of flowers. Go in with photos of flowers, colors, home accessories, or even clothing that you like. If you've got a photo of your wedding dress, that's invaluable to the florist in assessing your style. A photo of the bridesmaids' dresses is also helpful.

- Find out what's needed to reserve the date. Some florists require a signed contract, some require a deposit, and others require nothing more than your word.

contemporary than the traditional rosebud against a leaf and baby's breath. A compact orchid, coffee berries, or hypericum berries are stylish alternatives.

The boutonniere should share a common element with the bride's bouquet. As with the bouquet, you want to choose flowers that can hold up without water for the length of the wedding; if you must have chocolate cosmos, have a backup boutonniere ready if the flower wilts after cocktail hour. Also think about scent: Stephanotis simply smells wonderful, rosemary symbolizes remembrance and is a stimulant reported to improve memory, and lavender is renowned for its calming properties.

Fourteen Smart Flower Strategies

1. Be flexible about your flowers. Heavy rains can wipe out crops, and an early heat wave can shift a season. Transportation problems, labor strikes, and customs officials can delay them. Realize that you won't always be able to get exactly the flowers you want. Instead of being overly specific with a florist, focus on the quality that's most important to you—a particular hue, texture, or style—and allow your florist to choose the best available flowers.

2. You can get most flowers at any time of year from somewhere in the world, but flowers that are in season are heartier, more robust, more abundant, and far less expensive. Even better are locally grown flowers, which save you a bundle on transportation costs—cosmos trucked in from a local farm can cost as much as 40 percent less than those flown in from Holland.

3. If your budget is limited, concentrate your flower dollars where they'll show the most: the altar or ceremony area, the bridal bouquet, and the centerpieces. No one will notice if you don't have pew decorations.

4. If your wedding is in a house of worship, find out if you can share ceremony flowers with another couple. Or have your wedding near Christmas, when the church will be fully dressed for the season.

5. Ask your florist whether he has seen any "bargain" flora. A florist can buy two bunches of gladiolus for $10—you'll have a hundred blossoms easily mistaken for orchids when scattered on tables, floated in glass containers, or hung on fishing line from chandeliers. In winter, flowering branches provide a lot of drama for much less than cut flowers. Sheaves of wheat, tall grasses, and bamboo can supplement arrangements or be used in large urns in place of pricier posies.

6. Make inexpensive flowers look lush by sticking with one color and massing them together. Carnations and baby's breath can be striking when handled creatively.

7. Submerge long stems of flowers (orchids, gladiolus, and amaryllis are gorgeous) in tall glass cylinders. The stems are a statement all their own.

8. Stick to simple arrangements. Hand-tying bouquets for centerpieces is relatively simple, whereas pinning hundreds of carnation heads to foamboard to create a wall of flowers takes hours of manpower. Floral installations that have to be assembled on-site require more staffers at the location and cost more than those that can be made ahead. If the flower estimate is coming in too high, talk to the florist about ways to simplify the arrangements to reduce labor costs.

9. If the ceremony and reception are in the same place, design large arrangements to perform double duty. Big urns or columns marking the aisle or altar can flank the entrance to the reception or the stage for the band. A floral arch or chuppah can shelter the wedding cake. Just make sure arrangements are moved discreetly.

10. Choose a small wedding party. At the high end, eight bridesmaids can mean $800 in bouquets; if you have only two bridesmaids, you've saved $600.

11. Create centerpieces out of potted plants, such as orchids or hyacinths. They are cost-effective and can double as gifts to close relatives or members of the bridal party.

12. Think low. Low centerpieces cost less than tall ones—and your guests will get a better view.

13. Choose a location that you find beautiful. You'll spend far less to decorate it or hide its flaws. Botanical gardens and conservatories can often be rented for weddings, negating the need for flowers. Some florists and nurseries also rent out their studios for events.

14. Avoid having a wedding near dates where there is peak demand for flowers, namely Valentine's Day and Mother's Day. Around Valentine's Day, the price for roses can double.

Pay tribute to your heritage and make the floral accent more personal with bells of Ireland for the Irish, a snippet of tartan ribbon for the Scottish, and a red flower for the Chinese.

The groomsmen's boutonnieres should all match, but the groom's boutonniere is usually distinguished in some way to make him stand out. Don't forget to order boutonnieres for the fathers of the bride and groom, the ushers, and the ring bearer.

A floral wreath perfectly plays up a flower girl's charm and innocence. She may also carry a basket of petals, a pomander, a garland, or a hoop decorated with flowers and ribbons. And if your dog is in your wedding, don't forget about him: a floral leash or collar links him to the rest of the wedding party. (Make sure the flowers aren't toxic to canines.) To ensure that every bloom looks its freshest, keep any personal flowers refrigerated until the moment they're needed. The cool air will help them last longer.

Corsages

MOTHERS AND GRANDMOTHERS traditionally wear corsages, and stepmothers are usually accorded the honor as well. If you're particularly close to another female relative, a corsage can be a touching gesture.

Though they embody a lovely sentiment, corsages can look outdated, especially on a mother in a slinky Badgley Mischka gown. A small bouquet or some other floral accessory might be a better option; the best florists can turn flowers into a form of jewelry, fashioning a wristlet out of orchids, a pendant out of rosebuds, or a hair accessory out of buds, berries, and foliage.

Make sure you consult with the recipients to find out what type of outfit they're wearing and where they would like to wear flowers. If a woman is wearing a jacket, she'll

prefer flowers on her lapel to her wrist, and women wearing delicate fabrics won't want to damage them by poking a pin through them.

Ceremony Flowers

At a ceremony, nothing creates a romantic aura quite like flowers. Whether they're flowing from hanging containers, lining the aisle, or adorning a chuppah, flowers are a powerful reminder of the beauty of the day.

The type of flower treatment at your ceremony will depend largely on the ceremony's location. Churches often have strict rules about which decorations are allowed, so find out what they are before you proceed; in any case, most houses of worship feature fairly elaborate interior details, so they won't need a lot of adornment. Make sure to ask about altar arrangements to find out what you're required to provide, whether you can share the arrangement with someone getting married the same day, and whether you can take it to reuse at the reception.

Restrictions aside, the altar or ceremony area should be your primary area of focus; not only is that where you'll become husband and wife, it's also where all eyes will be.

Altar flowers should be to scale with the ceremony space. The bigger the wedding, the grander the ceremony flowers will need to be to hold their own. At a hotel or estate, in a tent, or outdoors, you'll probably need to create and define your aisle and ceremony area, which means you'll need more in the way of flowers and decoration.

The Chuppah

TRADITIONALLY, the chuppah is a temporary structure consisting of four poles with a canopy partially covering them; the poles are supported by four members of the wedding party, and the sides are left open. Alternately, the chuppah can be constructed as a more elaborate, freestanding structure with a fabric-covered roof. A central component of Jewish weddings, it represents

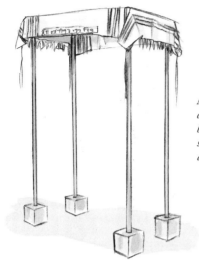

An unadorned chuppah topped by a prayer shawl called a tallith

A lush chuppah embellished with flowers and draping

The Aisle Runner

Though it's not a floral element, the aisle runner is one of those in-between items that falls under the florist's purview. If a house of worship allows an aisle runner, they'll usually provide it. Otherwise, you can rent one through your florist or a specialty runner source.

If you want an unusual color or custom-designed runner, you'll need to buy it, but if it's important to you, I think it's not a bad place to splurge—for a few hundred dollars, you can make a big impact. You can have a runner edged in crystals, you can have your monogram and wedding date painted on it . . . If you're a detail person, it's another area for you to play with.

Aisle runners should have a nonslip surface and shouldn't move around once they're placed on the ground; canvas is your best bet. Outdoors, you may be better off going without. (Fabric laid over an uneven surface has been known to trip up the occasional unsuspecting bridesmaid.) Those determined to have a runner on a less-than-cooperative surface can have an aisle made out of plywood and lay the runner on top of it. One thing I will say categorically is that aisle runners and sand are *not* a good mix! For beach weddings, I prefer to leave the aisle bare, bordering it with seashells or flower petals in graduated colors.

If you're using a basic runner, you can jazz it up inexpensively by scattering flower petals along the edges, but know that most churches don't allow this.

For an evening wedding, decorating the aisle with candles housed in glass hurricanes adds a gorgeous glow. (Just be sure that they're tall enough and placed in such a way that a long gown couldn't brush against them and start a fire—that's *not* the kind of excitement you want at your wedding.)

the couple's first home; these days, though, many non-Jews have found its symbolism appealing (especially at outdoor weddings). There are few religious rules governing the chuppah, leaving its decorative possibilities wide open. Many synagogues can provide a chuppah. Should you need to have one made, a floral designer should be able to do the job.

All manner of chuppah coverings, both ready-made and custom, are available from artisans at both Judaica shops and at online stores. The most traditional approach is to use a tallith (prayer shawl) or a lace veil from a family member for the canopy. You can also use a beautiful fabric of your own choosing. Some couples like to involve their family and friends by asking them to paint fabric squares, which are then stitched together to form the canopy—and become a lovely keepsake.

Flowers aren't required, but there's something magical about a lush floral chuppah. Flowers can ring the tops of the poles, edge the trim of the canopy, or cover the entire structure.

Floral Arches and Gazebos

A FLORAL ARCH OR ARBOR provides a romantic backdrop for the ceremony. Sometimes the opportunity presents itself; at one wedding I did in Napa Valley, the trees grew sideways and created a roof. We placed tables underneath and made the most of the natural canopy by adding lighting to the trees and hanging candles from the branches.

I love to see an arch at both the beginning and end of the aisle. It's more expensive, of course, but the dual arches define the area beautifully, particularly at an outdoor wedding.

Arches, arbors, and similar garden-like structures are handled by floral designers, who will rent or build them, install them on-site, and disassemble them after the ceremony.

If your site features a gazebo, consider draping garlands of flowers or foliage around the exterior or hanging pomanders or flower baskets from the ceiling. (If the vows will take place in the gazebo, just be sure that the florals don't block anyone's view.)

If your wedding is taking place outdoors or in an open space, consider renting columns or statues to help define the entrance to the aisle. Then have flowers tumble over the tops of the columns for a stunning, love-among-the-ruins effect.

Aisle Markers

AISLE OR PEW MARKERS are flowers, often enhanced with ribbons, attached to the ends of rows along the aisle. A lovely extra, they're not essential. If you love the look of pew markers but you're on a budget, place them every second or third row and ask your florist if you could save money by using foliage

A Wreath at the Door

Decorate the front door or gate of the church with a floral wreath and make guests feel immediately welcome. It's especially festive to hang a wreath on the front door at a home wedding. A circle is an ancient emblem of endless love, and a wreath announces a special occasion.

in place of flowers. For a lush, romantic look, you can add candles, housed in hurricanes for safety, placed on iron stands or hung from shepherd's hooks (also a lovely treatment for flowers).

A single flower can also be placed on chair seats or on the back of each chair. (Look for chair covers with a sheer organza pocket sized just right for holding a flower, fan, or program.)

Cocktail-Hour Flowers

As cocktail hour is not the main event, you don't want to devote too much of your floral budget to it. Instead, you can do clever things with candles and containers, using flowers as an accent rather than the central focus. For maximum impact, place the blooms you do use in some of the following spots:

Flanking the entrance. Rent trees and potted flowering plants such as azaleas to make a lush statement at a lower price.

On the seating-card table. (See page 318.)

On the buffet tables. First be sure to establish whether the florist, caterer, or venue is responsible for decorating these.

At the bar. These aren't usually necessary, but if you have the budget, flowers take some of the emphasis off pure function at a bar. You don't want arrangements to be knocked over by guests reaching for drinks, so they should be placed all the way to the sides, behind the bartender, or on the ground flanking the bar. Candles add a warm glow, but don't place them anywhere on the bar where guests could possibly set their sleeves on fire.

On trays of passed hors d'oeuvres. Try long-lasting blooms like orchids, or use a couple of striking leaves.

On cocktail tables. For high-top tables, small arrangements will do; or try a cluster of glass containers filled with candles and a bowl of water floating a gardenia.

Reception Flowers

Most couples earmark the majority of their floral budgets for centerpieces on the reception tables—and with good reason, as that's where guests will be spending much of their time. Here are a few things to consider when choosing your flowers.

Centerpieces shouldn't block guests' view across the table; their blooms, the widest part of the bouquet, should either be low enough or high enough to allow for eye contact and easy conversation. (In the world of centerpieces, you'll hear the words *high* and *low* bandied about frequently, and they always mean *tall* and *short*, not high-end and low-end.)

If your room has high ceilings, tall arrangements will probably work better. You don't want too much empty space between the tops of the tables and the ceiling. Tall arrangements tend to create a more formal look.

Low centerpieces are generally less expensive, because you don't need as grand an arrangement or as many flowers when they're closer to eye level. They lend themselves to a more intimate atmosphere and work well in a smaller room or restaurant; they also look very natural outdoors.

A low centerpiece can also be made up of a cluster of smaller containers, known as a "satellite" arrangement. Doing a satellite arrangement with a few stems in each

vessel keeps the labor costs down and makes for great favors—at one of my weddings, we placed ten mint julep cups filled with hydrangeas on each table, and each guest took one home at the end of the evening.

Beyond Flowers

Flowers are, of course, the mainstay of centerpieces at weddings, but sometimes you want something different, either to stand out from the throngs or to save money. Some creative nonfloral approaches:

- Fill tall glass cylinders with fruit (look for fruit with waxy skins such as lemons, limes, oranges, kumquats, and apples), then pour water over them. Float a candle on top.

- Create a still life out of fruits or ornamental vegetables. Use sugared fruit if you want to add a little sparkle; or try using only one type of fruit or vegetable per arrangement and let the repetition and quantity make the statement.

- Giant leaves in tall containers give a fresh and sophisticated effect. Best of all, an all-foliage arrangement can save you as much as two-thirds the cost of a floral display. Try areca palm fronds in seven-foot-tall arrangements, or a few stems of philodendron selloum leaves, or elephant ears.

- Candles can hold their own when clustered together in glass hurricanes. Make sure they're substantial enough to get attention—six tea lights won't be enough at a table for ten people, but six pillars could carry it—and vary their heights. Wrap the hurricanes in colored paper or fabric to echo your color scheme.

- Especially with a very low or simple centerpiece, you might consider ways to add interest to the table: scatter flower petals, crystals, seashells, or river stones. Or try seasonal decorations like pinecones and berries in the fall and Christmas ornaments and holly for a December wedding.

FLOWER SPOT-CHECK

The following are places to *think about* using flowers. You wouldn't use them in every place on this list, but if you've got this in hand, you won't forget to order flowers you wanted for an entryway or your "best dog."

CEREMONY

- Wreath on door of ceremony space
- In the bathroom at ceremony space
- On the guest-book table or table holding programs or yarmulkes
- Along the aisle, at ends of pews, or on backs of chairs
- Altar arrangements
- Bouquet to offer the Virgin Mary
- Petals for tossing
- Petals for defining aisle (outdoor wedding)
- Chuppah, arch, gazebo, or arbor decoration
- Garlands for trees
- Bridal bouquet
- Bride's tossing bouquet
- Bridesmaids' bouquets
- Groom's boutonniere
- Boutonnieres for groomsmen, fathers, ring bearer
- Corsages or nosegays for mothers, grandmothers, other honored women
- Garland or petals for flower girl
- Floral collar or leash for dog in wedding party

COCKTAIL HOUR

- Urns at entrance
- On trays of drinks or hors d'oeuvres
- On seating-card table
- On bars
- In restrooms
- Centerpieces for cocktail hour
- Buffet or station centerpieces

RECEPTION

- Urns at entrance
- Centerpieces
- On backs of chairs
- On cake and cake table
- Buffet or food station centerpieces
- Urns of flowers flanking stage for band
- Tiebacks for curtains
- Centerpieces on coffee tables in lounge area
- Rented trees for reception
- Hanging from ceiling or chandeliers
- On seating-card table
- In restrooms

OTHER

- Petals for honeymoon suite
- Decorations for getaway vehicle
- On favors table (reuse seating-card table flowers)
- Arrangements to send to parents
- Centerpieces for rehearsal dinner
- Arrangements for day-after brunch

Alternating high and low centerpieces ("high-low," in florist-speak) can be a wonderful way to break up a room and save it from looking flat, especially at a larger reception with twenty or more tables. As a general rule, centerpieces do not need to be identical from table to table, but they should share common elements that will tie your look together. Vary the flowers and keep the colors uniform, or vice versa; vary the containers; or vary the nonfloral elements. There are all sorts of wonderful touches your florist can incorporate, from fruits and berries to ornaments corresponding to the season.

Also consider the shape of the tables. Long, family-style tables look most dramatic with linear centerpieces that line up down the center—flats of wheatgrass punctuated with gerbera daisies, low boxes paved with flower heads, or a series of woven rectangular baskets packed with flowers and fruit. Round tables are complemented by round arrangements or clusters. (For an overall approach to table-top arrangements, including nonfloral elements that can be part of your centerpiece, see "The Tabletop," page 311.)

One last note: Avoid using highly scented flowers such as Casablanca and Stargazer lilies around food—a strong scent interferes with gustatory pleasures.

Vessels for the Centerpieces

YOUR CHOICE OF VASES and containers goes a long way toward setting the tone for the table. A classic silver bowl, a whimsical ceramic pitcher, and a woven basket all say very different things. Add character and save money by bringing in compotes, vases, and bowls that belong to your family, or use containers that reflect your interests. If you collect teapots or creamers or pitchers, why not incorporate your collection into the centerpieces? I collect lady head vases (just what it sounds like—vases shaped like women's heads), and like to add one per table as part of a satellite arrangement.

THE FLORIST'S CONTRACT

When interviewing a florist and working on details in the contract, make sure you cover these points:

- Establish who will find out about any restrictions at the venue in terms of décor and candles.

- Find out how much time your location allows for setup and breakdown and go over plans with your florist. How much time will he need? Some floral installations can take days, and if you won't have access to the venue until the morning of the wedding, that could present difficulties. If the florist is late breaking down, you could incur overtime fees on rentals.

- Find out when a deposit is due. Though deposit policies vary from florist to florist, you shouldn't have to put down more than 50 percent. Find out when the remainder is due (typically, two weeks before the wedding).

- Ask about the cancellation policy and changes to the order.

- Find out how many events the florist will be doing that weekend. If there are multiple weddings, find out who will be handling yours, since it may not be the person you've been dealing with.

When in doubt, go with clear glass vessels. They can look modern or traditional, at home on the beach or in the ballroom. Florists keep a variety of sizes and shapes in stock, and they're usually the least expensive option.

Even the area below the flowers can benefit from a creative approach. You can tint the water (only with certain flowers—otherwise, your white hydrangeas may turn a different color by the middle of the reception) or underlight it if you want to turn it purple or apricot. You can also line the glass with wide monstera or ti leaves, which gives it a whole different look.

Recycling the Flowers

Don't let all those beautiful blooms go to waste. Arrange to donate them to a nursing home, senior center, or hospice after the wedding. (This is definitely something to attend to in advance.) Or give local guests bouquets to take home with them. While guests are dancing, have someone deconstruct the centerpieces and set up a flower stand where people can stop on their way out.

Working with a Florist

After your initial meeting, the florist will prepare a proposal giving descriptions of each floral element and prices. Some will include options—a proposal is not an all-or-nothing proposition, and you can reject certain elements if they're pushing you over budget.

Once you accept the proposal, the florist will create a sample centerpiece and sketch out any other elements, free of charge; the timing of this follow-up can vary, depending on seasonal flower availability. This is the time to discuss any changes you'd like to make. Maybe you don't care for a particular flower or you realize that you don't want any yellow in the centerpieces or you decide that the table could really use some pillar candles mixed in with the votives. Bring a camera to photograph the samples; you can use the images to help coordinate other visual elements.

To the Table

At a sit-down meal, guests typically spend four hours at the table, so you want to make the tabletops as compelling as possible.

Think about how your tabletop elements will work together. If you've decided on clear glass containers for your centerpieces, you might want to keep the tableware clean and modern, rather than going for chargers with an aged patina. Aim for harmony. If you're going with a Tuscan theme, you would want gutsy tablecloths with texture rather than a glossy satin. Also think about your table service: If you're having family-style platters, use weighty bronze chargers and stemless wineglasses. They're more casual and less prone to tipping if people are reaching to serve themselves.

If you're having an on-site wedding, you can keep costs down by sticking with the venue's linen, china, flatware, and glassware offerings, though you do have the option of splurging on specialty rentals if you wish. For an off-site wedding, you'll generally be renting everything that goes on the table, from the dinner plates to the salt and pepper shakers. The caterer is likely to offer basic china, glassware, and flatware, but if you want any specialty items, you'll probably need to turn to a party rental company. Since you're already spending money to rent your china, glassware, and linens—even if they're basic white—it's actually less of a splurge to upgrade to specialty items at an off-site wedding.

If you bring in your own photos, candy dishes, cloth napkins, or plates, make sure you have a system to keep track of what's yours, and make arrangements for someone to gather them and take them home at the end of the night.

Talented bargain hunters have been known to find tableware on sale or at flea markets at similar costs to rentals, but this type of shopping is not for everyone.

China, Glassware, and Flatware

You can take a table from blah to wow with distinctive dishes, glassware, and flatware; some specialty rental companies offer amazing selections.

Consider the surroundings. At an outdoor garden party reception, you might evoke a picnic theme by using flatware with translucent plastic handles or checkered red-and-white napkins. Mixing and matching gives a warm, eclectic look to the table, so don't be afraid to add a floral bread and butter plate to ivory dinnerware or to use different patterns of crystal in the glassware. If you love red, why not rent red wineglasses? Silver chargers, white napkins bordered with red, and red tablecloths could complete the look.

China

YOUR CATERER will advise you as to what kind of china your menu will require. If you want something a little dressier than a solid plate, you can never go wrong with bone or white china edged in silver or gold. If your colors are warm, gold is a better fit, while silver complements cool colors.

To make a big impact without going overboard on your budget, rent one special plate. You'll get the most bang out of a special charger, but a striking salad plate also gets noticed because it comes out at the beginning of the meal, while guests are still paying attention.

Glassware

CONSIDER BOTH cocktail hour and the reception when making your choices in glassware. For the bar, consult with your bartender or caterer about which glasses you'll need and how many of each. You can certainly use all-purpose wineglasses for many a mixed drink, but if you're having a margarita or martini bar, or serving a signature cocktail, you'll want to play that up with drink-specific glasses. Don't forget cordial glasses if you're planning on serving after-dinner drinks. And if you're having an after-party or lounge, you'll need to factor that into your bar needs.

Are you going to offer beverages before the ceremony or at any other time? Make sure to order necessary glassware.

At the table, your glassware needs should be more obvious. Are you serving champagne? Are you distinguishing between wineglasses that hold red and white wine? (Doing so will add to your cost.) If it's within your budget, crystal adds sparkle to the tabletop. Make the most of it by varying pattern, height, or color among your water, wine, and champagne glasses.

Also consider table shapes and serving style. If guests are going to be passing platters family style, you're better off with solidly grounded glasses than easy-to-topple stemware. And always arrange to see a complete place setting before committing—you really need to see how the glassware relates to the dinnerware and the flatware before

you sign off on it. For more information on glassware and barware, see Chapter 10, "Spirits, Wine & Bubbly."

Flatware

CHOOSE YOUR FLATWARE LAST, after the dinnerware and the glassware. It should complement the other elements, not stand out as a separate statement. If your look is sleek and modern, choose streamlined flatware; if it's more traditional, you can opt for either ornate or basic flatware. Weightier utensils feel more luxurious, so if the flatware that the caterer offers feels flimsy, consider upgrading.

Your caterer should let you know what each dish will require in terms of utensils. Do you need fish forks, fish knives, steak knives, or soup spoons? You'll typically need extra teaspoons, especially if you're serving desserts that require a spoon. You'll need special coffee spoons, though you can also order additional teaspoons.

For cocktail hour, your caterer can advise on how many forks to order, based on the number of guests and the menu. If you're going heavy on finger food, you may not need much in the way of utensils.

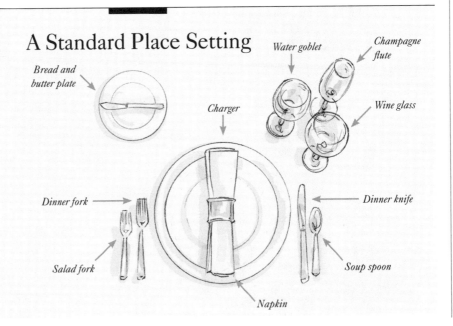

Discuss with the caterer what utensils the meal calls for before designing your place setting. This setting is fairly standard, but if you're serving fish, you may wish to add a fish fork and fish knife. If you're not serving champagne, you don't need a champagne flute. If the setting looks too cluttered, you can opt to put out champagne flutes, dessert forks, and spoons only as needed.

A Standard Place Setting

Bread and butter plate

Water goblet

Champagne flute

Charger

Wine glass

Dinner fork

Dinner knife

Salad fork

Soup spoon

Napkin

One question I hear often is whether it's acceptable to mix metals on the table, especially if you're using gold-rimmed dinner plates and silver flatware. I think it's perfectly fine, though consistency does unify a table.

Small Touches

Besides china, glassware, flatware, and centerpieces, loads of other interesting (and possibly unique) elements can grace your tables. Some are informational and some are decorative, but all can be incorporated seamlessly into the tablescape.

Table numbers. A 7-by-14-inch piece of paper in card stock folded into a tent shape is the classic way to go. You can have a calligrapher draw numbers and even embellish the cards with tiny crystals or hand-painted flowers. Or cover a hurricane lantern in tissue paper with the table number written on it—the glow from the flame will make the number easier to spot. Rather than numbering your tables, you might also name them after favorite songs or places you're planning to visit on your honeymoon.

Menus. If you don't have the budget to print individual menus but still want the effect, you can do up one menu per couple, or even one per table. Tucked into a napkin fold, placed in the center of the table, or wedged between two place settings, menus are a lovely touch and keepsake. (Though, truth be told, guests often leave them behind.)

Place cards. Should you want to designate exactly where each guest will sit (which isn't necessary, unless you're trying to play matchmaker or avoid igniting particular tensions), you'll need place cards. For details on table numbers, menus, and place cards, see chapter 20, "The Invitations."

Favors. I prefer handing out favors to guests as they leave, but you can also set them on the table above the place setting. (If there's not enough room, the bread plate is a fine receptacle.) See chapter 22, "Favors & Gifts," for ideas.

The Handmade Wedding

While some couples favor a traditional look for their wedding day, these days many brides and grooms are looking to bring in handmade, personal touches where they can. Some crafty brides opt to make elements of the décor themselves—likely candidates include programs, invitations, place cards and signage, one-off projects like display tables and photo booths (see page 93), and smaller scale baking or assembly projects like edible favors or welcome totes (see pages 328 and 331). But for many, the challenge of planning a wedding alongside a full-time job means there isn't likely to be much time left over for stringing up sixty paper lanterns the night before the wedding (when you'd rather be relaxing or spending time with out-of-town guests) or for hand-stenciling monograms on a towering stack of invitations.

Fortunately, you don't have to be a crafting queen or a time-management expert to bring a sweet, homemade flair to the proceedings. One of my favorite resources for unique handmade goods is the wedding section on Etsy, where you can find a staggering array of artisan-made goods for reasonable prices. Etsy is a storefront for a whole community of talented artists and artisans working in every discipline under the sun, and incorporating their creations can be a great way to personalize your décor without breaking the bank. What you may not realize is that many of these vendors will happily create custom goods upon request. If you see something you like, don't be afraid to ask. I've ordered custom hand-forged metal table numbers, adorable reception signage, and individual wooden dishes that we filled with chocolates and placed on reception tables. Those whimsical or slightly rough-hewn touches can go a long way toward warming up a space.

I love the site so much I've been known to visit for impulse shopping in the middle of the night!

Lamps. Cabaret table lamps with domed shades help create a supper club atmosphere.

Candy dishes. Pretty dishes to hold chocolates or nuts make guests feel as if they're in someone's home—they are that personal. (I like to use glass or porcelain candy dishes I buy at flea markets for as little as a dollar each.) They're more charming if they don't match, though you may want to stick with a single material like Depression glass.

Personal collections. Whether you collect glass fruit, vintage creamers, or whimsical salt and pepper shakers, work an item or two into your centerpieces and your tables will instantly come to life.

Ribbons

RIBBONS ARE ONE of the prettiest, most cost-effective flourishes you can add to your reception. They can be ultra-feminine or tailored, depending on their fabric, color, and texture.

Organza is one of my standbys, because it's sheer, shimmery, and romantic. Double-faced satin is classic and versatile and comes in a huge array of colors. For spring and summer weddings, I love to use grosgrain; the finely ribbed texture works in traditional, casual, and outdoor settings, and in a color like navy or chocolate, it isn't overly girly. In fall and winter, I love velvet for its richness and warmth.

There are many ways to use ribbon, but here are a few of my favorites:

- Around the rim of votive candle holders
- Hanging from a gazebo or chuppah
- Hanging from trees in the ceremony area
- Streaming from the backs of ceremony chairs
- Trimming the unity candle
- Wrapping the stems of bouquets
- Tied around napkins
- Banding glass vases in the centerpiece
- Tied around favors
- Running in strips across square or rectangular tables to dress up plain tablecloths

Candles

CANDLES ADD a warm glow to a wedding. They're cozy *and* glamorous, instantly creating that "special occasion" feeling. They also cast a flattering, warm light that your guests will thank you for. Obviously, you shouldn't waste your money on candles for a daytime event. But if your wedding will extend till sundown or later, I urge you to incorporate some.

One myth about candles: They're not necessarily the money saver people make them out to be. Tea lights and small votives are quite inexpensive (for a small event, some florists and caterers may even provide them at no charge), but a three-by-nine-inch pillar isn't cheap. By the time you buy four to six sizable pillars for each table—and rent the glass hurricanes to house them—you've made a significant investment.

Of course—it's worth repeating—before you proceed, you'll need to find out your site's rules and restrictions regarding candles. Your event space may have an ordinance requiring candles in public spaces be surrounded by glass, and you don't want the friendly fire marshal to have to stop by and blow out all the lights. (Yes, it *has* happened to me.) In any case, at an outdoor event, candles should *always* be housed in glass. If your site doesn't allow flame of any kind, battery-operated candles are a safe alternative and are carried by many florists.

Where to place candles? Think about whether people will be reaching across an area for a drink or the bread basket, or to serve themselves at a buffet. Don't put candles where they could set a guest's sleeve on fire, and stick with unscented candles in any area where people congregate or around food.

Some of my favorite ways to use candles:

Dollars and Sense

Florists can provide many candles, but should you want to purchase them yourself to save money, you can find good deals at warehouse clubs or large home-furnishing stores. If you have access to a wholesale flower district, look in any store where florists shop for supplies; it's bound to stock a good assortment of candles at attractive prices. For bargain prices, shop after the holiday season, when many retailers put their candles and containers on clearance.

- In glass votives or hurricanes wrapped in sheer fabric to bring out the colors of your wedding

- Placed in tall glass spheres of various sizes along the aisle. (Make sure they're not too low to the ground, so you don't risk setting anyone's clothing on fire.)

- Hung in glass candleholders from hooks along the aisle or walkways. (Just make sure they aren't blocking guests' view of the altar.)

- Scented, in restrooms

- Mixed in with the centerpieces

- Floated in a nearby fountain or pool; have your florist weight them so they stay in place.

- Adorning focal points like mantels, bars, or the guest-book table

THE FURNITURE

Seating

In many instances, you won't have much of a choice when it comes to ceremony seating. But if you're doing an off-site ceremony and supplying the seating —or if you're not satisfied with your venue's chairs and decide to bring in your own—you have a world of options.

If you're creating your ceremony area from scratch, figure out the layout first. Though it's the tried-and-true setup, you don't have to seat everyone in rows flanking a single aisle: Consider an intimate ceremony in the round, which gives everyone a better view of the couple.

If you're renting, make sure the chairs you rent for the ceremony also work for the reception. Folding chairs and Chiavari chairs most easily bridge ceremonies and receptions. The most common chair styles can be rented through party rental companies, event designers, and some florists and caterers. Specialty chairs can be found through prop houses or party rental companies specializing in high-end events.

During the Cocktail Hour

FOR HIGH-TOP TABLES, you'll need barstools. (Stools with backs tend to look more formal than those without.) People tend to stand around high-tops, but you still need four stools per table so things don't look too bare. Ideally, you would have one cocktail table for every twenty guests; if that's not possible, provide at least two tables with four chairs each. (If you have elderly guests, make sure you have some standard-height seating for them, as many of them find it difficult to clamber onto a barstool.)

At the Reception

SOMETIMES THE CHAIRS that hotels and other venues offer detract from the look you've worked so hard to put together while designing your wedding. If that's the case, look into renting chair covers before committing to chair rentals—you'll save a bundle. (See "Linens," page 318.) But if that won't work, renting chairs might make sense.

Wooden folding chairs. Often white wood with a padded seat, these are simple and economical. You can rent chair covers or colored seat pads if you want to change their look.

Chiavari chairs. This elegant chair, a classic for weddings and formal events, is identifiable by its bamboo-style wooden back. It can cost three times as much to rent as a basic folding chair, but its slim profile might allow you to fit more chairs at a table and save on table rental costs.

Bentwood. With a curved, open back and a padded seat, these chairs also have slim profiles. Reminiscent of café chairs, they're more suited to a dinner table than a ceremony.

Ghost chair. A clear polycarbonate chair designed by Philippe Starck, the Ghost chair fits in with a hip, modern, minimal aesthetic. It comes in versions with arms, which look great around a small table at cocktail hour, and without, which works better when you want to fit as many chairs as possible around a table for a meal. They're pricey and available only through specialty rental services, but they make a big statement.

The Bride's and Groom's Chairs

The bride's and groom's chairs shouldn't be confused with any others in the room. One way to make them stand out is to have the florist adorn them with garlands, ribbons, or other special floral touches. You can also rent an entirely different type of chair for the bride and groom—ask the rental company if there are any particularly regal styles available. The other way to set them apart is through a chair cover or fabric tie around the back of the chair. If the other chairs in the room have covers, consider using a different color for the bride's and groom's, or have them monogrammed with hand-painted or embroidered initials.

Lounge. If you're having a late-night lounge, consider springing for seating that looks relaxed and inviting. Upholstered chairs, chaise longues, ottomans, and sofas are all great, but high-top tables and barstools can work as well.

Lounge Furniture

IF YOU'RE IN A POSITION to splurge, wow your guests by renting residential seating like the chaise pictured above. For one outdoor wedding in Malibu, I set up white sofas and club chairs—very Shabby Chic. Everyone loved the change of pace and the comfortable seats. You can also bring in rattan garden furniture or mix in a few café tables. Break up rows of chairs at the ceremony by interspersing small statues or a few urns overflowing with flowers—just keep them low enough not to block anyone's view.

Rental furniture is most effective when used to create a clublike lounge, a place where guests can congregate and put up their feet. You can set up this kind of area by the bar, next to the dance floor, or in a separate room for the after-party.

Though you can sometimes rent furniture through a florist or a prop house, you may need to turn to a specialty furniture rental company. A wedding planner or an event designer should be able to supply sources. But large hotels and resorts can sometimes move furniture from another area to your reception space—so always ask before turning to outside rentals.

Tables

There's no law decreeing that a sit-down reception has to be filled with sixty-inch- or seventy-two-inch-round tables. In fact, deviating from the expected table configuration is one of the simplest ways to make your reception stand out and give the room a stylish, eclectic look. I often mix round and square tables, plus one long table for the bridal party. (If you're going this route, try to create some kind of pattern for harmony and balance.)

Square tables, more often associated with restaurant dining, lend an air of instant chic. Long tables also change the look of a space and are wonderful outdoors; depending on how they're dressed, they can look casual and rustic or ultrachic.

For a cocktail reception (meaning, no sit-down dinner), you don't need to provide seating for all of the guests; but if you're serving substantial hors d'oeuvres, you should provide seating for at least half of the guests. Try mixing high-tops and standard rounds (sixty-inch), which will break up the room nicely and provide for the comfort of your older guests.

A note on banquet tables: These long, rectangular tables come in four-foot, six-foot, and eight-foot lengths, and you can align several to create the length you need. Figure on at least one foot per person if you're using them as dining tables. They're narrow, not leaving much room for china and centerpieces, so I place two together lengthwise to create extra width. If you're renting specialty linens, know that long tables require more tablecloths than rounds.

The Head Table

THE HEAD TABLE is where, historically, the bride and groom sat with their parents and members of the bridal party. These days a large bridal party or complex family situation often makes that arrangement unfeasible. (Another tradition that's largely fallen by the wayside is seating the bridal party on a "dais," a long banquet table on a riser.)

The head table tradition still persists, but there's flexibility as to who sits there. Some couples sit with their bridal party and leave each set of parents to host their own tables. Other couples sit with their parents, their maid of honor, and their best man; or with their parents and the entire bridal party, if it's small enough to fit at one table (don't forget to count significant others).

ANCILLARY TABLES

You might find the need for a host of smaller tables other than dining tables to fulfill special purposes. Take a look at this list and see whether you've overlooked any. Most of these aren't mandatory; it all depends on what type of wedding you're having.

FOR THE CEREMONY
- Guest-book table
- Table to hold programs and yarmulkes
- Table at the altar (to hold a unity candle, prayer book, chalices) or under the chuppah (to hold the prayer book, kiddush cup, bottle of wine, glass for breaking)

FOR COCKTAIL HOUR
- Guest book table
- Table for photobooth props
- Gift table
- High-tops
- Tables for buffets, stations

FOR THE BAR AREA OR LATE-NIGHT LOUNGE
- High-tops
- Coffee tables

Many couples find that the best solution is to sit by themselves at a sweetheart table near the dance floor, eliminating awkward arguments over who is at the head table and who isn't. Each set of parents gets a table flanking the couple's, as does the bridal party. Couples typically don't get to spend much time at their table, but it may give them a chance to share a few moments alone while they eat.

Once you've figured out whom you want to sit with, take a look at the number and go from there. If it's ten or twelve people, you have a lot of choices, but if you have twenty-four people to seat, a long banquet table or a large oval is the best solution—I like to place it in the center of the room, near the edge of the dance floor.

At a small wedding with fifty or fewer guests, you can sidestep the entire issue by seating everyone at one long table. The bride and groom typically sit in the middle, with parents and members of the bridal party close by.

The Seating-Card Table

POSITION THE SEATING-CARD TABLE, also referred to as an escort-card table, near the entrance to the cocktail hour venue or in another highly visible spot. If there's a wait, guests can get a drink and come back. Don't set it up by the doors to the reception, where it can create a bottleneck.

Since this table is one of the first things guests see on their way in, treat it with care. Cover it with a cloth that fits your color scheme, and consider using swagging or an overlay for a bit of eye-catching detail.

Accent the table with flowers or a creative arrangement and candles. It's a great place to bring in touches from home, like framed photos of you and the groom or pieces from a personal collection.

Some of my favorite treatments for the seating cards themselves: laid on a table covered in moss; propped between blades of wheatgrass grown in flats; stuck in trays filled with sand and colored beach glass or pebbles; or suspended by ribbons from tree branches. I also like to put linen-covered risers on the table at different heights to vary the tablescape.

The Cake Table

COVER THE CAKE TABLE with a pretty cloth and overlay to set it apart. Bridesmaids' bouquets, votive candles, and framed photos of the couple's parents at their wedding all make great decorations. You can scatter rose petals or hearty blooms as well. If the ceremony took place in the same room and you had a special floral gazebo or chuppah made, turn it into a canopy for the cake.

Gift and Guest Book Tables

THE WEDDING GIFT TABLE isn't what it once was. Now most people send gifts ahead (and bless them for saving you the trouble of having to transport them home). But some will still bring gifts, so don't neglect to set up a gift table just inside the entrance to the reception. Cover it with a tablecloth that extends to the floor (you don't want to see metal legs poking out), and make it look attractive.

It's fine to put a box for checks on the table, but keep it low-key and elegant. Designate someone close to you to handle checks given directly to you during the wedding.

The guest-book table should also be set up near the entrance, but it should be separate from the gift table. so as to avoid creating a bottleneck.

The guest-book table should be attractive and welcoming, too, covered with a long cloth and decorated with flowers or a framed photo or two. No matter what form your guest book takes—you'll find creative ideas in chapter 20, "The Invitations"—make sure all necessary supplies are on the table. Appoint a friend to man the table and drum up participation. If it's an out-of-the-ordinary guest book, she can also offer guidance to those who aren't sure what to do. One increasingly popular choice is the photo booth guestbook, which enables guests to paste in a selfie along with their message; see page 93 for more about this.

Tablecloths

Nothing adds color and texture to your room more effectively than linens, one of the surest ways to bring out your color scheme. So indulging in spectacular overlays, chair covers, or even napkins can pay off in spades in terms of visual impact.

While color is naturally your first focus, don't forget to consider texture and weight. Unlike china and glassware, fabric is linked to a particular time of year. Velvet, damask, brocade, and dark satin should be saved for fall and winter months, while airy organza looks best in warm weather. Most cotton, linen, and silk can work year-round, depending on the color.

Unless they're made of wood, any tables you're using at the ceremony, cocktail hour, or reception will need some kind of cloth. You don't want guests to be staring at a bare wood-grain altar table during the ceremony.

The first order of business, however, is length. Many venues use tablecloths that extend only halfway to the

Common Table Sizes

TABLE SIZE	SEATS
36-inch round	cake display
48-inch round	cake display
58-inch round	6 to 8
60-inch round	8 to 10
66-inch round	10 to 11
72-inch round	10 to 12
48-inch square	8
60-inch square	8
72-inch square	12

floor, exposing those not-so-pretty table legs. This is one area where it's worth splurging on rentals—it's much more polished to have cloths that reach all the way to the floor.

Round cloths remain more common than square ones, so they're easier to rent. If you're using tables of an unusual size, however, you're likely to need custom linens. To determine the size of cloth you'll need for each table, consult with the rental service.

A Glossary of Linens

THE TERMS YOU'LL ENCOUNTER in linens may overwhelm you, so bone up on the lingo before you start shopping.

Pickups. Table skirt fabric is randomly "picked up" (think of fabric being pinched) and held in place with flowers, appliqués, or embroidery. It's the same technique used on wedding gowns to create volume.

Overlay. An optional, decorative cloth that sits on top of the underlay (see following) to provide contrast in color or texture. The overlay extends about halfway down the sides of the table. At weddings, an overlay is often sheer and decorated with light beading or embroidery.

Runner. A long strip of fabric that runs the length of the table but doesn't cover the full width. You would most likely use a runner down a long banquet table. It can be placed over bare wood or on top of an underlay.

Ruching. Fine pleating or tucking around the edge of the cloth.

Swagging. Two tablecloths are layered, and the top one is alternately gathered and draped into soft arcs.

Underlay. A full cloth that covers the entire table and falls to the floor.

Napkins

Napkins can provide wonderful bursts of color. If you love the look of specialty linens but can't afford to go all out, consider sticking with standard tablecloths and renting napkins in an eye-catching color or fabric. Do make sure that they'll

Monogram or Wedding Date

Your monogram or wedding date can create a visual element that provides continuity throughout your wedding. It can appear on the front of your program, on fans you hand out at an outdoor wedding, on the dance floor (using a gobo light—see page 324), on the side of your wedding cake, and on favor boxes. You could even go so far as to have the date printed on M&M's to hand out as favors. If you're going to use a monogram or date as a logo throughout, you'll want to have a graphic artist or invitation designer create a special version to reflect the style of your wedding—flourishes and serifs fit in with a romantic décor, but you'll want cleaner type if your wedding is more streamlined and minimalistic.

Triangle fold

1. Fold napkin into a triangle.

2. Fold lower corners up to meet top of triangle.

3. Fold top of "diamond" under to meet bottom point.

4. Pinch center fold so top corners move in toward each other.

5. Prop up napkin, adjusting as needed.

Goblet fan fold

1. Fold napkin in half to form a rectangle.

2. Fold rectangle in half to form a new square.

3. Begin to create a series of even accordion folds.

4. The completed shape should be long and thin.

5. Fold the lower quarter of the accordion to create an anchor.

6. Insert into glass and spread into fan shape.

Pocket fold

1. Fold napkin into a triangle.

2. Fold lower corners up to meet top of triangle.

3. Fold bottom third of new shape under itself.

4. Fold right corner in just past center line.

5. Repeat with left corner, tucking ends into fold as shown.

6. Flip napkin over and place on plate.

serve their purpose—double-faced satin napkins aren't very absorbent.

Determine where you'll be needing cloth napkins and where you'll be filling in with paper napkins. Typically, paper napkins are used at the bar and during cocktail hour. Order extra cloth napkins for guests who need theirs replaced and to decorate the bar, buffet, or stations.

If you rent napkins, be sure that someone, usually the caterer, is in charge of collecting them at the end of the reception. Napkins tend to get overlooked at breakdown time, and you certainly don't want to get billed for 250 of them.

Napkin Treatments

NAPKINS HOLD a decorative role in the place setting. You can position them to the left of the plate, in the center, or fanned into the water glass. There are plenty of ways to make the presentation stand out. Use napkin rings that fit your theme, and give them away as favors. Tie napkins with a ribbon printed with love poems or your names and wedding date. Or tuck a sprig of lavender or a single orchid into a napkin folded on top of the plate.

I often fold the menu into the napkin, which looks lovely and doesn't incur any extra costs for flowers or ribbon.

As for styles of napkin folds, start by asking the venue which ones they offer. Three of the most enduring folds are the fan (tucked into the water glass), the triangle, and the pocket fold, which is ideal if you want to tuck a menu, flower, or favor into the cloth.

Chair Covers

Covering chairs in fabric or accenting with colorful chair pads can add comfort and color to a room. Accessorizing chairs adds to the bottom line, to be sure, but if plain chairs are noticeably taking away from the look of things, it can be worth the investment.

Chair covers, which slip over a chair and cover it from top to bottom, come in several silhouettes; I prefer the tailored styles. A sash may be added around the top and tied or buttoned behind. For those who want to go all out, some chair covers have tulle skirts or corset-laced backs that neatly evoke wedding gowns.

For a less formal approach, chair pads or cushions take your guests' comfort into account. Coordinate them

If you want your napkins rolled up and tied with ribbon, don't assume the venue will do it for you. Ask the venue or the florist if they can take care of it. If they can't or if it's beyond your budget, arrange to get the napkins early and enlist some friends to help tie them up. Same goes for chair sashes and slipcovers—find out if the linen company can help out.

with the tablecloths to pull together the look of a space. A chair "cap" goes over the top of a ladderback chair, adding a hint of color to the room.

OTHER DESIGN ELEMENTS

Bring on the Props

Sometimes a space is too much of a blank canvas and calls for a little oomph. This is where props come in; you can generally rent them from prop houses or florists. If they fit into a particular retail category, sometimes stores selling the item will rent them to you for a percentage of the selling price.

These are a few of my favorites:

Chandeliers. Although they're expensive to rent and you'll need lighting professionals to install them, they're worth their weight in wow. I've even hung vintage chandeliers outdoors, from trees, to define an area—they have tons of impact outside because they're *so* unexpected. Besides crystal, consider shell-encrusted or wrought iron chandeliers.

Statues. Available at prop houses or garden supply stores, statuary can flank an entrance, add an unusual element to an outdoor ceremony area, or help set off the stage at the reception. (Cherubs, classical figures of men and women, and dogs are most common.)

Columns. If you're working with a wide-open space, either indoors or out, columns can help you define separate areas. Two rows of columns create an aisle, and two columns draped with flowers can outline a makeshift "altar."

Ice carvings. Though you may think of ice sculptures as a bit old-fashioned, these days you can turn to a cutting-edge sculptor for an entire bar made of ice or an eye-catching carving for the center of the room. Ice sculptures are a classic for cocktail hour and buffet tables, but today the ice may be carved into actual bowls or serving pieces.

Fabricking and Carpeting a Room

If your ballroom's walls are in need of a paint job, or the space feels cavernous, or your tent is just looking too bare, you can have the ceiling and walls draped with fabric to create an intimate enclave. Since fabricking can be done in any color, it has the power to totally change the look of the venue, but it's a pricey proposition and for safety reasons must be handled by professionals—typically event designers or florists.

Less drastic options include draping only the ceiling, looping fabric panels from the ceiling, or hanging panels along the walls. The latter two can bring down the height of a tall loft or help create defined areas in a vast warehouse. If your space is broken up by columns or poles, the designer can wrap them with fabric to help make them more decorative. But before you venture down this path, there are some questions you should be sure to ask:

- Ask the manager what you can do to the walls. Most venues have rules.

- Find out the local fire code standards. You'll need to use flame-retardant fabric and obtain a fire permit. (An event designer or planner usually handles this, but make sure they're on top of it.) Don't try to cut corners. I've had fire marshals show up at events to test the fabric; if your fabric isn't deemed up to code, they'll shut down the wedding.

- Determine whether you can access your venue early enough to do draping. It takes time and usually requires access to the space a day or more before the event.

Carpet, particularly in a hotel ballroom, is something brides love to hate. Yes, it's possible to hide an ugly carpet by laying a new carpet over the existing one with the venue's permission, but it's quite costly (anywhere from $4,000 to $15,000), and you'll need early access to the room.

Here's what you don't realize: By the time the tables and dance floor are in place, you'll hardly see the carpet. There are only a few feet of it exposed between each table. If you're still concerned, use decorating tricks to draw the eye up—hang flowers from the ceiling or rent chandeliers.

Sprucing Up the Great Outdoors

Mother Nature is often the best event designer of all. In a setting with a beautiful panorama, shade-giving trees, and colorful flowers, you really don't need to "decorate." Your focus, instead, needs to be on defining the space to make it feel less vast and more intimate—think of it as creating outdoor rooms. This can be accomplished by hanging chandeliers (the extravagant option) or paper lanterns (economical but stylish) from tree branches, creating cozy groupings of furniture, and outlining these areas with planters, topiaries, or rented palm trees.

If guests are going to be outside for any length of time and you expect it to be sunny, rent market umbrellas to shade the tables. The umbrellas themselves become a key accent, especially if you put a little time into finding colors or patterns that fit in with your color scheme. If the event will stretch into the evening, string twinkle lights or hang lanterns from the inside of the umbrellas, creating a glowing fairyland at each table.

Outdoor walkways become enchanting when accented with twinkle lights, lanterns hanging from above, or luminarias (candles placed in structured bags) alongside the path. Your florist can usually suggest ideas for lanterns, whether or not they're enhanced with flowers or greenery.

As with any other space, your outdoor room will need focal points. Work with what you have to highlight special features. Float candles in a fountain. If there's a swimming

MEETING AND GREETING

A RENTAL COMPANY

The term "rental company" encompasses a wide range of businesses—it can mean a linen rental service, a general rental company that offers everything from chairs to tents, or a specialty company offering high-end china. If your rentals include larger items such as a dance floor and portable toilets, be sure to also read the section on working with rental companies in chapter 11, "The Nitty-Gritty." Companies that rent china, linens, chairs, and tables are typically listed under "party rentals" in the Yellow Pages, and you can find myriad leads on the major bridal websites.

- Ask for references and check with the Better Business Bureau before signing a contract with a rental company.

- Make sure you get a cell phone or after-hours number for your contact in case some of the items you're expecting aren't delivered or arrive damaged on the day before your wedding.

- Try to deal with as few rental companies as possible, particularly if you're not working with a wedding planner. Otherwise, coordinating deliveries and pickups, which are usually broad windows, not specific times, and getting every fork and napkin back to the right source could turn into a horrible ordeal.

- If you are dealing with multiple companies and things look like they're getting out of hand, ask your florist or caterer to help coordinate the rentals.

- Be sure to talk to your contact at your venue about how to handle the arrival and pickup of rentals. They will usually pack up rental items for you, but you'll need to make arrangements in advance.

- If your venue requires a Sunday pickup after a Saturday event, find out if there will be a surcharge from the rental company.

---

pool, use it: Float candles in it (your florist can weight them so they don't drift to the sides), launch a decorative raft carrying candles and flowers, or project your monogram onto the surface with a gobo light. (See page 324.)

Lights, Please!

Lighting is the fairy dust at weddings, the unseen element that can transform a room from mundane to magical. In a problem space, it can hide faults—let's throw that peeling wallpaper into shadow—and accent strong points.

You don't need a $100,000 budget to be able to afford good lighting. While lighting can get pricey, there *are* simple, inexpensive lighting techniques out there. If your ceremony and reception are outdoors, entirely in daylight hours, natural light should be sufficient; but if the ceremony or reception will run into the evening, look up the time for sunset on your wedding date so that you can accurately size up the situation.

Many churches and houses of worship have restrictions on lighting, so check with the site before you proceed. Hotels should have basic lighting in place, and many will have an in-house technician to handle basics.

Visit the ceremony and reception sites at the time you'll be holding your event to assess the light, making sure to take seasonal variance into account. Think about the arrival time on the invitation, the ceremony end time, and the start and end times of the reception. Is there enough light? Will the setting sun be shining straight into guests' eyes during the ceremony? (If that's the case, you can either resituate the ceremony or hang fabric from the back of a canopy or chuppah to filter the light.) Will outdoor pathways require lighting?

Tricky Lighting

DON'T HAVE MUCH of a lighting budget? These techniques can improve the look of a space—and/or the people in it—without running up a big tab.

- At the reception, change white lightbulbs to amber or pink to cast everyone in a flattering glow. (But check with the venue in advance to determine any restrictions.) While you're at it, change the lightbulbs in the bathrooms to peach; they'll make the ladies happier when they're touching up their makeup.

- Shine a monogram or pattern onto a wall or dance floor.

- String twinkle lights in trees or on bushes.

- If the lights have dimmers installed, turn them down by about a third. You'll instantly get much more of a special-occasion feel.

- Make liberal use of candles. They automatically add up-lighting, giving a warm glow to faces. (Just make sure they're balanced by other lights in the room or your space will be too dark.)

A Glossary of Light

THESE LIGHTING TERMS and techniques are the ones that most often apply to weddings:

Color wash. A diffuse, even application of light (see Up-lighting and Gels), usually achieved by covering a light with a gel. It can warm up a room or create special effects. Typically, a wash is used on a dance floor or against fabric on a wall or ceiling. Color "wheels" can make the room slowly change colors over the course of the evening.

Gels. Layers of acetate placed over lights to change their color. A soft peach or pink gel casts a glow flattering enough to make everyone in the room look better. Gels can also be used to create special effects, turning white columns in a room to purple.

Gobos. One of the most popular lighting techniques for weddings, a gobo is a die-cut stencil that slides into a projection unit and casts an image onto the wall or the ground. Most commonly, couples have their monogram or names projected onto the dance floor, onto a wall, or

THE RENTAL COMPANY CONTRACT

Your contract with a rental company should cover the following points:

- When the deposit is due and how much is required. One-third to one-half down is common.

- When and where the goods will be delivered to the site. Make sure this corresponds with the window of time during which you have access to the site. Be specific about where the merchandise will be delivered and whether it will be unpacked and set up. Some companies charge different fees depending on the level of service involved in the delivery.

- When the rentals will be picked up. Again, make sure the timing agrees with your contract at the site.

- How the rentals should be prepared for pickup. Many companies want the dishes, glassware, and flatware washed and repacked in boxes and the linens shaken out and folded into one pile.

- Whether there is a delivery or pickup fee.

- What kind of insurance they carry.

- What will you be charged if any items are lost or damaged?

- Detailed descriptions and numbers of every item you're renting.

- Whether any overtime or extra charges apply to your proposed rental time frame. You may be paying extra if you want rentals delivered a day or two early or if you request a Sunday (instead of a Monday) pickup. Some of these extra charges are negotiable, especially if you're placing a large order.

Money and Power

If you're bringing in extra lighting, more and more venues—including some hotels—charge for the additional power required. If you don't know about this hidden cost, you can get blindsided by an unexpected expense. Some reception sites explain the charge in their contract. To avoid an unwelcome surprise, ask your lighting designer to contact the engineer at the site to figure out how much power is required. The catering director should then be able to give you the price so you can factor it into your budget.

onto the lawn. Gobos with stock images are inexpensive, but custom four-color gobos (made from an image you supply) get pricey.

Intelligent lights, aka automated lighting. A computerized lighting system that allows you to change color and texture at the touch of a button, intelligent lights can slowly move and change color, so they're great for late-night dance floors. They require a technician, part of the reason they're quite pricey.

Landscape lighting. Exterior lighting for pathways, trees, bushes, lawns, and swimming pools. It's often needed so guests can find their way, but can also be employed to create dramatic effects.

Pin spotting. A narrow field of light used to pick out and highlight an item. Frequently used on centerpieces, the cake, the altar, or the chuppah, pin spotting is also an effective way to draw attention to beautiful architectural elements in the room or to aisle markers.

Spotlights. Sometimes used to draw people's attention to special entertainment or to the couple during their first dance, a single, focused beam of light.

Twinkle Lights. Small golden lights usually strung in trees or shrubs. Can also be used indoors, either in trees or to wrap columns or accent fabric on the ceiling. They can create a romantic fairy-tale look when used with restraint; don't overdo it, as too many twinkle lights can give a Christmassy look.

Underlighting. Typically used to light a glass table from below. Can also be used under flower arrangements, particularly those where the water is visible, to give a warm glow.

Up-lighting. Soft lighting aimed upward, usually at tall props like a chuppah. With a colored gel, up-lighting is commonly used to add color to fabric draping the walls or ceiling of a room.

ASK MINDY

Q My parents are paying for the wedding, and my mother seems to think that this means my opinion doesn't count. She wants control over everything, down to my tablecloths and hair jewelry. I'm angry at her and scared I won't even like my wedding. What she's doing just isn't to my taste! Is she really allowed to run this whole thing?

A Sometimes I find that the moms who didn't have the wedding they wanted are reenacting at their daughter's wedding what they would have liked to have had. You have to be gracious because they're paying, but there's got to be a way to communicate that this is your dream and your memories—a way to come to a compromise with your mom—just like you'll have to compromise in your marriage. It's such a hard call.

Sometimes bringing Dad in—in an up-front way, not behind her back—can smooth things over, because he's a little more detached from the details. But the truth is, most of my moms don't ever give in. It's a control issue. They're losing control of their child, and they're acting out. Ultimately, my best advice is to pick your battles.

A Professional Lighting Designer

A LIGHTING DESIGNER in a major metropolitan area typically charges a minimum of $1,500, though some top-tier designers start much higher. Many hotels and clubs have in-house lighting technicians or contracts with an outside firm, so always ask about lighting at your venue before consulting an independent lighting designer.

A lighting designer will do a walk-through of your site and create what's called a lighting "plot"—a written description of the lighting and equipment he thinks the space calls for, along with a price quote. The bid will itemize the options, so if it's too high you can always eliminate some of the suggestions. Along with the general vendor questions you should cover (see page 49 for a refresher), determine whether a staffer will be present at your wedding. (It's not necessary for all lighting jobs, but I always pay extra to have one there in case of a problem—otherwise, guests could be left in the dark for a long stretch if you blow a fuse.)

Does the price include a generator, and a backup generator? Ask about power requirements for the lighting and determine whether your venue has adequate power. If extra power is needed, are there extra charges? Power can turn into a pricey last-minute surprise if you don't plan for it.

I've seen so many brides get carried away with the visual elements of the wedding that they give short shrift to the friends and family who've stood by their side. It's understandable; there's so much decorative stuff to consider. But as the world's great beauties have always known, there's more to style than meets the eye. Grace is of the essence, and that's why the next chapter focuses on the gifts *you'll* be giving to friends, family, vendors, and honored guests. ◆

DÉCOR SPOT-CHECK

Glance around and make sure you're not overlooking any area or surface in need of beautification:

- **At the ceremony:** entrance, aisle treatments, runner, chuppah or arch, altar, seating

- **In the cocktail space:** tables, chairs, bar, buffet, stations, seating-card table

- **At the reception:** tables, chairs, centerpieces, place settings, linens, buffets, stations, bar, dance floor, stage, light fixtures, walls, furnishings

- **At the post-reception party:** tables, chairs, bar, furniture

- **Other spaces:** walkways, anteroom, entrances, departure area/valet station, restrooms

CHAPTER TWENTY-TWO

Favors & Gifts

A WARM WELCOME AND A SWEET GOOD-BYE

Across cultures, the wedding favor—the parting gift given to guests at the end of the wedding—serves as a talisman designed to spread the happy couple's good fortune to their guests. When favors bring a moment of joy to the recipient, they have fulfilled their age-old mission. And they have also marked your graciousness as a host.

But I've seen far too many couples invest far too much time and money on impersonal trinkets that many guests leave behind.

So here's my rule, and it's one that I can't emphasize strongly enough: If organizing favors for your guests is becoming a burden or putting a strain on your budget, drop the idea and do not look back. You're under no obligation to hand out favors; veterans of the wedding circuit may even feel relieved not to be presented with yet another "keepsake."

Don't take this to mean that I'm opposed to favors. I love them when they're meaningful and personal to the couple—the most touching favors are often modest gifts that reflect an aspect of the couple's history, share a family tradition, or remind guests of a specific moment during the wedding. A favor should be a sweet token of appreciation, not an attempt to compete with Hollywood swag bags.

Favors are not to be confused with welcoming gifts, which are given to out-of-town guests upon their arrival at their hotels. Where favors are a nicety, I view welcome gifts (also known as "in-room gifts") as a necessity. They needn't be lavish; even bottled water with a few snacks, a local map, and visitor information will do.

Lastly, you should honor those who helped and supported you during the planning process and on your wedding day. Attendants should be at the top of the list, but there are others to consider as well, like the officiant, your parents, and even your spouse-to-be.

Great Ideas for Favors

A wedding favor should be either edible, drinkable, or useful—remember that! And while favors should be personal, bear in mind that outside of your immediate family, there's limited demand for keepsakes bearing your name and wedding date.

Send guests off with something to nibble on during their drive home. I've brought bags of specialty doughnuts to next-day brunches so that guests can pick up a bag of fresh, hot pastries on their way out. To make a package out of it, throw in a Sunday newspaper and a cheerful note.

If you have an especially talented baker in your family, you might go the DIY route or pass their unbeatable macaroon recipe to a pastry chef. One bride found in this a wonderful way to honor her late grandmother, who was famous for her beautifully decorated nutmeg cookies; she even had her grandmother's photograph and a copy of the recipe scanned onto a tag for the cookie bag.

The Numbers Game

How many favors to order or make? It depends on whether you're planning to give out one per guest or one per couple, with single guests receiving their own. If you're placing favors on reception tables, count on giving out one per person, as it will be too confusing to designate shared and individual favors. But if many of your guests are attending as couples, scaling back on favors can be an effective way to bring your budget in line.

ASK MINDY

Q I wanted a big wedding, but now that I begin to tally up the money that's being spent, I feel as if I want to give something back. What can I do?

A We're constantly trying to think of ways to incorporate giving back. We try to donate the flowers and leftover food, but often it's harder than people think—hospitals don't want flowers because of the fragrance, and when you're at a hotel you can't take the extra food out because of health codes. (Off-site, with caterers, you can sometimes donate.)

My favorite party favor is a donation in honor of your guests to a charity or foundation that's touched your lives. I did one wedding where the couple bought several trees and had them planted in areas that needed some greening up.

One of my brides created a delightfully fragrant favor by bottling and hard-labeling dried lavender she'd picked from her garden.

Chocolates are a classic gift. Look for shapes that relate to your interests; I've seen sailboat chocolates, golf club chocolates, car chocolates—there's a lot out there.

Candy shops bring out the inner child in every guest. Set up your very own by filling glass penny-candy jars with whatever your heart desires. Gummi Bears, Jelly Bellies, Tootsie Rolls, Red Hots, Bazooka gum, and mini candy bars are all fair game. Have bags and scoops ready so guests can create their own mix on their way out.

And then there's the lovely, simple tradition of offering guests leftover slices of wedding cake, packed up in little boxes. To save manpower, place bakery boxes on the dessert table so people can help themselves to a doggy bag.

Give out a specialty food related to the location along with a note explaining the connection. Honey, jam, wine, and olive oil all make excellent choices.

Photos make a terrific favor, too. For fun, campy portraits, rent an amusement-park-style photo booth and have guests go to town, or create a DIY photo booth complete with props—see page 93 for more on how.

Packets of flower seeds make a great living keepsake. Forget-me-nots are always popular, but any flower or herb associated with your wedding will do. You can attach notes to the packets asking guests to remember you when the flowers bloom, or find a company that creates personalized packets.

Fresh flowers also make a wonderful take-home favor that prevents the centerpieces from going to waste—though it only makes sense if many of the guests are local or are staying on for a day or two. Discuss the idea with your florist when planning the centerpieces so they can be designed for easy dismantling. After the reception, put the flowers into black buckets and have guests gather their bouquets. Have a staffer from the reception site on hand to wrap them up in paper.

Better to Give

A DONATION to an organization that's meaningful to you as a couple is a beautiful way to honor your guests. If you're stuck trying to come up with a meaningful favor, or if you can't find favors that meet your standards within your budget, consider taking your budget for favors—even if it's a small amount—and writing a check to an organization that can put the money to good use.

To let guests know about the donation, print out cards (you can do them yourself) and put one at each place setting.

Distributing Favors

ONE THING about placing favors on tables is that they often get left there. It's difficult to keep up with your favor while you're table-hopping or tearing up the dance floor!

TRADITION PRIMER

The Wedding Favor

Favors have been associated with weddings for centuries. Over the years, biscuits, sweet rolls, knotted ribbons, floral nosegays, and mementos like scarves and gloves have all had their moments in the spotlight.

Elizabethan brides would sew colored ribbons (actually called "favours") onto their gowns, each color representing a different kind of luck. Guests were so eager to grab a little good luck for themselves that they would swipe the ribbons, and in their frenzy, sometimes rip the bride's dress. It wasn't long before protective mothers-of-the-bride and bridesmaids staged an end run: They began to carry baskets of favours (usually knotted ribbons) so that guests could help themselves.

When it comes to the most enduring favor of all time, Jordan almonds—pastel, candy-coated, and tied in tulle—win the prize. In France, they're known as *dragées*, in Italy as *confetti*, and in Greece as *koufeta*. Why almonds? Their bittersweet flavor represents the bitter and the sweet in life; coating them in sugar is a ploy to tip the future toward the sweet.

At Italian weddings, five almonds are given to each guest, representing health, wealth, happiness, fertility, and longevity for the bride and groom. Traditionally, the five confetti are wrapped in tulle, a reference to the bride's veil. Borrow from this tradition and add a tag explaining the meaning of the five almonds, along with your names and wedding date, and you'll have a lovely favor that has stood the test of time. If you're planning to give out dragées, make sure you buy fresh, quality Jordan almonds so that your guests can truly enjoy them.

I prefer to distribute favors at the end of the reception. You can set them up on a table and have the wedding

In honor of our wedding day,
a donation to the
AMERICAN HEART ASSOCIATION
has been made on your behalf.

Thank you

for sharing this special moment in our lives.

AMY AND JOHN
September 7, 2018

A pretty card turns a donation into a gift.

coordinator or a hotel staffer hand them out. If most guests are driving, it's a delightful surprise when the valet leaves favors in their cars.

Always try to attach a message to the favor, though if the gift is physically tiny, you may have to stick with just the couple's name and wedding date. Clever notes that reference the gift always work.

A simple, straightforward wish also works well in a short message.

WE'RE STUCK ON YOU.

THANK YOU

FOR SHARING THIS SPECIAL DAY WITH US.

Rachel and Alyssa

MAY 13, 2017

A note attached to a box of saltwater taffy—so simple and so sweet

For any treats delivered in the evening, you can't go wrong with a note that says simply: "Sweet dreams. Love, Samantha and Jeremy."

A "wish" attached to a packet of cornflower seeds turns an everyday object into a very special goodie.

These seeds are for you to plant. As you watch these flowers grow, we hope you will think of us and this special day.

A Warm Welcome

When guests who've traveled to your wedding arrive, greet them with a gift, a welcome letter, and a detailed itinerary. It's nicest if packages are in their hotel rooms awaiting their arrival, but you may not want to pay the hotel to deliver them; you can also leave gifts behind the front desk to be given to guests when they check in.

Don't neglect out-of-towners who aren't staying at the main hotel. Find out in advance where all of your guests are staying and either deliver gifts to those staying with friends or relatives or at a different hotel, or give gifts out at the rehearsal dinner.

The Welcome Letter

A LETTER IS one of the most important ways to make your guests feel welcome. Although I've included a particularly eloquent sample, all you really need to do is convey your excitement and thank your out-of-town guests for coming to your wedding.

On the reverse of the letter or on a separate sheet of paper, include a personalized guide to the neighborhood. You might include a spot where guests can get a decent cup of a coffee, directions to an area that's good for strolling or window-shopping, and a few restaurant choices in case guests choose to extend their stay. Write up your suggestions with a personal touch to let guests know you've handpicked your selections: "The local hot spot for breakfast is the Waterfront Café. The Morning Glory muffins are to die for! To get there from the hotel, turn right, and walk three blocks to the harbor."

Dear Friends and Family,

We are so excited and grateful that you have traveled to Los Angeles to share this special time with us. Your presence will help make our wedding a truly memorable event.

It is said that all who attend a wedding have two obligations. The first is to "bear witness" to the marriage of the bride and the groom. The second is to partake in the festive meal, to dance, and to rejoice.

It is with these thoughts in mind that we look forward to having you share in a weekend filled with good food, music, laughter, and lots of love!

Love,
Max and Jessie

A really great welcome letter should be warm and personal; it should also get guests excited about the festivities to come.

Welcome Gifts

My MAIN GOAL in putting together gift bags is to include enough snacks and beverages so that guests never have to raid the minibar. When they've bought plane tickets and paid for hotel rooms to come to your wedding, they shouldn't have to spend three dollars for a bottle of water. Include some salty snacks such as pretzels, nuts, or trail mix, and a sweet treat such as chocolates, jelly beans, or cookies. If you have the budget for extra niceties, consider a candle, tote bag, and a local treat.

Take care with the presentation. Even a bag of simple niceties will seem more thoughtful when it's tied up with a pretty ribbon. Though they look great, don't use baskets to hold welcome gifts. They're attractive but costly, and most of them get left at the hotel because they're too bulky to pack in luggage. Instead, use gift bags decorated with wedding-themed stickers, canvas tote bags, or cardboard boxes.

Gifts of Appreciation

Far in advance of the wedding, try to start thinking about and budgeting for the personal gifts you need to give. With so many other last-minute details, you really don't want to be running around town five days before your wedding, frantically searching for eight matching necklaces. You'll also need to make time to wrap those gifts and write personal notes to go with them.

Besides your bridesmaids and groomsmen, you'll want to give gifts to the ring bearer, flower girl, and any other members of your wedding party. It's a thoughtful gesture to give a smaller gift to anyone who has a special role in the wedding or who helps by handing out programs, lighting candles, or manning the guest book.

Anyone who hosts an event in your honor, from an engagement party to a day-after brunch, also merits a special gift. It's a lovely gesture to thank your parents after the wedding, particularly if they are funding it—but even if they aren't, they're probably doing their fair share of work. (And even if they aren't, you wouldn't be where you are without them, so thank them!)

If you're inviting children to the wedding, you'll want to stock up on small gifts and activity packs (see page 333.)

Add to the list any vendors who have gone out of their way for you or to whom you feel especially grateful.

Brides and grooms have exchanged gifts for centuries, and though it's not a necessity—especially if your finances have already been overtaxed by the wedding—it's a sweet custom.

Great Gifts . . .

FOR BRIDESMAIDS

Engraved silver picture frames holding a photo of the bride and the attendant

Jewelry

Monogrammed makeup bag and goodies

Monogrammed robe

Personalized stationery

Spa day for all of the attendants, followed by lunch or dinner

FOR GROOMSMEN

Cigars in an engraved holder

Cuff links

Dopp kit

Monogrammed flask

Tie for wedding day

Watch

Small-batch bourbon or other high-end spirits

FOR USHERS AND OTHER HELPERS

Cosmetics pouch

Gift cards

Manicure

Personalized luggage tags

Special fragrance or scented candle or soaps

FOR HOSTS

A coffee-table book geared to their interests; ones related to entertaining are always appropriate

A spectacular vase

A subscription to a gourmet fruit service

A throw for the sofa

His-and-hers robes

Personalized stationery

A gift certificate for a massage

Gifts for Attendants

THE GIFTS for your bridesmaids and groomsmen typically require the most thought and planning, particularly if you have six or more attendants on each side.

Be generous with your attendants—they've spent countless hours helping you shop for your dress and assemble your invitations. Even long-distance friends have probably logged hours of phone time. In all honesty, I would be happy to see you skip the champagne toast if that's what it takes to treat your attendants right.

Remember, too, that attendants often have an idea of what you've spent on your wedding; think of what a slap in the face it would be if you knew a bride had spent $25 on each invitation but bought you a $5 candle as her sole thank-you. What you can spend on each gift will vary according to your budget and how many attendants you have, but I think that $30 per person is a good starting place, and Etsy is a great resource for unique gifts in that range. If you're treating them to manicures or other pampering services, that certainly counts for something, but you still want to make sure you're giving them something tangible as well.

I've also seen couples recruit relatives to create handmade gifts for the wedding party—one grandmother knitted yarmulkes for all the groomsmen, and a mother-sister team embroidered the bridesmaids' and groomsmen's names on vintage handkerchiefs.

Frequently, the bridesmaids' gifts are items they can wear to the wedding, such as jewelry, handbags, wraps, or monogrammed bathrobes or PJs for them to wear while they're getting their hair and makeup done; for the groomsmen, it might be cuff links or a shirt and tie. (One bride got the groomsmen bottle openers made from old pieces of train tracks, and had them embossed with their names.) Be sure to signal early on if you'll be giving them jewelry or anything else you expect them to wear for the wedding—you don't want them to waste time or money buying accessories on their own. The gifts to the attendants can be identical or slightly different. For bridesmaids, the jewelry can incorporate different stones or crystals (personalized to each bridesmaid's dress, birthstone, or skin tone), but the gifts usually share a unifying element—one necklace might have citrines and freshwater pearls, another might have pink topaz and freshwater pearls, but the pearls would be consistent from one necklace to the next. Cuff links are a discreet enough accessory for you to feel free to choose a pair that speaks to each groomsman's interests. Some couples with the means to do so pay for the bridesmaids' dresses or tuxedo rentals as their gift; that's always a welcome gesture, as it relieves the attendant of one of the major expenses associated with being in a wedding.

Don't think you have to find a single perfect gift. A themed bag of gifts is always a great alternative—it takes the pressure off finding *the* item and feels like a treasure trove to the recipients. For bridesmaids, it might be a monogrammed canvas bag containing yoga pants, a tank top, and flip-flops. For groomsmen, it could be a duffel bag with a travel alarm clock, collapsible valet tray, and sports sandals.

It's also nice to give the maid of honor and best man a gift that's slightly different to mark their status as honor attendants. The gift needn't be more expensive, though.

Bridesmaids' gifts are traditionally presented shortly before the wedding at a bridesmaids' luncheon, which can take place anywhere from a week before to the day of the wedding, depending on everyone's schedules. Groomsmen don't have this ritual, but if they're getting together for a joint activity before the wedding, the groom can present the gifts then. Gifts can also be presented at the rehearsal or at the rehearsal dinner, though it's preferable to carve out a few minutes to do this in private and not make a big spectacle of the gift giving—you don't want anyone feeling left out.

Gifts for Children in the Wedding Party

GIFTS FOR FLOWER GIRLS, ring bearers, and any other children included in the wedding party serve a dual purpose: You want to show your appreciation, of course, but well-chosen gifts can help keep children happily entertained (read: quiet) during the ceremony.

Kid Care

If you're inviting children to the wedding, prepare age-appropriate activity packs to keep them entertained at the reception. Most of mine are quite inexpensive and can be bought in bulk at party stores or online.

If children are attending the wedding ceremony, you might want to put a piece of candy that won't make too much of a mess on their seats. A lollipop usually does the trick. At the reception, put activity packs on their chairs and stock them with enough stuff to keep them busy for a few hours. Consider using canvas backpacks or tote bags to hold the goodies; buy a fabric pen and write each child's name on the bag to be sure they get the right one, especially if you're making different ones for each age and gender. Avoid any activities or candy that could create a stain-removal nightmare on party clothes or rented tablecloths. If you can tie the kids' favors and gifts into the wedding—say, giving them plastic leis and luau-type items at a Hawaiian wedding—all the better.

For the reception, if you have the budget, you can hire some kind of kid-friendly performer, such as a magician, or offer more activities like the ones you had at the ceremony to keep the kids busy. Offering babysitting at the venue is a generous gesture but not necessary. If you have guests who you know are bringing kids, you may want to discuss pooling child-care options with them so they can plan ahead and designate a time when the kids will leave the reception.

Children's Activity Packs

Coloring books or stickers and paper

Crayons or gel pens (washable)

Dolls and action figures

Game books like word searches or crossword puzzles

Inexpensive handheld video game (make sure it's on "silent" mode)

Magna Doodle or other "erasable" drawing toy

Simple costume jewelry kits

The biggest challenge is finding age-appropriate gifts. A great gift for a four-year-old will do nothing for an eight-year-old. If you're not familiar with the child's likes and dislikes, ask the parents or someone who has kids of the same age for guidance.

(If you're leaving gifts on children's seats at the ceremony, remove them from their plastic packaging ahead of time. You don't want crinkling to interrupt your vows.)

A Gift for Your Spouse

THE RINGS REMAIN the official gift between husband and wife, but many couples enjoy exchanging something more intimate as well. It's not necessary, especially if you're paying for your wedding and are already over budget. (And it's not necessarily reciprocal, either; sometimes, one spouse gets the other a gift, while the other may not be aware of the tradition.)

A gift from the groom to the bride most often involves jewelry—something spectacular to wear on the wedding day, or something personal or sentimental. The bride most often gives the groom a watch or cuff links. These gifts should generally be something that's built to last—a metaphor for your marriage, of course! The gifts can be presented in the week before the wedding or on the wedding day. If you get your groom something to wear at the wedding, have someone deliver it while he is getting dressed.

Guys should remember that most brides plan their outfit down to the last detail well in advance, so giving brides something to wear at the wedding is a risky proposition; consulting with her mother or maid of honor on this delicate matter is recommended.

Thanking Generous Hosts

ANYONE WHO HOSTS an event for you should get a gift that reflects your appreciation. The gift itself isn't nearly as important as adhering to my golden rule: The present should reflect the taste and interests of the recipient—and be accompanied by a likewise personal note. If you need a refresher, turn to chapter 15, "Saying Thank You."

These gifts are perhaps the most important grace note of all, so take care when selecting and wrapping them. If you're at a loss, think back to the event the person hosted for you. Do they have a taste for Limoges? Perhaps you could complement their tableware with a beautiful tea set. Is their garden a source of pride? A lovely watering can and set of garden tools could do the trick.

Now that we've taken care of your wedding karma, let's move on to a sweet and pretty indulgence: the cake. This might be the one time in your life when it's appropriate to shout, "Let them eat cake!" ♦

CHAPTER TWENTY-THREE

The Sweet Finale

LET THEM EAT CAKE!

P ure, unadulterated joy swathed in frosting, the cake is one of a wedding's sensory highlights. While many nuptial traditions are continually subjected to scrutiny and revision, it's rare to find anyone *not* salivating over the prospect of cake. So many of us associate frosted cakes with memories of childhood birthday parties and other joyous

events, and now this cake—the first official sweet you'll share as husband and wife—will become a key link in that continuum.

The cake cutting is such a pivotal moment in the reception that it's considered rude for anyone to leave before the first slice has been savored by the bride and groom. The cutting is usually preceded by the couple giving a short speech in which they thank key people for making the day

special, which gives the moment even more weight in the arc of the wedding.

The wedding cake itself can be traced back to the Victorians, who created towering confections as a means of signaling their wealth. It wasn't until then that the refined flour, baking powder, and baking soda necessary to create delicate, airy cakes was available. Before then, fruitcakes, which are hardier and don't need refrigeration, were the norm in both England and America. (They still are in the British Isles.)

The stacked silhouette of the iconic wedding cake reportedly mimics the spire of St. Bride's church in London. But the cake itself represents grain, an ancient symbol of fertility and of life. In ancient Rome, the couple broke bread together by sharing part of a dry biscuit during the ceremony; the remainder was crumbled over their heads to bring about fertility and prosperity, and guests dove for the crumbs in hopes of bringing some good fortune into their own lives.

In medieval England, as sugar became more readily available, dry biscuits evolved into sweet rolls stacked into mounds. If the couple managed to kiss across the pile of rolls without toppling them, they were in for a good life together and would bear many children. In America, industrious bridesmaids would later try to ensure a successful and happy union by cementing the rolls together with honey and applesauce. (And though the DIY bride may be tempted to make her own cake, she should know that doing so is believed to interfere with a woman's fertility.)

Cake lore has it that icing entered the picture when a French chef traveled to England in the seventeenth century, saw the tower of sweet rolls, and hit upon the idea of holding them together with a sugar glaze. White icing proved to be such a popular addition that it would forever alter the look of wedding cakes.

Cake Maker, Cake Maker, Bake Me a Cake!

Who should make your cake?

If you want a showstopping confection like the ones you see in bridal magazines and budget isn't a concern, your best option is a specialty cake maker. Many can furnish cakes that taste as scrumptious and sophisticated as they look. Some enjoy such an elevated status that they're practically household names; if you have your sights set on a cake superstar, you need to approach him early—typically six months in advance—to determine his availability.

The upper echelon of cake makers limit the number of cakes they'll take on at any given time and don't compromise by working ahead and freezing cakes. Most of them will either arrange to transport the cake to you or come to you to make the cake; either way, it will cost you.

There are plenty of quality cake makers across the country, and before you get hung up on a marquee name, it's worth your while to investigate local options. Working with a baker near your wedding location decreases the chances of the cake getting damaged in transit, and it will help keep costs from soaring. Some talented cake makers don't have retail bakeries and simply rent commercial kitchen spaces for baking—unless they advertise or you stumble upon their website, you may have to rely on word of mouth to find the good ones. They can be a great find (and well priced, because their overhead is low), but be sure to get solid references on their work and reliability before booking them to make sure that theirs is not a fly-by-night operation.

If you're having your reception at a hotel, country club, private club, or banquet hall, and your budget is more stringent, you should first try to work with the in-house pastry chef. He'll typically be well versed in the art of wedding cakes and can deliver a lovely cake that fits the setting and satisfies the taste buds. When evaluating the in-house baker, focus on the taste. If the style isn't to your liking, you can always order a plain cake covered in white icing—sometimes called a raw cake—in a basic flavor like vanilla and have it decorated with fresh flowers. If you want to bring in a cake from an outside source, you might pay a hefty cake-cutting fee that can range from $1 to $8 per slice; this can double the price of your cake. (It's a fee that you can try to eliminate or reduce when negotiating your contract with the venue.)

If you're working with a caterer, it's worth asking if he has a pastry chef on staff. Some full-service caterers have their own cake maker or regularly contract with an outside baker. Unlike a hotel, however, a caterer doesn't typically charge a cake-cutting fee.

Cake Referrals

I f you already have a florist in mind, ask him for cake referrals. Since florists are frequently involved in wedding cake decoration, they often become intimately acquainted with the abilities of area bakers. If you're working with a caterer, ask him for names as well. He has a vested interest in providing a good name, since guests often assume that the caterer is responsible for the cake!

Of course, many regular bakeries turn out luscious wedding cakes as part of their repertoire. If you have sweet memories of a bakery convenient to the wedding locale—say, they made all of your birthday cakes when you were growing up—by all means, consider turning to them for your wedding cake. Some bakeries may have dated ideas of what a wedding cake should look like, so study the photos closely before moving ahead.

Occasionally, friends or relatives will step forward to bake the cake as a gift. If you're looking for sentimental value or homemade goodness in a cake, there's no better way to go. But before you accept, be aware that a wedding cake can be a complicated feat of engineering. Unless the volunteer baker has experience in stacked cakes (see how they're constructed later in this chapter), this could be a disaster in the making. I strongly advise you to sidestep a potential problem by countering with one of these three alternatives:

- Arrange for the friend or relative to make multiple smaller cakes to be used as centerpieces on tables or displayed together on cake stands of varying heights.

- Have the pastry chef at the hotel try to replicate your friend's or relatives's famous lemon chiffon cake recipe.

- Divert her toward cookies (or another simple dessert) to send home with guests as special favors. Attach a note explaining who made them, along with the recipe, if she's willing to divulge it.

When to Book a Cake Maker

DECIDING ON A BAKER and a cake doesn't need to be high on your priority list *unless* you're after a major star in the cake world—in that case, you should try to line him up as soon as you've settled on a date, location, officiant, and photographer. Keep in mind that bakers may require nonrefundable deposits, so make sure you've got your logistics in place before committing.

Otherwise, cake vendors should be firmed up three to four months before the wedding, and you can often get a fantastic cake in less time.

ASK MINDY

Q I'm allergic to gluten, and my fiancé just isn't a sweets person. Is it okay to pass on the wedding cake? It just seems like such a waste of money.

A I'm all for having it your way, but I don't like to see couples bypass the cake tradition. If you're really an ice-cream sundae girl, put out a dessert buffet with a sundae and cookie bar. But the cutting of the cake is one of the all-time classic wedding photos—why not get a small cake to cut for ceremonial purposes? Then you can make it a children-only cake. They'll love having something just for them.

The Cake Tasting

T his is the one stage of wedding planning that no one wants to miss: Attending a cake tasting is like getting an extra birthday party without having to turn a year older.

You'll typically schedule a tasting about three to four months before the wedding. The baker will bring out a selection of cakes and fillings to try. Some will present full slices, others bites. You'll also look through photos in the baker's portfolio or see the dummy cakes the bakery has on display. Bring photos of cakes and other design elements you like.

The cake tasting is designed to show the baker's range. You don't need to be handed the perfect cake—if you feel confident that it's a good match, you can always tweak combinations and flavors later on.

Both the bride and groom should attend the tasting, and you may want to invite your mothers, maid of honor, or best man, mostly for their enjoyment.

Designing Your Cake

The cake design should be a collaboration between you and your cake maker. Consider the setting, the flavors you like, the meal you're serving, and (of course) the cost. Cakes are typically priced by the slice.

Your cake should look as if it belongs in its environment. For a reception in a raw loft space, a Victorian-inspired white tower of a cake would look out of place. And it's not just an aesthetic choice: A wedding cake sits on display for hours before it's served, and buttercream frosting, whipped cream, custard, or mousse are too delicate to withstand heat for any length of time—so you wouldn't want them featured in an outdoor wedding in the summer.

Cake Construction

LAYER CAKES are complex structures involving tiers. Separated tiers are broken up by pillars or flowers, while stacked tiers appear to sit on top of one another; the latter are kept from collapsing into each other by the use of either separator plates or dowel rods and cake plates.

Think about the shape you're after. Angled shapes tend to look cleaner and more contemporary than round tiers. Varying the shapes of the different tiers—alternating hexagons and squares or ovals and octagons, for instance—can also give a cake a modern edge. (Mix more than two shapes and the cake tends to look quirky and whimsical, which is perfectly fine, as long as that's what you want.)

Flavors and Fillings

THIS IS YOUR CAKE, to be sure, so you should choose flavors and fillings that you love. But if your taste runs to the exotic, it's thoughtful to alternate with tiers of a crowd-pleasing favorite. Ingredients that tend to inspire extremes of emotion include coconut, bananas, and peanut butter, so if you're using any of those, try to offer another choice as well.

Also consider your menu before deciding on a cake flavor. Do a taste test of the meal in your mind and try to imagine what type of cake would finish off such a meal. (If you're serving an Italian meal, a coconut-papaya cake would be a strange finish.)

Icing

SAD TO SAY, icing cannot be chosen by taste alone. It can be delicate and unstable, so climate conditions may trump taste. Here's what you need to know about icing options:

Fondant. Also called rolled fondant, this very smooth icing gives a clean finish. It's well suited to cakes with a tailored look. It's very sweet, and most people don't consider it as tasty as buttercream, but it holds up much better at an outdoor wedding or anywhere warm.

Buttercream. Just as it sounds, this wicked concoction is a blend of butter, cream, sugar, and vanilla, chocolate, or other flavoring. The simplest and the best, in many a cook's opinion, it can be spread smoothly or in peaks and valleys for a charming vintage look. But a buttercream cake can't stand for too long before the icing starts to run off into a puddle.

Royal icing. Egg whites and confectioners' sugar whisked together into a sugary paste that hardens as it sets, royal icing is mainly used as a sculptural element.

Crunchy and sugary, it's likely to appear in decorative touches like polka dots, small flowers, or piping.

Marzipan. Made of hardened almond paste and sugar, this confection is traditionally used to make realistic edible cake toppings, from flowers to bride and groom figurines. It can also be rolled and used as icing.

The Cake Toppers

A cake is an edible creation, so anything on it should be edible, or at least natural—flowers, for example. Many things can be placed atop a wedding cake, but to my mind, plastic should not be among them. That goes for figures, pillars, and urns as well. (Of course, anything that's a part of the cake's structure is another story.)

I do confess to a soft spot for vintage cake toppers. A plastic bride and groom from the 1950s is too retro to resist, and an icon that belonged to a parent would warm the heart of even the most adamant purist.

Decorative Touches

WHEN IT COMES to wedding-cake decorations, frosting is often just the beginning. Options abound, from fresh flowers to handmade sugar-paste flowers, crystallized fruit, gold and silver leaf, and crystal cake jewelry.

Tiered wedding cakes especially tend to need something near or on the top in order to look finished. Cake makers can create all manner of toppers out of sugar paste, though flowers remain the number one choice—when done well, they look astonishingly like detailed porcelain.

If you're feeling the budget pinch, stick with fresh flowers or fruit, which cost considerably less than their sugar-paste counterparts; just make sure the flowers are pesticide free (florists or cake makers usually order organic flowers for cakes). Purists believe that any fresh flowers on a cake should be edible, but as long as you're removing the flowers before serving the cake, I think it's better to keep your options open.

Crystallized flowers and fruit are delicate adornments that can help link a wedding to its season or its setting. Crystallized flowers are real flowers preserved with sugar to maintain their natural color and details; fruit is cooked in sugar syrup, then coated with sugar.

Making It Yours

THERE ARE AS MANY ways to make a cake all about you as there are flavors to choose from. Here are some of my favorite ways to tie the cake to the couple:

- Use a family heirloom as the cake topper. It could be the cake topper from your parents' cake, but it could also be a special china cup of your grandmother's.

- Have the baker use a family recipe. On your menu, or in your toast, make everyone aware of the connection.

- Choose your favorite cake flavor. If you're stumped, think back to what you loved as children. If the two of you can't agree, have the baker do alternating tiers.

- Adorn the cake with your favorite flowers, whether they're real or made of sugar paste. The flowers on the cake might also reference ones in the bouquet.

- Incorporate your favorite colors, either in the frosting or the decorations. A cake could even be your something blue, or it could reflect the colors of the wedding.

- Tie the cake to your theme, season, or location. For a beach wedding, consider gum paste seashells and starfish edging the layers.

- Choose a cake that reflects your cultural or ethnic heritage. Almonds are part of the wedding tradition in many Mediterranean countries, so if you're Italian or Greek, think about marzipan frosting or decorations.

- Incorporate your initials or monogram; sleek initials can top the cake, or an elaborate monogram can grace the bottom tier.

- Use your wedding dress as inspiration, borrowing the buttons, lace pattern, embroidery, sash, or corset lacing as a design element.

A Cake Glossary

CAKE MAKING AND DECORATING are artisanal skills with many complex techniques involved. You don't need to master them, but you do need to know their names.

Appliqué. A design rolled out of sugar paste and applied to fondant icing.

Beading. Pearl shapes piped around the edge of the cake.

Cake jewelry. A relatively new term that describes any stand-in for a cake topper involving bling. Some examples: the couple's monogram rendered in crystals, a crown, enameled flowers on individual stems, or a crystal heart.

Cornelli. A form of piping that creates a three-dimensional pattern of lace or squiggles.

Crystallized flowers. Edible flowers preserved with sugar to retain their vibrant appearance. Also known as candied or sugared flowers.

Dragées. Decorative silver-coated balls made of sugar. (Can also refer to a traditional candy; see page 329.)

Draping. A mixture of fondant and gum paste rolled out and positioned over the first layer of fondant for the effect of fabric or ribbons spilling over the cake. Icing swags can also be draped around the edge of a tier.

Ganache. A dark, rich combination of chocolate and cream used as a filling or icing. Additional flavors such as espresso can be added.

Genoise. A classic French sponge cake that's drier than American cakes. It's typically soaked in a liqueur syrup and layered with fruit fillings or flavored whipped cream.

Gum paste. Also known as sugar dough, gum paste is a moldable mixture of sugar and gelatin. It's used to create intricate edible flowers, fruits, seashells, and figures. Decorations made of gum paste have a long life span.

> If you're fixated on a chocolate cake, stick to a light-colored layer on the bottom—that's the layer you'll cut into for your photo op, and you don't want to risk having chocolate on your teeth or a dark smudge on your wedding dress.

Layer. When a cake is split and sandwiched with fruit filling or icing, that's a layer. Don't confuse it with a tier, especially when placing a cake order.

Marzipan. A paste of ground almonds, sugar, and egg whites that can be molded into fruit-shaped decorations or small, whimsical figures. It can also be rolled to ice or layer a cake.

Mousse, mousseline. Cake fillings flavored with chocolate or fruit that are lighter and airier than buttercream.

Petal dust. A type of decorating dust applied with an artist's brush to add shimmer to icing or gum paste. Gold dust and pearl dust achieve similarly lustrous effects.

Piping. A decorative technique in which icing is squeezed from a pastry bag to create a three-dimensional design on the cake. The pastry-bag tips come in a variety of shapes, allowing a pastry chef to pipe a border, swags, ropes, polka dots, flowers, or even an elaborate pattern like lace. Piped flowers (the kind you'd see on a supermarket birthday cake) aren't as finely detailed as flowers made of sugar or gum paste.

The Sheet Cake Trick

It's something of a myth that ordering a smaller cake for display (or building it up with fake layers) and supplementing with sheet cakes in the kitchen will save you a bundle. You'll save a bit, to be sure, but there's actually a better reason to take this route. Once a cake for two hundred guests is cut by the bride and groom and wheeled to the kitchen, it can take twenty minutes or more to cut and plate. The use of a display cake allows the catering staff to cut sheet cakes during dinner so slices are ready to go at dessert time. Delivering cake quickly keeps up a good flow and energy at this point in the reception, when you don't want guests to start petering out.

Spoon frosting. Think Duncan Hines. Old-fashioned, stucco look achieved by applying the icing with the back of a spoon.

Spun sugar, pulled sugar. An advanced technique that involves pulling or spinning caramelized sugar into threads that can be shaped into nests, bows, or domes. Used to top cakes or other desserts.

Sugared fruits. Small fruits such as grapes or kumquats coated with sugar for a frosty finish. They can serve as embellishments or cake toppers.

Tier. A complete cake that's iced and then stacked or separated by pillars from other tiers to form a wedding cake. For couples who can't decide, each tier can be made of a different kind of cake. Not to be confused with layers.

Outside the Cake Box

I f a large cake doesn't float your boat, take a look at some of these delightful and creative alternatives. But beware: While some can work in favor of an overstretched budget, others come with hefty price tags.

Table cakes. Individualized table cakes are a charming cure for the overgrown wedding cake. Supplemented by a minimalistic arrangement like mint julep cups filled with a few blooms, they can actually serve as centerpieces throughout the meal. Though the individual cakes will likely prove more expensive than a single large cake, you'll save on floral centerpieces, so you'll lower your total costs, often by up to $50 a table. Each cake should be placed on a

---

MEETING AND GREETING

THE CAKE MAKER

As you know from your other vendor meetings, you should bring photographs of cakes you like along with you. If your tastes run to extravagances that aren't within your budget, maybe your cake maker can find some way to create a compromise.

- Look at photos of cakes he's done for weddings and other big events. Study them to see if you like the proportion, colors, decorations, and overall aesthetic.

- If you have a photo of a cake similar to the one you want, ask if he's had experience with this type of cake and how he'd go about creating it.

- Ask how long he has been baking cakes, and find out if he's available for your wedding date.

- *When do you make your cakes in relation to the wedding? Do you freeze them beforehand or keep them fresh?*

- Ask about his choice of ingredients. In top-quality cakes, everything is natural, meaning there's butter (not shortening) in the buttercream icing, and fruit fillings are made by the baker.

- Find out if there's a delivery charge and what it is. No matter how tight your budget, get the cake delivered to the site. Cakes are delicate and tricky to transport, and you really don't want strawberry-filling stains in your car. (Trust me on this one; I have the stains to prove it.) Also, while the cake is in the baker's possession, he remains responsible for it; once it's in your hands, guess who's responsible if anything goes wrong?

- If you plan to decorate the cake with fresh flowers, ask who provides them and puts them on the cake. (Sometimes it's the cake maker, and sometimes it's the florist.)

- Put him in touch with the catering manager so he can find out the best way and time to access the reception room with the cake.

- Find out whether a deposit is required and its terms, and when the remainder of the payment is due.

- Ask how the pricing is established. *Is it strictly a per-slice charge, or are there extra charges for certain designs or an abundance of hand-rolled, gum paste flowers?*

riser or cake stand so that it's clearly visible, but it shouldn't be so high that it interferes with conversation. Two-tiered cakes, with a false tier at the bottom, can make stunning centerpieces, too. Someone at the table will cut the cake, so you can usually avoid a cake-cutting fee, though some hotels may charge a minimal plate fee.

Cupcakes. Everyone seems to have rediscovered this childhood favorite in recent years. Cupcakes work out to be less expensive than a large cake ($2 to $4 less per person), and they can be decorated with gum paste flowers or dusted monograms. They can be displayed on tiered dessert stands or passed around on silver trays. Since there's no cake cutting involved, many reception venues won't charge an extra fee.

Individual cakes. By far the most lavish and expensive option, individual cakes are commissioned for each guest. The painstaking process of decorating so many cakes drives up their price, which can range from $5 to $45 per cake. They can be served at the reception or sent home in favor boxes.

Multiple cakes. Cluster several medium-size cakes together on cake stands to create an enchanting display. With a lace tablecloth underneath, it will look like an ultra-elegant bake sale.

Dollars and Sense

Cakes can be expensive. A few ideas for slicing your costs:

- If you're having 150 or more guests, order a cake for 25 fewer people than you expect.

- Serve cupcakes or table cakes to avoid cake-cutting fees.

- Decorate cakes with fresh flowers instead of costly sugar paste imitations.

- Since much of the cost of a cake hinges on how much labor is involved in decorating it, order a simple frosted cake, then buy crystallized flowers online and go to town.

Groom's Cakes

White wedding cake was renamed bride's cake in the 1860s, and the traditional fruitcake that had been served at weddings for centuries became known as the groom's cake. Fruitcake aside, a groom's cake gives guys a chance to express their tastes, which may not run to whipped cream layers and strawberry filling. Long a southern tradition, it has grown popular across the country in recent years. Sometimes the bride surprises the groom with a cake, which can make for a memorable reaction and turn into a highlight of the reception. A groom's cake is by no means necessary, however, so skip it if you're on a tight budget.

For years, groom's cakes were made of chocolate (the dark cake providing a counterpoint to the bride's), but now they can be just about anything. I'm not one to pass up an opportunity to introduce chocolate, but I do like to see the flavor reflect the groom's preferences. If that's pineapple upside-down cake, why not?

The groom's cake is much smaller than the central cake—count half the number of guests when ordering—and is usually much more whimsical, reflecting a hobby, passion, or interest of the groom. Cakes bearing the logos and colors of professional or college sports teams are perennial favorites, as are cakes designed around golf and car themes. One of my favorite groom's cakes was an homage to the groom's bulldogs, shaped like two dog bowls and complete with sugar-dough dog food—not to everyone's taste, but perfect for this particular wedding.

The two cakes are generally displayed on separate tables, but they can also look wonderful side by side or even at opposite ends of the room.

Groom's cakes often go uneaten if served at the reception, even when a small slice is served next to the wedding cake. To make sure yours doesn't go to waste, have slices boxed up for guests to take home. (I like to attach a tag or sticker reading "Sweet Dreams," after a superstition that if single women put a slice of the groom's cake under their pillow, they'll dream of the man they're going to marry.) You can also save the groom's

THE CAKE MAKER'S CONTRACT

The contract with the cake maker should address the following points. If he presents you with a contract that leaves any of these out, draw up a letter covering them (label it "Addendum to Contract") and gently lobby to have him sign it. Make sure he attaches the letter to his copy so that he has all of the terms in plain view.

- The date, time, and location where the cake is to be delivered. Double-check the information to make sure it's correct—a transposed number is the kind of typo that can really cost you. There is often a two-hour window for delivering the cake.

- There should be a sketch or photo of the cake you're ordering, along with a written description of both the interior and exterior. The description should specify the type of icing, decoration, cake, and filling and the number of people the cake is to feed.

- The fee for the cake, along with deposit and final payment information, should be clearly stated, along with how much money has been received and how much is due. If there are any circumstances under which you would get a refund, those should be defined.

- Anything that the cake maker is supposed to provide, such as flowers for decorating the cake or a monogram cake topper, should be documented in the contract.

cake to serve at brunch the day after the wedding, or make sure it gets the attention it deserves by unveiling and serving it at the rehearsal dinner.

Do You Need Dessert, Too?

Though it's become very trendy to offer a cake, a dessert table, *and* a treat to take home, I think wedding cake is the only dessert you need. It's so special and imbued with meaning—why not let it be the star of the show?

If you're worried about the dessert plate looking bare, the cake can be dressed up a bit for serving. A coulis or sauce, a scoop of sorbet or ice cream, or even a chocolate truffle or two on the side can transform a slice of cake into a mini dessert platter.

If you're tied to the idea of doing more than just cake, an assortment of fruit is a nice complement or alternative for your health-conscious guests. You don't need anything too elaborate—plates of cookies or an ice-cream sundae station are popular choices. And then there's the perennial chocolate fountain (a gussied-up way of serving fondue), which can be a festive addition and a good gathering spot. I've even seen couples throw in bowls of their favorite candy—for the kids, and well, just because.

The cake cutting is the last of the many wonderful rituals encompassing your wedding celebration. So if you're coming to the end of this chapter, you're ready to go full steam ahead. From here on out, you'll be wrapping up details left and right. It may feel as though you can't stop for breath, but just remember that the fruit of all your labor is just around the corner. ◆

PART IV

THE BIG EVENT

CHAPTER TWENTY-FOUR

The Weeks Before

HITTING THE FINAL STRETCH

Once the vendors are in place, the dress has been ordered, and the major decisions have been made, you'll probably get to enjoy a short lull. But when you hit the two-month mark, it's time to ramp up again. You've got RSVPs to track, fittings to attend, flower arrangements to finalize, and entrées to taste. You'll need to stay on top of last-minute tasks both big and small, from preparing a schedule and seating your guests to writing a speech and packing an emergency kit. (The Week-by-Week Planner on page 395 should be a great help to you during this time.)

Don't throw your routine out the window during this flurry. Stick to your exercise plan if you've got a goal in mind; two months is plenty of time for those stress pounds to creep on. If anything, you should probably be *adding* an extra yoga class to your week—you'll need that centered feeling of calm.

It's likely that you'll be making a fair number of changes and adjustments to your plans during this time. Stay flexible, and don't be afraid of those tweaks—some of my best ideas have come out of last-minute emergencies.

The Schedule

The key to keeping your wedding day running smoothly is the schedule of events. Creating and fine-tuning this schedule is certainly a better use of your time than phoning the florist daily to see if he's found striped parrot tulips. None of your guests will know if the lavender tulips on the table were supposed to be ruffled red and yellow—but they *will* notice if the string quartet is still setting up as they walk into the ceremony or if they have to wait thirty minutes for a shuttle bus.

An exhaustive schedule will also help you feel calmer and more organized. Once you download all of the wedding flotsam and jetsam from your brain and put it in its logical place, you'll be able to stop worrying about it (to a degree).

The full schedule of events covers the entire wedding time line, from setup to breakdown. You'll extract different portions of it to give to attendants, parents, and the hair and makeup artists. The schedule is as much for the vendors as it is for you. It will tell the florist which entrance to use for delivery and ensure that your bridesmaids know when and where to show up for hair and makeup.

The more detailed the schedule, the better. If you have a wedding planner, she will take charge of it, but if not, you should start working on it six to eight weeks before the wedding. Use whatever computer program you're most comfortable with.

Put your names and the day and date of the wedding at the top of the file, then start walking through the complete event in your head, from the arrival of the out-of-towners to your honeymoon flight info. Anyone doing an involved setup—the catering company, possibly the florist, the musicians, etc.—should provide you with a schedule of their own; take what they give you and work it into yours.

For an off-site wedding, the schedule will be quite lengthy and involved. One tent wedding I arranged took about two weeks to set up and six days to break down . . . the schedule was twenty-eight pages! But that's not typical; most of my schedules are five to eight pages long.

On the following pages, you'll find sample schedules for a hotel wedding, an off-site tent wedding, and a destination wedding in Mexico, along with a schedule in letter form for the attendants. Read over the one that most closely represents your wedding. If you're doing the schedule yourself, it's a good idea to send a draft to the vendors in time for them to make adjustments as needed.

As details fall into place, you'll continue to add to the schedule and fine-tune it. Around the three-week mark, it should be pretty much set. Get a copy to each of your vendors, whether in person or by email. Bring extra copies to the rehearsal and wedding for any vendors who forget theirs.

Scheduling Photos

Allow enough time for all of the photographic permutations required. For a small bridal party with two attendants on each side, an hour and a half is usually enough. For a medium bridal party, allow two hours. If your party is large, with more than six bridesmaids, plan on three hours for photos. The more people in a photo, the longer it takes to set up, and the more frames the photographer needs to shoot to get one where everyone looks good. If you have a small bridal party but a large family, add more time for portraits. Your photographer will also advise you on how much time to budget.

On the schedule you give the attendants, give them a call time thirty minutes before they're actually needed. That way, if some of them are late, they won't hold everyone up.

Details, Details

On your schedule, include day-of contact information for all vendors and anyone involved with the wedding—from the florist to the limo driver; that way you can call the driver if there's no sign of him. If you booked a band, makeup artist, or anyone else through an agency, also have the agent's contact info. In case of a no-show, the agent may be able to rustle up a substitute. If you're picking up anyone at the airport or taking anyone to the airport, include airlines and flight numbers.

The Seating Chart

Though seating charts are considered mandatory only for formal events, I think that when you've put so much effort into planning a reception, it's a mistake to leave something so important to chance. Even at a casual event, you're risking mayhem by letting guests devise their own seating plans. Do you want them pulling up extra chairs to your carefully laid tables and squeezing in two extra place settings at your table for eight? Guests also don't want to feel they've been left to fend for themselves—they enjoy themselves more when they feel taken care of.

Cocktail receptions and dessert receptions are notable exceptions. If you're not providing seating for everyone, then you're excused from making a seating chart. It's thoughtful to reserve a few tables for the bridal party, parents, elderly relatives, or anyone else who needs to sit.

Devising a seating plan is like working on a puzzle—and the level of difficulty depends on the family dynamics and personalities involved. If a lot of family squabbles arose surrounding the guest list, you may be in for more of the same when it comes time to figure out who sits where. For couples with divorced parents, seating can be particularly challenging if not everyone is on good terms. In some cases, though, clear table groupings emerge organically from the chaos, and it's smooth sailing.

A note: When I talk about seating, I'm referring to placing people at specific tables, not at specific seats on those tables; when guests arrive, they'll pick up a card with their table number on it. Whether to take it a step further and assign them a seat at the table—which you would designate with a place card—is entirely optional. It's usually not necessary, but some people feel they can better direct the table chemistry by specifying who sits next to whom. If you're seating everyone at one long table, you definitely want place cards to facilitate easy interaction.

Seating Philosophy 101

THE MEAL IS WHERE guests spend the most time together, and whom they sit with contributes mightily to how good a time they have. Your two main goals are to encourage stimulating, comfortable conversation and to honor special guests.

Typically, you accomplish this by seating like people together. That means your college roommate sits with other college pals; that your colleagues from work sit together; and that your aunts, uncles, and cousins share a table.

Now if you've got a work friend you think would hit it off with a college friend, there's nothing wrong with manipulating the groupings a little to put them at the same table. (Just *please* don't make the mistake of seating all the single girls together—you may think you're setting them up for a rollicking good time, but they're going to feel like lepers!)

You might consider grouping by age rather than family unit. So instead of seating your aunt and uncle with their children, you could seat them with other aunts and uncles or friends of your parents, and seat the children with other cousins around their age. If you're inviting children to the wedding, they're likely to have a better time at a separate children's table. If the only children are the flower girl and ring bearer, however, seat them with their parents. But there's no one way to do things, so listen to your gut.

The Skinny on Seating

THE MORE TIME you leave yourself to work out the seating arrangement, the better. Putting the process off until the last minute won't leave you time to deal with the issues or disagreements that may arise. Start working on seating as soon as the response cards are in. When you sent out invitations, you should have asked guests to reply three or four weeks before the wedding (see page 284). If you don't have all of the replies by the deadline, call stragglers to find out if they plan to attend. If a large number of people didn't RSVP, enlist parents and attendants (or a wedding planner, if you're working with one) for help.

If a calligrapher will be doing the seating cards, find out when she needs names. Otherwise, make it your goal to finalize seating five days before the wedding.

(continued on page 358)

Schedule for a Hotel Wedding

Even when a seasoned professional is handling every detail, you still need to have a schedule. It structures the timing and flow of your event, ensures that all parties involved are informed of their responsibilities, and helps you keep track of any outside items you are bringing in. (Don't worry: Yours doesn't have to be as "pretty" as the ones I've included here. Just make sure everything is crystal clear.)

THE WEDDING OF

Jessica Sterrick and Michael Josephson

BEVERLY HILLS HOTEL

JULY 20, 2019

FRIDAY, JULY 19

1:00 p.m.	Stage extension built in ballroom
4:00 p.m.	Dance floor delivered 30 x 30 by School's Out Party Rentals [contact info]
5:00 p.m.	Wedding rehearsal
	Bridesmaids' and groomsmen's gifts brought to the hotel
7:00 p.m.	Rehearsal dinner

If the stage is too small for your band, you can build it out.

SATURDAY, JULY 20

8:00 a.m.	Setup begins in the ballroom
	Draping of the ballroom
	Lighting
	Flowers
	Rental company to deliver silver beaded chargers [contact info]
	Event planner arrives—to bring: Menus, cocktail napkins, table numbers, seating cards, programs, candy for tables
10:00 a.m.	Tables and hotel chairs to be set
	Crew arrives to put on chair covers and tie sashes—Resources Unlimited [contact info]
	Pick up dress at boutique
11:00 a.m.	Hair and makeup arrive at hotel (hair: Sara, contact info; makeup: George, contact info)
12:00 p.m.	Florist to set up moss place card table in foyer
	Lunch delivered to room

Specialty chargers usually come from a party supply company. The site supplied the rest of the china.

These were all specialty items we had personalized.

Hair and Makeup Schedule

	Hair (Sara)	Makeup (George)
11:00 a.m.	Laura	Mom
12:00 p.m.	Mom	Laura
1:00 p.m.	Jessica	
2:00 p.m.		Jessica

1:00 p.m.	Dresser arrives at hotel
1:30 p.m.	Bridesmaids ready but not dressed
1:45 p.m.	Photographer (contact info) and videographer (contact info) arrive
	Getting-ready pictures begin
	Videographer to set up ceremony sound
2:00 p.m.	Groomsmen arrive ready but not dressed
3:30 p.m.	Pictures begin
	Jessica and bridesmaids
	Michael and groomsmen
4:00 p.m.	Wedding cake delivered
	Photo-op! Jessica and Michael to see each other for the first time
	DJ to arrive for setup
4:30 p.m.	Extended-family pictures begin
5:00 p.m.	Family pictures
	Pictures with flower girl and ring bearer
	Table placed under canopy—use Resources Unlimited ivory linen
5:30 p.m.	Pictures complete
	Jessica to go back to room to freshen up

A "dresser" specializes in dressing the bride, bustling the gown, and dealing with any wardrobe malfunctions that arise (for the entire bridal party). She's like an emergency kit in a person, so it's a really nice splurge if you have the wiggle room. Sometimes you can hire a bridal salon's alteration person to fulfill this role.

See page 99 for possible shot lists to give to your photographer.

If the ceremony and reception are in the same space, I like to hand out the reception seating cards before the ceremony—it's easier than trying to get guests' attention once the wedding is underway. (With dual spaces, you can set up a table at the entrance to the reception, where everyone will see it.)

6:15 p.m. Prelude music begins

10-piece wind/string orchestra and fluegelhorn—classical

6:30 p.m. Ceremony invitation time

Wedding planners to assist guests with seating cards

6:50 p.m. Wedding planner to line up bridal party

7:00 p.m. Ceremony begins

Prelude: "Air on G String"

Officiant

Grandparents of the Groom

Grandparents of the Bride

Best man Joe Josephson

Groom Michael escorted by his parents, Mary and John Josephson

Groomsmen:
Rodney
Daniel
Aaron
Yossi
Diego
Brandon
Chris
David

Bridesmaids:
Melissa
Stacy
Alli
Candace
Dee
Patricia
Michelle
Amy

Maid of Honor Laura

Ring bearer Jonathan

Flower girls:
Danielle
Rosie

Bride's procession: "Life Is Beautiful"

Bride Jessica escorted by her parents, Lisa and David Sterrick

Recessional: "Book of Days"

Postrecessional: "All You Need Is Love"

7:30 p.m. Cocktail hour

Cocktail music is playing—solo pianist
Tray pass cocktails and hors d'oeuvres

Dresser to bustle Jessica's dress
Vendor buffet meal set up in Oak Room

8:30 p.m. Guests invited into the ballroom

Music is playing

8:50 p.m. Grand entrance and first dance

Song: "A Whole New World"

Introduced as Jessica and Michael Josephson

Midsong, emcee to invite
Parents
Bridal Party
Then all guests

Then 4 dance songs

9:10 p.m. Guests invited to be seated

Welcome by Lisa and David Sterrick

9:20 p.m. First course served

9:45 p.m. Dance set

10:05 p.m. Second course served

10:20 p.m. Best man toast—Joe

Maid of honor toast—Laura

10:30 p.m. Dance set

10:50 p.m. Entrée served

11:20 p.m. Father/daughter dance
Song: "Somewhere Out There"

Midsong, emcee to invite
Mary and Michael
Then all guests

Followed by high-energy dance set

11:55 p.m. Dessert served

Followed by cake cutting

Jessica and Michael to say something

12:05 a.m. Dancing continues

Bouquet and garter toss

Warm chocolate chip cookies served w/shots of milk

12:30 a.m. Band ends or overtime

2:30 a.m. Strike
Linens
Lighting
Florals
Fabric
Touch of Style to pick up chargers

SUNDAY, JULY 21

8:00 a.m. Dance floor removed

9:00 a.m. Stage extension removed

10:00 a.m. Brunch in the Sunset Room

Time to decide whether to have the band go into overtime—it can really add up—or call it a night. If the dance floor is full, it might be worth your while, but if only a few people are still going strong, it's better to end on a high note.

Schedule for a Tent Wedding

A tent wedding always requires extra setup time. You probably won't need the four days we had here—our setup was fairly involved. (P.S. You really don't have to hire a babysitter for your guests' children—but it's an extra, extra nice thing to do if you can.)

THE WEDDING OF

Jennifer Floria and Brandon Case

MAY 27, 2017

When you're putting in a subfloor, you might need to begin installation as early as five days before the wedding.

TUESDAY, MAY 23
Rentals to begin installation

WEDNESDAY, MAY 24
Begin subfloor installation at location

THURSDAY, MAY 25
Rental installation continues

FRIDAY, MAY 26
Rental installation continues
Décor and lighting install begins
Restrooms delivered
Welcome gifts delivered to out-of-town guests
3:00 p.m. Jennifer and Brandon check into hotel
6:20 p.m. Wedding Rehearsal—Beau Rivage

SATURDAY, MAY 27
9:00 a.m. Caterer arrives
10:00 a.m. Old-fashioned photo booth delivered

The staff arrives early and may need help parking.

Valet arrives for staff parking
Florist to deliver flowers to cake maker
11:30 a.m. Videographer arrives
11:45 a.m. Calypso band begins
Unlimited Party Rentals to set up (2) market umbrellas for band
12:00 p.m.–5:00 p.m

The rehearsal and rehearsal dinner don't have to be on the same night.

BBQ

SUNDAY, MAY 28
8:00 a.m. Floral installation begins

The driveway was very uneven, and I wanted a smoother surface for walking. Sometimes you have to get creative. . . .

AstroTurf placed on the driveway
Linens delivered

Round tables—lemongrass beaded embroidery overlay & multifloral overlay with lemongrass underlay

Alternating your napkin treatment from table to table is a great way to get in your two colors.

Alternate napkin treatment—½ lavender and ½ wreath
Chiavari chairs
9:00 a.m. Breakfast delivered to house for girls
Bagels, cream cheese, croissants, baked goods, fruit salad, and orange juice
9:00 a.m. Manicures and pedicures for Jennifer [bride] and Stacy [maid of honor]
11:00 a.m. Jennifer to begin hair and makeup

If you don't have time to do your mani-pedis the day before, do them really early in the morning so you have time to dry.

Hair and Makeup Schedule

	Hair (Marbella)	Makeup (Juan)
10:30 a.m.		Alli
11:00 a.m.	Alli	Stacy
11:40 a.m.	Jennifer	Debbie
12:20 p.m.	Terry	Jennifer
1:00 p.m.	Stacy	Terry
1:30 p.m.	Ashley	Melissa
2:00 p.m.	Debbie	Ashley
2:20 p.m.	Melissa	Kim
2:50 p.m.	Kim	

12:00 p.m. Dresser arrives
Videographer to set up ceremony sound
Wedding planners to deliver lunch:
Small sandwiches—vegetarian and turkey, side of hummus, grilled veggie wrap, 2 salads, Vitamin water, Diet coke, Coke, Sprite, mayonnaise and mustard on the side

12:30 p.m.	Videographer and photographer arrive for getting-ready pictures
1:00 p.m.	Caterer arrives
1:30 p.m.	Pictures begin—Jennifer and Brandon to see each other for the first time
	Reserved seating cards placed on chairs
2:30 p.m.	Family pictures
	Wedding cake delivered
	Parents' wedding pictures placed on cake table
2:30 p.m.	Shuttle to depart hotel [VIP 310-555-1111] Shuttle to proceed to location—24 passenger Charter 53469
2:45 p.m.	Shuttle departs—24 passenger Charter 53471
3:00 p.m.	Babysitter arrives for kids
3:30 p.m.	Prelude music begins (6 chairs)
	Pictures complete
4:00 p.m.	Invitation time for ceremony
	Waitstaff to tray pass lemonade and water
	Wedding planner to assist guests with seating cards
4:15 p.m.	Wedding planner to line up bridal party
4:30 p.m.	Ceremony begins
	Music: Harp
	Procession

This is such a sweet way to dress up your cake table.

This is a really nice thing to do. . . .

Officiant

Brandon with his parents, Debbie and Ken

Groomsmen:
Aaron
JJ
Michael
David

Bridesmaids:
Liz
Laura
Ashley
Kim

Melissa—flower girl

Jennifer with her parents, Terry and Paul

Recessional

5:00 p.m.	Cocktail hour begins
	Music is playing
	Tray passing of cocktails and hors d'oeuvres
6:00 p.m.	Guests invited into the reception tent
	Coleman Band is playing
6:15 p.m.	Grand Entrance—first dance as husband and wife, announced as Jennifer and Brandon Case
	First dance song: "How Sweet It Is"
	Emcee to invite up to dance: Parents—Terry and Paul Debbie and Ken Wedding party Then all guests
	Then 2 dance songs
6:35 p.m.	Guests invited to be seated
6:40 p.m.	Welcome by Terry and Paul
6:50 p.m.	First course served
	Dance set
7:45 p.m.	Entrée served
	Toasts during entrée JJ (brother) Aaron (brother) Stacy (bridesmaid)
8:30 p.m.	Father/Daughter Dance Song: "Unforgettable"
	Midsong, emcee to invite Brandon and Debbie Then all guests
	Followed by dance set
9:10 p.m.	Cake cutting—Jennifer and Brandon to say something
9:15 p.m.	Dessert served
10:00 p.m.	Band ends or goes into overtime

MONDAY, MAY 29

9:30 a.m. Brunch at Marguerite

TUESDAY, MAY 30

Strike all vendors

Schedule for a Destination Wedding

A cigar station, a pre-rehearsal dinner barbeque, three separate bands . . . this destination wedding was as elaborate as they come. With so much being planned long-distance, you need to make sure you're covering all your bases. It's all about the details.

THE WEDDING OF
Lianne Tocklas and Jed Pastek
GREEN PALMS RESORT, CABO SAN LUCAS, MEXICO
JUNE 15, 2019

TUESDAY, JUNE 11

Lighting arrives in Mexico

WEDNESDAY, JUNE 12

Wedding planner arrives in Mexico; will bring linens, cocktail napkins, seating cards, table numbers, leather folder for ceremony notes and vows, walkie-talkie radios

7:00 a.m.	Bahia #3 room available for storage
8:00 a.m.	Truck arrives in Mexico with fabric, furniture, floral supplies, and lighting equipment
	Images Light Co. and Mark's Garden florist to check truck and begin unloading
	Part of ballroom available for florist setup (Hotel to set up plastic on the floor and set with work tables, [8] 6-foot-long tables)
2:00 p.m.	Lianne and Jed arrive in Mexico
	Tocklas and Pastek families arrive in Mexico
	Hotel to have flowers sent to: Mindy and Robert Note to say: Happy Anniversary Love, Jed and Lianne
8:00 p.m.	Dinner in C Restaurant—under bride's name

> *Since the florists were doing the arrangements on-site, we needed to cover the floor to protect it from water damage.*

> *Don't forget to celebrate other people's special days—they will be so touched that you remembered.*

THURSDAY, JUNE 13

Welcome note delivered to hotel rooms

Photographer and videographer arrive

11:00 a.m.	Discuss time of setup for welcome party
	Hotel to set long tables on the beach with white folding chairs
2:00 p.m.	Lianne and Jed to do blood tests for marriage license and meet with the translator

7:00 p.m.	Green Palms to arrange transportation to pick up guests at Hilton Hotel
7:30–10:30 p.m.	
	Welcome party—beach BBQ
	Shoe check-in setup
	Guacamole station/margarita station
7:30–8:30 p.m.	
	Mariachis playing
	Photographer—coverage for 2 hours
	Tequila tasting
8:30–10:30 p.m.	
	Aqua Trio—3 Bolleros playing
10:30 p.m.	Green Palms to arrange transportation to take guests back to Hilton Hotel

> *Since people will be arriving on different flights, they'll be trickling in. Bring everyone together to kick off the festivities.*

FRIDAY, JUNE 14

Hair and makeup arrive
Hair: Eric B.
Makeup: Renee P.

8:00 a.m.	Setup begins in the ballroom: Fabric installed Lighting installed
10:00 a.m.	Golf for 24 people—Arroyo/mountain
	Surfboards at Costa Zaul for Jed
	Tee Times Group 1: Larry, Matt, Pete, Jed Group 2: Jerry, Andrew, JJ, Chris Group 3: Tommy, Peter, Matt, Greg Group 4: Alex, Carl, Steve, open
10:30 a.m.	Spa day for Lianne and bridesmaids
	Deluxe continental breakfast set up in spa for girls

> *This beach BBQ was barefoot, so we staffed an area where guests could check their shoes. We even gave them shells with painted-on numbers as claim stubs; and at the end of the night, we provided damp hand-towels so they could wipe the sand off their feet.*

Manicure and Pedicure Schedule

	Manicure	Pedicure
10:30 a.m.	Lianne & Lisa	
11:00 a.m.		Cara & Laura
11:15 a.m.	Allyson	
11:45 a.m.		Lianne
12:00 p.m.	Cara & Jill	
12:30 p.m.		Lisa & Heather
12:45 p.m.	Leslie	
1:15 p.m.		Jill

Be specific where there's room for confusion.

12:00 p.m.	Set up rehearsal dinner
	Blue linens with green florals
	Use hotel's plain white folding chairs
	Hotel to set up microphone for speeches
4:00 p.m.	Hotel to set up 2 rows of chairs for ceremony rehearsal on South Lawn (9 chairs in each row)
4:30 p.m.	Eric and Renee to do hair and makeup for Lianne and Marie
6:00 p.m.	Wedding rehearsal: South Lawn
6:30 p.m.	Green Palms to arrange transportation to pick up guests at the hotel
7:00 p.m.	Rehearsal dinner at Vista Point
	Photographer—coverage for 2 hours
8:00 p.m.	Guests invited to be seated
8:15 p.m.	Welcome by Allyson
	Buffets ready
9:00 p.m.	Toasts begin
	During rehearsal dinner—hotel to deliver chocolate chip cookies and milk to all wedding guest rooms
10:30 p.m.	Transportation ready to take guests back to Hilton Hotel

Talk through the order with your best man or maid of honor; they should start the toasts and hand off the mike.

SATURDAY, JUNE 15

8:00 a.m.	Setup continues in ballroom
9:45 a.m.	Breakfast delivered to Allyson's hotel room
	Bagels, muffins, orange juice, coffee, and water for 7 people

Hair and makeup will take a while when you have a large bridal party, so it's nice to feed everybody.

Hair and Makeup Schedule

	Hair (Eric)	Makeup (Renee)
9:45 a.m.	Jill	Lisa
10:25 a.m.	Lisa	Jill
11:05 a.m.	Cara	Leslie
11:45 a.m.	Leslie	Cara
12:25 p.m.	Heather	Allyson
1:00 p.m.	Allyson	Heather

Hair and Makeup Schedule continued

1:40 p.m.	Renee and Eric to move to Lianne's Room	
2:00 p.m.	Diane	Marie
2:30 p.m.	Marie	Lianne
3:30 p.m.	Lianne	
4:00 p.m.		Lisa
4:30 p.m.		Diane

11:00 a.m.	Massage for Lianne and Marie Conf # R-30683 (in a double villa)

Ceremony area—South Lawn

	Begin setup of ceremony area
	Chair covers placed on hotel's white folding chairs
	Hotel to set reception tables and chairs
	10 chairs set in dinner area for wind/string orchestra
11:30 a.m.	Reception linens placed
	Ivory satin underlays and lace overlays
	Ivory satin chair covers placed on ballroom chairs
3:00 p.m.	Lianne's bouquet delivered to Lianne's room
	Bridesmaids' bouquets delivered to Allyson Pastek's room
3:15 p.m.	Seating cards set up
	Menus and place cards put on tables
	Photographer and videographer arrive in Lianne's room for getting-ready pictures
4:30 p.m.	Pictures begin with Lianne and bridesmaids
	Jed and Lianne not seeing each other for pictures before ceremony
5:00 p.m.	Pictures begin with Jed and groomsmen
	Reserved cards set up in ceremony area
	Please set umbrellas over ceremony musicians
5:30 p.m.	Family pictures—discuss locations
	Hotel to try to turn off fountain in courtyard
	Candles put in fireplace
	Ceremony area complete
6:00 p.m.	All pictures complete
	Lianne to touch up hair and makeup
	Green Palms to arrange transportation to pick up guests at the Hilton
6:15 p.m.	Prelude music begins—wind/string orchestra
6:30 p.m.	Ceremony invitation time
	Waiters to tray pass white wine, lemonade, and water
6:50 p.m.	Wedding planner to line up bridal party
7:00 p.m.	Ceremony begins

It's good to note this so that everyone knows to keep the bride and groom separate.

This was a really noisy fountain!

Unless the ceremony is taking place in a church, I always plan to start a half hour later than the actual invitation time to give guests time to get there—but once it looks like everyone is there, you can just go ahead and start.

355

(continued on next page)

Bride's Side (Left Side)—First Row
Anna Tocklas, Lisa Tocklas, Michael Tocklas, Matt Tocklas, Diane Tocklas, Louisa Tocklas, Peter Tocklas, Marie Tocklas, Larry Tocklas

Bride's Side (Left Side)—Second Row
Lisa Berman, Jill McNamarra, Cara Evans, Leslie Evert, Heather McDonald

Groom's Side (Right Side)—First Row
Kathie Pastek, Jerry Pastek

Groom's Side (Right Side)—Second Row
Andrew Pastek, Aaron James, John Salter, JT Soon

Music—"Dances with Wolves"

Jed and groomsmen to walk out on side
Best Man—Andrew
Groomsmen—Aaron, John, JT

Walking Down Aisle
Lianne's grandpa—Larry Tocklas

Lianne's mom—Marie

Jed's mom—Allyson

Bridesmaids:
Jill
Lisa
Cara
Leslie
Heather

Ring bearers:
Michael—to ring bell
Joe—to ring bell (the bride is coming)

No pillow for ring bearer

Flower girl—Louisa

Music: Concerto for Clarinet in G—Mozart
Lianne escorted by her mom, Marie

CEREMONY

Recessional

After ceremony waiters to have trays of champagne, white wine, and water on the South Lawn

> *Write this down so it doesn't get overlooked in the heat of the moment.*

Witnesses to stay behind to sign the marriage license—Jill, Heather, JT, and Cara

7:30 p.m.   Cocktail hour begins
Wedding planners to assist with seating cards
Tray passing of cocktails and hors d'oeuvres
Cocktail music playing—jazz quartet
Strings to be reset for dinner near fountain

> *If you have to pay the musicians for a certain number of hours, get as much out of them as you can.*

Vendor meal set up in Palm Court suite

8:30 p.m.   Guests invited in to dinner
Strings are playing throughout dinner—Frank Sinatra medleys
Waiters to take entrée order

> *Don't forget—you have to feed the vendors.*

8:40 p.m.   First course served
Wild asparagus risotto, Parmesan crisp, truffle oil

8:50 p.m.   Best man toast—Andrew Pastek

9:10 p.m.   Second course served
Heirloom tomatoes, feta cheese salad, olive and caper salsa, mixed greens salad

9:20 p.m.   Toast by Marie Tocklas

9:40 p.m.   Entrée Served
Pan-seared salmon, zucchini, tomato, bouillabaisse
Or
Grilled aged prime New York strip, caramelized red onion chayote

10:15 p.m.   Ballroom opens—band is playing
Cigar roller in this area

10:20 p.m.   First Dance: "Never Tear Us Apart"—INXS
Introduced as Lianne and Jed Pastek

> *This timing is unusual for my weddings. I prefer to have the couple enter and do their first dance before sitting down to dinner, but Lianne and Jed wanted all the dancing to be seamless.*

Do-Not-Play list
"Come Away with Me"—Nora Jones
"YMCA"—Village People

Midsong, emcee to invite
Parents
Bridal Party
Then all guests

Followed by big dance set

> *This is a really short Do-Not-Play list.*

10:55 p.m.   Dessert buffet opens

11:15 p.m.   Cake cutting
Lindsay and Jed to say something

11:25 p.m.   Father/daughter dance
Song: "The Way You Look Tonight"
Midsong, emcee to invite
Jed and his mom
Then all guests
Followed by dance set

1:00 a.m.   Strike begins

Emcee Never to Say Mr. and Mrs. Jed Pastek

> *Make a note of how you want to be announced, or that you don't want to be announced at all.*

SUNDAY, JUNE 16

9:00 a.m.   Hotel to deliver to all guest rooms orange juice, muffins, and fruit
Vendors to load truck

MEXICO CONTACTS

Catering: Emma 555-555-1234
Band: Jorge 555-555-1245
Officiant: Juan 555-555-1111

Hand out a wedding-party schedule at the rehearsal dinner, or when the attendants arrive. You could do three separate schedules, but if everything fits on one page, save yourself the trouble.

To Our Wedding Party

We are so excited that our wedding day has finally arrived!
Below please find a time line for the day of our wedding.
If you have any questions or concerns please call Connie at 555-1212.

FOR THE GIRLS . . .

Please look below for your hair and makeup time. Please come to my hotel suite at the Regent Hotel 15 minutes before your assigned time with your hair washed and no makeup. Ask at the front desk for my room number.

A light breakfast and lunch will be served in my hotel suite.

Hair and Makeup Schedule

	Hair	Makeup
10:00 a.m.	Jen	Paige
11:00 a.m.	Paige	Jen
12:00 p.m.	Me	Janis
1:00 p.m.	Janis	Me

2:30 p.m. Pictures will begin in my room.
Please be dressed and ready to smile.

The photographer will be taking pictures for 2 hours. We will be able to come back to the room and freshen up before the ceremony. Transportation will be provided to the church and back to the hotel.

I'm so excited!
Thanks for sharing this time with me.

Mandie

FOR THE GROOMSMEN AND DADS

12:00 p.m. Groomsmen should meet in my hotel room.

We will have lunch and watch the football game!

3:00 p.m.   Pictures begin—everyone has to be dressed and ready to take pictures for a long 2 hours (hey, I did it for a lot of you guys!)

GRANDPARENTS:

Please be in the lobby of the hotel at 4:00 p.m. to take pictures.

You can go back to the room before the ceremony.

We will all go over to the church together.

Thanks!

Ben

(continued from page 349)

There are almost always last-minute cancellations—someone will get ill, or something else unexpected will happen. Finish the seating chart knowing that you'll have to make some adjustments. I've had to rejigger tables twenty minutes before the bride walked down the aisle! I hope that won't be the case for you, but seating is definitely one of those things you need to approach with a degree of *que sera, sera*.

First off, who will sit with the bride and groom? If you're having a head table (see page 317), you'll need to determine how to fill it.

If parents get their own tables, let them decide how to fill them. In general, ask parents to seat their own friends and relatives—it will be that much less for you to do, and they know better than you which great-uncle can't be anywhere near unaccompanied females after a few drinks.

ASK MINDY

Q The seating chart is making my head spin. Is there any easy way to go about it?

A I do seating the old-fashioned way: I use paper plates to represent the tables and write guests' names on Post-it notes so we can move everything around. I try to be very modern, but I always go back to the paper plates! I like to get couples to start thinking about it when the responses start coming in. Anchor tables with the first people to respond and go from there. It's hard on brides and grooms who wait to do this until the week of the wedding, on top of all the other stress. But do know that some things will change up until right before the wedding.

If the officiant accepted your invitation to the reception (remember, you invited him or her, plus spouse), he should be seated at the head table or with the parents. If the couple is having a sweetheart table, he sits with the bridal party or with the parents.

Who Does the Seating?

Seating is one area where a wedding planner, if you have one, can't take over. She won't know which people go together, and which people need to be put on opposite sides of the room. She may, however, sit with you to help figure things out once you've begun your groupings.

The bride and groom can do the seating together, or they can seat "their" tables of friends and have the parents do theirs. Sometimes the mother of the bride takes charge of the seating, especially if she's seasoned in this department.

Once the bridal party and parents are taken care of, you can move on to more general seating. This is where your groups come into play. To make it easier to explore the possible configurations, use my trademarked Post-it and paper plate method. (See Ask Mindy, this page.) I name the plates to remember the concept behind them, such as "Joe's school buddies," "Mallory's cousins," or the slightly indelicate "leftovers" for people who don't naturally fit into a larger category. Then I start playing around with the names and tables until I solve the puzzle.

The bride and groom's table is placed centrally, at the edge of the dance floor. Members of the bridal party, parents, and close members of the family sit with them or at tables nearby. In terms of precedence, the inner ring of tables, closest to the dance floor, is choice, and the best seats are those that face the dance floor. (Keep in mind that the tables near the speakers, where the music is the loudest, are best suited to a younger contingent.) Table numbers should be in sequence so guests can find their way. If you're naming tables instead of numbering them, plan on having extra staffers armed with seating charts at the entrance to help guests find their tables.

Once you've figured out your seating, type up a list of who is sitting at each table; when the seating is final, alphabetize the list for easy reference. (Use Excel or a similar program and you'll be able to sort the list either by table number or by last name.)

Seating Cards

SEATING CARDS can either be small cards tucked into envelopes or tented cards (the name goes on the outside, the table number on the inside); you may also hear these referred to as "escort cards," though the term isn't technically correct (see page 288).

Seating cards were traditionally handled by a calligrapher, but it's perfectly fine to print them yourself. The font should reflect the style of your wedding; if in doubt, mimic the font on your invitation. A calligrapher will charge anywhere from 50 cents to $5 per card. If a stationer prints them for you, figure on 25 cents to $1.25 per card. Or, if your handwriting is decent, handwrite the cards yourself.

Should you use first names or Mr. and Mrs. on your seating cards? If you sent out formal invitations that listed the parents as Mr. and Mrs. Jerry David, then the seating cards should match the style. But if the invitation listed the parents by first name, then the seating cards should follow suit (Marsha and Jerry David).

> Creative alternatives abound if you want to make a statement with your seating cards: for a beach wedding, write names on the insides of seashells; for an outdoor wedding, on postcards tied to tree branches; or, for a winter wedding, on holiday ornaments.

Planning the Toasts

Approaches to toasting vary. Some couples prefer their toasts to be spontaneous, inviting any willing parties to stand up and say a few words off the cuff, an approach that works best at small, informal weddings. But at a large, formal affair, you're likely to wind up with a lot of dead air if you call for speeches and people aren't prepared—they'll just be too intimidated.

A Bridesmaids' Luncheon

Thank your bridesmaids for all of their efforts by organizing a special get-together a day or two before the wedding. Tradition calls for a bridesmaids' luncheon, but there's no reason you couldn't do a breakfast, afternoon tea, dinner, or an afternoon of primping and pampering at a spa. The bride (and sometimes her mother) hosts and covers expenses for the event.

Besides the bridesmaids and your mother, you'll want to invite sisters, grandmothers, the groom's mother, and the groom's sisters, geography permitting. If you're particularly close to another female relative, or if someone went above and beyond (maybe she arranged the flowers or baked the cake), you'll want to invite her as well. Invitations can be informal fill-ins or even phone calls or emails.

The groom can choose to take the groomsmen on some kind of outing as well; we're not talking another bachelor party, though! A wholesome daytime activity a day or two before the wedding is a much safer bet.

This get-together can be a good time to give attendants their gifts (see page 332 for gift ideas). Be sure to toast and thank them for standing up for you.

The rehearsal dinner, on the other hand, is a great time for spontaneity (though it's a given that the hosts will toast). Rehearsal dinner toasts tend to be a lot more colorful than wedding toasts; with that in mind, if there's a specific incident or subject you don't want mentioned, it's best to do a preempt by talking to the potential toaster ahead of time.

Tradition dictates that the best man give the first toast at the reception; the maid of honor and one or more parent may wish to toast as well. In an ideal world, the onus would be on them to prepare themselves, but it's likely they'll need a gentle reminder. About two weeks before the wedding, you might casually ask them if they've started to think about their toasts yet.

It's also time to start working on your own toast or speech. You'll want to say a few words at the rehearsal dinner and the wedding. If there's an additional welcome party, you'll want to say something there, too. Talk to each other three weeks before to decide if one or both of you will be delivering the speeches.

The bride and groom usually make their reception speech when they cut the cake, unless they're hosting, in which case they would say something earlier to welcome everyone. Though a story about their first meeting or courtship usually makes for good material, these speeches are a time to honor parents and thank them for their help, and also to thank guests for coming.

Last-Minute Disasters

You can insure your wedding to the nines, check and recheck your seating plan until the cows come home, and map out your schedule down to the minute—there's still no insurance against life. I hope none of the following situations befalls you; but in the event that you do find yourself faced with some insurmountable disaster, know that a wedding can always be rescheduled. (But most of the time, there's a workaround.)

If There's a Death in the Family

THE COURSE OF ACTION depends on how close the family member is to the couple. I always think that life celebrations should go on, but this is a personal family matter, and your family may have a different take on it. In the Jewish religion, you're not supposed to postpone any celebratory occasions. Discuss with your immediate family whether or not to postpone the wedding. If it's a parent or sibling, most often the wedding does get postponed.

If a Vendor Backs Out

THE FIRST COMMANDMENT IS: Thou shalt not panic. At moments like these, people will pull together to help out. If you have a wedding planner, she should be able to round up a sub. If not, start calling your other vendors to

Get Your Tips Out

The week before the wedding, get your gratuities in order so you won't have to fumble around for them on your wedding day. Each tip should be put in a small envelope. You often won't know the full names of the people you'll be tipping, so you'll need cash. See page 27 for tipping guidelines.

Pack for Your Honeymoon

If you're leaving for your honeymoon within a day or two of the wedding, get the packing out of the way a week before the wedding, before things get too crazy and when you'll still have the ability to concentrate on what you'll need in Bora Bora or Bangkok. If you received luggage as a wedding gift, this is the time to break it in. And don't forget to pack all that lingerie from your shower.

see if they can recommend anyone—start with the manager of your reception venue, the florist, and the caterer, as they usually have large networks. You'll find someone to fill in or a creative way to get a cake, photos, food, or flowers.

If the Bride or Groom Gets Sick

UNLESS THE BRIDE OR GROOM needs to be hospitalized, most couples are able to tough it out. I've had brides and grooms make it through the wedding with flus and sinus infections—it's amazing how the adrenaline kicks in for that seven-hour period, and then you have the whole honeymoon to recover. Of course, if the bride or groom is in the hospital, you'll have to postpone the wedding.

If Your Finances Radically Change

IF AN UNEXPECTED DIP in your or your parents' finances is suddenly making your wedding look a whole lot more extravagant, it's time to make some alterations. Don't worsen your financial straits with a wedding you can't afford; it will start off your marriage with undue stress. To lower costs, you can reduce your orders with most of your vendors up until two weeks before the wedding. Cut back on flowers, order a smaller cake, switch from a full bar to a soft bar (wine, beer, soda), and prune the number of hors d'oeuvres. You may be able to change a full dinner to a cocktail or dessert reception—it's worth asking. For music, photography, and video, you'll have to refer to the cancellation policy in your contract, but some vendors will let you out of it if they can rebook the date. If that's not enough, it may be cheaper to elope (even with the cancellation fees you'll incur). Send a clever but sincere card or email to your guests to explain; people who love you will understand.

Finalizing Plans

You might have made initial arrangements with many of your vendors but left the final details until later. It's now time to nail down playlists, finalize menu choices, decide on your ceremony readings, create photo shot lists, and make last-minute changes.

These weeks are a key time for good organization—you may find you need a spreadsheet (or reminders on your electronic calendar) to help you track who owes you an answer about the dipping sauces for the shrimp, when to send the remainder of the deposit to the videographer, and what day you need to give the final head count to the caterer.

I've highlighted key points to go over in the major areas, but be sure to check in with each and every person you're doing business with—from the officiant to the chair rental company—about two weeks before the wedding to confirm their services and discuss any changes.

The Clothes

AT A FULL-SERVICE BRIDAL SALON, the gown should arrive about eight weeks before the wedding. If you haven't heard anything from the salon, call to determine whether they're on top of the order and when they expect to receive it.

As soon as it arrives, schedule your fittings. The salon should tell you how many to schedule, but three is standard at a high-end salon. Ideally, you want to have the last fitting two weeks before the wedding so there's still a little wiggle room in case the seamstresses are running behind schedule or the gown needs an additional nip or tuck. (Don't forget to invite a bridesmaid to one of the later fittings so she can learn how to bustle the gown.)

If the bridesmaids' dresses were ordered through a bridal salon, they should arrive around the same time as the gown. You or the maid of honor should check in to make sure that the dresses are on schedule and that the bridesmaids have allowed time for alterations. You should also be finalizing their accessories during these weeks.

ASK MINDY

Q I am worried that my fiancé is going to get tanked at the wedding. We both want to have fun, but I don't want him to make a mockery of this day. I've even thought of sneaking into the groomsmen's area and watering down their alcohol. What would you do?

A I let the groom have a beer before the ceremony if he wants one—it really does take the edge off the anxiety or excitement. But if you're really worried about it, just be up front. Assure him that there will be plenty of time for drinking, but tell him that you don't want him to pass out on the way to the altar—or to the honeymoon suite!

Ultimately, you can only be responsible for yourself. You can voice concerns, but he's an adult. You don't want to start fighting right before the wedding—you want to start your marriage with compromise.

If you haven't placed orders for the groom and groomsmen's formalwear rentals yet, do it pronto. Make sure that the groom and groomsmen have been fitted or have sent in measurements—the rental shop should have them at least four to six weeks before the wedding. You'll also need to coordinate accessories and buy any special shirts, ties, cufflinks, shoes, or socks.

The Flowers

IF YOU HAVEN'T ALREADY SEEN samples of your centerpieces, don't be alarmed; some florists prefer to do samples and setups closer to the wedding date, when they can work with flowers that are actually available. If you've already approved your setup, check in with the florist two weeks before the wedding. Find out which flowers he's likely to get and review your contract's details. Let the florist know of any changes—maybe you've added two tables and need two more centerpieces, or one of your groomsmen dropped out and you need one less boutonnière. Keep in mind that florists place their orders about two weeks before the event; try to notify them of any changes before then.

The Music

IT'S LIKELY YOU WON'T have had further contact with your band or deejay after having booked them. Touch base with your bandleader or DJ to remind him of your date, and set up a meeting four to six weeks prior to the wedding.

Meanwhile, add your musical preferences into your wedding-day schedule (see pages 348–357, for more detail). At your meeting, go over your choices and find out what the band or DJ needs in terms of equipment and when they need access to the venue. Even if it's already in the contract, make sure you review attire.

Photography and Videography

SET UP YOUR MEETING(S) about a month before the wedding. Review the details of the contract and go over timing and setup. Bring your preliminary wedding-day schedule (they may suggest changes) and your shot list and/or interview list. Find out the best means—email or phone—to convey updates and changes.

The Food

YOU SHOULD ATTEND a tasting about six to eight weeks before the wedding. Once you've finalized the menu, update the contract to reflect it. Together with the caterer, review the contract and make sure you're both clear on who's bringing what—the china, the chairs, the linens, etc.

Send the caterer a detailed preliminary schedule, then review it together and make changes as needed.

The Officiant

YOU'VE PROBABLY HAD some ongoing contact with your officiant; you may be working according to his schedule, but if not, get in touch two months before the wedding.

You should be choosing the readings and your music, writing your vows (if you're not going with standard ones), and discussing any personal touches you'd like to add to the ceremony. If you haven't already done so, ask to see the script the officiant plans to use for your ceremony. (This request might not be appropriate for a highly religious wedding, but if the officiant has leeway in his wording, make sure you're in accord with what is being said.) The most sensitive areas for couples generally involve gender roles (remember love, honor, and obey?) and the descriptions of a supreme being.

Paper Goods

IF YOU'RE HAVING any paper goods custom-made (other than the invitation, which already went out, of course), you'll need to settle on styles and place your order about eight weeks before the wedding. If your order includes items like seating cards and place cards, find out when you need to supply your stationer with a list of your guests' names. (Same goes if you're working with a calligrapher.) And don't forget to order any other peripheral goods like cocktail napkins or favor bags.

Q I have two aunts who hate each other with a passion. The story is too long and involved for me to even begin to explain, but let's just say one once accused the other of trying to poison her. They haven't seen each other in ten years and they're both coming to the wedding. Is there anything I can do to make sure we avoid some kind of scene?

A Obviously, you want to make sure they're not seated at the same table. But it might also be nice to open a dialogue before the wedding—you certainly wouldn't want their mutual presence to come as a surprise. Try this: "Aunt Sue, I want you to know that Aunt Kay is going to be there, and that I hope that there won't be any issues that day. Is there anything I can do to make things more comfortable for both of you?" The fact that you had to make that call might actually embarrass them into behaving.

Don't assign people to babysit your aunts—it's not a fair expectation. You can have someone subtly look in on them every once in a while, but that's about it.

Moving the Dress

When your alterations are done, a bridal salon will give your gown a final steaming, stuff it with tissue, and bag it so that it's ready to travel. Both the bodice and the sleeves should be stuffed with a form or tissue so they retain their shape. If you have several weeks until the wedding, take the dress out of the bag and hang it up to prevent wrinkles, letting down the train so it doesn't crease. If you got the alterations done by someone who did not stuff the dress, take it to a good dry cleaner to be steamed and prepped for the trip.

If you're traveling by plane to your wedding, take the dress on board with you. Never put it in checked luggage. Never ship it ahead. Both options are too risky—you don't want to be separated from your dress before the wedding. Ask the gate attendant if you can be seated next to an empty seat, or try to make arrangements with the airline to hang the dress in the first-class cabin.

Although it sounds like an extreme extravagance, many gown experts advise buying an extra seat on the plane for your dress, especially if it's a big ballgown. That way, you're assured of a space for it in transit, and the cost is much lower than having to replace a gown gone missing.

The Rehearsal

You may be wondering why ceremonies require rehearsals. True, you're not putting on a Broadway show, but there are musical cues to be heeded, lines to be learned, and a sequence of events to be followed. It's important that all members of the wedding party know what to expect and what is expected of them. Aside from all that, the main purpose of the rehearsal is to make sure that people aren't rushing around, harried and confused, during the actual ceremony. You want things to feel peaceful, and to flow. I once skipped a rehearsal, and everyone felt uneasy and unprepared.

If the rehearsal is in a house of worship, dress accordingly. That typically means no bare shoulders and no shorts. For rehearsals in other places, you can dress any way you like, even in tank tops and flip-flops. Most people go straight from the rehearsal to their rehearsal dinner, so they'll be dressed for that.

PACK YOUR EMERGENCY KIT

Touch-up and emergency kit in one, this troubleshooting stash has saved many a day—I bring one to every wedding. I do. Over the years, I've found that some items have unexpected uses: in a pinch, hairspray can make a sticky zipper glide, and baby powder is the best remedy for a splash of red wine on a white gown. You can buy most of the components at a drugstore, or you can purchase ready-made kits.

A hanging toiletry bag or large makeup bag with clear compartments makes an ideal home for your emergency provisions. No need to dismantle it after the wedding—you'll find that many of these items come in handy on your honeymoon, too.

You can stash your touch-up kit in a hotel room, the ladies' room, or wherever you are getting dressed—on the premises—for the wedding. Or ask your mother or maid of honor to keep track of it for you. (Ask your mom or best friend to keep an eye on you too, and let you know if your mascara is running, you have lipstick on your teeth, or just need a makeup refresher.)

HERS . . .

- Makeup, including powder, blotting papers, mattifying lotion for shine, lipstick, concealer, and mascara
- Baby wipes and Q-tips to remove smudges
- Band-Aids (clear)
- Breath mints and toothpicks
- Clear nail polish to repair runs in your stockings; nail polish in case yours chips
- Crochet hook (if there are buttons or loop closures on your gown or the bridesmaids' dresses)
- Deodorant
- Extra pads for shoes
- Extra pair of hosiery
- Fragrance
- Hairpins and an elastic to pull your hair back—just in case
- Hairspray and gel, comb or brush
- Lint brush or travel-size lint roller
- Lip balm
- Manicure set, including an emery board, nail scissors, and a nail clipper
- Moisturizer and hand cream
- Moleskin for uncomfortable shoes
- Mylanta or other antacid
- Redness-relief eyedrops
- Six safety pins in small and large sizes (for reattaching a strap or holding together an usher's waistband)
- Sewing kit
- Small pair of scissors
- Straws for sipping while you prep without messing up your lipstick
- Super-glue for reattaching beads or a heel
- Tampons
- Three strips of double-sided fabric tape for fallen hems and holding bra straps in place
- Tissues to remove lipstick from your cheeks
- Toothbrush and toothpaste
- Tweezers
- Two Oxiclean stain removal wipes
- Tylenol or Advil
- White chalk or baby powder—in case you get lipstick on your wedding dress or on his collar

. . . AND HIS

- Breath mints
- Cologne
- Comb
- Dental floss
- Extra pair of black dress socks (or whatever color socks the groomsmen are wearing)
- Extra pair of black shoelaces
- Hair gel
- Handkerchief
- Lip balm
- Razor
- Shaving cream
- Toothbrush and toothpaste

If you've hired a hairstylist and makeup artist for the bridal party, enlarge the hair and makeup schedule and put it somewhere visible in the dressing room (you can tape it to the mirror) for the stylists and the bridesmaids to check throughout the day. It will help everyone stay on track.

Who runs the rehearsal? If the ceremony is taking place in a house of worship, the church's or temple's wedding coordinator will take charge; otherwise, the wedding planner, if you have one, runs the rehearsal.

If you're not working with a planner, there are several options. If the officiant is able to attend the rehearsal, he will run things. If not, an involved catering manager might step up to the task. And barring that, you'll have to assign someone the job. I highly recommend that you not try to do this yourself—that's a recipe for a heart attack.

All members of the wedding party and anyone who's doing a reading or participating in any way should attend the rehearsal. If there's an opportunity to practice readings, it's helpful, but not a must. If the sound system is set up, anyone singing or playing music should practice; or they should arrive at the ceremony early to practice with the ceremony musicians. If you have ring bearers, flower girls, or other children in the wedding party, their parents should attend. And invite both your parents and the groom's.

The length of the rehearsal depends on who is running it. When I run a rehearsal, it's thirty minutes, no more. But I've been to church rehearsals that lasted more than an hour. The running time hinges on the practices of the church, the complexity of the service, and the size of the wedding party.

What Happens at the Rehearsal?

BECAUSE IT WOULD BE too costly to bring in the musicians, most rehearsals are conducted without music—though in churches, organists will sometimes join in.

Once everyone has arrived, you'll start going through paces and places. Instead of doing a ceremony run-through in order, start by showing people where to stand at the top of the aisle—that way, they'll understand their destination. (If space or time restrictions prevent you from holding the rehearsal at the ceremony site, set up chairs to designate an improvised aisle.) From there, practice the recessional. Then, start from the beginning and have everyone walk down the aisle in order. If any key players are still unsure what to do, you can practice again.

Have a complete wedding day schedule ready to hand out to the wedding party. The schedule should cover where and when they need to show up for hair and makeup, photos, and the ceremony, and should also give transportation details.

The rehearsal is a good time to give gifts to your attendants, since it's a little more intimate than the rehearsal

ASK MINDY

Q What do I do about my RSVP stragglers? Is it rude to call them up and let them know I need an answer? And if I still haven't heard, at what point is it safe to assume they're not coming?

A I don't think it's rude to call stragglers the day after the response period ends. Nine times out of ten they'll either tell you "I didn't get it" (sometimes out of embarrassment) or apologize. If they're not calling back after you've left two or three messages, assume they're not coming. They're the ones who will be embarrassed if they show up and there's no place for them.

If they do show up, the head of catering will tell you and you'll have to deal with it. It's a hassle, but you'll figure it out. Be gracious and find a seat for them. They'll be much more uncomfortable than you.

dinner. Some brides and grooms like to exchange their gifts for each other at the rehearsal as well.

If there's a wedding planner, make sure that everyone in the wedding party is introduced to her and given her cell phone number, email address, or pertinent contact information. If you're not working with a planner, have a designated contact for last-minute emergencies, and put her information on the wedding day schedule.

Spending the Night Apart

Everyone knows that couples are supposed to spend the night before their wedding apart—to prevent hanky-panky, of course! But really, does it still make sense, especially for couples who have been living together for two years prior to the wedding?

I think so. Spending the night apart won't restore anyone's virginity, but it will add an element of mystery and anticipation to the wedding day. And to the wedding night, too. There's a certain excitement that builds as the bride and groom anticipate laying eyes on each other for the first time in their wedding garb.

The time apart also allows the bride to hang out with her girlfriends, relax in the bathtub, and take care of any last-minute packing. The groom can enjoy bonding time with his friends and get organized for the next day.

But if you can't bear not to sleep in each other's arms the night before your wedding, that's okay, too. Do whatever will leave you feeling your best when you wake up on your big day. ♦

CHAPTER TWENTY-FIVE

Getting Ready

LET THE COUNTDOWN BEGIN . . .

After so many months of anticipation, it's *finally* time to start prepping and primping for the walk down the aisle—a life event unlike any other. And the way you approach getting ready for the wedding will affect how you look, feel, and act the rest of the day. First of all, try to get a good night's sleep the night before—it really can be done, I promise.

(The more organized you are, the easier it will be—you won't be panicking about all that is left to be done.) If you're getting married away from home, bring something along to soothe your nerves and make your hotel room more comfortable—a candle, a photograph, or a favorite book from childhood. However, this is not the time to try taking sleeping pills for the first time. Neither is it a good idea to think that an

extra nightcap might help you sleep better. A hangover is *not* the right condition in which to approach a lifetime together with the person you love best.

Remember to set the alarm and/or request a wake-up call; on this, of all days, you don't want to get a late start.

If you've got a regular morning routine, stick to it. So, if you run, do a series of yoga postures, or meditate every morning, don't

change things around on the day of your wedding.

You can often book a yoga or Pilates instructor for a private session through your hotel's health club. Some couples like to do this together, and some brides like to invite the bridal party for a group class. A workout is a great way to both energize and calm you. But if you haven't touched a free weight in four years, this is not the moment to suddenly decide to do six sets of arm curls—nobody needs a last-minute injury.

Although a massage sounds like the perfect antidote to pre-wedding jitters, it's often a waste of money. Brides and grooms are filled with too much anticipation about the day ahead to relax and enjoy it; it's much more effective to get a massage the day before.

> Feeling sentimental? (I hope so!) Send your beloved a love letter the morning of the wedding; have it hand-delivered by the maid of honor, the best man, or the wedding planner.

If the bridal party is getting made up and dressed together at midday, think ahead and order lunch for everyone, including the hairstylist and makeup artist. (The groom should order food to be sent to the guys if they're getting ready together.) A simple platter of sandwiches and wraps is a good choice, as is a garden salad. Have non-messy snacks like raw veggies and pretzels on hand. Simple cookies (oatmeal-raisin or sugar) satisfy a sweet tooth without risking a mess. It's really important to stay hydrated, so drink lots of water, and have a selection of soft drinks available in the room.

This should go without saying, but just in case: Eat *before* donning your wedding gown. And keep food and beverages far away from wedding clothing hanging in different parts of the room. Last but not least: Have plenty of drinking straws on hand to help bridesmaids keep their lipstick picture-perfect.

Eating Before the Wedding

You may feel nervous, so be kind to your stomach by eating a low-fat, nongreasy breakfast. Cereal, yogurt, or scrambled eggs and toast are all good choices. Stay away from juice, which is high in acid and can irritate a butterfly-laden stomach. If you need your caffeine in the morning, one or two cups of coffee or tea is fine, but more than that could also upset your stomach or make you jittery.

How much to eat before the wedding will depend on what time you're getting married. In general, though, eat small meals every three hours to keep your energy up without getting bloated. Stay away from greasy foods (that means no burgers and fries), and from foods that can linger on your breath, like garlic and tuna fish. Also steer clear of foods that cause bloating and gas, such as onions, cauliflower, and broccoli.

In-Between Time

If you've followed my advice thus far, you'll be lucky enough to have a little downtime on your wedding day—while the bridesmaids are in hair and makeup, or while you're sitting with your hair in hot rollers. Though there's likely to be a lot of buzz around you, take advantage of every free minute to ground yourself. (It's a shame we can't tack a few extra hours onto the day just for that purpose.) I think it's really important to try to have some contemplative moments in the time leading up to the wedding—and if you've got to do that with six bridesmaids, a hairstylist, and a makeup artist around you, so be it.

Another great thing to do with any downtime is to run through your vows. As I've said, I don't believe you need to memorize your vows and I think it's perfectly fine to have a cheat sheet, but practicing aloud (or just reading through the text a few times) will definitely help your delivery.

Dressing Room Confidential

Many brides indulge in loads of girl-bonding time before the wedding by getting their hair and makeup done with their bridesmaids. You can also invite your mother and the flower girl to get prettified, and if you have a close relationship to the mother of the groom, it's great to include her as well. But perhaps you know you're going to need alone time to steady your nerves; if that's the case, just be up front about it and arrange to get ready alone or with the person who always calms and reassures you—your maid of honor, your mother, your sister, whomever.

For same-sex couples, another question arises: Will you be seeing each other in your wedding best before the big moment? If so, you might decide to get festive and have everyone primp together. Should you prefer to take some space for yourselves on this important day, you'll need to stake out separate dressing areas, and brides should work out a hair-and-makeup schedule that leaves you both a comfortable time cushion. (I recommend this approach: There's nothing like walking down the aisle and seeing your beloved in their wedding-day finest for the very first time.) If your budget allows, hire two separate hair and makeup teams to make sure no one gets shortchanged.

If your makeup artist and hairstylist are coming to you, you want a room with good lighting; natural light is preferable. There should also be plenty of mirrors, at least one of which should be full-length. If you're getting your makeup done in a hotel, ask if they can send barstools to the room for the girls to sit on while getting their hair and makeup done. The hairstylist and makeup artist will need tables for laying out their tools, and you should have a steamer, an iron, and an ironing board on hand for dress touch-ups.

Bring some of your favorite music to play while you're in the room—you might be there a while. It's not unusual for bridesmaids to be asked to show up four or even five hours before the wedding. It may strike some as excessive, but it takes a long time to do everyone's hair and makeup and get them all dressed (especially if there are more than four bridesmaids).

Make sure you have instructions from the hairstylist on what condition everyone's hair should be in when they arrive—some will ask for clean, wet hair, and others for dry, unwashed hair (second-day hair makes for a better updo). If a makeup artist will be doing their makeup, the bridesmaids should come with clean faces. Otherwise, they may want to do their makeup before they come to the room.

You should all be wearing something comfy that can be slipped off without messing up hair or makeup. That means no shirts that need to be pulled over the head. Best bets: a robe, a zip-front hoodie and sweatpants, or a button-front shirt and jeans.

Lastly, you'll need to keep things moving. The bride shouldn't be stressing out about the time, but someone should be in charge of making sure the hair, makeup, photography, and departure schedule is maintained. If there's a wedding planner, she'll assume this responsibility. Sometimes the head of catering can fulfill this role. But if not, designate the most organized bridesmaid to be the keeper of the clock.

Prepping the Dress

WHEN YOU GET TO the changing room, all dresses should be taken out of their garment bags and hung up. Some fabrics will melt if they're ironed, and many embellishments shouldn't be ironed or steamed, so get care instructions from the store or alterations staff when you pick up the wedding dress and bridesmaids' dresses.

If the bridesmaids' dresses are looking wrinkled or flat, hang them in the bathroom and run a hot shower for ten minutes with the bathroom door closed; turn off the shower and leave the dresses hanging for another fifteen minutes. The steam should get rid of most of the wrinkles. Next, take a clean white towel and gently rub it down the length of the dresses to smooth out the fabric.

If there are still wrinkles, it's okay to touch up the dresses with a handheld steamer.

The wedding gown is higher maintenance, particularly if it's white or ivory, and particularly if it's satin. If the bodice and sleeves were stuffed properly when you had your alterations done, it should have traveled fairly well. Hang it high enough so that the skirt doesn't touch the floor. Most closet rails aren't high enough to do the trick, but often the door of an armoire, a door frame, or a window frame will work. (If your dress is heavy, be cautious about hanging it from a curtain rod—you don't want the rod, dusty curtains, and your dress to end up in a tangle on the floor.)

One of the biggest challenges with a white dress is keeping it pristine till the wedding. Inspect the area where you're going to hang the dress and wipe off any dirt or dust with a towel. Also lay a white towel on the floor underneath the dress to keep the hem clean. Hang up the veil at the same time; everyone tends to forget that veils wrinkle, too.

Many higher-end hotels have laundry service staff experienced in steaming wedding dresses. Make arrangements in advance, though—experienced steamers don't work 24-7. If there isn't a professional service around, apply the same steaming procedures described for the bridesmaids' dresses, taking care to put a white towel on the floor beneath the dress wherever you hang it.

Hair and Makeup

If you're springing for professional hair and makeup on your wedding day and have the budget, it's a wonderful gesture to let the bridesmaids and mothers get in on the action. If you have more than four bridesmaids, you may need to hire more than one hairstylist and makeup artist. If you need to streamline the process, limit the makeup to eyes and lips for bridesmaids, asking them to do their own foundation and cheeks. For a more detailed look at hair and makeup, see chapter 19, "Just Gorgeous."

If the same hair and makeup people will be working on you and your bridesmaids, schedule yourself right in the middle. You don't want to be first, because you want to look as fresh as possible, but you don't want to risk getting shortchanged at the end. Arrange to have your hair done before your makeup. Hair usually takes longer, and you want the makeup to look fresh for photos. (Plus, exposing your makeup to a hair dryer isn't a great idea.) If your hair is being set, the makeup artist can begin your makeup while the rollers are in.

Limit your beautification procedures on the wedding day to hair and makeup. Do not try a self-tanner the same day. Do not try a new facial mask containing some miracle acid. Never have a facial the day of the wedding. I don't even recommend getting your manicure and pedicure that day—brides think they're going to have perfect nails by doing them the day of, but more often than not, they don't let them dry completely, and the polish gets ruined.

Getting Dressed

When your hair and makeup are done and you're ready to put on your dress, stop—and go to the bathroom. Then, with all of the necessary undergarments on but no shoes—the heel might catch on delicate lace or tulle at the hem—have someone stand up the dress and hold it open so that there's a clear view of the floor. Then step into it. If the dress must go over your head, wear a mesh makeup protector hood (available at beauty supply stores) to prevent your makeup from rubbing off on

If the hairdresser and makeup artist are coming to you, schedule them to arrive thirty minutes earlier than the bridesmaids. This gives them time to create stations and set up their tools and equipment.

Wedding Day Don'ts

You can't plan for everything that happens on your wedding day (and that's half the fun), but some things *are* always under your control. Take my advice and steer clear of these wedding day don'ts:

Don't drink too much. During the preparations, many bridal parties like to break out the bubbly, but don't have more than half a glass before the ceremony. If you imbibe before your photos, it's going to show in your face, and you're not going to be happy with your portraits. And you're going to be in the spotlight for the remainder of the event, so you need to have your wits about you.

Don't take recreational drugs or pharmaceutical drugs you don't normally take to "steady your nerves." This is such a bad idea for so many reasons. Obviously, a wedding is really not the time for recreational drugs. But it's become disturbingly common for brides to dip into a bridesmaid's antianxiety prescription at the last minute, on a whim. First of all, you never know how you're going to react to someone else's prescription. Second, when your emotions are already running high, there's really no telling what kind of effect even a low dose of an unfamiliar drug could have. And last, think of the toasts—mixing pharmaceuticals and alcohol is a huge no-no.

Don't smoke in your wedding dress before the ceremony. You don't want to risk a burn on your gown, and you don't want to smell like cigarette smoke when hugging your guests.

Don't forget to take any regular medications, including your birth control pill (it's easy to forget quotidian matters on such an out-of-the-ordinary day).

Don't go ballistic and start yelling at everyone if you're stressed out or if something wasn't done exactly to your specifications. That's all anyone will remember when the day is over.

Don't fight with your fiancé. Yes, sometimes we take out our anxiety on those closest to us. But on a day that's already so fraught with emotion—and one that you are going to remember forever—I recommend closing the lines of communication if that's what it takes for you to keep your wits about you. (I know what I'm saying will get me in trouble with just about every psychiatrist there is, but I do think there are times and places for airing things out. Your wedding is not one of them!)

Don't skip meals and don't forget to drink water. This is not the way to look thinner in your wedding photos, and you need to eat and stay hydrated so that you won't faint, get a headache, or become inordinately irritable. You may not have a chance to eat during the reception, so you want to leave for the ceremony in top form.

the fabric. Now you can put on your shoes, though you might need help if they have buckles.

You'll need someone to zip, button, or lace you into the wedding dress. If there are lingerie straps for hanging it, have your helper make sure those are tucked well inside the armholes. If they keep reappearing, cut them off.

In order to avoid wrinkles, some people will advise you not to sit down once the dress is on, but if you're going to get nervous standing around, it's better to sit. Sit on a stool rather than a chair, and arrange your skirt to minimize the damage.

Attaching the Veil

IF YOU'RE ABLE to have your hairstylist on-site, he'll pin on your veil and touch up your hair at the last minute. If you're going to a salon to have your hair done, the hairstylist will attach your veil there.

Once the veil is pinned in place, it should feel secure, but shouldn't be digging into your scalp. Some brides pay the hairstylist to stay until *after* the ceremony to take out the veil properly and touch up or change their hair for the reception, but that's understandably not within everyone's means. If your hairstylist won't be with you after the ceremony, get instructions on how to remove the veil and rearrange your hair if necessary. Have your maid of honor or another helper with you when you're getting instructions. Once the veil and comb are secured, it's not always obvious how to remove them without wrecking the hairstyle. (More than one bridesmaid has had to cut a veil out of the bride's hair.)

Pre-wedding Photos

Some of the prettiest photos come out of the pre-wedding primping. Plan to have the photographer come to the dressing room while you are putting on your gown (or, if you can afford it, an hour earlier to capture you and the bridal party hanging out and getting your hair and makeup done). Don't forget to have the photographer pay a visit to the groom's headquarters to get equivalent shots of the guys.

The tradition of the bride and groom not seeing each other before the wedding is deeply ingrained in our culture. But there's really not anything behind the super-

stition that applies today. Although there are multiple theories about its origins, the most likely is that it dates back to the days of arranged marriages, when the groom never saw the bride until they were both at the altar. Families didn't want the groom messing up a perfectly good arrangement based on the bride's looks.

This is one area where I urge couples to cast superstitions aside and get photos out of the way before the ceremony. Often the light will be better. You'll have more time with the photographer, which leads to better pictures. And you can use the time after the ceremony to spend some quiet moments alone or mingle with your guests at the cocktail hour.

If you decide it's important to you to wait until the ceremony to see each other, at least get the individual portraits done beforehand, along with the photos of the bride and groom with their separate wedding parties.

Still not convinced? Ask a couple who has done it. Every one of my couples who took photos before the ceremony—even the ones who fought the idea—has thanked me afterward.

Even when the bride and groom plan to see each other before the ceremony, there should be a special moment for what's called the "reveal" in wedding planner lingo. Someone should be helping to time things so you don't just see each other at some unplanned moment, or when you aren't completely ready yet. The reveal is a wonderfully emotional moment. (Translation: You'll want to make sure the photographer is there to capture it.)

Walking in a Wedding Gown

Walking in a floor-length wedding gown takes a bit of practice, especially if a train or stairs are involved.

Stand up straight with your shoulders back so the gown hangs correctly. Keep your head up; lower your head, and the gown will hang longer in front, making you more likely to trip. If there's a train, do not attempt to back up! On stairs, or anytime you need to look down, lift the skirt a few inches off the floor, holding it lightly at the sides. (Don't clench the fabric in your fists; you don't want to leave a rosette of wrinkles on the sides.)

Arrive on Time

In the interest of looking perfect, brides sometimes ignore the clock. But you really ought to get to the church on time. For a service in a house of worship, that means planning to arrive thirty minutes before the time on the invitation (assuming you're already dressed). The groom and his groomsmen should arrive forty-five minutes early to see that everything is set up correctly and so that ushers are in place to seat guests.

|||||||||||||||||||||||||||||||||||||||||||||||||||||||||||||||||||||||||||||||||||||||||||||||||||||

WHAT TO BRING WITH YOU

Make sure you've got all of the items you need from the list below. Put a family member, a member of the bridal party, or the wedding planner in charge of bringing them. Ask the same person to collect anything that needs returning afterward.

TO THE CEREMONY...

- [ ] Wedding-day emergency kit (contents listed on page 360)
- [ ] Copy of the vows
- [ ] Programs
- [ ] Wedding rings
- [ ] Ring bearer's pillow
- [ ] Marriage license. The officiant will mail it in, so stamp the envelope and enclose a check to cover extra copies. (See chapter 12, "Making It Legal.")
- [ ] Guest book and pen
- [ ] Unity candle
- [ ] Chalice, goblets, or kiddush cup
- [ ] Glass to break (Jewish ceremony)
- [ ] Yarmulkes (Jewish ceremony)
- [ ] Ketubah (Jewish ceremony)
- [ ] Handkerchief (for bride)
- [ ] Anything that will be handed out to guests, such as bells or fans

- [ ] Family Bible
- [ ] Extra copy of shot list for photographer
- [ ] Schedule of events
- [ ] Boutonnieres
- [ ] Bouquets
- [ ] Corsages

TO THE RECEPTION...

- [ ] Wedding-day emergency kit
- [ ] Guest book and pen
- [ ] Box for gift envelopes
- [ ] Gratuities for vendors (already in envelopes)
- [ ] Tossing garter
- [ ] Tossing bouquet
- [ ] Cake-cutting knife
- [ ] Toasting glasses
- [ ] Challah knife and challah cover (Jewish ceremony)

- [ ] Any items such as family photos that you're using to personalize the space
- [ ] Personalized cocktail napkins
- [ ] Favors
- [ ] Seating cards
- [ ] Table numbers
- [ ] Place cards
- [ ] Menus
- [ ] Extra copies of shot list for photographer and "Do-Not-Play" list for musicians or DJ
- [ ] Extra copies of the schedule of events (for vendors)
- [ ] Extra pair of shoes for the bride to put under her chair
- [ ] Amenities for the restrooms such as breath mints, deodorant, safety pins
- [ ] A copy of any DVD or video you're showing
- [ ] Extra CD of the first-dance song
- [ ] MP3 player if you're providing music

Granted, Jewish ceremonies often start twenty minutes late, and in some cultures weddings are *expected* to start late. At a hotel or off-site wedding, the ceremony can start up to half an hour late without anyone getting too annoyed, but here are three prime reasons that the wedding should start within ten minutes of the appointed time:

- As a courtesy to your guests. They've gone to great lengths to get to your wedding. It's rude to keep them waiting.

- You could lose out on part of your service. In a Catholic church, you'll miss your mass if you're late.

■ You'll run into overtime charges from vendors. If everything starts an hour late, you're likely to face overtime for everyone from the photographer to the band. When you hire a DJ for four hours and ask him to show up at 8 p.m., his clock runs out at midnight, no matter what time he starts spinning music. If there's a short window for breakdown, you may also incur late fees on rentals. Overtime charges can bust a budget, especially one that's already maxed out.

Last-Minute Details

Always, always go to the bathroom one last time before the ceremony. You don't want to be standing in front of all those people at one of the most important moments of your life with your mind entirely preoccupied by how badly you need to pee.

Toilets—especially toilet stalls—and wedding gowns don't make for the friendliest of bedfellows. For brides who aren't overly modest, the best tactic is to have one or two bridesmaids hold the skirt up high while you relieve yourself. If the gown is very, very simple, you can probably manage things yourself. But this is just one of those times when you're going to have to throw your inhibitions out the window.

One last thing: Before your walk down the aisle, move your engagement ring to your right hand so that the groom can slip the wedding band onto your ring finger without special maneuvering. An application of hand cream will help it slide on without a hitch (but remove your engagement ring first so you don't leave a film on the stone and dull its sparkle).

Now that you've preened and primped within an inch of your life, there's nothing left to do but get out there and make this happen. One of my favorite grooms sent his bride flowers the morning of their wedding with the following words, which I think will aptly lead us into the next chapter: "Let's get married, baby!" ◆

CHAPTER TWENTY-SIX

Here Comes The Bride

FROM "I DO" TO "WE DID IT!"

You've gotten to the church, temple, hotel, or tent on time. You are strapped into your dress, your makeup is picture-perfect, and you are *R-E-A-D-Y.* You're nervous, excited, over the moon. Everything is etched in sharp detail, or it's all a big blur. Whatever you're feeling, you can be pretty sure that your wedding is going to be an out-of-body experience.

Before you start the walk down the aisle, close your eyes and take a few deep breaths. Then try to be in the moment—it will all be over in a flash. Take in the presence of all your loved ones and the beautiful scene around you. And let the details fade away. Try not to worry about whether the florist remembered to add that one last centerpiece or how the icing on the cake is holding up. Focus on the reason you're here: to pledge your commitment to the person you love, for the rest of your life.

Devise an advance strategy for retaining your calm. Maybe it's as simple as repeating a mantra like "Serenity and Grace." Maybe it's looking into the eyes of your spouse-to-be.

Mentally walking through the minutiae of your wedding day in advance will help you clear your mind of clutter in the moment. Of course, you will have physically walked through some of the paces at your rehearsal, which should also help steady your nerves.

Above all, know that there's really no way for you to mess up your own wedding. Sure, people forget vows, catch their heel on the aisle runner, or bicker with their mothers in the changing rooms. But what of it? I can honestly say that I've never seen a failed wedding. Even true disasters have their redeeming qualities—usually, a good dose of humor.

THE CEREMONY

The Walk Down the Aisle

Every ceremony, regardless of religion or culture, has an element of performance about it. And since we're talking choreography, I think you just can't be too detailed. Here's the lowdown on all those little moments nobody really tells you about. . . .

First of all, let's get into some sticky territory: the veil and your lips. You don't want them connecting. A matte or semi-matte lipstick will be less gooey than a gloss and less likely to adhere to the veil. A lipstick sealer can also help, but so can some good old-fashioned blotting.

If your veil has an extra-long blusher that covers the hands, carry the bouquet under the veil to create a buffer zone. With a mantilla veil, the bride traditionally carries her flowers under the veil—it gives the bouquet a romantic, soft-focus look.

One of the biggest mistakes brides make is carrying the bouquet too high, positioning the elbows at an odd angle and cutting off the line of the waist. The bouquet should be carried down at hip height, rather than at the waist. Practice in the mirror ahead of time so you can choose the most flattering placement. One exception: A very small bouquet, like a posy, will get lost at the hips and should be carried a bit higher, right around the belly button.

When you walk down the aisle, take slow, measured paces. Practice the walk ahead of time in your wedding gown. Forget the "step, together, step" routine—unflatteringly nicknamed the "hesitation step"—you may have seen in movies. It was designed to help slow the pace, but it looks comic and stilted. Instead, just focus on taking your time. This is your moment, so draw it out. Everyone has been waiting to see the beautiful bride—especially the groom!—so give them time to get a good look.

Whoever is walking you down the aisle will stop before he reaches the groom (the first row of chairs is a good visual marker); if you're wearing a veil with a blusher, he'll lift it to give you a kiss, then replace it. Then you step into place beside the groom.

Once you reach the altar or chuppah, you'll hand your bouquet to your maid of honor. If the dress has a train, this is the point when she also takes charge of arranging it behind you. (Since she'll need her hands free if she's on train duty, the maid of honor should hand your bouquet and her own flowers to another bridesmaid for safekeeping.)

The key thing to remember about wearing a train is that you cannot step backward in it or you'll get tripped up by the fabric. Wait for your maid of honor to lift up the train before going anywhere.

At the Altar

So you get to the altar. And surprise, surprise, there's the groom. You give each other a peck on the cheek, or join hands for a moment. And then what happens, while you stand there and the minister, rabbi, or whoever is marrying you begins to speak?

Well, it's sort of different for everyone. Some brides are absolutely blissed out, so overjoyed that they almost don't have room for conscious thought. Some describe a sense of tunnel vision—they are listening to the ceremony but also feel as if they're floating above it. Some are keenly aware that every eye in the place is fixed on them, and are wondering whether their veil is starting to slide to the right or where to put their hands. The lucky,

The What-Ifs

I know you're a worrier—these days, who isn't? So let's just tackle your stress head-on by looking at some of the things that can go wrong at the ceremony (and in the hours before), and what you can do about them. Be forewarned: Someone will forget something. There have been grooms who forgot to pick up their boutonnieres (no matter that the bride left them at the front desk of his hotel), brides who forgot their shoes or their handwritten vows, seamstresses who forgot to bustle the wedding gown, and makeup artists who forgot to show up.

None of these situations put a damper on the wedding. The bride was the only one who noticed the lack of boutonnieres; someone was dispatched to the bride's home for the shoes; the bride who forgot her vows spoke from her heart; safety pins were employed to create a rudimentary bustle; and we called a local salon to find a last-minute replacement for the makeup artist.

The officiant doesn't show. See if any of the guests (judge, Universal Life Church minister) are qualified to preside at the wedding. If the wedding is at a hotel or place with multiple weddings that day, approach the officiant at one of the other weddings to ask if he can help you out. To cut down on problems, remember to confirm with the officiant a day or two before the wedding.

The ring gets lost. First, never entrust a child with the real ring. Leave that to the best man, and give the ring bearer a faux ring. If the ring simply vanishes, ask to borrow a ring from one of your guests.

Someone faints during the ceremony. This happens more often than you might think. I always have an empty chair at both sides of the aisle so a member of the wedding party can sit down if they're feeling woozy. Have smelling salts on hand in case someone does faint. As long as it's not the bride, groom, or the parents, the ceremony should go on as soon as the person who has fainted is moved to a comfortable spot. The bride and groom should remember to eat that day and to drink enough water so they're not the ones down for the count. If it should happen, the congregation will simply wait for everyone to feel sure-footed again.

You flub the vows. No one will notice. Unless you say "I will *not* take this man," you're still going to be married. And those mistakes will just give you something to laugh about later!

The groom cuts his foot while breaking the glass. This actually happened at one of my weddings. Okay, maybe this is one of those things without a silver lining, but it's not the end of the world; the groom went and got his stitches and then returned to the reception. To prevent cuts, wrap the glass well in a cloth napkin and make sure anyone breaking it has good, solid soles on his shoes.

The wind starts blowing everything around at your outdoor wedding. First, try to anchor everything down ahead of time. If a strong gust of wind can find its way to your ceremony, it will. Don't stress out if it happens. Hold the edges of your veil and think about the amazing photos you'll have of it trailing in the wind. . . .

A bridesmaid shows up late for hair and makeup or not at all. Don't expend mental energy worrying about her—just concentrate on getting yourself ready on time. The wedding will go on, with or without the bridesmaid.

centered ones are totally in the moment, focused only on the enormity—and fabulousness—of the occasion.

One thing everyone seems to agree on is that it goes by really, really fast. And all of a sudden, it's time for you to say your vows.

If you wrote your own vows, have the officiant hold a copy in case you need prompting. It's totally acceptable to read from a piece of paper whenever needed. There will be so much on your mind that committing vows to memory can add stress you just don't need. And don't worry if your hands shake: Your guests will find it touching.

Speak more slowly than you think you need to—nervous public speakers always tend to rush—and take care to enunciate. Your guests will want to hear every word.

The Kiss

YOU'VE DONE IT! The officiant is saying, "You may kiss the bride." You're not alone if you're wondering what type of kiss works best under this type of public scrutiny. Many couples worry about their kiss being too short, too long, too passionate, or not passionate enough.

Just do what feels right. Throw in a hug! (But keep it PG-rated.)

Why the kiss at all? Well, "sealed with a kiss" isn't just a fanciful expression. For centuries, a kiss was how agreements were cemented and letters concluded: Signing off with a row of *x*s was actually common practice in the Middle Ages. Some believe that a man and woman exchange a piece of their souls during a kiss. A sign of love, tenderness, and affection, this kiss is a physical oath to honor the spoken vows.

Doggy Pit Stop

If your dog is taking part in the ceremony, have someone take him for a walk beforehand so he doesn't relieve himself halfway down the aisle. For a reluctant pooch, have treats on hand. A groomsman who's on good terms with your dog should keep the treats in his pocket for coaxing or rewards.

After the "I Dos"

Now that you're Mr. and Mrs. (or Mr. and Ms.), steal a few minutes of quiet time together. Go back to the bridal dressing room or another private space. You might arrange to have some food and drinks brought in to fortify you for the celebration ahead; many couples miss most of the cocktail hour, and some don't get a chance to eat at the reception. At Jewish weddings, this time alone together is called *yichud*, and it's where the bride and groom break their fast after the wedding, but anyone can co-opt the tradition.

If you're doing photographs with the bridal party and your families right after the ceremony, try to get at least fifteen minutes on your own. Trust me, you'll feel robbed if you don't.

ASK MINDY

Q If we finish our photos and there are only ten minutes left in the cocktail hour, should we go into the party?

A If you enter cocktail hour at that point, everyone will be so excited to see you that it will delay the start of the reception, which could throw off the whole schedule. (Not that you should be overly worried about the schedule on your wedding day, but you do want guests to be fed at a reasonable hour.) Stay out of the way and have someone bring you a drink and a few hors d'oeuvres. Then make your big entrance at the beginning of the reception.

THE RECEPTION

Receiving Lines and Table-Hopping

Once an integral part of weddings, receiving lines are one of those things people think they have to do, but they're actually considered optional even by the strictest etiquette experts. (I don't happen to like receiving lines—they seem too formal, they delay the start of the reception, and it's tiring for guests to stand in line for so long. Depending on the size of the wedding, the receiving line can easily last an hour or more.) What *is* important—and not at all optional—is finding a way to greet all of the guests and thank them for coming.

Some couples lose sight of the fact that guests really want to connect with them, even if they're relative strangers attending as someone's date. If they don't know you well, they're going to feel self-conscious approaching you when you're likely to be catching up with close family members and friends, so it's important to offer an equal-opportunity moment. Besides, you owe it to every guest to thank him or her for going to the effort and expense to be there on your wedding day.

I like to see couples spending five to ten minutes at each table to get in their face-time with guests. The parents, or whoever is hosting the wedding, can do the same. Start making the rounds early in the reception—during and after the first course, during the early dance sets, and after the main course. Do a few tables, sit down to eat, dance a little, then do some more.

The advantage of a receiving line is that you would have gotten all of the greetings out of the way at the beginning of the reception without missing anybody. If you're having a very large wedding with more than 250 guests, or you're not having a sit-down dinner, then a receiving line probably is your best option. (And realize that in some areas, they're more of an institution.)

Receiving Lines 101

SHOULD YOU DECIDE to have a receiving line, do it either right after the ceremony (in the church vestibule or outside the church), at cocktail hour, or at the entrance to the reception. It partly depends on the timing of your photos—if you're doing pictures following the ceremony and the reception starts soon after, you won't have time to do a receiving line at the church. I prefer to do them at cocktail hour.

Make sure there's enough room for everyone to line up. If your location allows it, offer guests tray-passed drinks and a few nibbles to keep them from getting cranky, and have a place where they can deposit their empty glasses before they start shaking hands and kissing people.

In a traditional receiving line, the female host of the wedding (typically the mother of the bride) is first in line, followed by either the father of the bride or the mother

A traditional receiving line

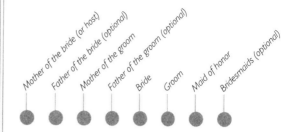

of the groom. Greetings should be kept short and sweet. If any guests start to get chatty, keep them moving along by telling them how glad you are to see them and asking if they've met the groom, or whoever is next in the receiving line.

Fathers and groomsmen may circulate among the guests and attend to other hosting duties instead of joining the lineup. To my mind, including the bridesmaids is overly formal and makes the line way too long, so I tend to leave them out.

Entering the Reception

No matter what your disposition, you shouldn't enter the reception quietly—it's your day! First off, everyone should be in the room by the time you make your entrance. If you have a bandleader or emcee, he can introduce you to the crowd. Discuss how you want to be announced in advance, and note it on their version of the schedule. Some people want to be called out as "Mr. and Mrs. Smith" while others might prefer "Mindy and Robert Smith." If the bride is keeping her name, it's best not to hit everyone over the head with a feminist statement. It's better to just use first names: "Let's welcome the newlyweds, Mindy and Robert!" (This is *not* meant as a slur on keeping your name, but older relatives are funny about it.)

Guests aren't supposed to dance until the bride and groom have, so I recommend going straight to the floor after your entrance; it gets things off to an energetic start.

If you plan to change into a different dress for the reception, you would generally do so after the first dance.

As for the veil, there's no need to leave it on. Everyone knows you're the bride, and it's likely to get in the way while you're dancing, eating, or drinking. Have your maid of honor remove it after the first dance—she should have directions from the hairstylist—or before, if you prefer. If you arranged to wear fresh flowers in your hair, she should know how to pin them in place.

The First Dance

MOST COUPLES are understandably nervous about the first dance. After all, how often are you alone on a dance floor, with all eyes trained on you? You may worry about forgetting the steps, treading on toes, or catching your heel on your hem. Just know that no matter what you do, everyone will be oohing and aahing. No one is waiting for you to trip up.

At a traditional wedding, the parents, then the wedding party, then the rest of the guests would gradually join the bride and groom after the first dance, but these days it's more likely to be a free-for-all. What comes next is up to you. Some couples follow the first dance with the father-daughter dance, then the mother-son dance, while others choose not to do those until after the main course is eaten. At a Jewish wedding, the first dance may be followed by the hora, which gets the party off to a rousing start; at a Greek wedding, this would be a perfect time to launch into the *kalamatiano*, another type of circle dance involving all of the guests. (See page 126 for a more detailed description of these and other traditional wedding dances.)

Someone Else's Special Day

Consider yourself extra fortunate if someone elects to spend their wedding anniversary or birthday attending your wedding. It's wonderful to acknowledge that it's a special day for them, too, either by sending them small cakes or raising a glass to them after the meal.

The Meal

You have a lot to be thankful for today. You've just married the love of your life, you're surrounded by friends and family, and there's an abundance of food and drink. Whether or not you subscribe to a particular religion, it's a perfect day to say a blessing before the first course. It also gives you an opportunity to give a special friend or relative an honorary role in leading the blessing; if your officiant is attending the reception, he would be the one to lead the prayer.

At a Jewish wedding, the challah (a braided bread) is traditionally blessed by the father of the bride or anyone to whom you want to give an honorary role—perhaps a grandfather, brother, or uncle. After he slices the bread, the loaf is passed around and everyone breaks bread together.

As for the meal itself: You may or may not have a chance to eat at your wedding. It's a pity to miss out on the food that you've taken so much time to choose, though. At the very least, try to taste everything you've chosen. You can always ask your catering manager to pack up a box for you to enjoy later in your room.

Toasts

EVEN IF YOU'RE SHY and don't relish the idea of being spoken about in public, trust me: Toasts are one of the highlights of a wedding, but too many can bog down a celebration. So can toasts that go on and on. I remember one wedding where the father spoke for more than thirty minutes! No toast should last for more than five.

As the first course is served, whoever is hosting the wedding stands up to welcome everyone and offer a toast. The bride's parents can start off and then invite the groom's parents to speak, or the bride and groom can lead the welcome and then call up both sets of parents.

After that, it's the best man's turn; he usually stands up toward the end of the first course or during the second course. He is followed by the maid of honor.

It's likely you'll get a few surprises in there as well—the mystery of who's going to stand up is all part of the fun!

The Cake Cutting

The cake cutting is an especially tender moment. I have to say, though, I'm not a big fan of the cake-in-the-face move. You're ruining the bride's beautiful makeup! And sometimes, her dress. Not to mention, it could be taken as a sign of latent aggression. (Okay, I'm no psychiatrist, but I've seen fights break out over this issue.)

Time the cake cutting to take place forty-five minutes to an hour after the main course is cleared. It's generally considered rude for guests to leave before the cake cutting, and some of your older attendees and parents of young children may be waiting for it as their cue to depart.

The bandleader or whoever is serving as your emcee should make an announcement, something along the lines of "And now, Jeffrey and Natalie will cut the cake." Waiters should pass out glasses of bubbly or refill wineglasses.

The bride's hands should be on the knife, with the groom's hands over hers. (It's thought to be bad luck to interrupt the bride's direct connection to the cake, which represents fertility.) Once the cake is cut, feed each other bites to show that you'll be caring for each other *and* sharing all of your possessions.

The groom—or the couple—then offers a toast, thanking everyone for being there, and thanking the parents and anyone else who helped make the wedding happen.

Waiters will then wheel the cake into the kitchen for plating, and dancing resumes until the cake is served. (It usually takes about twenty minutes, unless you're using the sheet cake trick; see page 340.)

Saving the Top Tier

IT'S A LONG-STANDING TRADITION for couples to save the top tier of their cake to eat on their first anniversary. A few hundred years ago in England, it would have been a fruitcake containing enough liquor to pickle itself quite nicely on its own.

Today, a freezer is probably in order, though cake purists would much rather you order a fresh cake to celebrate your first anniversary. However, if you wrap the cake very well before freezing, it can still be quite tasty a year later (see page 390). As for the rest of the leftover cake, why not serve it at brunch the next day?

ASK MINDY

Q Will the groom or I be required to speak at some point at the rehearsal dinner or reception? Should we prepare something?

A Yes. Traditionally, you will speak at the wedding as a response to all the toasts. Most of my couples speak at the cake cutting, but you can choose to do it any time. You could prepare, if you want to relay a specific anecdote or something, or you could go off the top of your head, which will be nice and warm and fuzzy. If someone is hosting you at the rehearsal dinner, stand up to thank them; that makes a nice beginning to the weekend. And some people really put a lot of time and effort into their rehearsal dinner toasts, so it's nice to acknowledge that. Basically, anytime someone is going to be saying something about you, be prepared to say a few words in response.

Bouquet and Garter Toss

Both the bouquet and garter toss are completely and utterly optional. Some brides love these rituals, some find them appalling, and others can't wait to toss the bouquet but wouldn't be caught dead even touching a garter.

Remember, this is your wedding. You can do one and not the other, neither, both, or devise some creative variation; to illustrate his departure from the single life, one of my grooms tossed his little black book to his single male friends. (Generally, it is the bride who does the tossing, though.)

Though the garter toss is obviously a light moment, it shouldn't be va-va-voom raunchy—I have seen one too many grooms remove the bride's garter with his teeth! Please, exercise a little restraint—this isn't the bachelor party. Have whoever is on emcee duty call the single men up for catching. Don't toss away that expensive silk La Perla garter; an inexpensive polyester "throw garter" is made just for this purpose. Wear it on your right leg, just above the knee. It's not the most comfortable thing, so slip it on right before the toss.

The bouquet toss, though still whimsical, is obviously a much less tongue-in-cheek moment. It's something I definitely see much more often than the garter toss . . . and it has a poignancy about it. When the bride tosses the flowers over her shoulder to her single friends, it's as if she's casting off her last tie to single life. It's also a gesture of generosity, sharing her bounty of love and commitment. The one who catches the bouquet, as we all know, is supposed to be the next to marry.

But the bouquet toss has gotten some bad press in recent years. It can be sort of embarrassing for the single women to be—for lack of a better word—singled out like that. Think about the number of single women at your reception, and take age into account. If you expect to have only six, and most of them are north of thirty, the bouquet toss could prove an acute source of embarrassment; it might be better to skip it. If you've got a large group of young, single friends and relatives, however, it could all be in good fun.

For sentimental reasons, most brides want to hold on to their actual bouquet; if you do, ask the florist for a tossing bouquet—some will even include one gratis, as they're smaller, less involved, and less expensive than a real bridal bouquet.

In the past, the bouquet toss was done right before the bride and groom departed, but now people extend the party longer and many guests leave before the end, so it makes sense to hold it while you've still got a substantial audience—and a photographer. If you're also doing a garter toss, it's traditional to hold that first, but there's no hard-and-fast rule.

Why We Toss Things

The traditions of tossing the bouquet and garter date back to the fourteenth century. As different as they seem today, they share the same roots. Any piece of the bride's attire was considered lucky, so guests were eager to claim their own bit of good fortune. Overeager well-wishers would rush the bride to grab at her bouquet, so to protect themselves from a mauling, brides started preemptively tossing their bouquets to the crowd.

The garter probably came from the (sort of creepy) "bedding ceremony." Guests would accompany the newlyweds to their bedchamber, and the groom's friends would try to remove the bride's garters. To avoid being groped by a bunch of drunk men, brides began tossing their garters in their direction.

The moral of the story? Watch out for those grabby singletons!

The End of the Night . . .

The clock has struck twelve and the bandleader is asking you if you would like to go into overtime. How do you decide? Overtime is costly, but you don't want to be a killjoy.

Here's my policy: If the dance floor is at least half full and you can afford it, keep the band playing for another thirty minutes, then reassess the situation every half hour. If there are only four people on the dance floor, it's time to let the band go home. With a DJ, overtime isn't as expensive, but you shouldn't keep him on if the party is petering out. The goal is to leave everyone sorry that the party is ending so soon!

Passing Out Tips

FOR THE VENDORS who get tips (see guidelines on page 27), you should have envelopes pre-prepared. Assign someone to the task of handing them out ahead of time—the wedding planner, the groom, the best man, or one of the fathers. Should you be giving any of your vendors a gift instead of a tip, send it after the wedding.

ASK MINDY

Q We just found out that I'm going to be four months pregnant by the wedding date. It's not public knowledge at this point. Would the reception be a good time to announce it?

A You'll never have another chance to get everyone together like this, so why not? It will hardly raise an eyebrow in this day and age. And if you're starting to show, it's better to put it out in the open rather than let people whisper. After you thank your families in your toast, go on to say that you have two reasons to celebrate today, and announce the happy news.

The Grand Exit

I ADORE THE IDEA of a bride changing into a chic suit with a corsage pinned to her lapel, tossing her bouquet to the girls, then stepping through a shower of rice into the getaway car. Sadly, that's a scene you see only in the movies nowadays. Most couples stay until the end of the party, not wanting to miss a moment of the fun.

But if you're a retro kind of girl, go ahead. You could even stage a big departure and reappear a bit later at your after-party! As for the vehicle, a horse-drawn carriage is timeless and romantic. If your reception is on a lake or harbor, consider taking your leave by boat. (One of my couples left on a tandem bike, and it was such a sweet moment.) For more getaway ideas, see page 150.

The best man typically heads up the efforts to decorate the departure vehicle. He and his helpers will duck out during the reception to tie on tin cans, festoon the vehicle with ribbons, and put on a JUST MARRIED sign. In lieu of shaving cream, which can damage the finish on cars and is expressly prohibited in some rental contracts, encourage them to order vinyl transfers that can be customized with your names or monogram. If you're planning a public exit and want picture-perfect results, involve the florist in decorating the car; don't leave it entirely to the groomsmen.

Beyond the Bouquet Toss

If the traditional bouquet toss doesn't work for you, consider these variations:

■ Present the bouquet (privately or publicly, depending on the situation) to a special friend or relative.

■ Skip the garter toss and invite single men to join the women in vying for the bouquet.

■ Order a breakaway bouquet, which dissolves into eight smaller bouquets in midair, potentially sending eight recipients to the altar.

■ Honor the woman who has been married the longest by presenting her with the bouquet.

■ Have the band do a "bouquet dance" or "anniversary dance" in which all married couples are asked to step onto the dance floor. As the dancing continues, the emcee asks couples who have been married five years or less to leave the dance floor, then ten years, fifteen years, and so on, until the longest-married couple is left standing.

The After-Party

IF YOU'RE HAVING an after-party, or even just a casual post-reception gathering at a local bar, it's likely you won't have mentioned it on your invitations. You can either surprise guests by announcing the after-party location toward the end of the reception, or include the information in your welcome note. Let local guests know through word of mouth. It's understood that the after-party is geared to friends of the couple and younger guests, so most of the older folks will take their leave.

The one downside to planning an after-party is that you won't be able to gauge in advance what your energy level will be like after getting through the whole she-bang. Some couples are exhilarated and want to stay up all night, and others are completely wiped out. If the latter is the case for you, you're totally within your rights to poop out. You definitely don't need to be the last two standing—if your friends have the fortitude, they'll keep the party going without you. Just don't sneak off without saying your good-byes.

And After the After-Party . . .

YOU'RE FINALLY ALONE. The room is lit with candles, and someone thoughtfully scattered rose petals on the bridal bed. It should be natural to feel amorous under these circumstances, right? After all, it's your wedding night.

But guess what? You're both tired. Bone tired. What you probably need most is something to eat, a glass of water (you're dehydrated after all that champagne), and a good night's sleep. Don't worry if you don't have great sex—or any sex at *all*—on your wedding night. After all, that's what the honeymoon is for!

When your wedding actually happens, I hope it's everything you dreamed of. No matter what turns out less than perfect or goes downright wrong, you'll be smiling fondly over your memories for weeks—and years—to come. But before we part ways, there are just a few more things you'll need to take care of. ♦

Last-Minute Details

You don't want anything to get left behind at your reception, so appoint bridesmaids, groomsmen, siblings, or parents to:

- Make sure nothing is left in the bride's and groom's changing rooms.

- Transport gifts to the car or honeymoon suite.

- Collect cash from a money dance or checks from the box on the gift table.

- Put gold jewelry presented to the bride (common at Muslim and Indian weddings) in a hotel safe or other secure place.

- Take the top tier of the wedding cake home to freeze. (Sometimes it gets left in the refrigerator of the hotel kitchen.)

- Take home personal items such as a cake-cutting knife, toasting flutes, guest book, the extra pair of shoes under the bride's chair, framed photos, and any tabletop or décor items. (Make a detailed checklist in advance.) If you brought your own MP3 player or CDs, don't forget those.

- Save your seating card—it may be the first time you see your name as Mr. and Mrs. (if that's what you opted for), and you'll want it for your memory box or scrapbook. If any speeches were written out, save those, too.

- Take the bouquet home to preserve it.

- Collect ceremony items such as the family Bible or unity candle.

CHAPTER TWENTY-SEVEN

Mr. & Mrs.

STARTING YOUR LIFE TOGETHER

You've sailed through the wedding with flying colors. You were gorgeous, the groom was dashing, and everyone declared it to be the best wedding ever. You've not only got a ring on your finger, but a marriage certificate to confirm your new status as husband and wife. Isn't love grand? Yes, but before you start playing your own version of the newlywed game,

you've got some unfinished business to handle. Some tasks will need to be delegated so they're taken care of the day after your wedding; you'll have to keep chipping away at others over the next couple of months. The gifts will keep on pouring in, and the thank-you notes should keep on pouring out. A few returns may be on the horizon as well. And for crafty types, there are tons of unique, homespun ways to commemorate your wedding experience; there are plenty of options for the craft averse as well.

You'll also need to begin tackling some big-picture questions as a couple. That may involve asking *yourselves* some tough ones.

How will you handle the merging of your finances? Are you saving at a sufficient rate to afford the future you envision together? Oh, and by the way, what does that future look like, if you haven't discussed it yet? Where will you live? Where you live now? The country, a suburb, or a city? How often will you visit family, yours and his? Many couples find that, once the initial glow has faded somewhat, early marriage is a time of serious introspection.

Don't avoid these conversations; a marriage is serious business, so some serious conversations are par for the course. Keep on polishing those rough edges, and treasure the memory of the day it all started.

Taking Care of Business

Figure out which of these housekeeping tasks you need to do now, which can wait till after the honeymoon, and which you can delegate to a parent or attendant.

The Returns

RENTED TUXEDOS usually need to go back the day after the wedding. If you're fortunate, your best man was deputized with the job of returning all of the rental tuxes, or at least the groom's. (Some wedding planners will handle the returns for you.) You can also charge each groomsman with returning his own tux. If you've got one person doing all of the returns and your wedding took place in a hotel, arrange to have each groomsman leave his tux in the hotel's baggage area under the name of the person picking them up.

If you had any other rentals for the wedding, from chandeliers to potted trees, they'll typically need to go back the day after the wedding. Remember, you may have to pay a premium for Sunday pickups.

Monetary Gifts

DON'T TREAT MONEY CARELESSLY and don't take it with you on your honeymoon. (Imagine if it was stolen.) If you're leaving for your honeymoon the day after your wedding, make a plan to have a close family member or friend hold on to the checks until you get back. If you're not leaving on your honeymoon right away, make a list of the gift givers along with the amounts, then deposit the checks and cash at the bank. (You'll allude to how you plan to use the money in your thank-you note, even though you wouldn't be so crass as to mention the amount.)

Saving the Bouquet

IF YOU'VE DECIDED to preserve your bouquet (see more details and other options on page 390), make arrangements in advance. For successful results, you'll need to keep the bouquet fresh and get it to the preservation place pronto. One service I use picks up the bouquet the same night. If you're sending it off instead of taking it to a local service, get instructions from the preservation service on how to store and ship the bouquet—they might advise putting it in a plastic bag in the refrigerator and shipping it via an overnight service in a cooler.

The Post-Wedding Blues

Once the wedding and honeymoon are over, you can finally start settling into married life. But what are those less-than-blissful feelings? Post-wedding blues are more common than you might think. Not everyone lets on that they're feeling down because they fear it reflects badly on their marriage, but it's perfectly natural to hit a slump after all the excitement leading up to your wedding day.

Brides, in particular, have a hard time accepting that their big day is over and, with it, their moment in the spotlight and—for many—their sense of purpose. A whole chapter of your life has ended, so it's also normal to go through a bit of a mourning period for your single days.

Don't deny or downplay your postnuptial letdown; the more you let yourself experience the feelings, the faster you'll process them. Try yoga, meditation, or other mind-body exercises to help you stay centered and relaxed while you're going through this adjustment—and try not to get too freaked out by it.

Handle the Gown

IF THE RECEPTION left visible stains on your gown, there's a better chance of removal if you can get it to the cleaner's right away. (Ask your mother or maid of honor to drop it off.) If there aren't visible stains, you can wait until after the honeymoon to get your dress to the cleaner's, but definitely get it there within six weeks. Read the section on cleaning and preserving your gown on page 389,

Wedding Announcements

Once commonplace, wedding announcements are no longer often sent out. They look very much like an invitation, only with different wording. Technically, they were meant to inform those who weren't invited to the wedding about the marriage, but they can end up looking like a request for gifts from those who didn't make the cut. The only time there's a real purpose to sending out announcements is if you had an extremely small wedding or if you eloped. Ideally, they should be mailed the day of the wedding or the day after the wedding, though you may send them out up to two months after the wedding. (Etiquette experts say you have up to a year, but I think it looks apathetic after two months.)

If the wedding was in a house of worship, you include the name of the church or synagogue after the date and before the town. If the ceremony was held at a hotel or other site, simply list the city and state where the wedding took place. Traditionally, formal announcements were mailed in double envelopes, but there's no real reason for an inner envelope today.

Jeremy Miles Akron
AND
Philip Elliot Jones
ARE PLEASED TO ANNOUNCE
THEIR MARRIAGE

SATURDAY, THE SIXTEENTH OF OCTOBER
TWO THOUSAND AND SEVENTEEN
BEL AIR, CALIFORNIA

A wedding announcement issued by the couple

Mr. and Mrs. Robert Smith
announce the marriage of

Sydnee Emily
AND
Max Henry Hersh

Saturday, the fourteenth of October
two thousand and seventeen
Bel Air, California

A wedding announcement issued by the parents

so you can better decide which process is right for you. Ideally, you should decide on the dry cleaner before the wedding; some high-end cleaners will even pick up the gown, so you may be able to leave it at the hotel. Make sure you point out any stains for the cleaner (leave a note with the dress) and any places you think you spilled white wine, soda, or champagne—these invisible stains oxidize over time and turn color. With dry cleaning, they won't be removed unless the area is pretreated with a cleaning agent. These would come out with professional "wet-cleaning," but not all gowns can be wet-cleaned.

Change Your Name

IF YOU'VE DECIDED to change your name, you can start the process once you receive your marriage certificate in the mail, usually a few weeks after the wedding. For pros and cons and how-tos, turn to page 151. And do it while you're still excited by the sound of your new name; the paperwork will only get more tedious with time.

If the wedding brought with it a move, let everyone know your new address by sending either snail mail or email moving announcements. Keep it simple by having small cards printed with your new info and inserting them into thank-you notes. You'll also need to change your address with your credit card companies, bank, employer, and so on.

Set Up Your Finances

THE QUESTION that all newlyweds face: to file jointly or singly at tax time? Married couples typically pay more in taxes, so minimize the financial whammy by talking to an accountant about what's best for you.

If you don't have one already, come up with a plan as to how you're going to handle household expenses and budgets. Will you each pay half? Dump everything into a joint account? Keep separate accounts and a joint account, with each of you contributing a predetermined percentage? Also try to agree on what percentage will go into savings, particularly if you are working toward buying a home. Proactively figuring out your approach to money will ward off a lot of petty arguments down the road.

Lastly, decide on general goals for monetary wedding gifts—will they go toward your honeymoon? A downpayment on a home? A sofa? Don't let the money ebb away.

Miscellaneous Paperwork

FIRST OFF, you will undoubtedly want to update the beneficiary or emergency contact and your marital status on insurance policies, wills, medical records, and investments. If you both have health insurance, evaluate your respective plans and decide whether it makes sense to maintain separate plans or for one spouse to be added to the other's policy.

Consider purchasing life insurance, especially if one spouse is dependent on the other's income. Evaluate your homeowner's or renter's insurance. If you've recently moved in together, you'll need to update your policy. Even if you've been living together, you probably will need to increase your coverage to reflect all of those lovely gifts. Make sure you have coverage for your engagement and wedding rings, which may require a rider.

It's also a good idea to create a living will, which assigns power of attorney for health care to a designated person, usually a spouse. The living will also states what medical measures you do and don't want taken should you become incapacitated. You can find living will forms for your state online, and they're relatively simple to prepare. Some states require witnesses, while others require the will to be notarized.

Of Course, the Thank-Yous

THE DAY AFTER the wedding, you won't be the only ones feeling a letdown. Your parents are bound to feel deflated after the big celebration. It was their party, too. Send a special thank-you to show your gratitude for all they did to make the wedding happen. I love to send a flower arrangement with a note, but if you've busted your bank account with the wedding, a heartfelt letter is just as special.

The day or two after your wedding, while it's still fresh in everyone's mind, is also the best time to thank your attendants for wearing those uncomfortable shoes all day long. If you worked exceptionally closely with any vendor, call and let him know you appreciated his efforts. Vendors also like a handwritten note, not only for its sentiment but

to share with potential clients, so add vendors who did fabulous work to your thank-you list for later.

Once the honeymoon is over, so is your grace period on thank-you notes. First up, if you haven't written notes to all of your attendants yet, do those first. And if you want to write any special notes of thanks to vendors, get those out within a month of the wedding.

As for wedding gifts, you're probably facing a mountain of notes. Writing thank-you notes doesn't qualify as anyone's favorite pastime, but you've got to get them done. Revisit chapter 15, "Saying Thank You," for etiquette, tips, and sample notes. To recap:

- In the age of IMs, the one-year rule no longer applies. You have three months, max, to get the notes out.

- Set a schedule for getting them done, and build in rewards along the way.

- Divvy them up. The groom can write his share.

- Promptness puts your note in a favorable light. A run-of-the-mill thank-you received three weeks after the wedding will be better regarded than a more eloquent note received three months later. And the sooner you write the notes, the shorter they can be.

Gift Returns and Exchanges

SO MANY LOVELY GIFTS . . . and a few not so lovelies. It's time to exchange or return the duplicates and the duds. Check the receipts for return policies, and then triage the gifts according to how long you have to return them. Remember that many independent boutiques have thirty-day limits on returns and exchanges; department stores and big-box retailers have more lenient policies, but some limit the return period to ninety days.

Check your registries to make sure there are some items left for stragglers. If you've been fortunate enough to have your registries stripped bare, go ahead and add more items. Find out how long the registry will remain active and extend it as long as possible. Then see if you can convert it to a "special occasion" or "gift" registry—very handy for anniversaries and birthdays.

Lasting Memories

All of those memories of your wonderful day are still freshly etched in your mind, but believe it or not, they will fade. You'll want to take advantage of traditional and more innovative ways to freeze-frame your memories, but don't feel obligated to preserve *everything*. Pick the things that are meaningful to you and concentrate on those.

Some items, like the bouquet, need to be preserved right away, while others, like a scrapbook, offer more leeway. Forge ahead now rather than putting it off. Working on a scrapbook or going through photos will help create closure. Besides, you don't want to be celebrating your tenth wedding anniversary still looking at an unfinished photo album.

Gown Cleaning and Preservation

BEFORE YOU AUTOMATICALLY spend hundreds of dollars to have your gown heirloomed in the hopes that your daughter will wear it someday, ask yourself: Did you have any interest in wearing your mother's wedding gown? Know going in that the heirlooming process is expensive, and there are no guarantees that the dress will be perfectly preserved twenty-seven years from now. And be prepared to hand over some serious closet space to the box, especially for a ballgown silhouette.

Whether you're going to keep it or sell it, you'll need to get the gown thoroughly cleaned after the wedding. Prices vary greatly according to region, the expertise of the cleaner, the fabric and embellishments on the gown, and staining. Count on spending between $200 and $800 for cleaning and preservation.

Find a cleaner before the wedding so you'll be prepared to get the dress in right after the big day. This is not a job for your neighborhood dry cleaner. To locate a specialist, ask for recommendations at the store where you bought your dress; if you purchased it out of town, call the toniest bridal boutique in your area and ask them where they send their gowns to be cleaned.

It's very important that you or whoever is dropping off the dress tell the cleaner about any and all stains. Treatment may vary, depending on the nature of the stain, and untreated invisible stains (such as Sprite or white wine) will emerge over time.

If the gown is being preserved, it should be placed in a pH neutral, acid-free paperboard box and stuffed with white, acid-free tissue paper.

Storing the Gown

Whether you had the gown preserved or simply cleaned, you want to store it away from direct sunlight and dampness, and where it's not subject to extreme changes in temperature. Attics and basements are the worst places to keep a gown. The best places: in your closet or under your bed. Any room you live in works well, since that's where you maintain a comfortable temperature range.

Use Your Dress to Do Good

If you're not absolutely attached to saving your dress, consider these "green" options, which keep it in circulation:

- Give it to a friend or family member who is getting married.

- Sell it on eBay or at a consignment shop to help pay off those wedding bills. Designer gowns from recent seasons fetch the most money. If you go the consignment shop route, you'll typically get half of the selling price. You probably won't be able to sell the dress ten years down the road when it's out of style.

- Donate it to a good cause. Thrift shops that benefit a hospital, women's shelter, or other charitable organization accept wedding gowns. Brides Across America accepts mail-in donations and will gift your gently used dress to a military bride-to-be.

If you're hanging the gown, even temporarily, hang it by the lingerie straps sewn into the underarms, not by the straps of the gown itself—the weight of the gown could stretch out the straps—and use a padded hanger. Here's the most important rule of all: Never cover the gown in plastic, which can lead to yellowing and mildew. Cover it in a clean white sheet or unbleached muslin cloth to protect it from dust and light (even if you're hanging it up just until you get it cleaned).

> Never take your dress to a place where gown preservation is guaranteed only if you don't break the seal on the storage box—you should open the box and check the dress every year. When you visit with your gown, wear disposable latex gloves so you don't leave oils on the fabric.

Freezing the Cake

ALTHOUGH CAKE MAKERS would much rather see you order a fresh cake to celebrate your first anniversary, the top tier of a wedding cake can often be frozen successfully. But cakes with whipped cream, custard, or fresh fruit fillings won't freeze well.

The trick to maintaining taste and texture is to keep moisture out and avoid freezer burn. First, remove any sugar flowers. (They can be saved, but be sure to wipe off any frosting.) Then refrigerate the cake overnight to harden the icing and prevent it from sticking to the plastic wrap. Wrap it in two layers of plastic, and cover with a layer of aluminum foil. If possible, place in a bakery box or plastic container to protect it from wayward roasting chickens. Label the outside of the package.

When it's time to celebrate, move the tier to the refrigerator, still in its wrappings, to defrost for a few hours—an abrupt temperature change will give you condensation on the frosting.

Oh, and don't forget to chill a bottle of champagne!

Saving the Bouquet

THE IDEA OF DRYING your bouquet carries a certain romantic appeal, but papery flowers and dried arrangements under glass aren't my thing. I'd rather see someone dry the flowers and turn them into sachets of potpourri—some flower-drying services will do this for you—or keep a framed black-and-white photograph of the bouquet at its prime on display.

If you do want to save the bouquet, you'll need to get it to a preservation service within a day or two of the wedding. Gently wrap the bouquet in paper, store in a plastic bag in the refrigerator, and, if shipping, pack into a cooler and send via an overnight service. Make arrangements in advance. Prices vary according to the preservation method and the size of the bouquet. (To keep costs down, select a few blossoms rather than the whole bouquet.) A framed bouquet of pressed flowers can run over $150, and a shadow box of a freeze-dried bouquet can easily cost $300. (But you can order a bag of potpourri made from dried petals for less than $20—hint, hint.)

Bouquets can be preserved in several ways, some of which are DIY and some of which require professional equipment:

Freeze-drying. The most effective method of drying flowers to retain a lifelike, three-dimensional shape. Flowers are flash frozen at –20°F, then reheated to room temperature over a four-week period. The end product is kept under glass.

Silica gel. Individual flower heads are covered with silica gel in an airtight container. The gel absorbs the moisture from the blooms in two days to a week.

Air-drying. Flowers are separated into small bunches and hung upside down in a dark, dry place—usually a closet. Drying time is one to four weeks.

Pressing. An age-old method of drying flowers by placing individual blooms between the pages of a heavy book or flower press. Once pressed, the flowers can be arranged into a display to be framed under glass or housed in a shadow box.

Microwave drying. You can dry a few blossoms at a time in the microwave by wrapping them in a paper towel and heating them on high for one to three minutes. Time and results vary, depending on the type of flower, so plan on experimenting. Set the timer for one minute and allow flowers to cool for a half hour; and if they need more drying, repeat the process.

Complete Your Photo Album

MANY PHOTOGRAPHERS and videographers have clauses in their contracts allowing you anywhere from six months to a year to choose images for your photo albums and finalize your wedding video. If you go beyond the specified time frame, you could be subject to extra fees. If you had your wedding professionally filmed, try to make your photo choices prior to finalizing your video, so you can incorporate some stills.

You may be tempted to skip the deluxe photo album package and try saving money by putting one together on your own, but just know that doing so can be a big job. Depending on how heavily your photographer shot and how many hours he worked, you could be wading through a few thousand frames. If your arrangement doesn't include an album and you're short on time, you can hire professionals to take over—typically, you'd find them at high-end stationery shops, or at photo studios with retail boutiques.

If you're going it alone, here are a few tips to get you started: Albums and paper should be of archival quality. Paper, photo corners, and adhesives need to be acid free, otherwise they can deteriorate over time

Photo Album Styles

When choosing an album, consider its coffee table appeal, price, size, and whether it allows you to arrange and display photos the way you want.

Commercial Digital Albums. You upload your digital photos to a website that produces a bound book for you. The initial book is expensive, but you'll get big price breaks on multiple copies. If you know you'll need ten copies of your album to keep the family happy, this is your best option.

DIY Digital Albums. With the rise of DIY photo printing, high-end albums with embroidered silk or patterned paper covers are now available. The albums are set up so that you can run the letter-size pages through your printer.

Scrapbook Albums. Not to be confused with scrapbooks, these albums feature plain paper pages, allowing for flexibility in the size and placement of photographs. Photos are mounted with photo corners or adhesives. The spine of handbound versions is often crisscrossed with ribbons for a beautiful, Old World feel.

Traditional Album. A leather-, suede-, or cloth-bound album with heavyweight paper pages. Photos are set into die-cut frames or mats, which means your layouts are predetermined by the size and shape of the frames.

Photo-Sleeve Albums. Plastic sleeves hold photos, making these albums the quickest to assemble. You usually can't vary the size of the photos within the album, so it's a great way to put together a quick look of four-by-six-inch photos, but not the most expressive choice for a main album. Don't get inexpensive albums if you want the photos to last—look for albums with PVC-free plastic and acid-free, lignin-free paper. Stay away from albums with self-stick pages, as these damage photos over time.

Photo Boxes. Not an album per se, a photo box offers an alternative for the chronically disorganized or those with an aversion to conventional albums. Some couples opt to get one to two dozen prints matted before storing them in a box. Make sure the paperboard used in the construction of the box is acid free and of archival quality.

Gift It

Wedding albums make treasured gifts for parents, and if you can time your delivery to the first Christmas or Hanukkah after the wedding, so much the better. Most companies offer a smaller album that's terrific for grandparents or other relatives. If you have digital rights to photos from your photographer, you can easily and economically create a book-bound album.

and cause photos to fade or discolor. Include detail shots, even though they may seem slightly mundane. A close-up of your shoes will stir up more memories and emotions than a table shot, and it nicely varies the flow of the book. An overhead shot likewise adds variety and often serves as an effective transitional image; an overhead of the reception space (shot before the guests arrived) could open the reception section of the album.

Don't overstuff albums. It's preferable to have multiple albums than to pack pages into a single album. Store out of direct sunlight in areas that aren't subject to a lot of humidity. (That rules out the basement, attic, or garage.) Ideally, albums should be kept flat—not upright—to keep pages from warping.

Last, when choosing and arranging photos, aim to create a narrative. A great album isn't an assemblage of images, but the story of your wedding day told in photos.

If you went the digital route, you should also share photos with the rest of your guests, which is quick and easy to do online. Many wedding photographers post photos to a site and send you a link and a password that you can then share with guests. They'll be able to place orders for any prints they like, without involving you as the middleman.

You can also upload the photographer's photos (but only if you bought digital rights) to your wedding website.

Beware, though, that digital makes it all too easy to upload 1,200 photos of the wedding. Not a single guest—not even your mom—wants to wade through that many. Find out if the photographer can edit the selection down to

a fixed number (no more than 250), or if you can designate a separate "top pics" section. If you're uploading photos to your own site, limit yourself to 25 to 30 of the best.

Video Tips

IF YOU HAD YOUR WEDDING professionally filmed, an edited product will be part of the package. You may have a say in the accompanying music, so start thinking of favorite tunes early on, as video editors need the music before they can start editing.

Once you have a finished product, upload the video to an online sharing site (make sure you have the rights in your contract with the videographer). Email the link to close friends and family and/or share it more widely on social media if you'd like to give those who didn't get a chance to attend a peek at the proceedings.

Creative Keepsakes

ONE OF THE UPSHOTS of the growing interest in weddings is the wealth of creative keepsakes now available. Every week, it seems, someone finds a new way to preserve wedding memories. These souvenirs are often quite pricey, but might be worthwhile for you if a particular element of your wedding is really close to your heart. Some bright ideas:

Bridal Gown. Instead of storing a huge box in your closet, get a fashion illustration made of you in your dress. Some designers will also craft miniatures of the dress (Kleinfeld's custom department does, but only for customers.) Prices are not for the faint of heart or weak of wallet: they start at $800.

Quilts, Blankets, Chuppah Covers. There are dozens of versions of commemorative chuppah covers, quilts, and blankets, using everything from fabric squares hand-painted by guests to photos of the happy couple. You can even invite guests to knit or crochet a square to be turned into a blanket; gather the girls together for a knitting party—some upscale knitting stores will lead classes and then turn the squares into a blanket for you.

Memory Boxes and Scrapbooks

A memory box is my favorite way to commemorate a wedding. If you lack an inner Martha, not to worry—the great thing about this keepsake is that it requires no skills whatsoever. I love an engraved silver box, but a leather or fabric-covered box works, too. Inside, stash items that bring back the day and any special events leading up to it. Possibilities include the save-the-date card, invitations, a brochure from the reception site, coasters or cocktail napkins, a copy of your menu, your program, your place cards, a champagne cork, sheet music from your first song, boarding passes from your honeymoon, ribbons, scraps of wrapping paper, love letters and special notes, and a copy of the wedding announcement. You can also turn the box into a time capsule by including the front page of the newspaper, the weather report, and your horoscopes for the wedding day.

A wedding scrapbook—or series of scrapbooks—is much more involved, but many brides relish the creative process. With thousands of scrapbooking stores across the country and abundant supplies available at craft chains, there's no shortage of materials. Some stores even offer workshops specifically focused on creating wedding scrapbooks.

Albums, paper, stickers, and add-ons need to be made of acid-free, archival-quality materials; write with archival-quality ink. You may not have time to start a scrapbook for months—you'll be writing thank-you notes—so save potential material (similar to what could go into a memory box) in large manila envelopes.

Collage. A collage artist can take your wedding ephemera (invitations, photos, coasters, cocktail napkins, place cards, newspaper wedding announcements, menu, fabric samples) and turn it into a sentimental journey for your wall.

In Closing

If there's one ending that's really a beginning, it's a wedding. You've gone through so much since you first slipped on that engagement ring, and you've grown stronger as a couple along the way. Think about all that you've experienced and learned about each other during this time. You've surely seen each other through family crises, bouts of adolescent regression (possibly complete with the occasional tantrum or two), and now you know that one of you packs four times as many shoes as the other for a week-long trip.

All of the wisdom, grace, maturity, and compassion that you've acquired on this journey can be channeled into building the foundation of a strong marriage. Vowing to love and cherish each other is one thing, but weaving that promise into daily life is another. So indulge his manic remote-control behavior, bring her coffee in bed (with two sugars, just the way she likes it), and call to say "I can't wait to see you."

I'd like to propose one final toast: May you live, laugh, and love happily ever after. ◆

Appendixes

The Year-Long Engagement

Week-By-Week Planner

Knowing you're on schedule will help keep you calm and ward off sleepless nights through the process of planning the wedding. Even if you normally resist organizational tools, a wedding involves far too many details to keep in your head, so start cozying up to your Google calendar, your day planner, your spreadsheets, your to-do list, or whatever system works for you.

The following time line is based on a one-year engagement. (If you don't have a year, not a problem. See page 401 if you're planning a wedding in six months or less; for destination weddings, see page 417.) Some items are purposely scheduled early to get them out of the way—you'll have so many things to tend to in the final weeks, and it's harder to make decisions when things get that hectic. So while you don't absolutely need to choose favors two months before the wedding or finish writing vows a month before, your life will be easier if you do.

No one's wedding will follow this schedule to the letter, and no wedding will require every item on this list. Adjust it as necessary. You may find you're ahead on a few things and behind on others. Just don't let yourself fall too far behind, especially when it comes to booking vendors and ordering custom-made merchandise. You can trim a month or two from the schedule by compressing meetings with vendors—many couples, for example, are able to make initial menu selections at their main meeting with the caterer and won't need a separate meeting.

Prepare for a big rush of planning between six and nine months before the wedding; once you have your vendors lined up and your dress ordered, there's a bit of a lull. Not everything can be finalized six months in advance, especially if it depends on seasonal goods like food and flowers, which is why you need to wait until the final couple of months to firm up centerpieces and menus.

One-Year Planning Time Line

Twelve Months

- Arrange for families to meet.
- Start cutting out pictures you like from magazines of dresses, color schemes, favors, and flowers.

Eleven Months

- Draw up preliminary guest list.
- Determine wedding budget.
- Agree on general time frame for wedding.
- Decide whether you want to hire a wedding planner; if you do, begin interviewing planners.
- Get engagement ring appraised and insured.

Ten Months

- Set wedding date.
- Book location for wedding and reception.
- For a wedding in a house of worship, schedule rehearsal time.
- Hire wedding planner if you decide you want a full-service planner.

Nine Months

- Hire photographer.
- Book officiant.
- Conduct site inspection of ceremony and reception locations; identify special needs that would call for a rental company or lighting designer.

Eight Months

- Choose the bridal party.
- Book blocks of rooms at hotels for out-of-towners.
- Negotiate group discounts with airline.
- Compile guest list.
- Start looking at wedding invitations.
- Choose save-the-date cards.
- Book band for reception and send deposit.
- Start looking at wedding gowns.

Seven Months

- Book caterer for off-site reception or rehearsal dinner.
- Send save-the-date cards.
- Send letter with travel and lodging information to out-of-towners.
- Hire videographer.
- Order thank-you notes for early gifts.
- Order wedding gown.
- Order veil.
- Set up wedding website.

Six Months

- Book florist.
- Book lighting company if needed.
- Select bridesmaids' dresses.
- Start interviewing/trying out hairstylists and makeup artists.
- Start a basic registry for gifts (shower and wedding); you'll continue to add to it.

- Evaluate whether you want wedding insurance; it's best to sign up soon after you start putting down deposits.
- Begin vaccinations if needed for wedding or honeymoon.
- Book or help coordinate location for rehearsal dinner.
- Reserve day-after brunch location.
- Create honeymoon wish list and start researching destinations.
- Book musicians or choir for ceremony.
- Book music for cocktail hour.
- Book musicians or DJ for reception.
- If you're hiring a day-of wedding coordinator, not a full-service planner, book now.

Five Months

- Order wedding invitations.
- Order maps to wedding or reception location.
- Order thank-you notes for after the wedding (if using married name on notes).
- Book calligrapher if using one.
- Order wedding announcements, if you plan to send them.
- Decide on tuxedo style, and place rental order for groom.
- If you want a jeweler to custom design your wedding bands, begin the process.
- As needed, book tent and other rentals through a rental company.
- Apply for passport or renewal if needed for honeymoon.

- Have engagement photo taken for use in newspaper wedding announcements, your website, or programs.
- Order flower girl's dress.

Four Months

- Schedule interviews/tastings with independent cake makers. (Note: If you're going for a star of the cake world, you should move this two months up; if you're getting your cake through your reception venue or caterer, you'll discuss the cake in conjunction with the rest of the menu.)
- Book hairstylist and makeup artist.
- Shop for gifts for the wedding party. For personalized gifts, allow eight weeks for special orders or engraving.
- Research marriage license requirements in the municipality where your marriage will take place; start obtaining documents, get any tests needed, and plan for any waiting periods or residency requirements. Determine best time to file your application—for a destination wedding, that may be during a planning trip.
- Review proofs of invitations.
- Shop for any accessories for the wedding gown, such as a handbag, wrap, costume jewelry, and shoes.
- Investigate travel insurance.
- Book hotel room for wedding night.
- Compile guest lists for showers.
- Order transportation to ceremony and reception for bridal party.
- Order shuttles or other transportation for guests, if needed.

- If you're thinking of a prenuptial agreement, start discussing it; try to have it signed six to eight weeks before the wedding.

Three Months

- Choose menus for wedding and rehearsal dinners.
- Meet with officiant to plan ceremony.
- See sample centerpiece from florist; see sketches or samples for ceremony area, including decorative elements like the chuppah.
- Order bouquets, boutonnieres, and other personal flowers.
- Choose table linens and napkin treatments.
- Place orders for any specialty tabletop rentals such as chargers, glassware, dishes, silverware.
- Buy wedding rings.
- Order wedding cake and groom's cake, if needed.
- Start choosing songs and making a Do-Not-Play list.
- Start thinking about favors; if you want personalized favors, you'll need to place orders eight weeks before wedding.
- Have groomsmen fitted for tuxes and place orders.
- Buy any necessary accessories for groom, such as cuff links, shirt, or shoes.
- Shop for outfits for bride and groom to wear to shower and rehearsal dinner.
- Check registries to make sure enough gifts remain at different price levels. (Do this every week or so until two weeks before the wedding.)

- Contact newspapers for guidelines about placing wedding announcements. (They are often found on newspapers' websites.)
- Buy any necessary undergarments for wedding gown and rehearsal dinner outfit.
- Make appointment for dress fitting.
- Choose gifts for shower hostesses.
- Schedule food tasting (six to eight weeks before wedding).
- Make arrangements, as necessary, for day-after brunch.
- Finalize guest list.
- Three weeks before mailing invitations, deliver envelopes and one invitation sample to calligrapher.
- Weigh one complete, stuffed invitation at post office to determine correct postage.
- Choose stamps for invitations.
- Stuff wedding invitations.
- Order rehearsal dinner invitations.
- Order day-after brunch invitations.
- Schedule rehearsal time and rehearsal dinner time.
- Choose ketubah for Jewish wedding.
- Book valet parking service, if needed.
- Choose first dance song, other special songs.
- If you are writing your own vows, start writing down your thoughts and checking various sources for inspiration.
- Schedule dance lessons.

(continued)

One-Year Planning Time Line (continued)

Eight Weeks

- Have final address list for invitations typed and ordered alphabetically.
- Mail wedding invitations (six to eight weeks before wedding).
- Send rehearsal dinner invitations, if separate from wedding invitations.
- Attend food tasting. With an in-house caterer, this will also be the wine tasting. With an outside caterer, bring wines to try with the meal.
- Choose seating cards and place cards.
- Order table numbers.
- Order cocktail napkins and guest towels.
- Buy gifts for anyone hosting showers.
- Send wedding announcement to newspapers. (Be sure to follow individual submission guidelines.)
- Buy wedding shoes; start wearing them around the house to break them in. Bring them to first gown fitting, and wear them to dance lessons so you'll look completely comfortable on the dance floor.
- Choose favors if you're doing them.
- Plan welcome gifts for out-of-towners.
- Choose headpiece or hair jewelry if you haven't already.
- Finalize honeymoon plans; double-check passport, visa, vaccination requirements.
- Get blood tests done, if needed, for marriage license.

Seven Weeks

- Create and implement system for keeping track of response cards to all events.
- Draft schedule of events for wedding weekend—fine-tune it as you have final meetings with vendors.
- Write thank-you notes for shower gifts within a week or two of shower.

Six Weeks

- Have final meeting with musicians or DJ to discuss schedule of events, special dances, and playlist. Review Do-Not-Play list and musicians' attire. Also go over "equipment loading" procedures—find out what time they need to set up the sound, microphones, and the instruments (drums often set up early), and when they plan to conduct sound tests.
- Draft shot list for photographer; refine as you get RSVPs.
- Make list of moments you want captured on video; draft list of guests you want interviewed on the video; refine as you get RSVPs.

Five Weeks

- Choose ceremony readings.
- Take rings to jeweler to be inscribed if needed (have them sized before engraving).

Four Weeks

- Obtain marriage license; make sure it's valid through the wedding day.
- Deadline for RSVPs to wedding. Contact stragglers who haven't replied.
- Create final schedule of events; send to musicians, DJ, caterer, photographer, videographer, florist, cake maker, venue manager, any other vendors who will need it, and officiant.
- Start working on seating chart.
- Meet with officiant to discuss procession and review order and contents of ceremony, arrival times, etc.
- Do trial runs with makeup artist and hairstylist.
- Print ceremony programs.
- Order menus for reception.
- Start gathering the following: guest book; pen; handkerchief; garter (if you're doing a garter toss); something old, new, borrowed, blue. If you need them for your ceremony, make sure you have: unity candle, kiddush cup, glass for breaking. Consider whether you want to buy a special cake-cutting knife and toasting flutes if you didn't receive them as gifts.
- Obtain instructions on how to change your name, if you plan to change it after the wedding.
- Meet with photographer to go over schedule and shot list. Follow up with seating chart once you've completed it.
- Meet with videographer to go over schedule and review details of contract. If you're doing interviews, give him a list of people you want interviewed. Follow up with seating chart once you've completed it.

- Review honeymoon travel reservations; make reservations for special restaurants, outings, or spa appointments.
- Make shopping list of anything you need for honeymoon.
- Send out rehearsal dinner invitations if they weren't part of initial invitation.
- Book manicure and pedicure appointments for the day before the wedding.
- Finish vows if writing your own.
- If moving, send change of address to post office.
- Have a blast at your bachelor/bachelorette party.

Three Weeks

- Set up final meeting with florist; discuss what flowers are actually available; go over schedule.
- If you have a pet, make arrangements for a pet sitter during wedding and honeymoon.
- Write toasts and speeches for rehearsal dinner and reception.
- If sending wedding announcements, address them and give to a family member to mail the day of or day after the wedding.
- Buy thank-you gifts for parents and wrap them. Or place order with florist. (Write the card so it's in your handwriting and give it to florist.)
- Stock up on any prescription medications (including disposable contact lenses, allergy meds, and birth control) you'll need for the honeymoon.

- Arrange for people to hand out seating cards and accept gifts at reception.
- Find out where all out-of-town guests are staying if delivering in-room gifts. (Include those staying with friends.)

Two Weeks

- Write as many thank-you notes as you can. Try to keep up before final deluge of gifts.
- Wrap gifts for bridesmaids and groomsmen.
- Have final dress fitting.
- Have final pre-wedding facial. (If you can't squeeze it in, skip it rather than having it closer to the wedding.)
- Have final pre-wedding hair color appointment. (It's okay to schedule up until one week before the wedding if it's your regular color or highlights.)
- Confirm hotel room for wedding night.
- Check registries to make sure enough gifts remain at different price levels (check every few days up until the wedding).
- Check in with anyone scheduled to make a toast at rehearsal dinner or reception.
- If traveling to another country for wedding or honeymoon, get $100 worth of foreign currency.
- Arrange to have someone check on your home and take in packages while you're away.

One Week

- Pick up wedding dress.
- Start packing for honeymoon if leaving within two days of the wedding.
- Prepare tip envelopes for vendors by putting cash into marked envelopes.
- Finalize seating arrangements.
- Deliver seating cards, place cards, and table numbers to calligrapher.
- Call transportation company to confirm reservations and pickup times; send explicit directions to driver; prepare a "call sheet" with all pickup and drop-off times, names, and addresses.
- Give ketubah (Jewish marriage contract) to rabbi if you're providing it.
- Check in with groom to make sure marriage license and anything he's in charge of is in order; remind him that things will soon be back to normal.
- Send seating chart to photographer to go with the shot list.
- Send seating chart to videographer to go with list of people to be interviewed.
- Start checking weather forecast for wedding day.
- Confirm food and bar menu details with caterer.
- Make arrangements to hold mail and stop newspapers for honeymoon.

Five Days

- Confirm all vendors the Monday before the event.

(continued)

One-Year Planning Time Line (continued)

Give final head count to hotel or caterer the Monday before the event. (Check your contract for actual deadline in case it's different.)

Prepare payment or donation for officiant and checks for vendors who get paid on wedding day.

Four Days

Arrange transportation to airport for honeymoon if you don't already have it.

Write thank-you notes to parents for all their support during the wedding planning.

Three Days

Confirm hotel reservations for honeymoon.

Check weather forecasts for wedding and honeymoon.

Practice vows.

Pack bag for wedding day, including emergency day kit—don't forget to include an extra pair of shoes for dancing.

Two Days

Deliver in-room gifts to out-of-towners on the day they arrive.

Give programs, yarmulkes, and anything else you're handing out at ceremony to person who will distribute them.

Give seating cards and place cards to person who will be putting them out.

Give guest book, cake knife, toasting glasses to person who will put them in place.

Give favors to person who will set them up or distribute them.

Pick up rental tuxes.

Make sure that bridesmaids have their outfits completely put together, including shoes and accessories.

Reconfirm wedding night hotel reservation.

One Day

Practice speeches and vows.

Get manicure and pedicure.

Review and finalize seating chart, adjusting for last-minute cancellations.

Confirm flight reservations for honeymoon.

Reconfirm pickup times and addresses with limo company; reconfirm any transportation you've arranged for guests.

Give tip envelopes to person assigned to distribute them.

Treat bridesmaids, mothers, sisters, and other very close female relatives to a luncheon, spa outing, or other special get-together.

Groom treats groomsmen, fathers, brothers, and other very close male relatives to a round of golf, dinner, or other outing.

Give gifts to members of bridal party.

Go over any specific jobs for members of bridal party such as manning guest book or taking gifts from the reception to your home.

Rehearse ceremony.

Enjoy rehearsal dinner.

Wedding Day

Get final steaming for wedding gown.

Relax and enjoy the day!

Have best man or maid of honor call airline to check on flight status for honeymoon.

In the excitement of the day, don't forget to take regular medications for allergies, birth control, etc.

Day After

Send thank-you notes to parents (and possibly flowers or a gift).

Thank attendants.

Return rental tuxedos.

Call any special vendors to thank them.

Deposit monetary wedding gifts or put them in safekeeping.

Freeze top layer of cake.

If preserving bouquet, send it to preservation service.

Make a note of any stains on wedding gown; if there are bad ones, don't wait to take it to the cleaner. Otherwise, hang it on a padded hanger (use the lingerie straps for this) in your closet and cover it with a clean sheet until you can get it to the cleaner.

Short Engagements

Week-By-Week Planner

Whether by choice or by circumstance, not everyone has a year to plan a wedding. If you have only four months, you need to approach it with a different mind-set than someone who has a year. It requires diving in, making the big decisions, and setting up the essential structure (date, location, budget, guest count) immediately.

Make no mistake—your choices will be limited, and that can get frustrating. The main hotel in town may already be booked. Your favorite photographer may have taken a deposit for that date months earlier. But these realities force you to either go with what's available or get creative. Seek out the off-season, the off-hour and -day, or the unexpected venue, and you'll find plenty of choices.

The time line below assumes a four-to-six-month engagement. If your engagement is shorter, follow the order and condense it to work within your schedule. You may find that it makes more sense to work with a venue where they handle a lot of the details for you or one that offers packages, cutting down on the number of meetings with vendors.

Prioritize! Don't get upset about details that don't alter the day. If you don't have time to get the rings engraved before the wedding, you can always do it after. You may not have time to order personalized gifts, favors, or cocktail napkins, which can take several weeks, but you can still get napkins in a great color, and no one will miss the monogram. Likewise, you may need to opt for a faster printing method on your invitations, skipping letterpress or engraving in favor of a lively flat printed invitation; it's far more important to get the invitations to guests in plenty of time than to follow formal etiquette guidelines to the letter.

Months Four, Five, and Six

- Arrange for families to meet.
- Decide if you want to hire a wedding planner; if you do, interview them ASAP.
- Nail down date and locations (for ceremony and reception), head count, and budget; schedule rehearsal time if wedding is in a house of worship.
- Book photographer.
- Book videographer.
- Book officiant.
- Book reception musicians or DJ.
- Choose wedding gown. (You may need to go with an off-the-rack gown, a floor sample from a bridal salon, or a designer gown in ivory rather than a bridal gown you need to order months in advance.)
- Choose bridesmaids' dresses. (Again, off-the-rack or the J.Crew catalog may be a better option than ones you order through a bridal salon.)
- Order flower girl's dress.
- Book caterer.
- Book florist.
- Set up wedding website.
- Choose outfits for groom and groomsmen and place rental orders.
- Compile guest list with addresses.
- Send save-the-date cards (optional); consider emailing.
- Schedule walk-through of ceremony and reception sites; identify whether you need to hire other vendors for rentals, lighting, etc.
- Choose the wedding party. (Hint: Smaller is easier.)
- Book blocks of rooms for out-of-town guests.
- Negotiate group discount with airline.
- Get engagement ring appraised and insured.

Three Months

- Order invitations, thank-you notes, maps to wedding or reception.
- Order wedding announcements, if you plan to send them.

(continued)

- Hire calligrapher, if using one.

- Proof invitations.

- Set up wedding registries.

- Book location for rehearsal dinner.

- Book day-after brunch location.

- Hire ceremony musicians or choir.

- Hire cocktail hour musicians.

- Choose cake maker.

- Order transportation to ceremony and reception for bridal party.

- Order shuttles or other transportation for guests, if needed.

- Send letter to out-of-towners with travel and lodging info.

- Order veil and headpiece.

- Evaluate whether you want wedding insurance; it's best to sign up soon after you start putting down deposits.

- Research honeymoon destinations.

- Renew passports if you think you may need them for honeymoon.

- Book day-of-wedding coordinator, if using one.

- Shop for wedding rings, either custom or ready-made.

- Reserve tents, chairs, other rentals.

- Have engagement photo taken, if doing one.

- Compile guest list for showers.

- Meet with officiant to plan ceremony.

- Shop for outfits for bride and groom to wear to showers and rehearsal dinner.

- If you're thinking of a prenuptial agreement, work out the details.

- Contact newspapers for guidelines, which are often found on newspapers' websites, about placing wedding announcements.

- Make appointment for dress fitting.

- Choose gifts for shower hostesses.

- Deliver envelopes (and one invitation sample if possible) to calligrapher or have stationery shop print them on laser printer.

- Order rehearsal dinner invitations.

- Order day-after brunch invitations.

- Hire valet parking service, if needed.

Two Months

- Stuff invitations.

- Weigh one complete, stuffed invitation at post office to determine correct postage.

- Choose stamps.

- Type and alphabetize final address list for invitations.

- Mail invitations (six to eight weeks before wedding).

- Choose menus for wedding and rehearsal dinner.

- Schedule food tasting.

- Book honeymoon.

- Investigate travel insurance for honeymoon.

- Book hotel room for wedding night.

- Check passport, visa, vaccination requirements for honeymoon.

- Hire hairstylist and makeup artist.

- Buy gifts for bridesmaids, groomsmen, flower girl, ring bearer.

- Research marriage license requirements in the municipality where the marriage will take place; schedule any follow-ups you need, such as blood tests. Determine when you're going to file your application.

- Buy undergarments, shoes, and accessories to wear with your wedding gown.

- See sample centerpiece from florist; see sketches or samples for ceremony area, including decorative elements like the chuppah.

- Order bouquets, boutonnieres, and other personal flowers from florist.

- Make lists of songs and prepare a Do-Not-Play list; choose a first dance song and songs for other special dances.

- Start wearing wedding shoes around the house to break them in; wear them at dance lessons and bring them to dress fittings.

- First dress fitting.

Seven Weeks

- Develop system for keeping track of response cards to all events.

- Draft schedule for wedding weekend; fine-tune it as you have final meetings with vendors.

- Begin dance lessons if needed.

Six Weeks

- Choose seating cards and place cards.

- Choose ketubah for Jewish wedding.

- Choose table linens and decide on napkin treatments.

- Order table numbers.

- Order cocktail napkins and guest towels.

- Place orders for any specialty tabletop rentals such as china, glassware, silverware.

- Attend food tasting. With an in-house caterer, this will also be the wine tasting. With an outside caterer, bring wines to try with the meal.

- Decide on favors.

- Select welcome gifts for out-of-towners.

- Order wedding cake; order groom's cake if needed.

- Send wedding announcement to newspapers. (Be sure to follow individual submission guidelines.)

- Get blood tests done, if needed for marriage license.

- Write thank-you notes for shower gifts within ten days of the shower.

Five Weeks

- Have final meeting with musicians or DJ to discuss schedule of events, special dances, and playlist. Review Do-Not-Play list and musicians' attire. Also go over "equipment loading" procedures—find out what time they need to set up the sound, microphones, and the instruments (drums often set up early), and when they plan to conduct sound tests.

- Make shot list for photographer.

- Make list of guests you want interviewed on the video and list of moments you want on video.

- Take rings to jeweler to be inscribed. Have them sized before engraving them.

- Mail rehearsal dinner invitations.

- Mail day-after brunch invitations.

Four Weeks

- Buy any accessories needed for groom, such as cuff links, shirt, or shoes.

- Choose menu for day-after brunch.

- If writing your own vows, collect quotes or readings and start drafting vows.

- Choose ceremony readings.

- Obtain marriage license if it's local; make sure it's valid through the wedding day.

- Deadline for RSVPs to wedding; contact anyone who hasn't replied.

- Create final schedule of events; send to musicians, DJ, caterer, photographer, videographer, venue manager, florist, cake maker, any other vendors who will need it, and officiant.

- Start working on seating chart.

- Have final dress fitting.

- Do trial runs with makeup artist and hairstylist. If doing your own makeup, make appointment at department store counter for makeup lesson.

- Print ceremony programs.

- Order menus for reception.

- Discuss procession with officiant; review the order and contents of the ceremony, arrival times, etc.

- Obtain information on how to change your name if necessary.

- Meet with photographer to go over the schedule and shot list; follow up with a seating chart once it's completed.

- Meet with videographer to go over the schedule and review the details of the contract. If you're doing interviews, give him a list of people you want interviewed. Follow up with a seating chart once it's completed.

- Check registries to make sure enough gifts remain at different price levels.

Three Weeks

- Start gathering the following: guest book; pen; handkerchief; garter (if you're doing a garter toss); something old, new, borrowed, blue. If you need them for your ceremony, make sure you have: unity candle, kiddush cup, glass for breaking. Consider whether you want to buy a special cake-cutting knife and toasting flutes if you didn't receive them as gifts.

- Review honeymoon reservations; make any special reservations for restaurants, spa appointments, activities.

- Make shopping list for anything you need for honeymoon.

- Book manicure and pedicure appointments for the day before the wedding.

- If moving, send change-of-address form to post office.

- If sending out wedding announcements, address them and give to a family member to mail the day of or day after the wedding.

- Buy thank-you gifts for parents and wrap them. Or place an order with the florist and include a handwritten card.

- Stock up on any prescription medications (including disposable contact lenses, allergy meds, and birth control) you'll need for the honeymoon.

(continued)

Short-Engagement Planning Time Line (continued)

- Find out where all out-of-town guests are staying, if delivering in-room gifts (include those staying with friends).
- Have a blast at your bachelor/bachelorette party.

Two Weeks

- Finish writing vows.
- If you have a pet, make arrangements for a pet sitter during the wedding and honeymoon.
- Write toasts and speeches for rehearsal dinner and reception.
- Arrange for people to hand out seating cards and accept gifts.
- Write as many thank-you notes as you can. Try to keep up before final deluge of gifts.
- Wrap gifts for bridesmaids and groomsmen.
- Have your final pre-wedding facial. (If you can't squeeze it in, skip it rather than having it closer to the wedding.)
- Final pre-wedding hair color appointment. (It's okay to schedule up until one week before the wedding if it's your regular color or highlights.)
- Have final meeting with florist; discuss which flowers are actually available; go over schedule.
- Confirm hotel room for wedding night.
- Check registries to make sure enough gifts remain at different price levels (check every few days up until the wedding).
- Check in with anyone scheduled to make a toast at the rehearsal dinner or reception.

- If traveling to another country for wedding or honeymoon, get $100 worth of foreign currency.
- Arrange to have someone check on your home and take in packages while you're away.

One Week

- Pick up wedding dress.
- Start packing for honeymoon if leaving within two days of the wedding.
- Prepare tip envelopes for vendors by putting cash into marked envelopes.
- Finalize seating arrangements.
- Deliver seating cards, place cards, and table numbers to calligrapher.
- Call limo company to confirm reservations and pickup times; send explicit directions to driver; prepare a "call sheet" with all pickup and drop-off times, names, and addresses.
- Give ketubah (Jewish marriage contract) to rabbi, if you're providing it.
- Check in with groom to make sure marriage license and anything he's in charge of is in order; remind him that things will soon be back to normal.
- Send seating chart to photographer to go with shot list.
- Send seating chart to videographer to go with list of people to be interviewed.
- Start checking weather forecast for wedding day.
- Confirm food and bar menu details with caterer.
- Make arrangements to hold mail and stop newspapers for honeymoon.

Five Days

- Confirm all vendors the Monday before the event.
- Give final head count to hotel or caterer the Monday before the event. (Check your contract for actual deadline in case it's different.)
- Prepare payment or donation for officiant and checks for vendors who get paid on wedding day.

Four Days

- Arrange transportation to airport for honeymoon if you don't already have it.
- Write thank-you notes to parents for all their support.

Three Days

- Confirm hotel reservations for honeymoon.
- Check weather forecasts for wedding and honeymoon.
- Practice vows.
- Pack bag for wedding day, including emergency day kit—don't forget to include an extra pair of shoes for dancing.

Two Days

- Deliver in-room gifts to out-of-towners on the day they arrive.
- Give programs, yarmulkes, and anything else you're handing out at ceremony to person who will distribute them.

- Give seating cards and place cards to person who will be putting them out.

- Give guest book, cake knife, toasting glasses to person who will put them in place.

- Give favors to person who will set them up or distribute them.

- Pick up rental tuxes.

- Make sure that bridesmaids have their outfits completely put together, including shoes and accessories.

- Reconfirm wedding night hotel reservation.

One Day

- Practice speeches and vows.

- Get a manicure and pedicure.

- Review and finalize seating chart, adjusting for last-minute cancellations.

- Confirm flight reservations for honeymoon.

- Reconfirm pickup times and addresses with limo company; reconfirm any transportation you've arranged for guests.

- Give tip envelopes to person assigned to distribute them.

- Treat bridesmaids, mothers, sisters, and other very close female relatives to a luncheon, spa outing, or other special get-together.

- Groom treats groomsmen, fathers, brothers, and other very close male relatives to a round of golf, dinner, or other outing.

- Give gifts to members of bridal party.

- Go over any specific jobs for members of bridal party, such as manning guest book or taking gifts from the reception to your home.

- Rehearse ceremony.

- Enjoy rehearsal dinner.

Wedding Day

- Get final steaming for wedding gown.

- Relax and enjoy the day!

- Have best man or maid of honor call airline to check on flight status for honeymoon.

- In the excitement of the day, don't forget to take regular medications for allergies, birth control, etc.

Day After

- Send thank-you notes to parents, and possibly flowers or a gift.

- Thank attendants.

- Return rental tuxedos.

- Call any special vendors to thank them.

- Deposit monetary wedding gifts or put them in safekeeping.

- Freeze top layer of cake.

- If preserving bouquet, send it to the preservation service.

- Make a note of any stains on wedding gown; if there are bad ones, don't wait to take it to the cleaner. Otherwise, hang it on a padded hanger (use the lingerie straps for this) in your closet and cover it with a clean sheet until you can get it to the cleaner.

Rings

Engagement Rings

The most visible public symbol of betrothal and marriage, rings represent both the initial jump-up-and-down phase and the quieter commitment of a lasting union. Though the concept of the engagement ring comes from the Romans, the pharaohs of ancient Egypt saw rings in general as a fitting way to represent eternity—circles have no beginning and no end.

Since I know that these days many couples forgo the element of surprise and take the safer route of going ring shopping together before getting engaged, I'm going to give you a crash course on engagement rings. You'll live with yours on a daily basis, and it's a considerable investment, so it's important to choose wisely.

What's so nuptial about diamonds? Well, they're the most resilient natural material known to man. Enduring, unbreakable, and brilliant, they were quick to become a metaphor for the bond of marriage. When first discovered in India around 400 B.C., the stones were believed to possess magical powers. The name derives from the Greeks, who called the gem *adamas*, which means "the unconquerable"; they believed diamonds were precious particles of stars that had fallen to Earth.

The first diamond engagement ring on record was offered by Archduke Maximilian of Austria to Mary of Burgundy in 1477. While sapphires (thought to represent the heavens) and rubies (the heart) were also hot contenders as tokens of love, diamonds were the rarest and costliest gems at the time, and they were believed to possess the power to ward off evils like snakes, fire, and poison. For the next four hundred years, only royalty and aristocrats would be able to afford the precious gems, but when large deposits of diamonds were discovered in South Africa in 1870, they became accessible to a much broader audience.

In 1947, an advertising agency representing De Beers coined the phrase "A diamond is forever"—and the rest is history. Today, more than 80 percent of engagement rings have diamonds.

Bling University

THERE ARE MANY FACETS to buying rings—you're dealing with precious gemstones *and* precious metals, for one. You've probably already heard of "The 4Cs" (cut, clarity, color, and carat). Those checkpoints cover the essentials, but before you get there, you'll need to think about the choice of stone (it doesn't have to be a diamond!), its shape and cut, the setting and mount, the metal, and, of course, your budget. You should also decide if you'd prefer to wear one ring or two on a daily basis. Do you want an engagement ring and band that can be worn together, or perhaps a jeweled band that stands alone?

The 4Cs

What sets true gems apart from the rest? In general, jewelers assess a diamond's dollar value first by its color, then by its clarity, cut, and carat. But when it comes to aesthetic value—think of it as a diamond's curb appeal—the cut is the most important factor, followed by color, clarity, and carat weight. Contrary to popular belief, anyone in the know will tell you that size is last on the list.

Cut

Cut is the only aspect of a diamond that's the result of human intervention. It refers to the shape of the stone and the cutting style, proportions, and finish. A good cut should enhance a stone's "fire" (rainbow-like flashes), brilliance, and scintillation (flashes of light in motion). If a stone looks lifeless, it's probably been poorly cut and its light is leaking out the sides or bottom.

There are two types of faceted cuts: brilliant cuts and step-cuts. Brilliant cuts take a round or curved geometrical shape and create the most sparkle; step cuts, also referred to as "emerald cuts," are shaped like stairs on the sides of a diamond and give a more streamlined look.

GIA Grading System

The Gemological Institute of America (GIA) established the internationally recognized "4C" grading system for judging diamonds. While prospective buyers aren't expected to be well versed in this detailed system of classification, it will behoove you to learn enough to be conversant when a jeweler tosses these terms around.

Clarity. There are eleven grades in the GIA's clarity scale, ranging from flawless (F or FL) to more prominent inclusions (I). Most flaws can be seen only under a jeweler's loupe. Contrary to popular belief, clarity will not affect a diamond's sparkle or brilliance, except at the lowest I grades. The "cleanest" stones are ranked F or FL (Flawless) and IF (Internally Flawless). Grades of VVS1 and 2 (Very Very Slightly Included) indicate a minute flaw that is difficult to see under a loupe, while VS1 and 2 (Very Slightly Included) tell you that very small

imperfections can be detected under a loupe. SI1, 2, or 3 (Slightly Included) suggest that several small flaws are present; while I1, 2, or 3, the lowest grades, denote a stone that exhibits obvious flaws, some of which are visible to the naked eye. Because imperfections in this category are so hard to see, this is a savvy place to compromise if you're on a tight budget, but anything below VVS2 can put you in dicey territory.

Color. When it comes to judging color, the GIA employs letters beginning with D (colorless) to Z (light yellow or brown). The most valuable gems are graded D–F, or Colorless, while those ranked G–J are Near Colorless, K-M are Faint Yellow, N–R are Very Light Yellow, and S–Z are Light Yellow. The tinge of a stone will be noticeable on a stone ranked from N–Z, making this the most affordable category. If a diamond's color is deeper than a Z, it's deemed a "fancy" or colored

diamond. A reputable jeweler will keep a set of master stones in the store so that you can see the range in color grade.

Cut. Unlike clarity and color, there are no internationally recognized grades for cut, and gem experts differ on the best way to judge this aspect of a stone. The GIA ranks a diamond's cut as Excellent, Very Good, Good, Fair, or Poor, but only for round brilliant cuts.

Carat. Diamonds are weighed on an electronic scale before the ring is set. One-carat diamonds, with a diameter of about 6 mm, are often purchased as engagement rings—it's a fine size for a solitaire setting, but you can do beautiful things with smaller stones and more elaborate settings. A two-carat stone, counterintuitively, isn't twice the size of a one-carat (it's around 8.2 mm in diameter), but it is quite substantial. Anything from three on up would fall into the "not-your-average-rock" category.

Mixed cuts, like the princess cut and Tiffany's Lucida, which have become more popular in recent years, use a combination of brilliant and step-cuts. An "ideal cut" is a round brilliant with fifty-eight precise cuts.

Clarity

Every diamond contains natural flaws. Internal flaws are called "inclusions," external ones "blemishes." Clarity is the degree to which a stone approaches flawlessness. (No stone, no matter how costly, will be totally free of imperfections.) Many of these inclusions and blemishes, which might include cracks, bubbles, specks, scratches, pits, or

chips, are invisible to the human eye and can be seen only with a jeweler's loupe. The number of such birthmarks determines a stone's value and allows individual gems to be identified, as no two diamonds will ever look exactly alike upon close inspection. The GIA Diamond Grading System (see box, this page) is widely used to assess clarity.

Color

Most diamonds contain slight traces of yellow or brown; only the rarest are colorless, or white. Color is rated on a graded scale, ranging from colorless to light yellow. Totally colorless gems, also known as exceptional white or rare white, are very difficult to come by and very pricey. Don't despair if you can't afford a rare or even a near colorless—the right setting can make a stone look whiter, and some people prefer a hint of color to cast the ring in a warm glow. Diamonds with a yellow, brown, or orange tinge are an attractive and more affordable alternative to white. Diamonds in pink, yellow, and other colors are called "fancy colored diamonds," and their color is evaluated differently.

Carat

The unit of measurement for a diamond's weight, a carat is divided into 100 points. One carat weighs about the same as a paper clip, 200 milligrams. (The carat system was actually invented in India and based on the uniform seeds of the carob tree: One seed equals one carat.) Diamonds of the same carat weight can have dramatically different monetary values based on cut, clarity, and color.

Anatomy of a Stone

Table. The flat plane at the top of the stone.

Girdle. The dividing line between the crown (top) and pavilion (bottom) of the stone. It's the widest part of the stone and forms the edge where the prongs or setting grips the stone.

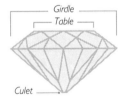

Girdle

Table

Culet

Culet. The point at the bottom of the stone.

Why the Fourth Finger?

With the exception of a few cultures—Greek and Polish, for instance—engagement and wedding rings are almost universally placed on the fourth finger of the left hand. There are various explanations as to how this tradition came about, but most historians trace it back to the ancient Egyptians, who believed that the *vena amoris* (vein of love) ran directly from the fourth finger to the heart.

Get It Certified

Don't fret if you can't tell a K-grade diamond from an N—many gems will look the same to the untrained eye. A diamond's true value is hidden in minute differences that only an expert can see. This is why it's important to buy from a reputable jeweler. Going with recommendations from friends or family is a good start; be sure to check for GIA diplomas or other verifiable evidence of training and education. Also consider how long the jeweler has been in business.

For diamonds weighing a carat or more, you'll want the jeweler to provide an independently produced lab report certifying its quality, weight, and cut. (The GIA Gem Trade Laboratory is one major source for such reports.) You'll need this document in order to get the ring insured.

Shapes and Cuts

MOTHER NATURE DETERMINES a stone's color and clarity, but the choice of shape and cut is up to you. Shape refers to the stone's silhouette (marquise, oval, round), and cut refers to the way the facets and steps are cut into the diamond (princess, cushion, Asscher). The choices are intertwined—many shapes, in fact, are only widely available in a single cut.

Even if you already have a favorite picked out (a round brilliant for a traditionalist, a marquise for an extrovert), try on a variety of shapes, as certain styles may be more flattering, depending on the size of your hands, the length of your fingers, and even the shape of your nail bed—a marquise will overly emphasize a pointy nail bed, for instance.

Round Stones

The most popular cut for engagement rings and the iconic cut for a solitaire, this traditional shape, also known as a brilliant cut, gets its unparalleled shimmer from fifty-eight perfectly angled and proportioned facets. If you're looking for maximum sparkle, this is the cut for you. While this versatile shape works well in both simple and more elaborate settings, it does have one drawback: Due to its 360-degree symmetrical shape, a round cut appears smaller than other diamonds of the same carat weight.

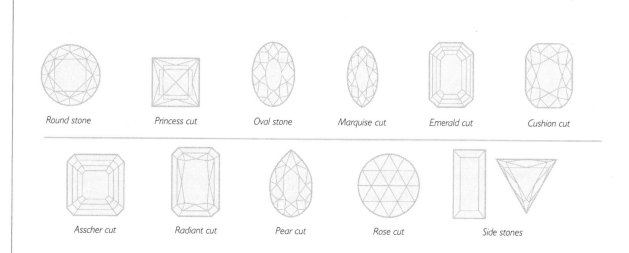

Round stone   Princess cut   Oval stone   Marquise cut   Emerald cut   Cushion cut

Asscher cut   Radiant cut   Pear cut   Rose cut   Side stones

The Princess Cut

A square-shaped stone whose intricate facets offer the brilliance of a round, this glittering, streamlined option may have anywhere from 49 to 144 facets, depending on the size of the gem; it is cut with the steps of an emerald shape and the triangular facets of a round. The shape works well as a center stone flanked by three or more stones or in an eternity band. Don't be misled by its regal name: This cut may be a relatively less expensive option because it closely follows a diamond's natural crystalline shape.

Oval Stones

An adaptation of the round, this cut offers optimal fire and brilliance in an elegant, elongated shape. Standard oval cuts will have a length-to-width ratio of 1.5:1, but other sizes and proportions are acceptable as well—it's really a matter of taste. The oval's best-kept secret is that it will look larger than a round stone of the same carat weight. While the shape is typically set along with other stones, it makes a wonderful solitaire for small hands, because it follows the line of the finger more naturally than a round brilliant.

The Marquise Cut

Reportedly created for Louis XV's renowned mistress, the Marquise de Pompadour—in homage to the shape of her mouth—it's no surprise that this oblong cut with fifty-six facets and pointed ends makes a strong statement. The length-to-width ratio is of primary importance, the general rule being that the length of the stone should be about twice the width to optimize sparkle. With its large surface area and shallow cut, a marquise appears bigger than its carat weight. It's a flattering shape, lengthening and slimming the fingers.

The Emerald Cut

If what you love about diamonds is their glassy sheen, this is the cut for you. Derived from the cut most commonly used on emeralds and created in the Art Deco era, this sophisticated, boxy shape can be either square or rectangular and has cut corners and step-cut sides. Because the emerald cut has only twenty-five facets, don't expect as much sparkle from this ring. Instead, the focus is on its long, clean surface, also known as the table. You'll want a stone with a high clarity grade (no lower than SI1 or SI2), as small imperfections will be more obvious. The emerald works well for a bride who doesn't want a flashy ring or one who is looking for a formal design.

The Cushion Cut

Women coveted this soft, pillow-shaped cut for much of the nineteenth century, when it reached the height of popularity. It has experienced a revival in recent years due to the visibility of estate jewelry, and it hasn't taken long for jewelers like Tiffany & Co. to introduce new variations on the shape. A rectangle with rounded edges, the cushion cut emits a soft glow, an effect achieved by large facets and a deep cut. Also known as the candlelight diamond, this cut is both nostalgic and modern.

The Asscher Cut

Created in 1900 by the Dutch Asscher brothers and popular through the 1930s, the Asscher is a square shape with cut corners and step-cut sides, similar to a square emerald. Its parallel step facets cast a beguiling pattern within the diamond that can be seen by looking directly into the stone. (This effect can only be achieved by top-notch precision cutting.) Like the cushion cut, the Asscher has made a comeback as Art Deco jewelry has become increasingly in vogue.

Dollars and Sense

You love a stone that looms large, but a 2.5-carat stunner isn't in the cards. Zero in on cuts that make a diamond look bigger. Oval, pear, and marquise shapes give you maximum mileage out of a diamond. (A round brilliant is smaller, when you compare side by side, carat for carat.) The choice of setting can also affect how big the stone appears; a bezel setting adds heft, making a diamond look more substantial.

Side stones flanking a center stone cause the light to bounce back and forth, upping the dazzle and making the center stone look more important. Another approach is to go for an elegant band covered with small diamonds—the total carat weight will cost much less than a single stone of the same size.

Finally, if the size doesn't quite add up to the diamond of your dreams, don't despair. You can trade up to a larger stone for your tenth anniversary, if not before. Some jewelers will even credit the price of your original stone against the purchase of a larger diamond down the road.

The Radiant Cut

A beautiful union between an emerald and a round cut, the impressive radiant is a rare find. Exuding the sparkle of a round, this shape is similar to a princess cut but more rectangular, and with trimmed corners. This unique design is achieved by a combination of step-cuts and facets.

The Pear Cut

Also referred to as a teardrop diamond, this shape is round on one end and pointed on the other, making it a feminine hybrid of cuts. While the shape itself is a cross between the oval and the marquise, the pear is cut like a round and features fifty-eight facets. Look for a length-to-width ratio of 1.5:1.75, and check that the shoulders of the stone (the round end) are even. The point is worn toward the fingernail, elongating the fingers.

The Rose Cut

One of the oldest cuts, the rose first emerged in fifteenth-century India. Unlike most shapes, where facets appear along the sides and bottom of the stone, the rose is domed and covered with facets that meet at a point on top of the stone—like the petals of a rosebud. This shape casts a soft, delicate glow and is a less expensive cut than other fancy shapes. It's most commonly found in antique and estate jewelry.

Side Stones

Certain cuts don't make the grade as main stones, but they add a certain something when used in a lesser role as side stones. For one thing, they channel more light into the main stone and enhance its sparkle. Baguettes, trillions, and trilliants are the most commonly used side stones, but almost all of the prime cuts described above—particularly princess cuts—are available in small sizes, in addition to specialty shapes such as trapezoids, kite shapes, and half-moons.

A baguette is a small, rectangular shape offered in both straight and tapered cuts; it's the most popular—and traditional—choice when it comes to side stones. Steplike facets along the sides lead the eye toward the center stone—typically a princess or round—like stairs leading to the main event.

Three-Stone Rings

Symbolizing past, present, and future, three-stone rings—also known as trinity or trilogy rings—have been around for thousands of years. The three matched stones are generally of similar size and shape. The cut is most often round, but a princess cut is another popular option. Part of their enduring appeal is the extra dazzle created by the light reflecting back and forth among the stones.

Cultured Diamonds

If your conscience reels at the thought of buying diamonds because of mining conditions, politics, or other issues, there are alternatives available to you. Man-made, or "cultured," diamonds are test-tube versions of the precious carbon crystals. They have soared in quality over the last few years, and the GIA began grading them in 2007, which conferred another level of acceptance within the jewelry industry.

These stones start with a sliver of diamond and are identical to natural diamonds in their chemical composition, but they're grown in artificial conditions, much like cultured pearls.

Cultured diamonds are available in white and in color (particularly yellow), with the yellow stones offering a staggering savings over natural diamonds. They may cost anywhere from 15 to 90 percent less than a mined diamond.

Another way to avoid buying into the diamond trade? Recycle. Take an old family diamond (or even diamonds from both families to represent your union) and have it remounted. You'll give new life to a beautiful stone that may have been wasting away in a jewelry box.

A trilliant is a triangular stone that serves as a bold partner to the main stone, combining step-cutting and brilliant faceting. (It's so spectacular, it's sometimes used as a center stone.) A trilliant will appear larger than its actual carat weight and makes a good companion to an emerald, radiant, or princess diamond, as the edges line up cleanly.

Beyond the Diamond

DIAMONDS AREN'T every girl's best friend. Some brides find them too expected and want to stand out by wearing a different gem stone. Others object to the politics associated with their mining.

Most people seeking an alternative gem choose it for either its color or meaning. Blue sapphires are a symbol of fidelity and the heavens, and rubies represent love and passion. A gem might also be a less expensive alternative to a colored diamond—you can get a hefty pink tourmaline for a fraction of the price of a rare pink diamond. You can also choose a stone that corresponds to your birthday, or combine two different stones to correspond to yours and his. The Victorians were fond of creating a hidden message by juxtaposing different gems, with the first letter of each standing for a secret word. One of the most popular was *dearest*, using diamond, emerald, amethyst, ruby, emerald, sapphire, and topaz.

When choosing a stone other than a diamond, do some research to make sure it can withstand the rigors of daily wear. Diamonds are the hardest substance, rating a 10 on the Mohs' scale of hardness. As a general rule, you should stick with stones that rate a 7 or higher on the scale. A jeweler will be able to tell you, or you can do a quick online search. But also take into account the toughness and brittleness of the stone, as that contributes to how likely it is to get damaged. Emeralds, for example, rate a 7.5 to 8 on the Mohs' scale, making them hard, but they're quite brittle and chip easily. If you love a particular color, ask a jeweler to suggest alternative choices; tsavorite, for instance, is a brilliant green stone that offers a more durable alternative to emeralds.

Once the news is out, you'll find yourself extending your hand several times a day to show off the ring. If ever there was a reason to get a regular manicure, this is it. You don't want uneven nails and raggedy cuticles to distract from the beauty of the stone.

Settings and Mounts

ALTHOUGH THE STONE accounts for as much as 90 percent of the cost of the ring, the setting is important, too. It's what holds your ring in place and protects your investment, but it also affects how your stones will look and how the ring itself will look on your hand.

When considering mountings, think about your plan for your wedding band. Do you want to stack the two rings on the same finger, or will you switch your engagement ring to the right hand after marriage? You'll find more details about what to consider in the section on wedding bands, opposite page.

The styles below apply to any ring with gemstones in it, which may also include wedding bands and men's rings.

Prong or claw. The most popular setting, it involves three to six claws that hold the stone and raise it up. The more prongs, the more secure the stone (but the less of it you see). On the downside, prongs can snag, making them more vulnerable than some other settings.

Bezel. A band of metal surrounds the stone, concealing the girdle. The stone is flush with the metal, which can protect a damaged girdle on an heirloom ring or hide imperfections. The color of the metal is reflected onto the stone, so a white metal can enhance a white diamond, while a yellow gold bezel can flatter a yellow diamond or a ruby.

Cluster. Multiple stones are set in a circular shape, usually a cluster of small diamonds around a larger one, often using prongs. It's one way to gather a lot of small stones into an impressive mass.

Tension. A contemporary setting that uses heavy pressure in the shank of the ring to hold the stone, so it looks as though it's floating, with no structural support on the underside. It allows a lot of light into the gem, but it is only suitable for the hardest of stones—diamonds, sapphires, and rubies.

Illusion. A built-up, ornate box of metal surrounding the stone to make it look larger.

Channel. Used on the band portion of a ring, stones are set between two parallel channels of metal, generally lying flat.

Bar. Stones are lined up on a band, with each one separated by a thin, vertical bar to hold it in place.

Bead/pavé. French for "paved," this setting features three or more rows of stones set into holes in the metal and held in place by metal beads to create a relatively smooth surface. Nearly always used for small stones.

Gypsy. Used primarily on bands and on men's rings, a gypsy setting sinks a stone so that it's flush with the metal band.

For guidance on choosing metals, see page 415.

Estate Jewelry

Though the term "estate jewelry" might sound upscale, it actually applies to any used jewelry, even the rings at your local pawn shop. "Antique" jewelry, on the other hand, must be at least a hundred years old to earn its designation. Estate jewelry with astonishing stones, a storied provenance, or a famous jewelry designer's name behind it will fetch a premium, but many older pieces of jewelry can turn out to be excellent buys.

A ring from the Edwardian, Art Deco, or Victorian period will definitely look unique, even if many modern jewelry styles echo cuts from those periods. The stones are generally smaller, with a softer glow (due not to aging, but to a difference in cutting techniques). The craftsmanship in vintage and antique jewelry is often finer and more detailed than in jewelry made today.

Though your main focus should be on finding a ring you love—rather than worrying about investment value—you still need to be a smart shopper. Don't buy on the spot, unless the ring comes from an impeccable source and is accompanied by a detailed report from a certified, independent gem appraiser. Even then, you should have your own appraisal done to make sure you're getting the real deal. (It wasn't unusual for Victorians to use cut glass in place of diamonds, so don't trust a ring simply because it's an antique and set in gold or platinum.)

A few precautions:

- Buy from a reputable jeweler, auction house, or dealer. Have the gems evaluated by an independent appraiser before committing to the ring, especially if you're buying from a pawn shop or a questionable source. Always check the return policy before buying.

- Look at the gems, setting, and the mounting under a jeweler's loupe or a magnifying glass. You're looking for well-matched stones, the condition of the prongs and metalwork, and any obvious inclusions, chips, or flaws in the stones. If there's an appraiser's report, you'll be able to see identifying characteristics under the loupe to determine if the report matches the ring at hand.

- Although other gems are very common, diamonds are your safest bet for two reasons: They're less prone to cracking than emeralds and rubies, and their universal grading system makes it easier to know what you're getting.

- The ring should be accompanied by a certified gemologist's report, along with a full written description from the jeweler. The description should include age, size, condition, flaws, and a list of any damages and repairs. (Repairs can change the value of the ring, especially if they weren't done properly.) If the ring came from a well-known designer, that should also be noted. If the ring's history is available, make sure that's included in the description as well.

- Prior to purchase, find out if the ring can be resized without incurring damage. And before wearing the ring, have a jeweler evaluate the settings to make sure they're secure.

Wedding Bands

Though there's a lot of focus on the engagement ring, since it's usually the one with the serious bling, in some ways, the wedding band is a more important choice—in theory, *this* is the ring you'll wear every day. The engagement ring serves as a promise of future commitment, while the wedding band enacts the commitment in the present tense; you're going from "Will you marry me?" to "With this ring, I thee wed."

It should be both beautiful and comfortable. Find out if there are any religious or cultural considerations for your bands—it's traditional for a Jewish band not to have gemstones or anything else that would break the circle, and people with African roots sometimes choose to incorporate an ankh, a symbol of eternal life and love.

Women have worn wedding bands throughout history. Though there have been periods when men wore bands, at other times they've gone bare-handed. But during World War II, the double-ring ceremony took off:

The Tiffany Setting

hat's so special about a Tiffany setting? The open, six-prong setting was introduced by Charles L. Tiffany in 1886 with the express purpose of maximizing the brilliance of diamonds. It raised the ring off the finger, allowed light to enter from all sides, and put more of the diamond on show, whereas prior settings had hidden more of the stone. When you see an illustration of a diamond solitaire—even a cartoonish one—it's invariably based on a Tiffany setting.

Soldiers returning to the front wanted to see a constant reminder of their beloveds. The percentage of Americans engaging in double-ring ceremonies soared from less than 15 percent in 1940 to 94 percent in 1944. After that, there was no turning back.

Choosing Bands

THE FIRST THING to establish is how you will wear the ring. Do you want to wear a stand alone band? Do you want the band to be worn on the same finger as your engagement ring, or do you plan to turn the engagement ring into a right-hand ring after the wedding? If you want to wear them on the same finger, tradition dictates that you wear the engagement ring above the wedding band so that the band remains closer to the heart. If you're not going to wear them together, coordinating the engagement and wedding ring isn't critical.

You should also think about whether you want gemstones on your band. This applies to guys as well, as there are more and more bands for men with diamonds, sapphires, and other precious stones. Do you have the type of lifestyle that demands a simple metal band? (Maybe you're an avid rock climber or work with your hands all day.) If you have sensitive skin or allergies, focus on metals (platinum chief among them) known for their hypoallergenic quality.

Jewelers can create wonderful engagement-ring-and-band combinations that blend together seamlessly, though it's easier to accomplish if you don't have your engagement ring yet and the jeweler gets to start fresh. Many engagement and wedding rings are available in "sets" designed to be worn together.

ASK MINDY

Q My beloved proposed to me with a ring that I find completely hideous. I said yes, of course, but what now? Do I have to look at this monstrosity every day for the rest of my life?!

A Okay, so he doesn't quite get your taste, or maybe it's a family heirloom. Wait a week, then broach the subject diplomatically. Try not to insult his taste. If it's a family ring, tell him how much it means to you but offer a practical reason why you should have the stone reset. Maybe the setting is too fragile for your active life—not uncommon with antique rings—and you fear it will get damaged. Or it's set in gold and you always wear silver and cool colors, so it would work much better if it were reset in platinum. (And yes, these definitely fall into the category of white lies!)

If the style (newly purchased or a family heirloom) doesn't reflect your personality, you might tell him you're not in love with the way it looks on your finger. If he bought it off the rack from a jeweler, you should be able to exchange it without a problem. Go to the jewelry store together to redesign or choose a new ring so that you're both involved in the process.

Shopping for Bands

START BY TRYING on a lot of bands to see what flatters your fingers and what feels comfortable. Anyone who works with their hands might do better with a thin "comfort fit." Band width is measured in millimeters, and a few millimeters can mean all the difference between a ring that's in the way and a ring you don't feel at all. If you plan to wear the band with your engagement ring, try them on together to see whether they complement each other or fight for attention.

Metals

FIRST, DETERMINE whether you prefer a warm or cool tone to your metal. Which is more flattering to your skin tone? (Warm metals look better on skin with a yellow undertone, while cool metals flatter skin with a pink undertone.) If the ring has gems in it, which metal pairs well with your stone? Is your other jewelry gold or silver? If you always wear gold, do you want to start over by choosing a platinum ring?

If you are choosing a band to be worn on the same hand as your engagement ring, you want matching metals.

If you go back and forth between gold and silver, a band that combines different metals might be just the thing.

Gold

This precious metal has history and tradition on its side. Its warmth suits people with yellow undertones to their skin. It's not always so great next to a white diamond, as it can make it appear more yellow; on the other hand, it can help balance the yellow that's already in a diamond, so it's essential to see your stone next to gold before making a decision.

Gold jewelry is made of an alloy, or compound. The amount of pure gold in the alloy is designated by its karat, or weight, with 24 karat being pure gold, brighter and more yellow in tone. In rings, though, 14 and 18 karat make the best choices; anything higher tends to be too soft to withstand daily wear. The inside of the ring should bear a stamp of its purity, either "14K" or "18K."

Yellow gold is an alloy of gold, copper, and silver. Other colors of gold are produced by varying the percentage and selection of other metals. White gold is yellow gold with a dose of nickel. Rose gold (also called pink gold) contains more copper and less nickel than white gold.

Platinum

The cool luster of platinum, rarer and more expensive than gold, brings out the brilliance of a white diamond. It's stronger than gold, tarnish resistant, and hypoallergenic. Those with fair skin and cool (or pink) undertones will find it particularly flattering. The platinum in jewelry is alloyed with other metals, but in the United States, it's traditionally 95 percent pure. (Though widely available, 585 platinum—an alloy with 58.5 percent platinum content—is not considered true platinum.) This elegance and durability doesn't come cheaply—expect to spend $500 more on a platinum band than you would on gold.

Palladium

A relative newcomer to wedding jewelry, palladium is a naturally white precious metal in the platinum family. In fact, it looks the same as platinum but weighs less. It can also be half the price, making it a bargain alternative to platinum or a smart trade-up from white gold.

Titanium

Strong as steel and light as aluminum, titanium is the superhero of metals, even though it's not considered precious. It's usually gunmetal gray and is suitable for sensitive skin. Titanium's durability and light weight make it a savvy choice for men who are hard on their jewelry; it doesn't have much of a following among women. Aircraft-grade titanium is not as pure as basic titanium, but it's much harder.

Inscriptions

A TRADITION that dates back to medieval times, an inscription adds something personal to even the plainest gold band, making it yours and yours alone. Keep inscriptions short—asking the jeweler to squeeze in too many words will make them nearly impossible to decipher—and find out how much time the jeweler needs for engraving. Have the rings sized first, or the inscription could be ruined by the sizing. Most couples have their initials and wedding date engraved inside the shank of the wedding band, but you can also use a phrase from a favorite song or poem, a nickname, or a phrase from your wedding vows.

Ring TLC

Diamonds are forever, but not if you don't take care of them. Same goes for your wedding bands. Since you're dealing with durable minerals and metals, the care is actually quite minimal.

The most common injury with any jewelry is scratching. That goes for both stones and metals. Diamond rings are not immune; although diamonds are the hardest substance on earth, diamonds *can* scratch other diamonds. They can also scratch the metal of other jewelry if they're jumbled together. To minimize scratching, don't let your ring touch other jewelry when you store it. When traveling, wrap it in a cloth and put it in a plastic bag, then tuck the bag into your jewelry roll.

A buildup of body oils will cloud your stone, so wipe it off regularly with a damp cloth. Metal shines up when you wipe it with a chamois cloth, which your jeweler can provide.

To clean a diamond ring or any newer ring with precious stones, squirt Ivory dish soap into a bowl and fill with warm water. Let the ring soak, then scrub it gently with a soft-bristled toothbrush that you use solely for this purpose. (You don't want traces of other cleansers on there.) Here's the real secret: Most of us concentrate on brushing the top of the stone, but much of the grime accumulates on the underside, so brush underneath and in the crevices around the mounting thoroughly. If you have a Water Pik, use it for cleaning your ring by squirting water into those hard-to-access crevices. Dry it off with a soft, lint-free cloth or towel.

Some rings can be cleaned in ammonia-based solutions or with ultrasonic cleaners, but it's safest to ask your jeweler for advice. Sapphires and rubies are nearly as hard as diamonds, so the care is similar. Emeralds, however, are softer and porous—which means they'll absorb perfume and cleaning chemicals—so ask your jeweler for cleaning advice.

This is common sense, but since it happens so often, I'll say it anyway: Don't wash your diamond ring over an open drain. You don't want to live out that sitcom scenario of the ring falling down the pipes.

It's a good idea to take off your rings before doing dishes (the stones can chip), and before going into a chlorinated pool or hot tub, because the chlorine can weaken or discolor the metal—and if metal prongs get damaged, you could lose your stone.

Take your ring to a jeweler once a year for a checkup. Schedule it around your anniversary to make it easier to remember—should you stumble across an anniversary gift at the jewelry store, so much the better. The jeweler will check to make sure the stones are secure and that the prongs are in place. He can also give it a good cleaning.

A Ring of One's Own

Going custom can get you a ring that's truly wonderful without much additional expense. You'll need to give the jeweler time to design the ring, so you should start the process at least five months before the wedding.

His-and-Hers

Your wedding bands certainly don't need to be identical, but it underscores the fact that the two of you belong together if the bands relate to each other in some way. That could mean sharing a common design element (such as a border with milgraining—beaded metalwork at the very edges of the ring), the same metal, or even the same inscription. If you want platinum and he wants gold, that's okay, too. The person wearing the band every day should feel comfortable wearing it.

Most jewelers don't charge for checkups and cleanings, though they would typically charge for repairs. Some insurance policies may require you to get the ring checked at certain intervals, so know your policy. (See below.)

In between checkups, occasionally jiggle your ring next to your ear. It shouldn't make any noise. Rattling is a sign that something is loose, and you should take the ring to your jeweler ASAP.

Appraisals and Insurance

IN THE EXCITEMENT of getting engaged, the hard realities of life sometimes get overlooked. One of the most terrible (and all-too-common) mistakes people make is not getting their ring insured immediately. A ring can get lost or stolen, or a faulty setting can cause a stone to fall out.

Renter's and homeowner's insurance policies typically exclude pricey jewelry. Call your insurance company to request a rider that will cover your new treasure. You can also shop around for a separate jewelry policy.

> **If your ring is extremely valuable or an irreplaceable family heirloom, consider having a cubic zirconium version made by a jeweler for daily wear. Keep the real one safe in a vault.**

When evaluating an insurance policy, find out if it covers the current value of the ring minus depreciation, or the replacement value. Will you receive cash or a new ring? How are irreplaceable heirloom rings treated? Make sure you know what's covered (such as loss versus theft and partial loss if the ring is damaged) and the cost of the deductible. Expect annual coverage to cost between 1 percent and 3 percent of the ring's appraised value.

Many policies will require you to get a professional appraisal of your ring so that it's insured for the correct amount—in addition to the gem report that comes with a diamond of a carat or more. You should have the ring reappraised every two years, since inflation can alter its value.

One newer way to add another layer of protection to your ring: a laser inscription on the stone. It's invisible to the naked eye, but can identify the ring in case of theft.

Destination Weddings

Destination Nation

You've decided that nothing could be more romantic than having palm trees, bougainvillea, and the cerulean blue of the Pacific Ocean as the backdrop for your wedding. Or a Tuscan hillscape, or the rolling hills of a Northern California vineyard, for that matter. You're not alone.

The destination wedding has skyrocketed in popularity in the last decade. And its appeal keeps growing.

First, it makes your wedding stand out vividly from the pack. You know how you ate the same tray-passed chicken satay at the last three weddings? And how you recognized the DJ? That won't happen at a destination wedding. When you take your wedding on the road, you automatically make it unique and memorable.

Second, it allows you to spend significant time with family and friends, not just a few minutes catching up. The shared meals and activities, ranging from golf to yoga, create a wonderful camplike atmosphere.

For a bride and groom feeling paralyzed by a sprawling guest list, a destination wedding can also be a welcome way out. Not only will you be able to count on more declines, you'll also be better able to explain your decision to keep things small and intimate.

Last, kept small and held at a resort with the help of a wedding coordinator, a destination wedding (paradoxically) can be less intensive to plan, allowing the bride to feel like all she has to do is show up. You're likely to be evaluating choices over email rather than running around to meetings. There's also the off chance that a time difference can work in your favor; more than one bride I know has felt blessed by the fact that she could make her wedding-related calls late at night, rather than during her workday.

With so many couples living somewhere other than where they grew up, it can be difficult to define a destination wedding. For our purposes, it needs to meet these three criteria:

- The bride and groom are planning the wedding long-distance.

- The events span a weekend or longer.

- At least half of the guests have to travel to the location.

This section is geared to help those who are fairly certain they want a destination wedding. For an overview of preliminary considerations, and to determine if you're suited to a destination wedding, see pages 37–39.

A destination wedding typically begins with guests arriving on a Thursday or Friday. If guests have to travel far, it kicks off with a welcome party on Thursday.

Dollars and Sense

Taking your honeymoon in the same spot as the wedding is a significant cost-saver. You won't have to pay additional airfare for the honeymoon, and the hotel may give you a break if you've already spent a lot of money there.

If your hotel offers a wedding coordinator (which should cost you nothing), you'll save on the cost of a planner. Some all-inclusive resorts offer complimentary weddings if guests book a specified number of rooms, and those can present a big savings *if* the hotel offers the type of wedding package you want (*package* being the operative word here—you can't expect much in the way of customization with this type of wedding).

Activities fill the days, and the ceremony and reception are generally held on Saturday evening. Guests get together on Sunday morning for a post-wedding brunch and possibly another activity before departing in the afternoon.

At many destinations, you won't have as great a range of choices in areas like flowers, food, music, and rentals, so it's important to remain flexible and take advantage of local resources rather than trying to import your vision. (In other words, if you want an English garden party, you have no business scouting locations in Mexico.) If money is no object, you can create anything you want anywhere in the world, but that is rarely the case.

A destination wedding will invariably involve compromises, last-minute substitutions, and a few things that don't go as planned. But it can end up being an amazing experience for everyone who attends, and one that isn't soon forgotten.

Who Pays for What?

Here's what everyone really wants to know about a destination wedding: Is it an indulgent extravagance or a bargain for the hosts? Here's the answer (and it's exactly the one you don't want to hear): It depends.

A destination wedding can cost you three times more than a similar bash in your hometown—or it can cut your costs in half. As with any other wedding, it all boils down to cost per head; the difference with a destination wedding is that you're going to be spending more per guest because you'll be entertaining them for three days, but you're likely to have a much smaller head count. Some couples spend the same amount of money they would have at home but find that they're able to have a much nicer wedding.

If by having a destination wedding, you're able to slash your guest list from 200 to 50, you'll probably save—assuming you stick to an on-site event at a resort. But if you end up hosting 200 people, it's going to cost a lot more. The destination weddings I plan tend to cost 20 percent more, but they often involve bringing in vendors from Los Angeles and flying in flowers and rentals. On average, destination weddings cost about 8 percent less.

Treating the Bridal Party

THERE'S NO RULE that the host of a destination wedding must pay airfare for guests or members of the bridal party. Some people with the necessary means do decide to pay the airfare for all of their guests, foot the bill for their hotel rooms, and host their meals, but they are, understandably, a small minority.

What happens more frequently is that the host helps defray expenses for members of the bridal party, paying either for their airfare or hotel rooms. Some couples who travel a lot are able to put frequent flyer mileage and hotel awards to good use. Other hosts pick up the cost of the bridal party's wedding attire.

There will be some people you really want at your wedding who can't afford to attend, so you should be prepared to help out with their costs.

As for how the costs are divided among families, there are no hard-and-fast rules there either. A destination wedding is more likely to be largely funded by the couple, with parents kicking in for the rehearsal dinner, the post-wedding brunch, or flying in the pastor. But some destination weddings follow tradition, with the reception paid for by the bride's parents, and the groom's family hosting the rehearsal dinner.

The Guest List

Though the size of your guest list might be radically different from what it would be on home turf, the process of preparing the list doesn't deviate all that much. (See chapter 5, "The Guest List.") One difference is that you can count on more declines, which means you can invite 20 percent more guests than you

Keeping Costs Down

These tricks apply to any wedding, but they're especially relevant to destination weddings.

- Book your wedding during the destination's shoulder season, when rates are lower than at high season. Low season offers even better rates, but the weather may prove too risky or unpleasant. There's usually a good reason the rates are low at that time of year—it may be hurricane season, monsoon season, or the average daily temperature may hover at 115°F.

- Plan an on-site wedding. Once you start getting into tents and rentals at a destination wedding, your costs skyrocket, and the planning becomes exponentially more complex.

- Host as much as you can at one place, usually a hotel. The more money you're spending with the hotel, the more clout you have to negotiate deals. (The hotel may throw in the day-after breakfast or the couple's room for the honeymoon.)

- Choose a beautiful location to keep décor costs down.

- Work with local vendors rather than importing your own.

- Keep the wedding party small. You'll want to do more for your attendants because they're doing more for you, but the costs add up, especially if you pick up the tab for lodging or airfare.

- Book an all-inclusive resort or cruise, so you'll have an accurate idea of costs up front.

can accommodate (as opposed to 10 percent at a local wedding). Other planners feel you can go 30 percent over with your invitations, but I see the acceptance rate rising, so I think that's asking for trouble.

Emotionally, though, the process may be more complex. I've seen many parents initially protest destination weddings out of a fear that their friends won't be able to make the trip, or that they will but will grumble about the

The Hidden Costs of Destination Weddings

I t's more challenging to estimate costs for a destination wedding, largely due to sneaky bills that can take you by surprise. When creating a budget, don't forget to account for:

- Significant data charges on your phone bill, especially if the wedding is out of the country. You'll be racking up hours with the planner on the phone.

- The cost of the planning trip (or trips) to the destination for the bride and groom.

- Hotel and meal costs for the bride and groom prior to the wedding. The bride and groom will likely need to allow several days on-site to handle last-minute planning; if the wedding is outside of the United States, they may need to arrive several days early for blood tests or to meet residency requirements. (See page 431 for more on the legal aspects of getting married abroad.)

- Shipping costs for sending items ahead to the site. If the rental selection is limited at the site, you may find yourself buying and shipping anything from tablecloths to votive candleholders. If the wedding is out of the country, expect to pay duty on the items to get them through customs.

- Baggage surcharges, if you're bringing things with you for the wedding and exceed the standard baggage allowance.

- Taxis or rental cars for local transportation. If wedding events are being held away from the hotel, it's courteous to provide local transportation for your guests.

- Travel costs for any vendors you're bringing in. You'll need to pay for their transportation, lodging, and food. And in many cases, vendors consider themselves on the clock during travel time.

- Delivery fees at the hotel. Many hotels charge to deliver welcome gifts to your guests' rooms or to deliver special notes and sweets at turndown. Count on $2 to $5 per delivery per room. (If the fees trouble you, circumvent them by having the gifts behind the reception desk or handing them out at the rehearsal dinner.)

---

hassle and expense. In my experience, once they get over their initial hesitation, they end up having a wonderful time and making new friends. I often find it's the parents and their friends who don't want to leave when Sunday afternoon rolls around!

But you should be prepared for the fact that not everybody is going to be a fan of your destination wedding. Some people will resent the money and the time commitment. Some will come grudgingly but end up having a grand time; some will send their regrets. A few will whine the whole time they're there about the flight, the rooms, the food, and the weather. Just remember: This is your wedding, not theirs, and not everyone is going to get it. (If you really are concerned that loved ones won't be able to attend, perhaps you should consider a wedding closer to home.)

One mistake that couples make is trying to sell the wedding to friends and relatives as *their* vacation. Sure, you chose a wonderful destination, but people already have their own ideas about where and when and how they want to spend their vacation time. Unless you're paying everyone's way and putting their vacation days back in the bank for them at work, this argument will make you sound like the type of self-involved bride you don't want to be.

Be forewarned that destination weddings with very limited guest lists can create lasting rifts when family members or close friends are excluded from the list. Before the wedding, try talking to people who are upset and tell them that you will miss sharing the day with them. But explain to them why it's important to you and your groom to have the type of wedding that you're having.

Choosing a Destination

If you're considering a destination wedding, chances are you already have a specific location in mind. If you're toying with the idea and looking for guidance, I can tell you that the best destinations are ones that hold some special meaning for the bride and groom. Some couples choose the spot where the groom proposed. Others choose an alma mater, the place where they met or spent their first vacation together, or a place where one of them vacationed growing up. It could also be a destination that's known for an activity they enjoy doing together, such as river rafting or scuba diving. Or it could simply be a place they've always dreamed of going together (especially if they're planning to honeymoon at the same site).

If you've chosen a general location but are at a loss as to how to locate a venue, turn back to chapter 3, "A Date & Place," for guidance. Look to travel books, websites, and/or a travel agent for suggestions and information. Since you may not be able to visit the venue before you book it, you're probably best off sticking with a safe, low-hassle place like a large hotel. And unless you are working with a top-notch wedding planner and a very large budget, I strongly advise against attempting an off-site destination wedding. It's complicated enough trying to wrangle tents, tables, chairs, china, silverware, and restroom facilities for a wedding in your own backyard; it all becomes that much more complicated when there are miles and language barriers to contend with.

Play Up the Destination

YOU NEED NOT SEARCH far and wide for a design inspiration at a destination wedding. The location itself flavors the wedding and should give it an overall structure and theme.

In Cabo San Lucas, I've thrown a full-blown Mexican fiesta as the welcome party. A mariachi band provided music and we threw serapes (colorful woven shawls) over the tables, covered the backs of chairs with ponchos, and filled sombreros with flowers for the centerpieces. In Hawaii, there's such an abundance of wonderful native flora that I always have a wonderful time working with bamboo, various greens, and gorgeous orchids. And you can forget about corsages; everyone gets a lei.

Of course, a place doesn't have to be exotic to be a "destination." I've found lovely local elements to work with in places like Maine, where I carried a mermaid logo from a lobster boat throughout a wedding weekend. In Austin, I've filled welcome bags with cowboy hats—a great icebreaker at the rehearsal dinner. I've even done a ceremony in Palm Springs where we flanked the aisle with two pink flamingos.

> Wedding insurance has saved more than one destination wedding when the site was damaged in a hurricane or experienced another unforeseen disaster. See chapter 12, "Making It Legal," for more information.

The Importance of a Planner

Unless you plan to be on-site for nine months, you're going to need a wedding planner to serve as your point person, local liaison, and source for vendors and area activities. That doesn't mean you'll have to shell out big bucks for a high-end wedding planner; you may, in fact, pay nothing at all.

Your options are:

- Hire a wedding planner where you live who has experience planning destination weddings. The advantage of this admittedly pricey option is that you'll be working together in person from the outset. You'll be paying her fee as well as her travel expenses for one or two advance visits, and for the wedding itself. Expect to pay travel time as well as the actual expenses. There may be multiple staff members who have to travel to the wedding as well.

- Hire an independent wedding planner at the location. She'll have relationships with local vendors, which will make them more accountable, and she'll be able to provide broader services if you plan to have events away from the host hotel.

- Choose a resort or cruise line that provides you with a wedding coordinator or "romance concierge." At a resort, their services are built into the fee structure and you don't pay extra. Many cruise lines subcontract wedding coordination to outside companies, so find out if there are additional fees beyond what you're paying for a wedding package. These planners will be able to coordinate anything you need on the property, including tent rentals, but they may not be able to help if you want to schedule off-site activities or a rehearsal dinner at a restaurant in town. Keep in mind that a wedding

coordinator at a hotel is handling many weddings at the same time, and possibly several weddings in the same weekend, so don't expect a lot of undivided attention. And always ask if the coordinator will be at your wedding—you definitely need a person you know and trust with you throughout the day to keep everything running smoothly. At an all-inclusive resort offering complimentary weddings with a weeklong stay, or otherwise aggressively marketing wedding packages, you probably won't get the same level of personalization as you would if you hire your own planner. As a local, however, the coordinator will be able to help you navigate through everything from blood tests to getting your favors through customs.

Planning Time Line

A destination wedding works with a unique planning schedule, because you have to make most of your decisions in a very concentrated time frame.

Some couples plan a destination wedding entirely from afar, but I always recommend visiting the site at least once. A lot of places look better in photos, and you don't want to arrive for your wedding and be disappointed by the reality. If you're extremely organized about it, you can plan a destination wedding with one visit. It's better for planning purposes if you can make two trips, but not everyone can afford to do that. Call the catering manager to set up a weekend-long visit. For such a scouting trip you can usually get a deeply discounted hotel rate from the catering department.

The One-Visit Planning Trip

WITH A ONE-VISIT PLANNING TRIP, there's a lot to pack in, so don't count on spending a lot of time by the pool. Take the trip about five months before the wedding.

In some areas, particularly islands, you won't have more than one florist or wedding photographer to choose from. If there is a choice of vendors, do everything you

---

ASK MINDY

Q *My fiancé and I are both African-American, and we've decided to go back to our roots for a destination wedding in Kenya. The guest list will be small, but we're planning a bit of a showstopper. Should we look into hiring a planner over there or bring one over with us?*

A First, I'd try to find someone great in Kenya, if not in the exact location where you're having the wedding, then nearby. You might find a planner in a populous city near your wedding location, for example, if you're getting married somewhere more rural. The venue where you're getting married might actually have someone, so check with them first. If you can't find anyone there, bring someone with you. I've been around the world! It all depends on your budget. But it is really nice to have someone local who knows the gist of things.

can to get CDs from prospective bands and DVDs from videographers in advance of your visit, viewing online portfolios from florists and cake makers as available. Check references with the hotel or a client.

If one of your goals is to hire a wedding planner at the destination during this visit, you'll need to have chosen one before you go so she can set up your appointments with other vendors. Try to avoid signing a contract, however, until you've met her and seen whether the appointments she set up went smoothly. Here's what your jam-packed to-do list will look like:

1. Site inspection. Walk the property and look at possibilities for each event. Consider the welcome and rehearsal dinners, the breakfast buffets, the ceremony, cocktail hour, the reception, and the post-wedding brunch.

2. Menu tasting. The catering manager will send you menus ahead of time so you can choose what you want to taste during your visit. You should also discuss the wedding cake ahead of time and see if they can make samples. Don't forget to talk about the types of cake that work at the destination, especially if it's a hot climate. After the tasting, you'll finalize the menu choices.

3. View the various room types. Visit a variety of rooms and a few suites. Find out what type of room or suite the bridal party will get and whether you will be comped a room for the wedding night. Don't forget to choose your room while you're there. If children will be invited, scope out which room configurations work best for families. Negotiate room rates based on your estimated guest count. If you need to offer less expensive lodging options, or if the host hotel isn't large enough to handle all of your guests, check out rooms at nearby hotels. Find out what kind of transportation you can arrange between the hotels.

4. Meet with the florist and band or DJ. You want to get as much done as you can during these meetings. Discuss ceremony and reception decorations, bouquets, centerpieces. What local flowers are available? Do they have access to imported flowers? If your heart is set on something that's not available, come up with a new, workable

idea. There may not be time to see a sample arrangement while you're there, but the florist can make one later and send you photos and measurements. (If your wedding planner is on-site, she should go see the sample in person.) Cover your music needs with the band or DJ.

5. Meet with the officiant. Discuss the type of ceremony you want and go through the legal questions. Are you a good match?

6. Meet with the photographer/videographer. You should have already reviewed samples of their work, so the meeting is about making sure your personalities are compatible and going over your specific needs.

7. Meet with hair and makeup artists. See photos of their work. If you have any photos you like, bring them along and gauge their reaction. If time allows, schedule a trial makeup or hair run while you're there.

8. Shop for in-room gifts. Scout stores for local products and specialty food items that might work as in-room gifts for guests. Also check the local price of flip-flops or sunscreen, or whatever else you plan to give out, to determine if you should buy them at the destination or ship them from home. (Warning: If you're sending goods to a foreign country, you could get slapped with customs fees, so it's better to buy things at the destination.) Look for eye-catching bags to hold the gifts for each guest. The stores don't have to be exotic—sometimes Target or Walmart can be your best friend. At the Mexico weddings I plan, the Costco in Cabo San Lucas is a prime source for in-room gifts. If you're planning to arrive a few days before the wedding, you can purchase the gifts then.

The Two-Visit Planning Trip

IF YOU'RE ABLE to swing two visits to the destination, the first visit (about six months before the wedding) focuses on establishing your vendors, and the second (three months before) is when you see samples, finalize choices, and go over the schedule. Any vendors not specifically mentioned below follow the same pattern. Also read the one-visit planning trip section for additional details.

On the First Visit

1. Meet florists and choose one to work with.

2. Plan menus with caterer.

3. Meet and decide on musicians or a DJ.

4. Do a site inspection. Establish areas for the ceremony, cocktails, and reception. Ditto for the rehearsal dinner and any other group events.

5. Preshop for local products. Are there specialty food items that might work as in-room gifts for guests?

6. Decide who will make the cake and discuss ideas.

7. Meet hairstylists and makeup artists.

On the Second Visit

1. View samples of flower arrangements. Tweak as needed.

2. Conduct food tasting. Finalize menus for all events.

3. Review schedule with musicians. Give them requests for the first dance, father-daughter dance, mother-son dance, and other special dances like the hora. Also go over the Do-Not-Play list and make any other special requests for songs.

4. At the site, repeat the walk-through. Make sure nothing has changed since your first visit.

5. Decide on the contents of the in-room gifts. Buy anything you intend to purchase locally (assuming it's not anything that will spoil in the next few months) and have the hotel hold it for the wedding.

6. Conduct the cake tasting.

7. Conduct style trials with hairstylist and makeup artist.

Back at the Ranch . . .

ONCE YOU'RE HOME from your trip, consider having a travel agent handle reservations for guests. An agent can usually negotiate upgrades or perks with the hotel, and the bride and groom have enough to do without acting

Is It Right for Me?

When evaluating potential destinations, consider these factors:

■ Do you like the destination's food, music, flowers, and general culture? If you don't care for Mexican food, stop looking at the Yucatán Peninsula—you don't want to be fighting the destination every step of the way.

■ Is it within a one-hour drive of a major airport? Expecting people to spend two and a half hours bouncing along a bumpy road after a long flight is asking a lot.

■ Do your homework on the weather for the time of year you're considering. If the room rates are particularly low during that period, there's probably a reason. Look at average air and water temperatures, precipitation, and humidity. Also ask about insects (blackflies, cicadas, and mosquitoes can make everyone miserable). There's no way to guarantee the weather, but you want to make sure you're not booking your wedding during hurricane, tornado, typhoon, or monsoon season.

■ Are there adequate medical facilities nearby in case of an emergency?

■ Are there language differences? Time differences? Can you work with them?

■ Does the destination fit your budget? Do the hotels seem in line with what your guests can afford?

■ Does the area seem safe?

■ Are there vendors at the destination offering products and services that appeal to you, or will you have to bring in vendors?

■ Is the cost structure clear, or are you hearing "don't worry" when you should be getting straight answers?

as the de facto travel agents for all guests. The agent gets paid commissions from the hotel and airlines, so there is no cost to you.

1. Reserve blocks of hotel rooms. (See chapter 3, "A Date & Place," for more details.)

2. Arrange discount group airfare.

3. Send out save-the-date announcements with travel info (six to twelve months before the wedding).

4. Send out invitations (eight weeks before the wedding).

You'll need to take care of last-minute details before you leave for the wedding. That means you'll need to prepare and pack programs and seating cards, and you may need to ship any larger specialty items you're planning to use for decoration—though I think you're better off keeping things as simple as possible.

Welcome gifts also need to be planned well in advance. You may buy them at home and ship them ahead, pack them in your luggage, or buy them at the destination. They can get stuck in customs, so allow extra time and be prepared to pay duty. Don't forget bags or totes for holding the gifts.

Special Considerations

This section emphasizes what's different about destination weddings—in particular, working with vendors. You should still read the chapter devoted to each vendor elsewhere in this book to get the complete picture and to know what points to cover in your meetings.

One of the main concerns when working with vendors long-distance is whether they're going to deliver what they've promised. To minimize the chances of a no-show or bad service, book vendors where you've got some kind of local connection—whether it's through the hotel, a wedding planner, or a local resident who has hired them. If they know there's future business tied to how well they perform at your event, they're more likely to do a great job for you. With long-distance vendors, it's extra important to thoroughly check references and get everything in writing. If you're working with vendors in a laissez-faire culture where written contracts aren't the norm, draw up a letter stating everything you've agreed upon and ask them to sign it.

As soon as you arrive for the wedding, have a last round of quick meetings with the vendors. It will cut down on disappointments—you'll *see* the flowers they're actually using—and it reaffirms expectations that they're going to be providing your food, administering your vows, or taking photos at your wedding in two days.

Invitations

HAVING A DESTINATION WEDDING with multiple events means you have a lot of information to convey in your invitation. A trifold or gatefold-style invitation with enclosures works best. If you've got the budget for it, a book format also suits the occasion, as do multiple cards stacked in a box. If you're having several events that weekend, such as golf outings or tours, you can create a single card with room to RSVP to each. "Taking Care of Guests," on page 428, covers the save-the-date announcement, which is a must at a destination wedding.

Bridal Attire

WHEN CHOOSING YOUR GOWN, take into account the weather at your destination. In general, you need a gown that can travel—one that can be folded (place layers of tissue paper between the folds), doesn't wrinkle excessively, and isn't too heavy. For a warm weather wedding, a breezy, sleeveless chiffon gown would be ideal. Trains

If you've taken my advice, your destination wedding is "on-site" and you should be working with a venue that has most everything you need—so rentals like tables, tents, and silverware shouldn't be an issue. To add visual pow, zero in on something easy to transport (think table runners or napkins) and bring that with you from home.

Gowns that Travel Well

Though a lot depends on the actual destination and the formality of the wedding, since so many destination weddings involve balmy weather and a beach backdrop, you want to look for a lightweight dress that travels.

An A-line, sheath, or mermaid silhouette is your best bet. If the weather will be warm, avoid fabrics like heavy satin. Stay away from long illusion sleeves and dresses with heavy crinoline underskirts. Polyester doesn't breathe the way a natural fiber does, so if you choose a dress in a synthetic material, make sure it's cut with plenty of room around the armholes to keep you cool. Silk charmeuse, embroidered cotton (think eyelet or dotted swiss), organza, chiffon, and lightweight silk satins are all good choices. So is lace, if it's light and airy.

You will probably be carrying this dress onto the plane yourself, so stay away from heavy beading and embroidery. A long train also adds weight and bulk—yet another reason it's not a good idea at a destination wedding.

Also think about easy maintenance. Is there anyone at the destination who knows how to properly steam a dress? When looking at dresses, ask yourself, "Can I steam this myself?" in case there isn't anyone to do it for you.

can be burdensome to pack, and they look out of place at a beach wedding, so it's best to get nothing longer than a sweep train. A long veil—consider one that's longer than the dress and serves as a train—can more than make up for the lack of train on your gown. When it blows in the breeze, it makes for gorgeous photos.

As for shoes, think about the surfaces at the ceremony and reception sites. Squishy surfaces and spiky heels are not a good combination. If you want to get married barefoot, but don't want your feet to look naked, some designers make jeweled "bottomless" sandals that serve as jewelry for your feet.

Have alterations done early so that you're picking up your dress at least a week before your departure date. If

you do have a train, make sure that you or your maid of honor know how to bustle it.

Choosing the Bridal Party

THE BRIDAL PARTY is typically very small at a destination wedding, and people often play dual roles. Brides have been known to have their grandmothers serve as the matron of honor, and many a groom has had his father as his best man.

Because costs for guests are so steep, it's kinder to not layer on the added expenses of dresses, rental tuxedos, and everything else that goes with being in the wedding party. Keep the number of attendants to a minimum, and invite your friends to come as guests. You'll also find that the care and feeding of the wedding party is more involved with a destination wedding—they may expect you to act as their travel agent, concierge, personal shopper, and tour guide—so you'll be grateful if there are only four people to deal with instead of eight.

If attendants are expected to pay their own way, it's essential to be up front about costs when you invite them to be in your wedding. Should you be picking up some of the tab, clearly state what you're covering. Before you invite people to be attendants, prepare an overall estimate that includes airfare, lodging, attire, and local transportation. You want them to accept the job with their eyes open, not turn into a bundle of resentment as the credit card charges pile up. Not everyone may be able to afford to participate, so be prepared for some people to decline.

Groom and Groomsmen's Attire

DO YOUR HOMEWORK to determine whether you should rent at the destination or bring tuxes with you. If there's a branch of a major formal-wear rental chain, you should be fine renting there. If there's a local formal-wear shop, check with locals you trust (a wedding coordinator, the concierge at the hotel, the florist) to find out if the shop is reputable, can deliver what it promises, and has a sufficient selection. If you're visiting the destination in advance, visit the shop to see the choices in person.

If you have any doubts about what you'll get at the destination, rent in your hometown and bring the suits with you. The longer rental will cost you a little more, but the peace of mind is priceless.

Many grooms choose something less formal than a tux for a destination wedding—anything from a sharp suit to a linen shirt and trousers. The groom should make sure he plans out every detail of his outfit in advance so he isn't madly scurrying about looking for sand-colored dress socks in Punta Cana.

The Officiant

YOU MAY NOT BE ABLE to find an officiant of a specific denomination at a destination. It's more common to have the ceremony performed by an interfaith minister or a local judge. If you have your heart set on a particular person, look into flying them in, though it might be difficult to convince anyone but a close friend to do this for you, even with expenses and travel time paid. Many couples also choose to have someone close to them become ordained through the Universal Life Church. (See page 77 for more guidance.)

Photography/Videography

THE PHOTOGRAPHER is the vendor that couples are most likely to fly in for the wedding. If you choose to do so, you'll need to pay for the photographer's travel, lodging, and food costs. Ditto for an assistant, if there is one. Make sure to find out whether travel time is billed and at what rate.

Some couples also bring a videographer with them, but more often they'll find one locally. Make sure the videographer is working with up-to-date equipment—if the video is important to you, you don't want to hire someone who's working with older technology.

Flowers

TALK TO THE FLORIST at the destination about the types of flowers that are available. On many islands, the selection is likely to be far more limited than it is in your hometown. On tropical islands, you can have all the exotic flowers you want, but you're going to have a hard time getting hydrangeas. Local flowers are your best bet, so make the most of them. Roses are available most everywhere in the world, but prices can be high.

Food

AT A DESTINATION WEDDING, play to the strengths of the local chefs and make the most of readily available ingredients. It's foolish to ask a chef in Jamaica to turn out a cream sauce for the red snapper when he could be preparing a wonderful *escabeche*. Besides, who wants a cream sauce sitting around in hot weather? Keep in mind that you're going to pay a premium price on islands for any food that needs to be imported. Local preparations are likely to make use of local ingredients. If you're on an island with abundant fruit, make the most of it by offering juices or smoothies as well as fruit-based sauces and fresh fruit at dessert.

Cake

AT A DESTINATION WEDDING, the wedding cake may involve compromise. Both the climate and local ingredients can wreak havoc on the chemistry needed to make a towering confection, especially in the tropics. Your two best bets: Design a very simple cake and have the florist decorate it with fresh flowers; or order a local specialty, such as a *tres leches* cake in Mexico (a white cake soaked in a mixture of three milks—usually sweetened condensed milk, evaporated milk, and whole milk or cream). Rather than bring in a photo of a cake to duplicate, ask the cake maker what he's best known for and choose something within that repertoire.

Before you leave home, be absolutely sure that your engagement and wedding rings are insured. You're traveling with a valuable piece of jewelry (or two), so act accordingly.

Top cake makers are accustomed to transporting cakes to a destination, but this level of service comes at a steep price, so it's worth investigating local options.

Music

LOCAL MUSIC IS one of the most joyous resources you can use to incorporate the destination into your wedding. If you don't want the local music for the main reception, use it at the recessional, cocktail hour, or the rehearsal dinner. If your wedding is outside of the United States but you want American standards for the reception, you're better off hiring a DJ than a live band. Many of my couples splurge on flying in a DJ in order to cut down on the number of unknowns.

Hair and Makeup

BIG HOTELS and resorts can often hook you up with talented hairstylists and makeup artists. Hair and makeup is so important to some brides that they fly in their team. But it's very common for brides to choose to do their own hair and makeup rather than deal with strangers.

Try booking a free makeover at a department store beauty counter. (Bobbi Brown is particularly good for weddings because of the emphasis on natural colors.) The makeup artist will teach you how to replicate what she's doing, and might draw you a map of your face with instructions. Be prepared to buy at least two products from the counter, since these makeup artists work on commission. A more expensive but more in-depth option is to book a session with either a makeup artist at a salon or an independent makeup artist who specializes in weddings. Ask questions and pay close attention to what she's doing; if possible, have an attendant come with you to help absorb the knowledge.

Hair is typically simpler for a destination wedding—romantic, loose locks rather than an elaborate updo. Plot out your wedding day hair with your hairstylist at home, and have him teach you or one of your attendants how to re-create it for the wedding. Take photos of the style to help you later. You can also use photos from home to

What If Everything Goes Haywire?

You're having a destination wedding and the weather is so bad that the airport has been closed down and guests can't get there. My advice? Take a deep breath and go ahead and get married, whether you've made it to your destination or are still at home. Go to city hall and arrange whatever kind of ceremony you can on short notice. And take the honeymoon as planned. This is one of those situations you just can't control.

If it's important to you to walk down the aisle in front of all your friends and family and you have the means to do so, reschedule your event and say your vows again. Or throw just the reception at a later date, on a smaller scale and in a more manageable location.

guide a hairstylist at the destination. Don't forget to bring your headpiece and veil to the salon so you'll know how to work them into your hair.

Taking Care of Guests

While a regular wedding means taking care of guests, a destination wedding means coddling them from the moment they arrive to the moment they depart. Not only have they spent hundreds or even thousands of dollars to attend your wedding, but they've ventured out of their comfort zone to get there; it's up to you to make them feel comfortable and to remind them at every turn how much you value their presence.

Save-the-Dates

THE WOOING STARTS with the save-the-date card, which you should send out as soon as you've chosen your date and agreed on your guest list—at least six months before the wedding, but the earlier, the better. (See pages 63–65 for more information.) For a destination wedding over a holiday weekend or in high season, it's not unusual to send out save-the-date cards a year in advance.

Save-the-date cards for destination weddings are often creative, fun, and lighthearted. They can be less formal and don't need to match the invitations in style. For a beach wedding, couples have drawn their names and wedding date in the sand and snapped a photo. An image of the location works well, as does a straightforward card topped by a dingbat that relates to the locale, like a pineapple or exotic flower for a wedding in Hawaii or a pair of skis for an Aspen affair. Some couples put their save-the-date announcements on the back of refrigerator magnets. Getting creative with the save-the-date is a good way to get guests excited about the idea of a destination wedding.

The Information Packet

THE SAVE-THE-DATE can also include the much more elaborate packet of hotel and travel information; if you're not ready to put that together in time, you can send the packet along later—preferably six to eight months before the wedding—but it will save you work to do it all in one go. It's also a nice touch because the packet can give guests an idea of some of the activities you're planning.

In addition to travel and hotel information, make sure it includes a list of things to do in the area; typical weather for that time of year; and times, places, and suggested attire for any other wedding-related events, from welcome cocktails to a post-wedding brunch. If you've got a wedding website, include the address. Even if it's not up and running yet, spread the word while you have the chance. Use the site to convey updates. (Should some guests

Once guests arrive at a destination wedding, you should take care of local travel for the weekend. Hotels can help arrange shuttle buses to outside events. If you don't have the budget to fund transportation, organize carpools so people can rent cars and ride together.

not have Internet access, be sure to contact them with updates.)

Keep guests informed every step of the way, and they'll feel more comfortable. It will also cut down on guests showing up late (or not at all) to wedding-related events.

As for the invitations, a trifold or gatefold is your best bet for presenting all of the information (see page 273). With a trifold, you might have one card for hotel and flight info, another for the events of the weekend, and a third with activities in the area and a map.

A Warm Welcome

FOR TIPS ON creating welcome baskets to greet your guests (an absolute necessity at a destination wedding), along with the type of information you'll need to include, see page 330.

Make sure your welcome letter includes a contact name (the wedding planner, best man, maid of honor, or a parent—never the bride or groom!) and room and cell phone numbers, in case guests have questions or problems.

As for the gift, think about something that can introduce them to the area or make their stay more pleasant. That might mean a bottle of sunscreen, a Frisbee, and flip-flops for a beach wedding. At a mountain wedding, you could include bug repellant or, for a winter wedding, some hand warmers for late-night revelers. Bottles of water, a split of wine, and snack food are always appreciated. Round everything out with local maps and tourist information, which you can get for free from the tourist office. A copy of the local city or regional magazine makes a great addition to the mix.

"Turndown gifts" are a very optional gesture but one that really ups the ante on the caretaking element. At the end of each evening, you can have the hotel deliver something to guests' rooms. Chocolate chip cookies and milk with

GREAT ACTIVITIES

Get the most out of your location by getting guests together for some fun—but optional—activities and outings. Consider some of these favorites to keep your guests occupied throughout the wedding weekend:

- [ ] Golf tournament foursomes
- [ ] Tennis tournament or round-robin
- [ ] Volleyball, softball, croquet, or badminton
- [ ] Spa treatments
- [ ] Hikes led by a naturalist
- [ ] Yoga class
- [ ] Guided bus tour

- [ ] Visit to an art museum, botanical garden, historic estate, or other local attraction
- [ ] Boat tour
- [ ] Snorkeling expedition
- [ ] Bingo games
- [ ] Movie night with popcorn (outdoors if weather permits)

- [ ] Game area set up with checkers, cards, bridge, and mah-jongg
- [ ] Poker tournament
- [ ] Winery tour or a tasting of local wines with the hotel's sommelier
- [ ] Cooking class with local flavor (can often be arranged at the hotel)

a "Sweet Dreams" note never fails to delight. Or send something for guests to use the next day, such as a shirt or hat to wear to the golf outing with a note that says you're looking forward to seeing them on the green. It's also a good time to send another copy of the following day's itinerary so they know when and where to show up. Want to go the extra mile? Add the updated weather forecast to help guests plan.

Keeping Guests Occupied

A DESTINATION WEDDING isn't just about the big event—it's typically about three or more days of togetherness. To foster the camp spirit, you'll want to organize activities for guests. This contributes to their sense that you're taking care of them for the whole weekend.

You don't need to pay for the activities, but you do need to clearly communicate any associated costs. When you send guests a list of activities, either note the prices or write "contact the concierge for pricing."

Let guests know about as many of the activities as you can when you send out the information packets. You may need to collect RSVPs to reserve golf and spa times.

Your planner or hotel contact can coordinate activities, arrange for transportation, and get head counts.

Activities should be optional, as some guests will just want to hang out by the pool. Don't schedule every minute, because everyone needs some downtime. And remember to think of all different ages when you plan. It's great to offer a morning hike, but you should also have some less active, indoor pursuits for those less able to get around. A bingo game in an air-conditioned room (with prizes!) appeals to both young and old.

If the destination has a well-known attraction, whether it's stingray petting, a perfume factory, or a popular open-air market, arrange a way for guests to visit it. They don't want to come home from your wedding feeling that they never saw the highlights of the destination.

If possible, set up a few gathering places at the hotel so family members have a place to go when they just want to hang out. Don't forget to let everyone know about them in the welcome packet. (In a tropical locale, have an area of the beach or pool sectioned off for your group, along with an indoor gathering area stocked with snacks and cool beverages for those who can't take the heat.)

Paperwork and Legalities

No matter where you're getting married, you'll have to follow the local marriage laws, which can differ from state to state, even from county to county.

Getting married in another country isn't for the faint of heart. Although some countries, including several Caribbean destinations such as the Cayman Islands, make it easy to get married on their soil, others are notorious for red tape and requirements that differ from one town to the next. (Mexico comes to mind.)

The headaches and the paperwork often aren't worth the hassle, so I recommend engaging in a little subterfuge. Most of my couples make a stop at city hall and get married in a civil ceremony before leaving for their destination wedding. The two of you should keep this your little secret. Guests don't like to think they're at a "fake" wedding—some may feel that they've traveled a long distance for nothing if they discover that you're already married. Conducting the legal ceremony stateside simplifies everything, and there will be no question that your union is legal and binding in the United States. So you don't feel as if you're cheapening the occasion, try to think of the ceremonial wedding as the one where you pledge yourselves to each other, and the courtroom procedure as a legal formality.

If you're determined to make your union legal under another country's flag, here are some general guidelines and strategies for choosing a destination that's friendly to conducting foreign marriages.

One complicating factor is that legislation regarding overseas ceremonies isn't consistent from state to state. There are varying degrees of legwork involved, depending on what state you're from and in what country you wish to get married. Check with the office that handles marriages or the state attorney's office. The US State Department's website gives basic guidelines under the section "Marriage of US Citizens Abroad."

If you choose to tie the knot in a foreign country, you're most often talking about a civil ceremony. Some countries don't permit foreigners to get married in a church or synagogue unless they have some kind of

Cruise Weddings

For those looking for the ultimate in amenities and activities, a cruise can be a fun and lively solution. Cruise weddings, with certain exceptions, don't usually take place out on the open water. The ceremony is more likely to take place at the point of embarkation or at a port of call, which means that the marriage license must be obtained from the appropriate office within the territory. Sometimes the legal marriage is performed at the port of embarkation by an officiant, with a ceremonial wedding following at sea—the latter officiated by none other than the captain. Many cruise lines have wedding planners on staff or on retainer to help you obtain the marriage license.

A downside of planning to get married at a stop on the cruise itinerary—though it's quite a romantic notion—is that your plans are subject to the vagaries of Mother Nature. If the ship can't dock at the island where you were set to get married and changes course, your plans could be jeopardized. The cruise's planner can certainly arrange for a ceremonial wedding on board (many ships have wedding chapels), but it won't be legally binding.

special connection. And even if you *can* have a religious ceremony, many foreign countries, including Mexico and France, require that it be preceded by a civil ceremony.

When evaluating places to get married, check with the country's US tourism office, consulate, or embassy for laws regarding marriage in that country. Look out for the residency requirement. France's thirty-day residency requirement for at least one member of the couple (plus another ten days for publishing the marriage banns at city hall) thwarts many a plan for a romantic Paris wedding.

Find out what documents you need to provide and whether you'll need witnesses. Documents may need to be authenticated (see the explanation of an apostille on the next page) and often need to be translated into the local language.

Determine what paperwork you'll need to provide. Countries that follow civil law (as opposed to common law, which is the primary legal system in the United States) require you to bring a certified document stating that you are free to marry (meaning that you're not already married and that nothing else stands in the way of your legal eligibility). This precise document doesn't exist in the United States, so what you typically have to do is request and pay a small fee for an "affidavit of eligibility to marry" at the American embassy or consulate in the country where you're getting married; alternately, the state where you live might provide you with a certificate stating that there exists no record of a previous marriage (a "no record statement").

On top of whatever documents are required, many countries will require that those documents be authenticated by what's called an "apostille"—a separate document that legalizes your paperwork internationally. (Check with your state bureau of records, part of the secretary of state's office, to obtain one.)

All this paperwork can be costly. Be on the lookout for hidden fees; in many countries, you will have to pay to have your documents translated into the local language. You may need to have blood tests done on-site, or publish a "notice of marriage" multiple times in the local newspaper. You may need to arrive several days early, which will up your lodging and food costs. And if you're taking out a wedding insurance policy, there's often a 10 percent premium for a wedding outside of the country.

Call your local marriage bureau to find out if you need to file any additional paperwork once you're home. If your overseas ceremony is religious, find out from your home church or synagogue whether you need to take any final steps to be sure the marriage is recognized on your home turf.

Don't forget to check up on your passports, visas, and vaccinations. For details and timetables (some of these processes should be started six months in advance) see "The Honeymoon," opposite.

On Home Ground

You got exactly the small, intimate wedding on the beach at sunset that you wanted. But you still want a party with all of your friends. Bring on the post-wedding party.

It's essentially an extra reception that you throw after you're back from the honeymoon and settled in a bit. There are no rules regarding when to have this gathering, but it usually takes place between one and three months after the wedding. You can invite your friends, coworkers, and family. Parents might want to weigh in on the guest list and include their friends. Spare those who came to the wedding, unless they were in the bridal party or they're immediate family members.

Three to six weeks before the bash, send out invitations. They're usually less formal than for a wedding.

Though the party can be hosted by anyone who's willing and still has the funds after the wedding, it's often the couple who picks up the tab. The party can be anything from cocktails and dessert to a five-course dinner, a beach barbecue, or a black-tie soiree—anything that expresses your style.

Part of the purpose of the party is to share the wedding experience with everyone, so display your wedding photos and roll your video. Put out a guest book, plan on having toasts, and order a great cake. I like to include a cake cutting because it continues the ancient tradition of breaking bread with friends and family when there's a cause for celebration. But don't go overboard on reception traditions or it's likely to make guests feel that they're at a wedding reenactment for B-listers: A garter or bouquet toss is a bit too literal. The bride and groom can get the dancing started, but you can't quite call it a first dance. Group dances, though, should absolutely be part of the festivities.

Some brides choose to wear their wedding dresses, which is fine, as long as they fit the setting. It works better if yours is the type of gown most often worn at a destination wedding—something simple, usually without a train. The headpiece and veil would be overdoing it, but do take yourself off to the hairdresser for a great blowout or updo.

Just Married!

Please celebrate our marriage
Cocktails, Dinner, and Dancing

Saturday, the third of November
at six o'clock in the evening

Hotel Bel Air
790 Stone Canyon Road
Bel Air, California

Sydnee and Max

It's fun to theme the party to the destination. If you got married in Hawaii, pass out leis and serve mai tais. If you had a Napa Valley wedding, set up wine-tasting stations. If you tied the knot in Bermuda, serve dark and stormys.

At some point in the evening—usually before you cut the cake—raise your glass, thank everyone for coming, and explain why you ran off to get married without them.

You shouldn't expect gifts at a post-wedding party, though some guests will undoubtedly send them. In case they're so inclined, check the state of your registries as soon as you send out invitations. Make sure there are plenty of choices remaining at different prices, and add items if they look picked over.

If you have the budget, hire a photographer, as it's bound to be a night to remember.

After a small destination wedding, it's perfectly legitimate to throw a post-wedding party on home ground.

The Honeymoon

Planning the Honeymoon

The honeymoon wasn't always the intimate getaway we think of today. From the late 1700s till the 1850s, it was commonplace for family members or friends to accompany the newlyweds on their bridal tour, which was partially designed to enable a visit to relatives who couldn't attend the wedding. How things have changed.

Today the honeymoon is about spending time as a couple and reveling in the newly married state. It's also a time to recover and recoup after the marathon of wedding preparations and the wedding itself.

A honeymoon isn't just another vacation. For one thing, you're going to be exhausted after the wedding.

For another, there's something special and different about the interlude just after you become married, when your relationship has been transformed into a legally sanctioned, till-death-do-you-part union.

Wait until your preliminary wedding vendors are in place before you begin planning the honeymoon. (I've seen brides use their honeymoon-planning as a procrastination tool. . . .) Still, you should have all of the arrangements in place months before the wedding—there will be too many other things to take care of as you get closer to the date, and you don't want to risk dropping the ball and forgetting something critical, like booking a hotel room for your wedding night. You should get the trip you want if you start planning six or seven months out and nail down reservations between four and six months ahead of time. If you're trying to go somewhere without a huge inventory of hotel rooms in high season—say, the French Riviera in July or August—you should start earlier.

The earlier you book, the more choices you'll have. That could mean the difference between a layover and a nonstop flight, a room with a view of the parking lot and an oceanfront bungalow. By planning ahead, you may also be able catch an airfare sale or claim an early-booking bonus (such as one free night) at a hotel.

Who Makes the Plans

THE GROOM used to be in charge of planning the honeymoon—and paying for it. (Remember, the bride's family was paying for the wedding.) Today, couples usually opt to plan their sojourn together.

This trip can benefit from the expertise of a travel agent. Even if you normally book trips online, a knowledgeable travel agent can suggest destinations that might not have occurred to you and point you to places that work with your budget and preferences. For example, for the same amount of money, maybe you'd rather have a luxury honeymoon in Las Vegas than stay in a so-so hotel in Hawaii.

Dollars and Sense

Airline miles and hotel rewards programs can help you pay for your honeymoon and might allow you to afford a more luxurious trip.

Throughout the planning process, look for ways to accumulate miles from wedding-related purchases. Some credit cards earn you miles or other rewards; programs such as Wedding Points earn you travel or cash awards when you work with member merchants; and some hotel chains allow you to accumulate credits.

If you're looking to economize on the honeymoon itself, beware of hotel terms like "honeymoon package" or "honeymoon upgrade"—price it out yourself to see if you're really getting a deal. You might be paying for things you don't really care about, like a keepsake photo album or a bottle of second-rate bubbly.

Every once in a while, I'll hear about a groom planning a surprise honeymoon for his bride. I have to tell you, most women like to know where they're going so they can prep for the trip and pack properly. How can you research activities or restaurants if you don't know the destination? But there are some women (or men, for that matter) who are willing to leave the decision in their spouse's hands and are excited about venturing into the unknown. If you want to go this route, follow two ground rules: (1) You both wholeheartedly agree to the surprise concept, and (2) The person doing the planning has to give good directions as to what to pack.

Setting a Budget

Some couples pay for the trip themselves; others receive contributions from one or both sets of parents; and still others sign up for a honeymoon registry—in effect getting all or part of the honeymoon as wedding gifts.

You'll need to determine your budget before you can pick a destination or start planning. Although it's generally safe to count on supplementing your funds with monetary gifts from the wedding, don't go into debt to pay for this trip. Create a trip you can afford, whether you do that by shortening the length of your stay, finding less expensive lodging, or choosing a destination that enables you to use frequent flyer miles. Remember, it's about spending time with the person you love, not adding a trophy stamp to your passport. When you're with the love of your life, you can create wonderful memories just about anywhere.

When figuring out your estimated costs, go beyond airfare, lodging, and meals. Don't forget to include the cost of getting to and from the airport, local transportation, gratuities, and special activities, such as guided tours, a round of golf, or a snorkeling trip. Do factor in an allowance to treat yourself to a few indulgences—a honeymoon shouldn't be a bare-bones trip where you're watching every penny. Think about massages at the hotel spa, a sunset sail, or a half-day trip to a deserted island.

Choosing a Destination

The ultimate destination is a highly personal choice, so I'm not about to tell you where to go. One person's paradise is another person's purgatory. One bride I worked with had planned a honeymoon to Fiji, complete with accommodations in a hut over the water.

Paradise, right? Not for this bride. As I got to know her, I learned that she hated sand, was terrified of bugs, and absolutely, positively had to have a television in the room. Eventually, she admitted to herself that this picture-perfect destination wasn't for her and switched her honeymoon to Italy. The moral of the story? Don't let yourself get caught up in anybody else's vision of a romantic destination.

Regardless of your tastes, here's one thing I will tell you: You can't even fathom how exhausted you will be after the wedding. There's nothing wrong with planning an active trip, but this isn't the time to try to see four cities in six days. You need time to rest and recharge, and you also need a break from planning, so stay away from destinations where figuring out the daily itinerary involves a ream of decisions and research.

Take travel time into account and make sure it allows for enough relaxation. The average honeymoon lasts eight days—if you spend two days getting there and another two getting home, that only leaves four at the destination.

You'll also want to research the weather for the time of your trip. Do you really want to risk getting trapped in the Caribbean at the height of hurricane season? You get the best prices during low season, but you're probably better off going during a destination's shoulder season, which is either right before or right after its high season.

Familymoons

FOR COUPLES who already have children—either with each other or from prior marriages—there is a trend toward the "familymoon," a honeymoon that includes the kids. I tend to think that a honeymoon is a time to

be alone with your new spouse, and children aren't very conducive to intimacy. You'll have plenty of time for family vacations later.

However, only you know the needs of your particular family situation, so if you decide to take a family trip, your best bet is a resort or cruise with on-staff child care or children's programs. That way, you won't be leaving the children behind, but you can still get some time for just the two of you.

All-Inclusive Resorts

IF YOU'VE EVER FLIPPED through a bridal magazine, you've surely seen a barrage of ads for all-inclusive resorts. While they're clearly popular with honeymooners, they're not for everyone.

The main advantage of an all-inclusive is that you know up front how much you're spending on the trip. Meals, drinks, activities, and gratuities are usually built into the price, but do read the fine print so you know what you're getting. Some all-inclusives may cover wine and beer but not hard liquor, and greens fees for golf may be included, but not the fee for the mandatory caddy. Airfare is usually an optional add-on.

Another big plus is that all-inclusives are no-brainers in terms of planning. For those who like to keep busy and enjoy group activities (think volleyball games and dance lessons on the beach), they can be a blast. If you loved the active pace and social aspects of sleepaway camp, an all-inclusive could be your ideal vacation.

All-inclusives aren't a great fit for independent travelers who like to take off and explore and experience local culture—they're really geared to people who are going to hang around the resort. And if you're the type who's perfectly happy to sit on a lounge chair at the beach all day with a good book, an all-inclusive might not be a good use of your money, since the price includes all kinds of water sports and activities that you wouldn't be using. However, if your spouse likes to be active, it could be a good compromise. If you don't drink alcohol, an all-inclusive probably is not your best deal, and the atmosphere may not be what you're looking for.

Cruises

THERE ARE CRUISE PEOPLE and noncruise people in this world. And you know who you are. But in case you're still in the undecided camp, the pluses: You get a taste of several different places but you only have to unpack once, planning is limited, but there's always something to do; and it can be a pretty good value.

The drawbacks? Prices don't include gratuities—which can add hundreds of dollars to the cost—and shore excursions; you don't get enough time in any port to get to know a place; and you may feel confined on board or find your particular cruise overly social. I happen to love cruises, but some people go stir-crazy with the heavy programming and the nonstop socializing.

There are a wide variety of cruises, from megaships that carry thousands to expedition ships that lodge fewer than a hundred. Some of the small ships and the very

high-end cruises create more of a sense of independent travel and steer clear of hokey entertainment. Work with a travel agent when booking a cruise—you are likely to get a better price, plus you need someone who knows the best cabins to book and understands the different "personality" of each ship.

When to Depart

When weddings were more commonly held in the morning, couples would leave for their honeymoon on the afternoon of their wedding day. As evening weddings became more popular, couples tended to leave the next day. Many wedding celebrations now extend to brunch the following day, and air travel isn't as carefree as it used to be. For these reasons, I prefer to see couples leave two or three days after their wedding. It allows them to enjoy more time with out-of-town guests, recover a bit from the wedding, deposit monetary gifts, pack for the trip, and tie up any loose ends, like dropping off the wedding gown at the cleaners. Some all-inclusive resorts and cruises run on schedules that begin and end on weekends, so if you have to choose between rushing out on your family to catch a flight or waiting for the following weekend, I recommend waiting if possible.

No matter when you're leaving, be sure to book a special place to stay for your wedding night, even if you need to stay near the airport for an early morning flight.

If you don't have time to take an immediate honeymoon, enjoy a few days locally at a country inn or a decadent hotel. Plan this "minimoon" just as carefully as you do the big honeymoon, because this time together immediately after the wedding is extra special. Schedule a couples massage, rent a tandem bike, choose a special bath from the hotel's bath butler—whatever will add to the romantic mood. If you're not able to honeymoon immediately, take the longer trip when your schedule allows, but get it on the calendar so it doesn't get put off indefinitely.

Getting Ready

Depending on your destination, you might need to pack more than a swimsuit and a sarong. And don't forget to take care of necessary travel documentation and other formalities: Waiting until the last minute could leave you with a mini crisis on your hands. Believe me, that's the last thing you need right before your wedding.

Passports and Visas

As soon as you settle on your honeymoon itinerary, determine whether you'll need a passport, visa, or vaccinations. If you already have a passport, check the expiration date to make sure it will still be valid. (Some countries require your passport to be valid for six months *beyond* your travel dates—check the "Foreign Entry Requirements" section of the US Department of State website or contact the destination's embassy or consulate.) Renewal can usually be done by mail.

If you don't have a passport, apply for one early to avoid rush fees. You will generally need an original birth certificate (look for a raised seal), and you'll have to visit a passport acceptance facility in person. You can search for the facility closest to you—often a passport agency, government office, or post office—on the US Department of State website. Leave plenty of time for passport applications, as they can take six weeks to process; if you don't have six weeks, rush options are available. And have the passport issued under your maiden name. (See page 438.)

Don't expect the airline or travel agent to inform you of whether you need a visa—it's up to you to find out. Go to the US Department of State website and look under "Foreign Entry Requirements," for the country to which you're traveling. Visas are typically issued by consulates or embassies, though some countries issue them to you directly upon your arrival.

Working the Honeymoon Angle

A lot of couples believe that announcing they're on their honeymoon can land them upgrades, champagne, and truffles at every turn. Well, it might. Or it might not.

Much has been made of the freebies awaiting honeymooners, and the generosity of airlines, hotels, and restaurants has started to wear thin, especially as some people lie about being on their honeymoon in hopes of landing upgrades. A lot depends on whether you're already a valued customer of the airline or hotel chain and how much you're spending—if you have platinum status with the airline, they're more likely to upgrade you, and if you're booking a suite at a hotel, you might be upgraded to a better suite. But if you're booking the least expensive room, don't expect them to hand you the keys to the presidential suite.

A lot also depends on your attitude. By all means, let people know it's your honeymoon, and if you're working with a travel agent, make sure the agent gets the word out. But don't *expect* any freebies, or act like you do. If you receive a basket of fruit with a note wishing you a wonderful honeymoon, be gracious about it.

Vaccinations

The fastest way to find out if any special vaccinations are required or recommended for your travels is to visit the travelers' health area of the Centers for Disease Control and Prevention website. Some vaccinations (such as those for hepatitis A and B) require multiple doses or need time to take effect, so investigate early. If you're past the recommended time frame, it's still worth checking with your doctor.

Some hospitals and health clinics have immunization centers that specialize in travelers' health, so it's worth an Internet search to see if you have such a center in your area, especially if you have any medical conditions that call for extra immunizations. You can also check with your regular doctor.

Stock Up on Medication

BEFORE LEAVING on your honeymoon, make sure you have a full supply of any prescription medications you take regularly. That includes birth control pills. If you wear disposable contact lenses, stock up ahead of time. If traveling abroad, it's also a good idea to bring along any over-the-counter medicines you use regularly, as they may not be available.

Travel Insurance

YOUR HONEYMOON might be the most expensive trip you've ever taken, so it's worth considering whether you should buy travel insurance (not to be confused with "wedding insurance," covered on page 160). If you've prepaid for accommodations or a tour package, you stand to lose if your honeymoon is derailed by bad weather, illness, or a missed connection. Some villa rentals may require prepayment and may not be forgiving of cancellations. If most of your trip can be canceled or changed with only small penalties, however, travel insurance could be an unnecessary expense.

The cost of travel insurance typically ranges from 4 to 10 percent of your total expenditure. The more situations covered by a policy, the more you'll pay; "cancel for any reason" insurance, which covers 75 percent of your

Wait to Change Your Name

Brides (and the occasional groom) planning to change their names postwedding should wait until after the honeymoon. The name on your airline ticket needs to match the name on your photo identification.

If you're applying for a passport for your honeymoon, use your maiden name. You can change the name on it within a year for no charge; after a year, there's a fee.

nonrefundable costs, often runs 40 percent higher than standard trip insurance. "Trip cancellation" insurance is the most common type of policy and may cover travel interruption, theft (identity or property), trip cancellation, severe weather, lost or damaged baggage (be sure to save baggage claim checks), accidents, medical or dental emergencies, and financial default (bankruptcy of airline, cruise line, tour operator, hotel, etc.).

Start researching options while planning your honeymoon, as travel insurance must often be purchased simultaneously with plane tickets. Although some policies can be purchased as late as the day before departure, you'll get more benefits if you plan ahead. Avoid buying travel insurance offered directly by a cruise line or tour operator—in short, anyone insuring their own product. If the company goes out of business, their insurance policy won't cover your losses.

Insurance can pay off if one of you gets sick or has an accident during the trip and needs medical attention, but if either of you has a medical condition, ask your insurance provider about any clauses regarding preexisting health conditions—you might not be covered.

Are You Already Covered?

Before buying a policy, call your health insurance and home (or renter's) insurance companies to find out what would already be covered on your trip; some policies cover medical emergencies and stolen property. Also check with your credit card company or bank to find out if they offer coverage. Always get the information directly from a company representative—don't rely on a website and don't try to interpret the fine print yourself—so you can make sure it applies to your particular policy.

For the record, I'll say it once: No amount of planning can ensure a hassle-free trip. The weather or airline gods are not always on our side. But come rain, sleet, or snow, your honeymoon will be a trip to remember. ◆

Sample Program

The program is an opportunity to communicate a heartfelt message to your guests—and to honor those whose presence is missed.

THE WEDDING CELEBRATION OF

Sydnee Smith

—AND—

Max Hersh

SATURDAY, THE FOURTEENTH OF OCTOBER
TWO THOUSAND AND SEVENTEEN

Hotel Bel Air

BEL AIR, CALIFORNIA

To our family & friends

We are so happy to share our special day with you. We have been blessed by your friendship, support, and love, and it's an honor to make this lifelong commitment to each other in your presence. We are so grateful to have you here today as we begin our life together as husband and wife. We hope you will enjoy this evening as much as we will.

A special thank you to our parents:
Without your unconditional love and support we wouldn't be the people we are today. You are not only our parents, but our friends, and we are so incredibly thankful for that.

Love,

SYDNEE AND MAX

Processional

Grandparents
Sydnee's grandmother, Annette Smith, escorted by Alex Doria
Max's grandmother, Madelyn Hersh, and grandfather, Thomas Hersh

Groom's Parents
Jeremy and June Hersh

Groom
Max

Best Man
Daniel Bowling

Groomsmen
Ryan Cavanaugh
Christopher Zimmerman
Jon Davenport

Bridesmaids
Jenny Spivey
Kendal Blackwelder
Kate Sederstrom

Maid of Honor
Amy Cook

Flower Girl
Gillian Balma

Bride's Parents
Sharon and Rick Smith

Bride
Sydnee

Order of Service

SEATING OF THE FAMILIES

PROCESSIONAL:
Gabriel's Oboe — Morricone
Bride, escorted by her father:
Canon in D — Pachelbel

WELCOME:
Rev. Robert Dorian

SCRIPTURE READINGS:
I Corinthians 13
Colossians 3:12 – 17

VOWS

EXCHANGING OF THE RINGS

PRAYER

DECLARATION OF MARRIAGE

BENEDICTION

RECESSIONAL:
Joyful, Joyful — Beethoven

In Loving Memory

As we begin the next stage of our lives together, we would like to lovingly remember those close to our hearts who are no longer with us.

Today we remember:

Grandparents of the Bride
Eleanor and Julius Pearson

Grandparents of the Groom
Jessie and Larry Flickinger

Your Wedding Budget

I recommend setting up your budget on a spreadsheet program that will automatically add up columns for you. (Why drag out the calculator if you don't have to?) Use the following worksheet as a guideline to create your own; or, if you're computer averse, cut along the dotted lines and do it the old-fashioned way. (Copy the pages first; your budget will go through many rounds of drafts.)

You won't necessarily need all the line items listed here. Likewise, you might need to add certain things that are personal to *your* wedding. Catholic brides might need rosary beads for the walk down the aisle; Jewish couples will want to budget for a ketubah.

ITEM	ESTIMATED COST	ACTUAL COST	DEPOSIT	NOTES
Essentials				
Ceremony location				
Reception location				
Food and service				
Beverages and bartenders				
Officiant fee or donation				
Marriage license				
Wedding night hotel room				
Honeymoon				
Travel				
Lodging				
Meals				
Other				
Gratuities				
Catering staff				

ITEM	ESTIMATED COST	ACTUAL COST	DEPOSIT	NOTES
Catering manager				
On-site coordinator				
Bartenders				
Coatroom attendants				
Bathroom attendants				
Drivers				
Musicians				
Hairstylist				
Makeup artist				
Miscellaneous tips				
Wedding planner				
Wedding insurance				
Honeymoon insurance				

Stationery

ITEM	ESTIMATED COST	ACTUAL COST	DEPOSIT	NOTES
Save-the-date cards				
Wedding invitations				
Wedding announcements				
Calligraphy				
Postage				
Thank-you notes				
Programs				
Menus				

ITEM	ESTIMATED COST	ACTUAL COST	DEPOSIT	NOTES
Seating cards				
Place cards				
Table numbers				

Rings

ITEM	ESTIMATED COST	ACTUAL COST	DEPOSIT	NOTES
Rings—his				
Rings—hers				

Attire

ITEM	ESTIMATED COST	ACTUAL COST	DEPOSIT	NOTES
Wedding gown				
Alterations				
Shoes				
Headpiece and veil				
Lingerie/foundation/hosiery				
Jewelry				
Handbag				
Other bridal accessories				
Tuxedo for groom				
Shoes for groom				
Shirt for groom				
Other accessories for groom				
Bridesmaids' dresses (if you're paying)				
Groomsmens' tuxedos (if you're paying)				

ITEM	ESTIMATED COST	ACTUAL COST	DEPOSIT	NOTES
Beauty				
Hairstylist(s)				
Manicure and pedicure for bride				
Makeup artist(s)				
Facials and other spa treatments				
Flowers				
Ceremony flowers				
Bridesmaids' bouquets				
Boutonnieres				
Corsages for mothers				
Cocktail flowers				
Reception flowers				
Postparty (lounge) flowers				
Wreath and petals for flower girl				
Miscellaneous flowers				
Chuppah				
Photography and Videography				
Photographer				
Additional prints and albums				
Videographer				
Additional copies of video				

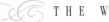

ITEM	ESTIMATED COST	ACTUAL COST	DEPOSIT	NOTES
Music				
Ceremony				
Cocktail hour				
Reception				
After-party				
Rentals				
Tent				
Chairs				
Tables				
China				
Glassware				
Flatware				
Dance floor				
Furniture				
Portable toilets				
Miscellaneous rentals				
Linen rentals				
Napkins				
Chair covers				
Chair sashes				
Seating-card table linens				

ITEM	ESTIMATED COST	ACTUAL COST	DEPOSIT	NOTES
Cocktail table linens				
Cake table linens				
Reception table linens				

Décor

Aisle runner				
Candles				
Lighting				
Other				

Reception

Coat check				
Paper cocktail napkins				
Guest towels for bathrooms				
Guest book and pen				
Cake				

Gifts

Bridesmaids' gifts				
Groomsmens' gifts				
Flower girl gifts				
Ring bearer gifts				
Parents' gifts				
Shower hostess gifts				

ITEM	ESTIMATED COST	ACTUAL COST	DEPOSIT	NOTES
Gifts for ushers and other helpers				
Favors				
Welcome gifts for out-of-towners				

Transportation

For couple				
For bridal party				
For guests				
Valet parking				

Other Entertaining

Bridesmaid luncheon				
Rehearsal dinner location				
Rehearsal dinner invitation				
Rehearsal dinner flowers				
Rehearsal dinner food				
Rehearsal dinner beverages				
Rehearsal dinner music and/or favors				
Additional rehearsal dinner expenses				
Day-after brunch location				
Day-after brunch catering				
Day-after brunch flowers (if not reusing)				
Other day-after brunch expenses				

ITEM	ESTIMATED COST	ACTUAL COST	DEPOSIT	NOTES
Destination Weddings *(additional costs)*				
Scouting costs				
Long-distance transportation				
Local transportation				
Lodging				
Shipping supplies to site				
Miscellaneous				

Your Wedding Contacts

WEDDING PLANNER

Name

Address

Office

Mobile

Email

OFFICIANT

Name

Address

Office

Mobile

Email

CEREMONY VENUE

Name

Address

Office

Mobile

Website/Email

RECEPTION VENUE

Name

Address

Office

Mobile

Website/Email

PHOTOGRAPHER

Name

Address

Office

Mobile

Website/Email

VIDEOGRAPHER

Name

Address

Office

Mobile

Website/Email

Your Wedding Contacts

FLORIST

Name

Address

Office

Mobile

Website/Email

CATERER

Name

Address

Office

Mobile

Website/Email

LIQUOR SUPPLIER

Name

Address

Office

Mobile

Website/Email

RENTAL COMPANY

Name

Address

Office

Mobile

Website/Email

HAIRSTYLIST

Name

Address

Office

Mobile

Website/Email

TAILOR/DRESSMAKER

Name

Address

Office

Mobile

Website/Email

Your Wedding Contacts

REHEARSAL DINNER VENUE

Name

Address

Office

Mobile

Website/Email

MUSIC

Name

Address

Office

Mobile

Website/Email

WEDDING CAKE BAKERY

Name

Address

Office

Mobile

Website/Email

TRANSPORTATION COMPANY

Name

Address

Office

Mobile

Website/Email

MAKEUP ARTIST

Name

Address

Office

Mobile

Website/Email

DAY-AFTER BRUNCH

Name

Address

Office

Mobile

Website/Email

Your Wedding Contacts

WEDDING-NIGHT HOTEL

Name

Address

Office

Mobile

Website/Email

HOTELS FOR OUT-OF-TOWNERS

Name

Address

Office

Mobile

Website/Email

HOTELS FOR OUT-OF-TOWNERS

Name

Address

Office

Mobile

Website/Email

HOTELS FOR OUT-OF-TOWNERS

Name

Address

Office

Mobile

Website/Email

HOTELS FOR OUT-OF-TOWNERS

Name

Address

Office

Mobile

Website/Email

HOTELS FOR OUT-OF-TOWNERS

Name

Address

Office

Mobile

Website/Email

Your Honeymoon Contacts

TRAVEL AGENT

Name

Telephone number

Email

DEPARTING FLIGHT

Date

Time

Airline   Flight number

RETURN FLIGHT

Date

Time

Airline   Flight number

PASSPORTS AND VISAS

Bride

☐ Country

☐ Country

☐ Country

Groom

☐ Country

☐ Country

☐ Country

ACCOMMODATIONS

Hotel

Telephone number

Confirmation number

Rate

Special arrangements (transportation, activities, etc.)

ACCOMMODATIONS

Hotel

Telephone number

Confirmation number

Rate

Special arrangements (transportation, activities, etc.)

ACCOMMODATIONS

Hotel

Telephone number

Confirmation number

Rate

Special arrangements (transportation, activities, etc.)

Your Rental Checklist

TABLES

Round:
☐ 48"   ☐ 54"   ☐ 60"   ☐ 66"   ☐ 72"

Long:
☐ 4'   ☐ 6'   ☐ 8'

CHAIRS

☐ Folding chairs   Color _____

☐ Chiavari chairs   Color _____

☐ Versaille chairs   Color _____

☐ Brentwood chairs   Color _____

LINENS

☐ Round table   Size _____   Color _____

☐ Long table   Size _____   Color _____

☐ Buffet linens   _____

☐ Cake-table linens _____

☐ Seating-card table _____

☐ Cocktail table   _____

☐ Dinner napkins   _____

☐ Cocktail napkins   _____

CHINA

☐ Dinner plate   _____

☐ Salad/cake plate   _____

☐ Soup bowl   _____

☐ Liner   _____

☐ Bread/butter plate   _____

☐ Coffee cup/saucer   _____

☐ Bowls   _____

☐ Chargers   _____

SILVERWARE

☐ Salad fork   _____

☐ Salad knife   _____

☐ Dinner fork   _____

☐ Dinner knife   _____

☐ Fish fork   _____

☐ Fish knife   _____

☐ Butter knife   _____

☐ Teaspoon   _____

☐ Tablespoon   _____

Your Rental Checklist

GLASSWARE

- ☐ White wine _____
- ☐ Red wine _____
- ☐ Champagne _____
- ☐ Water _____
- ☐ All-purpose _____

SERVICE TRAYS

- ☐ Round _____
- ☐ Oval _____
- ☐ Oblong _____
- ☐ Waiter trays/stands _____

SERVING PIECES

- ☐ Chafing dishes _____
- ☐ Bowls _____
- ☐ Coffeemaker _____
- ☐ Coffee urn _____
- ☐ Creamer and sugar set _____
- ☐ Coffee pitcher _____
- ☐ Tea set _____

- ☐ Salt/pepper shakers _____
- ☐ Ashtrays _____
- ☐ Water pitchers _____

TENT/CANOPIES

- ☐ Size _____
- ☐ Sidewalls _____
- ☐ Subfloor _____
- ☐ Carpet (color) _____
- ☐ Dance floor _____
- ☐ Heaters _____
- ☐ Air conditioning _____
- ☐ Stage dimensions _____
- ☐ Coat check _____

LIGHTING

- ☐ Generator _____
- ☐ Spot lighting _____
- ☐ Uplighting _____
- ☐ Stage lighting _____
- ☐ Dance floor lighting _____
- ☐ Ceremony lighting _____

Your Rental Checklist

OTHER RENTALS

Your Transportation Call Sheet

COMPANY

Contact

Telephone

Type of car

Passenger(s)

Pickup locations and times

Destination

COMPANY

Contact

Telephone

Type of car

Passenger(s)

Pickup locations and times

Destination

COMPANY

Contact

Telephone

Type of car

Passenger(s)

Pickup locations and times

Destination

COMPANY

Contact

Telephone

Type of car

Passenger(s)

Pickup locations and times

Destination

COMPANY

Contact

Telephone

Type of car

Passenger(s)

Pickup locations and times

Destination

COMPANY

Contact

Telephone

Type of car

Passenger(s)

Pickup locations and times

Destination

Notes

Notes

Notes

Notes

Notes

ACKNOWLEDGMENTS

Just as it takes a sizable team of people to pull off a wedding, it took the talents and expertise of dozens of people to give this book its depth and breadth.

We would like to thank Peter Workman and the visionary editors at Workman Publishing, especially Susan Bolotin and Savannah Ashour, who deftly ushered the manuscript through the publishing process with clarity and care. We're indebted to Jennifer Griffin, who first got the proposal off the ground. Thanks to Janet Vicario for creating a beautiful design, and to Munira Al-Khalili, Jodi Churchfield, Jarrod Dyer, and Lidija Tomas for all their hard work implementing it; thanks as well to Bunky Hurter, for her beautiful illustrations. We're thankful for the expert eyes of Melanie Bennitt, Judit Bodnar, and Katherine Camargo. We're already looking forward to working with Amy Corley, Amanda Pritzker, Marilyn Barnett, and everyone on the sales and marketing end. We're also grateful to our agent, Patty Sullivan of P.S. Ink, for seeing the project through from start to finish.

We are extremely fortunate to have benefited from the knowledge and experience of the professionals whose contributions enriched so many of the chapters. Rona Berg was especially gracious in sharing her vast knowledge of all matters of beauty and health. Kelly Bare was an indispensable resource in the realm of emotions and relationship dynamics. Our gratitude goes out to Mark Held of Mark's Garden and Casey Cooper of Botanicals for sharing a wealth of information about flowers; Ellen Black and Sol Lehr at Lehr and Black for guidance on invitations; Sam Godfrey at Perfect Endings for cake know-how; Julie Sabatino of The Stylish Bride for gown-shopping savvy; Jim Eppolito of West Coast Music; photographer Lara Porzak; Steve Dangcil at Vidicam Productions for videography; Edgar Zamora at Revelry for event design; Raymond Thompson and Curtis Stahl at Images by Lighting; Bentley Meeker at Bentley Meeker Lighting & Staging; Mark Anfangar at Classic Party Rentals; Pete Burra of John & Pete's for helping stock the bar in the cocktails chapter; Rebecca Grinnals of Engaging Concepts for destination wedding guidance; Michalena Lloyd of Vegas to Venice for tips on choosing destination wedding gowns; Kim Smith of David's Bridal; Rudi Steele of Rudi Steele Travel for honeymoon advice; and Steve Boorstein for his gown preservation counsel.

For sharing their approach to religious ceremonies, we are indebted to Minister Amar Nath Gupta, head priest of Rajdhani Temple in Chantilly, Virginia; Rabbi Elliot Cosgrove of Anshe Emet Synagogue; Rev. Bryan Siebuhr of the Midwest Buddhist Temple; and Marita McLaughlin of the Shambhala Meditation Center, all in Chicago.

Time and time again, we relied on The American Wedding Survey statistics kindly provided by Condé Nast Bridal Media to inform the book.

Brides across the country were gracious enough to serve on our "Bridal Board," generously sharing anecdotes, emotions, and insights about their weddings. Although there are too many to name, we would like to give special thanks to Shelley Beeler, Maureen Gainer, Nora Gainer, Megy Karydes, Stacey Koerner-Roney, Kylie Foxx McDonald, Cassie Murdoch, Megan Nicolay, Maggie Rhodes Shapack, and Alison Sonsini.

The staff at Mindy Weiss Party Consultants devote themselves to making every wedding beautiful and special, and they did the same for the book. We're very appreciative of Amy Bird Shapiro's intrepid research, and of Melissa Torre, Stacy Saltzman, Irene Boujo, Ashley Port, Kim Koral, Kristen Daniels, Sandie Bailey, and Alli Sims for helping out with all the odds and ends.

We are grateful for the excellent research assistance provided by Margaret Collins, Anne Halliday, Naomi Lindt, Carrie MacQuaid, Haley Pelton, and Sarina Rosenberg.

MINDY THANKS

Thanks to everyone at Workman, especially Savannah and Suzie, my fearless cheerleaders through the long haul of the writing process. We couldn't have finished without you!

My friend Janis, who listened to me talk about this book for years (literally!). You are the Ethel to my Lucy.

Ellen Black and Sol Lehr, whose beautiful invitations capture the spirit of all my weddings . . . you are my friends and family.

My hardworking publicist, Michele Shuman, who can find the funny in any situation. The Ultimate Party Team: Melissa, my double, who truly keeps the company running. Thanks, Meliss—I could not do it without you. Amy Weiss, who sticks by me and protects me like family; Valerie Lee, who never gets mad when I mishear a "no" as a "yes"; Mark A., Mark, Richard, Nancy, Cindy, Edgar, Curt and Ray, Jimmy, Steve, Lara, Jay, John, Simone, Barb and Corey, Peggy, and Brent . . . who knows if I could do it without you? I wouldn't want to even try.

To my sisters, Jaye and Dana . . . I love our singing, I love our craziness, and most of all I love that we have each other!

Auntie Sherry, thank you for taking care of me whenever I call, which is never enough.

In memory of Martin van Kempen, whose photography captured all the emotions and dreams of a couple starting their future together. Your kindness will long be remembered through the images you left behind.

To Mom and Dad, who are looking down on me every day. You raised me in a home full of laughter and parties galore. I miss you both.

LISBETH THANKS

Thanks to editors both past and present at *InStyle* magazine—Charla Lawhon, Honor Brodie, Jacqueline Goewey, Clare McHugh, and Janice Min in particular—for helping me build up wedding expertise by assigning me article after article.

I am indebted to Lisa Skolnik for her lending library, to Martha Barnette for her help with word origins, to Jennifer Lawler for her clear-headed wisdom, and to Bev Bennett, Margaret Littman, Maureen Gainer, Sophia Dembling, Jean Fain, Rachel Weingarten, and Amy Davis, who provided emotional and professional sustenance.

I am also profoundly grateful to Sister Muriel Brown and the other sisters at Cenacle Retreat and Conference Center in Chicago for recognizing and nurturing the spiritual aspect of this endeavor. Other supporters included Jack Levine and Jim and Lynne Frost, who freely opened their homes and cleared their desks for me, and Kerin Can, who kept things running smoothly on the home front and shuttled the kids wherever they needed to go.

My mother, Martha Levine, encouraged my writing early on. I learned much about the craft of journalism from my late father, Jerry Levine, who stringently line-edited everything I wrote while growing up.

For the encouragement, love, and forbearance of my husband, Scott Saef, and our beautiful children, Rachel and Jared, I will always be grateful.

Index